Child Psychology and Childhood Education

Child Psychology and Childhood Education

A Cognitive-Developmental View

Lawrence Kohlberg
Harvard University

with

Rheta DeVries
University of Houston

Greta Fein
University of Maryland

Daniel Hart
Rutgers State University of New Jersey

Rochelle Mayer
*National Center for Education in
Maternal and Child Health*

Gil Noam
McClean Hospital

John Snarey
Northwestern University

James Wertsch
Northwestern University

Longman
New York & London

Senior Editor: Naomi Silverman
Senior Production Editor: Ronni Strell
Text Design: Steven August Krastin
Cover Design: Steven August Krastin
Text Art: J & R Services, Inc.
Production Supervisor: Judith Stern
Compositor: Graphicraft Typesetters Ltd.
Printer and Binder: R. R. Donnelley & Sons Company

Child Psychology and Childhood Education

Copyright © 1987 by Longman Inc.

Longman Inc.
95 Church Street
White Plains, N.Y. 10601

Associated companies:
Longman Group Ltd., London
Longman Cheshire Pty., Melbourne
Longman Paul Pty., Auckland
Copp Clark Pitman, Toronto
Pitman Publishing Inc., New York

Library of Congress Cataloging-in-Publication Data

Kohlberg, Lawrence, 1927
    Child psychology and childhood education.

    Includes index.
    1. Child psychology. 2. Child development.
3. Educational psychology. 4. Education of children.
I. Title. [DNLM: 1. Child Development. 2. Child
Psychology. 3. Cognition—in infancy & childhood.
4. Psychology, Educational. WS 105 K788c]
BF121.K55   1987   155.4   86-15227
ISBN 0-582-28302-7 (cased)

87 88 89 90 9 8 7 6 5 4 3 2 1

Contents

264028

Preface

Thomas Kuhn, the historian and philosopher of science, has noted that science changes periodically through revolutions in theory and method rather than through the slow accumulation of findings. Kuhn calls these revolutions *paradigm shifts*. In child psychology and education such a paradigm shift has occurred during the past two decades. This shift was initiated by American awareness of the theory and research of Jean Piaget concerning the cognitive development of the child. As this book will indicate, this paradigm shift has not been simply in the cognitive domain but in the social-emotional domain as well. The central theme of this paradigm shift is the assumption that the child actively constructs his or her own world, the meaning of his or her actions in it, and his or her very instruments of knowing. The child's constructions pass through sequential qualitative stages, each representing a coherent viewpoint on the world. Development through these stages and the stages themselves are the result of processes of interaction between the child and his or her social and physical environment.

Although this cognitive-developmental paradigm has generated much research, as well as some programs in early education, it has not been used to review and integrate findings in all areas of child development or to review various programs in early education from the perspective of the general philosophy of educational practice to which this paradigm gives rise. This book is an effort to accomplish this, by presenting an integrated review of theories of development and selected areas of child development research. The book focuses on the child in the years from 3 to 10, the period in which basic developmental research relevant to education is most fully worked out and in which developmental programs of education have been created.

Part I seeks to clarify the three basic theories of development and their implications for education: the romantic-maturational theory; the environmental, or cultural-transmission, theory; and the cognitive-developmental, or interactional, theory. It presents a comprehensive argument for the cognitive-developmental theory while attempting to do justice to its alternatives. The second section of the book considers core problems or areas of child development research: intelligence, moral development, ego development, sex-role development, language and thought, and play and its role in development. The research findings in these areas are critical for operationalizing developmental educational aims and for assessing educational progress.

The book is meant for professionals and graduate students in both child development and education. It contains more child development research and theory than is customary for students in education because we believe that the most basic psychological concepts

and knowledge for the educator are those of child development. It also has more discussion of education than is customary for students of child development because we
believe that a developmental psychology useful to practice cannot be created without a
conscious concern for educational implications.

Our conviction that a review of developmental psychology research should include
an educational perspective is illustrated in both our selection of areas for review in Part
II and in the manner in which they are reviewed. As noted, Part II includes the basic
areas or dimensions of personality development relevant to educational goals. Each area
is reviewed with regard to the following issues:

1. How does each basic theoretical perspective define and measure the construct in
   question, for example, intelligence?
2. In what sense does the perspective define the construct as a basic "good" in human
   development and education?
3. In what sense is the area one that is open to possible educational intervention at
   various ages?
4. Within a general cognitive-developmental approach to the area, how do particular
   theories order the data? The major theories considered are the constructivist theory
   of Piaget, the symbolic-interactional theories of George Herbert Mead and Lev
   Vygotsky, and the neopsychoanalytic theory of Eric Erikson.

From the viewpoint we take, it is important to clarify the "success" of each theory,
not only in terms of its success in predicting and ordering the data, but in terms of
ordering the data in a way useful to education. As an example, we claim that both
biological-psychometric and Piagetian perspectives successfully order much data in the
area of intelligence but that the Piagetian perspective is useful to education in a way that
the biological view is not.

As a statement of cognitive-developmental theory, the book is novel more in breadth
than in basic concept. In part this breadth comes from the systematic application of
cognitive-developmental theory to "personal" and "affective" development as well as
to intellectual development. In part it comes from its statement of the theory as a
systematic philosophy of educational practice, a statement that leans heavily on the
philosophy of John Dewey.

Lawrence Kohlberg

PART I

A Theory of Early Education

The aim of Part I of this book is to set forth a *cognitive-developmental theory* of childhood education. Historically, this theory can be traced from its early philosophical formulation in America by John Dewey and James Mark Baldwin to its empirical elaboration in Switzerland by Jean Piaget and in Soviet Russia by Lev Vygotsky. Its most recent application is to American developmental education and research by writers such as the present authors. Cognitive-developmental theory is contrasted with two alternate theories or approaches to education. One of these is the romantic tradition commencing with Rousseau and advanced by modern free school theorists such as A. S. Neill. This approach has never generated a scientific or empirical psychology; it has simply provided a framework for criticism of the educational status quo. The second approach is the *environmental-learning*, or *cultural-transmission, theory*, which was developed by John Locke, elaborated in America by Edward Thorndike, and more recently propounded by educational theorists such as B. F. Skinner and Carl Bereiter. This theory has been the dominant influence on American educational psychology and American educational practice. Comparisons between the approaches are made in Part I.

In the first chapter, "Theory and Practice: Two Educational and Child Psychologies in Historical Perspective," the cognitive-developmental and environmental-learning approaches are compared with regard to the kinds of educational psychology they engender. Each has a different view of the relation of theory to practice or of the way in which psychological research may contribute to the progress or improvement of schooling.

The chapter briefly traces the history of the cognitive-developmental approach from John Dewey onward and the cultural-transmission approach from Edward Thorndike onward. These two approaches are contrasted, not only as two different psychological theories for ordering research data, but as two different views of the task of psychology in improving educational practice.

The Thorndike view of educational psychology attempts to be value-neutral. Starting with the goals of education as given in the schools, it attempts, through research on schooling as it is, to define better methods of instruction and better

1

methods of assessment of pupil achievement than previously existed.

In contrast, the Dewey view of educational psychology starts with the value assumption that development should be the aim of education. It does not study schooling as it is but the universals in cognitive, moral, and personal development. Because it sets up new aims for education, it cannot be based on research or the methods traditionally found in the schools. Instead, Deweyan methods require setting up new, experimental, or "progressive" schools, programs such as those described in DeVries and Kohlberg (1987).

In Chapter 2, the cognitive-developmental approach is considered in terms of its vision of the child's nature. The title of the chapter, "The Young Child as a Philosopher," expresses the child's nature as implied by the cognitive-developmental view and the unity of the child's mind that it presents.

In Chapter 3, each of the three approaches is considered as a total educational philosophy, a statement not only of psychology but of the values and goals of education each stresses. The title, "Development as the Aim of Education," states the cognitive-developmental view of educational aims, which was first clearly articulated by John Dewey.

The chapter progresses from psychological theories to total educational philosophies or ideologies and discusses both the psychological and philosophical positions underlying educational progressivism. The tenets of progressivism, most clearly identified with the work of John Dewey, are contrasted with those of two other educational ideologies, the romantic and the cultural-transmission theories, which historically have competed in the minds of educators as rationales for the choice of educational goals and practices. The authors claim that only progressivism, with its cognitive-developmental psychology, its interactionist epistemology, and its philosophically examined ethics, provides an adequate basis for defining the aims of education.

Whereas Chapters 1 and 2 elaborate a stage or cognitive-developmental psychology of the child and consider what this psychology implies for what early educators *can* do, Chapter 3 elaborates the philosophic, rather than the psychological, implications of stage development in terms of a theory of what educators *should* do. The issues dealt with in this chapter are issues of value instead of fact. Given the facts of stage development, which educators can stimulate, in what sense is it valuable or good to stimulate such development? How does the justification of the good of education as development compare with the justification of the good of education as educational achievement or as the cultivation of personality traits of mental health? The chapter deals with the general question of how psychological theories relate to educational ideologies, that is, how various psychological conceptions of what learning or development *is* translate into statements of educational aims of what learning ideally *ought* to be.

In analyzing this issue we focus on two related problems of value theory. The first is the problem of *value relativity*, the problem of defining some general ends of education whose validity is not related to the values and needs of each individual child or to the values of each subculture or society. The second is the relation of the ethical *ought* to the natural *is*. We claim that the cognitive-developmental approach can handle these issues because it combines a psychological theory of development with a rational ethical philosophy dealing with the issues first proposed by John Dewey. We claim that the psychological theories proposed by maturationists and environmental-training theorists cannot be translated into statements of educational aims free of the philosophic charge of being arbitrary and related to the values of the particular educator and school.

Chapter 1

Theory and Practice: Two Educational and Child Psychologies in Historical Perspective

Lawrence Kohlberg

A central purpose of this book and its companion volume, DeVries, *Programs of Early Education* (1987), is to bring the research and theory in child development of this generation (1965–1985) to students and professionals in developmental and educational psychology. It attempts to make students and professionals in child development more aware of the educational issues that we believe should determine the questions they should research.

Most child psychologists would agree that the long-range goal of their research is to provide guidance to educational and clinical practitioners working with children. While accepting the notion that research should have implications for practice, many researchers define the problems they research in terms of "pure" psychology. The assumption is that after a psychologist has answered these pure-psychology questions, deductions can be made to guide teacher practice. We call this assumption the *psychologistic fallacy* and identify it with Edward Thorndike, the founder of mainstream educational psychology, and his many successors. For them, experimental studies of teaching and learning in animals and children provided the basic laws of learning that could be translated into an educational technology the teacher was to follow. In Chapter 3, we will try to show the logical flaws of the psychologistic fallacy.

At the opposite extreme is the view of "teacher as artist," articulated by William James. A still different approach, identified with John Dewey and the one with which we concur, is that of the educator as experimenter. This view draws on conclusions from developmental psychology but uses these as the starting point to try innovations in the schools. It is committed to psychological theory but uses what is known to further a theory of education.

WILLIAM JAMES AND TEACHING AS AN ARTIST

Educational psychology was founded in America at the turn of the twentieth century by two intellectual giants, John Dewey and Edward Thorndike. These men had very different visions of the nature and purpose of educational psychology.

In their early intellectual years, both men were students of William James, the great philosopher-psychologist at Harvard. James's *The principles of psychology* (1890), was the first systematic American statement of psychology. The book was eclectic and foreshadowed the later statement of connectionistic habit theory by Pavlov, Thorndike, and Watson; Lorenz's ethological statement of instinct and imprinting; gestalt theories of perceptive and cognitive organization; and ego psychology's conception of a dynamic self. While providing an extremely sensitive introspective or phenomenological analysis of human consciousness, James's book viewed mind functionally, as an adaptive function of an organism evolved through Darwinian variation and selection, a view shared by both Thorndike and Dewey.

Although James helped begin the scientific study of psychology and was actively interested in its relation to education, his *Talks to teachers* does not come from a belief in a scientific educational psychology. Rather, he believed that education was an art, not a science, an art modeled by the gifted teacher. This art could draw on some basic concepts of psychology but could never be derived from it. He said, "Psychology is a science, teaching is an art, and sciences never generate arts directly out of themselves. An intermediary inventive mind must make the application by use of its originality" (James, 1958, p. 12).

From this perspective, James was able to make searching criticisms of still current educational practices. He gives the following example:

> A friend of mine visiting a school was asked to examine a young class in geography. Glancing at the book, she said, "Suppose you should dig a hole in the ground, hundreds of feet deep, how should you find it at the bottom, warmer or colder than on top?" None of the class replying, the teacher said: "I'm sure they know, but I think you don't ask the question quite rightly. Let me try." So, taking the book, she said "In what condition is the interior of the globe?" and received the immediate answer from half the class at once: "The interior of the globe is in a condition of igneous fusion." (James, 1958, p. 106)

James critiques this pattern of teaching from the standpoint of an understanding of the child's mind as organized and active, an understanding carried much further by Dewey and Piaget. For James, this implied teaching at the frontier of the child's mind, at a point just beyond the child's present point of comprehensions. "Start where the learner is and proceed" is a famous Jamesian dictum.

James's own approach to education was basically supportive and inspirational, reminding teachers to avoid "a certain blindness in human beings" preaching the "Gospel of Relaxation," saying, "Prepare yourself in the subject so it shall always be on top—then in classroom trust your spontaneity and fling away all further care" (James, 1958, p. 36).

The mainstream of American educational psychology was founded not by James but by Edward Thorndike, briefly a student of William James, who came to Columbia University before the turn of the century with a cage full of animals from whose learning patterns he hoped to establish a science of education. Thorndike thought this science would be based on the experimental establishment of basic *laws of learning* as influenced by punishment, reward, and practice. Educational science was also to be based on *measurement*, of the establishment of tests of intelligence and achievement based on psychometric methods and the normal curve. Since Thorndike, this line of educational psychology has been enhanced and enriched by learning psychologists like Skinner and Bereiter and pschometricians like Thurstone and Guilford.

Thorndikean educational psychology has had two foci that have powerfully affected American education: research on laws or methods of learning and instruction and research on tests of learning and of learning ability or intelligence.

Thorndike's work was based on a rigorous and positivistic view of educational psychology. He studied the behavior of cats in specially designed puzzle boxes and was interested in discovering how long it took the cats to solve the puzzles (which usually involved getting out of the boxes) and in learning what rewards were the most effective in achieving the objective. This procedure led to empirical studies documenting how many trial-and-error sequences took place before the cat finally "learned" to stick a paw through the grating and lift up the latch to open the cage. Thorndike was focusing on one aspect of learning—learning by trial and error. By putting a cat through this sequence often enough, a bond would be formed, a stimulus-response connection in the nervous system, so that the cat would "remember" what to do. Thorndike also studied human processes of learning. The classical curriculum of the secondary school (four years of Greek, four years of Latin, and so on) had been justified on the grounds that such exercise would "train" the mind: Spending time and effort on Latin, for example, made it easier to learn French, while Greek would improve your English. Using precise measurement procedures, Thorndike was able to show that little, if any, disciplining of the mind could be transferred from one subject to the other. Thorndike believed that transfer occurred only when elements in a situation were identical or at least similar to elements in a second situation.

In Chapter 3, we elaborate the fundamental philosophic and psychological assumptions of Thorndikean educational psychology as the *cultural-transmission* or *environmental-learning* educational theory. Here we need merely note that environmentalists assume that what is important in the child's development is the learning of intellectual, scientific, and moral knowledge and the rules of the culture; education's business is the direct instruction of such information and rules. Both specific concepts and general cognitive structures, such as the categories of time, space, causality, good, and evil, are reflections of structures that exist outside the child, that is, in the physical and social world. The structure of behavior is viewed as the result of the association of discrete stimuli with one another, the child's responses, and the child's experiences of pleasure and pain. Mental development is the result of guided learning; teaching, consequently, requires a careful statement of a behavior pattern considered desirable in terms of specific responses. Implied here is the idea that the child's behavior can be shaped by immediate repetition and elaboration of the correct response and by the use of immediate feedback or reward. Programmed text and teaching machines are developments of the principles of environmental learning theories.

The Thorndike stream of educational psychology was not necessarily completely behavioristic, as Skinner's work is. Thorndike and most of his followers admitted the existence of cognition, of conscious memories and thoughts in the child's mind. Their view of learning, however, still implied that the child's mind was a tabula rasa, a blank slate slowly filled with associations between perceptual stimuli and the organism's responses.

JOHN DEWEY, THE FOUNDER OF THE DEVELOPMENTAL APPROACH TO EDUCATIONAL PSYCHOLOGY

Like Thorndike, John Dewey was profoundly influenced by Darwin's theory of evolution. Like Darwin, Dewey took the biological view of human behavior as that of an organism sharing many attributes with subhuman animals, an organism whose behavior developed as an adaptive or *functional* response to an environment. Dewey and his followers and friends at the University of Chicago, C. Angell, H. Carr, and G. H. Mead, founded the functional school of psychology in opposition to what was then called the structural school of psychology founded by Wundt in Germany and led by E. B. Titchener in America.

At the turn of the century, *structuralism* meant the introspective analysis of perceptions and meaning into their component elements of sensation, where today it means the Piagetian exploration of structures as distinct from content.

Although deeply influenced by Darwinian evolution and psychology as a biologically rooted study of adaptive mental functioning, John Dewey began his intellectual career as a philosophic disciple of German Hegelianism. Prior to Darwin, and in the philosophic tradition of idealism (as opposed to the materialistic naturalism of Darwin), Hegel defined transformational stages in the mind of humans, using the material of historical changes in human culture, stages in philosophy, science, art, and religion.

Exposed to the pragmatic philosophies of Charles Peirce and William James, Dewey rejected Hegel's idealism for evolutionary naturalism. This naturalism retained a psychology of ontogenetic stages with some parallel to trends of sociocultural evolution, stages in scientific and moral thinking. Dewey's Hegelian sensitivity to stages within a naturalistic and evolutionary view of child development was shared with his early twentieth-century American colleagues, James

Mark Baldwin and George Herbert Mead. As a group, these theorists, pragmatists in philosophy, have held a psychological theory usually called *symbolic interactionism*. Central to this theory is the idea that mind and self arise through social dialogues, communication, and interaction. Social interaction leads to imitation and "taking the role of the other" in order to define the meaning of the self's own actions. Central particularly to Baldwin's thought was the assumption of developed mental stages as the formation of dualisms: first the real from the unreal, next the internal from the external, next the subjective from the objective. These differentiations came from actions that both assimulated objects and responses (often through play) into habits and accommodated to objects and persons through imitation. Exiled from America, Baldwin moved to Paris where he had weekly lunches with Eduard Claparede, the director of the Jean Jacques Rousseau Institute in Geneva. Claparede chose as his successor a young biologist and psychologist Jean Piaget. Taken up and richly elaborated in empirical studies by Piaget, the American functional-genetic theories of Dewey and Baldwin emigrated to Europe and returned to America when Piaget's work became widely known and accepted in American in the early 1960s. The continued fruitfulness of the theories of Baldwin and Mead as distinct from, though largely compatible with, Piaget's theory is elaborated in Part II, in which we also indicate their parallelism with that of Vygotsky, the Soviet psychologist. Stimulated by Marx's theory as a naturalistic or materialistic reworking of Hegelian stages, Vygotsky developed a cognitive developmental theory stressing the interactive relations between the individual and the social environment quite close to the theories of Dewey and G. H. Mead.

CONTRASTS IN THE RELATION OF THEORY TO PRACTICE

As approaches to educational psychology, even more fundamental differences exist between the Dewey and Thorndike schools than those between cognitive-developmental and associationistic or environmentalist theories. These more fundamental differences lie in assumptions about the nature of educational psychology truth and its relationship to practice. Dewey's claim to truth was that he presented a model of human development that was faithful to the facts of human nature as qualitatively observed. In contrast, Thorndikean psychology has less frequently claimed to show that its model of human nature fits the facts of development as qualitatively observed than that its model of human nature is the only one that can be scientific in its method. It has supported its notion that human nature can be adequately modeled by a system of general quantitative laws of learning less by appeal to quantitative facts explained by these laws than by the notion that no other model of human nature can be "scientific."

With regard to practice, Dewey attempted to show that the model of human development he believed was supported by the facts implied new educational ideals and practices. These educational ideals, in turn, required support by a systematic account of values. In contrast, Thorndikean psychology attempted to relate to practice in a "value-neutral" way, without philosophically constructing or defending a set of educational aims or ideals. Thorndikean scientific laws and facts were intended to be of use to educators, regardless of their aims or values.

The claim of Thorndikean psychology is to be value-neutral, to define methods of instruction and measurement relevant or valid for educational practice without specific prior value assumptions. Following Dewey, we would question the applicability of Thorndikean knowledge of methods of intruction and measurement to educational practice without prior acceptance of the "cultural transmission" of "traditional" educational values that Thorndikean psychology tacitly assumes. Stated slightly differently, Thorndike's value-neutral educational psychology does not use its facts and methods to define new educational ends, but defines its facts relative to the ends of the school as they are. To the extent to which the going aims of schools are to be questioned, so is the usefulness of Thorndikean facts and methods.

The implications of these points for research are significant. Most research on educational practice, on methods of instruction, and on the social psychology of the classroom is research on the schools as they are, with the aims they already have. If the schools require new formulations of aims, they also require new practices. Such new practices cannot be formulated on the basis of research findings on the old practices. The research base for a new kind of educational practice can only be evolved through (1) studying the nature of human development and (2) experimentally establishing new educational practices based on what human development research suggests in the way of new aims or new understandings of development and its formation.

Basic knowledge in human development is the necessary but not sufficient condition for improved educational practice. Following Dewey, we would hold that one cannot have a science of bridge building without building bridges. Dewey says:

> There was, I take it, no definite art or science of modern bridge building until after bridges of the new sort had been constructed. It was impossible that the new art should precede the new achievement. Nevertheless the pioneers had something to go upon and go ahead with, even if they had no specific art of bridge building to rely upon. They had a certain amount of dependable knowledge in mathematics and physics. The difficulty they suffered from was that no one before them had employed this knowledge in building the kind of bridge that new social conditions called for. If earlier mathmaticians and physicists had attempted to anticipate the result of inventive experimentation in bridge building by deducing from their sciences the rules of the new art, it is certain that they would have retarded the day of the new type.

> We take the statement to mean two things. First, research cannot discover important cause-effect relationships in education without engaging in an educational effort to cause a given effect. In this sense research on educational practices must ultimately be research on experimental education. Second, this implies that the educational researcher must have a philosophy and psychology of education which

can lead to a critical commitment to an experimental education worth researching. (1940, pp. 152–154)

Dewey committed himself to experimentally creating new educational practices by founding the University of Chicago Laboratory school. Commitment to starting a new school was based on his belief that the current schools were not addressing developmental aims and methods. The companion volume to this book, *Progress in early education*, considers more recent experimental efforts based on the same vision. The creators of those programs have been developmental psychologists as well as practical educators. In that book, formative educational research is discussed that bridges general developmental psychology research and practice. Developmental levels in educationally meaningful activities from reading to playing with shadows are discussed. A mixture of the study of "natural development", educational experimentation creating new activities meaningful to the child, and a concern for the changing demands of society for outcomes of education underlies this work.

In focusing on the historical originators of two strains of educational psychology, we have ignored many of the major figures in both developmental psychology and education from Freud to Bruner. We are pointing to a continuing tension as to the underlying assumptions of contemporary developmental and educational psychology and of the historical roots of our own position, the educational philosophy of John Dewey, elaborated in Chapter 3. The next chapter outlines what we believe to be the core contribution of Jean Piaget to developmental and educational psychology. But Piaget's work and the more recent research we discuss in this volume still needs to be seen in light of Dewey's vision.

In this vision, Dewey notes:

> . . . nutrition and reproduction are to physiological life, what education is to social life. This education consists primarily in transmission through communication. Communication is a process of sharing experience till it becomes a common possession. It modifies the disposition of both the parties who partake in it. That the ulterior significance of every mode of human association lies in the contribution which it makes to the improvement of the quality of experience is a fact most easily recognized in dealing with the immature. That is to say, while every social arrangement is educative in effect, the educative effect first becomes an important part of the purpose of the association in connection with the association of the older with the younger. As societies become more complex in structure and resources, the need of formal or intentional teaching and learning increases. As formal teaching and training grow in extent, there is the danger of creating an undesirable split between the experience gained in more direct associations and what is acquired in school. This danger was never greater than at the present time, on account of the rapid growth in the last few centuries of knowledge and technical modes of skill. (1916, p. 9)

The gap between "natural" experience and communication and formal learning and teaching is even greater today than when Dewey wrote his classic *Democracy and education.* It is the need to bridge this gap that is the center of Part I. In the next chapter we present the way in which Piaget's theory of children as philosophers constructing their world through stages can help close the gap between the "naturally" developing and the needs of formal teaching, and how the ability of educators to hear and communicate with the child require attention to the child's stage.

REFERENCES

Baldwin, J. M. (1906). *Social and ethical intepretations in mental development* (4th ed.). New York: Macmillan.

Dewey, J. (1916). *Democracy and education.* New York: Macmillan.

Dewey, J. (1940). In J. Ratner (Ed.), *Education today.* New York: Putnam.

James, W. (1890). *The principles of psychology.* New York: Holt.

James, W. (1958). *Talks to teachers on psychology, and to students on life's ideals.* New York: Norton.

Chapter 2

The Young Child as a Philosopher

Lawrence Kohlberg

The spirit is never at rest but always engaged in every progressing motion, in giving itself a new form. The gradualness of the merely quantitative progression becomes a qualitative leap as the spirit that educates itself matures slowly and quietly toward the new form, dissolving one particle of the edifice of its previous world after the other. This gradual crumbling which did not alter the physiognomy of the whole is interrupted by the break of day that, like lightening, all at once reveals the edifice of the new world.

—Hegel, Preface to the *Phenomenology*

Behold the child among his blisses. . . .
See, at his feet, some little plan or chart,
Some fragment from his dream of human life,
Shaped by himself with newly-learned art;
   A wedding or a festival,
   A mourning or a funeral;
   And this hath now his heart,
And unto this he frames his song:
   Then will he fit his tongue
To dialogues of business love or strife;
   But it will not be long
   Ere this be thrown aside,
   And with new joy and pride
The little Actor plays another part;
Filling from time to time his "humorous stage"
With all the Persons down to palsied Age,
That Life brings with her in her equipage;
   As if his whole vocation
   Were endless imitation.

Thou whose exterior semblance doth belie
    Thy Soul's immensity;
Thou best Philosopher, who yet does keep
Thy heritage, thou Eye among the blind,
That, deaf and silent, read'st the eternal deep,
Haunted forever by the eternal mind. . . .
The thought of our past years in me doth breed
Perpetual benediction: not indeed
For that which is most worthy to be blest;
Delight and liberty, the simple creed of Childhood. . . .
    Not for these I raise
    The song of thanks and praise;
    But for those obstinate questionings
    Of sense and outward things,
    Falling from us, vanishing,
    Blank misgivings of a Creature
    Moving about in worlds not realized. . . .
                —Wordsworth, *Ode. Intimations of Immortality*

The center of this book is the effort to see the world from the child's point of view, and to formalize this effort through the cognitive-development theory of Piaget, his predecessors, and his followers. Basic to the revolution of child psychology produced by Piaget were his interlocked assumptions or insights that the child was a philosopher and that the child's philosophy went through stages. Freud found that, just like grown-ups, children were interested in birth and death and sex. But Piaget found that children were largely interested in birth and death and sex because they were bothered by the origins of things, by what is space and time and causality and reality and good and evil, by all the things that are the concerns of the grown-ups called philosophers. To be a philosopher is to be concerned about the basic terms or categories of experience, and this is just what young children are interested in. To go through stages is to have qualitative transformations in world view or philosophy. I say that Piaget discovered the child as a philosopher and observed qualitative stages in the child's world view, but the discovery was really far earlier than Piaget.

The two quotations that open this chapter are the manifesto of the early nineteenth-century "romantic" discovery of the child's mind and of stages in human development. Hegel first saw parallel stages in the development of cultural ideas or philosophies and in the child's development, viewing both child and culture as engaged in constructing philosophies. Stages, as the quotation from Hegel suggests, are self-constructions of the mind, new forms which dissolve old forms and which lead to the perception of new worlds. Wordsworth expresses the romantic vision of the dual nature of the child as constructor, artist and philosopher. First Wordsworth's child is player, artist, dreamer, whose creed is "delight and liberty." The child's apparent "vocation" of "endless imitation," of learning his culture and its role, is really the playful and spontaneous enactment of roles "shaped . . . with newly learned art" representing "fragments from his dream of human life." If the more obvious side of the child's mind is that of imaginative player, artist, dramatist, its deeper side is that of a "Philosopher," "haunted forever by the eternal mind," full of "obstinate questionings of sense and outward things, fallings from us, vanishings."

THE CHILD AS PHILOSOPHER: THE IDEA OF CONSTANCY

Let us try to illustrate the dual nature of the child as player and philosopher by considering the child's dealings with constancy and change; the "fallings" and "vanishings" and "obstinate questionings of sense and outward things," which Piaget has studied.

Piaget saw that very young children's excitement at a game of peek-a-boo or hiding was due to interest in What is reality?—the problem of differentiating appearance and reality. Children love peek-a-boo because they are differentiating subjective and objective; because they are constructing a world of permanent, unchanging objects. Infants under ten months do not have a conception of a permanent object. If, when they are reaching toward a bright toy, it is covered with a handkerchief, they stop reaching; the toy no longer exists for them. By eighteen months they know objects permanently exist although they cannot always see them, but it is not until they are about 6 years old that they view the physical nature and identity of an object as unchangeable. Things that change in appearance change in reality.

It is part of the charm of young childhood that objects can change their identity and that young children can play at being, and feel they really are, a variety of persons and creatures. Sometimes this fluidity in the identity of things is a source of anxiety, sometimes a delight. One Halloween, we bought my boy, just turned 3, a dog costume. We put it on him in front of the mirror and he said, "I'm a doggie," and laughed delightedly. I asked him, "Are you a doggie or are you really a boy?" "I'm a doggie, real doggie," and he ran to the kitchen, took a dog biscuit, and half-pretended, half-tried, to eat it. To say the child is a philosopher is to say children are interested in the basic terms or categories of experience; to say the child *develops* as a philosopher is to say that children's original basic terms are different from our own. We are forced to reflect that we are philosophers, too, that our conceptions of reality, truth, and goodness are basic to understanding our own minds.

We have used as an example of basic terms the category of substance, constancy, or identity. We have used the concept of constancy as a category because it is present in a new form at each new general era of thought (defined in Table 2.1). The major cognitive constancies or invariances of the adult's world develop

TABLE 2.1
Piaget's Eras and Stages of Logical and Cognitive Development

---

Era I (Age 0–2)—The Era of Sensorimotor Intelligence

Stage 1—Reflex action
Stage 2—Coordination of reflexes and sensorimotor repetition (primary circular reaction)
Stage 3—Activities to make interesting events in the environment reappear (secondary circular reaction)
Stage 4—Means/ends behavior and search for absent objects
Stage 5—Experimental search for new means (tertiary circular reaction)
Stage 6—Use of imagery in insightful invention of new means and in recall of absent objects and events.

Era II (Age 2–5) Symbolic, Intuitive, or Prelogical Thought

Inference is carried on through images and symbols that do not maintain logical relations or invariances with one another. "Magical thinking" is the sense of (a) confusion of apparent or imagined events with real events and objects and (b) confusion of perceptual appearances of qualitative and quantitative change with actual change.

Era III (Age 6–10) Concrete Operational Thought

Inferences carried on through system of classes, relations, and quantities maintaining logically invariant properties and which *refer to concrete objects*. These include such logical processes as (a) inclusion of lower-order classes in higher-order classes; (b) transitive seriation (recognition that if $a > b$ and $b > c$, then $a > c$); (c) logical addition and multiplication of classes and quantities; (d) conservation of number, class membership, length and mass under apparent change.
Substage 1—Formation of stable categorical classes
Substage 2—Formation of quantitative and numerical relations of invariance.

Era IV (Age 11 to Adulthood) Formal-Operational Thought

Inferences through logical operations upon propositions or "operations upon operations." Reasoning about reasoning. Construction of systems of all possible relations or implications. Hypothetico-deductive isolation of variables and testing of hypotheses.
Substage 1—Formation of the inverse of the reciprocal. Capacity to form negative classes (e.g., the class of all not-crows) and to see relations as simultaneously reciprocal (e.g., to understand that liquid in a U-shaped tube holds an equal level because of counterbalanced pressures).
Substage 2—Capacity to order triads of propositions or relations (*Ex.:* Understand that if Bob is taller than Joe and Joe is shorter than Dick, then Joe is the shortest of the three).
Substage 3—True formal thought. Construction of all possible combinations of relations, systematic isolation of variables, and deductive hypothesis-testing.

---

through three levels: the sensorimotor, the intuitive-concrete, and the formal-abstract levels. At the end of the sensorimotor period the child has mastered the constancy of objects in place and time. The child has not, however, established which attributes of an object can change and which cannot. The child at the intuitive-concrete level, like my son, has not mastered all the basic invariances. These are established at around age 6 or 7, when the child is capable of reasoning with concrete operations, that is, logical operations of addition, subtraction, inclusion, reciprocity, and so forth. At the formal-operational level, the invariances established are those of underlying physical laws. Through hypothetico-deductive reason, the adolescent child can grasp the invariance of lawful variance. When left with a pendulum and asked what determines its period, adolescents can discover the invariant relations of the period of the pendulum to the length of the string and realize the irrelevance of all other variance. They do so because they are now capable of hypothetico-deductive reasoning and systematic experimentation to test hypotheses.

FANTASY AS PLAYFUL THOUGHT IN CHILDHOOD

Many are not used to thinking of the child as a philosopher or as establishing constancies and other categories of experience. Instead, they hear these things as "fantasy," the expression of the child's desires and wishes uncontrolled by outer reality.

Although the cognitive-developmental view of children does not deny their "fantasy," it interprets it differently. "Fantasy" is play and children move easily from play to sober attitudes toward objects. Their play attitude, however, is not ignoring of reality, it is not "primary process," nor is it primarily motivated by untamed drives of sex and aggression. Rather, children's play, like their "work" attitudes toward the world, is directed toward mastering reality. The play of the child is, of course, not the sober pondering of the adult philosopher, it is not "pure reason." Here we need to note that whether children are playful, sober, or fearful, their basic level of orientation to reality and its categories is maintained, and that even in play they are dealing with reality.

When my son pretended to eat the dog biscuit it was not because of any oral need; rather, it was his effort to master the reality-appearance distinction through a playful attitude. Children's playful attitudes, like their more serious attitudes, reflect their general way of thinking, their conception of reality. To illustrate this point, I shall discuss a study with an element of play as well as seriousness in it. A doctoral study by Rheta DeVries (1969) that I supervised started from the observations of the young child's sense of the constancy of identity, which I have just described in terms of reactions to a Halloween costume. Because children vary too much in their reactions to people in costumes and masks, we chose another situation for systematic study of children's constancy reactions. Instead of putting a mask on a human, we put a mask of a small, fierce dog on a live and well-trained cat named Maynard. In response to this masking of the cat, children of 3 and 4, when asked what the animal is, tend to say it is now a dog and feed it dog food when given a choice. Children of 6 tend to be firmly aware of what is going on, as do many of the 5-year-olds.

Of most interest are the reactions of the 5-year-olds who can't make up their minds as to what is going on. For example, Janice pets the cat with warmth before the mask is put on. She withdraws sharply after the mask is put on, but looks closely at the animal. When asked, she says the animal is a dog, but adds, "If I put my finger near his mouth, he really won't bite me, will he?" She doesn't try the experiment. When pressed, she says the cat turned into a dog, but when pressed further, says it's not a real dog; it just has on a dog face. Finally, she agrees to pet it and does so very gingerly. Again, she is asked whether it is a real dog, and she answers, "That's the problem, is it a cat or a dog? I think it's a dog. I'll feel his ears. It is a dog...but still it has cat's eyes so how can it be a dog? I think it's a dog."

Janice has a true scientific open-minded and exploratory attitude toward the animal's identity, soon to be discarded for a closed-minded view that cats are cats and dogs are dogs and cats can't be dogs, no matter what.

Why did Rheta DeVries do the study? To show that children really thought differently than adults. The critics of Piaget argue that Piaget asks children silly questions and gets silly answers. As elaborated by psychoanalytic critics, the theory is that what children say to Piaget is not due to a different logic or reality orientation but rather to their giving fantasy responses to unreal or abstract questions. However, we found that children's behavior and emotion in this situation were consistent with what they said. Only these children who said, "He is a real dog," refused to pet the animal and were generally fearful. The children's fear in this situation, like my son's play with the dog biscuit, reflected their level of thinking about realities, not their deeper fears or fantasies.

CHILDREN THINK FOR THEMSELVES; THEIR BASIC IDEAS DO NOT COME DIRECTLY FROM TEACHING

To say children are philosophers is to say that they think for themselves. The basic ideas of children do not come directly from adults or other children and will be maintained in spite of adult teaching. A classroom example will illustrate this.

A potted cactus stood before the class and the children were asked to discuss whether it was a plant or an animal and how they could tell. Eventually all of the children but one agreed it was a plant and that plants didn't move, didn't ingest food, and so on. This one boy held out and said he still thought it was an animal disguised as a plant. "One could never tell, however," he said, "because every time the animal saw someone coming it would instantly turn back into a plant." He had the teacher and class buffaloed; in this case, it wasn't an experiment that had caused him to believe things could change identity, the idea was his own. And this idea is quite resistant to efforts to impose adult cultural realities upon the child.

Teachers have little trouble accepting the notion that children are thinking for themselves when they make mistakes or when they are saying "fantastical" things. They have more trouble recognizing that children are thinking for themselves when they think correctly or give the right answer. The teacher likes to believe that the child has the right answer because the teacher taught it to him or her. But basic right answers are as much created by children as the wrong ones are. As an example, I'll use some findings on another reality task, the dream. Following Piaget, I asked children if they had ever had a bad dream and if they were frightened when they woke up from their bad dream. Susie, aged 4, told us she dreamed about a giant and answered, "Yes, I was scared, my tummy was shaking and I cried and told my mommy about the giant." Then I asked, "Was it a real giant or was it just pretend? Did the giant just seem to be there or was it really there?" "It was really there, but it left when I woke up. I saw its footprint on the floor."

According to Piaget, Susie's response is not to be dismissed as the product of a wild imagination but represents the young child's general failure to differentiate subjective from objective components of experience. It is easy to see that Susie's thinking about the dream is her own, not something taught by adults. It is harder to see that the more realistic thought of the older child about the dream is also not taught. A realistic concept of the dream, however, reflects a stage, a developing cognitive structure, just as does the unrealistic thinking of the child. Table 2.2 specifies the actual steps or stages of development found in children's beliefs about dreams. The first step, achieved before 5 by most American middle-class children, is the recognition that dreams are not real events. The next step, achieved soon thereafter, is that dreams cannot be seen by others. By age 6 children are clearly aware that dreams take place inside them, and by 7 they are clearly aware that dreams are thoughts caused by themselves.

The steps we have mentioned form an invariant order or sequence in development. If there is an invariant order in development, children who have passed a more difficult step in the sequence should also have passed all the easier steps in the sequence and get pluses (on the table) on all the easier items. For instance, all children who pass on Step 3, recognizing the dream's internal origin, should also pass Step 2 and Step 1. The fact that only 18 out of 105 children we studied did not fit one of these patterns is acceptable evidence for the existence of invariant sequence in the development of the dream concept. The stepwise development of the dream concept does not in itself indicate that the later stages are not the result of teaching from adults or from the culture. To document this fact I had to go to a culture where dreams were believed by adults to be real or external. While studying moral development among the Atayal, a Malaysian aboriginal group in Taiwan, I found that like many preliterate tribes the Atayal believed in the reality of dreams. An example is provided by an informal interview I had with the 70-year-old village medicine woman. I went to her because I had a bad cold and asked her to treat me. In the course of her diagnostic interviewing, I told her I had dreamed of a snake the

TABLE 2.2
Sequence in Development of Dream Concept in American and Atayal Children

Step	Scale Pattern Types						
	0	1	2	3	4	5	6
1. *Not Real*—Recognize that objects or actions in the dream are not real or are not really there in the room.	−	+	+	+	+	+	+
2. *Invisible*—Recognize that other people cannot see their dreams.	−	−	+	+	+	+	+
3. *Internal Origin*–Recognize that the dream *comes from* inside them.	−	−	−	+	+	+	+
4. *Internal Location*—Recognize that the dream *goes on* inside them.	−	−	−	−	+	+	+
5. *Immaterial*—Recognize that the dream is not a material substance but is a thought.	−	−	−	−	−	+	+
6. *Self-caused*—Reconize that dreams are not caused by God or other agencies but are caused by the self's thought processes.	−	−	−	−	−	−	+
Median age of American children in given pattern or stage (Range = 4 to 8)	4,6	4,10	5,0	5,4	6,4	6,5	7,10
Median age of Atayal of given pattern. (Range = 7 to 18)	8	8	10	16	12	11	

Number of American children fitting scale types = 72; not fitting = 18.
Number of Atayal children fitting scale types = 12; not fitting = 3.

night before. She told me, "Maybe you're sick because of what you dreamed last night and the snake made you sick." I asked, "Was it a real snake?" "No, it was a ghost using a snake's form—if you do some bad thing in the daytime the ghosts punish you at night—your body stayed in bed but your soul went to the mountains with the ghost."

The medicine woman, like most adult Atayal I talked to, equated the soul, the dream, and ghosts. Dreams, like ghosts, are neither thoughts nor things, dreams are caused by ghosts and during the dream the soul left the body and experienced things in far places.

Until the age of 11, the Atayal boys seem to develop toward a subjective conception of the dream through much the same steps as American children, though more slowly. In other words, the Atayal children tended to develop naturally toward a subjective concept of the dream up to age 11 even though their elders hold a system of religious belief that makes them think dreams are not subjective. This surely indicates that the children's discovery of the subjective nature of the dream is their own and not determined by what is taught.

THE CHILD AS A MORAL PHILOSOPHER

Most early educators don't altogether reject Piaget's cognitive stages, but they do find them limited. They speak to the child's logic and conceptions of the physical world, but they do not seem to speak to the child's social and emotional world. The position taken here is that the basic stage logic of Piaget can be applied to the child's social and emotional development. The position holds that there are *parallel* features or stages of cognitive and social development. Social and moral development is more than cognitive development; social development has a more complicated logic, but it is one that includes the logic of concepts of the physical world. The most compelling social stages that have their own logic are moral stages. The reason the most compelling social stages are moral is that the child is not only a philosopher about the physical world but a moral philosopher concerned about the categories of good and evil. To indicate what this means, let me briefly go over the four stages of moral thinking we have found in childhood. I'll begin with an example from one of my sons at age 5, which illustrates Stage 1 in morality. It also illustrates that children generate their own morality in spite of all the efforts of fond parents.

At the age of 5 my son joined the pacifist and vegetarian movement and refused to eat meat because (he said) it's bad to kill animals. In spite of his parents' attempts to dissuade him by arguing about the difference between justified and unjustified killing, he remained a vegetarian for six months. However, like most Doves, he did recognize that some forms of killing were "legitimate." One night I read to him from a book about Eskimo life which included a description of a seal-killing expedition. While listening to the story he became very angry and said, "You know, there is one kind of meat I would eat, Eskimo meat. It's bad to kill animals, so it's all right to eat them."

Now first I want to point out that although he was Stage 1, it was still Stage 1 *morality*. Basic to morality is a concern for the life of others, not because such concern is taught but because of an immediate empathic response. Children's concern for animal's lives is not taught. I quoted earlier my other son saying, "I really am a doggie"; such self-projection naturally leads to empathy. Pain at death is a natural empathic response, though it is not necessarily universally and consistently maintained. In this example, the value of life led both to vegetarianism and to the desire to kill Eskimos. This latter desire comes also from a universal value tendency, a belief in justice or reciprocity (here expressed in terms of revenge or punishment—an eye for an eye, a tooth for a tooth—at higher levels, the belief that those who infringe upon the rights of others cannot expect their own rights to be respected). Empathy and justice, then, are the basis of morality; each higher stage is a new stage in the sense of empathy and justice. Because it reflects this sense of value and of justice, Stage 1 is clearly already a moral stage. Piaget called Stage 1 the stage of heteronomous obedience to adults and rules. Though it does typically have this emphasis on obedience and punishment, it is still the child's own moral construction. Preschool children we talk to are often at an earlier, more egocentric stage in their thinking about good and bad. This earlier stage we call "Stage 0." At this stage, good is what I like and bad is what I don't like. Children at this stage are uncertain about how "good" as it is labeled by others is "good." For them good is what they like themselves, what is pleasurable and exciting. At Stage 0, one of my sons said, "I'm rough and when I'm big I'll shoot. We can be bad guys, robbers—they shoot. Or we can be nice guys, the nice guys shoot the bad guys." At Stage 0, the difference between "good guys" and "bad guys" is that "good guys" are more powerful and win, not that they act differently. Stage 0, then, is egocentric.

At Stage 1, labels of good and bad dominate what I like, "Killing is bad," "Good" and "bad" are qualities "out there." Things are just good and bad. There is a sense of justice as eye-for-eye, tooth-for-tooth reciprocity; good acts should be rewarded and the bad punished. The basis of rules and punishment is the power of authorities. Stage 1, then, is the stage of labeling, punishment, and obedience. At Stage 2 (around age 7 or 8) good is instrumental, it's what achieves a purpose or serves the interests of the self or others close to the self. Something is good for me but it may not be good for you. The good is relative; what's good for me may not be the same for you. Accordingly, when what is good differs for each, let's swap, let's trade, let's make a deal. Fairness or reciprocity is exchange to the advantage of each. We call this Stage 2 morality a morality of instrumental relativism and exchange. Piaget called it the morality of cooperation, which makes it sound a little loftier than it is, though cooperation does involve a Stage 2 sense of purpose and exchange. Following a developmental timetable, my son moved to this instrumentally relativist Stage 2 orientation when he was 7, a stage sometimes expressed in a very expedient view toward morality. At that time he told me, "You know, the reason people don't steal is because they're afraid of the police. If there were no police around, everyone would steal." I told him that I (and most people) didn't steal because we thought it wrong, because we wouldn't want other people to take things from us, and so on. My son's reply was, "I just don't see it, it's sort of crazy not to steal if there are no police." Of course I said all the right things, all the reasons I didn't steal even when the police weren't around, but he just thought I was a sucker. Luckily he moved on to the next stage, Stage 3, the "be nice," "be concerned about other people" stage at age 9. The core of Stage 3 is the ability to put yourself in the other person's place and see things from the other's point of view. At Stage 2 my son could see stealing from the point of view of other expedient people like himself but couldn't put himself in the place of the victimized property-holder. Now at Stage 3, fairness is the Golden Rule. When I asked my son, now Stage 3, "Is it more important to be nice, or to be smart?" he said, "To be nice, because if you're selfish, you won't be happy—if you're a pig, other people won't be nice to you." Here he generalizes the instrumental reciprocity of Stage 2 to a kind of social contract requiring altruism by putting himself in the place of others and thinking of why he is nice to others and they to him.

Now I want to show why a parent or educator really has to be a moral philosopher. At age 9, one of my sons still hadn't given up his concern for animals, and he told me it's just as nice to risk your life to save an animal as a person. I said, "But animals aren't worth as much as people." And he replied, "You think that just because you're selfish, you're a person. The animal doesn't think that, the animal thinks he's worth as much. You're selfish, you're a person, so you like people better but the animals don't think so." Now, how do you argue with that? You really have to be a philosopher. But if you are, you may decide he's right. If you're not, at some point you'll break down as I did and invoke Stage 4 law, order, and parental authority.

MORAL DEVELOPMENT AND COGNITIVE GROWTH

I said at the beginning of this section that moral and social development is more than cognitive development but depends upon it. The child at Stage 0 in morality is also prelogical or preoperational. At 4, my son was Stage 0 in morality; when he did something bad and was told it was bad, he answered, "You're bad, not me." This "defensive" statement had a Stage 0 moral logic behind it; if you do something the child doesn't like, for example, calling him bad, then you are bad because you "hurt" him. (At Stage 1 he would recognize that if he were bad, it is not bad to punish him or call him bad; he has an eye-for-eye, tooth-for-tooth sense of justice.) At the same time that he was Stage 0 in moral judgment, he was also "prelogical" on Piaget's stages. For example, he went on to say, "When I get big and you get small, I'll call you bad and spank you." His thinking was based on a prelogical notion that an adult's size can't be maintained; as he gets big, we get small. While moral stages parallel cognitive stages, a given cognitive step always precedes the parallel moral step. Moral thinking requires more than the logic of objects; it involves the more subtle and complex logic of subjects, or other people's viewpoints and claims. For this reason, moral and social development and education depend upon cognitive development and education but also require much more in the way of distinctively social, not cognitive, experience.

THE EGO STAGES

In addition to distinct strands of development like the cognitive and the moral, intuition tells us that there is a unity of the personality that ties all experience together called the ego, or self. Somehow the self is, and develops as, a whole; it does not just develop as a cognitive function and stage, a moral function and stage, and so on. The unitary self or ego is basically adaptive and oriented to the outside world, seeks for truth about the world, and is more or less aware of itself. In psychoanalytic theory, the developing and adaptive ego is more or less the cognitive ego. It is not the principle of moral or sexual development; it is somewhat at war with its irrational superego morality and its sexual id. In contrast, we would stress the unity of cognitive, moral, and psychosexual strands of development. This unity is integrated around a conception of the self in relation to others. In part the notion of ego development, then, represents the tendency of the child to be at closely parallel levels in cognitive and moral development; it represents the objective unity of development. In part, however, ego stages represent something more than cognitive and moral development; they represent conceptions of the self in relation to physical and social reality.

Different but related theoretical frameworks for defining ego development in these terms have been proposed by many: Erikson (1950), Fromm (1947), Sullivan (1953), Loevinger (1976), van den Daele (1968) and Kegan (1982). Regardless of differences in conception of ego stages, however, there is a fairly good correlation between measures of ego maturity based on the different schemes (Sullivan, McCullough, & Stager, 1964; van den Daele, 1968). As Loevinger has pointed out, all measures of ego development will correlate regardless of theory because all ego development schemes are based upon certain large regularities in the age-development of the self and of social attitudes, regardless of the theoretically proposed causes of these developments.

While there is broad agreement theoretically and empirically upon levels of ego development, there has been no clear, acceptable refined definition of ego stages. This is for two reasons. First, because ego stages, unlike cognitive and moral stages, are not defined by what the child thinks or puts into words directly; they are defined as the varying states of the self lying behind use of words and ideas. Insofar as theorists have different conceptions of the self or ego, then, they will come up with somewhat different definitions of ego stages. The second cause of disagreement is different assumptions about the relation of ego stages to cognitive and moral stages. Empirically, a good relation has been found between cognitive level and various measures of ego level, and between ego level measures and moral judgment level (Sullivan, McCullough, & Stager, 1964; van den Daele, 1968). Accordingly, it is difficult to know which aspects of development to include in defining ego stages and which to define separately as cognitive or moral development as opposed to ego development. In our view, ego stages would be something more than cognitive stages but would depend upon them. Indeed, the evidence available using various ego stage schemes suggests that a Piagetian cognitive stage is a necessary but not sufficient condition for attainment of the parallel ego stage. All children at a given ego stage must have attained the parallel cognitive stage, but not all children at a cognitive stage will have organized their self-concept and experience at the corresponding ego stage.

To clarify the relation of cognitive stage to ego stage, it is helpful to think of cognitive stages as logical stages and ego stages as stages in orientations to reality, physical and social. This is a "structural" conception of ego development. We have already described the child's orientation to reality as part of his or her cognitive stage. However, the core of cognitive stages is logic and the relations of causality, space, and time. It is a somewhat distinct problem for the child as a philosopher to ponder how his or her self or the mind is related to the external world and to other selves, that is, to physical and social "reality." Piaget's earliest and strongest view of the child as a philosopher was expressed in his early book "The Child's Conception of Reality"; his later work takes up the development of the child, not as a philosopher, but as a logician and scientist concerned with explaining physical experience. The adult philosopher ponders, What is reality, what is mind or self and what is the relationship between them? Piaget's early work explored children's answers to these questions, not directly given by their logic. Logical operations make possible certain distinctions of subjective and objective in the child's conception of reality, but they do not directly give rise to them. These growing distinctions between the subjective and objective, in turn, redefine the self as well as the outer world. The self is a composite of thoughts and feelings in a body. In part, developmental redefinitions of the self depend upon changing ideas of the relation of thoughts and feelings to the body and to the outside world. Considered in terms of the development of concepts of mind and self in relation to reality, ego stages represent a series of differentiations of the subjective (mind and self) from the objective (the material and sensational-empirical) with correspondingly better integrations of the relations of the self to nonsubjective reality. To some extent, these epistemological stages redefine the child's knowing, feeling, and moral judgment. For example, at an early stage, children confuse their wishes with what is right and good, part of a wider confusion of inner fantasy and outer reality. At a later stage, they confuse the "moral ought" with the moral beliefs and rules held by their society, part of a general epistemological confusion of the validly true or good with what the group believes in. At a still later stage, in adolescence, the morally ideal is distinguished from social reality, and ideal truth is distinguished from what others believe or from factual knowledge itself.

The first distinction the child makes is between "real" and unreal "events." In the case of the child's conception of the dream, we saw that the first aspect of the subjectivity of the dream discovered is that it's not "real." The real is what can be touched and handled, what is forceful and lasts over time.

At this early point in development, the real is more or less equated with what is outside. What is real is outside my body, what is not real is inside my body. The child first understands dreams to be unreal and soon thereafter thinks of them as physical but unreal events inside the body. When the child equates the real with the outside, the real is something outside and immediate, not something thought about or felt. The self is the body itself, and what the body does. At around age 6–7 children reorganize their experiences around the distinction between the mind (or mental) and the body (or physical). Heretofore, mind is treated as bodily activity (thinking, talking), or as something inside of but part of the body. This new clear distinction of two separate entities in each person, the mental and the physical, gives rise to many important changes in children's relation to reality, to the values they attach to themselves and to other people. In regard to reality, the child now has a "mind"; to relate to reality requires thinking, being smart; it requires mental

TABLE 2.3
Levels of Natural Philosophy across Four Major Categories

Level	Self—World	Mental—Material	Reality—Appearance	Knower—Known
1. Objective (age 4–7)	*Presumptive:* Self-evident, bodily self. Not differentiated from reflexive "itself."	*Adualist:* Gross head/body distinction. Visible and invisible not differentiated. Mind and body mutually permeable.	*Objective:* Reality presumed. Simple and immediate existence of external things. Real undifferentiated from nonartificial. Reality confounded with life.	*Dogmatic:* Thought and its objects undifferentiated. Direct, automatic knowing. Single extrinsic truth, known and handed down by authority.
2. Individual (age 8–12)	*Individual:* Self is specific person, me or you. Perceiving, acting person. Source or agent.	*Organic:* Mind differentiated from body as brainlike organ controlling rest of body. Discrete, nonvisible mental contents.	*Naive realist:* Certainty of reality directly sensed. Appearance is the way something "looks" and this is reality. Real differentiated from imaginary as persistent.	*Empirical:* Thought/object differentiation. Experience directly caused by object. Truth is absolute fact, is opposed to lie, and is individually apprehended and asserted.

3. Divided (age 12+)	*Divided:* Self is mind (mental self) more than body (physical self). Unique subjective traits, opinions, beliefs, or values. Authentic inner self differentiated from false outer appearance (social personality or role self).	*Immature dualist:* Abstract mental differentiated from concrete physical as a fluid and invisible medium. Mental and physical as overlapping classes.	*Realist:* Appearance generally realistic, but mind may add personal distortion (opinion or value). Mental is belief rather than reality.	*Social:* Concrete facts known by individuals. Truth as interpersonal demonstration and plausibility (overlap). Nascent skepticism.
4. Dualist (age 18+)	*Substantial:* Self as system: soul, intellect, logic, identity, or "cogito" (self-control). Self has mental and physical attributes. Self-concept, or "me," rather than "I." Generalized self or perspective.	*Cartesian:* Dualism between objective mechanistic system of scientific cause/effect, and subjective or spiritual world of belief, purpose, and reason. Unconscious differentiated from conscious.	*Dualist:* Reality assumed. Noumenon differentiated from phenomenon. Substantial reality is lawlike system generating appearances (data).	*Postivist:* Knowledge is inductive generalization of observation-constructive copy of world. Truth, which subordinates reality, is replicable and is achieved through social-conventional testing of models. Impartial "generalized other" defines objective standpoint.

activity. Values are not simply "out there" in objects, they are related to the child's mind, that is, the child's use and enjoyment of them. The child now sees his or her "self" as both a body and a mind, with some sense that the mind controls the body and bodily emotions. Thus children are led to differentiate will and self-control from physical power and coercion.

The next reorganization of reality, typically taken in adolescence, views both the mental and the physical as possible objects of thought and experience and draws the distinction between what is subjective and what is objective. This leads to the notion of "the transcendental self," a self as knower or experiencer distinct from anything it knows. This "transcendental self" can question everything it knows and believes, it it not bound by its "empirical self" of ideas, beliefs, and purposes.

Though the transcendental self may be the most real thing to the adolescent, this new differentiation of the subjective or transcendental self from the empirical self of body, mind, and role raises the puzzle or crisis of identity described by Erikson (1964). The transcendental self must choose which of many possible selves it is to be. In the dawning adolescent differentiation of the subjective and objective we have stressed the possibility of subjectivizing everything. To establish a balanced relation between subjective and objective requires a new distinction, that between the rational and the irrational. At this point of ego maturity, universal and rational principled ethics are differentiated from the "subjective" or culturally relative; arbitrary, universal, and rational scientific method is differentiated from arbitrary, subjective, and changing knowledge; and the self as rational decision-maker is differentiated from the emotional, uncertain self paralyzed by freedom. The self is no longer seen as unique but as striving for and attaining social universality in values, truth, and aesthetic experience. This differentiation defines the final clear-cut stage of ego development, the sense of a self committed to rationality, rational morality, and social creativity.

In describing the development of ideas of the mind and self, we have drawn on the empirical work of Broughton (1982), inspired by J. M. Baldwin's (1906) theory of genetic epistemology. Broughton's levels are summarized in Table 2.3.

IN WHAT SENSE ARE STAGES TRUE?

Let us summarize what has been said about the child as a philosopher in terms of the existence of cognitive and moral stages. What do I mean by the existence of cognitive stages? In most sophisticated discussion of stages, they are viewed as more or less useful theoretical fictions. We have stages described by Freud, by Erikson, by Gesell, and by Piaget. All these stages may be more or less useful abstractions from developmental process; they certainly cannot all be true or real, and perhaps it is useless to expect any to be. Flying in the face of such logical sophistication, I and others have engaged in research designed to show that stages are real structures to be found in development.

The conceptual and empirical criteria for structural stages include

1. Qualitative change in form of response
2. Invariant forward sequence in development except under extreme conditions
3. Each stage integrates the stage before it and logically requires the elements of the prior stage
4. Each stage forms a logically and empirically consistent "structured whole"

I stress that Piaget's cognitive stages can be said to "exist" because they meet these criteria reasonably well. Because Piaget's stages exist, they offer a definite guide to the educator. Freud's stages, Erikson's stages, and Gesell's stages capture important aspects of the child's development, but they do not exist in the same sense as Piaget's stages. Children cannot be directly observed in every culture going through an invariant sequence of consistently organized responses when observations are organized in terms of Freud's, Gesell's, or Erikson's stages. In part, this is because these other stages are theoretical; they derive from hypothetical constructs which cannot be directly observed. In the case of maturational stages like those of Gesell and Freud, the underlying theoretical construct is a neurophysiological structure which matures. The actual behavior of the stage derives from the actuation of this hypothetical physiological structure. In addition to physiological structures, unobservable and unconscious psychological tendencies and motives are typically assumed to underly other stages.

In contrast, cognitive and moral stages are defined independently of any particular psychological or physiological theory. One can accept Piaget's cognitive development. Structural stages *are* what they refer to, patterns of thought revealed in what the child says and does, they do not need to "diagnosed." Obviously, certain assumptions must be made to observe structural stages, primarily the assumption that there is a pattern or consistency to what the child thinks, that it has a *logic*, though not our adult logic. The description of the logic of the child's mind, however, does not depend upon espousal of a particular psychological theory or of any hypothetical constructs. The task of the definer of stages is like that of the literary critic or humanist trying to analyze the pattern of ideas involved in the work of Aristotle or Shakespeare. The child psychologist's interviews are the humanist's texts. The test of accuracy of interpretation is that, if it is claimed that certain ideas are related in certain ways in the text, this relationship makes sense in other places in the text or in the text as a whole. Acceptance of a humanistic analysis of the structure of Aristotle's thought does not depend upon acceptance of a theory of the psychology of Aristotle's personality. Acceptance of a structural analysis of the child's stage also does not imply a commitment to a theory of the child's personality.

Of course there is a step of generalization made by the stage psychologist not made by the literary critic. The critic analyzes the pattern of one person's mind, the stage psychologist analyzes the pattern common to *all* children at a certain level of development. To make this generalization the stage psychologist must distinguish between culturally or individually variable *content* of the child's thought and the reasoning pattern or *structure* of the child's thought. For example, in responding to a moral dilemma about whether a husband should steal a drug to save his wife, Taiwanese children at a certain level (Stage 2) typically say that he should steal the drug because if his wife died, it would cost a lot of money for her funeral. American children at this level never mention this specific *content*, expensive funerals, but the same pragmatic structure of reasoning is used with content like "He needs his wife to cook and take care of the children." Correctly distinguishing between "structure" and "content" in stage description is a difficult and lengthy process. If you take out too much as "content," you have stages without meat for the understanding of the individual child and his or her development. If you leave in too much as content, you have a picture of the stage true for some but not for all individuals assigned to that stage rather than a pattern found in every individual. This problem is serious, because stage theory is a theory about *all individuals*, not about groups or averages for children. Stage theory holds that every single individual, studied longitudinally, should only move one step at a time through the stage sequence and always in the same order. Any deviation from this order not due to obvious errors in observation or to dramatic regression-inducing stress or damage questions the validity of the stage conception itself. A stage sequence disregarded by a single child is no sequence, just as a law of learning disobeyed by a single rat is no law. In this sense, the deviation of 4 percent of our longitudinal subjects from the moral stage sequence in terms of downward movement is only acceptable because it is within the bounds of test-retest measurement error.

In summary, structural stages are descriptions of a number of interlocked features of thought. If the stages are valid, all individuals ought to fit consistently into one of these stages (or be a mixture of adjoining stages). Furthermore, all individuals must proceed in stepwise order through the stages. If these conditions can be met, the stages may be said to be "true," regardless of theoretical presuppositions.

STRUCTURAL STAGES AND PSYCHOANALYTIC STAGES: THOUGHT STRUCTURES AND FREUDIAN CONTENT

In claiming that the structural stages we have described are true, I am in some sense claiming that other theoretical stages are not true, though I am not claiming they are completely false. Other stage approaches differ in looking at the developing content of thought and emotion, not its structure. Accordingly, they are not contradictory in the sense that two competing sets of stages of cognitive structure are competitive. Stages defined in terms of mental content may, and often do, identify many important concerns in development missed by structural stages. We will argue, however, that insofar as the development of this content is truly sequential and regular for all individuals, it is so because it is content to which a given structural stage sensitizes the child. In writing about the child's cognitive and moral stage, I have used examples which are familiar from psychoanalytic descriptions of fantasy. In psychoanalytic stage-thinking, the preoperational and morally Stage 0 Child is "phallic" or "Oedipal." His moral remarks are full of vengeance. His remarks about Eskimos are oral-aggressive "cannibalism." His remarks that his Daddy gets small when he gets big is "Oedipal." His denial that he is bad is the "defense mechanism" of denial.

In discussing fantasy as playful thought, I tried to show that the structure or *pattern* of children's thought, even where its content is emotionally "loaded," is determined not by "primary process fantasy" but by adaptive reasoning (at a certain level) serving to organize their experience and to communicate it to others. I cited as evidence the DeVries study, which showed that children's behavior and emotional reaction to the change of a cat to a dog was largely determined by their general level of thought about constancy, rather than by emotions and fantasy. To say this does not deny that the content of children's thinking has Freudian elements, but it does imply that this Freudian content must be understood as consistent with, and in part generated by, young children's prelogical thought— that this Freudian content is not the intrusion of "primary process" fantasy into "secondary process" adaptive thought. To clarify this point let us use another example, one that suggests a psychoanalytic interpretation of the intrusion of fantasy: a spontaneous response made by Jimmy, a boy just turned five, "I can be a girl, you know. I can. I can wear a wig and have my throat so I can talk like a girl." It would seen plausible to attribute the immature logic of this statement to the fact that the boy's wishes and conflicts in this area were strong enough to override his interests in being realistic or correct. On another occasion, however, the writer (experimenter) had the following conversation with Jimmy:

Experimenter: Do airplanes get small when they fly away in the sky?
Jimmy: Yes, they get real tiny.
Experimenter: Do they really get small, or do they just look small?
Jimmy: They really get small.
Experimenter: What happens to the people inside?
Jimmy: They shrink.
Experimenter: How can they shrink and get small?
Jimmy: They cut their heads off.

These statements might also be taken as motivationally determined, rather than as a reflection of Jimmy's general level of thinking. Obviously, in the second conversation, Jimmy doesn't care about being correct, and ends up making a "fantasy" response. Sometimes Jimmy may care too much (sex-role), sometimes too little (airplane query), but if his general level of thinking is the same, it is hard to maintain that this level is a product of affective rather than cognitive-structural factors. The point is that Jimmy's belief that he can be a girl is consistent with his general prelogical thought pattern rather than being a specific fantasy in conflict with his "reality-oriented" thought.

A final example may also be used to clarify the way in which Freudian content may be introduced at a given level of thought. I had an experience testing a child on conservation which would delight Freudians who object to the supposed Piagetian view of the child as "purely cognitive." I demonstrated to a 5-year-old girl the problem of "conservation of mass," in which two balls of clay of equal size are changed in shape. The experimenter made his into a "hot dog" and asked the girl to make hers into a "pancake." He then asked whether they were still the same size or whether one was bigger that the other. Quite excitedly, the girl said, "Mine is bigger; look, I can cover yours all up," and proceeded to wrap her pancake around the hot dog, completely enclosing it. A Freudian has little difficulty in seeing the response as symbolic of the "Oedipal" girl's sexual attitude, one of demonstrating the quality of her genitals and sexuality to the more prominent genitals or sexuality of the male. We would not deny this interpretation but would point out that in spite of the presence of this Freudian content, her level of thinking on this task in which she failed to conserve mass was consistent with her level of thinking on other Piagetian tasks which she seemed to approach as "purely cognitive."

In this section, then, we shall try to show that some of the content of thought and concern attributed to the preschool "Oedipal" child by Freudians is not only compatible with the Piagetian notion of the structure of the preschool child as "preoperational" or "prelogical" but is actually generated by the child's preoperational thought structure and by the adaptive motivation to assimilate reality assumed by Piaget. In particular, the generation of Freudian content results from prelogical children's efforts to relate features of their bodies to social and physical reality. As we stated earlier, Freud found that children, like grown-ups, were interested in birth and death and sex, but Piaget found that children were largely interested in birth and death and sex because they were philosophers concerned about the basic terms or categories of experience. The basic categories of experience focused upon in Piaget's studies of children are the formal categories of experience, logic, space, time, causality, substance, and so forth. There are, however, also basic content categories of experience, categories such as that of sex and gender-identity or death-and-life. A consideration of these categories helps to bridge the gap between structural stages and the stages of thought-content presented by Freud and others.

Thought Structure and Emotion

Related to the problem of relating thought structure to thought content is the problem of relating thought structure to affect or emotion. If cognitive-structural stages seem to ignore content, so too do they seem to ignore the emotion. Without denying the structural stages give only a very abstract rendition of emotions and their development, it is important to note that, like "cognitions," "emotions" are organized structures. In fact, the distinction between cognition and emotion is only an abstraction, we have no cognition without emotion and no emotion without cognition. Every emotion involves some perception of the world and the self. As these perceptions change with development, so do emotions. New moral emotions develop with changes in the structure of moral judgment. Anger becomes moral indignation in childhood with the development of moral thought, and fear of punishment becomes guilt at a somewhat later age. The difference between fear of punishment and fear of guilt is not the bodily quality or origin of the painful feeling, it is in how the painful feeling is thought about. "Fear of punishment" implies that anticipation of pain is connected with a series of external events leading to punishment, guilt implies the painful feeling is the result of an internal process of self-judgment. The qualitative difference between fear and guilt, then, is "cognitive" or, better, "structural." By this we mean that as emotions develop, they change in structure or in organization just as cognitions do. The development of thought and emotion, then, is that of parallel structural development, in which structural change in emotions is largely parallel to cognitive-structural change.

In saying that emotions have a structural component, we are not saying that emotional development is reducible to cognitive development or that developmental changes in content are reducible to changes in structure. We are saying that we cannot have two theories: one for cognitive development, another for emotional development. In the earlier days of psychoanalytic theory, there was an effort to derive the development of thought from the theory of drives used to explain emotional development. According to these early theories, logical and realistic thought (secondary process) was a watered-down form of drive-determined fantasy (primary process), a dilution resulting from frustration, delay, countercathexes, defenses, and so on. We have seen that the view of the young child's thought as watered-down fantasy is untenable. Recognizing this, most analysts today recognize an "autonomous conflict-free" sphere of ego development but do not recognize that the basic processes of its development must also apply to the more intense emotional life of the child, which they see as largely determined by biological drives.

We would argue that while basic physical drives like hunger and thirst exist, they do not directly generate or develop into the deeper social emotions. Instead, we believe that social-emotional and cognitive development have the same basic motivational nature, what Robert White (1959) calls effectance motivation. This is the tendency to adapt to or master the environment, to seek novelties and incongruities and to enhance or expand the self. Far from being creatures who can only act in response to basic drives, infants actively seek to explore their world, master or assimilate it, and adapt or accommodate to it. The infant's earliest social emotions and activities arise from the same effectance motivation, not from oral drives and gratifications. As Kagan (1971) has shown, the infant's social smile is a smile to a complex perceptual stimulus (facial or nonfacial) which must have a certain balance of familiarity and incongruity. Infants smile at the sudden recognition of the familiar. What they smile at changes regularly with age as their cognitive-processing structures change.

The Cognitive-Developmental Approach to Psychosexual Development

What we propose, then, is that the more emotionally loaded areas of ego and moral development are determined by the same general cognitive structures and motivational tendencies we have discussed (though we are not saying that development in these areas is sheer cognitive development). To illustrate our meaning, let us turn to the area of development in which psychoanalysis has made its greatest contribution, psychosexual development. We shall try to retain many of the Freudian observations but show that psychosexual development involves the consistent operation of cognitive and moral thought patterns and that the child's development in this area is determined by competence motivation, not by drives. This "cognitive" approach does not imply that the child is not intensely interested in the issues Freud described. Are young children not interested or concerned with eating and being eaten? We believe they are. Are young children not interested in their genitals and body and those of others and how they relate to each other? Yes, they are. We do not believe, however, that we need to assume libidinal drives to explain these interests. It seems doubtful that young children have very powerful sexual drives, like those of adolescents; they cannot, by physiology. What they do have is a concern or fascination with certain thoughts which may be said to be "sexual." This is because their conceptions of the social world centers around their ideas of their bodies and their ideas of the bodies of others. Social acts are bodily acts; affection means physical contact and, in that sense, is "libidinal." Anger means physical fighting and physical destruction. Because children's thinking is concrete, ideas and emotions center around thoughts of the bodily activities which Freudians call "sexual" and "aggressive" (Kohlberg, 1966). If we ask for the significance of these activities or of the child's sex-role to which it relates, we must turn to a matter of fundamental concern to the child, the matter of seeing oneself as boy or girl. It is at first difficult to believe that a child's cognitive identity as boy or girl can help explain the child's sexuality or sexual concerns. There is, however, dramatic evidence of the importance of this cognitive identity for psychosexuality. This evidence comes from the studies of Money, Hampson, and Hampson (1957) of the psychosexual development of hermaphrodites, individuals of one sex hormonally and of the opposite sex in terms of external genital characteristics. In general, these individuals make a good adjustment to the role or identity they are assigned, regardless of their "true" genetic or hormonal sex. However, often when it is discovered that children are "truly" of the opposite sex genetically or hormonally, surgical intervention has been used and the child's gender identity as male or female has been reassigned. The studies indicate that if this reassignment of identity occurs before age 2–4, the individual adapts to it and in adolescence sexually functions normally in terms of the assigned gender identity. If reassignment occurs after age 2–4, however, the individual grows up to have deep conflict and disturbance about functioning sexually in terms of the assigned gender identity. Clearly, what is critical for normal sexual functioning is that the individual assigns him- or herself a gender identity as male or female in early childhood. This gender identity is a cognition, it is not something given either by biology or by emotional complexes such as the Oedipus complex and its resolution. This gender identity is not relatively stabilized until the age of four. Because gender identity depends upon general cognitive growth of constancy, it is changeable by reassignment before this period. Children's gender identity, however, is not important simply for adult sexuality. Sex-category or gender identity is the most salient category to which young children assign themselves. Gender identity is usually thought of as a salient characteristic of how the parents treat the young child. It is terribly salient to some parents, not very salient to others. It is always terribly salient to children, because it is the only basic general category or role to which they assign themselves. The other basic category of self-identity for children is that of child as opposed to adult. Unlike gender, however, age identity is not fixed; children know they will become adults, so issues of constancy of age identity do not arise in the same form.

Because gender is the only fixed general category into which children can sort themselves and others, it takes on tremendous importance in organizing their social perceptions and actions. Accordingly, we need to attend to the actual development of this basic gender identity. It seems to be absent in the first year or two of life, but by age 3, children will label themselves correctly and will label others' gender with partial accuracy. By age 4, children label gender correctly and show some awareness that gender cannot change. For example, Johnny, a 4½ year-old, points out gender constancy to young Jimmy, who is just turning 4. Here is the conversation:

> *Older Johnny:*   I'm going to be an airplane builder when I grow up.
> *Younger Jimmy:*   When I grow up I'll be a mommy.
> *Older Johnny:*   No, you can't be a mommy, you have to be a daddy.
> *Younger Jimmy:*   No, I'm going to be a mommy.
> *Older Johnny:*   No, you're not a girl; you can't be a mommy.

While constancy of gender identity starts to be asserted at 3 or 4, this constancy does not have a clear logical basis, nor is it linked to genital differences until about age 6 or 7. The child's gender identity becomes a perceptually or logically unchangeable identity, then, at the same age at which the child develops other unchangeable cognitive identities. This coherence was demonstrated when we asked the same questions about gender that DeVries did about masked dogs and cats. We asked whether a girl could turn into a boy if she wished to, if she wore a boy's haircut or a boy's clothes. Not until age 6 or 7 were most children quite certain that a girl could not be a boy regardless of changes in appearance or behavior. Children showing constancy of identity on one task were likely to do so on the other.

So far we have talked about the growth of a single concept, gender identity. Our structural approach implies that developmental changes in the cognitive structure of a child's gender identity would be reflected in developmental changes in the sex-role attitudes more usually studied in young children. Consider the attitude of masculinity-femininity assessed by various tests of preference for sex-typed objects and activities. Not surprisingly, as a boy becomes sure he is immutably a boy, and learns that boys like certain activities and girls like others, he will come to prefer boy-things. By age 6 or 7, when children reach the ceiling on gender identity, they also reach a ceiling on these masculinity-femininity preference tests, making 80 to 100 percent same-sex choices on them. This is not a response to cultural training or reward any more than the development of constancy of gender identity is. Rather, it can be attributed to two things. The first is their belief that they have little choice about sex-typed activities and roles. When our 4-year-old Jimmy abandons the belief he can be a mother, he also abandons the belief he can be a nurse or a secretary or someone who can wear girls' clothes or someone who can play with feminine dolls. At age 6 or 7 children equate the "I am" of their sex-identity with what they value. You can't be a girl so you don't want to; you can't be a nurse so you don't want to. Second is the natural tendency to like oneself and think well of oneself, of what is connected to the self or is like the self. If other boys are like the self, you like them more than you like girls. A boy aged 4 expressed a preference for a male babysitter. Asked why, his 7-year-old brother intervened to say, "Because he's a boy himself." To prefer the same sex in a consistent or categorical manner required conceptual growth and the development of fixed logical classes. For boys under 5, liking the same sex applies only to peers. By age 6 or 7 it applies to both father and strange adults. At this age, measures of preference and imitation for the father over the mother indicate the first gender cross-over to same-sex preference. Thus, what is often called father-identification, as well as what is called masculinity of values, grows with and out of the cognitive growth of a boy's gender identity.

Now that the child has organized his identity and his attitudes and values around his gender identity, we must ask what these attitudes and values are. When we enter into the attributes children assign to male and female roles and issues of the superiority of one over the other we find almost as much cognitive-developmental regularity as we did for gender-identity. By age six almost all boys see males as more powerful, aggressive, authoritative and intelligent than females. In part, this is also the old tendency of the boy to attribute value to what is like himself. This is not all, however, because most girls of the same age agree with him. Cross-cultural studies suggest that these stereotypes are universal. In our work we found that father-absent black boys developed the same stereotypes of a father at the same age as did father-present black and white boys. How do we explain this? By returning to the notion that for the young child sex-linked roles and attributes are linked to body attributes. Because males are perceived as physically bigger, stronger and more active than females, they are also thought to have what we would consider psychological rather than physical attributes, such as, aggressiveness, fearlessness, smartness and dominance. The child does not distinguish physical and psychological attributes; physical strength and energy are equated with intelligence, aggression and dominance. This tendency to derive psychological attributes and values from physical attributes is compounded by the child's categorical view of sex-role assignments. Boys can't be nurses, girls can't be soldiers. Roles we believe that both sexes can play but are more commonly played by males are categorically assigned to the male sex, roles from doctor to policeman to President. A boy cannot be a nurse any more than he can be a mother. We might say that the 6 year old boy is a full-fledged male chauvinist, much more so than his parents, and he is that way pretty much regardless of how he is brought up in a society which does do some sex-role-differentiation. Fortunately later phases of cognitive growth qualify, moderate or undo this chauvinism.

The next phase of cognitive growth in sex-role concepts takes place because the child redefines roles in terms of their place in a moral order called society rather than in terms of their physical characteristics. When first-graders are compared with fifth-graders in sex-role concepts and attitudes we see great differences related to the development of sociomoral concepts. By the fifth grade, psychological distinctions between males and females are seen as deriving from differences in wishes or intentions rather than from physical-body differences. More basically, differences between males and females are seen in terms of the differences in the social roles they play instead of in terms of physical or biological characteristics. Fifth-graders see sex roles as defined by social or shared expectations and norms. Differences in role-expectations are due to the social function of the role, its function for other people or society. The fifth-graders' intentions and wishes are dictated by social sex roles they are expected to play in the future. At this age, then, the child's sex identity and values are largely determined by conformity to social roles, and this conformity to social roles has a heavy basis in the distinction by sex. Eventually, in adolescence, many or most children develop independence of conformity to fixed social sex-role stereotypes and develop personal images and ideals of masculinity and femininity which they relate to their own aspirations.

In summary, many aspects of children's psychosexual development may be understood as elaborations of general cognitive, moral, and ego development trends. These generate very specific concerns about being a boy or a girl, about relating to others of the same or the opposite sex, and about one's future roles.

We have stressed the more or less "positive" or "moral" ways in which development of sex-role concepts channels the child's motivation for esteem and mastery. The psychoanalytic view stresses the dark side of the child's psychosexual attitudes, being concerned as it is with drawing links between childhood thoughts and experiences and adult psychopathology. As is discussed elsewhere (Kohlberg, Lacrosse, & Ricks, 1970), the Freudian effort to relate adult psychopathology to childhood thoughts and experiences has not been very successful, judged by longitudinal research evidence. Nevertheless, there is a dark side to the child's thoughts and feelings more or less neglected in the cognitive-developmental account. From our point of view, one can see the Freudian child as having the dark side of the positive interests of the Piagetian child. The child has a positive sense of justice which may have a dark side as a preoccupation with vengeance or punishment. The child has an interest in life and its origins which can shade into a dark interest in death. To clarify this point let us turn to the dark side of moral development discussed by psychoanalysis as the superego. The Freudian concept of morality was grounded on the popular Christian concept of conscience as a little agency inside the head that warns and punishes the self. It stressed, then, that (a) morality was punishment and self-punishment (b) by an agency distinct from the self or ego (c) from the self's perception of its surrounding social situation. In addition Freud stressed the analogy between the morality of the young child and the morality of the adult depressive, paranoid, or neurotically guilty.

Turning to these points, there is a sense in which a child's Stage 1 morality is recognizable in the psychoanalytic picture of the "punitive superego." Stage 1 children do believe that parents and authorities are always right, that punishment (even cruel punishment) is justified. Rules are obeyed in the absence of authority because of a vague sense of inevitable punishment. The child may believe in immanent justice, that a bad act will be punished by God or nature even if no human sees it. In the sterner Calvinistic religious tradition, this sense of immanent justice is encouraged in the child by the doctrine of predestined damnation and hell-fire. Under such considerations it is not surprising if the Stage 1 child displays features of "a stern superego."

The young child, however, does not have the capacity for deep guilt that Freudian theory implies. Studies indicate that clear guilt, as distinct from fear, first appears in preadolescence at the conventional stages of morality. Furthermore, the irrational moral feelings young children have tend to pass away as they develop. At age 5, my Stage 1 son had a "severe superego" which forbade him to eat living things. By age 7, he had become a "psychopath" who would steal if he could get away with it.

In perspective, the development of "conscience," of ideas and feelings about punishment and guilt, is only one of many issues touched by the development of the child's moral sense and is closely related to a developing sense of fairness, awareness of relations of affection and authority, conceptions of law, and so on. This "development" can in some children have a dark side, but this dark side does not define development itself.

In summary, other "stages," like the psychoanalytic, offer important insights and observations missing from the structural view. In large part these insights can be successfully recast in a way that can be integrated with cognitive-developmental theory. Such an integration is largely a task for the future. The task is not essential for the educator, but it is for the clinical understanding of the individual child.

STRUCTURAL STAGES AND THE PROCESS OF EDUCATION

For a long time the implications of stages for early education were thought to entail a passive approach, an approach of providing the child with the security and freedom to spontaneously grow. The metaphor of growth was that of the plant which needed only to be watered to grow and whose growth could not be forced. This metaphor was based on the notion that the stages were innate or wired into the nervous system and that they unfolded in a regular relation to age and physical or neurological growth. In contrast to this metaphor of growth was an opposed metaphor, that of behaviorism and environmental associationism. In this metaphor, mind was a machine, a switchboard emitting output after receiving input and associating input with output. The more information the environment put in through appropriate teaching, the more output there would be in terms of academic skills and appropriate social habits. In contrast to either view, Dewey and Piaget argue that the existence of stages requires that we think of development as a dialogue between children and their environment. Stages depend upon certain universal biological features of the child but they also depend upon universal features of the child's experience or environment.

A cognitive stage, a stage of knowing, cannot develop without something known, an object or a world. The nature of stages, then, is determined as much by the nature of the physical and social world as it is by the nature of the biological organism. Since the stages are universal, the aspects of experience of the world that our stages relate to are universal features of the world, features the world has in any culture or family. These include the experiences with physical objects which follow the universal laws of nature and the social experiences which have universal features, features arising from universals of social interaction, out of the fact all children are selves in a world of other selves organized in families, groups, and nations with certain universals of rules and justice. If social and physical worlds have these universal features of experience, why are they perceived so differently at different stages and why do some children move faster than others from one stage to the next? The world is seen differently at different stages because these universal features of experience, for example, physical laws or moral laws, are organized in different ways at each stage. At each stage, thought patterns are not direct reflections of patterns of the environment but are the result of the interaction between the child's active thought pattern and the pattern of the environment. Development occurs through dialogue or interaction. The child responds to the world and the world responds to the child, with the pattern of interaction working toward balance or equilibrium. An attained pattern of balance is called a stage. This pattern or balance of a lower stage is disrupted by a lack of fit between the stage structure and experience, leading to a new pattern of action and reaction with the world, leading to a new stage, a new balance or equilibrium.

Environments vary in the amount of stimulation they provide and in the degree to which the stimulation matches the child's level of development and his or her activities. The role of experience in education, then, is to provide stimulation for movement to the next stage of development and for consolidation of an attained stage into a firm organization that makes the world a coherent, meaningful, and intelligible place.

A concrete example of developmental moral education may clarify the ideas presented in this chapter. As we have indicated, young childhood (age 3 to 10) may span moral stage development from Stage 1 to Stage 3. In the ages 7 to 10, a single classroom may include students from Stage 1 to Stage 3. Jean Gill, a New Jersey librarian, led a hypothetical dilemma discussion dramatized on a filmstrip series called *First Things: Values* (Kohlberg & Selman, 1973) that presents dilemmas appropriate for children aged 6 to 10. Jean Gill's second grade discussion was in turn made into a filmstrip (*A Strategy for Teaching Values*) (Kohlberg & Selman, 1973).

Jean Gill had taken a workshop on moral education at Harvard before leading the discussion. Aware of the stages, the teacher, Jean Gill, aims to lead a discussion that will stimulate her children's thinking to move to the next stage. Stage 1 children are challenged by the Stage 2 thinking of the other children and tend to understand and assimilate it. Stage 2 children learn in turn from the reasoning of Stage 3's. So Jean Gill asks questions that elicit these reasoning stages.

Besides awareness of the stages, Jean Gill is aware of the Piagetian principle of cognitive conflict. Piaget and his followers claim that children move to the next stage through experiences of cognitive conflict, through facing problems that lead to self-contradiction and difficulty for thinking at their stage, and to reorganization at the next stage.

Jean Gill's efforts to use this principle are made easier by having available the filmstrip dilemmas constructed by Bob Selman and myself. The dilemma Jean Gill will have the students discuss is called "You Promised." Its heroine is Holly. Holly likes to climb trees, but after she has fallen and gotten hurt, her father asks her to promise not to climb any more. She promises, but then a situation comes up presenting Holly with a dilemma. A friend's cat climbs a tree and won't come down. The friend can't climb and asks Holly. It's late and she may have to climb if the kitten is to be saved. It's not dangerous, this particular time, to climb, but Holly made a promise. What should Holly do—save the kitten or keep her promise? Holly's dilemma arouses cognitive conflict because it is a moral dilemma. A moral dilemma asks a person to choose between two conflicting moral values. In most situations, the moral value of keeping a promise is not in conflict with another moral value of saving life. In Holly's dilemma, it is. Holly must choose between two good but opposing values. Choosing between them requires considering reasons for each basic value and better reasons for each. This means that a useful dilemma is controversial. Many teachers and parents ask, "Why present a dilemma in which it can be right not to keep a promise?" Such teachers do not believe moral behavior should be based on reasoning. Rather, it should be based on the adult's preaching and on stories and situations that reaffirm the child's faith in the adult's authority. Research since the days of Hartshorne and May, however, shows that preaching does little to influence either moral reasoning or moral action. What children learn from pious preaching is to preach to others. It is accommodative learning.

Holly's dilemma is not controversial to most adults because they agree that it's all right for Holly to break the promise to save the kitten's life. But is it for Jean Gill's children?

Let me summarize what went on in the discussion. After getting some first opinions, Jean Gill then broke the class into small groups. Each group contained some children who thought Holly should climb the tree, some who thought she should not. Then she moved from group to group asking them to listen to each other's reasons.

In one group, Harold, Nicole and Cathy were discussing. Harold said, "It's all right if she's going to break her promise. Well, she's not really breaking a promise exactly, because she's saving the kitten's life. It's a lot better than just the word promise." Without hearing more from Harold, we don't know whether his reasoning is Stage 2 or Stage 3. Clearly he has been through Stage 1 and rejects it. At Stage 1, labels like stealing or breaking promises are magical no-no's. Stage 2 and 3 know that sticks and stones can break your bones but in themselves words like "stealer" or "promise-breaker" can never hurt you. "Promise," says Harold, is just a word, and words aren't as good as kittens.

Nicole doesn't quite follow Harold's reasoning. She doesn't agree that Holly should climb the tree. Why? She answers, "So what, Harold. She's gonna get in trouble." Nicole's response is Stage 1 in moral reasoning. What is right for Nicole is obedience to authority, the father. The reason why something is right is punishment, "She's gonna get in trouble." Nicole has faith not only in the authority of Holly's father but also of her heavenly Father. She says, "But if she's Catholic, God will help her. If she isn't, if you're Jewish, you won't get help."

After Stage 1 is Stage 2, Cathy doesn't agree with Harold that Holly should climb the tree. She says, "But, Harold, the cat isn't hers and she shouldn't worry about it. It's not her problem."

After Stage 2 comes Stage 3. We said that Harold's thinking a live kitten is better than the word promise was rejection of a lower stage, Stage 1 thinking. But we couldn't tell what stage Harold's own positive thinking was. Some things he says later concern others' feelings and expectations. Harold says, "If she doesn't help the kitten and the friend, she'll be hurting someone else's feelings. And her father would understand." Harold is concerned about the consequences of actions to others' feelings and has an empathic concern for the kitten's life.

Harold's Stage 3 centering of moral judgment on empathy means he judges, and expects others to judge, the intention behind the action. The father should be empathic, too, so the prospect of disobedience and punishment is not frightening. Harold's Stage 3 thinking understands and refutes Nicole's Stage 1 thinking. It also can deal with Cathy's Stage 2 thinking. Cathy says, "The cat isn't hers and she shouldn't worry about it. It's not her problem." Harold answers, "But she'll feel real bad in her mind because she hurt her friend's feelings."

The filmstrip then suggests why moral dilemma discussion can lead to moral development: first, because dilemmas and disagreement arouse conflict and rethinking; second, because exposure to the reasoning of other children at a higher stage leads to some assimilation. Exposure to the dilemma and to Harold's Stage 2 and Stage 3 thinking helps Nicole to move from Stage 1 to Stage 2. When Jerry says, "What if it stays up in the tree? It'll die, and Nicole comments, "Okay, Cathy, what are you gonna say about that?" Nicole has picked up some of Harold's concern about value consequences to the cat and changes her mind.

We have collected clear research evidence that discussions like Jean Gill's do lead to moral development, development not found in elementary classrooms without this focus.

In the fall of 1974, Bob Selman ran a brief workshop for Cambridge, Massachusetts, second grade teachers and then asked them to present filmstrip dilemmas to their classes and to lead discussions of them as Jean Gill did. There were ten periods of filmstrip discussions, over a period of five weeks. Some of the teachers were sufficiently excited by the moral discussions that they continued them for the remainder of the year, bringing in their own dilemmas or having the students bring in theirs. The children in the three experimental classes were interviewed just before the discussions. They were interviewed about the dilemmas they would later discuss as well as some test dilemmas. At the end of the year they were reinterviewed. Those interviews were used to define the children's stages before and after the discussion experiment. Before the discussions all the children in the classes were at our first stage of moral reasoning. After the discussions one-third of the children in the experimental classes had moved ahead one stage. They were at our second stage. Selman picked as controls two additional classrooms where the children had no moral discussion during the year. In these control classes, all the children were still in Stage 1 at the end of the year. No one in the control group had moved ahead a stage, as had one-third of the experimental children. So developmental moral discussion does make a difference.

Now that we know moral education can lead to stage development, let's ask whether it's good. This is a question not only of psychology, but of philosophy or theology. Why is moral development good? To answer this philosophic question, we must listen to the children themselves. Because they are philosophers they prefer development; they prefer the highest stage they can understand.

Why do children prefer the next stage up to their own? Because each higher stage is a better stage in its ability to solve moral problems or to answer moral questions. Stage 1 starts with a concern about getting in trouble. Stage 2 asks, "But how is the father going to know?" Stage 1 can't answer that question. Stage 2 has trouble answering its own question, "Why keep a promise if the father won't know?" Stage 3 has an answer to Stage 2's question, "Why be moral if there are no immediate selfish consequences?" Stage 3 reasoning is also better because it leads to a better or more fair solution to Holly's dilemma, one that is fair to the father, to the kitten, and to the friend. Harold's Stage 3 thinking is fair because it implicitly uses the Golden Rule: putting yourself in the shoes of another. Using the Golden Rule leads to a solution, a right answer to this dilemma.

While moral education does not need to be grounded in a definite theology, there is one moral principle all theologies share. Nicole said that God won't help you if you're Jewish, not Catholic. But the Jewish prophets, Jesus, Buddha, and Confucius alike preached the Golden Rule. The Golden Rule—putting yourself in the other's place—is the empathic foundation of morality. The Golden Rule is also justice. Justice is fairness, equality, and reciprocity between persons. All cultures and all religions ground morality on empathy and justice, on the Golden Rule. Each of our moral stages is a higher stage in the understanding of these moral universals.

REFERENCES

Baldwin, J. M. (1906). *Social and ethical intepretations in mental development* (4th ed.). New York: Macmillan.

Broughton, J. M. (1982). Genetic logic and the developmental psychology of philosophical concepts. In J. M. Broughton & D. J. Freeman-Moir (Eds.), *The cognitive developmental psychology of James Mark Baldwin.* Norwood, NJ: Ablex.

DeVries, R. (1969). Constancy of generic identity in the years 3 to 6. *Monograph of The Society for Research in Child Development, 34,* No. 127.

Erikson, E. (1950/1963). *Childhood and society.* New York: Norton.

Erikson, E. (1964). *Insight and responsibility: Lectures on the ethical implications of psychoanalytic insight.* New York: Norton.

Fromm, E. (1947/1955). *Man for himself: An inquiry into the psychology of ethics.* New York: Holt, Rinehart.

Kagan, J. (1971). *Change and continuity in infancy.* New York: Wiley.

Kegan, R. (1982). *The evolving self.* Cambridge: Harvard University Press.

Kohlberg, L. (1966). A cognitive developmental analysis of children's sex-role concepts and attitudes. In E. Maccoby (Ed.), *The development of sex differences.* Stanford: Stanford University Press.

Kohlberg, L., Lacrosse, J., & Ricks, D. (1970). The predictability of adult mental health from childhood behavior. In B. Wolman (Ed.), *Handbook of child psychopathology.* New York: McGraw-Hill.

Kohlberg, L., & Selman, R. (1973). *First things: Values.* Pleasantville, NY: Guidance Associates.

Kohlberg, L., & Selman, R. (1973). *A Strategy for teaching values.* Pleasantville, NY: Guidance Associates.

Loevinger, J., with Blasi, A. (1976). *Ego development: Conceptions and theories.* San Francisco: Jossey-Bass.

Money, J., Hampson, J., & Hampson, J. (1957). Imprinting and the establishment of gender role. *Archeological Neurological Psychiatry, 77,* 333–336.

Sullivan, H. S. (1953). *An interpersonal theory of psychiatry.* New York: Norton.

Sullivan, E. V., McCullough, G., & Stager, M. (1964). A developmental study of the relationship between conceptual ego and moral development. *Child Development, 35,* 231–242.

van den Daele, L. (1968). A developmental study of ego-ideals. *Genetic Psychology Monongraphs, 78,* 191–265.

White, R. (1959). Motivation reconsidered: The concept of competence. *Psychological Review, 66,* 297–333.

Chapter 3

Development as the Aim of Education*

Lawrence Kohlberg and Rochelle Mayer

An extremely important issue confronting educators and educational theorists today is the choice of ends for the educational process. Without clear and rational educational goals, it is impossible to decide which educational programs achieve valid and useful objectives and which teach incidental facts and attitudes of dubious worth. There is no lack of studies comparing the effects of various educational methods and programs on outcome measures such as IQ and achievement tests, but very little has been done to clarify the worth of the outcome measures themselves by which research facts can help generate and substantiate educational objectives and measures of educational outcomes.

Three prevalent strategies for defining objectives and relating them to research facts are considered: the desirable trait or "bag of virtues" strategy; the prediction of success or "industrial psychology" strategy; and the "developmental-philosophic" strategy. It will be our claim in this chapter that the first two strategies: (1) lack a clear theoretical rationale for defining objectives which can withstand logical and philosophic criticism; and (2) that as currently applied they rest upon assumptions which conflict with research findings. In contrast, we claim that the developmental-philosophic strategy for defining educational objectives, which emerges from the work of Dewey and Piaget, is a theoretical rationale which withstands logical criticism and is consistent with, if not "proved" by, current research findings.

This presentation begins by making explicit how a cognitive-developmental *psychological* theory can be translated into a rational and viable progressive *educational ideology*, that is, a set of concepts defining desirable aims, content, and methods of education. We contrast the progressive ideology with the "romantic" and the "cultural transmission" schools of thought, with respect to underlying

*The position presented in this chapter was elaborated in a different form in *Proceedings of the Conference on Psychology and the Process of Schooling in the Next Decade: Alternative conceptions.* Washington, D.C.: U.S. Office of Education, 1971.

45

psychological, epistemological, and ethical assumptions. In doing so we focus on two related problems of value theory. The first is the issue of *value-relativity*, the problem of defining some general ends of education whose validity is not relative to the values and needs of each individual child or to the values of each subculture or society. The second is the problem of relating psychological statements about the actual characteristics of children and their development to philosophic statements about desirable characteristics, the problem of relating the natural *is* to the ethical *ought*. We claim that the cognitive-developmental or progressive approach can satisfactorily handle these issues because it combines a psychological theory of development with a rational ethical philosophy of development. In contrast, we claim that other educational ideologies do not stem from psychological theories which can be translated into educational aims free of the philosophic charge that they are arbitrary and relative to the values of the particular educator or school.

Subsequently, we look at the ways in which these ideologies form the basis for contemporary educational policy. We evaluate longitudinal evidence relevant to the "bag of virtues" definition of education objectives favored in maturationist models of education, and the academic achievement definition of objectives favored in environmental learning models. We conclude that the available research lends little support for either of these alternative educational strategies. More specifically:

1. The current prevalent definition of the aims of education, in terms of academic achievement supplemented by a concern for mental health, cannot be justified empirically or logically.
2. The overwhelming emphasis of educational psychology on methods of instruction and tests and measurements which presuppose a "value-neutral" psychology is misplaced.
3. An alternative notion that the aim of the schools should be the stimulation of human development is a scientifically, ethically, and practically viable conception which provides the framework for a new kind of educational psychology.

THREE STREAMS OF EDUCATIONAL IDEOLOGY

There have been three broad streams in the development of Western educational ideology. While their detailed statements vary from generation to generation, each stream exhibits a continuity based upon particular assumptions of psychological development.

Romanticism

The first stream of thought, the "romantic," commences with Rousseau and is currently represented by Freud's and Gesell's followers. A. S. Neill's Summerhill represents an example of a school based on these principles. Romantics hold that what comes from within the child is the most important aspect of development; therefore the pedagogical environment should be permissive enough to allow the inner "good" (abilities and social virtues) to unfold and the inner "bad" to come under control. Thus teaching the child the ideas and attitudes of others through rote or drill would result in meaningless learning and the suppression of inner spontaneous tendencies of positive value.

Romantics stress the biological metaphors of "health" and "growth" in equating optimal physical development with bodily health and optimal mental development with mental health. Accordingly, early education should allow the child to work through aspects of emotional development not allowed expression at home, such as the formation of social relations with peers and adults other than his parents. It should also allow the expression of intellectual questioning and curiosity. To label this ideology "romantic" is not to accuse it of being unscientific; rather it is to recognize that the nineteenth century discovery of the natural development of the child was part of a larger romantic philosophy, an ethic and epistemology involving a discovery of the natural and the inner self.

With regard to childhood, this philosophy involved not only an awareness that the child possessed an inner self but also a valuing of childhood, to which the origins of the self could be traced. The adult, through taking the child's point of view, could experience otherwise inaccessible elements of truth, goodness, and reality.

As stated by G. H. Mead (1936):

> The romantic comes back to the existence of the self as the primary fact. That is what gives the standard to values. What the Romantic period revealed was not simply a past but a past as the point of view from which to come back at the self. . . . It is this self-conscious setting-up of the past again that constitutes the origin of romanticism. (p. 61)

The work of G. Stanley Hall, the founder of American child psychology, contains the core ideas of modern romantic educational thought, including "deschooling."

> The guardians of the young should strive first to keep out of nature's way and to prevent harm and should merit the proud title of the defenders of the happiness and rights of children. They should feel profoundly that childhood, as it comes from the hand of God, is not corrupt but illustrates the survival of the most consummate thing in the world; they should be convinced that there is nothing else so worthy of love, reverence and service as the body and soul of the growing child.
>
> Before we let the pedagog loose upon childhood, we must overcome the fetishes of the alphabet, of the multiplication tables, and must reflect that but a few generations ago the ancestors of all of us were illiterate. There are many who ought not to be educated and who would be better in mind, body and morals if they knew no school.

What shall it profit a child to gain the world of knowledge and lose his own health? (1901, p. 24)

Cultural Transmission

The origins of the cultural transmission ideology are rooted in the classical academic tradition of Western education. Traditional educators believe that their primary task is the transmission to the present generation of bodies of information and of rules or values collected in the past; they believe that the educator's job is the direct instruction of such information and rules. The important emphasis, however, is not on the sanctity of the past, but on the view that educating consists of transmitting knowledge, skills, and social and moral rules of the culture. Knowledge and rules of the culture may be rapidly changing or they may be static. In either case, however, it is assumed that education is the transmission of the culturally given.

More modern or innovative variations of the cultural transmission view are represented by educational technology and behavior modification.* Like traditional education, these approaches assume that knowledge and values—first located in the culture—are afterwards internalized by children through the imiation of adult behavior models, or through explicit instruction and reward and punishment. Accordingly, the educational technologist evaluates the individual's success in terms of his ability to incorporate the responses he has been taught and to respond favorably to the demands of the system. Although the technologist stresses the child as an individual learner, learning at his own pace, he, like the traditionalist, assumes that what is learned and what is valued in education is a culturally given body of knowledge and rules.

There are, of course, a number of contrasts between the traditional academic and the educational technology variations of the cultural-transmission ideology. The traditional academic school has been humanistic in the sense that it has emphasized the transmission of knowledge considered central to the culture of Western man. The educational technology school, in contrast, has emphasized the transmission of skills and habits deemed necessary for adjustment to a technological society. With regard to early education, however, the two variations of the cultural transmission school find an easy rapprochement in stressing such goals as literacy and mathematical skills. The traditionalist sees literacy as the central avenue to the culture of Western man, the technologist sees it as a means to vocational adaptation to a society depending on impersonal information codes. Both approaches, however, emphasize definition of educational goals in terms of fixed knowledge or skills assessed by standards of cultural correctness. Both also

---

* The romantic-maturationist position also has "conservative" and "radical" wings. Emphasizing "adaptation to reality," psychoanalytic educators like A. Freud (1937) and Bettelheim (1970) stress mental health as ego-control, while radicals stress spontaneity, creativity, etc.

stress internalization of basic moral rules of the culture. The clearest and most thoughtful contemporary elaboration of this view in relation to preschool education is to be found in the writing of Bereiter and Engelmann (1966).

In contrast to the child-centered romantic school, the cultural transmission school is society-centered. It defines educational ends as the internalization of the values and knowledge of the culture. The cultural transmission school focuses on the child's need to learn the discipline of the social order, while the romantic stresses the child's freedom. The cultural transmission view emphasizes the common and the established, the romantic view stresses the unique, the novel, and the personal.

Progressivism

The third stream of educational ideology which is still best termed "progressive," following Dewey (1938), developed as part of the pragmatic functional-genetic philosophies of the late nineteenth and early twentieth centuries. As an educational ideology, progressivism holds that education should nourish the child's natural interaction with a developing society or environment. Unlike the romantics, the progressives do not assume that development is the unfolding of an innate pattern or that the primary aim of education is to create an unconflicted environment able to foster healthy development. Instead, they define development as a progression through invariant ordered sequential stages. The educational goal is the eventual attainment of a higher level or stage of development in adulthood, not merely the healthy functioning of the child at a present level. In 1895, Dewey and McLellan suggested the following notion of education for attainment of a higher stage:

> Only knowledge of the order and connection of the stages in the development of the psychical functions can insure the full maturing of the psychical powers. Education is the work of supplying the conditions which will enable the psychical functions, as they successively arise, to mature and pass into higher functions in the freest and fullest manner. (p. 207)

In the progressive view, this aim requires an educational environment that actively stimulates development through the presentation of resolvable but genuine problems or conflicts. For progressives, the organizing and developing force in the child's experience is the child's active thinking, and thinking is stimulated by the problematic, by cognitive conflict. Educative experience makes the child think—think in ways which organize both cognition and emotion. Although both the cultural transmission and the progressive views emphasize "knowledge," only the latter sees the acquisition of "knowledge" as *an active change in patterns of thinking* brought about by experiential problem-solving situations. Similarly, both views emphasize "morality," but the progressive sees the acquisition of morality as an active change in patterns of response to problematic social situations rather than the learning of culturally accepted rules.

The progressive educator stresses the essential links between cognitive and moral development; he assumes that moral development is not purely affective, and that cognitive development is a necessary though not sufficient condition for moral development. The development of logical and critical thought, central to cognitive education, finds its larger meaning in a broad set of moral values. The progressive also points out that moral development arises from social interaction in situations of social conflict. Morality is neither the internalization of established cultural values nor the unfolding of spontaneous impulses and emotions; it is justice, the reciprocity between the individual and others in his social environment.

PSYCHOLOGICAL THEORIES
UNDERLYING EDUCATIONAL IDEOLOGIES

We have described three schools of thought describing the general ends and means of education. Central to each of these educational ideologies is a distinctive educational psychology, a distinctive psychological theory of development (Kohlberg, 1968). Underlying the romantic ideology is a maturationist theory of development; underlying the cultural transmission ideology is an associationistic-learning or environmental-contingency theory of development; and underlying the progressive ideology is a cognitive-developmental or interactionist theory of development.

The three psychological theories described represent three basic metaphors of development (Langer, 1969). The romantic model views the development of the mind through the metaphor of organic growth, the physical growth of a plant or animal. In this metaphor, the environment affects development by providing necessary nourishment for the naturally growing organism. Maturationist psychologists elaborating the romantic metaphor conceive of cognitive development as unfolding through prepatterned stages. They have usually assumed not only that cognitive development unfolds but that individual variations in rate of cognitive development are largely inborn. Emotional development is also believed to unfold through hereditary stages, such as the Freudian psychosexual stages, but is thought to be vulnerable to fixation and frustration by the environment. For the maturationist, although both cognitive and social-emotional development unfold, they are two different things. Since social-emotional development is an unfolding of something biologically given and is not based on knowledge of the social world, it does not depend upon cognitive growth.

The cultural transmission model views the development of the mind through the metaphor of the machine. The machine may be the wax on which the environment transcribes its markings, it may be the telephone switchboard through which environmental stimulus-energies are transmitted, or it may be the computer in which bits of information from the environment are stored, retrieved, and recombined. In any case, the environment is seen as "input," as information or energy more or less directly transmitted to, and accumulated in, the organism. The organism in turn emits "output" behavior. Underlying the mechanistic metaphor is the associationistic, stimulus-response or environmentalist psychological theory, which can be traced from John Locke to Thorndike to B. F. Skinner. This psychology views both specific concepts and general cognitive structures as reflections of structures that exist outside the child in the physical and social world. The structure of the child's concepts or of his behavior is viewed as the result of the association of discrete stimuli with one another, with the child's responses, and with his experiences of pleasure and pain. Cognitive development is the result of guided learning and teaching. Consequently, cognitive education requires a careful statement of desirable behavior patterns described in terms of specific responses. Implied here is the idea that the child's behavior can be shaped by immediate repetition and elaboration of the correct response, and by association with feedback or reward.

The cognitive-developmental metaphor is not material, it is dialectical; it is a model of the progression of ideas in discourse and conversation. The dialectical metaphor was first elaborated by Plato, given new meaning by Hegel, and finally stripped of its metaphysical claims by John Dewey and Jean Piaget, to form a psychological method. In the dialectical metaphor, a core of universal ideas are redefined and reorganized as their implications are played out in experience and as they are confronted by their opposites in argument and discourse. These re-organizations define qualitative levels of thought, levels of increased epistemic adequacy. The child is not a plant or a machine; he is a philosopher or a scientist-poet. The dialectical metaphor of progressive education is supported by a cognitive-development or interactional psychological theory. Discarding the dichotomy between maturation and environmentally determined learning, Piaget and Dewey claim that mature thought emerges through a process of development that is neither direct biological maturation nor direct learning, but rather a reorganization of psychological structures resulting from organism-environment interactions. Basic mental structure is the product of the patterning of interaction between the organism and the environment, rather than a direct reflection of either innate neurological patterns or external environmental patterns.

To understand this Piaget-Dewey concept of the development of mental pattern, we must first understand its conception of cognition. Cognitions are assumed to be structures, internally organized wholes or systems of internal relations. These structures are *rules* for the processing of information or the connecting of events. Events in the child's experience are organized actively through these cognitive connecting processes, not passively through external association and repetition. Cognitive development, which is defined as change in cognitive structures, is assumed to depend on experience. But the effects of experience are not regarded as learning in the ordinary sense (training, instruction, modeling, or specific response practices). If two events which follow one another in time are cognitively connected in the child's mind, this implies that he relates them by means of a category such as causality; he perceives his operant behavior as causing the reinforcer to occur. A program of reinforcement, then, cannot directly change the child's causal structures since it is assimilated by the child in terms of his present mode of thinking. When a program of reinforcement cannot be assimilated to the child's causal structure, however, the child's structure may be reorganized to obtain a better fit between the two. Cognitive development is a dialogue between the child's cognitive structures and the structures of the environment. Further, the theory emphasizes that the core of development is not the unfolding of instincts, emotions, or sensorimotor patterns, but instead is cognitive change in distinctively human, general patterns of thinking about the self and the world. The child's relation to his social environment is cognitive; it involves thought and symbolic interaction.

Because of its emphasis on ways of perceiving and responding to experience, cognitive-developmental theory discards the traditional dichotomy of social *versus* intellectual development. Rather, cognitive and affective development are parallel aspects of the structural transformations which take place in development. At the core of this interactional or cognitive-developmental theory is the doctrine of cognitive stages. Stages have the following general characteristics:

1. Stages imply distinct or qualitative differences in children's modes of thinking or of solving the same problem.
2. These different modes of thought form an invariant sequence, order, or succession in individual development. While cultural factors may speed up, slow down, or stop development, they do not change its sequence.
3. Each of these different and sequential modes of thought forms a "structural whole." A given stage-response on a task does not just represent a specific response determined by knowledge and familiarity with that task or tasks similar to it; rather, it represents an underlying thought-organization.
4. Cognitive stages are hierarchical integrations. Stages form an order of increasingly differentiated and integrated *structures* to fulfill a common function. (Piaget, 1960, pp. 13–15).

In other words, a series of stages form an invariant developmental sequence; the sequence is invariant because each stage stems from the previous one and prepares the way for the subsequent stage. Of course, children may move through these stages at varying speeds and they may be found to be half in and half out of a particular stage. Individuals may stop at any given stage and at any age, but if they continue to progress they must move in accord with these steps.

The cognitive-developmental conception of stage has a number of features in common with maturational-theory conceptions of stage. The maturational conception of stage, however, is "embryological," while the interactional conception is "structural-hierarchical." For maturational theory, a stage represents the total state of the organism at a given period of time; for example, Gesell's embryological concept of stage equates it with the typical behavior pattern of an age period, for example, there is a stage of "five-year-olders." While in the theories of Freud and

Erikson stages are less directly equated with ages, psychoanalytic stages are still embryological in the sense that age leads to a new stage regardless of experience and regardless of reorganizations at previous stages. As a result, education and experience become valuable not for movement to a new stage but for healthy or successful integration of the concerns of the present stage. Onset of the next stage occurs regardless of experience; only healthy integration of a stage is contingent on experience.

By contrast, in cognitive-developmental theory a stage is a delimited structure of thought, fixed in a sequence of structures but theoretically independent of time and total organismic state (Kohlberg, 1969b; Loevinger et al., 1970). Such stages are hierarchical reorganizations; attainment of a higher stage presupposes attainment of the prior stage and represents a reorganization or transformation of it. Accordingly, attainment of the next stage is a valid aim of educational experience.

For the interactionist, experience is essential to stage progression, and more or richer stimulation leads to faster advance through the series of stages. On the other hand, the maturational theory assumes that extreme deprivation will retard or fixate development, but that enrichment will not necessarily accelerate it. To understand the effects of experience in stimulating stage-development, cognitive-developmental theory holds that one must analyze the relation of the structure of a child's specific experience to behavior structures. The analysis focuses upon discrepancies between the child's action system or expectancies and the events experienced. The hypothesis is that some moderate or optimal degree of conflict or discrepancy constitutes the most effective experience for structural change.

As applied to educational intervention, the theory holds that facilitating the child's movement to the next step of development involves exposure to the next higher level of thought and conflict requiring the active application of the current level of thought to problematic situations. This implies (1) attention to the child's mode or styles of thought, that is, stage; (2) match of stimulation to that stage, for example, exposure to modes of reasoning one stage above the child's own; (3) arousal, among children, of genuine cognitive and social conflict and disagreement about problematic situations (in contrast to traditional education which has stressed adult "right answers" and has reinforced "behaving well"); and (4) exposure to stimuli toward which the child can be active, in which assimilatory response to the stimulus-situation is associated with "natural" feedback.

In summary, the maturationist theory assumes that basic mental structure results from an innate patterning; the environmentalist learning theory assumes that basic mental structure results from the patterning or association of events in the outside world; the cognitive-developmental theory assumes that basic mental structure results from an interaction between organismic structuring tendencies and the structure of the outside world, not reflecting either one directly. This interaction leads to cognitive stages that represent the transformations of early cognitive structures as they are applied to the external world and as they accommodate to it.

EPISTEMOLOGICAL COMPONENTS OF EDUCATIONAL IDEOLOGIES

We have considered the various psychological theories as parts of educational ideologies. Associated with these theories are differing epistemologies or philosophies of science, specifying what is knowledge, i.e. what are observable facts and how can these facts be interpreted. Differences in epistemology, just as differences in actual theory, generate different strategies for defining objectives.

Romantic educational ideology springs not only from a maturational psychology, but from an existentialist or phenomenological epistemology, defining knowledge and reality as referring to the immediate inner experience of the self. Knowledge or truth in the romantic epistemology is self-awareness or self-insight, a form of truth with emotional as well as intellectual components. As this form of truth extends beyond the self, it is through sympathetic understanding of humans and natural beings as other "selves."

In contrast, cultural transmission ideologies of education tend to involve epistemologies which stress knowledge as that which is repetitive and "objective," that which can be pointed to in sense-experience and measurement and which can be culturally shared and tested.

The progressive ideology, in turn, derives from a functional or pragmatic epistemology which equates knowledge with neither inner experience nor outer sense-reality, but with an equilibrated or resolved relationship between an inquiring human actor and a problematic situation. For the progressive epistemology, the immediate or introspective experience of the child does not have ultimate truth or reality. The meaning and truth of the child's experience depends upon its relationship to the situations in which he is acting. At the same time, the progressive epistemology does not attempt to reduce psychological experience to observable responses in reaction to observable stimuli or situations. Rather, it attempts to functionally coordinate the external meaning of the child's experiences as *behavior* with its internal meaning as it appears to the observer.

With regard to educational objectives, these differences in epistemology generate differences with respect to three issues. The first issue concerns whether to focus objectives on internal states or external behavior. In this respect, cultural transmission and romantic ideologies represent opposite poles. The cultural transmission view evaluates educational change from children's performances, not from their feelings or thoughts. Social growth is defined by the conformity of behavior to particular cultural standards such as honesty and industriousness. These skill and trait terms are found in both common-sense evaluations of school grades and report cards, and in "objective" educational psychological measurement. Behaviorist ideologies systematize this focus by rigorously eliminating references to internal or subjective experience as "non-scientific." Skinner (1971) says:

> We can follow the path taken by physics and biology by turning directly to the relation between behavior and the environment and neglecting...states of mind....

We do not need to try to discover what personalities, states of mind, feelings,...intentions—or other prerequisites of autonomous man really are in order to get on with a scientific analysis of behavior. (p. 15)

In contrast, the romantic view emphasizes inner feelings and states. Supported by the field of psychotherapy, romantics maintain that skills, achievements, and performances are not satisfying in themselves, but are only a means to inner awareness, happiness, or mental health. They hold that an educator or therapist who ignores the child's inner states in the name of science does so at his peril, since it is these which are most real to the child.

The progressive or cognitive-developmental view attempts to integrate both behavior and internal states in a functional epistemology of mind. It takes inner experience seriously by attempting to observe thought process rather than language behavior and by observing valuing processes rather than reinforced behavior. In doing so, however, it combines interviews, behavioral tests, and naturalistic observation methods in mental assessment. The cognitive-developmental approach stresses the need to examine mental competence or mental structure as opposed to examining only performance, but it employs a functional rather than an introspective approach to the observation of mental structure. An example is Piaget's systematic and reproducible observations of the preverbal infant's thought-structure of space, time, and causality. In short, the cognitive-developmental approach does not select a focus on inner experience or on outer behavior objectives by epistemological fiat, but uses a functional methodology to coordinate the two through empirical study.

A second issue in the definition of educational objectives involves whether to emphasize immediate experience and behavior or long-term consequences in the child's development. The progressive ideology centers on education as it relates to the child's experience, but attempts to observe or assess experience in functional terms rather than by immediate self-projection into the child's place. As a result the progressive distinguishes between *humanitarian* criteria of the quality of the child's experience and *educative* criteria of quality of experience, in terms of long-term developmental consequences. According to Dewey (1938),

Some experiences are miseducative. Any experience is miseducative that has the effect of arresting or distorting the growth of further experience.... An experience may be immediately enjoyable and yet promote the formation of a slack and careless attitude...(which) operates to modify the quality of subsequent experiences so as to prevent a person from getting out of them what they have to give.... Just as no man lives or dies to himself, so no experience lives or dies to itself. Wholly independent of desire or intent, every experience lives on in further experiences. Hence the central problem of an education based on experience is to select the kind of present experiences that live fruitfully and creatively in subsequent experience. (pp. 25–28)

Dewey maintains that an educational experience which stimulates development is one which arouses interest, enjoyment, and challenge in the immediate experience of the student. The reverse is not necessarily the case; immediate interest and enjoyment does not always indicate that an educational experience stimulates long-range development. Interest and involvement is a necessary but not sufficient condition for education as development. For romantics, especially of the "humanistic psychology" variety, having a novel, intense, and complex experience is *self-development* or self-actualization. For progressives, a more objective test of the effects of the experience on later behavior is required before deciding that the experience is developmental. The progressive views the child's enjoyment and interest as a basic and legitimate criterion of education, but views it as a humanitarian rather than an educational criterion. The progressive holds that education must meet humanitarian criteria, but argues that a concern for the enjoyment and liberty of the child is not in itself equivalent to a concern for his development.

Psychologically, the distinction between humanitarian and developmental criteria is the distinction between the short-term value of the child's immediate experience and the long-term value of that experience as it relates to development. According to the progressive view, this question of the relation of the immediate to the long-term is an empirical rather than a philosophic question. As an example, a characteristic behaviorist strategy is to demonstrate the reversibility of learning by performing an experiment in which a preschooler is reinforced for interacting with other children rather than withdrawing in a corner. This is followed by a reversal of the experiment, demonstrating that when the reinforcement is removed the child again becomes withdrawn. From the progressive or cognitive-developmental perspective, if behavior changes are of this reversible character they cannot define genuine educational objectives. The progressive approach maintains that the worth of an educational effect is decided by its effects upon later behavior and development. Thus, in the progressive view, the basic problems of choosing and validating educational ends can only be solved by longitudinal studies of the effects of educational experience.

The third basic issue is whether the aims of education should be universal as opposed to unique or individual. This issue has an epistemological aspect because romantics have often defined educational goals in terms of the expression or development of a unique self or identity; "objectivist" epistemologies deny that such concepts are accessible to clear observation and definition. In contrast, cultural transmission approaches characteristically focus on measures of individual differences in general dimension of achievement, or social behavior dimensions on which any individual can be ranked. The progressive, like the romantic, questions the significance of defining behavior relative to some population norm external to the individual. Searching for the "objective" in human experience, the progressive seeks universal qualitative states or sequences in development. Movement from one stage to the next is significant because it is a sequence in the individual's own development, not just a population average or norm. At the same time, insofar as the sequence is a universally observed development it is not unique to the individual in question.

In summary, the cognitive-developmental approach derives from a functional or pragmatic epistemology which attempts to integrate the dichotomies of the inner versus the outer, the immediate versus the remote in time, the unique versus the general. The cognitive-developmental approach focuses on an empirical search for continuities between inner states and outer behavior and between immediate reaction and remote outcome. While focusing on the child's experience, the progressive ideology defines such experience in terms of universal and empirically observable sequences of development.

ETHICAL VALUE POSITIONS
UNDERLYING EDUCATIONAL IDEOLOGIES

When psychologists like Dewey, Skinner, Neill and Montessori actually engage in innovative education, they develop a theory which is not a mere statement of psychological principle, it is an ideology. This is not because of the dogmatic, non-scientific attitude they have as psychologists, but because prescription of educational practice cannot be derived from psychological theory or science alone. In addition to theoretical assumptions about how children learn or develop (the psychological theory component), educational ideologies include value assumptions about what is educationally good or worthwhile. To call a pattern of educational thought an ideology is to indicate it is a fairly systematic combination of a theory about psychological and social fact with a set of value principles.

The Fallacy of Value Neutrality

A "value-neutral" position, based only on facts about child development or about methods of education, cannot in itself directly contribute to educational practice Factual statements about what the processes of learning and development *are* cannot be directly translated into statements about what children's learning and development *ought to be* without introduction of some value-principles.

In "value-neutral" research, learning does not necessarily imply movement to a stage of greater cognitive or ethical adequacy. As an example, acquisition of a cognitively arbitrary or erroneous concept (e.g., it is best to put a marble in the hole) is considered learning in the same general sense as is acquisition of a capacity for logical inference. Such studies do not relate learning to some justifiable notion of knowledge, truth, or cognitive adequacy. Values are defined relative to a particular culture. Thus, morality is equivalent to conformity to, or internalization of, the particular standards of the child's group or culture. As an example, Berkowitz (1964) writes: "Moral values are evaluations of actions generally believed by the members of a given society to be either 'right' or 'wrong'" (p. 44).

Such "value-free" research cannot be translated into prescriptions for practice without importing a set of value-assumptions having no relation to psychology itself. The effort to remain "value-free" or "non-ideological" and yet prescribe educational goals usually has followed the basic model of counselling or consulting. In the *value-free consulting model*, the client (whether student or school) defines educational ends and the psychologist can then advise about means of education without losing his value-neutrality or imposing his values. Outside education, the value-free consulting model not only provides the basic model for counselling and psychotherapy, where the client is an individual, but also for industrial psychology, where the client is a social system. In both therapy and industrial psychology the consultant is paid by the client and the financial contract defines whose values are to be chosen. The educator or educational psychologist, however, has more than one client. What the child wants, what parents want, and what the larger community wants are often at odds with one another.

An even more fundamental problem for the "value-free" consulting model is the logical impossibility of making a dichotomy between value-free means and value-loaded ends. Skinner (1971, p. 17) claims that "a behavior technology is ethically neutral. Both the villain and the saint can use it. There is nothing in a methodology that determines the values governing its use." But consider the use of torture on the rack as a behavior technology for learning which could be used by saint and villain alike. On technological grounds Skinner advises against punishment, but this does not solve the ethical issue.

Dewey's logical analysis and our present historical awareness of the value consequences of adopting new technologies have made us realize that choices of means, in the last analysis, also imply choices of ends. Advice about means and methods involves value considerations and cannot be made purely on a basis of "facts." Concrete, positive reinforcement is not an ethically neutral means. To advise the use of concrete reinforcement is to advise that a certain kind of character, motivated by concrete reinforcement, is the end of education. Not only can advice about means not be separated from choice of ends, but there is no way for an educational consultant to avoid harboring his own criteria for choosing ends. The "value-neutral" consulting model equates value-neutrality with acceptance of value-relativity, that is, acceptance of whatever the values of the client are. But the educator or educational psychologist cannot be neutral in this sense either.

Values and the Cultural Transmission Ideology

In an effort to cope with the dilemmas inherent in value-neutral prescription, many psychologists tend to move to a cultural transmission ideology, based on the value premise of *social relativity*. Social relativity assumes some consistent set of values characteristic of the culture, nation, or system as a whole. While these values may be arbitrary and may vary from one social system to another, there is at least some consensus about them. This approach says, "Since values are relative and arbitrary, we might as well take the given values of the society as our starting point and advocate 'adjustment' to the culture or achievement in it as the educational end." The social relativist basis of the Bereiter-Engelmann system, for example, is stated as follows:

> In order to use the term cultural deprivation, it is necessary to assume some point of reference. . . . The standards of the American public schools represent one such point of reference. . . . There are standards of knowledge and ability which are consistently held to be valuable in the schools, and any child in the schools who falls short of these standards by reason of his particular cultural background may be said to be culturally deprived. (1966, p. 24)

The Bereiter-Engelmann preschool model takes as its standard of value "the standard of the American public schools." It recognizes that this standard is arbitrary and that the kinds of learning prized by the American public schools may not be the most worthy; but it accepts this arbitrariness because it assumes that "all values are relative," that there is no ultimate standard of worth for learning and development.

Unlike Bereiter and Engelmann, many social relativist educators do not simply accept the standards of the school and culture and attempt to maximize conformity to them. Rather, they are likely to elaborate or create standards for a school or society based on value premises derived from what we shall call "the psychologist's fallacy." According to many philosophical analysts, the effort to derive statements of *ought* (or value) directly from statements of *is* (or fact) is a logical fallacy termed the "naturalistic fallacy" (Kohlberg, 1971). The psychologist's fallacy is a form of the naturalistic fallacy. As practiced by psychologists, the naturalistic fallacy is the direct derivation of statements about what human nature, human values, and human desires ought to be from psychological statements about what they are. Typically, this derivation slides over the distinction between what is desired and what is desirable.

The following statement from B. F. Skinner (1971) offers a good example of the psychologist's fallacy:

> Good things are positive reinforcers. Physics and biology study things without reference to their values, but the reinforcing effects of things are the province of behavioral science, which, to the extent that it concerns itself with operant reinforcement, is a science of values. Things are good (positively reinforcing) presumably because of the contingencies of survival under which the species evolved. It is part of the genetic endowment called "human nature" to be reinforced in particular ways by particular things. . . . The effective reinforcers are matters of observation and no one can dispute them. (p. 104)

In this statement, Skinner equates or derives a value word (good) from a fact word (positive reinforcement). This equation is questionable; we wonder whether obtaining positive reinforcement really is good. The psychologist's fallacy or the naturalistic fallacy is a fallacy because we can always ask the further question, "Why is that good?" or "By what standard is that good?" Skinner does not attempt to deal with this further question, called the "open question" by philosophers. He also defines good as "cultural survival." The postulation of cultural survival as an ultimate value raises the open question too. We may ask, "Why should the Nazi culture (or the American culture) survive?" The reason Skinner is not concerned with answering the open question about survival is because he is a cultural relativist, believing that any non-factual reasoning about what is good or about the validity of moral principles is meaningless. He says:

> What a given group of people calls good is a fact, it is what members of the group find reinforcing as a result of their genetic endowment and the natural and social contingencies to which they have been exposed. Each culture has its own set of goods, and what is good in one culture may not be good in another. (p. 128)

The Fallacy of Value-Relativism

Behind Skinner's value-relativism, then, lie the related notions that: (1) all valid inferences or principles are factual or scientific; (2) valid statements about values must be statements about facts of valuing; and (3) what people actually value differs. The fact that people do value different things only becomes an argument for the notion that values are relative if one accepts the first two assumptions listed. Both assumptions are believed by many philosophers to be mistaken because they represent forms of the fact-value confusion already described as the naturalistic fallacy. Confusing discourse about fact with discourse about values, the relativist believes that when ethical judgment is not empirical science, it is not rational. This equation of science with rationality arises because the relativist does not correctly understand philosophical modes of inquiry. In modern conceptions, philosophy is the clarification of concepts for the purpose of critical evaluation of beliefs and standards. The kinds of beliefs which primarily concern philosophy are normative beliefs or standards, beliefs about what ought to be rather than about what is. These include standards of the right or good (ethics), of the true (epistemology), and of the beautiful (esthetics). In science, the critical evaluation of factual beliefs is limited to criteria of causal explanation and prediction; a "scientific" critical evaluation of normative beliefs is limited to treating them as a class of facts. Philosophy, by contrast, seeks rational justification and criticism of normative beliefs, based on considerations additional to their predictive or causal explanatory power. There is fairly widespread agreement among philosophers that criteria for the validity of ethical judgments can be established independent of "scientific" or predictive criteria. Since patterns for the rational statement and justification of normative beliefs, or "oughts," are not identical with patterns of scientific statement and justification, philosophers can reject both Skinner's notion of strictly "scientific" ethics and Skinner's notion that whatever is not "scientific" is relative. The open question "Why is reinforcement or cultural survival good?" is meaningful because there are patterns of ethical justification which are ignored by Skinner's relativistic science.

Distinguishing criteria of moral judgment from criteria of scientific judgment, most philosophers accept the "methodological non-relativism" of moral judgment just as they accept the methodological non-relativism of scientific judgment (Brandt, 1956). This ethical non-relativism is based on appeal to principles for making moral judgments, just as scientific non-relativism is based on appeal to principles of scientific method or of scientific judgment.

In summary, cultural transmission ideologies rest on the value premise of social relativism—the doctrine that values are relative to, and based upon, the standards of the particular culture and cannot be questioned or further justified. Cultural transmission ideologies of the "scientific" variety, like Skinner's, do not recognize moral principles since they equate what is desirable with what is observable by science, or with what is desired. Philosophers are not in agreement on the exact formulation of valid moral principles though they agree that such formulations center around notions like "the greatest welfare" or "justice as equity." They also do not agree on choice of priorities between principles such as "justice" and "the greatest welfare." Most philosophers do agree, however, that moral evaluations must be rooted in, or justified by, reference to such a realm of principles. Most also maintain that certain values or principles ought to be universal and that these principles are distinct from the rules of any given culture. A principle is a universalizeable, impartial mode of deciding or judging, not a concrete cultural rule. "Thou shalt not commit adultery" is a rule for specific behavior in specific situations in a monogamous society. By contrast, Kant's Categorical Imperative— act only as you would be willing that everyone should act in the same situation—is a principle. It is a guide for choosing among behaviors, not a prescription for behavior. As such it is free from culturally-defined content; it both transcends and subsumes particular social laws. Hence it has universal applicability.

In regard to values, Skinner's cultural transmission ideology is little different from other, older ideologies based on social relativism and on subjective forms of hedonism, for example, social Darwinism and Benthamite utilitarianism. As an educational ideology, however, Skinner's relativistic behavior technology has one feature which distinguishes it from older forms of social utilitarianism. This is its denial that rational concern for social utility is itself a matter of moral character or moral principle to be transmitted to the young. In Skinner's view, moral character concepts which go beyond responsiveness to social reinforcement and control rely on "prescientific" concepts of free will. Stated in different terms, the concept of moral education is irrelevant to Skinner; he is not concerned with teaching to the children of his society the value-principles which he himself adopts. The culture designer is a *psychologist-king*, a value relativist, who somehow makes a free, rational decision to devote himself to controlling individual behavior more effectively in the service of cultural survival. In Skinner's scheme there is no plan to make the controlled controllers, or to educate psychologist-kings.

Values and the Romantic Ideology

At first sight the value premises of the romantic ideology appear to be the polar opposites of Skinner's cultural transmission ideology. Opposed to social control and survival is individual freedom, freedom for the child to be himself. For example, A. S. Neill (1960) says:

> How can happiness be bestowed? My own answer is: Abolish authority. Let the child be himself. Don't push him around. Don't teach him. Don't lecture him. Don't elevate him. Don't force him to do anything. (p. 297)

As we have pointed out, the romantic ideology rests on a psychology which conceives of the child as having a spontaneously growing mind. In addition, however, it rests on the ethical postulate that "the guardians of the young should merit the proud title of the defenders of the happiness and rights of children" (G. S. Hall, 1901, p. 24). The current popularity of the romantic ideology in "free school," "de-school," and "open school" movements is related to increased adult respect for the rights of children. Bereiter (1972) carries this orientation to an extreme conclusion:

> Teachers are looking for a way to get out of playing God.... The same humanistic ethos that tells them what qualities the next generation should have also tells them that they have no right to manipulate other people or impose their goals upon them. The fact is that there are no morally safe goals for teachers any more. Only processes are safe. When it comes to goals, everything is in doubt.... A common expression, often thrown at me, when I have argued for what I believed children should be taught, is "Who are we to say what this child should learn." The basic moral problem...is inherent in education itself. If you are engaged in education, you are engaged in an effort to influence the course of the child's development...it is to determine what kinds of people they turn out to be. It is to create human beings, it is, therefore, to play God. (pp. 26–27)

This line of thought leads Bereiter to conclude:

> The Godlike role of teachers in setting goals for the development of children is no longer morally tenable. A shift to informal modes of education does not remove the difficulty. This paper, then, questions the assumption that education, itself, is a good undertaking and considers the possibilities of a world in which values other than educational ones, come to the fore. (p. 25)

According to Bereiter, then, a humanistic ethical concern for the child's rights must go beyond romantic free schools, beyond de-schooling, to the abandonment of an explicit concern for education. Bereiter contrasts the modern "humanistic ethic," and its concern for the child's rights, with the earlier "liberal" concern for human rights which held education and the common school as the foundation of a free society. This earlier concern Bereiter sees expressed most cogently in Dewey's progressivism.

The historical shift in the conception of children's rights and human rights leading Bereiter to reject Dewey's position is essentially a shift from the liberal grounding of children's rights in ethical principles to the modern humanistic grounding of children's rights in the doctrine of ethical relativity.

Bereiter is led to question the moral legitimacy of education because he equates a regard for the child's liberty with a belief in ethical relativity, rather than recognizing that liberty and justice are universal ethical principles. "The teacher may try to play it safe by sticking to the middle of the road and only aiming to teach what is generally approved, but there are not enough universally endorsed values (if, indeed, there are any) to form the basis of an education" (Bereiter, 1972, p. 27). Here, he confuses an ethical position of tolerance or respect for the child's freedom with a belief in ethical relativity, not recognizing that respect for the child's liberty derives from a principle of justice rather than from a belief that all moral values are arbitrary. Respect for the child's liberty means awarding him the maximum liberty compatible with the liberty of others (and of himself when older), not refusal to deal with his values and behavior. The assumption of individual relativity of values underlying modern romantic statements of the child's liberty is also reflected in the following quote from Neill (1960):

> Well, we set out to make a school in which we should allow children freedom to be themselves. In order to do this, we had to renounce all discipline, all direction, all suggestion, all moral training, all religious instruction. We have been called brave, but it did not require courage. All it required was what we had—a complete belief in the child as a good, not an evil, being. For almost forty years, this belief in the goodness of the child has never wavered, it rather has become a final faith. (p. 4)

For Neill, as for many free school advocates, value relativity does not involve what it did for Bereiter—a questioning of all conceptions of what is good in children and good for them. Neill's statement that the child is "good" is a completely non-relativist conception. It does not, however, refer to an ethical or moral principle or standard used to direct the child's education. Instead, just as in Skinner's cultural transmission ideology, the conception of the good is derived from what we have termed the psychologist's fallacy. Neill's faith in the "goodness of the child" is the belief that what children *do* want, when left to themselves, can be equated with what they *should* want from an ethical standpoint. In one way this faith is a belief that children are wired so as to act and develop compatibly with ethical norms. In another sense, however, it is an ethical postulation that decisions about what is right for children should be derived from what children do desire— that whatever children do is right.

This position begs the open question, "Why is freedom to be oneself good; by what standard is it a good thing?"

The question is raised by Dewey as follows (1938):

> The objection made [to identifying the educative process with growing or developing] is that growth might take many different directions: a man, for example, who starts out on a career of burglary may grow in that direction...into a highly expert burglar. Hence it is argued that 'growth' is not enough; we must also specify the direction in which growth takes place, the end toward which it tends. (p. 75)

In Neill's view it is not clear whether there is a standard of development, i.e., some standard of goodness which children who grow up freely all meet, or whether children who grow up freely are good only by their own standards, even if they are thieves or villains by some other ethical standards. To the extent that there is a non-relativist criterion employed by Neill, it does not derive from, nor is it justified by, the ethical principles of philosophy. Rather, it is derived from matters of psychological fact about "mental health" and "happiness."

> The merits of Summerhill are the merits of healthy free children whose lives are unspoiled by fear and hate. (Neill, 1960, p. 4)
>
> The aim of education, in fact, the aim of life is to work joyfully and to find happiness. (Neill, 1960, p. 297).

Freedom, then, is not justified as an ethical principle but as a matter of psychological fact, leading to "mental health and happiness." These are ultimate terms, as are the terms "maximizing reinforcement" and "cultural survival" for Skinner. For other romantic educators the ultimate value terms are also psychological, for example, "self-realization," "self-actualization," and "spontaneity." These are defined as "basic human tendencies" and are taken as good in themselves rather than being subject to the scrutiny of moral philosophy.

We have attempted to show that romantic libertarian ideologies are grounded on value-relativism and reliance on the psychologist's fallacy, just as are cultural-transmission iedologies, which see education as behavior control in the service of cultural survival. As a result of these shared premises, both romantic and cultural-transmission ideologies tend to generate a kind of elitism. In the case of Skinner, this elitism is reflected in the vision of the psychologist as a culture-designer, who "educates others" to conform to culture and maintain it but not to develop the values and knowledge which would be required for culture-designing. In the case of the romantic, the elitism is reflected in a refusal to impose intellectual and ethical values of libertarianism, equal justice, intellectual inquiry, and social reconstructionism on the child, even though these values are held to be the most important ones:

> ...Summerhill is a place in which people who have the innate ability and wish to be

scholars will be scholars; while those who are only fit to sweep the streets will sweep the streets. But we have not produced a street cleaner so far. Nor do I write this snobbishly, for I would rather see a school produce a happy street cleaner than a neurotic scholar. (Neill, 1960, pp. 4–5)

In summary, in spite of their libertarian and non-indoctrinative emphases, romantic ideologies also have a tendency to be elitist or patronizing. Recalling the role of Dostoievsky's Grand Inquisitor, they see education as a process which only intends the child to be happy and adjusted rather than one which confronts the child with the ethical and intellectual problems and principles which the educator himself confronts. Skinner and Neill agree it is better for the child to be a happy pig than an unhappy Socrates. We may question, however, whether they have the right to withhold that choice.

Value Postulates of Progressivism

Progressive ideology, in turn, rests on the value postulates of ethical liberalism.* This position rejects traditional standards and value-relativism in favor of ethical universals. Further, it recognizes that value universals are ethical principles formulated and justified by the method of philosophy, not simply by the method of psychology. The ethical liberal position favors the active stimulation of the development of these principles in children. These principles are presented through a process of critical questioning which creates an awareness of the ground and limits of rational assent; they also are seen as relevant to universal trends in the child's own social and moral development. The liberal recognition of principles as *principles* clears them from confusion with psychological facts. To be concerned about children's happiness is an ethical imperative for the educator without regard to "mental health," "positive reinforcement," or other psychological terms used by educators who commit the "psychologist's fallacy." Rational ethical principles, not the values of parents or culture, are the final value-arbiters in defining educational aims. Such principles may call for consultation with parents, community, and children in formulating aims, but they do not warrant making them final judges of aims.

The liberal school recognizes that ethical principles determine the ends as well as the means of education. There is great concern not only to make schools more just, that is, to provide equality of educational opportunity and to allow freedom of belief but also to educate so that free and just people emerge from the schools. Accordingly, liberals also conscientiously engage in moral education. It is here that

---

*There are two main schools of ethical liberalism. The more naturalistic or utilitarian one is represented in the works of J. S. Mill, Sidgewick, Dewey, and Tufts. The other is represented in the works of Locke, Kant, and Rawls. A modern statement of the liberal ethical tradition in relation to education is provided by R. S. Peters (1968).

the progressive and romantic diverge, in spite of a common concern for the liberty and rights of the child. For the romantic, liberty means non-interference. For the liberal, the principle of respect for liberty is itself defined as a moral aim of education. Not only are the rights of the child to be respected by the teacher, but the child's development is to be stimulated so that he may come to respect and defend his own rights and the rights of others.

Recognition of concern for liberty as a principle leads to an explicit, libertarian conception of moral education. According to Dewey and McLellan (1895),

> Summing up, we may say that every teacher requires a sound knowledge of ethical and psychological principles.... Only psychology and ethics can take education out of the rule-of-thumb stage and elevate the school to a vital, effective institution in the *greatest of all constructions—the building of a free and powerful character.* (p. 207)

In the liberal view, educational concern for the development of a "free character" is rooted in the principle of liberty. For the romantic or relativist libertarian this means that "everyone has their own bag," which may or may not include liberty; and to actively stimulate the development of regard for liberty or a free character in the child is as much an imposition on the child as any other educational intervention. The progressive libertarians differ on this point. They advocate a strong rather than a weak application of liberal principles to education. Consistent application of ethical principles to education means that education *should* stimulate the development of ethical principles in students.

In regard to ethical values, the progressive ideology adds the postulates of *development* and *democracy* to the postulates of liberalism. The notion of educational democracy is one in which justice between teacher and child means joining in a community in which value decisions are made on a shared and equitable basis, rather than non-interference with the child's value-decisions. Because ethical principles function as principles, the progressive ideology is "democratic" in a sense that romantic and cultural transmission ideologies are not.

In discussing Skinner we pointed to a fundamental problem in the relation between the ideology of the relativist educator and that of the student. Traditional education did not find it a problem to reconcile the role of teacher and the role of student. Both were members of a common culture and the task of the teacher was to transmit that culture and its values to the student. In contrast, modern psychologists advocating cultural transmission ideologies do not hold this position. As social relativists they do not really believe in a common culture; instead they are in the position of transmitting values which are different both from those they believe in and those believed in by the student. At the extreme, as we mentioned earlier, Skinner proposes an ideology for ethically relative psychologist-kings or culture designers who control others. Clearly there is a contradiction between the ideology for the psychologist-king and the ideology for the child.

Romantic or radical ideologies are also unable to solve this problem. The romantic adopts what he assumes are the child's values, or takes as his value premise what is "natural" in the child rather than endorsing the culture's values. But while the adult believes in the child's freedom and creativity and wants a free, more natural society, the child neither fully comprehends nor necessarily adheres to the adult's beliefs. In addition, the romantic must strive to give the child freedom to grow even though such freedom may lead the child to become a reactionary. Like the behavior modifier, then, the romantic has an ideology, but it is different from the one which the student is supposed to develop.

The progressive is non-elitist because he attempts to get all children to develop in the direction of recognizing the principles he holds. But is this not indoctrinative? Here we need to clarify the postulates of development and democracy as they guide education.

For the progressive, the problem of offering a non-indoctrinative education which is based on ethical and epistemological principles is partially resolved by a conception that these principles represent developmentally advanced or mature stages of reasoning, judgment, and action. Because there are culturally universal stages or sequences of moral development (Kohlberg & Turiel, 1971), stimulation of the child's development to the next step in a natural direction is equivalent to a long range goal of teaching ethical principles.

Because the development of these principles is natural they are not imposed on the child—he chooses them himself. A similar developmental approach is taken toward intellectual values. Intellectual education in the progressive view is not merely a transmission of information and intellectual skills, it is the communication of patterns and methods of "scientific" reflection and inquiry. These patterns correspond to higher stages of logical reasoning, Piaget's formal operations. According to the progressive, there is an important analogy between scientific and ethical patterns of judgment or problem-solving, and there are overlapping rationales for intellectual and ethical education. In exposing the child to opportunities for reflective scientific inquiry, the teacher is guided by the principles of scientific method which the teacher himself accepts as the basis of rational reflection. Reference to such principles is non-indoctrinative if these principles are not presented as formulae to be learned ready-made or as rote patterns grounded in authority. Rather, they are part of a process of reflection by the student and teacher. A similar approach guides the process of reflection on ethical or value problems.

The problem of indoctrination is also resolved for the progressive by the concept of democracy. A concern for the child's freedom from indoctrination is part of a concern for the child's freedom to make decisions and act meaningfully. Freedom, in this context, means democracy, that is, power and participation in a social system which recognizes basic equal rights. It is impossible for teachers not to engage in value-judgments and decisions. A concern for the liberty of the child does not create a school in which the teacher is value-neutral and any pretense of it creates "the hidden curriculum" (Kohlberg, 1969b). But it can create a school in which the teacher's value-judgments and decisions involve the students democratically.

We turn, now, to the nature and justification of these universal and intrinsically worthy aims and principles. In the next sections we attempt to indicate the way in which the concept of development, rooted in psychological study, can aid in prescribing aims of education without commission of the psychologist's fallacy. We call this the developmental-philosophic strategy for defining educational aims.

STRATEGIES FOR DEFINING EDUCATIONAL OBJECTIVES AND EVALUATING EDUCATIONAL EXPERIENCE

We have considered the core psychological and philosophical assumptions of the three major streams of educational ideology. Now we shall consider these assumptions as they have been used to define objectives in early education.

There appear to be three fundamental strategies for defining educational objectives, which we call "the bag of virtues" or "desirable trait" strategy, the "industrial psychology" or "prediction of success" strategy and the "developmental-philosophic" strategy. These strategies tend to be linked, respectively, with the romantic, the cultural transmission, and the progressive educational ideologies.

The romantic tends to define educational objectives in terms of a "bag of virtues"—a set of traits characterizing an ideal healthy or fully-functioning personality. Such definitions of objectives are justified by a psychiatric theory of a spontaneous, creative, or self-confident personality. This standard of value springs from the romantic form of the psychologist's fallacy. Statements of value (desirability of a character-trait) are derived from psychological propositions of fact, for example, that a given trait is believed to represent psychological "illness" or "health."

The cultural transmission ideology defines immediate objectives in terms of standards of knowledge and behavior learned in school. It defines the long-range objective as eventual power and status in the social system (e.g., income, success). In Skinner's terms, the objective is to maximize the reinforcement each individual receives from the system, while maintaining the system. In defining objectives, this focus on prediction of later success is common to those whose interest lies in maintaining the system in its present form and those whose interest lies in equalizing opportunity for success in the system.

Within the cultural transmission school there is a second strategy for elaborating objectives which we have called the "industrial psychology" approach (Kohlberg, 1972). Psychologically, this strategy is more explicitly atheoretical than the "bag of virtues" approach; with regard to values it is more socially relativistic. Adopting the stance of the value-free consultant, it evaluates a behavior in terms of its usefulness as a means to the student's or the system's ends, and focuses on the empirical prediction of later successes. In practice, this approach has focused heavily on tests and measurements of achievement as they predict or relate to later success in the educational or social system.

The third strategy, the developmental-philosophic, is linked to the progressive ideology. The progressive believes that a liberal conception of education pursuing intrinsically worthy aims or states is the best one for everyone. Such a conception of objectives must have a psychological component. The progressive defines the psychologically valuable in developmental terms. Implied in the term "development" is the notion that a more developed psychological state is more valuable or adequate than a less developed state.

The developmental-philosophic strategy attempts to clarify, specify, and justify the concept of adequacy implicit in the concept of development. It does so through: (a) elaborating a formal psychological theory of development—the cognitive-developmental theory; (b) elaborating a formal ethical and epistemological theory of truth and worth linked to the psychological theory; (c) relating both of these to the facts of development in a specific area; and (d) describing empirical sequences of development worth cultivating.

Now we need to critically examine the three strategies. Our task is both logical and empirical. Logically, the chief question is, "Does the strategy define objectives which are intrinsically valuable or universally desirable? Can it deal with the charge that its value is relative or arbitrary?" Empirically, the major question is, "Does the strategy define objectives predicting to something of long-term value in later life?"

The Bag of Virtues Strategy

The "bag of virtues" strategy for choosing objectives is the approach which comes most naturally to educators. An example is the formulation of a Headstart list of objectives—as cited in Dr. Edith Grotberg's review (1969) offered by a panel of authorities on child development. One goal is "helping the emotional and social development of the child by encouraging self-confidence, spontaneity, curiosity and self-discipline." We may note that development is defined here in terms of trait words. From the point of view of the philosophic-developmentalist, the qualification of the term "social development" by such trait words is superfluous and misleading. The developmentalist would chart universals in preschool social development empirically and theoretically with implications for later development and would indicate the conditions which stimulate such development. Such a charting of development would make trait words like "spontaneity" and "self-confidence" unnecessary.

The justification for using trait words to qualify development as an educational end has usually been that development is too vague a term. We consider this question later. Here we need only note the arbitrariness and vagueness which underlies all efforts to use the positive connotations of ordinary trait terms of personality or character to define educational standards and values. This arbitrariness and vagueness exists in lists of mental health traits such as the Headstart list and also in lists of moral virtues composing moral character, such as the Hartshorne and May (1928–1932) objectives of "honesty, service, and self-control." Arbitrariness exists first in composing the list or "bag" of virtues itself. One member of the committee likes "self-discipline," another "spontaneity"; the committee includes both. While both words sound nice, one wonders whether cultivating "self-discipline" and cultivating "spontaneity" are consistent with one another. Second, we may note that the observable meaning of a virtue-word is relative to a conventional cultural standard which is both psychologically vague and ethically relative. The behavior that one person labels "self-discipline" another calls "lack of spontaneity." Because the observable meaning of a virtue-word is relative to a conventional cultural standard, its meaning is psychologically vague, a fact which was first demonstrated by Hartshorne and May for the virtue-word "honesty." Hartshorne and May were dismayed to discover that they could locate no such stable personality trait as honesty in school children. A child who cheated on one occasion might or might not cheat on another: cheating was for the most part situationally determined. In a factor analysis, there was no clearly identifiable factor or correlation pattern which could be called "honesty." Furthermore, "honesty" measurements did not predict to later behavior. This contradicts the commonsense notion underlying the bag of virtues approach. It turns out that dictionary terms for personality do not describe situationally general personality dispositions which are stable or predictive over development.

Related to the problem of psychological definition and measurement is the problem of the relativity of the standard of value defining "honesty" or any other virtue. Labeling a set of behaviors displayed by a child with positive or negative trait terms does not signify that they are of adaptive or ethical importance. It represents an appeal to particular community conventions, since one person's *"integrity"* is another person's *"stubbornness,"* one person's *"honesty* in expressing your true feelings" is another person's *"insensitivity* to the feelings of others."

We have criticized the "bag of virtues" approach on the grounds of *logical* questions raised by a procedure of sorting through the dictionary for trait terms with positive meaning. We need next to question two "scientific" or *psychological* assumptions, the concept of the personality trait and the concept of mental health, as they relate to the development of children. With regard to the trait assumption, longitudinal research findings lead us to question whether there are positive or adaptive childhood personality traits which are stable or predictive over time and development, even if such traits are defined by psychological rather than lexical methods. The relatively general and longitudinally stable personality traits which have been identified in earlier childhood are traits of temperament—introversion-extroversion, passivity-activity—which have been shown to be in large part hereditary temperamental traits without adaptive significance (research reviewed in Ausubel & Sullivan, 1970; Kohlberg, 1969b; Kohlberg, La Crosse, & Ricks, 1971). The longitudinal research indicates that the notions of "mental health" or "mental illness" are even more questionable as concepts defining the meaning and value of personality traits. Unlike development, the term "mental health" has no clear psychological meaning when applied to children and their education. When the clinician examines a child with reference to mental health, he records the child's lags (and advances) in cognitive, social, and psychomotor development. Occasionally such lags are indicative of "illness," for example, of an organic brain condition. But, in general, if "illness" means anything beyond retarded development it means a prognosis of continued failure to develop. Considering the child's development as an aim of education, the metaphors of health and illness add little to detailed and adequate conceptions of cognitive and social development. This also is indicated by empirical longitudinal findings (Kohlberg, LaCrosse, & Ricks, 1971). We are led to ask whether early childhood traits with apparent negative mental health implications like dependency, aggression, or anxiety, have predictive value as indicators of adult difficulties in "life adjustment" or "mental health." The answer at present is no: the mental health traits listed among the Headstart objectives, as well as those commonly included among the goals of other early education programs, have failed to show their predictive value for positive or negative adult life adjustment. Even if the behavior changes sought in such programs were achieved, the child would be no more likely than before to become a well-adjusted adult.

Secondly, from the philosophic point of view, those who espouse the mental health bag of virtues commit the psychologist's fallacy and a related fallacy, that a panel of psychiatrists or child psychiatrists such as the one defining Headstart objectives are "experts" on ethical principles or values.

In educational practice, a concern for mental health has at least meant an ethical concern for the happiness of the child; this was neglected by the cultural transmission school. But ethical principles based on a concern for the child's liberty and happiness can stand on their own without a mental health bag of virtues to rationalize them.

The Industrial Psychology Rationale

Translating educational objectives into a "bag of virtues" (skills) in the intellectual domain does not run into all the difficulties which it has encountered in the social-emotional domain. This is because reasonable precision has been attained in defining and measuring intellectual skills and achievements, because there is some-degree of predictability over time in these skills, and because the questions of value-relativity raised by concepts of "moral character" and "mental health" as educational objectives are not as obvious when school aims are defined in terms of intellectual skills. But concepts of intellectual skills have only appeared satisfactory because of the high empirical overlap or correlation of these skills, with cognitive development (in the developmental-philosophic sense) and because of the overlap with the non-educational or "biological" constant of general intelligence. Once cognitive skills are defined and measured by educational *achievement* measures, they have little clear use in defining educational objectives.

The "achievement skills" conception is a joint product of the "bag of virtues" and "industrial psychology" approach to educational aims. We have noted that the industrial psychology approach rests on identifying and measuring relative individual success in meeting the task demands of a current job or work-position, and on identifying characteristics predicting to later success or mobility in the job system. Its major application in education has been the development of achievement tests. While not originally developed to define operational educational goals, achievement tests have frequently been used for this purpose. The massive Coleman Report (1966) rested its entire analysis of the quality and effects of schooling on variations in achievement test scores. A number of academic early education programs, including the Bereiter and Engelmann program (1966) previously quoted, essentially define their objective as the improvement of later achievement scores.

From the ethical or philosophic point of view, the use of achievement tests to measure educational objectives rests on a compounding of one type of relativism on another. The items composing an achievement test do not derive from any epistemological principles of adequate patterns of thought and knowledge, but rather represent samples of items taught in the schools. The information taught in the schools is relative and arbitrary: Latin and Greek for one hour, computer programming for another. There is no internal logical or epistemological analysis of these items to justify their worth. Another relativistic aspect of achievement tests is "marking on the curve." This leads to what Zigler has called "defining compensatory education objectives as raising the entire country above the 50th percentile in achievement tests" (unpublished comment).

Finally, and most basically, the relativism underlying achievement tests involves predicting to success in a system without asking whether the system awards success in an ethically justifiable manner, or whether success itself is an ethically justifiable goal. The original ethical impulse in constructing the achievement test was to equalize educational opportunity by a more impartial selection system than teachers' grades, recommendations, and the quality of schools the child has previously attended. This was done with relativistic acceptance that the content and demands of the school serve as social status gating mechanisms. It is hardly surprising that the whole desire to equalize opportunity, or increase educational and occupational justice through raising educational achievement scores, has failed in every possible sense of the word "failure" (Jencks, et al., 1972).

On the psychological and factual side, there have been two basic and related flaws in the assumption that achievement tests represent something of educational value. The first is the notion that correlation or prediction can be substituted for causation. The second, related notion is that success within an arbitrary system, the schools, implies success in other aspects of life. With regard to the first assumption, advocates of the industrial psychology strategy and achievement tests based on it feel that the relation between causation and prediction is unimportant. We can efficiently select those who will do well in college, become successful salesmen, or become juvenile delinquents without facing the causation issue. But if we shift from using a test or a measure of behavior as a selector to using it as the criterion for an educational objective, the problem is quite different. Unless a predictor of later achievement or adjustment is also a causal determinant of it, it cannot be used to define educational objectives.

As an example of the confusion between correlation and causation, we know that grades and achievement scores in elementary school predict to comparable scores in high school which in turn predict to comparable scores in college. The assumption is then made that the *cause* of particular achievement scores is the earlier achievement. It is assumed that a child who does not attain a second grade level of performance on reading achievement will not attain an adequate level of reading later because he is low in reading achievement at second grade.

In fact, the prediction of early to later achievement is mainly due to factors extraneous to achievement itself. Longitudinal studies show that the stability or predictive power of school achievement tests is largely due, first, to a factor of general intelligence and, second, to social class. Achievement scores correlate with IQ scores and both measures predict to later school achievement; early elementary achievement does not predict to later achievement any better than does IQ alone. In other words, bright children learn what they're taught in school faster, but learning what they're taught in school does not make them brighter nor does it necessarily mean that they will learn later material faster.

Achievement tests also fail to predict to success in later life; in fact, longitudinal studies indicate that school achievement predicts to nothing of value other than itself.

For example, in terms of future job success, high school dropouts do as well as graduates who do not attend college; high school graduates with poor achievement scores and grades do as well as those with good scores; and, college graduates with poor grades do as well as those with good grades (see Kohlberg, LaCrosse, & Ricks, 1971; Jencks, et al., 1972).

In summary, academic achievement tests have no theoretical rationale. Their practical rationale is primarily an industrial psychology "prediction for selection." But even by industrial psychology standards the tests do not do well since they fail to predict to later life achievement.

These criticisms do not imply that schools should be unconcerned with academic learning. They do suggest: (1) a heavy element of arbitrariness in current school objectives in academic learning; (2) the inability of educational testing methods endorsed by the industrial psychology school to make these objectives less arbitrary; and (3) the invalidity of assuming that if academic achievement is good, early achievement is best. Schools should teach reading, writing, and arithmetic, but their goals and success in teaching these subjects should not be judged by skill or achievement tests.

The Development-Philosophic Strategy

The developmental-philosophic strategy, as opposed to the other two, can deal with the ethical question of having a standard of non-relative or universal value and with factual questions of prediction. The concept of development, as elaborated by cognitive-developmental theory, implies a standard of adequacy *internal* to, and governing, the developmental process itself. It is obvious that the notion of development must do more than merely define what comes later in time. It is not clear that what comes later must be better. As an example, if anal interests mature later in time than oral interests, this in itself is no reason for claiming that the anal interests are better than the oral interests.

Cognitive-developmental theory, however, postulates a formal internal standard of adequacy which is not merely an order of events in time. In doing so it elaborates the ordinary-language meaning of the term "development." Webster's Dictionary tells us that to develop means "to make active, to move from the original position to one providing more opportunity for effective use, to cause to grow and differentiate along lines natural of its kind; to go through a process of natural growth, differentiation, or evolution by successive changes." This suggests an internal standard of adequacy governing development; it implies that development is not just any behavior change, but a change toward greater differentiation, integration, and adaptation. Cognitive-developmental psychological theory postulates that movement through a sequential progression represents movement from a less adequate psychological state to a more adequate psychological state. The existence of this "internal standard of adequacy" is suggested by studies which show that the child prefers thinking at the next higher moral or logical stage to thinking at his own stage (or at lower stages) (Rest, 1973), and that he moves in that direction under normal conditions of stimulation.

The concept of development also implies that such an internal standard of adequacy is different than notions of adaptation based on culturally relative success or survival. As a case, we may take stages of morality. Being at the highest moral stage led Socrates and Martin Luther King to be put to death by members of their culture. Obviously, then, moral development cannot be justified as adaptive by standards of survival or of conformity to cultural standards. In terms of developmental psychological theory, however, King's morality was more adequate than the morality of most people who survive longer. Formally, King's morality was a more differentiated and integrated moral system than that of most people. It was more adequate because if all people adopted King's morality, it would resolve for everyone moral problems and conflicts unresolved by lower-stage moralities.

As the example of King suggests, the formal standard of cognitive-developmental psychological theory is not itself ultimate, but must be elaborated as a set of ethical and epistemological principles and justified by the method of philosophy and of ethics. The distinctive feature of the developmental-philosophic approach is that a philosophic conception of adequate principles is coordinated with a psychological theory of development and with the fact of development.

In contrast to "value-free" approaches, the approach suggested by Dewey and Piaget considers questions of value or adequacy at the very start. Piaget begins by establishing epistemological and logical criteria for deciding which thought structures are most adaptive and adequate for coping with complexity. Similarly, our work on ethical stages has taken a philosophic notion of adequate principles of justice (represented especially in the work of Kant and Rawls) to guide us in defining the direction of development. Epistemological and ethical principles guide psychological inquiry from the start. Thus, the strategy attempts to avoid the naturalistic fallacy of directly deriving judgments of value from judgments about the facts of development, although it assumes that the two may be systematically related. It takes as an hypothesis for empirical confirmation or refutation that development is a movement toward greater epistemological or ethical adequacy as defined by philosophic principles of adequacy.

The progressives' philosophical method differs from the approaches of philosophers of other persuasions in that the progressive or developmental method is partly empirical rather than purely analytic. It combines a prior conception of development with a prior notion of an ethical standard of adequacy; but these notions can be revised in light of the facts, including the facts of development. If the facts of development do not indicate that individuals move toward philosophically desired principles of justice, then the initial philosophic definition of the direction of development is in error, and must be revised. The analytic and normative "ought" of the developmental philosopher must take into account the facts of development, but is not simply a translation of these facts.

This method of "empirical" or "experimental" philosophy is especially central for an educational philosophy prescribing educational aims. Philosophical principles cannot be stated as ends of education until they can be stated psychologically. This means translating them into statements about a more adequate stage of development. Otherwise the rationally accepted principles of the philosopher will only be arbitrary concepts and doctrines for the child. Accordingly, to make a genuine statement of an educational end, the educational philosopher must coordinate notions of principles with understanding of the facts of development.

DEVELOPMENT AS THE AIM OF EDUCATION

We have attempted to clarify and justify the basic claim that developmental criteria are the best ones for defining educationally important behavior changes. We need now to clarify how the psychological study of development can concretely define educational goals. A common criticism is that the concept of development is too vague to genuinely clarify the choice of the curricular content and aims of education. A second, related criticism is that the concept of development, with its connotation of the "natural," is unsuited to determine actual educational policy.

With regard to the issue of vagueness, if the concept of development is to aid in selecting educational aims and content, this assumes that only some behavior changes out of many can be labeled developmental. We need to justify this assumption and to clarify the conditions for developmental change.

Our position has been challenged by Bereiter (1970), who claims that determining whether or not a behavior change is development is a matter of theory, not an empirical issue. For example, Piagetian research shows that fundamental arithmetical reasoning (awareness of one-to-one correspondence, of inclusion of a larger class in a sub-class, of addition and subtraction as inverse operations), usually develops naturally, without formal instruction or schooling, that is, it constitutes development. Such reasoning can also be explicitly taught, however, following various non-developmental learning theories. Accordingly, says Bereiter, to call fundamental arithmetical reasoning developmental does not define it as a developmental educational objective distinct from non-developmental objectives like rote knowledge of the multiplication tables.

In answer, the cognitive-developmental position claims that developmental behavior change is irreversible, general over a field of responses, sequential, and hierarchical (Kohlberg, 1970). When a set of behavior changes meets all these criteria, changes are termed stages or structural reorganizations. A specific area of behavioral change like fundamental arithmetical reasoning may or may not meet these criteria. Engelmann claims to have artificially taught children the "naturally developing" operation of conservation, but Kamii (1971) found that the children so taught met Engelmann's criteria of conservation without meeting the criteria of development, for example, the response could be later forgotten or unlearned, it was not generalized, and so forth.

When a set of responses taught artificially do not meet the criteria of natural development this is not because educational intervention is generally incompatible with developmental change. It is because the particular intervention is found to mimic development rather than to stimulate it. The issue of whether an educational change warrants the honorific label "development" is a question for empirical examination, not simply a matter of theory.

We have claimed that development can occur either naturally or as the result of a planned educational program. As was discussed earlier, development depends on experience. It is true, however, that the way in which experience stimulates development (through discrepancy and match between experienced events and information-processing structures) is not the way experience is programmed in many forms of instruction and educational intervention. It is also true that the kinds of experience leading to development must be viewed in terms of a stimulation which is general rather than highly specific in its content or meaning.

Because the experiences necessary for structural development are believed to be *universal*, it is possible for the child to develop the behavior naturally, without planned instruction. But the fact that only about half of the adult American population fully reaches Piaget's stage of formal operational reasoning and only 5 percent reach the highest moral stage demonstrates that natural or universal forms of development are not inevitable but depend on experience (Kuhn, Langer, Kohlberg, & Haan, 1971).

If this argument is accepted, it not only answers the charge that development is a vague concept but helps answer the charge that there are kinds of development (such as growth in skill at burglary) which are not valuable.

Such questionable types of "development" do not constitute development in the sense of a universal sequence or in the sense of growth of some general aspect of personality. As stated by Dewey (1938): "That a man may grow in efficiency as a burglar...cannot be doubted. But from the standpoint of growth as education and education as growth the question is whether such growth promotes or retards growth in general" (p. 75).

While a coherent argument has been made for why universal developmental sequences define something of educational value, we need to consider why such sequences comprise the ultimate criteria of educational value. We also need to consider how they relate to competing educational values. How does universal structural development as an educational aim relate to ordinary definitions of information and skills central to the educational curriculum? It seems obvious that many changes or forms of learning are of value which are not universals in development. As an example, while many unschooled persons have learned to read, the capacity and motivation to read does not define a developmental universal; nonetheless, it seems to us a basic educational objective. We cannot dispose of "growth in reading" as an educational objective, as we could "growth in burglary," simply because it is not a universal in development. But we argue that the ultimate importance of learning to read can only be understood in the context of more universal forms of development. Increased capacity to read is not itself a development, although it is an attainment reflecting various aspects of development. The value or importance of reading lies in its potential contribution to further cognitive, social, and aesthetic development. As stated by Dewey (1898),

> No one can estimate the benumbing and hardening effect of continued drill in reading as mere form. It should be obvious that what I have in mind is not a Philistine attack upon books and reading. The question is not how to get rid of them, but how to get their value—how to use them to their capacity as servants of the intellectual and moral life. To answer this question, we must consider what is the effect of growth in a special direction upon the attitudes and habits which alone open up avenues for development in other lines. (p. 29)

A developmental definition of educational objectives must not only cope with competing objectives usually defined non-developmentally, but with the fact that the universal aspects of development are multiple. Here, as in the case of evaluating non-developmental objectives, the progressive educator must consider the relation of a particular development to development in general. As an example, Kamii (1971) has defined a program of preschool intervention related to each of the chapter headings of Piaget's books: space, time, causality, number, classification, and so on. Kamii's intent in making use of all the areas of cognitive development discussed by Piaget is not to imply that each constitutes a separate, intrinsic educational objective. Rather, her interest is to make use of all aspects of the child's experience relevant to *general* Piagetian cognitive development. Such a concept of generalized cognitive-stage development is meaningful because Kohlberg and DeVries (1971) and others have shown that there is a general Piagetian cognitive-level factor distinct from psychometric general intelligence.

In contrast to the psychometric concept of intelligence, the developmental level concept of intelligence does provide a standard or a set of aims for preschool education. It does not assume a concept of fixed capacity or "intelligence quotient" constant over development. In this sense, developmental level is more like "achievement" than like "capacity," but developmental level tests differ from achievement tests in several ways. While the developmental level concept does not distinguish between achievement and capacity, it distinguishes between cognitive achievement (performance) and cognitive process (or competence). Developmental tests measure level of thought process, not the difficulty or correctness of thought product. They measure not cognitive performance but cognitive competence, the basic possession of a core concept, not the speed and agility with which the concept is expressed or used under rigid test conditions.

Psychometric and developmental level concepts of intelligence are quite different. In practice, however, the two kinds of measures are highly correlated with one another, explaining why clear theoretical and operational distinctions between the two concepts of intelligence have not been made until recently. Factor-analytic findings now can provide an empirical basis for this distinction (Kohlberg & DeVries, 1971). While psychometric measures of general intelligence and of "primary mental abilities" at mental age six correlate with Piagetian measures of cognitive level, there is also a common factor to all developmental level tests. This factor is independent of general intelligence or of any special psychometric ability. In other words, it is possible to distinguish between psychometric capacity and developmental level concepts or measures of intelligence. Given the empirical distinction, cognitive stage measures provide a rational standard for educational intervention where psychometric intelligence tests do not. This is true for the following reasons:

1. The core structure defined by stage tests is in theory and experiment more amenable to educational intervention—Piagetian theory is a theory of stage movement occurring through *experience* of structural disequilibrium.
2. Piagetian performance predicts later development independent of a fixed biological rate or capacity factor, as demonstrated by evidence for longitudinal stability or prediction independent of IQ. Because Piaget items define invariant sequences, development to one stage facilitates development to the next.
3. Piagetian test content has cognitive value in its own right. If a child is able to think causally instead of magically about phenomena, for instance, his ability

has a cognitive value apart from arbitrary cultural demands—it is not a mere indicator of brightness, like knowing the word "envelope" or "amanuensis." This is reflected in the fact that Piaget test scores are qualitative; they are not arbitrary points on a curve. The capacity to engage in concrete logical reasoning is a definite attainment, being at mental age six is not. We can ask that all children reason in terms of logical operations; we cannot ask that all children have high IQ's.

4. This cognitive value is culturally universal, the sequence of development occurs in every culture and subculture.

The existence of a general level factor in cognitive development allows us to put particular universal sequences of cognitive development into perspective as educational aims. The worth of a development in any particular cognitive sequence is determined by its contribution to the whole of cognitive development.

We must now consider the relation of developmental aims of education to the notion of developmental acceleration as an educational objective. We indicated that a concept of stages as "natural" does not mean that they are inevitable; many individuals fail to attain the higher stages of logical and moral reasoning. Accordingly, the aim of the developmental educator is not the acceleration of development but the eventual adult attainment of the highest stage. In this sense, the developmentalist is not interested in *stage-acceleration*, but in avoiding *stage-retardation*. Moral development research reviewed elsewhere suggests that there is what approaches an optimal period for movement from one stage to the next (Kohlberg & Turiel, 1973). When a child has just attained a given stage, he is unlikely to respond to stimulation toward movement to the next stage. In addition, after a long period of use of a given stage of thought, a child tends to "stabilize" at that stage and develops screening mechanisms for contradictory stimulation. Accordingly, it has been found that both very young and very old children at a given stage (compared to the age-norm for that stage) are less responsive or less able to assimilate stimulation at the next higher stage than children at the age-norm for that stage. The notion of an "open period" is not age-specific, it is individual. A child late in reaching Stage 2 may be "open" to Stage 3 at an age beyond that of another child who reached Stage 2 earlier. Nevertheless, gross age-periods may be defined which are "open periods" for movement from one stage to the next. Avoidance of retardation as an educational aim means presenting stimulation in these periods where the possibility for development is still open.

We need to consider a related distinction between *acceleration* and *decalage* as an aim of education. Piaget distinguishes between the appearance of a stage and its "horizontal *decalage*," its spread or generalization across the range of basic physical and social actions, concepts, and objects to which the stage potentially applies. As a simple example, concrete logic or conservation is first noted in the concept of mass and only later in weight and volume. Accordingly, acceleration of the stage of concrete operations is one educational enterprise and the encouragement of *decalage* of concrete reasoning to a new concept or phenomenon is another. It is the latter which is most relevant to education. Education is concerned not so much with age of onset of a child's capacity for concrete logical thought, but with the possession of a logical mind—the degree to which he has organized his experience or his world in a logical fashion.

It is likely that the occurrence of such horizontal *decalage*, rather than age of first appearance of concrete operations, predicts to later formal operational thought. Formal reasoning develops because concrete reasoning represents a poor, though partially successful, strategy for solving many problems. The child who has never explored the limits of concrete logical reasoning and lives in a world determined by arbitrary unexplained events and forces, will see the limits of the partial solutions of concrete logic as set by intangible forces, rather than looking for a more adequate logic to deal with unexplained problems.

We have so far discussed development only as general cognitive development. According to cognitive-developmental theory there is always a cognitive component to development, even in social, moral, and aesthetic areas. Development, however, is broader than cognitive-logical development. One central area is moral development, as defined by invariant stages of moral reasoning (Kohlberg & Turiel, 1971, 1973). On the one hand, these stages have a cognitive component; attainment of a given Piaget cognitive stage is a necessary, though not sufficient, condition for the parallel moral stage. On the other hand, moral reasoning stages relate to action, principled moral reasoning has been found to be a precondition for principled moral action (Kohlberg & Turiel, 1973). For reasons elaborated throughout this paper, the stimulation of moral development through the stages represents a rational and ethical focus of education related to, but broadening, an educational focus upon cognitive development as such (Kohlberg & Turiel, 1971). Programs effective in stimulating moral development have been successfully demonstrated (Blatt & Kohlberg, 1973).

While developmental moral education widens the focus of cognitive-developmental education beyond the purely cognitive, there is a still broader unity, called ego-development, of which both cognitive and moral development are part (Loevinger, Wessler, & Redmore, 1970). Particularly in the earlier childhood years, it is difficult to distinguish moral development from ego-development. Cognitive development, in the Piagetian sense, is also related to ego development, since both concern the child's core beliefs about the physical and social world. Much recent research demonstrates that the development of the ego, as attitudes and beliefs about the self, involves step-by-step parallel development of attitudes and beliefs about the physical and social world. Further, it indicates definite stages of ego-development, defined by Loevinger et al. (1970), van den Daele (1970) and others, which imply step-by-step parallels to Piaget's cognitive stages, although they include more social emotional content. In general, attainment of a Piagetian cognitive stage is a necessary but not sufficient condition for attainment of the parallel ego stage. All children at a given ego stage must have attained the parallel cognitive stage, but not all children at a cognitive stage will have organized their self-concept and social experience at the corresponding ego stage. Thus, a general concept of ego-development as a universal sequential phenomenon is becoming an empirically meaningful guide to defining broad educational objectives. Furthermore, experimental educational programs to stimulate ego-development have been piloted with some definite success at both the preschool and the high school levels (van den Daele, 1970; Sprinthall & Mosher, 1970).

Thus, education for general cognitive development, and perhaps even education for moral development, must be judged by its contribution to a more general concept of ego-development. In saying this, we must remember that "ego-development" is the psychologist's term for a sequence which also must have a philosophic rationale. One pole of ego-development is self-awareness; the parallel pole is awareness of the world. Increasing awareness is not only "cognitive," it is moral, aesthetic, and metaphysical; it is the awareness of new meanings in life.

Finally, we need to note that in the realm of ego-development, a focus upon "horizontal *decalage*" rather than acceleration is especially salient. The distinction reflects in a more precise and viable fashion the concern of maturational or romantic stage-theorists for an educational focus upon "healthy" passage through stages, rather than their acceleration. In maturational theories of personality stages, age leads to a new stage regardless of experience and reorganizations at previous stages. As a result, education and experience become valuable not for movement to a new stage, but for healthy or *successful integration* of the concerns of a stage. Onset of the next stage occurs regardless of experience; it is only healthy integration of the stages which is contingent on experience and which should be the focus for education. Without accepting this contention, cognitive-developmental theory would agree that premature development to a higher ego stage without a corresponding *decalage* throughout the child's world and life presents problems. In psychoanalytic maturational terms, the dangers of uneven or premature ego development are expressed as defects in ego-strength with consequent vulnerability to regression. In cognitive-developmental terms, inadequate "horizontal *decalage*" represents a somewhat similar phenomenon. While the relation of "ego-strength" to logical and moral *decalage* is not well understood, there are many reasons to believe they are related. A child who continues to think in magical or egocentric terms in some areas of cognition and morality is likely to be vulnerable to something like "regression" under stress later in life.

In conclusion, if a broad concept of development, conceived in stage-sequential terms, is still vague as a definer of educational ends, it is not due to the inherent narrowness or vagueness of the concept. Rather, it is due to the fact that researchers have only recently begun the kind of longitudinal and educational research needed to make the concept precise and useable. When Dewey advocated education as development at the turn of the century, most American educational psychologists turned instead to industrial psychology or to the mental health bag of virtues. If the results of the cognitive-developmental research of the last decades are still limited, they indicate real promise for finally translating Dewey's vision into a precise reality.

SUMMARY AND CONCLUSIONS

The present chapter essentially recapitulates the progressive position first formulated by John Dewey. This position has been clarified psychologically by the work of Piaget and his followers; its philosophic premises have been advanced by the work of modern analytic philosophers like Hare, Rawls, and Peters. The progressive view of education makes the following claims:

1. That the aims of education may be identified with development, both intellectual and moral.
2. That education so conceived supplies the conditions for passing through an order of connected stages.
3. That such a developmental definition of educational aims and processes requires both the method of philosophy or ethics and the method of psychology or science. The justification of education as development requires a philosophic statement explaining why a higher stage is a better or a more adequate stage. In addition, before one can define a set of educational goals based on a philosophical statement of ethical, scientific, or logical principles one must be able to translate it into a statement about psychological stages of development.
4. This, in turn, implies that the understanding of logical and ethical principles is a central aim of education. This understanding is the philosophic counterpart of the psychological statement that the aim of education is the development of the individual through cognitive and moral stages. It is characteristic of higher cognitive and moral stages that the child himself constructs logical and ethical principles; these, in turn, are elaborated by science and philosophy.
5. A notion of education as attainment of higher stages of development, involving an understanding of principles, was central to "aristocratic" Platonic doctrines of liberal education. This conception is also central to Dewey's notion of a democratic education. The democratic educational end for all humans must be "the development of a free and powerful character." Nothing less than democratic education will prepare free people for factual and moral choices which they will inevitably confront in society. The democratic educator must be guided by a set of psychological and ethical principles which he openly presents to his students, inviting criticism as well as understanding. The alternative is the "educator-king," such as the behavior-modifier with an ideology of controlling behavior, or the teacher-psychiatrist with an ideology of "improving" students' mental health. Neither exposes his ideology to the students, allowing them to evaluate its merit for themselves.
6. A notion of education for development and education for principles is liberal,

democratic, and non-indoctrinative. It relies on open methods of stimulation through a sequence of stages, in a direction of movement which is universal for all children. In this sense, it is natural.

The progressive position appears idealistic rather than pragmatic, industrial-vocational, or adjustment-orientated, as is often charged by critics of progressivism who view it as ignoring "excellence." But Dewey's idealism is supported by Piagetian psychological findings which indicate that all children, not only well-born college students, are "philosophers" intent on organizing their lives into universal patterns of meaning. It is supported by findings that most students seem to move forward in developmentally oriented educational programs. Furthermore, the idealism of the developmental position is compatible with the notion that the child is involved in a process of both academic and vocational education. Dewey denied that educational experience stimulating intellectual and moral development could be equated with academic schooling. He claimed that practical or vocational education as well as academic education could contribute to cognitive and moral development; it should be for all children, not only for the poor or the "slow." Our educational system currently faces a choice between two forms of injustice, the first an imposition of an arbitrary academic education on all, the second a division into a superior academic track and an inferior vocational track. The developmental conception remains the only rationale for solving these injustices, and for providing the basis for a truly democratic educational process.

REFERENCES

Ausubel, D., & Sullivan, E. (1970). *Theory and problems of child development*. New York: Grune and Stratton.

Bereiter, C. (1970). Educational implications of Kohlberg's cognitive-developmental view. *Interchange, 1*, 25–32.

Bereiter, C. (1972). Moral alternatives to education. *Interchange, 3*, 25–41.

Bereiter, C. (1973). *Must we educate?* Englewood Cliffs, NJ: Prentice-Hall.

Bereiter, C., & Engelmann, S. (1966). *Teaching disadvantaged children in the preschool*. Engelwood Cliffs, NJ: Prentice-Hall.

Berkowitz, L. (1964). *Development of motives and values in a child*. New York: Basic Books.

Bettelheim, B. (1970). On moral education. In T. Sizer (Ed.), *Moral education*. Cambridge, MA: Harvard University Press.

Blatt, M., & Kohlberg, L. (1973). Effects of classroom discussion upon children's level of moral judgment. In Kohlberg & Turiel (Eds.), *Recent research in moral development*. New York: Holt, Rinehart.

Brandt, R. B. (1956). *Ethical theory*. Englewood Cliffs, NJ: Prentice-Hall.

Coleman, J. S. et al. (1966). *Equality of educational opportunity*. Washington, D.C.: U.S. Dept. of Health, Education and Welfare, Office of Education.

Dewey, J. (1898). The primary-education fetish. *The Forum*. Washington, D.C.: U.S. Government Printing Office.

Dewey, J. (1968). *Experience and education*. New York: Collier (originally written in 1938).

Dewey, J., & McLellan, J. (1964). The psychology of number. In R. Archambault (Ed.), *John Dewey on education: Selected writings.* New York: Random House.

Freud, A. (1937). The ego and the mechanisms of defense. London: Hogarth Press.

Grotberg, E. (1969). *Review of research, 1965 to 1969.* Office of Economic Opportunity Pamphlet 6108–13. Washington, D.C.: Research and Evaluation Office, Project Head Start, Office of Economic Opportunity.

Group for the Advancement of Psychiatry. (1966). *Psychopathological disorders in childhood: Theoretical considerations and a proposed classification.* Formulated by the Committee on Child Psychiatry, GAP Report, *62*, 173–343.

Hall, G. S. (1901). The ideal school based on child study. *The Forum, 32.*

Hartshorne, H., & May, M. A. (1928–1930). *Studies in the nature of character.* Vol. 1. Studies in deceit. Vol. 2. Studies in service and self-control. Vol. 3. Studies in organization of character. New York: Macmillan.

Jencks, C. et al. (1972). *Inequality: A reassessment of the effect of family and schooling in America.* New York: Basic Books.

Kamii, C. (1971). Evaluating pupil learning in preschool education: Socio-emotional, perceptual-motor, and cognitive objectives. In B. S. Bloom, J. T. Hastings, & G. Madaus (Eds.). *Formative and summative evaluation of student learning.* New York: McGraw-Hill.

Kohlberg, L. (1968). Early education: A cognitive-developmental view. *Child Development, 39* (December), 1013–1062.

Kohlberg, L. (1969a). The moral atmosphere of the school. Paper delivered at Association for Supervision and Curriculum Development Conference on the "Unstudied Curriculum." Washington, D.C., January 9, 1969 (printed in A.A.S.C. Yearbook, 1970).

Kohlberg, L. (1969b). Stage and sequence: The cognitive-developmental approach to socialization. In D. Goslin (Ed.), *Handbook of socialization theory and research.* New York: Rand McNally.

Kohlberg, L. (1970). Reply to Bereiter's statement on Kohlberg's cognitive-developmental view. *Interchange, 1,* 40–48.

Kohlberg, L. (1971). From is to ought: How to commit the naturalistic fallacy and get away with it in the study of moral development. In T. Mischel (Ed.), *Cognitive development and epistemology.* New York: Academic.

Kohlberg, L. (1973). The contribution of developmental psychology to education: Examples from moral education. *The Educational Psychologist, 10,* 2–14.

Kohlberg, L., LaCrosse, R., & Ricks, D. (1971). The predictability of adult mental health from childhood behavior. In B. Wolman (Ed.). *Handbook of child psychopathology.* New York: McGraw-Hill.

Kohlberg, L., & DeVries, R. (1969). Relations between Piaget and psychometric assessments of intelligence. In C. Lavatelli (Ed.), *The natural curriculum.* E.R.I.C., 1971.

Kohlberg, L., & Turiel, E. (1971). Moral development and moral education. In G. Lesser (Ed.), *Psychology and educational practice.* Chicago: Scott Foresman.

Kohlberg, L., & Turiel, E. (Eds.) (1973). *Recent research in moral development.* New York: Holt.

Kuhn, D., Langer, J., Kohlberg, L., & Haan, N. (1971). *The development of formal operations in logical and moral judgment.* Unpublished mimeo monograph, Columbia University.

Langer, J. (1969). *Theories of development.* New York: Holt.

Loevinger, J., Wessler, R., & Redmore, C. (1970). *Measuring ego development*. San Francisco: Jossey-Bass.

Mead, G. H. (1936). *Movements of thought in the nineteenth century*. Chicago: University of Chicago Press.

Neill, A. S. (1960). *Summerhill*. New York: Hart.

Peters, R. S. (1968). *Ethics and education*. Chicago: Scott Foresman.

Piaget, J. (1960). The general problem of the psychobiological development of the child. In J. M. Tanner & B. Inhelder (Eds.), *Discussion on child development*. Vol. 4. New York: International Universities Press.

Rawls, J. (1971). *A theory of justice*. Cambridge, MA: Harvard University Press.

Rest, J. (1973). Comprehension preference and spontaneous usage in moral judgment. In L. Kohlberg & E. Turiel (Eds.), *Recent research in moral development*. New York: Holt, Rinehart.

Skinner, B. F. (1971). *Beyond freedom and dignity*. New York: Knopf.

Sprinthall, N. A., & Mosher, R. L. (1970). Psychological education in secondary schools: A program to promote individual and human development. *American Psychologist, 25* (October,) 911–924.

Turiel, E. (1969). Developmental processes in the child's moral thinking. In P. Mussen, J. Langer, & M. Covington (Eds.), *New directions in developmental psychology*. New York: Holt, Rinehart.

van den Daele, L. (1970). Preschool intervention with social learning. *Journal of Negro Education, 39* (Fall), 296–304.

PART II

Critical Areas of Child-Development Research

In the first chapter of this book, we claim that one of two most important kinds of knowledge for a developmental education arose from research in the various areas of universal or "natural" development. The research areas selected for Part II were chosen with four criteria in mind. First, the area is considered a basic area of development for all children in all cultures. Second, development in the area can be defended philosophically as an intrinsic good defining the aims of a developmental education. Third, there is reason to believe that experience and education can actually stimulate development in the area. Fourth, there is a body of cognitive-developmental theory that can help order data in the area, a consideration personally important to the authors.

We can illustrate our manner of approach to each area of research by considering the issues dealt with in the first chapter of Part II, Chapter 4, "Psychometric and Piagetian Measures of Intelligence: Their Nature and Educational Uses." The chapter reviews the three major theoretical approaches to the nature of intelligence. The first theory described is the classic "British" biological view of intelligence, the view of Galton (1869) and Spearman (1930). This view treats intelligence as primarily a general cognitive capacity transmitted by heredity and developing through maturation. The second theory reviewed is Piaget's interactional theory of the development of intelligence. Also considered is a third view of intelligence as environmentally determined skill learning.

In reviewing the three conflicting theories of intelligence, we point out how each is wedded to a certain method. The British approach, striving for assessment of innate capacity, attempts either to provide the child with thoroughly novel tasks or to widely sample more familiar tasks. It does so to randomize out the effects of specific experience, leaving a factor of general intelligence or cognitive capacity. In contrast, while distinguishing competence from performance, Piaget does not distinguish innate capacity from attained competence. He replaces the distinction between general intelligence as capacity, distinct from specific learning, with the notion of intelligence as that which changes as a result of general and self-initiated forms of experience. This is assessed, not by an addition of right answers of what the child knows or can do, but by a determination of the level, quality, or structure of the child's acts of thought and adaptation with regard to tasks universal to every child's thought and experience.

In the chapter we conclude that if investigators use the psychometric method, they must eventually reach conclusions similar to those of the British. We report that results achieved with the Piagetian method are sufficiently distinct (in terms of factor analysis) as to yield the possibility of reaching conclusions closer to Piaget's.

We point out that allied to the kinds of theory employed in measuring intelligence are the kinds of philosophic assumptions about the value of intelligence. In America, major objections to the British conception of intelligence come from its natural linkage to an aristocratic view of tests, one used for social selection for intelligence. We argue that the Piagetian view of intelligence helps define it as an aim of education for everyone rather than as an aim of educational selection. The chapter goes on to discuss a third type of intelligence in addition to the psychiatric and Piagetian cognitive-style assessments of intelligence. These, we suggest, may relate to the Piagetian concept of decalage of development, a possible educational aim, as well as to notions of ego development or ego strength. In summary, the chapter argues that the stage-developmental approach allows us to define a general dimension of cognitive developmental intelligence distinguishable from IQ, which has value in its own right and is subject to educational stimulation.

Chapter 4 compares Piaget's cognitive-developmental theory with both biological-maturational theory and environmental-learning theory, and method, in the study of intellectual growth. Finer contrasts between biology and culture in cognitive growth are taken up in Chapter 5, "Language and the Development of Thought." Two extreme theoretical positions about the development of language in its relation to thought are briefly considered and rejected. The first is Chomsky's nativistic theory that universal grammar is an innate biological capacity that simply matures. The other extreme theory rejected is the cultural-learning theory of cognition, which sees cognitive categories as simply the reflection of culturally relative variations in language, a form of the "Sapir-Whorf" view. Furth's finding that Piagetian concrete operational categories of logico-mathematical reasoning develop roughly on schedule among the deaf is one of many findings supporting Piaget's claim for a partial autonomy of cognitive development from language learning. A subtler theory of the role of language and communication, and hence of culture, in the development of thought is then considered: the symbolic interactionist theory of G. H. Mead (1934) in America and of Lev Vygotsky (1962) in the Soviet Union. This theory is presented and contrasted with Piaget's theory. Like Piaget's theory, the theories of Mead and Vygotsky are cognitive-developmental stage theories. Both, like Piaget, see cognitive and symbolic development as having roots in sensorimotor action independent of language. Both, however, see thought as developing new structures, and new functions, as linguistic dialogues are internalized, first as private or "egocentric" speech (speech to the self), and then as inner thought. The chapter is particularly novel in stressing the neglected but important theory of G. H. Mead (1934) on the socialization of thought through the internalization of the social dialogue, and in providing illustrative observations supporting the theory. The presentation of the symbolic interactionist theories of Mead and Vygotsky, and their comparison with Piaget's theory in Chapter 5 and elaboration in Chapter 6, lays the groundwork for a later discussion of the way these theorists treat the development of play in Chapter 9.

The first two chapters of Part II (Chapter 4 and 5) deal with cognitive development. The remaining chapters (6, 7, 8, 9) deal with social and emotional development. The approach taken in these chapters is called *cognitive-developmental*, not because it holds that cognitive development is more important than social and emotional development, but because it claims that an understanding of cognitive stages and principles of cognitive growth are part of what is required for an understanding, or theory of, the more complex and elusive phenomena of social and emotional growth. A central criticism of the classical Freudian theory of social and emotional growth is that its account of drives and defenses provides no direct way of understanding the complexities of cognitive growth. Accordingly, it cannot fully account for the even more complex story of social growth, which must include cognitive growth and more besides. If understanding normal social development presupposes some understanding of cognitive development, an understanding of socioemotional psychopathology ultimately presupposes an understanding of normal social development.

Chapter 7 focuses on moral development because morality has been most directly researched and interpreted both by Piaget's (and our own) cognitive-developmental theory and by the other classical theories of social development, psychoanalytic theory, and social learning theory. This chapter is important because moral development is the most basic aspect of social development for education, in the view of educational philosophers from Plato to Dewey. Moral development has been studied by cognitive-developmental theory primarily as moral *judgment*, by social learning theory primarily as moral *behavior* ("resistance to temptation" and "prosocial behavior"), and by psychoanalytic theory primarily as the *emotion* of guilt. Starting with studies of moral behavior, we suggest that the general and internal or "character" component of moral behavior is best defined as ego development and ego strength. Related to ego development and ego strength, but still distinguishable from it, is the development of moral judgment. Piaget's theorizing and observations of moral judgment development are reviewed in light of the research evidence. While Piaget's two stages of childhood moral judgment, the heteronomous-authoritarian and the autonomous-democratic, are not exactly supported by the evidence, most of the dimensions of development that Piaget hypothesizes are found to characterize childhood moral development.

In Chapter 7, Kohlberg's own moral judgment stages, built on this prior work on Piaget's stages, are then described and their "inner logic" or structure presented.

The method used to assess moral stage is described. Results with longitudinal data are reported verifying the sequential nature of the stages. Relations of moral judgment to action and to other aspects of development are reviewed. The author's moral judgment stages are primarily based on data from children 10 and older. (Accordingly, Damon's stages of earlier childhood moral judgment are also presented in depth.) The role of environmental factors in moral judgement is next discussed. Following G. H. Mead's symbolic interactionist theory of sociomoral development, "role-taking opportunities" as differential contributions to moral development are stressed. In developing this theory, it is proposed that families, schools, and institutions may themselves have a collective moral atmosphere with stage-like properties.

Finally, the chapter considers the development of guilt and its functioning in delinquency and childhood neuroses, which are centers of interest in psychoanalytic thought about morality. Psychoanalytic, social-learning, and cognitive-developmental interpretations of the findings on guilt and social psychopathology are compared.

Our next chapter on social development (Chapter 8) reviews theory and research on ego development. As Loevinger says, ego development is a name for the general factor in social development (once intelligence has been held constant), as intelligence is a name for the general factor in cognitive development. Loevinger's own work on the topic is treated in depth, since her thinking and method have done the most to confirm that there is stage progression, in projective test data sufficiently general to justify the term ego development. Loevinger's work, while basic, is in our opinion not necessarily definitive, because in a sense it is a hybrid of two approaches, the cognitive-structural or cognitive-developmental or Piagetian approach, and the ego-functional or neopsychoanalytic approach of Erik Erikson. Loevinger derives her formal stage model from Piaget and stresses cognitive complexity as one aspect of ego development. At the same time, her theoretical model and her method of test construction rely heavily on neopsychoanalytic theory. Because her model of ego development is mixed, it is necessary to understand each of the two more "pure" approaches to the area, as well as Loevinger's own approach, though the others are not as well developed on the measurement and research side. This is particularly true of Erik Erikson's neopsychoanalytic theory, which we attempt to cover in some depth. The broad sweep of his theory, the observational insights behind it, and its compatibility with other developmental views compel attention to it. In Chapter 9, our treatment of Erikson's theory is elaborated in its application to play.

On the opposite pole, a stronger commitment to a cognitive-structural approach to ego development than Loevinger's is displayed by the work of others reviewed in the chapters, propounders of stage schemes in the child's conceptualization of self and of social relations. These include Selman's work on childrens' concepts of interpersonal relations, Broughton's work on the self, van den Daele's work on the ego ideal, and Fowler's work on the development of faith-systems. Each of these researchers' stages of social-cognitive development in childhood is described. As yet, no single measure or assessment of general ego development in childhood has claim to solidity. We believe that if such a measure is eventually developed, it will represent something along the lines of these researches into social-cognitive development.

Chapter 9, "Play and Constructive Work as Contributors to Development," is the final chapter of Part II. Play is the central phenomenon of early childhood on which developmental education builds. To deal constructively with play, the educator must become familiar with its development. The stages of pretend play sketched by Piaget and elaborated in research by Greta Fein are charted. The major theories of childhood play are reviewed. Chapter 5, on language and thought, compares Piaget's theory with the more cultural or symbolic interactionist theories of Mead and Vygotsky. These theories are taken up again in their interpretation of the development of play. Finally, Erikson's theory of play is considered in depth. The implications of theories and findings on play for early education are elaborated.

REFERENCES

Galton, F. (1869). *Hereditary genius*. London: Macmillan.

Mead, G. H. (1934). *Mind, self, and society*. Chicago: University of Chicago Press.

Spearman, C. (1930). The psychology of 'g'. In C. Murchison (Ed.), *Psychology of 1930*. Worchester, MA: Clark University Press.

Vygotsky, L. (1962). *Thought and language*. Cambridge: MIT Press.

Chapter 4

Psychometric and Piagetian Measures of Intelligence: Their Nature and Educational Uses*

Lawrence Kohlberg
Rheta DeVries

In Chapters 2 and 3, we discussed three psychological and philosophical streams in the history of educational thought: the maturationist or romantic view, the cultural-transmission view, and the cognitive-developmental view. In this chapter, we will consider in detail how the assumptions implicit in these views lead to different concepts about the nature and origins of intelligence and to different operational definitions in assessments of intelligence.

THREE APPROACHES TO INTELLIGENCE

By *intelligence* we mean both cognitive development as well as intellectual functioning conceived as a personality trait (as something on which individuals vary in a way that is relatively consistent across situations and relatively stable over time).

In comparing different conceptual approaches to intelligence, we will examine the following issues:

1. Theoretical assumptions about the nature and origin of heredity and environment
2. Method of assessing intelligence
3. Philosophic value of intellectual assessments—educational uses

---

*An elementary understanding of factor analysis is needed to follow some of the issues raised in this chapter. We present a minimal orientation, and refer the reader to Thomson (1946) who probably still provides the simplest and clearest entries into these issues.

Discussion on these issues is organized in terms of two distinctly different approaches—the psychometric and the Piagetian. The Piagetian view is also supplemented by the view of Vygotsky. We begin with an overview to provide the reader with a general orientation.

Two psychometric approaches are distinguishable. The first is the classic British biological view of intelligence as hereditary and maturational. This view is represented by Galton (1869), Spearman (1904, 1923, 1930), and Cattell (1972). With regard to the *theoretical* issue of nature and origin, they believed "intelligence is defined as innate general cognitive ability" (Spearman, 1904). With regard to the issue of assessment of cognitive functioning, the British school developed a *method* that maximized the chances of observing intelligence as a general biological capacity relatively independent of experience. The method is one of using novel cognitive tasks (or a broad sample of cognitive tasks) in such a way as to cancel out the effect of specific experience in individual scores. With regard to the *philosophic* issue, the British view leads to the use of intelligence tests for social selection, with a value stance of justice as intellectual meritocracy. Since intelligence is conceived of as fixed capacity by this approach, the educational use of intelligence tests must be for educational selection, not for assessing educational progress or change.

The second psychometric approach we will consider is the environmental-learning view. With regard to theory, an environmental-learning conception of intelligence is reflected in various American writings. One definition is that of Hayes (1962) that "manifest intelligence is an accumulation of learned facts and skills." Environmental-learning approaches have not provided a clear conceptual distinction between "intelligence" and specific skills of school achievement. With regard to method, the environmental-learning approach has not led to a method of assessing intelligence distinguishable from that provided by the Spearman "biological" approach. The methodological approach inspired by the environmental-learning view has been primarily an effort to rework the test of general capacity through differentiation of test scores into multiple mental skills or abilities. In our view and that of McClelland (1973), this elaboration has added little theoretical or practical meaning to psychometric scores. The value of intelligence as defined by the environmental-learning view is relative to its prediction of success in a particular culture. From this standpoint, tests of intelligence do not stand up well except where they are used to gate further education as in the British test selection of those going on to academic (grammar) schools and later to universities and university-required careers (McClelland, 1973; Kohlberg, Ricks, and Sharey, 1984).

At still other points, the cultural-learning view of intelligence suggests that except in the metier of middle-class Western culture, it is impossible to distinguish capacity or competence from performance in psychometric test scores. Rather than representing a different method or approach to intelligence from the British psychometric view, the environmental-learning view has essentially represented a different interpretation of results obtained with tests originated from the biological view. In the cultural-learning view, the nature and meaning of intelligence are viewed as being largely determined by the content of knowledge valued in a particular culture.

The third approach to intelligence we consider is that of Piaget. In regard to theory, Piaget's position is interactionist; it is not a doctrine about the quantitative contribution of heredity and environment to intelligence, but a doctrine about the origins of the structure of intelligence and its development. While he acknowledged both biological rate and environmental learning factors, Piaget's (1972) position is that intelligence is the product of the individual's active construction and interpretation of experience through a process of equilibration. Thus Piaget adds to the customary consideration of the two factors of (1) biological heredity and maturation and (2) cultural and social learning a third factor (3) *equilibration*, a balance of assimilation and accommodation that represents intelligence as adaptation itself. Equilibration, in turn, is a function of the interaction of biologically maturing structures or schemata with the general structures of the physical and social world. Piaget's stages of logico-mathematical, physical, and sociomoral/cognition then are not the result of either biological maturation or cultural and educational learning; rather, they are the result of the interaction between the developing child's structures and the universal structures of his or her physical and social world. Therefore, the underlying structure of thought undergoes progressive qualitative changes through an invariant sequence of stages. According to Piaget, the nature or form of intellectual competence thus changes with development.

In summary:

1. The terms *cognition, thought,* or *intelligence* basically refer to adaptive actions upon objects or internalization of such actions. Mature or adequate cognition is defined by an equilibrium or reciprocity between action and object. Intelligence is defined as function (as modes of action) evolving through qualitative structures (stages) rather than as content (as sets of words, "verbal responses," associations, memories, etc.) or as a faculty or ability (a power of producing words, memories, etc.). The encouragement of cognitive development, then, is the provision of opportunities for activities of an organized or equilibrated form.

2. Cognition proceeds through stages of structural reorganization. While cognitive functions are present from birth, cognitive structures are radically different from one stage to the next.

3. The implication of structural reorganization in development is that the source of cognitive structure and cognitive development is to be found neither in the structure and maturation of the organism nor in the teaching structures of the environment but in the structure of the interaction between organism and environment.

4. The optimal conditions for such structural organization entail some optimal balance of discrepancy and match between the behavior structures of the child and the structure of his psychological environment.

Associated with Piaget's theory of intelligence is a unique method for its study. Piaget's career in psychology began with qualitative explanations of children's wrong answers to the Binet test. His interest lay not in the quantitative analysis of correct content, "right answers," but in the qualitative analysis of the development of the forms of the children's reasoning, forms that could be characterized as developmental stages. The Piagetian method of studying intelligence involved tasks whose content is not novel but is universally experienced by all children and universally structured through various developmental levels. We shall elaborate on Piaget's method of studying intelligence later in this chapter.

Piaget also took a different stand on the philosophic issue of the value of scores on assessments of intelligence from the British biological- and American cultural-learning views of intelligence. The British biological- and the American cultural-learning views started as Binet did, with the notion that the value of a measure of intelligence was the ability to predict something external, for example, school achievement or success and the later success of occupational mobility and achievement in life. This view we called in Chapter 3 "the industrial psychology view." The disagreement between the British and American views was that the cultural-learning view held that what was valuable as cognitive ability varied from culture to culture while the biological view held that general cognitive ability "noesis" was equally valuable in any culture. The British view was largely self-fulfilling, because until recently, the British educational system weeded out at grade 11 those who did not pass tests of general intelligence and achievement. Those weeded out were denied further academic education and access to universities and thus to middle-class or upper-middle-class careers. Accordingly, the predictive validity or value of high test performance was largely artifactual. In the name of social utility—the greatest good for society—the system denied justice to the culturally and biologically disadvantaged insofar as they performed poorly on psychometric tests from age 10 on.

In contrast, the Piagetian, or cognitive-developmental view, held that intelligence as equilibration (cognitive development) was a good in itself, the "progressive" view of development as the aim of education described in Chapter 3. As we noted in Chapter 3, development is not always culturally rewarded and does not always lead to individual survival. Those at the highest stages of moral development, the Gandhis and Martin Luther Kings, have been assassinated. The justification for the value of cognitive development, as for moral development, is philosophic; a higher cognitive stage is a better stage on philosophic logical or epistemologic grounds. Formal operational thinking is better than concrete operational thinking from the point of view of philosophic epistemology and logic—not because it predicts school or career success. As stated by Piaget (1972), "In the first place, every human being has the right to be placed in a scholastic environment during his formation which will enable him to build until completion the basic tools of adaptation which are the processes of logic. If logic itself is created rather than being inborn, it follows that the first task of education is to form reasoning." In summary, Piaget's view is that intelligence represents adaptation and has intrinsic value in itself. The development of intelligence through education in its broadest sense is then a human value to which all children have a right; it is not the privilege of the biologically gifted.

ENVIRONMENTAL LEARNING THEORIES OF PSYCHOMETRIC INTELLIGENCE

Any conception of intelligence must distinguish between intelligence as *capacity* or *competence* and actual test performance. If a biological conception of capacity is not accepted, then some alternative environmental conception must be worked out. If this is not done, the notion of intelligence loses any conceptual meaning, and intelligence is simply whatever intelligence tests measure. An example of an aconceptual approach to intelligence is that of Bayley (1970), an outstanding empirical worker in the field. Bayley reviews definitions of intelligence ranging from Spearman's to Hayes's without committing herself to any of the definitions. She believes that commitment to a theoretical or conceptual view of intelligence involves "the danger of personal bias and preferences made and in the consequent conclusions." Not only does Bayley refuse to opt for any particular conceptual definition of intelligence, she also refuses to accept the assumptions necessary for one or another conceptualization of intelligence. She does not differentiate between intellectual capacity or competence and test performance or between cognitive and noncognitive components of ability tests. As an example of this, she notes that baby-test intelligence scores have no stability or predictability over time. She concludes that

> It is now well established that test scores earned in the first year or two have little predictive validity although they may have high validity as measures of the children's cognitive abilities at the time. (Bayley, 1970, p. 24)

The fact that the correlation between eight-month intelligence and four-year intelligence is .08 does not lead Bayley to question whether the eight-month test is validly measuring "cognitive ability" since cognitive ability is whatever a test of cognitive ability measures. A more conceptualized conception of intelligence would lead to the conclusion that there is very little in the eight-month baby test that reflects intelligence or cognitive ability.

While Bayley's aconceptual approach to intelligence is extreme, it is typical of most writers who do not accept a biological concept of intelligence as capacity. It is easy to point out environmental effects on performance, effects that make it difficult to establish a biological capacity component of any given performance. It is difficult, however, to work out an alternative environmental conception of capacity or competence.

Until the 1960s, environmental accounts of intelligence and its development were based on the "cultural transmission" theories of learning described in Chapter 3. In contrast to either the maturational view of Spencer and Isaacs, or the structural-interactional theory of Piaget, environmental-learning theories have either denied the existence of mental structure or have seen them as the *mirrors* of external physical and mental structure.

In contrast to nativistic theories, learning theories may allow for genetic factors in ease of learning of a complex response, but they assume that the basic structure of complex responses results from the structure of the child's environment. Both specific concepts and general cognitive structures, like the categories of space, time, and casuality, are believed to be reflections of structures existing outside the child, structurings given by the physical and social world.

Almost of necessity, the view that structure of the external world is the source of the child's cognitive structure has led to an account of the development of structure in associationistic terms. From John Locke to J. B. Watson and B. F. Skinner, environmentalists have viewed the structure of behavior as the result of the association of discrete stimuli with one another, with responses of the child, and with experiences of pleasure and pain.

At its extreme, this conception of mental structure has the following implications:

1. Mind or intelligence is a set of specific responses to specific stimuli in the environment. Cognitive development is the result of guided learning, of recurrent associations between specific discriminative stimuli in the environment, specific responses of the child, and specific reinforcements following these responses.
2. "Cognition" is a matter of discrimination and generalization learning. Conceptual development occurs through learning overt or covert verbal labeling responses to discriminated and generalized classes of stimuli. Training in discrimination of the stimulus attributes implied by cultural concepts and generalization of response to these attributes leads to concept learning.
3. The child is born with very little patterning of personality or of mind. Accordingly, it is possible to teach a child almost any behavior pattern, provided one teaches in terms of the laws of association learning and provided one starts at an early age before competing response patterns have been learned.

It is important to recognize that all these postulates of environmentalist theories of learning are not inconsistent with the innate determination of IQ or other traits of ability or temperament. These postulates do, however, suggest that teaching can go on without much prior understanding of the structure of a given desired behavior pattern as it "naturally" develops and as it relates to prior organismic behavior structures. Teaching instead requires primarily a careful statement of a behavior pattern considered desirable (e.g., a skill such as reading or arithmetic) in terms of specific responses. This pattern is then to be taught in accordance with general laws of learning believed applicable to the learning of all organisms (old or young, human or nonhuman) and to the learning of all behavior patterns.

In general, such a program implies a plan for shaping the child's behavior by successive approximation from responses he is now making to the desired end responses. At every step, immediate feedback or reward is desirable and immediate repetition and elaboration of the correct response is used. A careful detailed programing of learning is required to make sure that (*a*) each response builds on the preceding, (*b*) incorrect responses are not made since once made they persist and interfere with correct responses, and (*c*) feedback and reward are immediate.

Since the 1960s, cultural-learning views of intelligence have rejected these associationist conceptions and have accepted notions of cognitive level as developed by Vygotsky and his followers (see Chapter 5) but have questioned Piaget's stage theory and stressed the role of cultural-linguistic coding and specific cultural experience as cognitive development. Particularly important is the work of Bruner and his colleagues, Cole and his colleagues, and Feldman. Their themes are largely based on the theory of Vygotsky, which we shall consider in the next chapter.

In part, however, it is in our opinion extreme in its endeavor to completely challenge the British biological theory of psychometric intelligence that we have just reviewed on psychometrics' own ground.

This approach generates somewhat conflicting claims: (*a*) that intelligence as competence is cultural, (*b*) that intelligence as competence is biological but is expressed differentially in different performances according to culture, and (*c*) that one cannot distinguish between intellectual capacity or competence and performance.

The first claim, that intellectual competence is cultural, is stated by Greenfield and Bruner (1966) as "Intelligence is to a great extent the internalization of tools provided by a given culture. Thus culture-free means intelligence-free." They go on to interpret the considerable variation in test performance they find from culture to culture as indicating a cultural conception of intelligence. It is, of course, not really possible to dismiss the many culturally universal aspects of intellectual performance as not representing intelligence. Accordingly, Cole and Scribner (1974) at some point shift to the more plausible and common position that biological culture-free competence components of intelligence are very difficult to separate from culturally determined performance measures. Bruner and Cole end up suggesting that one can distinguish between a capacity that is constant across cultures from a capacity of variation from culture to culture in the context of the expression of this competence. They say, "When we systematically study the situational determinants of performance, we are led to conclude that cultural differences reside more in differences in the situations to which different cultures apply their skills than to differences in the skills possessed by the groups in question" (p. 274).

We now turn to a more detailed treatment of the characteristics and critical differences among these three approaches to conceptualizing and assessing intelligence.

PSYCHOMETRIC INTELLIGENCE AND ITS ASSUMPTIONS

The history of the psychometric approach to intelligence represents a dialectical argument around two issues: (1) the "number of factors" issue, that is, the conflict between the view of intelligence as a unitary general capacity and the view of intelligence as a sum of various factors, faculties, or abilities, and (2) the heredity versus environment issue.

General Intelligence in the Psychometric Tradition

The history of psychometrics started with the effort to identify a number of elementary or simple faculties like reaction time, memory, and sensory thresholds. Tests constructed on these lines showed no consistent relation to one another and yielded no meaningful interpretations. Testing was revitalized by Binet, who approached the matter from a more practical point of view. Binet (1910) wrote:

> Our goal is to make a measurement of the child's intellectual capacities, in order to learn whether he is normal or retarded. We need concern ourself with neither his past nor his future, we will not make a distinction between acquired and congenital feeblemindedness. Our goal is not to analyze the aptitudes of those inferior in intelligence, here we confine ourselves to measuring their *intelligence in general.* (p. 4)

Behind Binet's point of view were two assumptions. The first was the notion that there was an "intelligence in general." While Binet originally believed that there were separate mental "faculties" such as memory, imagination, attention, and judgment, he believed that these "faculties" were only revealed in complex performances calling for a number of these faculties at the same time. The Binet test, then, was a test of diverse contents or "faculties" combined to provide an *average level.* As stated by Terman:

> The assumption that it is easier to measure one aspect of intelligence that all of it is fallacious in that the parts are not separate parts and cannot be separated by any refinement. The reader will understand that no single test used alone will determine accurately the level of intelligence. A great many tests are required: (1) because intelligence has many aspects, and (2) in order to overcome the accidental influence of training or environment. As stated by Binet: "Let the tests be rough, if there are only enough of them." (1916, p. 24)

The second assumption behind the Binet approach was that "intelligence in general" could be represented by an average "mental age." The individual's intelligence was defined as his or her mental age relative to the average age level in a normative sample for passing specific items. Thus Binet equated intelligence with cognitive development, that is, with the average level of any cognitive task that showed regular age-development trends.

In summary, Binet assumed that there was an intelligence in general that could develop normally or be retarded or advanced, and which was distinct from, though related to, school learning or achievement. While Binet had his eye on what teachers considered "intelligence," he did not wish to develop a test of school learning. From Binet's practical notion of a general cognitive level, a more theoretical notion of general intelligence soon emerged—the notion of biological cognitive capacity elaborated by Spearman (1904, 1930) and his descendants. Spearman introduced two basic, interrelated novelties. The first was to claim that it was meaningful to talk not only about *"intelligence in general"* as Binet did, but to talk about *"general intelligence"* as a unitary cognitive function or ability. For Binet, "intelligence in general" was an average of various intellectual abilities and skills involved in complex mental performance. For Spearman, it was a single unitary power of "cognition" or "noesis." The second novelty introduced by Spearman was that of identifying "general intelligence" (as opposed to "average performance" or "intelligence in general") with a *biological capacity* varying quantitatively with heredity, with age-maturation, and with biological conditions.

For Binet's "intelligence in general," average performance could be due to both components of innate capacity and of experience. For Spearman, experience could affect skill in any specific task included in an intelligence battery, but it could not affect level of general intelligence, a construct that could be distinguished from a mere average of test performances. A statistical method was thus required to differentiate "general intelligence" from "intelligence in general," or average performance. This method, called "factor analysis," involved extracting the general factor involved in each specific test performance by analyzing the correlations among tests. The more determined by specific experience a test was, the less it measured capacity or general intelligence and the more it measured specific learning. The sum of a person's factor scores on good measures of general intelligence could be distinguished from the individual's average on all tests and would represent a better estimate of his or her innate capacity.

With regard to conceptualization, the first thing to note is that Spearman equates general intelligence with cognition, with all performances involving cognitive activity. This is a different notion from the one that an individual's general intelligence represents the sum of all his or her readinesses to learn. Intelligence as cognitive activity, however, is broader than the notion of intelligence either as the logical reasoning central to the Piagetian concept, or as the verbal abilities central to environmental-learning concepts. According to Spearman, perceptual tasks may require cognitive activity, though they are not reasoning tasks and do not involve language. At the same time, however, not all learning or patterned response depends on cognitive activity. As stated by Stout (1894), Spearman's intellectual predecessor:

> The varying degrees of noetic synthesis correspond to the degree of the intelligence of the individual. The more developed it is, the less conspicuous by comparison is the part played by mere association. A person of intelligence in narrating an occurrence

brings the relevant points together as a systematic whole. Another person seems unable to proceed otherwise than by casual associations of proximity in time and space. (p. 34)

In this view, the essence of noncognitive/associative processes is the governing of mental acts or responses by relationships *external* to the stimulus or the response, for example, by relationships of contiguity or associative learning, a distinction experimentally documented by Jensen. There is awareness of stimuli but not direct awareness of the relations between them, independent of their contiguity in space or time. The essense of cognitive processes in this view is the governing of responses by awareness of *internal* relationships between ideas or stimuli. As stated by Spearman (1930):

When a person has in mind any two or more ideas or perceptions, he has more or less the power to bring to mind any relations that essentially hold between them. (p. 348)

This cognitive process is called "the eduction of relations" by Spearman. It is exemplified, for instance, by the Binet "similarities" test items (such as "In what way are a hat and a coat the same or alike?"). A second major process, according to Spearman, is the "eduction of correlates," "when a person has in mind any idea together with a relation, he has more or less the power to bring to mind the correlative idea" (Spearman, 1930, p. 115). This process is exemplified by an analogies test item (e.g., "A glove is to a hand as a boot is to what?"). To answer the question, the person first has to see how a glove is related to a hand (eduction of relations) and then has to apply this relation to a new idea (boot) and so arrive at the idea of a foot (eduction of correlates). These processes are also reflected in nonverbal tasks designed to measure *g*, such as the Raven (1956) matrices, a nonverbal analogies test. In its board form for children, each item consists of a square divided into four parts. The two top squares present two designs with a certain relationship. The lower left square presents a third design, and the lower right square is empty. The child must choose from six designs to fill the fourth hole, the one that relates to the third design as the second design relates to the first. For instance, the first two designs might be circles, the second larger than the first, and the third design a square the size of the larger circle. The correct completion for the fourth box would be a larger square.

In equating general intelligence, *g*, with cognition of relationships, or "noesis," Spearman claimed that the same basic process or power is involved in cognizing relationships, whatever the type or *form* of relationship (e.g., spatial, temporal, causal, resemblance, etc.), whatever the media in which the relationship is presented (verbal, visual-spatial, etc.), and whatever kind of task or response to the relationship is expected (e.g., judgment or evaluation, recall, as in vocabulary, production of new responses, etc.). This conception of general cognition is thought to be culturally universal or "culture free." The Raven matrices were intended to be a particularly good example of a culture-free test of g in part because no verbal instructions are given, no verbal stimulus is required, and no verbal response is needed. The shapes are assumed to be familiar to all children. The child responds actively by putting a piece into the fourth hole.

Factor Analysis and the Issue of
General Intelligence Versus Specific Abilities

In summary, Spearman's claim was: (1) that correlational analyses indicate a general intelligence factor varying from test to test in quantity, not quality, (2) that what is included in this factor is given by his conception of cognition; and (3) that the nature and distribution of this factor are relatively culturally invariant. On the whole, these claims are supported by research. More extensive test elaboration and factor analytic work indicated the existence of specific factors.

Spearman's claim for a general factor then rested on his finding of correlations among all tests involving "noesis." Some examples may clarify how relationships are expressed quantitatively with a correlation. The correlation between height and weight is approximately .60. As a general rule, taller people are heavier than shorter people, but the correlation is not perfect (that is, 1.00), reflecting the existence of short, heavy persons as well as tall, thin ones. An example of negative correlation is the relationship between age and running speed in adults. Typically, adults run slower as they get older. This correlation is negative because increases in one variable (age) are associated with decreases ($-.74$) in the second variable (running speed).

If intelligence is general and global, the result would be consistently large positive correlations among scores on mental tests. In fact, correlations among measures were low and not nearly so large as was expected according to the generalist view, seeming to give support by default to the separatist notion of multiple intelligences. This conclusion was altered when Spearman (1904) showed that the size of correlation is limited by the reliability of the two measures being correlated. Reliability refers to the consistency or reproducibility of a set of results. A measure or test is considered reliable if it produces consistent scores for the same individual and consistent differences among individuals when administered at two different times. Spearman showed that the maximum possible correlation between two measures decreases as the reliabilities of the measures decrease.

Spearman presented correlations among test scores for children. He concluded that when the correlations were evaluated in light of the reliabilities of the tests, there was evidence for a two-factor theory of intelligence. A general factor, or g, was involved in performance on all measures. In addition, test-specific intellectual factors, referred to as s (for specific), were thought to be involved at some level in all measures of intelligence.

If human intelligence is general and global, correlations should be uniformly high; if human intelligence consists of separate, specific abilities, we expect performance on certain tests to be highly correlated but unrelated to scores on tests that measure other abilities. If, for example, verbal ability is a separate component of human intelligence, performance on tests of verbal ability should be highly correlated but unrelated to measures of quantitative skill. The two types of test, quantitative and verbal, should define two clusters of correlations, one between quantitative tests and one between verbal tests, with the two clusters uncorrelated with each other.

Spearman's (1904) two-factor theory of intelligence, with its emphasis on the general factor *g*, initially appeared to account for correlations between scores on cognitive tests. This was true, however, only so long as the mental tests involved dissimilar types of problems. If there were several tests of one type, for example, verbal, and another set of tests of another, for example, quantitative, they appeared to define separate clusters of intercorrelations.

Accordingly, Thurstone (1938) proposed an alternative theory of intelligence based upon his analysis of performance on a large battery of mental tests administered to undergraduates at the University of Chicago. He rejected the idea of a general factor and proposed instead a theory that focused on independent, primary mental abilities. Rather than postulating a general factor, he argued the general factor was unnecessary to account for correlational data. In his research on mental abilities, he found evidence for a set of primary mental abilities that were labeled Space, Verbal Comprehension, Word Fluency, Number Facility, Induction, Perceptual Speed, Deduction, Rote Memory, and Arithmetic Reasoning. The 57 individual tests administered could be mapped on to these separate factors, and his data indicated that these factors, or abilities, were independent.

To give some idea of what the factors illustrate, we need to examine some of the tests defining separate factors. For example, Spatial Ability was assessed by tasks that required the individual to judge whether two items rotated in space were the same or different. The items compared were letters, abstract shapes, or flags. The space factor was thought to represent the ability to visualize how parts of objects fit together, what their relationships are, and what they look like when rotated in space. This is in contrast to the Perceptual Speed tests, where items also had to be compared to determine if they were identical. However, the items were not rotated. This difference led to two different factors or clusters of correlations.

Let us consider the original group of students tested by Thurstone—University of Chicago undergraduates, a highly select intellectual group. All possessed superior general intellectual ability; what differentiated them were specific abilities, such as verbal, numerical, and spatial reasoning. Thus, the data Thurstone (1938) collected from these individuals could readily be accounted for by a set of independent primary mental abilities; a general factor was unnecessary mathematically and psychologically.

The situation becomes very different, however, if we test a less select group of individuals on a set of mental tests. Our data will tend to show a pattern in which performance on each test is correlated with performance on all other tests; that is, there are no zero correlations in the correlation matrix, supporting Spearman's thesis. The data are more consistent with the idea that the individuals in our diverse group not only possess specific abilities but that these specific abilities are themselves correlated, giving rise to the notion of an overall ability.

Such a conclusion arose when Thurstone administered his primary-mental-abilities test battery to a group of schoolchildren (Thurstone & Thurstone, 1954). His data forced him to abandon a solution involving orthogonal or independent factors. He chose instead a set of correlated or oblique factors that best approximated his "simple-structure" mathematical criterion for factor analysis. In choosing a solution with correlated specific factors, one is left with the problem of explaining the pattern of correlations of the factors extracted from the pattern of correlations of the original tests. In Thurstone's case, he chose to resolve the problem in terms of a second-order general factor, derived from factoring again his oblique specific factors with the various specific or primary mental abilities loading differentially on this general factor. Ultimately, Thurstone agreed that such a second-order factor, obtained by factoring the correlations between the primary factors, was very similar to Spearman's g.

The outcome is partial agreement between the theories of Spearman and Thurstone. Both were forced to accept a hierarchical theory of intellectual abilities, a type of theory advocated by those of the British school.

From the 1940s to the present, factor theories have been developed that represent a reconciliation of the Spearman and Thurstone positions. Two major hierarchical theories have been proposed. The first of these, specified by Vernon (1965), represents an extension of the British emphasis on the general factor. The second, described by Cattell (1963, 1971), represents an emphasis on primary abilities characteristic of the American approach of Thurstone but ends with one or more general factors.

The theory proposed by Vernon (1965) is based upon a factor analysis approach that starts at the top of the hierarchy. The general factor is first determined for a correlation matrix. Relationships among tests based upon this general factor are factored out. The resulting residual correlations—that is, correlations between tests after the general factor is eliminated—are then factored further. This type of top-down approach can proceed through a number of successive levels, each level having less general significance than the preceding one. At the top of the hierarchy is g. Below g are two major group factors representing verbal-educational ability ($v:ed$) and spatial-practical-mechanical ability ($k:m$). The $v:ed$ factor can be further decomposed into more specific abilities, such as verbal and numerical ability. Similarly, the $k:m$ factor is further decomposed into specific abilities such as perceptual speed and spatial ability. In addition, there are certain cross-links, such as mathematical ability, which are influenced by both spatial and numerical ability.

At each level of the hierarchy, some of the specific sources of variance associated with each test item are sifted out, so to speak, so the *g* factor cannot be described in terms of the face characteristics of any single test of group tests. The *g* factor is neither verbal, nor numerical, nor spatial, nor mnemonic, nor mechanical, etc. The sources of variance specifically associated with what can be properly described by terms such as these are ascribable to the group factors, leaving to *g* only that source of variance shared in common by all such abilities, as evidenced by the positive correlation among them.

R. B. Cattell's bottom-up approach to a hierarchy of factors leads to the distinction between *crystallized* and *fluid* general intelligence. The theory proposed by Cattell (1963, 1971) represents a major attempt to synthesize Thurstone's and Spearman's views of intellect. Cattell accepts the idea of primary abilities as well as the derivation of higher-order abilities from the relationships among the primary abilities or factors as second-order factors. Given a set of results such as Thurstone's correlated primary abilities, the next step is to conduct a second-order factor analysis utilizing oblique rotations. The result is a set of correlated second-order factors that can be further analyzed to determine more general third-order factors. Thus, a hierarchy is built up from the bottom, in contrast to the type of top-down procedure advocated by British theorists such as Vernon.

Horn and Cattell (1967) reported the results of a second-order factor analysis of several primary abilities. They derived five second-order factors. Cattell's theory places primary emphasis on the second order *gf* and *gc* factors, where *gf*, fluid intelligence, is interpreted as representing the basic biological capacity of the individual and *gc*, crystallized intelligence, represents the effects of acculturation upon intellectual ability. The *gf* factor is best defined by primary abilities that closely follow Spearman's interpretation of *g*, the ability to educe and apply relations. The *gc* factor is best defined by verbal comprehension ability, which is heavily dependent on cultural context and prior experience.

Of interest is the fact that *gc* and *gf* are themselves correlated. The substantial correlation between them can be interpreted as support for the Spearman and Vernon position of a single higher-order *g*.

Cattell and Horn, however, theorize that general intelligence takes two forms, termed by them *fluid* and *crystallized*. Fluid intelligence is reflected from inference and reasoning on tests that are relatively free of cultural or informational content. On the other hand, crystallized intelligence is manifested in the results of tests that are strongly influenced by the trappings of a culture, such as tests of vocabulary, facts, and information. Thus, by definition, fluid intelligence is more culture-free than crystallized intelligence and corresponds more closely to Spearman's *g*.

Another important recent development of the British theory of general intelligence is that by Eysenck (1967) and his colleagues (Jensen, 1986). This development started with the work of a colleague of Eysenck, Furneaux (1960), who focused on "mental speed" as one of the major dimensions of general intelligence. Furneaux and Eysenck (1967) focused on the notion that general intelligence represented a biological capacity growing with maturation, speed of information processing. As an example, speed of complex reaction time to lights going off in a situation when the subject had to respond to configurations of lights was found to correlate highly with measures of general intelligence (Eysenck 1967, Jensen 1982). The next step for Eysenck was to relate general intelligence and speed of complex reaction time to a neurophysiological process, the Average Evoked Potential. John P. Ertl (1966, 1968) and his co-workers are credited with discovering the first essential link between intelligence and brain physiology by measuring the electrical activity of the cerebral cortex, recorded as the average evoked potential, or AEP. The latency and amplitude of the brain's reaction on the EEG (electroencephalogram) to a simple visual or auditory stimulus, such as a flash of light or a sharp "click," were found to be significantly correlated with IQ.

One of Eysenck's doctoral students, Hendrickson (1972), had as her thesis topic the relationship between auditory evoked potential (AEP) and individual differences in verbal and spatial abilities. Hendrickson's results revealed that simple latencies of the AEP were correlated significantly (values ranging between 0.30 and 0.50) with the composite psychometric scores. These results become more impressive after correction for attenuation due to measurement error as discussed earlier in connection with Spearman's (1904) correction for attenuation. After such correction, the correlations between the AEP and the psychometric test scores increase to about 0.70. A correlation of this magnitude is nearly as large as the *g* loadings of the psychometric tests themselves.

Hendrickson subsequently developed a method of measuring the AEP, not in terms of latency or amplitude of the EEG per se, but in terms of the overall complexity of the multiple-wave reaction following the evoking stimulus (as determined by computer-integrating the total set of waves within a given time-locked epoch). This measurement of the AEP yields larger correlations (in the range of 0.70 to 0.80) with IQ than do other measurements. When the AEP is measured in this way, moreover, its correlation with a given subtest of the Wechsler scale is directly related to the subtest's *g* loading, indicating that the AEP primarily reflects the physiological basis of psychometric *g*. Indeed, the size of these reported correlations even suggests the possibility that virtually all of the true variance in *g* might be measurable by the AEP, a finding which, if it should stand up under repeated replications in various laboratories, would be of great theoretical and practical importance. For one thing, this would mean that Spearman's characterization of *g* as a capacity for abstraction and for the eduction of relations and correlates may be too restrictive. The stimuli used to trigger the evoked potentials are far too simple to evince higher mental processes figuring in Spearman's description of *g*. Returning to Cattell's distinction between fluid and crystallized intelligence, complex choice reaction time for Auditory Evoked Potential represents a measure of fluid intelligence, as opposed to crystallized intelligence measured by comprehension and vocabulary.

HEREDITY AND ENVIRONMENT IN PSYCHOMETRIC INTELLIGENCE

Having examined Spearman's notions of general intelligence as noesis, we need now to consider how this notion connects with a biological capacity notion of intelligence. We have described the formative work of Eysenck and his students relating *g* to neurophysiological measures. We turn now to the biologic heredity component of *g*.

As biological capacity, general intelligence would be determined by heredity, by age-maturation, and by freedom from physical injury or malnutrition. This claim we also view as correct within certain limits. Spearman's view of intelligence is an abstraction from the data, an abstraction that ignores some variation in performance in order to organize better the remaining elements of regularities in the variation in performance. To say that intelligence is general cognitive ability is not to say all reliable variance in cognitive tests is accounted for by a single general factor. Likewise in this interpretation, to say that intelligence is biological capacity is not to say that all reliable individual variation in general level of intelligence tests is due to hereditary factors. The correct interpretation of the Spearman claim is that (1) most of the common variance in cognitive performance tests is attributable to *g*, (2) most of the variance in general intelligence is due to heredity, and (3) heredity and *g* are more closely linked than are heredity and nongenetic factors of cognitive performance. Almost all serious reviews of the empirical literature agree that (1) a first factor accounts for 50 percent or more of the common variance in correlations among intelligence tests and (2) heredity accounts for 50 percent or more of the variance in measures of general intelligence in studies comparing monozigotic twins and fraternal twins raised apart. As stated by Cattell in the 1970 Encyclopedia Britannica (Vol. 12, p. 345):

> The usually accepted figures based on the soundest and most extensive studies employing verbal intelligence tests assign 75 percent to 80 percent of the observed test variation in the general population to genetic factors and the rest to environmental conditions in home, schools and society.

Eysenck (1971, 1979) also estimates that 80 percent of general intelligence is hereditary using the estimates of correlation corrected for attenuation as described earlier in Spearman's (1904) work. This estimate is based on synthesis and reanalysis of data on monozygotic-dizygotic twins reared together and apart, correlations between IQs of nontwins living in the same house, correlations between foster parents and adopted children, correlations between natural parents and their natural children given up for adoption at birth, and inbreeding studies.

The high estimates of the hereditary component of intelligence given by Cattell and Eysenck have recently been called into question partly because the data of Cyril Burt on the hereditary component of intelligence have been called into question. Burt fudged or made up data on his twin studies designed to prove the conclusion accepted by Cattell (1972) and Eysenck (1979). Burt's data, however, are not necessary to make the points made by Eysenck and Cattell. The evidence for the claims on the hereditability of IQ come not from the studies by Burt, but from those of Holzinger. Holzinger, a teacher of this writer at the University of Chicago, was a man of unquestionable integrity with no particular bias toward hereditarian conclusions before starting his studies.

Holzinger was a statistician who worked with Newman, a geneticist, and Freeman, a psychologist. The study by Newman, Freeman, and Holzinger (1937) is definitive and representative of other studies of this time. The principal study uncovered 19 pairs of identical twins, most of whom had been separated since their first years of life. They were compared with pairs of fraternal twins, some raised together and some raised separately. The study found that the correlation between identical twins reared apart was .77. The correlation between fraternal twins reared together was .63. This suggests that being identical twins is a more important factor than growing up in the same environment. A closer picture is provided by a look at the effect of environment on the identical twins reared apart. Holzinger and his colleagues divided the identical twins reared apart into two groups, those raised in homes and schools providing good education and those raised with poor educational opportunities.

The difference in the Stanford-Binet IQ of the twins reared apart ranged from 24 IQ points to 1 point. Holzinger compared the IQs of the identical twins reared apart when one twin had good educational opportunities and the other did not. The mean difference in IQ was 16 points in favor of the better educated. He then compared the identical twins reared apart who had similar educational opportunities. The mean differences were essentially 0 for these twins. A correlation of .79 was found between a rating of (discrepancy in) educational opportunities and (discrepancy in) IQ.

Thus the Holzinger study shows the effect of environment and also gives some support to the claim of Cattell and Eysenck that 75 percent of the variance in general intelligence is due to heredity (Anastasi, 1965, p. 295–300; Brown and Herrnstein, 1975).

QUANTITATIVE INTERACTION BETWEEN HEREDITY AND ENVIRONMENT

So far our treatment of the quantitative constitution on heredity and environment has been simplistic, as if one could define all the amounts of reliable covariance due to hereditary (estimated at 75 percent) and that due to environment (estimated at 25 percent) and arrive at a total variance of 100 percent. In fact, one must consider the factor called in analysis of variance, *interaction*. Besides the quantitative factor of heredity and the quantitative factor of environment, there is a quantitative factor of interaction representing the fact that the amount of effect of the environment depends on conditions of biological heredity and vice versa. This interaction factor is more like a factor of multiplication than of addition. The individual's IQ is better conceived as the product than the sum of the heredity and environment factors. Related to the multiplicative relation of interaction is the variable range of variance in either the heredity or environment variance in the equation. Any estimate of the relative contribution of hereditary and environmental factors to individual differences obviously depends upon the range or extent of both hereditary and environmental differences within the population under consideration. If, for instance, all the subjects of a study are restricted to mongoloid children who by heredity have a limited range of biological variation, the environmental factor will appear greater. In contrast, if all the subjects are subject to severe school and home cognitive deprivation, there is little range in environment and heredity will loom large. Thus in the Holzinger study, the effect of good educational opportunities interacted with the biological factor of twins as monozygotic or dizygotic.

Accordingly, as stated by Anastasi (1965, p. 68), the most widely accepted view of the heredity-environment relationship is that of interaction. This means primarily that the effects of hereditary and environmental factors are not cumulative or additive but rather that the nature and extent of the influence of each type of factor depends on the contribution of the other. In other words, any one environmental factor will exert a different influence depending on the specific hereditary material upon which it operates.

In summary, the British biological view of general intelligence appears to be the interpretation of the intelligence concept most consistent with the psychometric research data. The limits of the British position, however, are that its validity rests on the prior assumptions involved in the psychometric method of assessing intelligence. The psychometric search for general intelligence started with a set of tests designed to minimize the role of experience in performance. This was done by either presenting the child with a novel task for which prior experience was assumed to be irrelevant (Raven's matrices) or by averaging over a wide sample of incidental learnings (e.g., vocabulary) to which all individuals might be expected to be equally exposed. Such a procedure is bound (as it was intended) to maximize the biological capacity component of the performances assessed. Given the assumptions under which IQ tests have been developed, it is impossible to give any general worthwhile meaning to the experientially determined portion of IQ scores. Because IQ tests were created to measure general capacity inherited and stable or fixed over time, the hereditary portion of test-variation is meaningful—it is what the test was intended to measure. Because of these same assumptions behind the tests, the experience-determined portion of the variance is only random noise, that is, residual and unstable variance with no clear meaning within the initial assumptions of meaning by which the tests were constructed. Insofar as experience changes test scores, it is an intrusion on the concept of intelligence, something that must be treated almost as error. If, for instance, a child is coached on the Binet, the child's IQ will go up. This effect of experience is sheer error, however; the child's intelligence has not changed. We will expect that the increase will neither generalize to a new test nor lead to better performance at a later age. This is because the tests were initially designed so that the only general and longitudinally stable component of performance would be the capacity component.

In summary, Spearman's conception of experience-free general intelligence is supported by psychometric data, but that data involves a methodology that can only isolate as general what is relatively experience-free. Using the results of the psychometric methodology, one does indeed conclude that the solid bulk of intelligence variation is hereditary or native. An alternative conception and methodology of testing cognitive development might lead to other conclusions.

HOWARD GARDNER'S THEORY OF MULTIPLE INTELLIGENCES

We have summarized the evidence for the British biological heredity approach to general intelligence. A new approach to multiple intelligences in the Thurstone or American tradition but stressing biology and ignoring correlational and factor analytic approaches to the subject has been proposed by Howard Gardner (1983).

An ambitious theory is described by Howard Gardner in his book *Frames of Mind* (1983). As implied in the names of both the theory and the book, Gardner's theory is in the tradition of multifactor theories like those of Thurstone (1938) and Cattell (1971). Furthermore, Gardner is not far from the traditional view in arguing that

> a human intellectual competence must entail a set of skills of problem solving—enabling the individual *to resolve genuine problems or difficulties* that he or she encounters and, when appropriate, to create an effective product—and must also entail the potential for *finding or creating problems*—thereby laying the groundwork for the acquisition of new knowledge (p. 62, emphasis in the original).

These skills or competencies should collectively cover "a reasonably complete gamut of the kinds of abilities valued by human cultures" (p. 62).

The scope of Gardner's work emerges in the way he establishes distinct intelligences, for here he goes far beyond the garden-variety psychometric evidence to develop his theory. Gardner proposes several "signs" that can be used to identify distinct intelligences. They are signs rather than exact criteria because "this undertaking must be provisional; I do not include something merely because it exhibits one or two of the signs, nor do I exclude a candidate (i.e., possible) intelligence just because it fails to qualify on each and every account" (Gardner, 1983, p. 62). The signs are these:

1. *Isolation by brain damage*. Often injury to the brain results in the loss of a specific intellectual skill. Such *selective impairment* indicates that the affected intellectual skill is at least partially independent of other skills that remain intact following brain damage.

2. *The existence of individuals with exceptional talent.* Some individuals are truly extraordinarily skilled in one intellectual domain but ordinarily skilled—or even retarded—in most other domains. Idiot savants, for example, are retarded persons who have one extraordinarily well-developed talent, often in the areas of musical or numeric ability (Hill, 1978). Such selective competence, like selective impairment following brain injury, suggests autonomy of that particular competence.

3. *A distinct developmental history.* If an intelligence is autonomous, it should develop in a distinct manner and in much the same way in all people. That is, we should see a reliable sequence of development in which skills progress through a standard set of initial, intermediate, and advanced stages of development.

4. *Encoding in a symbol system.* Symbols such as words and pictures are fundamental to communication and thought in all human cultures. This universal human proclivity to use symbols leads to Gardner's (1983) final sign of an intelligence. Specifically, he suggests that "while it may be possible for an intelligence to proceed without its own special symbol system...a primary characteristic of human intelligence may well be its 'natural' gravitation toward embodiment in a symbolic system" (p. 66).

These signs function collectively as a screening device; any given intelligence will show many but probably not all of the signs. By the same token, some phenomena may show a few signs but not enough to qualify as a distinct intelligence. Suppose, for example, that we proposed solving crossword puzzles as a distinct intelligence. We would probably be able to provide some empirical support for its independence, and one could well imagine a set of distinctive hurdles that a budding crossword puzzle solver would pass en route to completing her first puzzle in the *New York Times*.

Yet on the other signs, solving crossword puzzles fails as an intelligence, and fails miserably. Brain damage does not impair only crossword ability; instead, other language skills are usually lost as well. Crossword puzzle aficionados are usually not completely ordinary in other skills; most often they are articulate persons who have also acquired the odd argot of the crossword puzzle. Finally, there is no reason to believe that a unique set of cognitive processes is in operation when individuals solve these puzzles; on the contrary, the retrieval of words to solve a crossword puzzle is not unlike the retrieval of words in conversation or thought. The retrieval in solving crossword puzzles is simply slowed considerably because the cues in the puzzles that aid retrieval are often unorthodox.

Solving crossword puzzles may seem like a contrived example, because no one would seriously propose such a specific form of intelligence. Using the signs in a manner not unlike our use in these two examples, Gardner (1983) concludes that the cumulative evidence points to six distinct intelligences. Some of these intelligences are not new, including linguistic intelligence, a logical-mathematical intelligence, and a spatial intelligence. In addition to musical intelligence, Gardner lists two other intelligences not considered by psychometric and factor-analytic approaches—bodily kinesthetic intelligence (dance) and personal intelligence (self-understanding). A musical intelligence may seem at best a secondary or adjunct intelligence in comparison to verbal, logical, and mathematical skills. Gardner is opposed to this view; he believes that the appropriate relationship would be for musical intelligence to be as central as logical-mathematical skills:

> For most of humanity, and throughout most of human history, the processes and products involved in artistic creation and perception have been far more pervasive than those enshrined in the sciences. In fact, logical scientific thought can be considered an invention of the West in the wake of the Renaissance—an invention which is still restricted to a small enclave of thinkers; participation in the literary, musical, or graphic arts, on the other hand, has been widespread for thousands of years (p. 299).

Gardner has marshaled an array of evidence to buttress this claim for a musical intelligence.

The key components of music are *pitch*, the highness or lowness of a sound, *rhythm*, the grouping of successive pitches, and *timbre*, the quality of a tone (i.e., the same notes played on a saxophone and violin produce quite different experiences for a listener, reflecting differences in timbre). Comprehending music, then, involves making sense of pitch, rhythm, and timbre.

Several fascinating case studies of the sequelae to brain damage attest to the independence of musical intelligence. One such case was the Russian composer Shebalin. He was afflicted with Wernicke's aphasia, in which speech remains fluent but comprehension is impaired. Nevertheless, his ability to understand and compose music remained entirely intact.

Probably no area of accomplishment is so rich with legends of prodigies as musical talent. Undoubtedly the best-known is Mozart, whose talent as both a musical performer and composer was evident early in childhood. Less widely known are *idiot savants*, whose mental retardation is accompanied, inexplicably, by musical talent. Gardner (1983) describes "Harriet [who] was able to play 'Happy Birthday' in the style of various composers, including Mozart, Beethoven, Verdi, and Schubert.... At the age of three, her mother called her [i.e., got her attention] by playing incomplete melodies, which the child would then complete with the appropriate tone in the proper octave" (p. 121).

For most children living in Western cultures, musical ability develops little after the preschool years. Individuals learn more songs and sing them with greater precision and feeling, but we see no further qualitative changes of the Piagetian variety. For musically talented youngsters, however, there is a clear progression during childhood and adolescence. In the early elementary-school years,

> the child proceeds on the basis of sheer talent and energy: he learns pieces readily

because of his sensitive musical ear and memory, gains applause for his technical skill, but essentially does not expend undue effort. A period of more sustained skill building commences around the age of nine or so, when the child must begin to practice seriously even to the extent that it may interfere with his school and his friendships (Gardner, 1983, pp. 111–112).

A second change occurs in adolescence, when blossoming musicians must "supplement their intuitive understanding with a more systematic knowledge of music lore and law" (Gardner, 1983, p. 111).

The developmental pattern, then, has two tiers. One tier is for all individuals; the second, for the musically talented. Nevertheless, Gardner (1983) speculates that these tiers exist only because most Western cultures tolerate "musical illiteracy." Unlike instruction in reading, science, or math, instruction in music is not emphasized in schools. Perhaps more individuals would progress to the second tier of development if systematic musical instruction were the rule instead of the exception.

Gardner's theory of multiple intelligences represents a sophisticated effort to bridge the gaps between the traditional approaches to intelligence. It is probably best viewed as a general theoretical framework rather than as a fully elaborated, final theory. As George Miller (1983) wrote in evaluating Gardner's work, "For his attempt to integrate diverse approaches, Mr. Gardner deserves everyone's gratitude. The fact that he calls his proposal a theory should not frighten off a general reader. It is less a scientific theory than a line on which he hangs out his intellectual laundry" (p. 5).

PIAGET'S QUALITATIVE CONCEPT OF INTERACTION
BETWEEN BIOLOGY AND ENVIRONMENT

The purely quantitative concept of interaction of biology and environment elaborated in the last section should be sharply disentangled from Piagetian or a constructivistic theoretical concept of interaction. As stated earlier, Piaget's theory of intelligence includes a biological factor, an environmental learning factor, and an equilibration or interactional factor with emphasis laid on the last. This emphasis is allied on the structure rather than the content of cognitive development. The British theory of noesis is primarily hereditarian-maturationist as elaborated in our earlier quote from Isaacs, leaving the remaining factor-specific learning *s* and allowing no place theoretically for an interactional view of general intelligence.

In Chapters 2 and 3, we contrast the maturationist assumption that basic mental structure results from an innate patterning with the learning theory assumption that basic mental structure is the result of the patterning or association of events in the outside world. In contrast, the cognitive-developmental assumption is that basic mental structure is the result of an interaction between certain organismic structuring tendencies and the structure of the outside world, rather than reflecting either one directly.

This interaction leads to cognitive stages, which represent the transformations of simple early cognitive structures as they are applied to (or assimilate) the external world and as they are accommodated to or restructured by the external world in the course of being applied to it.

We outlined Piaget's theory of intelligence as making the following assumptions:

1. The terms *cognition, thought,* or *intelligence* basically refer to adaptive actions on objects or internalizations of such actions. Mature or adequate cognition is defined by an equilibrium or reciprocity between action and object. Cognition is defined as function (as modes of action) rather than as content (as sets of words, "verbal responses," associations, memories, etc.) or as a faculty or ability (a power of producing words, memories, etc.). The encouragement of cognitive development, then, is the provision of opportunities for activities of an organized or equilibrated form.

2. Cognition proceeds through stages of structural reorganization. While cognitive functions are present from birth, cognitive structures are radically different from one stage to the next.

3. The implication of structural reorganization in development is that the source of cognitive structure and of cognitive development is to be found neither in the structure and maturation of the organism nor in the teaching structures of the environment but in the structure of the interaction between organism and environment.

4. The optimal conditions for such structural organization entail some optimal balance of discrepancy and match between the behavior structures of the child and the structure of his psychological environment.

We stressed that the core of the cognitive-development position, then, is the doctrine of cognitive stages. Cognitive stages have the following general characteristics (Piaget, 1960):

1. Stages imply distinct or qualitative differences in children's modes of thinking or of solving the same problem at different ages.

2. These different modes of thought form an invariant sequence, order, or succession in individual development. While cultural factors may speed up, slow down, or stop development, they do not change its sequence.

3. Each of these different and sequential modes of thought forms a "structured whole." A given stage-response on a task does not just represent a specific response determined by knowledge and familiarity with that task or tasks similar to it; rather it represents an underlying thought-organization. An example is the stage of "concrete operations," which determine responses to many tasks which are not manifestly similar to one another on the "ordinary" dimensions of stimulus generalization. According to Piaget, at the stage of

concrete operations, the child has a general tendency to maintain that a physical object conserves its properties on various physical dimensions in spite of apparent perceptual changes. This tendency is structural; it is not a specific belief about a specific object. The implication is that both conservation and other aspects of logical operations should appear as a consistent cluster of responses in development.

4. Cognitive stages are hierarchical integrations. Stages form an order of increasingly differentiated and integrated *structures* to fulfil a common function. The general adaptational functions of cognitive structures are always the same (for Piaget the maintenance of an equilibrium between the organism defined as a balance of assimilation and accommodation). Accordingly, higher stages displace (or rather reintegrate) the structures found at lower stages. As an example, formal operational thought includes all the structural features of concrete operational thought but at a new level of organization. Concrete operational thought or even sensorimotor thought does not disappear when formal thought arises but continues to be used in concrete situations where it is adequate or when efforts at solution by formal thought have failed. However, there is a hierarchical preference within the individual, that is, a disposition to prefer a solution of a problem at the highest level available to him. It is this disposition which partially accounts for the consistency postulated as our third criterion.

It is extremely important to test whether a set of theoretical stages does meet the empirical criteria just listed. If a logical hierarchy of levels did not define an empirical sequence, the hierarchy would tell us little about the process of development nor would it justify our notion that the sequence is interactional in nature. If empirical sequence was not found, one would argue that the "stages" simply constituted alternative types of organization of varying complexity, each of which might develop independently of the other. In such a case, the "stages" could represent alternative expressions of maturation or they could equally well represent alternative cultures to which the child is exposed. It would hardly be surprising to find that adult physical concepts are more complex, more different-iated and integrated in educated Western culture than in a jungle tribe. The fact that the Western and tribal patterns are at different levels of structural organiza-tion, however, in itself tells us little about ontogenesis in either culture and leaves open the possibility that ontogenesis in either culture is simply a process of learning cultural content.

In contrast, if structural stages do define general ontogenetic sequences, then an interactional type of theory of developmental process must be used to explain ontogeny. If the child goes through qualitatively different stages of thought, his basic modes of organizing experience cannot be the direct result of adult teaching or they would be copies of adult thought from the start. If the child's cognitive responses differed from the adult's only in revealing less information and less complication of structure, it would be possible to view them as incomplete learnings of the external structure of the world, whether that structure is defined in terms of the adult culture or in terms of the laws of the physical world. If the child's responses indicate a different structure or organization than the adult's, rather than a less complete one, and if this structure is similar in all children, it is extremely difficult to view the child's mental structure as a direct learning of the external structure. Furthermore, if the adult's mental structure depends upon sequential transformations of the child's mental structure, it too cannot directly reflect the current structure of the outer cultural or physical world.

If stages cannot be accounted for by direct learning of the structure of the outer world, neither can they be explained as the result of innate patterning. If children have their own logic, adult logic or mental structure cannot be derived from innate neurological patterning because such patterning should hold also in childhood. It is hardly plausible to view a whole succession of logics as an evolutionary and functional program of innate wiring.

It has just been claimed that it is implausible to view a succession of cognitive stages as innate. This claim is based on an epistemological assumption, the assumption that there is a reality to which psychology may and must refer, that is, that cognition or knowing must be studied in relation to an object known.

The invariant sequences found in motor development (Ames, 1937; Shirley, 1931, 1931–1933) may well be directly wired into the nervous system. The fact that the postural-motor development of chimpanzees and man proceed through the same sequence suggests such a maturational base (Riesen & Kinder, 1952). The existence of invariant sequence in cognition is quite a different matter, however, since cognitions are defined by reference to a world. One cannot speak of the development of a child's conception of an animal without assuming that the child has experience with animals. Things become somewhat more complicated when we are dealing with the development of categories, that is, the most general modes of relating objects such as causality, substance, space, time quantity, and logic. These categories differ from more specific concepts, for example, the concept of "animal," in that they are not defined by specific objects to which they refer but by modes of relating any object to any other object. Every experienced event is located in space and time, implies or causes other events, etc. Because these categories or structures are independent of specific experiences with specific objects, it has been plausible for philosophers like Kant to assume that they are innate molds into which specific experiences are fitted. If structures or categories like space and time were Kantian innate forms, it is difficult to understand how these structures could undergo transformation in development, however.

The interactional account assumes that structural change in these categories depends upon experience. The effects of experience, however, are not conceived of as learning in the ordinary sense, in which learning implies training by pairing of specific objects and specific responses, by instruction, by modeling, or by specific practices of responses. Indeed, the effects of training are determined by the child's cognitive categories rather than the reverse. If two events which follow one another in time are cognitively connected in the child's mind, it implies that he relates them by means of a category such as causality, for example, he perceives his operant behavior as causing the reinforcer to occur. A program of reinforcement, then, cannot directly change the child's causal structures since it is assimilated to it.

If cognitive development occurs in terms of stages, then, an understanding of the effect of experience upon it requires three types of conceptual analysis customarily omitted in discussions of learning.

In the first place, it requires an analysis of universal structural features of the environment. While depending on structural and functional invariants of the nervous system, cognitive stages also depend upon universal structures of experience for their shape. Stages of physical concepts depend upon a universal structure of experience in the physical world, a structure which underlies the diversity of physical arrangements in which men live and which underlies the diversity of formal physical theories held in various cultures at various periods.

In the second place, understanding cognitive stages depends upon a logical analysis of orderings inherent in given concepts. The invariance of sequence in the development of a concept or category is not dependent upon a prepatterned unfolding of neural patterns; it must depend upon a logical analysis of the concept itself. As an example, Piaget postulates a sequence of spaces or geometrics moving from the topological to the projective to the Euclidean. This sequence is plausible in terms of logical analysis of the mathematical structures involved.

In the third place, an understanding of sequential stages depends upon analysis of the relation of the structure of a specific experience of the child to the behavior structure. Piaget (1964) has termed such an analysis an "equilibration" rather than a "learning" analysis. Such an analysis employs such notions as "optimal match," "cognitive conflict," "assimilation," and "accommodation." Whatever terms are used, such analyses focus upon discrepancies between the child's action system or expectancies and the experienced event, and hypothesize some moderate or optimal degree of discrepancy as constituting the most effective experience for structural change in the organism.

In summary, an interactional conception of stages differs from a maturational one in that it assumes that experience is necessary for the stages to take the shape they do as well as assuming that generally more or richer stimulation will lead to faster advances through the series involved. It proposes that an understanding of the role of experience requires (*a*) analyses of universal features of experienced objects (physical or social), (*b*) analysis of logical sequences of differentiation and integration in concepts of such objects, and (*c*) analysis of structural relations between experience-inputs and the relevant behavior organizations.

PIAGET'S VIEW OF HEREDITARY CAPACITY AND OF
PSYCHOMETRIC TESTS

Piaget then approached the question of intelligence with an agenda entirely different from that of Spearman and other psychometricians. Piaget wanted to find universal similarities in human knowing, in contrast with psychometric efforts to measure individual differences. Table 4.1 summarizes the contrasts between the views of Spearman and Piaget. Spearman was concerned with the general intellectual capacity of individuals that remains stable over time relative to that of other individuals. Piaget was concerned with the universal character of specific changes in individual intellectual capacity over time. Spearman focused on quantifying differences among individuals, Piaget on describing qualitative changes within individuals. Spearman's method was to study individual differences with tasks that *minimized* the role of experience in performance (novel tasks or tests on information presumed equally accessible to all). Piaget studied universal changes with tasks that *maximized* the role of experience in performance. For example, he probed children's constructions of many aspects of the physical world (e.g., object permanence, causality of shadows, wind, night, dreams, spatial and temporal relations), and the social world (e.g., familial and age relationships, social and moral rules). In studies of conservation, Piaget and his collaborators focused on children's construction of the idea of invariance—that is, the logical reasoning that enables a child to deduce that transformations in shape do not change the quantity of a given number, weight, volume, and so on. Piaget focused the bulk of his efforts on studying the development of logical reasoning, including the role of mental imagery, perception, and memory.

TABLE 4.1
Contrasts between the Views of Spearman and Piaget

Spearman	Piaget
Concerned with identifying general hereditary individual differences in intelligence	Concerned with identifying universal similarities in forms of intelligence
Concerned with individual potential or capacity for knowing in the future, relative to other individuals	Concerned with universal character of human intellectual experience, in a present age period, relative to past and future knowledge
Quantified individual differences and relative stability within specified age groups	Described qualitative differences in the individual over time from birth to adolescence
Studied individual differences with tasks that minimized the role of experience in performance	Studied universal changes with tasks that maximized the role of experience in performance

Piaget acknowledged heredity as one factor in the development of intelligence. In this respect, we find a convergence with the view of Spearman. However, Piaget had a more limited notion of the role of heredity. In this regard he commented:

> First, obviously genetic factors play a role in the development of intelligence. But they can do no more than open certain possibilities. They cannot do anything about actualizing these possibilities. That is, there are no innate structures in the human mind which simply come into being. . . all our mental structures must be constructed. So genetic factors or maturational aspects are not adequate for explaining what really takes place at any given stage. (Evans, 1973, pp. 31–32)

> . . .at the sensori-motor level, the coordination between grasping and vision seems to be clearly the result of the myelinization of certain new nervous paths in the pyramidal tract as physiologists have shown. This myelinization seems to be the result of hereditary programming. However, in the domain of higher, representative and especially operational structures, these structures are not innate. (Piaget, 1972, pp. 8–9)

For Piaget, the role of biology in intelligence was not an amorphous *g*, but an active mechanism of knowing. He said:

> I would conclude in discussing the role of biology as a factor of development that what is important for us to take from biology is not the notion of hereditary programming. . . .We should take the more general notion of self-regulating mechanisms. (Piaget, 1972, p. 12)

As noted earlier, in addition to the genetic factor, Piaget pointed out three other factors: (1) general physical logico-mathematical and social experience, (2) social transmission, and (3) resulting equilibration.

Definition of Intelligence

While Piaget did not discuss Spearman's biological assumption directly, he did distinguish his own definition of intelligence from that of Spearman:

> But we find less rigid forms of empiricism. . .especially in Spearman's interesting theory, which is both statistical (factor analyses of intelligence) and descriptive; from this second point of view, Spearman reduces the operations of intelligence to the "apprehension of experience" and to the "eduction" of relations and "correlates," that is to say, to a more or less complex reading of immediately given relations. These relations, then, are not constructed but discovered by simple accommodation to external reality. (Piaget, 1950, p. 16)

Thus we see that Piaget's theory of operations differs significantly from Spearman's eduction of relations and correlates. Spearman's conception of intelligence as the ability to "educe" relations and correlates does not go far enough for Piaget who commented:

> ...the fundamental error of empiricist theories of "mental experiment" is that they concentrate on the isolated operation....
> To take other examples: a "correlate" in Spearman's sense (dog is to wolf as cat is to tiger) has meaning only as a function of a matrix. A relation of kinship (brother, uncle, etc.) refers to the whole constituted by a family tree. (Piaget, 1950, pp. 34–36)

Piaget described Spearman's "eduction of correlates" in terms of multiplication of classes "that never exist singly, but always form a group or system of relations"— what Piaget calls "operations." For Piaget, Spearman's theory lacked two characteristics crucial to his own view: operations and constructivism:

> ...when Spearman reduces intelligence to three essential activities, the "apprehension of experience," the "eduction of relations" and the "eduction of correlates," we must add that experience is not apprehended without the intervention of constructive assimilation. The so-called "eductions" of relations are to be thought of, then as genuine operations (seriation or the grouping together of symmetrical relations). (Piaget, 1950, p. 93)

Quoting Spearman's (1923) definition of correlates ("the presenting of any character together with any relation tends to evoke immediately the knowing of the correlative character," p. 91), Piaget said:

> this is compatible with certain definite groupings, namely those of multiplication of classes and relations. (Piaget, 1950, p. 93)

Limited Usefulness of Psychometric Tests

On a more practical level, Piaget saw psychometric tests as fulfilling a limited purpose:

> I.Q. tests probably do serve a purpose in providing, as Inhelder ([1943] 1968) suggested, a "first approximation" to assessment of a child's intelligence.
> It is indisputable that these tests of mental age have on the whole lived up to what was expected of them: a rapid and convenient estimation of an individual's general level. But it is no less obvious that they simply measure a "yield," without reaching constructive operations themselves. As Pieron rightly pointed out, intelligence conceived in these terms is essentially a value-judgment applied to complex behavior. (Piaget, 1950, pp. 153–154)

On the other hand, Piaget thought that the psychometric approach focused on performance without reaching competence and that his approach to operational reasoning promised greater success in understanding the nature of general intelligence. He asked:

Is intelligence measured only on the basis of some performance, or are we really getting at the competence, the internal structure? I am afraid that in studies of this sort (Jenson, 1969) people have always measured performance, and it is quite obvious that performance will vary according to the social environment. For my part, I have no faith in measures that are based on intelligence quotients or on any other performance measure. (Evans, 1973, pp. 31–32)

Inhelder ([1943] 1968) concluded that "Although the Binet-Simon test is an excellent means for the rapid detection of mental anomalies, it cannot meet the demands of a psychological 'diagnosis' of thought" (p. 44).

Although Piaget did not dismiss psychometric tests completely, he felt that such quantitative measures were premature, as they purported to measure intelligence without knowing what it was. He commented:

In working out his intelligence tests, Binet had the excellent idea of applying them to the most diverse functions, convinced that intelligence is everywhere and constitutes a sort of summation of all cognitive activities. But when afterwards he was asked what intelligence was, he replied with ready wit: "It is what my tests measure," a very wise reaction but a little disturbing when one thinks of the theoretical knowledge acquired by the instrument of measurement thus constructed. A physicist, on the contrary, does not measure a form of energy until a far more thorough theoretical study has been made of what is to be measured and of the instrument of measurement itself. ...it is important to diagnose not so much what the subject can do when undergoing the test, as what he would be capable of doing in many other situations. Intelligence was therefore "measured" long before it was known what it consists of, and we are only just beginning to have some inkling of the complexity of its nature and functioning. (Piaget, 1966, p. 59)

Still, Piaget recognized the research value of psychometric tests, yet considered them an experimental method that ought not to be used as a practical selective or educational measure of individual differences in intelligence. This is clear when he said that

in particular, his (Binet's) practical achievement in devising intelligence tests has led to innumerable research projects involving the measurement of mental development and individual aptitudes. And though the tests have not produced all the results expected of them, the problems they raised are of far greater interest than could have been foreseen at the time they came into use: either we shall one day find good tests or else intelligence tests will go into history as an example of a fruitful error. (1970, p. 150)

As we have noted, Binet and Spearman looked at different kinds of performances from those that interested Piaget. Binet and Spearman looked behind correct bits of trivial knowledge and right answers with a narrow focus on reasoning products. Piaget examined incorrect as well as correct knowledge and reasoning, and probed well beyond surface products to structures behind the products or performances. Piaget criticized psychometric performances, in contrast to the performances he was interested in, in the following way:

> In fact, nearly all intelligence tests are based on a postulate which is certainly limitative and consists in measuring only the resultants or "performances" and not the actual processes which have produced them. In physics, of course, processes can be judged by their results, but this is because they are homogeneous and the results of a given process constant. In mental activity on the contrary, the same resultant can be obtained by different paths and above all, *an operative structure is the source of a great many possible resultants which cannot be deduced from the performance observed but presuppose a knowledge of the underlying operative mechanism* [italics added]. The latter is therefore the objective to be reached in judging an individual's intelligence, particularly since it is important to diagnose not so much what the subject can do when undergoing the test, as what he would be capable of doing in many other situations. (Piaget, 1966, p. 59)

Thus we see that for Piaget intellectual competence is not just achievement, but also has a generality that goes beyond specific performance. This generality does not require a concept of biological capacity. For Piaget, intelligence is the child's actually attained level of structure. To call a child's cognitive stage "intelligence," implies that intelligence is not a constant characteristic of the child over development, that is, it is not a capacity or rate factor.

Stages and Constructivism

In contrast with Spearman's noesis, Piaget's theory is interactionist or constructivist. Psychometric tasks and their interpretation by both biological and environmental theorists in effect present cognition as static, as correct information, performance judged by concordance with the culturally correct answers. Noesis is static in that it is correct apprehension of a set of relations "out there" in the stimulus or task. We described above how Piaget's conception of intelligence is active assimilation or fitting of the stimulus to the organism's activities and structures insofar as such assimilation is accompanied by accommodation to the unique characteristics of the stimulus. The relations known by the intelligence are not in stimuli, but are constructed in the mind of the knower in the course of interaction with objects (including people). Logical relations are not read from stimuli, but are constructed from actions and reflected in actions, including play.

Piaget replaces the distinction between general intelligence as capacity distinct from specific learning or experience with a notion of general intelligence as that which changes as a result of general and self-initiated forms of organizing action, as opposed to that which changes with specific content learning. We have said that Piaget derives the generality of intelligence as something inside the organism, not from "capacity" but from "structure." In addition, Piaget ascribes the generality of cognitive development to general features of the organism's experience.

Essentially, Piagetian intelligence differs from school achievement not in the sense that it exists or develops without experience as capacity, but in the sense that it develops through universal experiences, experiences that occur with or without schooling of one sort or another. All children have recurrent experiences of time, space, causality, substance, number, and so on. The children's structure of reasoning about number or causality cannot be attributed to something out there that they have learned through specific experience, like the word "envelope." Neither is it a motor pattern like creeping, which matures from within. A cognitive structure is, rather, an interaction between neurological structures and environmental structures that is not reducible qualitatively or quantitatively to either. Insofar as differences exist in individual children's general cognitive levels, they are differences largely due to environments, rich or poor in general experience rather than differences resulting from a capacity independent of experience.

The problems in comparing the biological capacity and Piagetian views of intelligence are different from the problems of comparing biological capacity and environmental psychometric views. The biological and environmental views are alternative theories about the set of facts, the facts of psychometric variation. Some writers have treated the comparison of Piagetian and biological views of intelligence in the same fashion. In particular, Hunt (1961) seemed to suggest that Piaget's theory of the interactional origins of mental structure might provide us with a new interactional view of the quantitative contributions of heredity and environment to general intelligence. Hunt's review of various transformations in behavioral science (Piaget's work being the most central) led him to seriously question "the immutability of the IQ," and suggest that

> ...instead, the IQ is regarded as a phenotype, like height or weight, for which the genes set limits of potential development but which is finally developed through encounters with the environment. (Hunt, 1961, p. vi)

This idea is problematic because it leaves Piaget's theory of intelligence in the same field of empirical reference as that of the psychometricians. Piaget's new theory of cognitive development, however, could not be expected to change any of the old facts or theory about hereditary and environmental contributions to psychometric measures of intelligence.

PIAGETIAN AND PSYCHOMETRIC INTELLIGENCE AS OVERLAPPING FACTORS

In discussing psychometric intelligence, we pointed out that a meaningful conceptualization of intelligence requires: (1) a distinction between cognitive competence and performance, and (2) a conception of intelligence as general, as more than the sum of specific performances. For the British, these two requirements of an intelligence concept were based on distinguishing between *general capacity* and *specific performance.* For Piaget, general competence is distinguished from specific performance, but without the assumption of a fixed capacity factor. Piaget did distinguish between a specific "*achievement*" (like conservation in a specific task) and a more general *process* or *structure* of reasoning underlying the achievement. Binet and Spearman looked behind the child's achievements (such as bits of knowledge and problem-solving) for a general capacity. Piaget looked for general thought process or structures behind logical products or achievements. These thought processes or structures are, of course, defined in terms of qualitative stages. The stage of "concrete operations" refers to a dynamic network or system of interdependent processes of reasoning reflected over the whole field of logico-mathematical aspects of thought. For Piaget, intelligence as something general derives from the notion that thinking is organized in terms of general structures or systems of operations characterizing a stage. We saw that the Binet-Spearman approach used generality as a criterion of intelligence and achieved generality by removing the effects of experience on task performance.

We will hold that Piagetians, like psychometricians, are also bound by the notion of generality if they are to say they are assessing intelligence. If Piagetian tasks of class inclusion, conservation, and so on are said to assess intelligence, they must be assessing more than the sum of a set of items called conservation, class inclusion, and so on. The notion of generality implied by the Piagetian, however, is not that of capacity. The distinction between psychometric capacity or intelligence and achievement is largely that intelligence is more general than achievement. Piagetian intelligence, however, is not more general than the observable sum of the child's operational activities or structures of reasoning, a field of reasoning in such scientific domains as mathematics, physical causality, and spatiotemporal relations. In a sense, Piaget's conception of intelligence, though it is a concept of general intelligence, is *narrower and more specific than Spearman's.* Spearman said that all cognitive performances that correlated with one another reflect or define intelligence. Piaget would not agree. Only those performances that reflect a certain general level of thought structure are "intelligent" in his narrower sense. Piaget would not attempt to explain the fact that there is a certain small g factor in all Binet performances by positing that they all reflect a general structure. Those facts can be left to the Spearman approach. However, he would anticipate a further or greater generality or consistency to performance on tasks that fairly directly involve structures of concrete operational reasoning. Piaget then postulates a competence-performance distinction and a notion of intelligence as general without centering these distinctions on a concept of biological capacity.

Our own point of view is not that the Piagetian and biological views are different orderings of the same facts, but different orderings of different systems of facts that overlap. The Piagetian notion of intelligence as reasoning structure dependent on universal experience does not directly contradict the psychometric notion of general capacity, nor need it be entirely empirically distinct from it. Piaget would neither deny the existence of a general factor in psychometric tests nor explain it as deriving directly from either heredity or environment. He also would not deny that this general biological capacity factor might have an influence on a child's level of operational reasoning. While general forms of universal experience are required to attain concrete operations, children may be born with different rates or powers of assimilation, different levels of general activity that help determine the age of achievement of Piagetian structures. This in no way contradicts the interactionist theory of mental structures. The theory that a genuine cognitive structure is neither a direct reflection of a pattern in the genes nor a direct reflection of a pattern in the environment, but is an equilibrational patterning of the interaction between the two, need not deny an innate capacity factor. However, while hereditary g may affect rate of cognitive-structural development, this fact tells us little about the nature, development, or value of structural intelligence.

The notion of a partial empirical overlap between psychometric intelligence and Piagetian intelligence is necessary if the latter concept is to have meaning. For Piagetian theory to persuade us of this new view of intelligence, however, performance on Piagetian tests of intelligence must be correlationally or factorially distinct from performance on the psychometric tests. This distinctness, neverthe-less, cannot be complete. It is a problem of "damned if it is, damned if it isn't." No impartial review of research could deny a general intelligence factor. Accordingly, a failure of Piagetian tests to correlate with psychometric tests would indicate a failure of such tests to involve intelligence. If a Piagetian conservation task was unrelated to other intelligence items, the child's performance on a conservation task would be a relatively useless focus for intellectual assessment or intervention. On the other hand, if a conservation item were so highly correlated with psy-chometric intelligence items that it was just another test of g, it would also cease to be of interest in either theory or in educational intervention or assessment.

The Distinctiveness of Piagetian and Psychometric Intelligence

There were two reasons we thought factor analysis would distinguish Piagetian intelligence from psychometric intelligence test factors. First, responses in Piaget-ian tasks are assessed in terms of the form or structure of reasoning while responses in psychometric tests, in contrast, are assessed in terms of correctness of content. For example, in the WISC Similarities subtest, classification is assessed with such questions as "In what way are an apple and a banana alike?" The child who says they are both fruit receives a higher score than a child who says they are both foods. From a structural point of view, the question is inadequate to assess classificatory reasoning because the use of one or the other verbal labels does not reveal whether this content is organized in a hierarchical inclusive system of classes. This is an example of how psychometric tests fail to provide a basis for assessing the structure of reasoning behind correct answers. The psychometric focus on correctness in content also leads to failure to provide a basis for assessing reasoning underlying incorrect answers. From the structural perspective, this is important because some wrong answers are more advanced developmentally than others. For example, the child who believes dreams are real events that occur in the physical world is less advanced than a child who views dreams as internal events, yet believes in their causality by some external agency. Many psychometric test items could be analyzed from a structural point of view, but this would necessitate research of the sort Piaget did with his tasks. Qualitative analysis of psychometric test items would also make it possible to determine whether the factorial distinction between psychometric and Piagetian tasks is due to a difference in the form of scoring, or to the content of the tasks. This structure-content difference suggests that the consistency across Piagetian tasks of structure of reasoning might be expected to be higher than the consistency across psychometric tests based on content-focused assessment of success or failure.

The second reason we expected a factor analysis to distinguish Piagetian from psychometric intelligence was that the two approaches differ in their assumptions about the role of general experience in determining level of intelligence. The psychometric approach to general intelligence attempts to either get at capacity independent of experience by picking tasks whose content is novel (such as Raven's matrices) or average across tasks requiring specific cultural learning (such as vocabulary and information). In contrast, Piaget's approach to general intelligence attempts to get at capacity resulting from interaction between the organism's structuring tendencies and universal features of the physical and social environment. For example, regardless of schooling or culture, all children have dreams, observe discrete and continuous qualities, and notice adults in different sex and age roles.

Thus, our expectation of consistency among Piagetian tasks reflects an assumption that such consistency springs not from a dependence of each task on biological capacity, but from structural similarities in the organization of various features of experience. These similarities are denoted by the notion of stage as a structured whole, although this does not imply absolute evenness in the structure of thought across all content domains.

In summary, a hypothesized generality of Piagetian intelligence has a different theoretical basis than that involved in the idea of general intelligence as biological capacity. It comes, in the first place, from the formal similarity involved in scoring tasks in stage terms. It springs also from the nature of the Piagetian tasks that involve specific knowledge that is not arbitrary. The tasks require the child to actively reason about kinds of experiences to which the child has access across a variety of cultural and educational environments.

THE PSYCHOMETRIZATION OF PIAGETIAN TASKS: THE DREAM

In an effort to approach these issues empirically, we were led to psychometrize Piagetian tasks and attack the questions on psychometric grounds of factor analysis (DeVries and Kohlberg, 1977b; DeVries, 1974). Our studies took Piaget's notion of stage as a hypothesis that children's reasoning progresses through an invariant sequence of qualitative transformations of the child's interpretation of his experience. In Chapter 2 we cited an empirical study using scalogram analysis of children's responses to the dream interview (adapted from Piaget's procedure). The rationale for this approach was that a successful scalogram analysis of qualitative responses, indicative of sequentiality, would challenge an alternative interpretation of developing conceptions of the dream as verbal learning by social transmission. In this section we discuss in more detail the assessment of the developmental level of the dream concept.

The Concept of the Dream

Among the various areas of the child's belief studied by Piaget, and reported in *The child's conception of the world* (1929/1960), the concept of the dream is of special interest. On the one hand, the dream has an immediate and emotional significance to the child. On the other hand, Piaget views the development of the concept of the dream as explained by a very general cognitive change in the child's attitude toward reality, a change from an attitude of "realism" to one of relativistic objectivity. Piaget (1929/1960), following the seminal theories of J. Mark Baldwin (1895, 1906), believed that in the young child, the subjective and the objective are not distinguished from each other so that sensations or experiences are taken as givens rather than as deriving from selves or objects.

In *The child's conception of the world*, Piaget (1929/1960) endeavors to show that such confusions persist in the child until about age 11 with regard to the child's conception of thought, of the names of things, and of dreams. Piaget divided the development of the child's concept of thought, names, and dreams into four rough general stages:

i) Absolute realism (under age 5)—No attempt to distinguish the instruments of thought from objects and objects alone appear to exist.
ii) Immediate realism (Age 5–6)—Instruments of thought are distinguished from things but are situated in the things thought about.
iii) Mediate realism (Age 7–8)—Instruments of thought are regarded as a kind of thing and are situated both in the body and in the surrounding air.
iv) Subjective relativism (Age 9–10)—Instruments of thought are situated within ourselves. (1929/1960, p. 126)

Underlying this set of stages are the following set of differentiations, which Piaget believes take place in necessary sequential order. In Chapter 2 we discussed the logic of this order in terms of Baldwin's theory. The sequence as defined by Baldwin and Piaget is as follows:

a) Differentiation of a thought or a sign from the thing thought about. This distinguished stage ii) immediate realism, from stage i) absolute realism.
b) Differentiation of the internal from the external. This distinguishes stage iv) from

stages ii) and iii). Presumably awareness of errors and illusions of thought as in
a) leads to a location of thought as "inside."

c) Differentiation of thought from matter. (This also is used to distinguish stage iv)
from stage iii).) Presumably location of thought as inside the body eventually
leads to recognition that it cannot be located as a definite substance or object
within the body. (1929/1960, pp. 120–121)

Piaget did not interview children under the age of 5 concerning dreams, and did
not deal with the stage of "absolute realism" in the dream concept. He believed
that all his subjects were past the first stage in which it is believed that dreams are
"real" or "true." However, the existence of such a stage is suggested by the
following responses which we have observed in reading stories to children 2 or
3 years old:

Pam: Ooooh, there's a bee. Will the bee sting me?

  E: No, it can't sting you, it's only a picture of a bee."

Pam: The bee will sting me. (Moves away from the book.)

  E: (Moving book toward Pam.) Here comes the bee.

Pam: (Gets up and moves to the other side of the room.) No don't, the bee'll sting me.
         (Said in a tone that was half upset, half playful.)

Piaget's youngest subjects, he believed, think that dreams are deceptive, but that
they are deceptive external realities like the deceptive pictures in a book by Dr.
Seuss. At this stage, the stage of immediate realism (age 5–6), the child believes
that dreams are physical events that come from outside and take place in the
child's room while the child is dreaming. At the next stage, that of mediate realism
(age 7–8), the child believes that the dream is a physical image or picture that
comes from inside but takes place in the room in front of the child. At the stage of
subjective relativism (age 9–10), the child realizes that the dream takes place
within and is a product of thought.

Laurendeau and Pinard (1962) developed a form of Piaget's dream interview
that was standardized and objective and yet preserved the subtleties of Piaget's
procedure. This interview was administered to 50 children of age 4, 50 children of
age $4\frac{1}{2}$, and 50 children at each succeeding year of age up to the age of 12. The
children constituted a representative sample of French Canadian children.

Laurendeau and Pinard found that the responses of their subjects could be fitted
into Piaget's general stages of "realism." The greater adequacy of their data and
procedure led them to refine Piaget's stages into the following scheme, presented
with the median age in years and months of the children found to be at that stage.

Stage 0:   *Lack of comprehension or refusal.* (Age 4,2)

Stage 1:   *Complete realism.* (Age 4,8) Dreams have an external (though vague)
              origin. They take place in front of the dreamer. The dreamer's eyes are
              often believed to be open when dreaming. The dream can be seen by
              anyone else in the dreamer's room.

Stage 2: *Modified realism,* or *partial interiorization of the dream.*

  Sub-stage 2A: (Age 5,0) The dream may have an internal origin, or take place within. However, the child is very uncertain about any internality of the dream and goes on to contradict or ignore it.

  Substage 2B: (Age 5,8). Subjective or interiorized replies play a sure role in the child's response but confusion between the internal and external nature of the dream remains definitely present.

  Substage 2C: (Age 7,1). Dreams have an internal origin, take place within the dreamer, and are invisible to others. However, dreams are believed to be made of some material things and could be seen if the head were opened up.

Stage 3: *Complete subjectivity.*

  Substage 3A: (Age 8,6). Dreams are internal, individual, and immaterial. However finalistic or artificial causes for dreams are given. God makes us dream, we dream "to give us lessons," etc.

  Substage 3B: (Age 10,1) Complete subjectivity. The causes of dreams are naturalistic or psychological.

This scheme differs from Piaget's largely in labeling the degree of internal origins, on the materiality of the dream, and on the use of finalistic causality. The major discrepancy between the two sets of stages is based on the fact that Laurendeau and Pinard do not assign a sequential order to awareness of the internal origin of the dream as occurring prior to awareness of its internal locus, as did Piaget. Laurendeau and Pinard found no such temporal order and distinguished stages on the basis of degree of belief in the internality of dreams.

In a sense, the work of Laurendeau and Pinard seems definitive, as far as developmental description goes. They have been able to observe the phenomena discussed by Piaget objectively in a large sample of children and have ordered those phenomena in terms of a set of stages generally similar to Piaget's. They also claim a temporal order or sequence for their stages, as Piaget claimed for his. However, it seemed to us that Laurendeau and Pinard's analysis left open certain theoretical questions requiring analysis of stage sequentiality. From the perspective of the environmentalist, both Piaget's three stages and Pinard and Laurendeau's seven stages could to some extent be viewed as reducible to a bipolar dimension in which one pole is ignorance of the "adult" or culturally accepted concept and the other pole is knowledge of the concept. It could be said that each stage differs from the preceding one only in that more of a set of questions are answered with correct or "nonrealist" answers. To the extent to which such an interpretation is correct, it would imply that the development of the dream concept merely reflects the child's learning of more "right answers" as he or she grows older. In contrast to such an interpretation, Piaget believed that his data showed that the dream concept develops through successive transformations in the child's basic attitude toward experience, not through accumulation of ideas reflecting a primitive-to-adult continuum. Partly, to study the sequentiality issue, we conducted our own research on children's conceptions of dreams.

The Dream Interview

Our interview began by ascertaining that S knew what a dream was, by establishing that the subject of discussion was dreams occurring while asleep, and by eliciting an account of a dream experience. E said:

1. You know what a dream is, don't you? Do you dream sometimes during the night?
2. Can you have a dream if you stay awake and don't go to sleep? What did you dream about last time? Tell me a dream you had.

Subsequent questions pertain to the substantiality of a dream object and to whether S recognizes a difference between waking and sleeping experiences. E asked:

3a. What happened after the dream was over? What did you think and do? What happened to the (object) after you woke up? Where did it go? Where was it after you woke up?
        (If S said it disappeared): Could you see it leaving? (If S did not say it disappeared): Could you see it when you woke up?
        When you see a dog in a dream, is it the same as when you are awake at night and see a dog?

S's differentiation of real and unreal was explored at a very low level, partly to ascertain that some verbal distinction was made prior to probing beliefs about reality of dream. E said:

What is this (showed color photograph of dog)? Is this a real dog you see here, or is it a picture, just something that looks like a dog?
      (If S said real): Can this dog you see here bark or run? Can he come out of the picture and run away?

3b. Was the (object) you saw in your dream just pretend, just something that looked like a (object), or was it a real (object)?
3c. Was the (object) in your dream really there where you were, really close to you, or did it just seem to be there?
      (If S said really there): Could you touch the (object) and (smell or other appropriate sense) it?

Beliefs about the visibility of the dream to others were investigated by asking:

4. If your mother is in your room while you are asleep and dreaming, can she also see your dream?

(If S said no): Why not? How about me? Could I see your dream if I were in your room while you were dreaming?

Beliefs about the origin of the dream were probed by asking:

5. Tell me, where does a dream come from?
   Where are dreams made, where do they come from?
   Do they come from inside you or outside of you?
   Who makes the dreams come out? Is it you or somebody else?

Beliefs about the location of the dream were explored by inquiring as follows:

6. While you are dreaming, where is your dream; where does it go? Is it inside of you or in your room?
   (If S said dream was in the head thoughts, etc., indicating internal location): If we could open your head (or other location mentioned by S) while you are dreaming, if we could look into your head without hurting you, could we see your dream?
   (If S said no): Why do say that we could not see your dream?
7. (If S said dream was in the room, on the wall, close to his eyes, under the bed, etc.): Is it only that the dream seems to be in your room (or wherever S said), or is it really in your room?
   (If S said not really there): Where is the dream then?

Beliefs about the materiality of dream substance was probed by asking:

8. What is a dream made of?
   Is it made of paper?
   Then, what is it made of?
   Can we touch dreams?
   Is a dream a thought or is it a thing?

Beliefs about the causality of dreams was investigated by asking:

9. When you had the dream about the (object), why did you have that dream? What made you have that dream?
   Then do you know why we dream, why there are dreams?

If S said he didn't dream at the beginning of the interview, he was again asked to tell a dream. If he still did not, E said:

Let's make believe that you dream during the night about a monkey. Would it just seem that the monkey was there, or would the monkey really be there?
Let's make believe you dream about a monkey during the night. What would make you dream about that? Why would you have that dream?
Then do you know why we dream, why there are dreams?

Scale Scoring and Case Examples

Dichotomous (pass-fail) items were composed to include each of the qualitative aspects found by Piaget and Laurendeau and Pinard. Nine scale items were conceptualized and operationally defined as follows:

1. *Knows what a dream is*
   +: Says he knows what a dream is
      Gives an example of a dream that clearly is not an account of real experience
      Says he can't have a dream if he stays awake and doesn't go to sleep
      Says he can have a dream if he stays awake, but differentiates a daydream from a nightdream
2. *Partly aware of the unreality of the dream*
   +: Makes some statement to indicate that dream object or event is not real Answers either Q3c or Q3d to indicate that dream object is not real
3. *Fully aware of the unreality of the dream*
   +: On Q3c, says object was not a real object *and* on Q3d, says object was not really there and that he could not sense it
4. *Dream is not visible to others*
   +: Says mother and E could not see his dream
      Says mother or E could only see it if they went to sleep and dreamed the same thing
      (Score "–" if says another can't see the dream because it would run under the bed, or suggests another obstacle indicating belief that if the obstacle weren't present, the dream would be visible.)
5. *Dreams have some internal origin or locus*
   +: Says dreams come from inside
      Says he makes the dreams come out
      Names some internal location of dream
      Says dream just seems to be there
6. *Dreams are entirely internal in origin and may take place inside*
   +: All responses concerning origin indicate belief in internality and at least one response suggests some belief in internality of locus
7. *Sure dreams take place inside*
   +: Replies correctly to all questions about the location of the dream—where it takes place. May believe that dreams come from God or heaven, but, if so, believes that the dream goes inside the body or head before its occurrence
8. *Dreams are immaterial*
   +: Names no physical substance in response to "What are dreams made of?"
      Says dreams are not made of paper
      Says he can't touch dreams
      Says dream is a thought, not a thing
      Says cannot see dream if head is opened
      Says dreams are invisible in response to "Why couldn't we see your dream?"
9. *Dreams are caused in a purely subjective or immaterial fashion by the child*
   +: Responds to "Who makes dreams come?" by referring to self, mind
      Gives some explanation of having perceived or heard about the dreamed about object or event; some explanation of its having made an emotional impression or its having been thought about prior to the dream.

These nine scale items are designed to reflect seven attributes of dream beliefs. Items 2 and 3 both deal with the reality of the dream, but distinguish qualitative differences among children who are convinced that the dream is a real event, who are only partly aware of its unreality, and who understand perfectly well that dreams are not real events. Like Laurendeau and Pinard, we found beliefs intermediary between conceptions of dreams as external and internal. Items 5 and 6 permit distinction of children who believe dreams have some internal origin or locus from those who know that dreams are entirely internal in origin and take place inside. Let us turn to some examples of children's responses. The following interview with 5-year-old Ken is an example of reasoning scored as passing only the first two scale items and thus is level 2.

    E: You know what a dream is, don't you? Do you dream sometimes during the night?

Ken: Yes. I dream about bears and flying through the air.

    E: Can you have a dream if you stay awake and don't go to sleep?

Ken: Yes.

    E: What happened after that dream was over? What did you think and do?

Ken: I fighted with them and they got dead and didn't get up any more. I always have dreams and put the cover over my head. I wake up Mom and tell her I have a bad dream. I see it in my eyes, too.

    E: What happened to the bears after you woke up? Where did they go? Where were they after you woke up?

Ken: By me—close to me.

    E: Could you see them when you woke up?

Ken: Yes.

    E: When you see a dog in a dream, is it the same as when you are awake at night and see a dog?

Ken: Yes.

    E: What is this (picture of dog)

Ken: A dog.

    E: Is this a real dog you see here, or is it a picture, just something that looks like a dog.

Ken: It just looks like a dog.

    E: Can this dog you see here bark or run?

Ken: No.

    E: Was the bear you saw in your dream just pretend, just something that looked like a bear, or was it a real bear?

Ken: Play bear—big one.

    E: Was the bear in your dream really there, where you were, really close to you... or did it just seem to be there?

Ken: Yes. Really there. Then he went away.

    E: Could you touch the bear?

Ken: No, 'cause I think he'll take me away.

E: If you wanted to touch the bear, could you?

Ken: No, 'cause I'm scared. I don't like bears.

E: Tell me, where does a dream come from?

Ken: Don't know—up North—up in the skies. They'll get down from a parachute.

E: Where are dreams made, where do they come from?

Ken: They'll come in one of your houses.

E: Do they come from inside you or outside you?

Ken: Outside me.

E: Who makes the dreams come out?

Ken: I do. It comes out of my eyes and I can't kill it.

E: While you're dreaming, where is your dream?

Ken: In my eyes.

E: If we could open your eyes while you are dreaming, if we could look into your eyes, could we see your dream?

Ken: No.

E: Why do you say that we could not see your dream?

Ken: 'Cause it's too far down.

E: Where?

Ken: (Points to stomach) It's little.

E: If we could open your stomach there, could we see your dream?

Ken: Yes.

E: What is a dream made of?

Ken: Plastic.

E: Can we touch dreams?

Ken: Yes.

E: Is a dream a thought or is it a thing?

Ken: I dream it. I make it, put it by my bed and I don't want to touch it and when Donnie sees it he'll run back to his bed when he sees the bear.

E: When you had the dream about the bear, why did you have that dream? What made you have that dream?

Ken: Don't know.

E: I wonder why.

Ken: 'Cause I want to dream about it—'cause I like dreaming about 'em.

E: Then do you know why we dream, why there are dreams?

Ken: 'Cause you can't stop the dream. I can't, either.

E: Why is that?

Ken: 'Cause it's too hard. It can't get in my eyes. When I do like this (closes eyelid halfway). There's two—three bears, and then they'll fly away. I think they have feathers and they're not made of wood. They're made of skin.

For Ken, although the flying bears are made of feathers and skin, they are "play bears." They were really there by his bed, and would frighten his brother Donnie back to his bed. Ken believes that dreams come down in a parachute into his house, and go in his eyes and down to his stomach where they have a physical existence. Although he says he can't stop the dream, he feels that he has some control over creating it ("I make it and put it by my bed") and that he dreams because he wants to.

The following case of 7-year-old Robert is an example of reasoning scored as passing the first five scale items and failing the rest, and thus is level 5.

E: You know what a dream is, don't you?

R: Yes.

E: Do you dream sometimes during the night?

R: Yes.

E: What did you dream about last time. Tell me a dream you had.

R: The army and cannons and me and—just had a toy cannon and started firing back and forth and we won and I woke up.

E: What happened to the big army cannon after you woke up?

R: It got blown up on the other side of the flower garden in our front yard with two or three army men. It was blown to pieces.

E: Could you see it when you woke up?

R: No.

E: Why not?

R: Because you can't have a dream when you're not asleep.

E: When you see a dog in a dream, it is the same as when you are awake at night and see a dog?

R: Yes (uncertain tone).

E: Is this (picture) a real dog you see here, or is it a picture, just something that looks like a dog?

R: Just something that looks like a dog.

E: Can this dog you see here bark or run?

R: No.

E: Was the cannon you saw in your dream just pretend, just something that looked like a cannon, or was it a real cannon?

R: Pretend.

E: Was the cannon in your dream really there where you were, really close to you, or did it just seem to be there?

R: Just seemed to be there.

E: Could you touch the cannon?

R: No.

E: Where does a dream come from?

R: Hmmm.

E: Where are dreams made, where do they come from?

R: Up in heaven.

E: Do they come from inside you or outside of you?

R: Outside.

E: Who makes the dreams come out?

R: Angels.

E: While you are dreaming, where is your dream?

R: In my bed.

E: Is it only that the dream seems to be in your bed, or is it really in your bed?

R: Seems to be.

E: Where is the dream, then?

R: Outside?

E: Where do you think?

R: On my front sidewalk.

E: If your mother is in your room while you are asleep and dreaming, can she also see your dream?

R: No.

E: Why not?

R: Because she's awake.

E: If she went out to the front sidewalk, would she see it?

R: No.

E: Why not?

R: It's inside, but it just looks like it's outside.

E: So where is the dream?

R: Inside my house in my bedroom.

E: Is it really there, or does it just seem to be there?

R: Just seems to be there.

E: Then where is the dream?

R: Not in my brain—or is it?

E: Do you think it might be?

R: Yeah.

E: If we could open your brain while you are dreaming, we could look into your brain, could we see your dream?

R: No.

E: Why do you say that we could not see your dream?

R: Maybe it's invisible—No, it couldn't be because I'm seeing it in my dream.

E: How do you think that works?

R: Maybe it comes from my brain, goes in front of my eyes and I see it when I'm asleep.

E: If your mother came into your room while you were asleep and dreaming, could she see your dream?

R: No.

E: Why not?

R: Because it's invisible.

E: What is a dream made of?

R: Hmmm.

E: Is it made of paper?

R: No.

E: Then what is it made of?

R: It looks like a cloud out around it.

E: Is it made of cloud?

R: No.

E: What do you think?

R: You might say it's made out of cloud.

E: Can we touch dreams?

R: No.

E: Is a dream a thought or is it a thing?

R: A thought.

E: When you had the dream about the cannon, why did you have that dream?

R: Hmmmm...my thought.

E: How did that happen?

R: (No response)

E: Then do you know why we dream, why there are dreams?

R: Because they want something to watch every night.

Robert's interview is particularly interesting because it inspires him to actively struggle with the internal-external issue. His responses give evidence for the direction of development from belief in the external locus of the dream to an inner locus. He first says the dream comes from outside himself—from angels—and is in his bed, but later says that it only seems to be there. The questions about whether others can see his dream seem to make him feel a contradiction between his belief that they are not visible to others and his belief they are to some extent external. He tries to resolve this contradiction by hypothesizing that dreams are invisible, but rejects this idea because, after all, *he* can see it. Another contradiction is felt between the fact that the dream content is an event outside his house and his belief that the dream is really inside his house in his bedroom. This is resolved by figuring that it just looks like it's outside. When pressed about where the dream is, Robert spontaneously states that it is "not in my brain," and is immediately struck by this possibility—or is it? Asked if he thinks it might be, Robert decided that "maybe it comes from my brain and I see it when I'm asleep."

These interviews illustrate the qualitative changes in children's reasoning that distinguish a later stage or level from an earlier one. Now let us turn to the statistical analysis of our empirical findings.

The Guttman Scalogram Technique and Its Application to the Dream-Concept Scale

In Chapter 2, we presented some different data on the development of the dream concept. The statistical concepts involved may be summarized in conjunction with presentation of results obtained for 115 children 5 to 7 years of age (DeVries, 1971). Table 4.2 shows the ten perfect scale patterns of response to the nine attributes of the mature dream concept assessed in our interview. The pattern of response characterizing a given scale score is indicated by the set of pluses (indicating possession of the attribute) and minuses on the nine items. Thus, Scale Type 0's ideas about dreams would display none of the nine attributes of the mature concept, Scale Type 1 displays only the first attribute (e.g., he knows what a dream is, but is naive in all other ways). Scale Type 2 is only partly aware of the unreality of the dream, and so on. Table 4.3 presents only ten patterns of response, although there are 2^{10} or 1024 patterns of response that would be possible if success in terms of any one attribute were independent of success in terms of each other attribute.

If the nine attributes form a perfect Guttman scale (Guttman, 1954), the only pattern of response that should be found in a group of subjects would be the ten patterns or scale types listed. These patterns would occur if the nine attributes constituted an order of difficulty, such that success on an item (e.g., internal origin or locus) presupposes in all subjects the ability to succeed on all five easier items. Table 4.2 indicates that in fact other patterns of response occurred. Thirty of our 115 subjects displayed fifteen patterns of response other than the scale-type patterns. These nonscale types are scored in terms of the number of + 's.

In a world in which responses always include some error variance, it is unlikely that a perfect Guttman scale will ever be found. Guttman formulated a concept of the "reproducibility" of a scale, which is measured by the percentage of scale-type responses to individual scale items among the total number of responses made by all the subjects to all the items. Guttman arbitrarily defined 90 percent as being an adequate level of reproducibility.

The concept of reproducibility springs from the fact that in a perfect scale, the pattern of responses for all subjects could be perfectly predicted or reproduced simply from a knowledge of the number of correct responses made by each individual. Each failure on an item followed by a success on a more difficult item constitutes an error. A single individual who displays a nonscale type pattern will

TABLE 4.2

Median Age and Frequency of Scores at Ten Levels
on the Dream Concept Scale ($N = 115$)

| Scale score | Items | | | | | | | | | High-, Average-, and Low-12 Subjects | | |
	1	2	3	4	5	6	7	8	9	Scale type	Nonscale type	Median age scale score*
9	+	+	+	+	+	+	+	+	+	31	—	88
8	+	+	+	+	+	+	+	+	−	14	5	80
7	+	+	+	+	+	+	+	−	−	10	9	68
6	+	+	+	+	+	+	−	−	−	6	4	78
5	+	+	+	+	+	−	−	−	−	11	7	75
4	+	+	+	+	−	−	−	−	−	6	2	67
3	+	+	+	−	−	−	−	−	−	2	1	66
2	+	+	−	−	−	−	−	−	−	4	2	63
1	+	−	−	−	−	−	−	−	−	1	0	—
0	−	−	−	−	−	−	−	−	−	0	—	—
										85	30	
n	115	111	103	99	99	74	64	59	45			
$\bar{n}$	0	4	12	16	16	41	51	56	70			
$-+$	0	0	3	9	0	0	13	8	—			
$--++$	0	1	0	0	0	4	—	—	—			

Reproducibility = .963
Chance reproducibility = .831
Index of consistency = .78

generate one or more errors. In Table 4.2 there are 33 such ($-\ +$) errors, and 5 second-order errors ($-\ -\ +\ +$). The number of these errors divided by the total number of responses (115 subjects $\times$ 9 attributes) is subtracted from 1 to obtain the reproducibility of the scale ($1\frac{38}{1035} = .96$). It thus meets Guttman's criterion. However, a high level of reproducibility for a set of items could occur even if the items were independent of one another. That is, one could compose a "scale" made up only of items varying greatly in the number of persons passing them. Therefore, it is necessary to take into account the reproducibility that would be expected by chance. If, for example, attributes 4 and 5 were actually independent of one another, we would expect by chance 13 individuals to fail attribute 4 and pass attribute 5 (the number failing attribute 4 while passing attribute 5 is 13).

In fact, only nine Ss showed this pattern. Similarly, we would expect by chance 22–23 Ss to pass attribute 7 but fail item 6, whereas no Ss, in fact, did so. The chance reproducibility of the matrix of responses is .83, considerably below the actual reproducibility of .96, as determined by Green's (1956) formula.* Green recommends considering a set of items as a scale if the Index of Consistency is greater than .50, and our scale thus meets all the statistical criteria for scalability. We may conclude that the attributes of the dream concept formulated by Piaget, by Laurendeau and Pinard, and by us do form a satisfactory Guttman scale.

Interpretation of the Dream Scale as a Developmental Sequence

The mere fact of adequate scalability does not allow us to say a set of items constitutes a developmental sequence. A Guttman scale might be composed of items expressing various degrees of antipathy toward war, but such a scale would obviously not represent a developmental sequence. A set of vocabulary items of varying difficulty, starting with "orange" and ending with "amanuensis" might also form a Guttman scale reflecting relative frequency of word usage in the culture, but it would not define a developmental sequence. Knowledge of one word is clearly not a necessary precondition for knowledge of another, less frequently used word.

Only a large-scale longitudinal study in divergent cultural groups could firmly establish the existence of a developmental sequence. However, criteria other than longitudinal ones can be brought to bear in interpreting whether a scale is developmental. These criteria include the following:

a. The Guttman scale should order the attributes in the same hierarchy formed by the age of appearance and of completion of each attribute.

b. The attributes should be scalable in the same order, and the age of appearance of the attributes should form the same order, in divergent cultures.

c. The order of the attributes should follow from a plausible theory as to why each attribute is a prerequisite to other attributes.

Table 4.3 presents results of the DeVries study indicating the age of appearance and of predominance (e.g., at last 50 percent passing each dream attribute). Thus understanding of the internal origin and locus of the dream's unfolding (attributes 5 and 6) first appears in our 5-year-old group and is fairly complete among our 7-year-old group. The higher the attribute is in our dream scale the more difficult it is within each age level, and the later the age level at which it appears and is mastered. The percentages of successes increase as one goes down the columns and decrease across the rows. Table 4.3 shows that mean scale scores increase with age, and Table 4.2 illustrates a general increase in median age for scale scores.

The second criterion of a "true" developmental scale is that the sequence of

---

*To determine whether the actual reproducibility is significantly higher than the chance reproducibility, we calculate Green's Index of Consistency (I), which is the proportion of the difference between the actual and chance reproducibilities, to the difference between perfect reproducibility and chance reproducibility. The I is equal to zero if the scale items are independent, and it is 1.00 if the items are perfectly scalable. For the Dream Scale, the I is .79.

TABLE 4.3

Percentage of Subjects Succeeding on Scale Items
of DeVries Study and Kohlberg Study

	Age		
Scale item	5	6	7
DeVries Study ($N = 97$)			
1 = Knows what dream is	100	100	100
2 = Partly aware not real	94	94	100
3 = Fully aware not there	88	88	100
4 = Not visible to others	81	88	97
5 = Some internal origin or locus	65	97	94
6 = Internal origin and may occur inside	50	76	81
7 = Sure occur inside	38	60	69
8 = Immaterial	28	60	69
9 = Subjective cause	16	42	56
Mean scale score	5.63	7.11	7.87

development should be the same in spite of divergencies of training and culture. A comparison of our data with that of Laurendeau and Pinard, and of Piaget shows this to be true; we qualified this universality in Chapter 2 by showing that while it existed in an aboriginal group (the Atayal) there was culturally learned "regression."

The third criterion for determining whether a scale defines a developmental sequence stated that the order of attributes in the scale should be based on a plausible theory as to why one attribute should be a developmental prerequisite to the next. This criterion is met by our scale since the order of attributes forming our dream scale partly follows Piaget's and Baldwin's conceptualization of the following sequence of differentiations, and a "rationale" we have derived from this:

a. Differentiation of a thought, symbol, or fantasy from the object referred to by the thought. The differentiation of the existence of the image from the existence in reality of the object of reference.
b. Differentiation of the internal from the external. Once the child has become aware of the fact that the dream image is not real and that the dream image cannot be seen by others, the child must tend to locate it in a place inaccessible to others but accessible to him or her.
c. Differentiation of matter from thought.

It seems fairly self-evident that the real existence of the dream must be questioned before it is located inside the self. Insofar as a perceived object is "real", it must necessarily be external, though the reverse is not true. An event may be deceptive in its meaning, "not real," but external (e.g., a toy dog is not a "real dog"). In our scale the knowledge that the dream cannot be seen by others forms an intermediate step between saying the dream is unreal and recognizing that it is an internal event. Awareness of privacy of the dream experience precedes the well-established belief in its internal origin and locus. This accords with Piaget's conception, a conception Pinard was unable to confirm. We encountered a number of children who had fairly well-worked-out theories representing dreams as having an internal origin and an external unfolding, and we encountered no children with theories of the reverse sort.

With regard to immateriality of the dream, it seems intuitively plausible that this should be preceded by awareness of the dream's internality. Some of our Ss were sure that dreams take place inside but claimed they were made of substances such as wool, dust, paper pictures, and stuffed things, or of more ephemeral substances such as clouds and smoke. It is possible to think of a thought or dream as internal but material, but it is more difficult to conceive of a dream as external but material. As such, it would lose the characteristic of privacy that immateriality, taken together with internality, guarantees.

Psychological causality means that the dream is caused by the dreamers themselves and that it is caused by nonphysical means. Almost by definition, psychological causality implies some notion of the immateriality of the dream. At a much earlier level, children may believe that their actions and wishes cause dreams. An example is Stevie, who believed that by rocking he could bring on or ward off dreams. The causality involved is still magical, however. For Stevie, his wish has a causal impact on the dream through a physical action that presumably has a physical effect on the physical airy substance that is the dream. However, a substantial number of children (20 in the DeVries study) understood the immateriality of dreams but believed them caused by something or someone else. It is therefore clear that the idea of psychological causality is the last dream attribute to be constucted by the child because of the difficulty in making pertinent observations of personal experience.

Classification

A second example of our psychometrization of a Piagetian task is our analysis of classification or object sorting or grouping. The object-sorting technique was developed by Goldstein (Goldstein & Sheerer, 1941) and Weigl (1941). In Goldstein's studies, the subjects were presented with small objects, real or in miniature. The subject was asked to "put the ones together that belong together" and so was free to group the objects in any way.

The task has proved to elicit age-differential modes of concept formation in children (Weigl, 1941; Reichard, Schneider, & Rapaport 1944). Within the gestalt framework of Goldstein and Weigl these modes of sorting have been viewed as representing a concrete to abstract developmental hierarchy. This hierarchy has been most explicitly defined operationally by Rapaport (1945). Rapaport's approach involved an effort to break down Goldstein's "concrete-abstract" dichotomy of attitudes into a developmental hierarchy of actual modes of grouping objects. He described the following developmental hierarchy of responses to a sorting task.

Fabulated. Concepts starting with one attribute of an object and marking the object part of a story that includes other objects to compose a group. The objects are not united by a common attribute but rather by attributes in which they differ, but that figure in the action. An example is "the screwdriver belongs to a carpenter who uses the other tools and eats the sugar for lunch."

Concrete. Concepts based on a single physical attribute the objects have in common. An example is "a dog and a lion are alike because they both have tails."

Functional. Objects are grouped because they have a common use or function. Examples are: "A wagon and a bicycle are the same because you ride them both," "the hammer and pliers are things you use to make something."

Abstract-Conceptual. Concepts subsuming the objects under a culturally established general term. Examples are: "a dog and a lion are both animals," "the hammer and pliers are tools."

Vygotsky and Luria (1976) defined a similar set of levels.

Subsequently, Inhelder and Piaget (1958) used a variety of object sorting and classification procedures (involving such materials as colored geometric designs and such small objects as dolls, animals, utensils, furniture, trees, etc.) to study the early growth of logic in normal children 4 to 9 years of age. They found groupings, such as Rapaport's "fabulated," "concrete," and "functional," to characterize a certain stage in the child's development of logical classification. They also found a prior stage not noted by other investigators where children "put together things that go together, that are alike" by making spatial arrangements termed "graphic collections." That is, when children at this stage think about similarities and differences among objects, the part-whole relations they construct are highly influenced by spatial perceptions. One type of graphic collection is an arrangement of objects in a line where the criteria for belonging together fluctuate. For example, a blue triangle is followed by a blue square, then a yellow square, and other colored squares. All the objects would end up being included in a chain with no discrete groups or classes emerging. Such graphic collections are characterized by successively recognized similarities. These are not anticipated beforehand and, if criteria do not fluctuate, only accidentally result in homogeneous segments (e.g., all circles followed by all semicircles) that may or may not be recognized as groups.

In making graphic collections, children sometimes seem to lose sight of the original task of classification and are compelled by an overall geometric shape to combine heterogeneous objects or to view an arrangement as representational (e.g., a line may become a "bridge" or a "long trolleybus"). Inhelder and

Piaget refer to this type of graphic collection as "complex objects," which are the precursors of classification. When materials to be grouped are small toys, complex objects based on spatial patterns reflect preconceptual representational associations (e.g., putting a baby and a crib together, trees beside a house, "some men in a house"). Inhelder and Piaget saw associative graphic groupings as characteristic of a preconceptual stage in the sorting task. Sortings at the stage of graphic collections have the following attributes:

1. Failure to include all members of a class in the class.
2. Failure to maintain a constant criterion of the class as new objects are included in it (e.g., chain groupings).
3. Failure to distinctly separate one class from another.
4. Grouping objects on the basis of associative relations between them rather than on the basis of a common attribute.

Put somewhat differently, at the preconceptual stage the child does not differentiate the general class from the particular objects that are members of the class. Piaget quotes as an example his 2-year-old daughter's remark on a walk on which she had seen a snail for the first time. When she encountered a second snail she said, "There is the snail again." If such a differentiation of class and member is not clearly made, then grouping is a matter of bonding individual objects rather than subsuming a number of objects under a single class. It is clear how such a bonding set can lead to the stage-characteristics just mentioned.

Inhelder and Piaget point out that graphic collections do not reflect part-whole relations of inclusion that are necessary for true classification. In contrast to the graphic collections of Stage I, classification (Stage III) is characterized by an exhaustive differentiation and coordination of similarities and differences. That is, a group of objects is conceptualized as a whole class made up of subordinate and complementary classes that include all objects. Such a conception involves two kinds of properties or relations. The first are

(1) (a) Properties which are common to the members of the given class and those of other classes to which it belongs.
  (b) Properties which are specific to the members of the given class and which differentiate them from members of other classes. (Inhelder & Piaget, 1958, p. 17)

Inhelder and Piaget refer to this set of properties of a class as "intensive properties." The second kind of property or relation consists of

(2) Part-whole relations of class-membership and inclusion. These are conveyed by the quantifiers "all," "some" (including "one") and "none," when applied to the members of the given class and to those of the classes to which it belongs, insofar as they are qualified under (1a) and (1b). (Inhelder & Piaget, 1958, p. 17)

Inhelder and Piaget refer to this set of properties as "extensive properties" of a are quantitative relations that can be expressed algebraically (e.g., $A + A' = B$, where A and A' are subclasses such as "boys" and "girls" that make up the superordinate class B of "children"). True classification at the operational level has ten characteristics:

(1) There are no isolated elements, i.e. elements not belonging to a class. This amounts to saying that all the elements must be classified, and that, if an element (x) is the only one of its kind, it must give rise to its own specific (but singular) class: $(x) \ \varepsilon \ (A_x)$.

(2) There are no isolated classes, i.e. every specific class A characterized by the property a, implies its complement A' (characterized by not-a) within the closest genus $B(A + A' = B)$.

(3) A class A includes all the individuals having the property a.

(4) A class A includes only individuals having the property a.

(5) All classes of the same rank are disjoint: $A \times A' = O$ or $An \times Am = O$.

(6) A complementary class A' has its own characteristics a_x (thus $A' = A_x$), which are not possessed by its complement A: the individuals having the property a are thus not-A_x, just as individuals having the property a_x are not-a.

(7) A class A (or A') is included in every higher ranking class which contains all its elements, starting with the closest, $B: A = B - A'$ (or $A' = B - A$) and $A \times B = A$, which amounts to saying that "all" A are "some" B.

(8) Extensional simplicity: the inclusions in (7) are reduced to the minimum compatible with the intensional properties.

(9) Intensional simplicity: similar criteria (e.g. colours) distinguish classes of the same *rank*.

(10) Symmetrical subdivision: if a class B_1 is subdivided into A_1 and A_1' and the same criterion is applicable to B_2, then B_2 must likewise be subdivided into A_2 and A_2'. (Inhelder & Piaget, 1958, p. 48)

These characteristics enable an individual to think flexibly to shuffle and reshuffle classes using different criteria, with hindsight and foresight in reorganizing and anticipating reorganizations.

In between the stage of graphic collections and operational classification are found various Stage II types of transitional reasoning having some but not all of the ten characteristics. For example, Inhelder and Piaget found young children grouping objects in terms of perceptual belonging (e.g., same color, same shape, but not exhaustive or subdivided groupings) and functional belonging (e.g., things for making supper). They were careful to distinguish groupings by association from more advanced groupings by relations of belonging when the content of these groupings is parallel. Examples of graphic collections of objects grouped on the basis of association are "the boy eats from the plate" or "the plate and the fork." Examples of nongraphic collections grouped on the basis of belonging are "things you eat with" or "things for the dining room." The latter functional concepts still reflect associative relations, but show an advance over nongraphic associations based on use because they are determined by a common attribute. Inhelder and class. Intensive properties are qualitative characteristics, and extensive properties

Piaget note that during Stage II there is a steady growth in the extent to which most of the operational characteristics are recognized. However, the last structure in classification activity that distinguishes Stage II from Stage III is inclusion. The third stage of concrete operations in classification is reached at around age 8 with the development of hierarchical concepts that are inclusive or "nesting." Inhelder and Piaget recognized that children of 3 to 6 use and understand hierarchical concepts to some degree, as Welch has shown (1940). They recognize that boys and girls are also "people" or "children," that potatoes and apples are also "food." The young child does not conceptualize the higher-order concept (children) as including the lower-order concepts (boys and girls). If the child is presented with a group of children dolls, the child knows they are children and can divide them up into the subclasses, boys and girls. However, if asked to compare one of the subclasses with the whole (the question asked is "Are there more dolls or more girls?"), the higher-order class ceases to exist in the child's mind as a whole consisting of both subclasses. An example is provided by one of the tasks we used. The child was presented with four girl dolls and one boy doll and asked "Are there more girls or more dolls here?" Young children say that there are more girls than dolls. In another task, we tried to heighten motivation by using four chocolate M&M's and a white mint. Young children still said there were more chocolates than candy. Inhelder and Piaget concluded that these responses indicate that the child does not really differentiate the higher-order concept from the subclasses it includes. In other words, the child does not conserve the higher-order concept when focusing on a subclass. After focusing on the concept "girls" as a distinct class, and then asked to compare this class "girls" with the class "dolls," the child fails to include the girls within the class of "dolls," which is now unconsciously reduced to the subclass "boys."

Piaget (1941) and Inhelder and Piaget (1958) discussed hierarchical classification not only in terms of conservation of the whole but also in terms of reversibility of thought and the existence of a group of classification operations. Reversibility is indicated by the capacity to "undo" in thought—that is, the ability to think of the girls as a separate class while simultaneously thinking of the class of dolls, including the girls. The simultaneous conception of the girls as part of both the "girls" and the "dolls" classes requires such reversibility. Piaget and Inhelder also saw hierarchical inclusion as indicating that the classification operations of logical addition, subtraction, and multiplication form a group of operations, as indicated in the foregoing quotation listing the characteristics of classification. That is, when the young child is asked, he or she knows that the class of girls (A) and the class of boys (A') make up the class of dolls ($A + A' = B$). However, the child cannot reverse this addition operation and use its inverse, logical subtraction, in the situation. When he or she cannot do this, the child thinks, in effect, that when the girls are taken out, there is still the boy left over. Logically, the child is reducing the class of dolls (B) to the class of a single boy (A') when the girls (A) are subtracted or removed ($B - A = A'$), and then falsely concluding than A is greater than B.

In addition to class inclusion, there is another attribute of operational classification—flexibility of hindsight and foresight that makes possible shifting the basis for classification. Both Inhelder and Piaget and American workers (Reichard, Schneider, & Rapaport, 1944) have found a sizable minority of children of ages 5 to 11 capable of "shifting" the criterion they are using for grouping objects, when requested. Piaget and Inhelder say, however, that children do not engage in spontaneous planned shifting until the operational stage at around the age of 7 to 8 years. At this stage children, confronted with objects of varying forms and of varying colors, ask, "Do you want it sorted by color or shape?" Such a response indicates the capacity for logical multiplication and for the use of two classifications in a conceptual fourfold table. The phenomenological differences between such spontaneous conceptual shifting behavior and shifting behavior at a practical level are graphically presented in Weigl's (1941) work. According to Weigl, when shifting from form to color occurs, objects may "cease to be" triangles and circles and "become" red things and blue things, rather than remaining simultaneously in two alternative categories.

In our study of the sorting and inclusion tasks as cognitive variables, we wanted to test empirically whether the sequence outlined by Piaget for concept formation is, in fact, a sequence, that is, that the various attributes of concept formation dealt with by Inhelder and Piaget formed a Guttman scale.

The Sorting and Inclusion Tasks

The child was confronted with a randomly arranged cluster of miniature objects composed of the following:

3 infant dolls

3 father dolls (1 jointed plastic Renwall, 2 cloth and rubber Flagg dolls)

3 mother dolls (1 Renwall, 2 Flagg)

3 boy dolls (1 Renwall, 2 Flagg)

3 girl dolls (1 Renwall, 2 Flagg)

3 chairs

3 dogs, 2 spotted china and one green plastic

The first part of the task focused on eliciting the child's spontaneous classification. The child was asked to "Put them in order. Put the ones together that go together." Even the youngest of our children seemed to feel they comprehended the instruction and would start to group the objects. After the child finished sorting the dolls, the question was asked, "Why do these go together? Why did you put them together?" for each grouping. If the child grouped most of the objects in associative collections (membership in group not resulting from shared characteristics of objects), then the dolls were mixed again and the child was asked to "Put the ones that are the *same* together."

The second part of the sorting task was designed to explore whether the child could utilize a superordinate class and whether he or she could shift his bases for groupings. The dogs were removed and two sheets of paper were placed before the child, one to the right and one to the left. The child was told:

> Now make just two piles out of all the dolls. Put some of the dolls here and some of them there. Put all the ones that are the same, that go together, here. Put all the other ones that go together, that are the same, over here.

If the child still seemed uncertain as to what to do and did not respond, the child was told:

> We're going to take all these dolls that are together and make two piles out of them. Let's take this boy doll and put it on the paper. Now put all the other ones that go with the boy on this paper. Put the others ones that go together on this paper over here.

The child was asked why the dolls in each group went together.

Two forms of the class inclusion test were used. The first was Laurendeau and Pinard's (1966) standardization of Piaget's (1941) task with wooden beads. The child is shown 20 red and 2 blue beads, and asked, "Are there more wooden beads or more red beads?" "Why?" Our second form of this task employed four girl dolls and one boy doll in a play "schoolroom." The child was asked, "Are there more dolls or more girls?" "Why?"

For the second form of our class-inclusion task, Piaget's procedure was varied by using as the higher-order class "dolls" rather than "children." Pretesting with 4 year olds indicated, to our surprise, that the concept "children" or "kids" was not a really usable or familiar concept for many of them. While the word was familiar, some 4 year olds did not understand that both boy and girl dolls were children, but adult dolls were not. The inclusion question was therefore modified in terms of the children's language. The child was simply presented with three girl dolls and one boy doll, randomly mixed. The procedure was first to affirm that the child used the label "girls," "boys," and "dolls" correctly. The interviewer said:

> Here are some dolls. Here are some girls. Here is a boy. Are these girl dolls? Is the boy a doll?

Then the child was asked the inclusion question:

> Then are there more dolls or more girls? Why do you say there are more _____?

Scale Scoring and Case Examples

Our scoring of developmental level on the sorting task made use of some of the conceptual content criteria just defined as well as the other extensional and logical features of classification discussed by Piaget and Inhelder. The attributes scored and their scale positions are presented below. (The definitions of associative and true categorical groupings employed in the scale are those from the previous section.)

Object Sorting Scoring

1. *Makes some similarity groupings spontaneously or on request*
   +: Not all groups formed are associative.
2. *Most groupings are not associative*
   +: More than 50 percent of the groups formed are not associative (not based on weighted percentage; count all groups formed, including "forced sorts").
3. *Includes all objects*
   +: Spontaneously includes all 21 objects in groups (more than one group must be formed: a line of the 21 objects would not be scored as passing). A single object may form a "group" if the child makes some positive statement about it, e.g., "He goes by himself because there's no other one like him," "He's left over, so he can be the policeman," "These go together because they don't have any like them." A single object is considered excluded if no statement is made or if the child says she intends it not to be included, e.g., "I can't put him anywhere," "He doesn't go with anybody," "I don't need these."
4. *Uses complementary classes*
   +: Can construct a system of two complementary classes (including all human objects). Examples: males and females; children and adults. Question 2 is specifically designed to elicit this ability, but it may spontaneously appear prior to this. A verbal statement of opposite or bipolar classes may also be taken as indicative of this ability, e.g., "You mean put all the girls together and all the boys together?"

   Note: Where babies are excluded from male-female dichotomy because of uncertainty about sex, credit is also given on this item; however, score "–" if subject merely says, "There's nowhere to put them."
5. *Includes all members of a class in more than 50 percent of the spontaneous groupings*
   +: All objects are included that could be, on the basis of the child's reason for grouping; also, no inappropriate objects are included. Groupings of identical objects and groupings based on associative reason are considered to fail in including all members.
6. *More than 50 percent of weighted groupings are true categorical concepts*
   +: Spontaneous groupings are given one point each, but groupings made in response to "Put the ones together that are the same" and "Make two piles out of all the dolls" are given only one-half point. Any group

constructed a second time in response to a new instruction is scored only once.

7. *Uses overall system of inclusion*

    +: Entire set of spontaneously grouped objects is grouped according to' general criteria so that groups form a hierarchical system, e.g., age, sex, species criteria result in an overall system of subclasses. In the class-inclusion task, says there are more dolls than girls and gives an intelligible reason.

8. *Shifts from one system of classification in spontaneous groups to another in the forced sort*

    +: Set of objects can be viewed as grouped according to more than one set of criteria, e.g., age groups may be formed as well as sex groups. The shift is from one categorical grouping to another categorical grouping; changing from family groupings to age or sex groupings does not constitute a shift. Shifting may occur spontaneously or in response to request to compose two complementary classes. Verbalization of awareness of more than one possible categorical arrangement is also scored " + ", whether or not the arrangement is actually made, e.g., "Do you mean boys and girls or children and grown-ups?"

FACTOR ANALYTIC RELATIONS BETWEEN PIAGETIAN AND PSYCHOMETRIC INTELLIGENCE: DON'T THROW OUT THE PIAGETIAN BABY WITH THE PSYCHOMETRIC BATH

Our discussion of Piagetian intelligence has stressed its theoretical differences from "British" biological psychometric intelligence. Differences in theory should be reflected in differences in empirical data, differences of the sort that Spearman (1904) invented factor analysis to determine. Factor analysis has today become a complex and abstruse statistical technology, but its ideas, particularly as related to intelligence and elaborated by Spearman (1927) and Thomson (1946), are easy to grasp. To make the technical issues more interesting, we will place them in the context of a recent controversy. This took place in a set of exchanges in the journal *Intelligence* (1980, v.4, No. 2) and at a 1981 symposium during the biennial meeting of the Society for Research in Child Development.

Briefly, the history behind this controversy began with Kohlberg's design of an empirical study of the factor-analytic relations between psychometric and Piagetian task performance (first reported by Kohlberg & DeVries in 1969; published by DeVries & Kohlberg in 1977). DeVries (1974) continued this work with young children by refining the psychometrization of Piagetian tasks and considering relations with psychometric tests used in schools—group intelligence tests and achievement tests. Stephens and her colleagues (Stephens, McLaughlin, Miller, & Glass, 1972) studied the issue using a much wider age range. In these studies, Stephens, Kohlberg, and DeVries had a theoretical "bias." That is, they expected

Piagetian factors to appear that were distinct from already known psychometric factors, and used a factor-analytic method that favored their theoretical bias—rotation of factors to simple structure. Such rotation, invented by Thurstone (1947), is "biased" against the British or Spearman assumption of a single general factor in intelligence. Humphreys and Parsons (1979) did not accept the conclusion of these studies that Piagetian and psychometric intelligence overlap but have distinctiveness, and they reanalyzed the Stephens' data. Humphreys and Parsons concluded that the distinctiveness was a statistical artifact and that Piagetian tasks and psychometric tests are interchangeable assessments of intelligence. DeVries and Kohlberg then organized a symposium in which the issue could be further discussed. Beth Stephens, Rheta DeVries, and Lawrence Kohlberg argued for the separability of Piagetian and psychometric intelligence, and Lloyd Humphreys argued the "British" position that Piagetian tasks were simply reflecting Spearman's *g*. John Carroll, noted for his expertise in factor analysis, was invited to be the discussant and to reanalyze the data from the two studies by Kohlberg and DeVries.

Study by Stephens, McLaughlin, Miller, and Glass

In 1972, Stephens, McLaughlin, Miller, and Glass reported a factor-analytic study of intelligence tests, achievement tests, and 27 Piagetian reasoning tasks.
They summarized their study as follows:

> The purpose of the study was to determine relationships which exist among 27 Piagetian assessments and standard measures of intelligence and achievement. Data were available from an ongoing longitudinal study of the development of reasoning in normals and retardates. The random sample ($N = 150$) was comprised of 75 normals, IQ 90–110, and 75 retardates, IQ 50–75. These two subsamples, normals and retardates, were further divided into three age ranges, 25 subjects ages 6–10 (13 males, 12 females), 25 subjects ages 10–14 (12 males, 13 females), and 25 subjects ages 14–18 (13 males, 12 females). Factor-analytic techniques were used to determine relationships among the scores for the total group ($N = 150$) on 27 Piagetian reasoning variables and subscores from the Wide Range Achievement Test and the Wechsler intelligence scales, MA, and CA. *Five interpretable factors* were obtained. Review of the factor matrix indicated that Piagetian reasoning tasks involve abilities separate from those measured by standard tests of intelligence and achievement. (Stephens et al., 1972, p. 343)

The conclusion drawn by Stephens and her collaborators is based on a rotated, oblique factor analysis. The wide range in chronological age in this study (6 to 18 years) creates a problem. Since all developmental measures will correlate with one another if age is not limited or controlled by partial correlation, the correlations among Piagetian tasks are somewhat spuriously inflated. Oblique rotation again somewhat spuriously gives the appearance of separate Piaget factors when these factors are correlated with one another and with psychometric tests.

In 1979, Humphreys and Parson reanalyzed the Stephens et al. data with the results summarized as follows:

> A reanalysis of the intercorrelations of Wechsler subtests, achievement tests, and Piagetian tasks originally published by Stephens et al. (1972) has corrected errors in the original design and has used models which allow both differences and similarities to appear. Unit weighted composites of the two sets of tests were formed after first partialling chronological age out of the complete table of intercorrelations. The correlation between the composites is .876 which corrects, using split-half estimates of reliabilities, to .918. Next the matrix of partial correlations was factored and the factors rotated to a hierarchical structure. Piagetian tasks contribute almost equally to the definition of the general factor in intelligence along with the Wechsler subtests and the achievement tests. The general factor, furthermore, makes the single largest contribution to the variance of most of the measures of both sets. The smaller group factors consist of an Academic Achievement factor and three Piagetian factors. Of the latter the largest and most clearly identified is the factor called Operational Thought in the earlier analysis, but is here described simply as Conservation. It is concluded that the evidence of communality in function far outweighs the differences between intelligence tests and Piagetian tasks. (1979, p. 369)

Humphreys and Parsons basically criticize two features of the Stephens et al. study. The first is the use of rotated factors where a rotation process exaggerates the independence of a Piagetian cluster from psychometric measures. Second, they criticize the failure to control for, or partial out, chronological age from correlations before performing a factor analysis.

Most readers of the interchange up to this point will probably be inclined to lean to the conclusion of Humphreys and Parsons—that Piagetian intelligence is just another measure of *g*. However, there is more to the research story. Another study of ours and a reanalysis of the DeVries (1974) data provide a fairer test of the issue.

Studies by Kohlberg and DeVries

Data for the first study was collected in 1964 and reported by DeVries and Kohlberg (1977). After considering the criticisms of Humphreys and Parsons in relation to the Stephens study, we asked John Carroll to reanalyze the data from this and from the DeVries (1974) study (Carroll, Kohlberg, & DeVries, 1983). The DeVries and Kohlberg (1977) study had some advantages over the studies already discussed. The sample was limited to 67 middle-class kindergarten and first-grade children, presumably reflecting the age period in which children attain concrete operations. Subjects differed in mental age by no more than a year and in chronological age by no more than a year. In addition, this study was designed to sample the six distinguishable factorial tests of psychometric ability. In describing this study, we begin with theoretical considerations that led to this research.

Our data for this study was collected with the central purpose of testing a Piagetian versus a British theoretical interpretation of the correlations between and among psychometric and Piagetian tests. This meant in the first place that we wanted to restrict the range of chronological age and mental age of the sample so as not to have to partial out correlations due to age itself. We knew that we had to try to avoid the problem pointed out by Humphreys and Parsons—that many correlated changes with age cannot be interpreted as related in a meaningful theoretical sense. For example, if one takes children ranging widely in age, one would find Piaget tests correlating not alone with one another but with dentition or "dental age." We thus chose children between ages 5 and 6 whose mental age was 6 or above, that is, of average to above average IQ.

The second reason we gathered this kind of data was that we wanted to give psychometric intelligence a fair chance to explain intercorrelations on clusters of Piaget tests. Therefore, we selected psychometric tests that sampled widely the various abilities tapped by distinct psychometric tests. To make sure that we got an adequate assessment of Spearman's *g*, we followed the advice of psychometricians who recommended combining a general vocabulary test and a nonverbal test of general intelligence. We therefore included the Quick Test (Ammons & Ammons, 1962) and the Raven Progressive Matrices, colored board form (Raven, 1956). We wanted, however, not only a measure of *g*, but measures of all the distinguishable psychometric factors found at age 6. Otherwise, any Piaget factor we found might be simply one of these psychometric factors under another name. Six distinguishable psychometric factors have been found at age 6 by Thurstone (1938), Meyers et al. (1962), and McCartin (1963). We selected tests to represent each of these six factors, and these are listed in Table 4.4. Piagetian tasks are listed in Table 4.5.

In selecting Piagetian tests for our battery, we also kept a number of criteria in mind. In the same way that we wanted to include the whole psychometric domain in our study, we also tried to include a broad range of the domain of Piagetian development, rather than only tests of concrete operations or of specifically logico-mathematical structures. The Piaget-type tasks varied from "verbal" to the "nonverbal." Piaget's early studies involved very verbal procedures like the dream task described previously, procedures that he later abandoned in favor of tasks that were both more focused on strictly logico-mathematical aspects of reasoning and were more assessable by the child's actions and responses to concrete physical demonstrations such as the classification task already discussed. We were not satisfied with Piaget's efforts to minimize the verbal components, even in these later tasks, however. We went even further in the sense that we tried to define the child's level of response to the task by actions of pointing and choice without verbal explanation. For instance, we developed a procedure by which we could be relatively sure that a child was a conservor of liquid quantity if the child showed a consistent pattern of nonverbal choice between two unequal quantities of Coke when these were poured into variously shaped beakers.

In addition to reducing the verbal requirements of the tasks, we also tried to

TABLE 4.4

Tests Representing Primary Mental Abilities* at Mental Age 6

I.   Linguistic

V.   Vocabulary and comprehension of verbal meaning

     1. Quick Test—a picture vocabulary test (Ammons & Ammons, 1962; McCartin, 1963)

     2. W.I.S.C. Information Subtest (Wechsler, 1963; McCartin, 1963)

W. Verbal fluency

     3. Monroe classification test (Monroe, 1935)

        "Tell me as many things to eat (toys, etc.) as you can (in 30 sec)" (McCartin, 1963; Meyers et al.)

M. Immediate memory (P)

     4. Digit Span, Stanford Binet Form L-M (Terman & Merrill, 1960)

II.   Reasoning

R.   Verbal reasoning

     5. W.I.S.C. Comprehension (McCartin, 1963)

     6. W.I.S.C. Similarities (McCartin, 1963)

R.   Spatial reasoning

     7. Raven's Matrices, colored board from (Raven, 1956; Meyers et al.)

III. Psychomotor

M. Hand-eye psychomotor

     8. Line Drawing (Thurstone & Thurstone, 1954)

        "Draw lines from the top dot to the bottom dot as quickly as you can—timed 60 sec"

P.   Perceptual speed

     9. Pacific Perceptual Speed (Meyers et al., 1962)

        "Mark the one geometric figure that looks like that one"—60 sec. Meyers et al.

    10. Total mental age (sum of tests 1–9 based on converting raw scores on each task to mental age equivalents)

---

*Abilities defined by studies of Thurstone (1938), Meyers, Dingman, Atwell, and Orpert (1962), and McCartin (1963).

Source: DeVries and Kohlberg, 1977, p. 123.

heighten motivation to give correct responses. As noted in Chapter 2, critics of Piaget have often suggested that children give silly answers to silly questions. Some questions, or tasks, were made less "silly" by using activities with goodies children could eat. For instance, in the liquid conservation task questions related to conservation of continuous quantity were presented in terms of picking the container having more Coke to drink.

Finally, we tried to vary tasks across the physical and the social domain. Constancy tasks involved not only physical characteristics (length, quantity) but social roles (age, sex). (One of these tasks, constancy of sex identity, was discussed in Chapter 2.) Tasks involving awareness of the distinction between the mental and

TABLE 4.5

Piaget-Type Tasks

IV.	Conservation tasks
	11. Length conservation—movement
	12. Area conservation—ring segment illusion
	13. Liquid conservation
	14. Number conservation
V.	Generic identity tasks
	15. Sex
	16. Age
VI.	Classification
	17. Object-sorting tasks
	18. Class inclusion
VII.	Causal thinking
	19. Dreams
	20. Magic
VIII.	Moral judgment
	21. Objective versus subjective responsibility
	22. Sanctions versus rules orientation

Source: DeVries and Kohlberg, 1977, p. 124.

the physical (or of subjective appearance versus reality) were sampled in both the domain of nonsocial causality and in the field of moral or social causality or responsibility (e.g., intentions versus consequences). We reported our factor analysis of the intercorrelations among these tasks, and interpreted the results as supporting the notion of a first general factor in intelligence, including both psychometric and Piagetian tests, and a second bipolar factor that divided the Piagetian and the psychometric tasks from one another. Discovery of defects in the computer program led to a reanalysis reported by Carroll, Kohlberg, and DeVries (1984).

The results of Carroll's reanalysis are shown in Tables 4.6 and 4.7. As Table 4.6 shows, the correlations between and among the tests varied widely. The correlations among psychometric tests ranged between $-.03$ (comprehension and line drawing) and .64 (perceptual speed and information). The correlations among Piaget-type tasks ranged from .51 (conservation of ring segment area and of gender identity) to $-.30$ (liquid conservation and length conservation). Correlations between the psychometric and Piagetian tasks were somewhat lower (ranging from $-.23$ to .47).

For us, the most easily understood factor analysis addressing the question of whether Piagetian tasks are distinct from general intelligence is the procedure used by Spearman in his initial attempt to show that there was a single general factor of intelligence. Spearman and his British followers have used unrotated factors to

TABLE 4.6

Intercorrelations Among Psychometric and Piagetian Variables (Recomputed from DeVries & Kohlberg, 1977, data)
(Zero-order below diagonal; partial correlations above diagonal)* (N = 47)

	Age	A1	A2	A3	A4	A5	A6	A7	A8	A9	A10	A11	A12	A13	A14	A15
Psychometric variables																
A1: Quick test	.59	—	.45	.10	.18	.22	.17	.30	.19	.32	-.13	.11	.10	.12	.20	.18
A2: Information	.53	.62	—	.11	.32	.25	.40	.35	.21	.46	-.06	.35	.43	.12	.15	.44
A3: Monroe classification	.45	.34	.32	—	-.02	.11	.22	.17	.01	.14	-.05	.29	.05	-.04	.31	.08
A4: Digit span	.17	.24	.36	.06	—	.20	.38	.26	.45	.38	.05	.25	.25	.11	.42	.29
A5: Comprehension	.18	.28	.31	.18	.23	—	.21	.15	-.15	.10	-.06	.20	.16	.23	.32	.45
A6: Similarities	.35	.33	.50	.34	.41	.26	—	.34	.23	.51	-.32	.34	.45	.25	.31	.40
A7: Matrices	.53	.52	.53	.37	.31	.22	.45	—	.00	.30	-.16	.22	.40	.21	.23	.33
A8: Line Drawing	.55	.45	.43	.25	.47	-.03	.37	.29	—	.48	.05	.13	.23	.03	.13	.16
A9: Perceptual Speed	.62	.57	.64	.38	.40	.19	.59	.53	.65	—	-.13	.32	.45	.17	.11	.33
Piagetian variables																
A10: Length conservation	-.19	-.22	-.15	-.13	.01	-.09	-.36	-.23	-.06	-.22	—	-.09	-.05	-.26	.17	-.16
A11: Area segment	-.28	-.08	.14	.12	.19	.13	.21	.03	-.05	.06	-.03	—	.27	.25	.48	.32
A12: Liquid conservation	.14	.17	.44	.11	.26	.18	.47	.42	.27	.44	-.08	.22	—	.12	.28	.37
A13: Number conservation	.35	.30	.28	.12	.16	.28	.34	.35	.21	.34	-.30	.13	.16	—	.31	.37
A14: Sex identity	-.23	.02	.00	.16	.37	.27	.20	.07	-.02	-.06	.20	.51	.24	.20	—	.31
A15: Adult identity	.05	.17	.40	.09	.29	.45	.40	.31	.16	.29	-.17	.29	.37	.37	.31	—

*Partialing was with the (point-biserial) correlations with age.

156

TABLE 4.7

Unrotated Principal Factor Solutions for the DeVries-Kohlberg data ($N = 47$)

		Based on Raw Correlations				Based on Correlations with Age Partialed Out		
		I	II	h²		I	II	h²
Psychometric variables								
Quick	A1	.633	*.301*	.491	A1	.397	.026	.158
Inform	A2	.765	.146	.606	A2	.638	.062	.410
Monroe	A3	.414	.061	.175	A3	.231	−.127	.070
Digit	A4	.510	−.183	.294	A4	.541	.206	.335
Comp	A5	.386	−.253	.213	A5	.388	−.424	.330
Sim	A6	.722	−.069	.527	A6	.678	.012	.460
Raven	A7	.668	.126	.463	A7	.505	−.116	.268
Lines	A8	.554	.267	.378	A8	.375	.607	.509
Speed	A9	.816	*.309*	.762	A9	.675	.388	.606
Piagetian variables								
Length	A10	−.273	−.151	.097	A10	−.175	.113	.043
Ring	A11	.222	*−.544*	.346	A11	.531	−.140	.302
Liquid	A12	.531	−.152	.306	A12	.575	.085	.338
Number	A13	.459	−.087	.219	A13	.362	−.267	.203
Sex	A14	.248	−.759	*.638*	A14	.504	−.227	.305
S. Rosp.	A15	.528	−.344	.397	A15	.636	−.237	.461
Sum of Squares		4.465	1.445	5.910		3.805	.994	4.799

examine the *g* hypothesis, with *g* being indicated by their first general unrotated factor.

To understand the pattern of results, shown in Table 4.7, let us start by examining the first unrotated factor, Spearman's general factor. The values listed under this first factor for each test are the "loadings" of that factor, the proportion of the variance in each test attributable to this first general factor. The actual correlations between any two tests due to this factor are estimated by multiplying the two loadings together. Vocabulary (Quick Test) loads .63 and information loads .76 on the factor so that their expected correlation equals .48. Subtracting .48 from Table 4.6 (below diagonal) observed correlation of .62 leaves .14, a slight basis for helping to define the second factor in Table 4.7. Multiplying the second factor loading on Vocabulary (Quick) of .30 with the second factor loading on Information of .15 leads to an expected correlation of .05. Subtracting .05 from 14 leaves a correlation of .09, which could be a basis with other remaining correlations for a third factor. No such third factor was found, suggesting that the remaining correlation of .05 was an error or was specific to the two tests. In general, there were few correlations between pairs of psychometric tests that were not accounted for by the first general factor. Table 4.7 indicates that the psychometric tests are well accounted for by Spearman's *g*.

If, after extracting a first general factor, there are second or third unrotated factors, these contradict the hypothesis that a test battery can be understood as representing a single general intelligence factor. Second or third unrotated factors are always bipolar—that is, half the variables have negative and half positive loadings. The first-factor loadings essentially represent the average correlation of a test with all the other tests in the battery. When the correlations obtained from multiplying factor loadings with one another from the first general factor are subtracted from the remaining correlations of each test with the others, one always obtains factors equally composed of negative and positive loadings (i.e., a bipolar factor).

When the unrotated factors were extracted by John Carroll (Table 4.7), a first general factor appeared highly loaded on all the psychometric tests and with small loadings on all the Piaget tasks. Only one additional factor is significant (clearly higher than an eigen value of one), which is bipolar. Almost all the Piagetian tasks are negatively loaded on this factor, most especially the ring segment illusion and the sex-role identity tasks. Most of the psychometric tests are positively loaded on this second factor, particularly the vocabulary and perceptual motor speed tasks.

We may summarize the results as a tree with a first general intelligence factor branching into a second Piagetian versus psychometric factor.

Carroll et al. report an orthogonally rotated (by Varimax) table of loadings on the two factors that is not conceptually interpretable. Carroll also reanalyzed a larger study by DeVries (1974) because there was reason to think that the data could be reexamined in such a way as to delineate more clearly and validly the relationships between Piagetian, IQ, and achievement assessments. In this study, the Stanford-Binet (S-B) test, the California Test of Mental Maturity (CTMM), 15 Guttman-scaled Piaget-type tasks, and the Metropolitan Achievement Test (MAT) were administered to all or some of 143 bright, average, and retarded children chronologically (or mentally, in the case of the retarded children) aged 5, 6, and 7 years.

By one criterion Carroll found two significant factors; by another criterion he found three. We will stress the first two factors, which are fairly similar to those found in Table 4.7. A first, general intelligence factor loads on psychometric, Piagetian, and achievement tests alike. A second, bipolar factor loads negatively on ten of the Piaget tests and positively on the four achievement tests. The marginal, third factor divided psychometric intelligence tests from school achievement tests.

Carroll et al. (1984) conclude: "The net result of the two reanalyses might be said to be that Piagetian intelligence, especially as measured by conservation tasks, is somewhat distinct from psychometric intelligence. The narrow age ranges used in the studies here analyzed, and the appropriateness of the age range to development in Piagetian concrete operations may account for the difference between our conclusions and those of the reanalysis of the Stephens et al. data by Humphreys and Parsons (1979)." (p. 89)

THE CONSISTENCY OF STAGE ACROSS TASKS: DECALAGE

One can look at the Piagetian factor(s) in two ways. From the point of view of the empirical study of intelligence, the findings indicate that the Piagetian approach is capturing an "intelligence" narrower in range than Spearman's *g*, but relatively distinct from *g*. It indicates that Piaget is onto something more distinct from general intelligence than any special psychometric aptitude or abilities such as those listed in Table 4.4. The general element in Piagetian tasks is even broader than the notion of concrete operations or logico-mathematical thought and is consistent with what Piaget (1971c) terms the "broad period" hypothesis:

> Each time that a specific problem is studied, as for instance that of causality which is currently receiving our attention, the analysis of the responses and reactions of children of different ages seems to point to the existence of relatively well-defined stages in this limited area. The important point, however, is to discover whether the different stages found in these more limited and specific areas contain any elements in common. In other words, is it possible to detect broad periods in development with characteristics that can be applied in a general manner to all the events of these periods? This is the hypothesis that we are trying to investigate. (p. 111)

In terms of our findings we may say there is some empirical support for the "broad period" interpretation of Piaget's stage of concrete operations, an interpretation about which Piaget himself was hesitant. In earlier days, before Piaget formulated his theory of concrete operations, he was not so hesitant about a broad period interpretation. He was struck by the general qualitative changes in children's cognitive functioning occurring in the years 5 to 7. The preoperational 5 year old was "egocentric" and "realistic"; the operational 7 year old was (or was becoming) "social" and "subjectivistic" in thought. As noted, because we were interested in the "broad period" issue, we included tasks defined by Piaget's earlier theorizing as well as tasks representing concrete-operational structures in the narrow sense. Our study indicated that all these Piagetian tasks were somewhat tied together in the factor analysis, although specifically conservation tasks defined a more or less distinct factor or characteristic within the general cognitive shifts during the years 5 to 7 described by Piaget.

While there is thus some generality to Piagetian performance, it is also clear that the consistency of a Piagetian stage across tasks is not very high. Many psychologists believe Piaget's stage concepts are refuted when they find that children cannot be divided into two classes: those who perform all concrete operational tasks and those who fail them all. When a child passes one task and fails another, it appears that the child's task performance was not due to possession or absence of a stage-structure, but to various factors of situational learning plus general psychometric intelligence. Our findings indicate greater consistency to Piagetian performance than that. They do, however, pose the difficult problem that Piaget called the problem of "horizontal decalage"—that is, "spread" of application of the stage structure to a range of concepts or problems. Piaget assumed that when concrete operations appear in a given domain, they appear more or less as a whole—that is, as a network of interrelated operations. One does not have one logical operation, addition, without another, subtraction, or a third, reciprocity. Piaget argues, however, that the appearance of a structure in one content domain does not mean that it will then appear in all content domains. Piaget's view was that stage structures are general but that it takes additional time from the first appearance of the stage to its application to other content domains that differ in their "resistance" to structuring. According to Piaget (1971c):

> At certain ages the child is able to solve problems in quite specific areas. But if one changes to another material or to another situation, even with a problem which seems to be closely related, lags of several months are noted, and in some cases even of one or two years. Let us take one example: the problem of class inclusion. The problem is solved at approximately the age of eight years for flowers. But Barbel Inhelder and I have noted that if one uses animals, for example, the problem becomes more complicated. If you ask, "If you look out of the window, can you tell me whether there are more sea gulls or more birds in Geneva?" the child finds this more difficult to answer than for the flowers. Why is this? Is it because one cannot make a bunch with the sea gulls as with the flowers? I do not know.
>
> I have often been reproached for not having produced a sufficiently precise theory of these time lags in the same way as one can try to produce a theory of the overall structures or of the positive characteristics of stages. But time lags are a negative characteristic which form an obstacle to the construction of the overall structures.
>
> Time lags are always due to an interaction between the person's structures on the one hand, and the resistances of the object on the other. The object may be flowers, which offer little resistence; one places them on the table, and one makes a bunch of them. But there are other objects which offer more resistance, as for instance the birds. One cannot put them on the table. Some resistances of objects are unpredictable. When one encounters them, one can explain them, but always after the event. It is not possible to have a general theory of these resistances.
>
> I should like to find some sort of an excuse for this failure by a comparison with friction in physics. Physicists explain the role of friction in such and such a situation, but they have not yet come up with a general theory for this phenomenon. Time lags are somewhat analogous; they are comparable to all the concrete situations where friction is involved. (p. 125)

What Piaget is saying is that the problem of the generalization of concrete-operational structures (of "decalage") is not a problem that can or must be solved by the theory of concrete operations itself. The existence of decalage does not itself put the existence of a stage, or structure, of concrete operations in doubt if there is sufficient consistency in individual pattern of decalage to warrant the notion of concrete operational stage. Children showing operational reasoning on some tasks and not on others do not do so randomly. Piaget's interpretation of decalage in terms of "resistence of objects" implies that while a child may pass one operational task and fail another, the general order of difficulty of tasks should be the same, that is, all children should find class inclusion of birds more difficult than that of flowers. Such an order of difficulty or of "horizontal decalage" would then constitute a horizontal Guttman scale just as stages constitute vertical Guttman scales or vertical decalages. Sometimes such scales might represent varying degrees of resistances of objects to an operation, as in Piaget's quoted example of resistance of objects to class inclusion. In other cases, decalage represents an order of complexity in the operations themselves. Piaget found that conservation is established first with regard to substance, then weight, and later volume. Our data suggests that conservation develops earlier than either class inclusion or transitivity. While all three of these tasks require multiplication of relations, one must still conserve classes before including one class in another and one must conserve length before maintaining a transitive ordering of length. These and other Guttman-scaled "horizontal decalages" have been reported by Smedslund (1964), Uzgiris (1964), Nassafat (1963), and others.

The empirical study of decalage is extremely complex, and while evidence exists for order in extension of concrete operations across some content domains, it is difficult to establish a universal order for some content domains in which concrete operations appear at about the same time. DeVries (unpublished data) did not find a regular order of decalage for conservation of substance, length, number, and liquid. More research needs to be done on this issue. Nevertheless, while Piaget has no complete theory to account for decalage, there is enough order in the variation in presence of concrete operations to allow us to talk about children as varying in extent of decalage of concrete-operational thought. This seems more parsimonious than allowing the fact of decalage to throw the whole concept of concrete operations into question.

Horizontal Decalage and Ego Strength

While the existence of horizontal decalage is not an obstacle to Piaget's theory, Piaget provides little of the interpretation needed to make stage notions useful in defining measures of intelligence. The problem is critical for any use of Piagetian tasks for educational assessment. Important variations among children are not between those who show operational patterns and those who do not. Instead, they are differences in the extent of decalage of concrete operations across tasks. How are individual differences in decalage to be explained and in what sense is it better to have a more extensive decalage of operational thought? One interpretation of decalage would hypothesize that full decalage of concrete operations is a prerequisite to appearance of the next stage of thought, i.e., formal operations. This hypothesis does not appear to be completely plausible. There is anecdotal evidence for thinking that at least some adolescents and adults (e.g., "disturbed" or psychotic adolescents) may show formal operational thought and still be *preoperational* in some areas (Linden, 1970).

Insofar as extent of decalage is distinct from sheer rate of attainment of new stages, it would seem to be a somewhat more "motivational" or "cognitive style" matter, a matter of having a "logical mind." In the case of logico-mathematical tasks, the issue of "resistance" is the issue of the logical difficulty of the task. In many Piagetian tasks, however, the "resistance" to logical solution is not so much task difficulty as it is the overwhelmingly powerful perceptual and/or situational evidence for an illogical solution.

We developed some tasks in which tricks are presented in favor of preoperational or magical reasoning. An example was our magical causality task. In this task the experimenter performs a magic trick with a professional magician's change bag with a handle that reverses a double lining. A toy dog is placed in the bag and is transformed into a toy cat. Young children (aged 4 and 5) get very excited by this and insist it is "real magic," sometimes even after the mechanism is demonstrated to them.

This task can produce Guttman-scale-type levels ranging from a pure magical to a pure mechanistic causal explanation of what happened. To "pass" the magic task the child must not only have the logical structure or notion that "a toy cat cannot become a toy dog" but must maintain this notion in the face of unusual perceptual evidence to the contrary. The disposition to maintain a logical belief despite apparent experiential contradiction would seem to involve something more "volitional," which Piaget calls the "feeling of necessity." According to Piaget (1971c):

> Here we touch upon the real problem of overall structures: the problem of the appearance at a particular point in development of the feeling of necessity.
>
> My personal feeling is that there is only one acceptable psychological explanation: his feeling of necessity comes from the closure or completion of a structure....
>
> The feeling of necessity is an idea which is constructed at the same time as the overall structures. As soon as a structure is sufficiently complete for closure to occur, or, in other words, once the internal compositions of the structure become interdependent and independent of external elements and are sufficiently numerous to allow for all types of arrangements, then the feeling of necessity manifests itself. (p. 142)

To explain what Piaget means, we may note that preoperational children can readily be persuaded of either choice in a conservation problem. In contrast, almost no matter what one says or does with a child who has fully attained concrete operations, you cannot get him to make a nonconserving response. Because the structure is in "equilibrium" it is endowed with a certainty lacking in a less equilibrated structure.

Nevertheless, it is not completely convincing to reduce differences in "will" to differences in "skill" or cognitive level as such. To take an extreme example, the tendency to act in accordance with one's highest level of reasoning is not only a function of skill at one's moral judgmental level, but it is also a function of will, of ego-strength factors like stability of attention (Krebs, 1967). To some extent, the ability to use one's highest level of logical reasoning in the face of situational "pulls to regression" would also seem to involve something like a volitional component. Some findings supporting such a contention come from a study by Linden (1970) who compared a group of psychotic children with normal children of the same mental age using our tasks. The most marked lags of the psychotic children behind the normals were in the magical causality test. These children, presumably particularly deficient in ego strength, showed this deficit particularly in a task in which appearances most strongly violated expectations derived from a mature level of thought. Put in slightly different terms, one dimension of decalage may be sheer difficulty in the task. Another dimension, however, may be a characterological ability in the child to resist the "regressive" pull of a situation toward a lower level of thought. Children may not be orderable in the same way on these two dimensions of horizontal decalage.

As noted, Linden (1970) found preadolescent schizophrenics often believed that the task involved "real magic" even though they passed all the more traditional Piagetian conservation tasks. In a very interesting book, *The Tyranny of Magical Thinking*, Serban (1982) attributes many neurotic and psychotic symptoms in adolescents and adults to the persistence of preoperational magical reasoning in emotionally loaded content areas.

Rather than stating a decalage factor as a matter of ego strength, one might use somewhat comparable cognitive-style terminology. There is some evidence that Piagetian development is related to field-independence with IQ controlled. Specifically, for instance, field independence is related to Piagetian development of spatial concepts (LaCrosse, 1967). It seems plausible that a construct like field independence might relate closely to the child's ability to resist situational pulls toward preoperational responses that are involved in many of the Piagetian tasks.

A Note on Cognitive Style Conceptions of Intelligence

We have considered two major approaches to intelligence: the psychometric and the Piagetian or cognitive-developmental approach. In the previous section, we noted a third approach to intelligence, the cognitive-style approach, and suggested a loose relationship between Piagetian decalage and concepts of ego strength and cognitive style.

At the present time, the concept of cognitive style has not attained either the theoretical clarity or the empirical coherence achieved by both the biological-psychometric view of intelligence or the Piagetian-developmental concept of intelligence. There are a number of different approaches to cognitive style: "analytic-nonanalytic" (Kagan & Kagan, 1970), field-independent versus field-dependent (Witkin et al., 1962), and reflective-impulsive (Kagan & Kagan, 1970). While each of these traits is empirically distinguishable, each relates to age, IQ, and to some extent to one another. We will consider one cognitive style in detail, the most thoroughly studied trait of field independence or psychological differentiation. The core measures of field independence are the Body Adjustment Test and the Rod-and-Frame Test, both requiring adjusting to the true vertical when the room, the body, or the frame are tilted. Correlated with this perceptual proprioceptive measure are tests of ability to find embedded figures, that is, to separate them from the field in which they are embedded. A final correlate includes certain psychometric tests of spatial relations, for example, WISC block design, picture completion, and object-assembly. As is typical of cognitive-style measures, field independence is correlated with psychometric intelligence but can still be distinguished from it. Field independence and other cognitive style variables have their own lines or trends of development, not simply derivative from an increase in psychometric mental age with time. Field independence increases with age fairly continuously until age 17, though increase is most rapid in the period from 5 to 10. Further, field independence and other cognitive style variables reflect lines of individuality fairly stable or continuous over development. Although older children are more field-independent than younger children, field-independent children retain their relative advantage over field-dependent children as they grow up. Correlations in the 60s and 70s are reported between preadolescent (ages 10 to 12) field independence and adult field independence. It appears that after a period of rapid development in the early years (ages 4 to 10) field dependence or independence becomes a relatively stable characteristic of the individual. Of perhaps greatest interest, field independence has many personality or social behavior correlates that would not be expected if field independence were simply an aspect of psychometric intelligence.

Field-dependent persons are more oriented to the standards of others in social situations, more attentive to social cues and reinforcers, and more accommodative to the wishes and preferences of others. Field-independent persons are more "autonomous" in social situations. It seems likely that this autonomy goes beyond social situations, that field-independent persons are generally more stable—that their behavior is more independent of the pulls and pressures of the particular situation. As an example, it has been found that field-independent people are more consistently at the same stage of moral reasoning across tasks than field-dependent people. Field-dependent people at a given stage were more likely to vary in their stage of moral reasoning on hypothetical dilemmas and on a verbal presentation of a real-life dilemma they had faced.

It appears that field independence, while it is a variable related to cognitive development, also represents something that might be characterized as an ego-strength dimension distinguishable from intelligence or cognitive maturity as such.

If situational autonomy is one dimension of ego strength, attention and what used to be called will are others. In our own work with first graders and adolescents, we have found that brass-instrument and psychophysiological measures of attention relate closely to moral will in the sense of resistance to the temptation to cheat (Grim, Kohlberg, & White, 1968). Brass-instrument measures of attention (of reaction time) themselves define a developmental variable increasing with age and correlated with IQ. In addition to relating to what might be called will, the development of selective attention is of great importance in various tasks and learnings. After IQ, minute-to-minute schoolroom ratings of attention are the single best predictors of school achievement (Jackson, 1967).

If situational autonomy (field independence) and attention are major dimensions of ego strength, so is reflectivity, delay of gratification, and internal locus of control. A solid conceptualization that would integrate ego-strength dimensions and cognitive-style dimensions into a coherent whole remains to be constructed. From a Piagetian point of view, an integration is suggested by experimentally found relations between attention and decentering in perceptual and conceptual tasks. It has been found that the development of perceptual constancies and logical conservation are related to the development of systematic visual scanning of attention in a field. A child who scans the field "decenters" from the stimulus or any single aspect of it and puts it in comparative perspective. Decentering is both a mechanism for attaining cognitive stability and overcoming egocentricity of perspective and a mechanism of attention. Presumably, some process of attentional deployment is involved in the differentiation of figures from ground involved in field independence as well as in "analytic" or "reflective" cognitive problem-solving sets.

In summary, cognitive styles are variables of cognitive task performance that cannot readily be considered cognitive abilities (in the psychometric sense) or as levels of reasoning (in the Piagetian sense). As abilities they are more like ego abilities than cognitive skills. In relation to level of reasoning, they resemble stability of reasoning level, or extensiveness of the decalage of the reasoning level than they are, themselves, a level of reasoning. While not as purely cognitive as other approaches to intelligence, these variables are not motivational in the usual sense; they are not dependent on specific goals, intentions, or need states. At the same time, the development of such variables as field independence seems to be influenced by social and family factors in a clearer and more direct way than psychometric ability variables are. In summary, work on cognitive style offers the promise of an enriching addition to the assessment of intelligence in its widest sense, one that broadens the conception of intelligence to include the adaptive dimension suggested by the term ego strength.

THE EDUCATIONAL IMPLICATIONS OF PSYCHOMETRIC AND PIAGETIAN ASSESSMENTS OF INTELLIGENCE

We discussed at the start three different assumptions about the nature and origin of intelligence—the hereditary view, the environmental learning view, and the adaptational or interactional view. We showed how each of these views led to a different approach to the assessment of intelligence. Now we would like to discuss the different educational implications of psychometric and Piagetian assessments in relation to two broad issues. The first issue is the moral question of how the different philosophic positions lead to different educational uses. The second issue is the pragmatic question of how well the two kinds of assessments serve educators. We argue that whether one takes the hereditary or environmental view of intelligence, IQ tests provide neither a just nor a useful basis for differential educational treatment or for evaluating educational programs.

The Hereditary View

As we discussed above, research evidence supports the view that heredity makes a contribution to individual differences in IQ. The biological view is an empirically warranted theoretical interpretation of data gathered by the psychometric method. This method of making an intelligence test yields a generality in performance that is largely biological. To the extent that a biological conception of intelligence is true, a psychometric test is useless as a measure of educational progress. That is, the hereditary view is that educational experiences affect not general capacity, but specific experience-determined test performance.

Although the biological view rules out the use of psychometric intelligence tests to assess educational progress, it does suggest its use as a basis for social and educational selection. The use of intelligence tests for selection means selecting those who will most profit from educational experience or those who will be most effective in later positions of social leadership, for which education is required. Carried to its logical extreme, this view led to advocacy of eugenic selection by IQ. Kelley (1930) introduced a chapter on intelligence by stating: "What more complete social life can there be than one in which the somatic structures of one generation are so full of wisdom that they determine the germ cells of the generation to be?" Thorndike is quoted as saying: "Until the last removable impediment in man's own nature dies childless, human reason will not rest." A shade less extreme was the British use until recently of 11 + aptitude tests to select students for academic secondary education.

It is clear that the use of intelligence tests for social selection rests not only on the premise that intelligence is biological, but also on certain value premises or ethical postulates. Selection by intelligence presupposes a conception of social justice in which power and rewards are merited by intelligence. In one form this conception of justice is the Platonic notion of governance by the wise because such governance is best for the social whole; in another form the doctrine is one of social Darwinism. In addition to these assumptions about social justice, the use of intelligence tests for social selection reflects an assumption that intelligence is intrinsically adaptive or valuable regardless of role or culture—that its meaning and value are not culturally relative.

The moral issue to be confronted arises from the value assigned to individual differences in IQ. When IQ is assigned a high value, what is implied for education? Should innate differences imply different educational treatments? Should all be treated equally—receive equal opportunity—regardless of variations in natural endowment? If one assumes that differences in IQ accurately reflect differences in innate intellectual endowment, the social policy issue is thus whether it is fair to use these scores to determine the kind of educational opportunity available to an individual.

From an egalitarian perspective, hereditary differences are irrelevant for general social policy decisions. Differential treatment or tracking of lower-class or black children based on their low group means—that is, because they are lower class or black—is unjust. Such discrimination is unfair, whether mean IQ differences among social and racial classes are hereditary or whether they are environmental. Similarly, it is unjust to provide fundamentally different educational opportunities to a "dull track" than to a "bright track"—when these limit future educational progress. The fact of a hereditary component in intelligence cannot make unjust social policies just. An egalitarian position implies some degree of compensation for those with less endowment—for example, early or remedial education.

The fact that brightness is socially prized does not serve as a justification for considering it a merit to be rewarded or a demerit to be punished. In this sense, innate intelligence is not so different from innate beauty or innate physical strength. A strong person may more likely make a good football player and a bright person may more likely make a good scholar, but there is no ground for saying that it is fair to select football players just by strength or scholars just by IQ. If selection is required, a fair selection process rests on criteria of relevant achievement, not of native capacity. Indeed, as McClelland (1973) has noted, one can argue that if two individuals are of equal scholarly achievement, it would be fair to select the less bright individual for advanced educational opportunity, since it may be more legitimate to reward conscientious effort than effortless displays of capacity. In summary, the justification of the use of IQ tests for selection rests on the notion that it is fair to assign inequalities of opportunity or reward on the basis of hereditary intelligence. While such a distribution is perhaps fairer than awarding opportunity directly to inherited rank and wealth, it is still open to the objection that it is an unfair perpetuation of an aristocracy of hereditary talent.

Turning to the social utility of selection by psychometric intelligence, the assumption of utility rests on a further assumption—that general cognitive ability predicts to "good" vocational or social achievement or contribution. It is true that the primary practical prediction from IQ tests is to school grades and school achievement. And there are a number of things to note about these positive correlations between IQ and school achievement. The first is that it does not justify IQ tests as a general measure or predictor of adaptation. Intelligence as adaptation implies the ability to organize one's experience, to define realizable and nonconflicting ends, and to find means to realize those ends. As documented in Kohlberg,

Ricks, and Snarey (1984), school achievement itself does not predict life adaptation. Although IQ does have some value for predicting adult life success or adjustment, the correlations are rather low and uncertain in their meaning. The small predictive value of IQ for later achievement may be largely circular. That is, after favoring the bright, we find that to some extent the better achievers are favored later. The substantial correlation of IQ with school achievement does not justify it as predicting something of real practical value.

In the sense just discussed, the culturally relativistic critique of intelligence is justified. The value of psychometric intelligence is more or less contingent on the culture's evaluation of its correlates. A culture that values a certain type of scholastic achievement will value the capacity that contributes to it, but this valuing is arbitrary if the valuing of scholastic achievement is arbitrary. School achievement as currently measured by grades and achievement scores is itself an arbitrary value. Psychometric IQ tests and psychometric achievement tests are similar in that they represent, in the main, a random sample of specific items of trivial skills or bits of information added together to assign an individual a relative place on a normal curve. The difference between the two kinds of tests is that one consists of trivial items not stressed by school or society and (IQ tests), the other consists of items more or less arbitrarily stressed by the schools (achievement tests). IQ is a good index of a fixed or innate capacity to think about and learn trivial material. It is hardly surprising that capacity to learn such material is not very much related to life adaptation and it is thus our belief that the utility of psychometric tests for educational selection is seriously challenged on moral, empirical, and logical grounds.

The Environmental View

Advocates of the environmental-learning view cannot clearly distinguish a concept of intelligence from a concept of a set of learned specific skills or bits of information. Accordingly, it has not been able to provide a concept that gives some order to the generality of intelligence test performance. From this environmental perspective, conventional IQ tests primarily reflect the abilities or opportunities for learning provided by middle-class Western cultures to its members. The value of intelligence is relative to its prediction of cultural success, and even this prediction can be questioned on grounds of justice, as discussed above. Insofar as intelligence is valuable from this perspective, its value is not intrinsic but relative to the culture's valuing of the individual who possesses it. In our view, however, social selection by intelligence is not a just reward for merit but a self-perpetuation of status advantages in which a society that provides greater learning opportunities to the socially advantaged child then selects these children for leadership or status roles.

The environmental-learning conception of intelligence does not, we conclude, give rise to a standard of value for assessing educational progress. An educational program might, for instance, lead to passing an average of five more items on the Binet. From an environmental-learning point of view, the value of such an increase in Binet performance must be evaluated in terms of the specific learnings involved and their predictive value for later social success. To call the learnings involved in passing the items a "change in intelligence" adds nothing to the value that might be attributed to these items as educational outcome measures.

Our questioning of the practical value of psychometric intelligence tests cannot be resolved by an environmental-learning interpretation of their meaning. From this point of view, not only is the value of differential ability culturally relative, but a lower score on ability reflects primarily unfair "cultural disadvantage." A fair and effective compensation for disadvantage in learned cognitive ability would rest not on trying to bring the disadvantaged child to a higher relative rank in IQ, but attempting directly to provide the child with greater social opportunities and achievements, when IQ is such an uncertain or poor predictor of later success or social achievement.

In conclusion, we believe there are no justified uses of psychometric intelligence tests for making decisions of educational policy or evaluation. The tests offer an important and useful research instrument and a potentially useful tool for individual counseling and guidance. They do not provide a viable conception of intelligence for education. The elaboration of such a conception requires a different theory and method—what we call the cognitive-developmental.

The Piagetian View

Our empirical studies reported above indicate that Piagetian intelligence is a construct relatively distinct from the British biological construct of general intelligence, yet meaningfully related to it. This basic finding contradicts Hunt's (1961) theoretical marriage of psychometric and Piagetian conceptions of intelligence, and calls into question his expectation that early stimulation and education will necessarily bring increases in children's *psychometric* intelligence. In fact, most of the research in recent years on the effects of preschool programs has indicated that changes on IQ scores do not persist beyond the second or third grade (see DeVries and Kohlberg, 1987; White, Day, Freeman, Hantman, & Messenger, 1972, for review and summary of these studies).

The psychoeducational issue concerns the meaning and use of Piaget-type tasks for assessing individual differences. We should note first that our results suggest that Piagetian tasks will not be better tests of psychometric intelligence than psychometric tests themselves. The fact that the Piagetian tasks do not well define *g* indicates that they will not cover the correlational ground that a good test of *g* does. Piagetian tasks would not be expected to match psychometric tests with regard to their success in long-range prediction of IQ and school success. However, by using items linked with school achievement, Binet opened a Pandora's box in the culture's conception of cognitive growth or cognitive education. Essentially, the IQ tests introduced a relativistic criterion of intellectual competence. Intellectual competence is not defined by a basic set of operations or achievements, but by position on the normal curve. As noted in Chapter 3 the rudderless nature of educational aims that results from this conception of intelligence is well expressed by Edward Zigler's facetious statement that the official aim of compensatory education in the United States is to bring 100 percent of the population above the 50th percentile on IQ and achievement tests.

Despite the predictive success of psychometric tests, McClelland (1973) challenged the validity of IQ tests as measures of intelligence. His review of the literature led him to argue convincingly that the high correlations between IQ scores and various measures of occupational success or life adjustment are likely the result of social class and educational opportunity rather than intelligence.

It should be noted, too, that the kinds of achievement tests used to validate IQ tests have also been under attack recently. It might seem that school achievement test items are more significant than psychometric items because achievement tests are intended to assess whether children have learned what teachers have tried to teach them. However, as indicated in Chapter 3, the reviewed literature shows that school achievement only predicts further school achievement and fails to predict anything else of value (such as occupational success).

Thus, if the value of the kinds of school achievement used to validate the IQ is questioned, then the validity of the IQ itself must be questioned. It appears that the crumbling assumptions that an IQ score represents intelligence and that school achievement prepares children for later success lead to a demand for alternatives in testing theory and practice. Chapter 3 and Kohlberg, Ricks, and Snarey (1984) suggest that Piagetian measures provide a more rational basis for cognitive evaluation of educational intervention than psychometric intelligence tests. This alternative suggestion is congruent with McClelland's (1973) less specific advocacy of tests with scores that "change as the person grows in experience, wisdom, and ability to perform effectively on various tasks that life presents to him (p. 8)." Therefore, the Piagetian alternative to psychometric methods seems worth examining.

We earlier noted that the British biological school is centrally a doctrine as to the theoretical origins of cognitive structure or process, not a quantitative doctrine that all the empirical variance in IQ is due to heredity-biology. Even more clearly, Piaget's claim is the theoretical one that the developing structure of intelligence depends on structural features of interaction with the environment, not the claim that individual variation in intelligence-test performance is primarily environmental. While Piaget's doctrine is not quantitative, it does imply that enough variation in performance on Piagetian tasks is due to interaction with the environment, to make the interactional concept one that does order data. Piaget's method is consistent with his assumptions about biology and environment. That is, Piaget-type test items involve experience that can be structured at various levels of maturity. In the Binet-Spearman approach the search for general cognition led to the use of different novel or trivial task content at different age levels, scored as pass-fail. In contrast, Piaget-type test items concern the same experiential content across age levels, scored as qualitative levels of thought. As an example, the child who is familiar with the content or verbal definition of "the dream" and would pass a Binet-type vocabulary test on which this was an item, might view the dream as external and real. At every age the Piaget task asks the child about the dream, but each new maturity level is expressed in a new way of thinking about it. A good Piaget item is not novel; it is one that shows the cumulative restructurings of experience.

The fact that Piagetian intelligence does not claim to be biological capacity and that it has a ceiling (most people evidently reach early or basic formal operations) means it is not a device for social selection. Neither does it claim to predict school achievement or "life success" in industrial-psychology terms. Rather, developed intelligence claims to be a good in itself, it claims to be adaptation, not to externally predict to adaptation (as an external criterion). An act of developed Piagetian intelligence (on a test or in life) is an act of adaptation, of equilibration or reciprocity between the organism and the environment. To illustrate, we may contrast defining "envelope" on the Binet, and conserving on a Piagetian test. Knowing "envelope" is a bit of information, it is not per se an adaptative interaction with the environment. In contrast, compensating length and width to maintain conservation of mass is an act of adaptation to environmental change, producing a veridical balance or order between the world and the child.

Piagetian tasks are significant because they represent natural and culturally universal general sequential organizations of the child's world. They are important because they reflect the child's construction of his or her world. Because the Piagetian notion of intelligence is relative to an individual's place in a universal sequence of development rather than being relative to the performance of other individuals, it may provide a much more serviceable guide to education. A study by Kuhn, Langer, Kohlberg, and Haan (1977) indicates that at least on the pendulum and probability tasks, only about 60 percent of adults are able to use formal operational reasoning and that many adults with high IQ are in this group. If formal operational reasoning is considered a desirable educational goal, then Piaget's theory and research may provide helpful guides to curriculum development and educational evaluation.

Whether it is possible or even desirable to develop a Piagetian scale of intelligence is debatable. Perhaps it is not possible to develop *any* single meaningful scale of intelligence. As researchers continue to ponder the problem of psychoeducational evaluation, however, we would like to point out Piaget's emphasis on the importance of knowing what it is we are trying to measure before we attempt to measure it. As Piaget put it:

> . . . it is important to diagnose not so much what the subject can do when undergoing the test, as what he would be capable of doing in many other situations. Intelligence

was therefore "measured" long before it was known what it consists of, and we are only just beginning to have some inkling of the complexity of its nature and functioning. (Piaget, 1966, p. 59)

In summary, a growing body of literature indicates the need to reassess the widespread use of psychometric measures such as IQ for educational purposes and to provide a broadened perspective on intelligence testing that will generate better methods of educational evaluation.

REFERENCES

Ammons, R. D., & Ammons C. H. (1962). *The Quick test*. Missoula, MT: Psychological Test Specialists.

Anastasi, A. (1958). Heredity, environment and the question 'how?'. *Psychological Review*, 65, 197–208.

Anastasi, A. (1965). *Differential Psychology*. New York: MacMillan.

Baldwin, J. M. (1895). *Mental development in the child and the race*. New York: Macmillan.

Baldwin, J. M. (1906). *Functional logic or genetic theory of knowledge*. New York: Macmillan.

Bayley, N. (1970). Development of mental abilities. In P. Mussen (Ed.), *Carmichaels' manual of child psychology*. New York: Wiley.

Bentler, P. (1969). Monotonicity analysis: An alternative to linear factor and test analysis. Paper presented at Symposium on Ordinal Scales of Development. Montorey, CA.

Binet, A. (1910). *Les idees modernes sur les enfants*. Paris: E Flommoriar.

Binet, A., & Simon, T. (1912). *A method of measuring the intelligence of young children*. Lincoln, IL: The Courier Co.

Brown, R., & Hernnstein, R. J. (1975). *Psychology*. Boston: Little, Brown.

Bruner, J. S., Oliver, R. R., & Greenfield, P. M. (1966). *Studies in cognitive growth*. New York: Wiley.

Carroll, J., Kohlberg, L., & De Vries, R. (1984). Psychometric and Piagetian intelligence. *Intelligence, 8*, 67–91.

Cattell, R. B. (1963). Theory of fluid and crystallized intelligence: A critical experiment. *Journal of Educational Psychology, 54*, 1–22.

Cattell, R. B. (1971). *Abilities: Their structure, growth, and action*. Boston: Houghton Mifflin.

Cattell, R. B. (1972). *Abilities: Their structures, growth and action*. Boston: Houghton Mifflin.

Cole, M., Gay, J., Glick, J. A., & Sharp, D. W. (1971). *The cultural content of learning and thinking*. New York: Basic Books.

Cole, M., & Scribner, S. (1974). *Culture and thought*. New York: Wiley.

Dasen, P. (1977). *Piagetian psychology: Cross cultural contributions*. New York: Gardner Press.

De Vries, R. (1969). Constancy of generic identity in the years 3 to 6. *Monograph at the Society for Research in Child Development, 34*(3, Serial no. 127).

De Vries, R. (1974). Relationships among Piagetian IQ and achievement assessments. *Child Development, 45*, 746–756.

De Vries, R., & Kohlberg, L. (1977). Relations between psychometric and Piagetian assessments of intelligence. In L. Katz (Ed.), *Current topics in early childhood education,* Vol. 1. Norwood, NJ: Ablex.

De Vries, R., & Kohlberg, L. (1987). *Programs of early education.* White Plains, NY: Longman.

Dudek, S. Z., Lester, E. P., Goldberg, J. S., & Dyer, G. B. (1969). Relationship of Piaget measures to standard intelligence and motor scales perceptual and motor skills. *Perceptual and Motor Skills, 28,* 351–362.

Ertl, J. P. (1966). Evoked potentials and intelligence. *Revue de l'Université d'Ottawa, 36,* 599–607.

Ertl, J. P. (1968). *Evoked potentials, neural efficiency, and IQ.* Paper presented at the International Symposium for Biocybernetics, Washington, D.C.

Evans, R. I. (1973). *Jean Piaget: The man and his ideas.* New York: Dutton.

Eysenck, H. J. (1967). Intelligence in assessment: A theoretical and experimental approach. *British Journal of Educational Psychology, 37,* 81–98.

Eysenck, H. J. (1971). *Race, intelligence, and education.* London: Temple Smith.

Eysenck, H. J. (1979). *The structure and measurement of intelligence.* New York: Springer-Verlag.

Furneaux, W. D. (1960). Intellectual abilities and problem solving behavior. In H. J. Eysenck (Ed.), *Handbook of abnormal psychology.* New York: Basic Books.

Galton, F. (1869). *Hereditary genius.* London: Macmillan.

Gardner, H. (1983). *Frames of mind: The theory of multiple intelligences.* New York: Basic Books.

Ginsburg, H., & Ofper, S. (1979). *Piaget's theory of intellectual development* (2 ed). Englewood Cliffs, NJ: Prentice-Hall.

Goldstein, K. (1939). *The organism.* New York: Appleton.

Goldstein, K., & Scheerer, M. (1941). Abstract and concrete behavior: An experimental study with spacial tests. *Psychology Monographs, 53,* No. 2.

Gieco, P. (1959). *Etudes d' epistomologie genetique. VII Apprentissage et connaissance.* Paris: Presses Universitaires de France.

Green, B. (1956). A method of scalogram analysis using summary statistics. *Psychometrika, 21*(1), 79–88.

Greenfield, P. M., & Bruner, J. S. (1966). *Studies in cognitive growth.* New York: Wiley.

Grim, P. F., Kohlberg, L., & White, S. H. (1968). Some relations between conscience and attentional processes. *Journal of Personality and Social Psychology, 8*(3), 239–252.

Guilford, J. P. et al. (1954). A factor analysis study on human interests. *Psychology Monographs, 68,* No. 4.

Guttman, L. (1954). The basis of scalogram analysis. In S. A. Stougger, et al. (Eds.), *Measurement and prediction.* Princeton: Princeton University Press.

Hathaway, W. E. Jr. (1973, March). The degree and nature of the relations between traditional psychometric and Piagetian developmental measures of mental development. Paper presented at annual meeting at the American Educational Research Association. Chicago.

Hayes, K. J. (1962). Genes, drives and intellect. *Psychological Reports, 10,* 299–342.

Hendrickson, D. E. (1972). *An examination of individual differences in cortical evoked response.* Unpublished doctoral dissertation, University of London.

Hill, A. L. (1978). Savants: Mentally retarded individuals with special skills. In N. R. Ellis

(Ed.), *International review of research in mental retardation*, Vol. 9. Orlando, Fla.: Academic Press.

Horn, J. L. (1968). Organization of abilities and the development of intelligence. *Psychological Review, 75*, 242–259.

Horn, J. L., & Cattell, R. B. (1967). Refinement and test of the theory of fluid and crystallized intelligence. *Journal of Educational Psychology, 57*, 253–270.

Humphreys, L. G., & Parsons, C. K. (1979). Piagetian tasks measure intelligence and intelligence tests assess cognitive development: A reanalysis. *Intelligence, 3*, 369–382.

Hunt, J. Mc V. (1961). *Intelligence and experience*. New York: Ronald Press.

Inhelder, B. (1943, 1968). *The diagnosis of reasoning in the mentally retarded*. New York: Day.

Inhelder, B. (1943/1968). *Le diagnostic di raisonnement chez les debiles mentaux*. Neuchâtel: Delachaux and Niestlé. *The diagnosis of reasoning in the mentally retarded*. English translation. New York: Day.

Inhelder, B., & Piaget, J. (1958). *The growth of logical thinking from childhood to adolescence*. New York: Basic Books.

Inhelder, B., & Piaget, J. (1958). *The growth of logical thinking from childhood to adolescence*. New York: Basic Books.

Isaacs, S. (1930). *Growth in young children*. London: Routledge Kegan Paul.

Jackson. P. (1967). *Life in classrooms*. New York: Holt, Rinehart.

Jenson. A. (1969). IQ and scholastic achievement. *Harvard Educational Review, 39*(1), 1–123.

Jensen. A. R. (1982). Reaction time and psychometric *g*. In Eysenck, H. J. (Ed.), *A model for intelligence*. Heidelberg: Springer-Verlag.

Jensen, A. R. (1986). The theory of intelligence. In S. Modgil & C. Modgil (Eds.), *Hans Eysenck: Consensus and controversy*. London: Falmer.

Kagan, J., & Kagan. N. (1970). Individual variation in cognitive processes. In P. Mussen (Ed.), *Carmichael's manual of child psychology*. New York: Wiley.

Kail, R., & Pelligrino, J. W. (1985). *Human intelligence*. New York: Freeman.

Kelley, T. (1930). The measurement of intelligence. In C. Murchisan (Ed.), *Psychologies of 1930*. Worcester, MA: Clark University Press.

Kohlberg, L. (1968). Early education: A cognitive-developmental view. *Child Development, 39*(4), 1013–1062.

Kohlberg, L., Ricks, D., & Snarey, J. (1984). Childhood development as a predictor of adaptation in adulthood. *Genetic Psychology Monographs, 110*, 91–172.

Kohlberg, L., & De Vries, R. (1969). Concept measurement kit: Conservation: Review. *Journal of Educational Measurement, 6*, 263–266.

Kohlberg, L., & DeVries, R. (1980). "Don't throw out the Piagetian baby with the psychometric bath." *Intelligence, 4*(2), 175–179.

Kohlberg, L., & Mayer, R. (1973). Development as the aim of education. *Harvard Educational Review, 42*(4), 449–496.

Krebs, R. (1967). *Some relations between moral judgment attitudes and resistance to temptation*. Unpublished doctoral dissertation, University of Chicago.

Kuhn, D. (1969). *Comprehensions and preferences for levels of conceptualization other than one's own*. Unpublished doctoral dissertation, University of California, Berkeley.

Kuhn, D., Langer, J., Kohlberg, L., & Haan, N. (1977). The development of formal operations in logical and moral judgment. *Genetic Psychology Monographs, 95*, 97–188.

LaCrosse, J. (1967). *Relations between field independence and Piagetian Spatial reasoning.* Unpublished doctoral dissertation, University of North Carolina, Chapel Hill.

Langer, J. (1969). *The role of disequilibrium in children's learning.* Paper presented at conference on the National Curriculum of the Child. Urbana, IL.

Laurendeau, M., & Pinard, A. (1962). *Causal thinking in the child.* New York: International Universities Press.

Laurendeau, M., & Pinard, A. (1966). *The development of intelligence.* NY: International Universities Press.

Linden, J. (1970). *Piagetian reasoning in childhood psychosis.* Unpublished doctoral dissertation, University of Chicago.

Luria, A. R. (1976). *Cognitive development: Its cultural and social foundations.* Cambridge, MA: Harvard University Press.

McCartin, R. (1963). *Primary mental abilities at age 6.* Paper presented at the Society for Research in Child Development. New York.

McLelland, D. C. (1973). Testing for competence rather than for "intelligence." *American Psychologist, 28*(1), 1–14.

Meyers, C. E., Dingman, H. P., Attwell, A. A., & Orpert, R. E. (1962). Primary abilities at mental age 6. *Monograph of the Society for Research in Child Development, 27* (1,Serial No. 82).

Miller, G. A. (1983, December 25). Varieties of intelligence. [Review of *Frames of mind*, by H. Gardner.] *New York Times Book Review*, p. 5.

Monroe, M. (1935). *Reading aptitude tests.* Boston: Houghton Mifflin.

Morf, A., Smedslund, J., Vinh, Bang, & Wohlwill, J. (1959). *Etudes de epistemologie genetique v le apparatssage des structures logiques.* Paris: Presses Univertaue de France.

Nassefat, M. (1963). *Etude quantitative sur l'evolution des operations intellectual.* Neuchâtel: Delachaux and Niestlé.

Newman, H., Freeman, F., & Holzinger, K. (1937). *Twins: A study of heredity and environment.* Chicago: University of Chicago Press.

Piaget, J. (1950). *The psychology of intelligence.* New York: International Universities Press.

Piaget, J. (1952a). *The child's conception of numbers.* London: Routledge & Kegan Paul.

Piaget, J. (1952b). *The origins of intelligence in children.* New York: International Universities Press. (First published in 1936.)

Piaget, J. (1960). *The child's conception of the world.* Totowa, NJ: Littefield, Adams and Company. (First published in 1929.)

Piaget, J. (1966). *The psychology of intelligence.* Totowa, NJ: Littefield, Adams, and Company. (Originally published in 1947.)

Piaget, J. (1970). "Piaget's theory" in P. Mussen (Ed.), *Carmichael's manual of child psychology.* New York: Wiley, pp. 703–732.

Piaget, J. (1968). *Memory and identity.* Barre, MA: Clark University Press with Barre Publishers.

Piaget, J. (1971a). *Biology and knowledge.* Chicago: University of Chicago Press.

Piaget, J. (1971b). *Science of education and the psychology of the child.* New York: Viking.

Piaget, J. (1971c). The theory of stages in cognitive development. In D. R. Green, M. P. Ford, & G. B. Flaver (Eds.), *Measurement and Piaget.* New York: McGraw-Hill.

Piaget, J. (1972). Problems of equilibration. In C. F. Nodine, J. M. Gallagher, & R. D. Humphreys (Eds.), *Piaget and Inhleder on equilibration.* Philadelphia: The Piaget Society.

Piaget, J. (1973). *Main trends in psychology.* New York: Harper & Row.

Piaget, J., & Inhelder, B. (1959). *Le structure elementaire de la classification chez l'enfant.* Neuchâtel: Delachaux et Niestlé.

Price-Williams, D. (1981). Concrete and formal operations. In R. H. Munroe, R. L. Mussan, & B. Whiting (Eds.), *Handbook of cross-cultural human development.* New York: Garland.

Rapaport, D. (1945). *Diagnostic psychological testing,* Vol. 1. Chicago: Yearbook Publishers.

Raven. J. C. (1956). *Raven progressive matrices.* New York: The Psychological Corporation.

Reichard, S., Schneider, M., & Rapaport, D. (1944). The development of concept formation in children. *American Journal of Orthopsychiatry, 14,* 156–161.

Riesen, A., & Kinder, E. (1952). *The postural development of infant chimpanzees.* New Haven: Yale University Press.

Russel, R. W. (1940a). Studies in animism, II: The development of animism. *Journal of Genetic Psychology, 56,* 353–366.

Russel. R. W. (1940b). IV: An investigation of concepts allied to animism. *Journal of Genetic Psychology, 57,* 83–91.

Serban, G. (1982). *The tyranny of magical thinking.* New York: Dutton.

Shirley, M. (1931–1933). *The first two years* (2 Vols.). Minneapolis: University of Minnesota Press.

Sigel, I. E., & Hopper, F. M. (Eds.). (1968). *Logical thinking in children.* New York: Holt, Rinehart and Winston.

Smedslund, J. (1961a). The acquistition of conservation of substance and weight in children, III: Extinction of conservation of weight acquired normally by means of control as a balance. *Scandinavian Journal of Psychology,* 85–87. (Reprinted in Sigel & Hooper, 1968.)

Smedslund, J. (1961b). The acquisition of conservation of substance and weight in children, V: Practice in conflict situations without external reinforcement. *Scandinavian Journal of Psychology, 2,* 156–160, 203–210. (Reprinted in Sigel & Hooper, 1968.)

Smedslund, J. (1964). Concrete reasoning: a study of intellectual development. *Monograph Society of Research in Child Development, 29,* No. 2 (Whole No. 93).

Spearman, C. (1904). "General intelligence" objectively determined and measured. *American Journal of Psychology, 15,* 201–293.

Spearman, C. (1923). *The nature of intelligence and the principles of cognition.* London: Macmillan.

Spearman, C. (1927). *The abilities of man.* New York: Macmillan.

Spearman, C. (1930). The psychology of 'g'. In C. Murchison (Ed.), *Psychology of 1930.* Worcester, MA: Clark University Press.

Stephens, W. B. (1972). *The development of reasoning, moral judgment and moral conduct in retardates and normals: Phase II.* Mimeographed report, Temple University, Philadelphia.

Stephens, W. B., McLaughlin, J., Miller, C. K., & Glass, G. U. (1972). Factional structure of selected psychoeducational measures and Piagetian reasoning assessments. *Developmental Psychology, 6,* 343–348.

Stout, G. A. (1894). *Psychology.* Cambridge: Cambridge University Press.

Terman, L. M. (1916). *The measurement of intelligence.* Boston: Houghton Mifflin.

Terman, L. M., & Merrill, M. (1960). *Stanford-Binet intelligence scale.* Boston: Houghton Mifflin.

Thomson, G. H. (1946). *The factorial analysis of human ability*. Boston: Houghton Mifflin.

Thorndike, R. L. (1963). Some methodological issues in the study of creativity. *Proceedings of the 1962 invitational conference on testing problems*. Princeton, NJ: Educational Testing Service, pp. 40–54.

Thurstone, L. L. (1938). Primary mental abilities. *Psychometric Monographs*, No. 1.

Thurstone, L. L. (1947). *Multiple factor analysis*. Chicago: University of Chicago Press.

Thurstone, T. G., & Thurstone, L. L. (1954). *SRA primary mental abilities for ages 5 to 7*. Chicago: Bureau of Child Study of the Chicago Public Schools.

Tuddenham, R. D. (1969). Intelligence. In R. L. Ebel (Ed.), *Encyclopedia of Educational Research* (4th ed.). New York: Macmillan.

Tuddenham, R. D. (1971). Theoretical regularities and individual idiosyncrasies. In D. R. Green, M. P. Ford, & G. B. Flamer (Eds.), *Measurement and Piaget*. New York: McGraw-Hill, pp. 64–74.

Uzgiris, I. C. (1964). Situational generality of conservation. *Child Development, 35*, 831–841.

Vernon, P. E. (1950). *The structure of human abilities*. London: Methuen.

Vernon, P. E. (1969). *Intelligence and cultural environment*. London: Methuen.

Wechsler, D. (1944). *The measurement of adult intelligence*. Baltimore: Williams & Wilkins.

Wechsler, D. (1949). *Wechsler intelligence scale for children*. New York: The Psychological Corporation.

Weigl, E. (1941). On the psychologic of the so-called processes of abstraction. *Journal of Abnormal Social Psychology, 36*, 3–33.

Welch, L. (1940). A preliminary investigation of some aspects of the hierarchical development of concepts. *Journal of General Psychology, 22*, 359–378.

Werner, H. (1948). *Comparative psychology of mental development*. Chicago: Follett.

White, S. H., Day, M. C., Freeman, P. K., Hantman, S. A., & Messenger, K. P. (1972). *Federal programs for young children: Review and recommendations*. Washington, DC: U. S. Government Printing Office.

Witkin, H. A., Dyk, R. B., Faterson, H. F., Godenugh, D. R., & Karp, S. A. (1962). *Psychological differentialism*. New York: Wiley.

Wohlwill, J. A. (1968). A scalogram analysis of the number concept. In I. Sigel, & F. Hooper (Eds.), *Logical thinking in children: Research based on Piaget's theory*. New York: Holt, Rinehart.

Chapter 5

Language and the Development of Thought

Lawrence Kohlberg
James V. Wertsch

This book has focused on the most important research direction of recent child psychology, the study of developmental change in cognitive structures. A second parallel major direction of recent child psychology has been the study of structural change in language development. For example, Brown (1973) has carried out several empirical studies on the development of grammar, conceived in structural terms. He has found invariant sequential stages in English-speaking children, just as the Piagetians have found invariant stages in their cognitive development. Brown also reports that some of the features of his stages are linguistically universal—the same sequences are found for children learning any language. The very existence of universals in grammatical development suggests that these universals have some sort of base in cognitive development. In this literature on language development, however, relatively little has been said about the relationship between language and thought. Brown (1973) suggests some possible bases of grammatical stages in Piagetian infant cognitive stages, but these relations remain to be studied empirically.

In this chapter we will not describe the development of language or the development of thought in isolation, and we will not limit ourselves to describing the details of simple parallelisms between language and cognitive development. Assuming some general parallelisms, we ask the next question. This involves causal relationships: "Does language development cause cognitive development or does cognitive development cause language development or can one occur without the other?" The question is of direct significance to the educator. Almost any approach to early education will include a place for the stimulation of language development and use, for the oral and written "language arts." Such early language education does not require a rationale in terms of its uses in stimulating cognitive development. The question of causal direction arises, however, as soon as language

179

stimulation is seen as furthering cognitive-developmental goals of education. Some early education theories, like the Montessori, deny a major causal influence of language on cognition and minimize oral language in relation to cognitive skills. Other theories and programs, like the Bereiter-Engelmann (and the Bereiterian new math), see cognitive developments like classification and number as a matter of learning formal linguistic classification and number schemes.

In terms of an overall position on this issue, we will clarify Piaget's view that congnitive development is largely independent of language. Piaget and his followers have been the first researchers to systematically observe thought development independently of language, observations that support Piaget's view that language does not play a large role in logical-structural development. This evidence suggests that the parallelisms between the structural development of language and cognition do not indicate a major causal role for language.

Although we conclude that the Piagetian structural view of the independence and primacy of thought is correct in many important respects, we also conclude that this view slights significant areas in which language is integral to thought development. These areas are of particular importance to education, which is centrally communicative interchange. In considering these special areas where thought and language fuse, we draw on the ideas of two major cognitive-developmental theorists, Vygotsky (1956, 1960, 1962, 1978, 1981a, 1981b, 1981c) and Mead (1924–1925, 1934). From Vygotsky we draw the insight that the way to study the contribution of language to thought is by studying areas of "emergent interactionism" between the two. As Vygotsky (1962) phrased the question:

> Are there particular phases of development of language and thought in which the two interact in such a way as to create qualitatively new forms of thought-and-speech?

We consider this question with regard to two issues studied by Vygotsky: first, the cognitive-structural development of verbal or "scientific" concepts, and, second, the development of "inner speech" or self-directed verbal thought.

Following Mead (1934), we claim that an understanding of these areas of thought and speech rests on defining language development in terms of dialogic communication and we define the contribution of language development to thought as the growth of self-communication and inner dialogue. Our focus on the two general issues of scientific concepts and inner speech or self-communication is based on their inherent interest for understanding children and on their educational importance, as well as on their importance for a general theory of thought and language.

RELEVANT DEFINITIONS OF LANGUAGE AND THOUGHT

In order to evaluate and compare various accounts of the relationship between language and thought, we must begin by asking what is meant by "language" and what is meant by "thought." Because investigators have often failed to provide clear answers to these questions, research on this issue has progressed slowly. Instead of producing an increasingly detailed and integrated picture of the relationship between language and thought, it has often produced arguments and misunderstandings that stem from a confusion over what question is being asked.

To identify points of similarity, conflict, and complementarity and thus to "locate various theories on the conceptual map," we begin our discussion with a brief outline of various interpretations of the terms language and thought. First, we introduce the distinction between language as representation and language as communication. This will help us identify points at which various approaches differ in what is meant by language. Second, we examine the distinction between unmediated psychological processes and mediated psychological processes. This will allow us to identify points at which various approaches differ in what is meant by thought.

Language as Representation and Language as Communication

The first question we ask when considering any theory of language and thought is: What is meant by "language?" Many distinctions can be used to compare various accounts of language, but for the purposes of comparing theories of language and thought, one general distinction is of particular importance. This is the distinction between language as representation and language as communication. It is of critical significance because theories of language and thought are often based on the implicit assumption that one or the other focus is the key to defining language. Even though such assumptions have a powerful impact on a theory's definition of language, they are seldom made explicit. The result is that unnoticed differences on this point produce misunderstandings about what view of language is being proposed and related to thought.

Approaches that view language as a means of representation focus on the fact that linguistic units such as words and sentences can be used to represent events and objects. Of particular importance in this connection is the claim that such linguistic representation makes it possible for the individual to plan and reason about events and objects that are not present in the immediate perceptual field. Indeed, such representation makes it possible for an individual to reason about events and objects that he or she has never experienced. Investigators such as Luria (1976), Scribner (1977), and Tulviste (1978) have studied these processes in their examination of syllogistic reasoning. As we will see, Piaget and Vygotsky also argue that language as representation plays a role in thought processes.

When investigators study language as representation, they often focus on the linguistic code as a formal system. For example, they may focus on the options in a language for combining words into clauses or for coordinating several propositions into a sentence. The options available in a language are defined by a grammar. For this reason, researchers sometimes assume that the study of the child's emerging mastery of the grammatical system of a language can provide insight into the development of thought.

Much of the current interest among linguists and psycholinguists in grammar can be traced back to Chomsky's (1957, 1965) formulation of transformational generative grammar. Chomsky's main interest was syntax (a description of how words combine to form sentences). He argued that an account of the syntax of a language can be provided by a finite system of rules that can generate all the acceptable sentences of that language and no unacceptable ones. Some of the assumptions that underlie most grammatical analyses are similar to assumptions that guide Piaget's investigations of cognitive structures. For example, like Piaget's analysis of cognition, Chomsky's analysis of language distinguishes content and structure. It assumes that the development of formal systems of grammatical relationships can be studied relatively independent of the meaning of language. It also assumes that a structure can be formulated as a logic, as a system of invariant relationships under apparent transformation of content. Finally, it assumes that language development is to be studied as a cognitive competence distinct from specific performances.

Given these assumptions, one would expect a broad parallelism of cognitive and grammatical development. However, attempts to document this parallelism have met with limited success, at least partly because the "logics" involved in grammar and in Piaget's approach are related, if at all, only at a very general level of abstraction. For example, the principles of reversibility that concern Piaget are quite different from the rules of linguistic transformation proposed by Chomsky and his colleagues. As a result, such parallelisms which at first might seem to be natural candidates for relating language and thought do not stand up under scrutiny.

In contrast to those who have focused on the grammatical properties of language and its use as a means of representation, some theorists have viewed language primarily in terms of its use in human communication. In such cases the term language is employed to refer to communicative processes. It often has little to do with properties of the linguistic code and their potential for respresentation. A focus on language as communication might lead an investigator to examine the processes of dialogue and role-taking. These are processes that involve language, but their focus is not on representation and formal linguistic structure. Rather, the focus is on properties of collaborative activities that happen to use language as a medium.

A focus on language as communication need not be incompatible with a focus on representation. Those who study language as communication do not deny that it has formal structural properties or that language can be used to represent objects and events. Conversely, those who study language as representation do not deny that language is used in communication. However, theories of language and thought often focus on one interpretation of language and essentially ignore the other. Such a focus has a powerful impact on the kinds of questions asked and the research methods used. In order to make accurate comparisons among such theories it is therefore essential to recognize their respective emphases on this matter. In our review of Piaget, Vygotsky, and Mead we will ask in each case what is meant by language.

Unmediated and Mediated Psychological Processes

The second major question we must ask when examining accounts of language and thought is, "What is meant by thought?" We will argue that there are major differences in how theories answer this question. In particular, we will see that they differ in their assumptions about the origins and properties of the representational means used in thought.

As with analyses of language, analyses of thought invoke many different distinctions. However, one distinction that plays a role in virtually all theories of cognitive development is of particular interest for our purposes. This is the distinction between psychological processes that rely on perceptual and sensori-motor activity in the immediate context and psychological processes that utilize representational means that allow them to be carried out in the absence of such contextual support. The key to this distinction is the presence or absence of some system of mediation.

Such a system provides the representational means that make decontextualized psychological processes possible. Because of the centrality of mediation, we term these processes that are tied to the perceptual and sensorimotor context "un-mediated psychological processes" and those processes that are not context bound in this way "mediated psychological processes."

One or another version of this general distinction has been proposed by many philosophers and psychologists. For example, in developing a schema-based cognitive psychology Neisser (1976) has introduced the notion of the "detachment of schemata" to deal with the differences between what we call unmediated and mediated psychological processes. While Neisser's primary concern when analyz-ing schemata is perception, he notes that

> ...schemata can be detached from the cycles in which they are originally embedded; such detachment is the basis of all the higher mental processes. What happens then is not perceiving, however, but imagining, planning, or intending. (1976, p. 23)

Neisser illustrates this general claim with the following example of a detachment of a schema.

> Perceiving [a] dog (or anything) takes time, it involves schematic anticipation as well as information pickup.... Later on, the process of detachment will begin: the word *doggie* will create a visual readiness even when [the child] knows that the dog is nowhere nearby and is not really to be expected. Thus the names of things become able to evoke images of them, with incalculable consequences. (1976, pp. 166–167)

The "incalculable consequences" Neisser has in mind here are the emergence of mediated, decontextualized psychological processes.

Any theory of cognitive development must deal with the fact that the child initially operates only on objects and events that are spatiotemporally present and later develops the ability to deal with these phenomena in their absence. Theories differ, however, in exactly how and why mediated psychological processes develop. First, they disagree about what form of representation or mediation is involved. In particular, some theories view language as playing a central role in this representation, while others do not. Second, theories of cognitive development differ over the time when mediated psychological processes begin to emerge in ontogenesis. This, of course, is tied to the first point. Third, theories hold differing views on whether the emergence of mediated psychological processes occurs in the form of a single qualitative change or as a continuum of several steps. In one sense a continuum interpretation is compatible with all theorists we will examine; all of them argue that mediated processes develop over an extended period in onto-genesis, not fully maturing until early adolescence. In another sense, however, their approaches argue for a dichotomy. This stems from the fact that each theorist tends to emphasize some single source of mediated processes and to view other developmental events and trends as less important and/or as extensions of this qualitative change. For this reason it is possible in each case to identify a single qualitative change in ontogenesis that the theorist views as being responsible for the emergence of mediated psychological processes.

PIAGET'S OBSERVATIONS OF COGNITION AND LANGUAGE

In considering the relation of language to thought we must start by noting the problem of circularity that is involved in much of the thinking about the subject. This circularity has arisen because some theorists have defined thought in terms of language. In particular, there has been a tendency to interrelate or even equate mediated psychological processes and a knowledge of the structure of language. If the two are identified, the question of causal relationships or interrelationships cannot arise.

This identification of cognitive development with language has been character-istic of certain Soviet cognitive psychologists combining the Pavlovian tradition with a Marxist sociology. (As we will see, this comment does not apply to Vygotsky.) For these psychologists, higher mental processes are equated with language or "the second signal system" and its internalization. As the doctrine of the second signal system is applied to child development, it holds that the chief features of cognitive development are caused by "internalization of language." Soviet investigators such as Luria (1959, 1969) have argued that very young children initially respond to language by others as "signals" or stimuli much like other external signals, and emit verbal responses as signals or stimuli for others. With development, language becomes distinct from external stimuli, is used for self-direction, and facilitates inferences between the external situations and responses. This, as "the internalization of language," is assumed by writers like Sokolov (1969) to cause or be the essence of cognitive development.

According to Sokolov (1969),

> The theoretical point of departure...[is] the principle of the unity and reciprocity [of thought and speech] in the process of human cognitive activity.
>
> According to this principle, thought is not only expressed in speech but is formed and carried out in it. Language not only gives names to objects, but permits the abstraction of their properties and relationships. Language leads to generalization in the form of concepts and their objectification in the form of words and other symbols. It is therefore concluded that abstract thinking is impossible without language (in the broad sense of the word) and that in man all thinking is based on language. (pp. 531–532)

Related to the Soviet assumption about the unity of thought and speech is the assumption that higher mental processes are a product of, or internalization of, the culture through social learning. Sokolov (1969) says:

> As the individual assimilates the socially reinforced system of words and the grammatical rules of their changes and combinations in sentences, he also assimiliates all the associated logical forms and thought processes. (p. 532)

This statement equates thought with language as representation. The circularity in this conception is partly due to a materialist epistemology. If human cognition is not a Pavlovian physiological connection, it at least has a physical substratum, the word. The objectivity or substantiality of the word is also guaranteed by a sociological epistemology—by the view that social structure and its language culture are "real" in a sense that individual phenomena are not. Aside from epistemological presuppositions, however, there is a natural tendency toward a circular equation of the social contribution toward cognition with the social medium of language itself. Insofar as cognition and cognitive development are distinctively related to culture, it is easy to interpret the cause of cultural influences on cognition as being the language medium through which cultural influences on cognition are largely coded and transmitted.

In summary, most theories that identify thought with language and its internalization rest on circularities in the definition of language and thought. They start with a valid observation, that thought is universally influenced by society. They illegitimately reduce the causal influence of society on cognition to the linguistic medium of society's influence, and they reduce the cognitive effect of socialization to its linguistic products.

To avoid this pitfall and to validly talk about relationships between thought and language, we must first define and observe the two in independent terms and than relate them. The major problem in doing this involves the difficulty of observing thought apart from language (of inferring thought patterns in a way that is not dependent on what the child says). Piaget was the first psychologist to work out systematic methods of observing cognitive development without relying on language. Based on these methods, he concluded that thought development in children is largely independent of language.

To consider Piaget's conclusions, we must examine in more detail what it means to observe cognition or thought independently of language. The first point to emphasize in this regard is that Piaget's claims about the role of language in thought should not be confused with his claims about the role of representation or mediation in thought. Indeed a major point of his argument is that a fundamental change occurs in ontogenesis because of the emergence of representation, representation that is not, however, dependent on language. According to him, the origins of representation are to be found in play and imitation. The following quotation from Piaget (1962) reveals the essential role of this representation in the transition from sensorimotor intelligence (Piaget's version of unmediated psychological processes) to representational intelligence (Piaget's version of mediated psychological processes).

> At an earlier stage, the development of sensory-motor intelligence is. . .determined by the equilibrium between these two functions [i.e., assimilation and accommodation]—the two poles of any adaptation—but it is then only present assimilation and accommodation that are in question. . . . Representation, on the contrary, is characterized by the fact that it goes beyond the present, extending the field of adaptation both in space and time. In other words, it evokes what lies outside the immediate perceptual and active field. (p. 273)

This statement reveals that Piaget makes a clear distinction between unmediated and mediated psychological processes. At this general level his ideas parallel those of other theorists. However, important differences between his and others' accounts arise when we consider how representation is defined. Therefore, we need to examine more closely what Piaget means by representation. For Piaget, the problem of representation is a problem of individual psychology. He views the child's mastery of the collective signs of language as an extension of more fundamental representational activity that emerges in the individual independently of the development of language. This early representational activity appears in the form of play, dreams, and imitation. In the first pages of his major work on this topic Piaget (1962) is quite clear about his views on the individual origins of representation and its independence from language.

> We shall. . .try to show that the acquisition of language is itself subordinated to the working of a symbolic function which can be seen in the development of imitation and play as well as in that of verbal mechanisms. Our study of the beginnings of representation in the child will mainly be in those fields where the individual processes of mental life dominate the collective factors, and we shall emphasise these individual

processes particularly in the case of imitation, which though it leads to inter-individual relationships does not necessarily result from them. (pp. 1–2)

Piaget's claims about the individual, nonlinguistic origins of representation are extremely important when trying to make comparisons between his ideas and the ideas of other theorists such as Vygotsky and Mead. While Piaget admitted that "the collective institution of language is the main factor in both the formation and socialization of representations" (1962, p. 273), he emphasized that he saw the real origins of representational intelligence in the individual processes of assimilation and accommodation. He viewed the emergence of language and verbal communication as introducing no qualitative change in the representational activity of the child. Instead of focusing on any fundamental change that might emerge with the mastery of language, Piaget argued that the major transition (i.e., from sensori-motor to representational intelligence) occurs without the involvement of language. Furthermore, since he accounted for this transition in terms of the functional constants of assimilation and accommodation, he emphasized the continuity rather than the fundamental change that occurs with the advent of representational activity.

> ...in the field of play and imitation it is possible to trace the transition from sensori-motor assimilation and accommodation to the mental assimilation and accommodation which characterise the beginnings of representation. Representation begins when there is simultaneous differentiation and co-ordination between "signifiers" and "signified." The first differentiations are provided by imitation and the mental image derived from it, both of which extend accommodation to external objects. The meanings of the symbols, on the other hand, come by way of assimilation, which is the dominating factor in play and plays an equal part with accommodation in adapted representation. Having progressively separated at the sensory-motor level and so developed as to be capable of going beyond the immediate present, assimilation and accommodation finally come together in a combination made necessary by this advance beyond the immediate present.... Our first hypothesis...will therefore be that there is functional continuity between the sensory-motor and the representational, a continuity which determines the construction of the successive structures. (1962, pp. 2–3)

To summarize, Piaget viewed language as only one aspect of representational intelligence and viewed representational intelligence itself as emerging through nonlinguistic forms of representational activity (e.g., symbolic play and deferred imitation). Furthermore, he emphasized the continuities rather than the qualitative differences between sensorimotor and representational intelligence. With this in mind, let us turn to some of his specific claims.

In making his claim that representational intelligence emerges without language, Piaget was particularly concerned with the later phases of the sensorimotor period when early forms of representation are beginning to emerge. The period in question is one without genuine communication.

Given these facts, the only question to be raised about Piaget's conclusion is whether sensorimotor actions really reflect thinking (when defined as a mediated psychological process). The first implication of the notion that a child is thinking is that the child in able to represent objects or events not immediately present. A second implication that emerges from this representational ability is that the child can make inferences, that is, can use these representations to construct or combine relationships not previously perceived together in a single perceptual field. A third criterion of thinking is that the child can generalize, that is, can treat perceptually distinct objects as functionally equivalent. At Piaget's higher sensorimotor stages, the infant clearly demonstrates these attributes of generalization, representation, and inference implied by the concept of thinking. As an example, the child will seize a rake to use as a tool to pull in a toy that is out of reach. Thus mediated psychological processes, at least in their early forms, can be seen in operation at these later stages of the sensorimotor period. For this reason, we would argue that Piaget's claim that early forms of genuine thinking can develop without language is relatively noncontroversial.

The second claim that Piaget made about language and thought is more controversial. This is the claim that logical thinking or concrete operations can be accounted for without recognizing any unique and inherent contribution of language. The two chief areas of concrete operational thought are classification and quantitative relations. It is particularly astounding that Piaget should claim that classification can develop its concrete logical features without requiring language. Almost all students of classification prior to Piaget assumed that these logical features emerged from the apprehension of the verbal classes and the relations between classes (complementarity, inclusion, etc.) given by the language. In contrast, Piaget argued that these logical features of concrete-operational classification represent reversible coordinations of these classifying actions.

Assessment of the validity of Piaget's claim that concrete-operational logic develops without direct reliance on language depends on our ability to observe concrete-operational thought apart from verbal indicators. It has been shown that some concrete-operational tasks such as a conservation task can be passed "nonverbally." These tasks or observations of concrete operations are not completely devoid of language usage as are Piaget's sensorimotor tasks. Some instructions must be communicated to the child and absolute certainty that the response is concrete-operational usually requires a verbal response to the question, "Why?" Nevertheless, experience administering these tasks to children lends conviction that they represent an assessment process that does not simply measure the language skills of the child.

Given the possibility of observing concrete operations without relying on language, several potential tests of Piaget's claims present themselves. For example, one could observe how the emergence of certain linguistic skills in children affects their performance on concrete operational tests. A second approach would be to examine the performance of deaf children on concrete operational tasks. Both of these approaches have been used by Piagetians.

For example, Sinclair (1969) has conducted a study in which she assessed the impact of verbal training on concrete operational abilities. She began by pointing out that "correct" linguistic usage of certain relational or logical terms is correlated with the attainment of concrete operations in conservation and seriation. She then went on to examine whether or not this correlation of language and logic is to be explained as language development causing cognitive development. The answer seems to be "No." Sinclair was able to train "correct" discrimination and application of several specific linguistic terms of relationship, but this led to no increased attainment of logical operations on Piagetian tasks.

Sinclair's study is an attempt to examine the causal relationship between an aspect of the grammatical organization of language and a mediated psychological process. She focused on a specific aspect of the abstract semantic system and its relationship with concrete operational abilities—that is, she focused on one aspect of language as representation. While her study provides a response to one type of question that can be posed about language-cognitive relationships, it leaves other questions open, especially those about other aspects of language as representation and language as communication.

As we noted earlier, a second way to examine the influence of language on concrete operations is to observe the logical development of deaf children without language. This is just what Furth (1966, 1971) has undertaken. If mastery of language is critical for the development of the logical aspects of thinking, deaf children should be retarded on concrete operational tasks. In fact, however, Furth found that concrete-operational thought develops almost on schedule among the deaf.*

Although Furth has presented impressive evidence in support of his claims,† several questions remain unanswered. First, it is not always clear what is meant by language in this research. It seems that the primary concern is with language as representation (e.g., syntactic and semantic structure). If this is the case and spoken language is not used by the children, the question then arises as to whether alternative forms of language as communication such as manual signing could introduce the child to equally complex forms of language as representation. Based on recent studies of signing systems, linguists have come to argue more and more that its grammatical organization, while different, may be no less complex than what is found in spoken language. Thus it is not necessarily the case that deaf children have failed to master a form of language as representation.

---

* The findings on the deaf are particularly striking when they are compared with a study of some aspects of concrete-operational thinking in the blind (Nordin, 1968). While of average intelligence on a verbal intelligence test, these blind children were three to four years retarded on the Piagetian tasks. These finds at least suggest the importance of visual observation of physical objects and one's actions upon them for attainment of concrete logic.

† The Furth studies suggest that language is not even a necessary, much less a sufficient, condition for logical operations.

Second, it is important to note that many children in Furth's studies were not entirely deaf and/or had not been deaf from birth. This raises the question of early (and "partial") experiences with spoken language.

These questions identify potential problem areas for Furth's studies. However, we should note that these questions have only been raised at this point. No one has produced solid evidence to refute Furth's argument. Therefore, we would argue that his research presents a formidable challenge to those who would argue that mediated psychological processes are heavily dependent on language. Furth's findings on the deaf are surprising because they do not fit our ordinary experience with "normal" children in whom language and thought development are linked. In part, our experience with normal children is specious because we do not observe thought independently of language. In part, however, our observations of normal development are correct and there are basic parallelisms or correlations between language development and thought development observed independently.

Our usual interpretations of these correlations are incorrect, however. We assume that correlation is causation, that language (development) causes thought or that it is a necessary condition for thought development. A crude example of this kind of interpretation is the often repeated claim that verbal intelligence tests tap the verbal learning favored in middle-class settings. The basis of such an interpretation is the fact that vocabulary tests—tests of the number of words known by a child—correlate well with total intelligence test performance. Although verbal exposure does enter into vocabulary performance, nonverbal general intelligence (in the British biological sense of Chapter 5) is also a major determinant of vocabulary performance. Smart children (in IQ test terms) learn more words; learning more words does not make children smart. The Raven's matrices, a relatively nonverbal and culture-free test of general intelligence, predicts to vocabulary; the reverse (that vocabulary contributes to matrices performance) is much less clearly the case.

When we focus on the development of skills in the grammatical organization of language and the relationship of these skills to thought, we can draw the following conclusion. There is a general, as yet undefined conception of cognitive development underlying both grammatical-linguistic stages and Piagetian logical-intellectual stages. In this interpretation, the specific cognitive attainments of a given Piagetian logical stage are not necessary for attainment of the parallel linguistic stage, nor is the specific attainment of a linguistic stage necessary for attainment of the parallel logical stage, but these are more general cognitive features of both linguistic and logical stages that link the two.

This conclusion has been reached by several researchers concerned with early language development. For example, there are parallelisms between independent observations of the mastery of the grammatical organization of language and of Piagetian cognitive development. These parallelisms or correlations are best understood as due to a general factor of intelligence or cognition underlying both of them. As stated by Brown (1973),

Though the order of acquistion of linguistic knowledge will prove to be approximately invariant across children learning one language. . .the rate of progression will vary radically among children. . . . I will. . .predict that. . .the rate will. . .be dependent on what the intelligence testers call *g* or general intelligence. . . . Studying the early I.Q. items of Binet and Simon and Terman, I have been fascinated by several linguistic subsets but especially by one that involves imitating sentences, with more and more syllables as chronological age advances. The authors of these items thought in terms of syllables but. . .I see also an order of increasing cumulative [grammatical] complexity. (p. 408)

What interpretation are we to make of parallelisms in language and cognition if language development is neither a necessary nor sufficient condition of cognitive development? One alternative is that Piagetian cognitive stages and activity cause or determine language development. This appears to be true, but only partly true. Brown (1973) interprets his first stage of language as reflecting the achievements of Piaget's highest stage of sensorimotor intelligence. He says:

. . .the linguistic process does not start from nothing and can build on data that are not linguistic. Agent, object, datives of indirect object, and person affected constructions. . .presuppose the knowledge that the self, other persons and objects are all potentially "sources of causality," or initiators of forces and also, potentially, recipients of forces. Piaget judges this knowledge to be entirely lacking in the early sensori-motor stages. . . . In sum, I think that the first sentences express the construction of reality which is the terminal achievement of sensori-motor intelligence. (Brown, 1973, p. 200)

Piaget (1967) advanced a second interpretation that sees language and thought as two related sides of a more general developmental process.

In the last analysis, both [language and thought] development depend on intelligence itself, which antedates language and is independent of it. (p. 98)

In saying this, Piaget meant that a full description of intelligence and its development would include the cognitive features of language development as well as the cognitive features of the child's direct actions on objects and persons given in Piaget's sensorimotor stages. He meant also, however, that for him sensorimotor development is more essential than language development for a core concept of intelligence as adaptive organization of action.

In addition to viewing intelligence as underlying both language and thought, Piaget also sees language and thought as independent terms in interaction with one another. Piaget says (1967):

Language is. . .a necessary but not sufficient condition for the construction of logical operations. . . . [L]anguage and thought are linked in a genetic circle where each necessarily leans on the other in interdependent formation (p. 98).

Overall, Piaget's view of the interaction of language and thought stresses the primacy of thought development in this interaction. He says:

> As language is only a particular form of the symbolic function and as the individual symbol is certainly simpler than the collective sign, it is permissible to conclude that thought precedes language and that language confines itself to profoundly transforming thought by helping it to attain its forms of equilibrium by means of a more advanced schematization and a more mobile abstraction. (1967, pp. 91–92)
> ...the structures that characterize thought have their roots in action and in sensorimotor mechanisms deeper than linguistics. (1967, p. 98)

Piaget stresses that language aids cognitive development mainly by providing tools for the cognitive organization the child is striving toward in any case. Piaget also believes that the importance of these tools becomes greater the higher or more abstract the logical organization the child is striving toward. He says:

> ...the more the structures of thought are refined, the more language is necessary for the achievement of this elaboration. (1967, p. 98)

Piaget believes that language is irrelevant to the formation, consolidation, and use of sensorimotor intelligence, is of more importance for concrete operations, and is still more critical for formal operational development. This is because most formal operational thought depends on a formulation in terms of abstract classes and propositions as the material for thought. Although not all formal operational solutions of problems depend on formulation in linguistic propositions, many problems do require linguistic formulations for formal operational solutions. It is important to recognize that when Piaget speaks of language, his focus is strictly on language as representation.

We have discussed at length Piaget's view of the interaction of thought and language as independent elements, and it is almost inevitable that one arrives at Piaget's view of thought or cognition as primary. Language is the tool of thought and thought development in a much more real sense than thought is the tool of language.

VYGOTSKY'S APPROACH TO RELATIONS OF LANGUAGE TO THOUGHT—"EMERGENT INTERACTIONISM"

During the years when Piaget was beginning to develop his approach in Geneva, the Soviet psychologist Lev Semenovich Vygotsky (1896–1934) was outlining an important alternative position on the relationship between language and thought. Vygotsky was familiar with Piaget's early research on egocentrism. In fact, he was the editor of a volume of translations of Piaget's early works, and he wrote a long introductory essay in which he outlined a critique and an alternative to Piaget's early ideas. This essay, originally published in 1932, later served as a chapter in

Vygotsky's most important book, *Thought and Language* (1934). Piaget did not read Vygotsky's work until the English translation of *Thought and Language* appeared in 1962. Since this was long after Vygotsky's death, the two authors did not have the opportunity to engage in direct debate.

Like Piaget, Vygotsky made a fundamental distinction between unmediated and mediated psychological processes. Instead of using Piaget's distinction between sensorimotor and representational intelligence, however, he contrasted "elementary" (or "lower," "rudimentary," "natural") and "higher" (or "cultural") mental functions. Vygotsky (1978) used the following criteria to distinguish these functions:

> The central characteristic of elementary functions is that they are totally and directly determined by stimulation from the environment. For higher functions, the central feature is self-generated stimulation, that is, the creation and use of artificial stimuli which become the immediate causes of behavior. (p. 39)

This quotation reveals that at a very general level Vygotsky and Piaget shared a common concern for the distinction between unmediated and mediated psychological processes. Both investigators were concerned with representational means that make it possible for humans to operate on objects and events that are not part of the immediate perceptual or sensorimotor field. However, major differences between the two become apparent as soon as we consider the mechanisms they cited as giving rise to mediated psychological processes. For Piaget, the crucial event in the development of mediated psychological processes is the emergence of representation in play and imitation. As we noted earlier, he acknowledged the role of language in representational intelligence, but viewed language as just one of several forms of representation. For him, the development of language produces no qualitative change in the development of representation and thought.

For Vygotsky (1978), on the other hand, the integration of linguistic mediation into the child's general functioning causes a major qualitative change.

> ...*the most significant moment in the course of intellectual development, which gives birth to the purely human forms of practical and abstract intelligence, occurs when speech and practical activity, two previously completely independent lines of development, converge.* Although children's use of tools during their preverbal period is comparable to that of apes, as soon as speech and the use of signs are incorporated into any action, the action becomes transformed and organized along entirely new lines. (p. 24)

This statement reflects a major critical difference between Vygotsky and Piaget. While both theorists agreed that language plays a role in mediated psychological processes, Vygotsky argued that the development of language itself produces a qualitative change in the development of such processes, whereas Piaget did not. Thus the two differed over the nature of mediated psychological processes and their causes.

To understand more fully the differences between these two theorists, we must place Vygotsky's claim in the broader context of his general theoretical approach. We begin by pointing out that Vygotsky did not equate thought and language. As we noted earlier, any coherent account of the relationship between thought and language must begin with an examination of the two in independent terms. Instead of equating them, Vygotsky viewed thought and language as being connected through what we shall call "emergent interactionism." In his theory, emergent interactionism is what produces mediated psychological processes. Vygotsky (1956) outlined the general tenets of this process as follows:

1. We find different roots in the ontogenetic development of thought and speech.
2. In the development of the child's speech we clearly can identify a preintellectual stage, and in the development of thought a prespeech stage.
3. Up to a certain point the two develop along separate lines, independently of one another.
4. At a certain point, the two lines meet, whereupon thought *becomes* verbal, and speech *becomes* intellectual. (1956, p. 134)

These basic tenets of emergent interactionism reflect the differences between Vygotsky and Piaget. Piaget asked, "What in general is the interaction of thought and speech conceived as independent elements?" and concluded that insofar as they interact, thought is primary. Vygotsky, instead, asked the question, "Are there particular phases of development of language and thought in which the two interact in such a way as to create qualitatively new forms of thought-in-speech?"

We would emphasize that the essential feature of "emergent interactionism" is the claim that at certain points in ontogenesis qualitatively unique forms of verbal thought arise that cannot be reduced to prior thought or prior speech as independent elements. Vygotsky started by objecting to theories that identify thought and speech, whether by reducing thought to inner speech (Watson's behaviorist notion that thought was "speech minus sound") or by reducing speech to the expression of thought (the Wurzberg school). He also objected to efforts to define language and thought independently of one another rather than defining a unity of thought-and-speech. Vygotsky was not objecting to the general definition and study of language and thought as independent terms as in Piaget's approach. He was objecting to carrying these independent definitions over to the special areas in which the interaction of thought and speech is "emergent." He proposed, instead, to study as a single irreducible unit "verbal thought" or "word meanings." A word meaning, he claimed, cannot be defined independently of a thought element (since it implies a concept or generalization) nor can it be defined independently of a language element. Vygotsky took as his program the study of the development of verbal thoughts or verbal concepts conceived as this indissolvable union of language and thought.

For Vygotsky, prespeech intellect is a general term for elementary mental processes (i.e., Vygotsky's version of unmediated psychological processes). His account of elementary functions was largely borrowed from the developmental and comparative psychology of his day. For example, he often relied heavily on Kohler's (1925) ideas about the unmediated problem-solving behaviors in apes, and he is very interested in the ideas of Buhler (1930) about the similarities between early "technical thinking" in children and the thinking of chimpanzees. This research was conducted before Piaget had made many of his major discoveries about the nature of sensorimotor intelligence. However, the following passage from Vygotsky (1978) reveals that his notion of unmediated "technical thinking" shares some important traits with what Piaget would later describe as part of the later stages in the sensorimotor period.

> Buhler interpreted the manifestations of practical intelligence in children as being of exactly the same type as those we are familiar with in chimpanzees. Indeed, there is a phase in the life of the child that Buhler designated the "chimpanzee age." One ten-month-old infant whom he studied was able to pull a string to obtain a cookie that was attached to it. The ability to remove a ring from a post by lifting it rather than trying to pull it sideways did not appear until the middle of the second year. (p. 21)

For Vygotsky, a major point of such elementary mental functioning is that it is relatively context bound because it is not mediated by speech. For him it is important that Buhler was led to conclude "that the beginnings of practical intelligence in the child . . . as well as actions of the chimpanzee, are independent of speech" (1978, p. 21).

When considering Vygotsky's account of elementary functions and prespeech intellect, it is important for us to recognize that it is quite unsophisticated by today's standards. At the time when he was writing, no one understood the complex developmental changes that Piaget (1952) was later to outline in the sensorimotor stage. As a result, Vygotsky's account of elementary mental functions stands in need of revision in light of contemporary research. For example, by taking into account the emergence of the early forms of representation identified by Piaget (1952, 1962) in play and imitation, Vygotsky's account could be strengthened. First, it could be revised so that it recognizes changes in representational capacity that occur independently of language acquisition. Furthermore, because he says so little about the natural line of development or prespeech intellect, Vygotsky cannot specify its role in the development of higher mental functions. Recall that his account is based on emergent interactionism, and thereby calls on him to specify how speech interacts with, and transforms, aspects of prespeech intellect. While he focused on what transforms this intellect, he said very little about the nature of what it is that is transformed, a criticism that has been raised by Soviet theorists such as Rubinshtein (1957). In general, therefore, we would argue that Piaget's account of development in the sensorimotor period is a superior alternative to Vygotsky's notion of elementary mental functions and should be incorporated into Vygotsky's account of emergent interactionism.

This does not mean, however, that Piaget's overall approach can replace

Vygotsky's. To do that, Piaget's approach would have to be able to provide an alternative to Vygotsky's account of the emergent interaction between such speech and preverbal intellect, an interaction that leads to higher mental functions. Whereas Vygotsky devoted relatively little effort to understanding the complexities of elementary mental functions, his account of the role of speech in the ontogenesis of higher mental functions is unique and insightful even by today's standards.

The key to understanding Vygotsky's ideas about higher mental functions and the role of language in their development is to realize that for him higher mental functions have social origins. By this we mean that in order to understand Vygotsky's account of the nature and development of higher mental functions we must examine the communication in which the child participates and how this communication reflects the broader sociocultural milieu.

Along with Vygotsky's emphasis on language, this is a second point on which his approach differs fundamentally from Piaget's. As we saw earlier, Piaget insisted that we must understand processes in the individual before we can understand processes in the social milieu. When Vygotsky considered elementary mental processes, he too argued that the individual is the sole focus of investigation. However, when he considered higher mental processes, his argument was the opposite; he argued that in order to understand the psychological processes of individuals we must begin by going *outside* the individual and studying social interaction and communication. This is a point on which Vygotsky (1981b) criticized much of the psychological research of his day.

> Formerly, psychologists tried to derive social behavior from individual behavior. They investigated individual responses observed in the laboratory and then studied them in the collective. They studied how the individual's responses change in the collective setting. Posing the problem in such a way is, of course, quite legitimate; but genetically speaking, it deals with the second level in behavioral development. The first problem is to show how the individual response emerges from the forms of collective life. In contrast to Piaget, we hypothesize that development does not proceed toward socialization, but toward the conversion of social relations into mental functions. (pp. 164–165)

Thus we see that for Vygotsky, the development of higher mental functions is primarily a matter of participating in, and gradually mastering, social interaction. He made it quite clear that this was his major interest.

> We place this transition from a social influence outside the individual to a social influence within the individual at the center of our research and try to elucidate the most important factors that give rise to this transition. (1960, p. 116)
>
> It is not nature, but society that above all must be considered to be the major factor in the determination of human behavior. It is in this that the whole idea of the cultural development [i.e., the development of higher mental functions] of the child is comprised. (1960, p. 118)

So far, we have identified two points that distinguish Vygotsky's approach from Piaget's. First, Vygotsky argued that the development of linguistic mediation creates a qualitative change in the development of thought, whereas Piaget saw it as only one aspect of another qualitative change. Second, Vygotsky argued that certain individual psychological processes can be understood only by understanding the social and communicative processes that give rise to them, whereas Piaget focused on individual processes (e.g., assimilation, accommodation) as the key to explanation.

These two points are of course not unrelated in Vygotsky's approach. Indeed, Vygotsky was concerned with language and speech precisely because their interaction provides the mechanism for "the conversion of social relations into mental functions." Instead of viewing language simply as one of several forms of representation that mediate individual psychological processes, Vygotsky began by focusing on its role in communication and social interaction. For him, language is primarily a means of social interaction and only secondarily a means for mediating individual psychological processes.

> The initial function of speech is the function of communication, social connection, influencing others (children influencing adults as well as being influenced by them). Thus the initial speech of the child is purely social. To call it socialized would be incorrect since this word is tied to the presupposition of something that is initially nonsocial, something that becomes social only in the process of its change and development. (1956, p. 86)

This does not mean that Vygotsky was uninterested in the role of speech in mediating individual processes. Indeed, this was his main focus of research. It does mean, however, that he emphasized that the developmental analysis of higher mental processes must begin with an examination of their linguistically mediated social origins. He made this point in a variety of ways, but his most general statement of it can be seen in his formulation of the "general genetic law of cultural development" (i.e., the development of higher mental functions).

> Any function in the child's cultural development appears twice, or on two planes. First it appears on the social plane, and then on the psychological plane. First it appears between people as an interpsychological category, and then within the child as an intrapsychological category. This is equally true with regard to voluntary attention, logical memory, the formation of concepts, and the development of volition. (1981b, p. 163)

Vygotsky viewed the use of language (or, more generally, the use of signs) as central in this transition from interpsychological to intrapsychological functioning.

> The history of signs, however, brings us to a much more general law governing the

development of behavior. Janet calls it the fundamental law of psychology. The essence of this law is that in the process of development, children begin to use the same forms of behavior in relation to themselves that others initially used in relation to them. Children master the social forms of behavior and transfer these forms to themselves. With regard to our area of interest, we could say that the validity of this law is nowhere more obvious than in the use of the sign. A sign is always originally a means used for social purposes, a means of influencing others, and only later becomes a means of influencing oneself. (1981b, p. 157)

These comments by Vygotsky reflect an important point about his notion of language. He did not assume that one must choose between a focus on language as representation and language as communication. Instead of examining one or the other in isolation, he worked on the assumption that human communication is possible *because* of representation; or, stated conversely, he assumed that linguistic representation emerges *because* of the demands of communication. Thus, unlike Piaget who focused on language as representation, Vygotsky argued for an approach to language that combines its representational and communicative powers.

There are two particular phenomena Vygotsky studied in connection with his notion of emergent interactionism: the development of word meanings or concepts and the internalization of speech. In both cases, he argued that intrapsychological functioning in higher mental processes can be understood only by examining its interpsychological origins, and he argued that language plays a unique and necessary role in this transition.

Vygotsky's Account of the Development of Word Meaning

For Vygotsky, one of the most important things a child masters in learning a language is a system of word meanings or concepts. He sees the process of mastering concepts as occurring over a long period of time, not being complete until early adolescence. This process has great importance for him since by mastering and coming to operate on this aspect of the representational system of language (i.e., semantics), the child obtains a way to regulate and organize activity independently of any immediate context. That is, the child can operate on the basis of a highly developed form of mediated psychological functioning.

The key to Vygotsky's argument in this case is his distinction between a word's meaning (znachenie) and its reference (predmetnoe otnesenie).

...it is necessary to distinguish...the meaning of a word or expression from its referent, i.e., the object designated by the word or expression. There may be one meaning and different objects or conversely, different meanings and one object. Whether we say "the victor of Jena" or "the loser at Waterloo," we refer to the same person (Napoleon). The meanings of the two expressions, however, are different. (1956, p. 191)

For Vygotsky this distinction "provides the key to the correct analysis of the development of early stages of children's thinking" (1956, p. 192). Its importance derives from the fact that it allowed Vygotsky to deal with the function of referring, or picking out particular objects independently of the function of classifying or categorizing these objects in terms of a context independent meaning category (i.e., in terms of the grammatical organization of language).

Vygotsky (1981c) argued that the ontogenetic origins of reference and meaning are to be found in the "indicatory function" of speech. By this he meant that words are first used and understood by the child as indicating or pointing out objects in the immediate context of speech. If the original function of speech in Vygotsky's account is the indicatory function, what mechanism does he propose for explaining how the child begins to develop word meanings or concepts? His answer is that the child goes through a series of developmental phases characterized by various levels of generalization and that the motivating force for change is social interaction with more mature members of a culture. His attempt to specify the nature of these changes constitutes an attempt to provide a detailed interpretation of his claim that "the levels of generalization in a child correspond strictly to the levels of development in social interaction." Of course this is a claim that is based on the assumption that language as representation and language as communication are inextricably linked. In his account of concept formation Vygotsky (1956) outlines an ontogenetic progression from "unorganized heaps" to "complexes" and then to "concepts" on the basis of a block sorting and classification task. In collaboration with several colleagues he used this task in a series of studies on concept formation. Vygotsky's main finding from this study was that the criteria and operations used in making block selections change during ontogenesis. It is only at later stages that children use stable categories in carrying out this task. Thus only then could one expect subjects to select a series of blocks on the basis of a stable criterion such as yellowness, tallness, largeness, yellowness and tallness, and so on.

One of Vygotsky's major contributions to this line of research was to demonstrate that development does not simply consist of switching from random selection to selection based on stable criteria. Instead, he proposed a developmental account that identifies the stages leading up to the stable functioning found in adults' performance. Vygotsky identified three basic levels in this development. First is the use of "unorganized heaps" by preschool children. At this level there is no criterion or set of criteria that an adult observer can discern as guiding the child's selection. In describing children's performance at this stage, Vygotsky wrote of the diffuse, unstable, syncretic image that unites the objects. The criteria used at this stage for selecting objects are often subjective and hence not obvious to an outside observer, but a few objective criteria may be in evidence at this early stage. Thus a child may group a tall, small, black cylinder with a short, large, yellow cube because the child sees the two as a chimney and a building. Then the child may add a yellow block that matches the yellow one already selected, and may add a red cube because it is pretty, and so on.

The second period in Vygotsky's account of concept development is the period of "thinking in complexes." Vygotsky (1956) wrote that

> ...the generalizations created with the help of this mode of thinking are *complexes of various concrete objects* or things. The objects are no longer related on the basis of the child's subjective ties or impressions, but *on the basis of objective connections that actually exist among the objects.* (p. 168)

Vygotsky outlined several types of complexes on the basis of the criteria that guide subjects' selection of blocks. Although he noted important differences among the forms of thinking in complexes, he emphasized that they are united by the fact that they are tied to the concrete context in which the subject carries out the task.

An examination of what he called a "chain complex" illustrates this point.

> A chain complex is constructed in accordance with the principles of *a dynamic, temporary combination of various links into a single chain and the transmission of meaning through the individual links of this chain....* For example, when given a yellow triangle as the original block, the child may select several triangular blocks and then, if the last of these is blue, he may add other blue figures, say semicircles and circles. This in turn is sufficient to change to a new feature again and make subsequent selections on the basis of being round. During the process of forming a complex the subject constantly switches from one feature to another. (1956, p. 173)

From this example, we can see that rather than being governed by a single stable category throughout the task the subject is governed by properties of the concrete objects in the task setting. Specifically, he or she is governed by the iconic relationships among these objects in the context. This means that some feature or features of the objects themselves have taken on the role of the sign that regulates the subject's activity. Rather than the subject's using signs to structure the context, signs (icons) in the context are structuring the subject's activity.

The third period in Vygotsky's schema of conceptual development is when "genuine concepts" appear. Vygotsky argued that experience in educational activity is an important force that guides the development of genuine concepts, hence his distinction between the genuine or "scientific" concepts learned as a result of schooling and the "everyday" or "spontaneous" concepts learned by the child elsewhere. He argued that "the *absence of a system* is the cardinal psychological difference distinguishing spontaneous from scientific concepts" (1962, p. 116). The system he has in mind is the semantic system of language. In the case of spontaneous concepts, the child's attention "is always centered on the object to which the concept refers, never to the act of thought itself" (1962, p. 92). In contrast:

> In the scientific concepts that the child acquires in school, the relationship to an object is mediated from the start by some other concept. Thus the very notion of scientific

concept implies a certain position in relation to other concepts, i.e., a place within a system of concepts. (1962, p. 93)

With the development of scientific concepts, a child not only can use words such as "table," "chair," and "furniture" appropriately in connection with the objects to which they can be used to refer; the child can also operate on statements of logical equivalence, nonequivalence, entailment, and so on, such as "All tables are furniture."

For Vygotsky, the criterion that distinguishes scientific concepts from everyday concepts is the fact that the former are learned in a school setting, whereas the latter emerge on the basis of children's experience in the everyday world. He argued that schooling's emphasis on using language to talk about language, as opposed to talking only about nonlinguistic reality, is an important force in the emergence of scientific concepts.

Vygotsky argued that the development of scientific concepts has great significance for the evolution of higher psychological processes because these concepts necessarily involve conscious realization and hence voluntary control. For him this was a natural consequence of the systematicity imposed on scientific concepts by the nature of their presentation and mastery in instruction.

This interpretation of the role of scientific concepts in the development of conscious realization and voluntary control is of great importance in Vygotsky's account of the higher forms of human consciousness. It is through scientific concepts that humans can carry out mental activity in a way that is maximally independent of the concrete context. This does not mean that such mental activity is somehow purer or less bound by some form of constraints. After all, the semantic organization of language plays an important role in this respect. It does mean, however, that sociohistorically evolved semiotic mechanisms come to play an increasingly important role in mental functioning while the concrete context plays a decreasing role. This "trade-off" in the sources of control of mental activity is the topic of Vygotsky's research on complexes and concepts.

Thus we see that Vygotsky's account of concept development fulfills the criteria he established for the emergence of mediated psychological processes. First, development begins with social interaction (and hence language as communication). Thus, the account of concept development is framed in accordance with the general genetic law of cultural development. Second, this approach focuses on a specific aspect of language as representation—generalization and categorization—that produces changes in the individual child's psychological functioning.

Vygotsky's Analysis of the Internalization of Speech

The second area of development that Vygotsky studied from his emergent interactionism approach is the development of inner speech, or thought in the form of internalized speech. This development takes place, Vygotsky held, in the years 3 to 8. Before age 3 speech does not seem to play a unique cognitive function and verbal concepts have a structure and function much like concepts that do not center on words. During the 4-to-8 developmental era, however, children begin to talk to themselves overtly, then to think in words to themselves or silently. At this point of internalization, speech is first used for self-stimulation, to serve "thinking" functions (rather than expressive and communicative functions), and thinking first becomes heavily dependent on language. At this point, in Vygotsky's view, the two lines of development of thought and speech meet whereupon thought becomes verbal and speech rational (cognitively structured thought).

The phenomenon of "speech internalization" is a limited but fascinating and critical portion of the story of the relations between language and thought development. As Vygotsky (1962) wrote:

> No matter how we approach the controversial problem of the relationship between thought and speech, we shall have to deal extensively with *inner speech*. . . . But psychology still does not know how the change from overt to inner speech is accomplished. (p. 44)

In dealing with this problem, Vygotsky took up Piaget's (1926) work on "egocentric speech." Egocentric speech was defined by Piaget (1926) as speech "which is not addressed or adapted to another person and which is carried on with apparent satisfaction in the absence of any signs of understanding by a listener." Piaget showed that such speech is extensive among preschool children and declines from ages 5 to 10. He interpreted the decline as the result of the child's increased communicative competency. Corresponding to the preschool child's prelogic is the child's "egocentricity," the inability to differentiate one's own perspective from that of others or to take a perspective other than one's own reflected in one's own language and communication. As the child's ability and desire to take the other's point of view develops, "egocentric" speech declines. Piaget's label "egocentric speech" of course prejudges the interpretation of such speech. A more neutral term is "self-directed speech," assuming that at least part of the purpose of, or auditor for, the spoken words is the self.

Vygotsky started by questioning Piaget's interpretation of self-directed speech as egocentric. Piaget's interpretation implies that the child intends to communicate to another person but lacks either the skill or the will to take the other person's point of view and hence fails in communication. Vygotsky, instead, believed that the appearance of self-directed speech reflects the emergence of a new, self-regulative function that eventually produces inner speech; for him, self-directed speech is "a speech form found in the transition from external to inner speech" (1956, p. 87). It is because self-directed speech provides insight into the development and nature of inner speech that Vygotsky (1956) saw it as having "such enormous theoretical interest" (p. 87).

In his analysis of speech functions Vygotsky often stressed the transitional nature of self-directed speech. He viewed it as sharing characteristics both with external social speech and with internal self-regulative speech. Its external form is a reflection of the fact that the child has not fully differentiated this new speech function from the function of social contact and social interaction, and its emerging self-regulative function reflects its affinity with inner speech. Thus Vygotsky (1956) described self-directed speech as "inner speech in its psychological function and external speech in its physiological form" (p. 87). Roughly at the age of 7, self-directed speech disappears, a fact that Vygotsky attributed to its "going underground" to form inner speech. For him this is a product of the fact that the self-regulative function of speech has become clearly differentiated from its other functions (communication, contact, expression).

Data gathered by Vygotsky and subsequent researchers lend strong support to his interpretation of self-directed speech. These data specifically deal with two major questions he raises in his attempt to provide an alternative to Piaget's interpretation of egocentric speech. These two questions are: What is the function of self-directed speech? (i.e., self-regulation or manifestation of egocentric thinking); and what are the origins and fate of self-directed speech? (i.e., social origins and "going underground" to form inner speech or individual origins and atrophying with socialization). The data from several studies support his interpretation in both cases (i.e., the first alternative in each case).

Vygotsky's contention that the function of egocentric speech is to plan and regulate human action led him to argue that an increase in the cognitive difficulty of a task should result in an increase in children's use of self-directed speech. To test this hypothesis he used a technique in which an experimenter surreptitiously introduced an impediment into the flow of a child's action in order to observe the effect this would have on the child's use of self-directed speech. Vygotsky reported that

> Our research showed that the coefficient of children's egocentric speech, calculated for those points of increased difficulty, was almost twice the normal coefficient established by Piaget and the coefficient calculated for these same children in situations devoid of difficulties. (1956, p. 79)

This finding has received corroborative support in a study by Kohlberg, Yaeger, and Hjertholm (1968). These researchers compared the amount of overt directed speech that children (4, 6–5, 0) used in four task settings (bead stringing, easy jigsaw puzzle, building a block tower, hard jigsaw puzzle) and reported a statistically significant increase in the mean number of self-directed speech comments with an increase in task difficulty.

On the basis of his findings about the relationship between task difficulty and incidence of egocentric speech Vygotsky concluded that "egocentric speech very early...becomes a means of the child's realistic thinking." (1956, p. 84). He argued that his data clearly refute Piaget's claim that egocentric speech reflects egocentric thinking (and hence serves no useful function) and support his own claim about its role in planning and regulating action.

If Vygotsky's first criticism of Piaget's account of egocentric speech concerns the function of this speech form, his second criticism concerns the related issue of its origin and fate. In this connection he and his colleagues carried out a second set of studies. Vygotsky reasoned that if self-directed speech is "a speech form found in the transition from external to inner speech" (1956, p. 87), one should be able first of all to document a close relationship between social speech and early forms of egocentric speech. Then, with the development of egocentric speech, one should be able to document an increasing divergence between it and social speech and an increasing approximation to inner speech. These hypotheses about the origin and fate of egocentric speech contrast sharply with those generated by Piaget's position since according to him self-directed speech reflects egocentric thinking and should therefore lose its egocentric quality and disappear with progressive socialization.

As already noted, the specific semiotic mechanism that Vygotsky posited as giving rise to self-directed speech is the differentiation of speech functions.

> ...the process of growth in the child's social speech, which is multifunctional, develops in accordance with the principle of the differentiation of separate functions, and at a certain age it is quite sharply differentiated into egocentric and communicative speech. (1956, pp. 86–87)

On the basis of this claim about the differentiation of speech functions, Vygotsky outlined the development of self-directed speech in the following terms:

> The structural and functional properties of egocentric speech grow with the child's development. At three years of age the distinction between this speech and the child's communicative speech is almost zero. At seven years of age we see a form of speech that is almost 100% different from the social speech of the three-year-old in its functional and structural properties. It is in this fact that we find the expression of the progressive differentiation of two speech functions and the *separation of speech for oneself and speech for others out of a general, undifferentiated speech function* which, during the early years of ontogenesis, fulfills both assignments with virtually identical means. (1956, p. 346)

This understanding of functional differentiation during the period when self-directed speech is used provides the foundation for specific empirical hypotheses. The first issue Vygotsky addressed concerns the relationship between social and self-directed speech. According to his line of reasoning, one should find a lack of differentiation or even a thorough confusion between social and self-directed speech in young children's verbal behavior. In this connection Vygotsky carried out three "critical experiments" that were designed to determine the degree to which children's use of self-directed speech is affected by phenomena that influence the use of social speech (e.g, the presence or absence of an interlocutor). His argument was that if the use of self-directed speech is sensitive to the same factors that affect the use of social speech it is not egocentric in the sense that Piaget had in mind. Furthermore, it would reflect a close connection between self-directed speech and its developmental precursor, social speech.

Each of the three studies conducted by Vygotsky focused on a requirement of self-directed speech that reflects its lack of differentiation from social speech. The three requirements he examined are: the illusion of understanding by others, the presence of potential listeners, and vocalization. In all cases the procedure was to create a relatively high incidence of self-directed speech in children and then to change the context such that one of the requirements for such speech is no longer present.

For example, in the study concerned with the illusion of understanding by others, Vygotsky placed children whose coefficient of self-directed speech had already been established in a situation where the illusion of being understood by others was no longer tenable. Thus, he put individual subjects in a group of deaf mute children or in a group of children who spoke a foreign language (one not known by the subject). In all other respects the child collective and the activity remained the same as it had been in the setting in which the baseline of self-directed speech had been established. Vygotsky reported that when the illusion of understanding by others is removed, the coefficient of self-directed speech falls drastically. In the majority of cases self-directed speech disappeared altogether, and in the remaining cases its mean coefficient was only one-eighth what it had been under normal conditions.

Vygotsky summarized the results of his studies on this issue as follows:

> In all three studies we were pursuing the same goal. We focused on the three phenomena that appear with almost all egocentric speech by the child: the illusion of understanding, collective monologue, and vocalization. All three phenomena are common to egocentric and social speech. We experimentally compared situations in which these phenomena were present with situations in which they were absent and found that the exclusion of these features...inevitably results in the dying out of egocentric speech. On the basis of these findings we can legitimately conclude that although the child's egocentric speech is already becoming distinguished in function and structure it is not definitively separated from social speech, in whose depths it is all the while developing and maturing. (1956, pp. 353–354)

Thus we see the kind of evidence that Vygotsky provided in support of his claim that self-directed speech grows out of social speech.

Kohlberg et al. (1968) have introduced an additional form of evidence that supports Vygotsky's interpretation of the function and fate of self-directed speech. They argue that since Vygotsky's interpretation calls for self-directed speech first to be differentiated from social speech and then to be internalized, one could predict an initial *increase* followed by a decrease in its use. In contrast, they point out that Piaget's interpretation calls for a steady decline in the use of self-directed speech; in his account there is no reason to expect an increase in the use of self-directed speech at any time. In a standardized situation Kohlberg et al. (1968) found that self-directed speech increased in children of average intelligence from age 4 through 6 and declined thereafter. That is, instead of a steady decrease in its use, they found its use to be curvilinear. In accordance with Vygotsky's interpretation, this curvilinear development of self-directed speech reflects first the differentiation and growth of the self-regulative use of overt speech, and then the internalization of self-regulative speech into inner speech or verbal thought.

In addition to carrying out studies on the level of use of self-directed speech, Vygotsky examined its structural properties. In particular, he was concerned with the way in which this speech form diverges more and more from social speech as it develops toward inner speech. He argued that the quality of self-directed speech changes in a way that supports his interpretation and not Piaget's. Specifically, he argued that if the development of self-directed speech represents the progressive differentiation of speech for oneself from speech for others, it should become less intelligible to others with age. Such a prediction contradicts the prediction generated by Piaget's interpretation of self-directed speech. On the basis of Piaget's contention that self-directed speech is a manifestation of egocentric thinking, one would expect its intelligibility to increase with age. This follows from the fact that progressive socialization should result in the child's being more likely to take others' perspectives into account, therefore producing self-directed speech (and speech in general) that is more intelligible to others. Vygotsky found that his analysis of self-directed speech supported his prediction and not Piaget's.

> One of the most important and decisive factual results from our research is that we established that the structural characteristics of egocentric speech which distinguish it from social speech and make it incomprehensible to others do not decrease, but increase with age. These characteristics are at a minimum at the age of three and are at a maximum at the age of seven. Thus they do not die away but evolve, their development is inversely related to the coefficient of egocentric speech. (1956, p. 345)

The research of Kohlberg et al. (1968) again supports Vygotsky's claim on this point. These researchers report that with an increase in age there is an increase in the proportion of self-directed speech that is unintelligible. Specifically, they found that the proportion of all self-directed speech that falls in the category of "inaudible muttering" ("statements uttered in such a low voice that they are indecipherable to an auditor close by") rose from about .24 to about .50 between the ages of 5 and 9. This increase in the proportion of unintelligible self-directed speech was offset by a decrease in the proportion of self-directed speech in categories such as "describing own activity," categories made up of speech that could be understood by others.

Studies of the quantitative course and qualitative distribution of self-directed speech in the years 3 to 8 support Vygotsky's view that it is a way station to inner speech or verbal thought. Research studies have shown that children who use self-directed speech use it to give themselves directions: to do arithmetic, to remember and plan future acts, and to maintain sequences in memory (Kohlberg et al., 1968; Levina, 1981; Luria, 1969; Meacham, 1979; Wertsch, 1979a, 1979b, 1980). Finally, studies suggest that self-directed speech is not just a by-product of cognitive activity but actually improves cognitive functioning. Children who use self-directed speech tend to do better on tasks where such self-stimulation is functional than do same-age children who do not (Flavell, Botkin, Fry, Wright, & Jarvis, 1968; Luria, 1959). (The exception are children who report completely silent inner speech in such tasks.) Thus we would argue that Vygotsky's interpretation of self-directed speech as a way station to inner speech or verbal thought is confirmed. As in the case of concept development, the "general genetic law of cultural development" guides Vygotsky's account of social, self-directed, and inner speech.

> ...the child's egocentric speech is one of the phenomena in the transition from interpsychological to intrapsychological functioning, i.e., from forms of social, collective activity to individual functioning. (1956, p. 343)

Inner speech is a form of intrapsychological functioning that derives from interpsychological functioning (i.e., social speech), and overt self-directed speech links the two. The self-regulative function of the latter reflects its emerging status as an intrapsychological process, and its overt form and sensitivity to communicative parameters reflects its interpsychological origins.

For Vygotsky, mediated psychological processes are possible because of the development of forms of linguistic mediation such as genuine concepts and inner speech. His notion of linguistic mediation is based on an account of language that integrates its communicative and representational properties. While he argued that such linguistic mediation grows out of speech *and* elementary psychological processes, he actually said very little about how these processes are involved. In this, he contrasts with Piaget, who identified a close and theoretically motivated connection between his version of unmediated and mediated psychological processes. In general, Vygotsky's approach would stand to benefit if it were to incorporate many of Piaget's ideas about sensorimotor intelligence. Where Vygotsky made his major contribution is in his account of the unique properties that linguistic mediation brings to human thought. His analyses show that such linguistic mediation cannot be reduced to Piaget's notion of representation. In the case of concepts or word meanings, the distinction between reference and meaning and the possibility of relating word meanings *qua* meanings are properties unique to linguistic mediation. In his analysis of social, self-directive, and inner speech, Vygotsky again seemed to be making the claim that there is something unique about linguistic mediation, something that cannot be reduced to a more general notion of representation *à la* Piaget. However, he was less precise about what this unique property is. In order to explicate the implications of his arguments, we must extend it in light of yet another theorist who was concerned with thought and language: George Herbert Mead.

LANGUAGE AND THOUGHT AS COMMUNICATION: MEAD'S VIEW

As we have already noted, Vygotsky argued that self-directed speech is grounded in social communication. However, he said relatively little about the specific properties of communicative activity that are introduced into intrapsychological functioning as speech is internalized. We have also noted that approaches that focus solely on the grammatical organization of language (i.e., language as representation), like those of Brown and Chomsky, cannot carry us further. Such approaches provide no way to understand how some distinctively linguistic functions can contribute to cognition. To address the issue of how language makes a distinctive contribution to thought, we must focus on the specifics of its use in communication. We will do this by using the ideas of Mead. As we will see, some of his ideas can be used to extend Vygotsky's basic approach.

Like Vygotsky, Mead (1934) started with the assumption that the primary function of language is communication, and that new structures of language and thought develop as the communicative function develops. This similarity between the two theorists' approaches has been noted by authors such as Bruner (1962), Hood (in press), and Wertsch (in press). From Mead's point of view, there are two general structural features of mature thought that are largely dependent on language. The first is that mature or logical thought is socialized thought, it is thought that proceeds through a process of influence that can be shared. The logical or scientific method is public. This means that logical thought is reversible across various social perspectives and that the universality of logical thought is attained through taking a generalized social perspective, what Mead calls "the perspective of the generalized other" on a universe of discourse. Although this claim is compatible with Vygotsky's approach, Vygotsky did not recognize all the implications identified by Mead. The second related characteristic of mature thought is that it is self-conscious, it is aware of the steps through which it proceeds. Again, this claim is compatible with Vygotsky's ideas, especially his formulation of higher mental functions, but Mead's interpretation goes beyond Vygotsky's in certain important respects.

Both these qualities of mature thought were also recognized by Piaget, but are given somewhat derivative status in his theory, especially in its later versions. In addition to allocating a less central role than Mead to these social aspects of thought-development, Piaget treated language as less central to the socialization of thought. According to Piaget, the child develops reciprocity in social interaction, and this development parallels the child's abandonment of egocentricity for logic. Piaget, however, stressed that development of social reciprocity developed through social *interactions* and treated language merely as the medium for reciprocal social interaction rather than as a critical constituent of reciprocal social interaction.

In contrast, for Mead, language (or, more generally, the "significant symbol") is more than a neutral medium for "taking the role of the other," for seeing the other's view of the self, and for establishing reciprocity between the other's view and one's own. The child can and does engage in reciprocal interaction before and without language, in what Mead called the conversation of gestures. What the child cannot do without language, said Mead, is to hold both his own and the other's perspective in his mind simultaneously. Language allows this because a word uttered by the self is heard by the self and arouses in oneself the attitude one strives to arouse in the other; it allows us to "take the point of view of the other" on our own words or acts. It also creates reciprocal awareness, because the word uttered by the other arouses in the other the same meaning or attitude aroused by the word in the self. This reciprocal awareness is largely unique to speech acts as opposed to other social acts. In a speech act, unlike such social gestures as giving a gift or striking a blow, at least some of the meanings attached to the verbal act of the speaker are the same for the listener. Neither a gift nor a blow presuppose that any meaning is the same for speaker and listener.

In this respect, Mead's line of reasoning is strikingly similar to Vygotsky's ideas about the transition from inter- to intrapsychological functioning. For both authors, the key to this transition is language since language mediates both social and individual functioning. Furthermore, like Vygotsky, Mead (1934) did not reduce thought to language.

> The identification of language with reason is in one sense an absurdity, but in another sense it is valid. It is valid, namely, in the sense that the *process of language* [i.e., speech] brings the total social act into the experience of the given individual as himself involved in the act, and thus makes the process of reason possible. But though the process of reason is and must be carried on in terms of the process of language—in terms, that is, of words—it is not simply constituted by the latter. (1934, p. 74) [italics added]

For Mead, the unique properties that language brings to social interaction and individual reasoning distinguish humans from animals and adults from children. Although he did not make an explicit contrast, such as Piaget's distinction between sensorimotor and representational intelligence or Vygotsky's distinction between elementary and higher mental functions, Mead's interpretation of language makes it clear that he saw it as differentiating his version of unmediated and mediated psychological processes. For him, language is a necessary mechanism for role-taking, for reciprocal interaction and the consequent socialization of thought.

The basic mechanism that makes the socialization of thought possible according to Mead is the process of dialogue. We change our beliefs or ideas through social dialogue in a way different from how we change our ideas through interacting with things. The view of experience stressed by Piaget is one in which action on objects leads to feedback until equilibrium of interaction is reached. The view of experience stressed by Mead is the Hegelian experience of dialogue. In this experience, shareable attitudes and meanings confront conflicting shareable attitudes until some synthesis is reached. In dialogue we accept the other's modification of our ideas only as it takes account of our original statement, as it is based on some prior sharedness. Communication between two selves is the precondition of the process of cognitive development through dialogue.

For Mead the role of language in cognitive development is to allow the process of dialogue. Words are not unique as instruments for solving problems, they are unique as instruments for dialogue. This focus on dialogue reflects the fact that Mead was primarily involved with language as communication. Specifically, he was concerned with the relationship between an utterance and the context created by preceding and subsequent utterances. Virtually all his analyses focus on this aspect of "intralinguistic" contextual relations. It is worth pointing out that Mead's notion of language as communication presupposes a notion of language as representation. Only through its representational capacity can linguistic units function as significant symbols. However, Mead did very little to develop this notion of language as representation. His major focus was always on language as communication.

The internalization of language allows the further progress of a dialogue with the self. Language or inner speech is a necessary medium for inner dialogue—it is not a necessary medium or tool for adaptation to most external cognitive task situations. Inner dialogue itself has unique functions, not shared with other forms of thought. It is the unique vehicle for the self's "taking a position," for self-definition, for self-change, and for posing problems as opposed to answering them. The "internalization of speech" leads to the possibility of an internal dialogue, to the modification of hypothesis and attitude through confrontation with an opposed hypothesis or attitude, presented by the self to itself "in the role of the other." Closely related to the dialogue function of language in cognitive development is its role in causing self-awareness. The early self-directed speech of preschool children suggests that they must talk to themselves to be aware of their own activities. At a somewhat later stage self-dialogue seems necessary for awareness of thought. An example we cited earlier of the developed self-dialogue for self-awareness was the journal or diary of adolescence.

Ultimately the self-awareness of thought, its reflectiveness, coincides with its maturity in terms of the epistemological and ego stages discussed in the preceding chapter. To understand this side of cognitive maturity, if not to understand sheer logical operations, we believe that it is necessary to postulate a critical role to language.

EXTENDING VYGOTSKY'S APPROACH IN LIGHT OF MEAD'S IDEAS ABOUT THE DIALOGIC PROPERTIES OF SELF-DIRECTED SPEECH

We said that Vygotsky was correct in defining self-directed speech as a way station to inner speech. We have also said that Mead's view of communication and reciprocity identifies some unique features of social interaction that have important implications for the nature of inner speech. Mead's treatment of these issues is compatible with Vygotsky's account, but it goes beyond what Vygotsky actually said. Therefore, in this section we will integrate the two theorists' ideas into a more comprehensive approach. We will draw on studies of self-directed speech by Kohlberg et al. (1968), Berner (1971), and Wertsch (1970a, 1980).

Our starting point is Vygotsky's claim about the dialogic nature of inner speech. Drawing on the ideas of Yakubinski (1923), Vygotsky (1960) produced the following formulation of self-directed speech, a formulation that assumes self-directed speech is dialogic:

> Speech is first a communicative function. It serves the goals of social contact, social interaction, and the social coordination of behavior. Only afterwards, by applying the same mode of behavior to oneself, do humans develop inner speech. In this process, they, as it were, preserve the "function of social interaction" in their individual behavior. They apply the social mode of action to themselves.
>
> Under this condition, the individual function becomes in essence a unique form of internal collaboration with oneself. (pp. 450–451)

As Ivanov (1976) and Bibler (1975) have pointed out, Vygotsky's statement about "internal collaboration with oneself" reveals that in his opinion inner speech is necessarily inner dialogue.

Such a claim about inner speech leads us to ask what the developmental processes are that lead up to its dialogic nature. To answer this question we must turn once again to the forms of social and self-directed speech that precede inner speech. When examining self-directed speech, we can begin with the question, "why does the child direct speech to himself at all?" Vygotsky provided one answer: the child is thinking out loud, guiding his or her own activity. Piaget provided another: the child is responding to the stimulus of another person as someone to talk to, but fails to take the other's point of view.

Vygotsky's interpretation seems appropriate for certain forms of self-directed speech in which the child engages. These forms have been categorized as "cognitive self-guidance" (Kohlberg et al., 1968). Examples of self-guiding speech come from Observation 1 of David, a 4 year old engaged in play with tinker-toys with the adult observer across the room. In this observation David makes such self-guiding utterances as: "We need to start it all over again," and "We have to cover up the motor just like a real car."

While much of the child's self-guiding speech fits this category, much does not. It fits instead other categories that reflect what Vygotsky sees as the incomplete differentiation between speech functions evidenced in self-directed speech. This incomplete differentiation also provides an interpretation of what Piaget calls "collective monologue." Of such speech, Piaget (1926) wrote:

> ...an outsider is always associated with the action or thought of the moment, but is

expected neither to attend nor to understand. The point of view of the other person is never taken into account; his presence serves only as a stimulus. (1926, p. 33)

Piaget's characterization imputes a lack of will to share, but also suggests some will to share attitudes or information without the skill for doing so appropriately. An example is provided by Observation 2 of 4-year-old David, playing with Brian, also 4.

David: Episode 2—Collective Monologue

Brian: I'm playing with this.
David: A what's, a what's.
Brian: Oh nuts, oh nuts.
David: Doodoodoo, round, round up in the sky. Do you like to ride a (toy) helicopter?
Brian: Okay. I want to play in the sandbox.
David: Much fun. Do you want to ride the helicopter?
Brian: I'm going outside.

David seems to have a will to share activities or ideas, but fails to differentiate perspectives in the sense of discriminating imagined sharing from real sharing. He persists in asking Brian to share ("Do you want to ride the helicopter?") but the activity is private and imagined since the toy helicopter cannot be ridden. In contrast, Piaget's characterization of a noncommunicative intent seems appropriate to Brian's responses, which describe what he is doing without actually inviting David to share the activity, or to respond to it. If we break the statements in this collective monologue down, most fall under the category, "Describing own activity" (Kohlberg et al., 1968). One of Vygotsky's students, Levina (1981), identified such descriptive speech as a precursor to the clear-cut "cognitive self-guidance" that seems to be Vygotsky's primary focus.

To label describing one's own activity simply as "egocentric" fails to define its function. On the other hand, to call word play for Observation 2, "A what's, a what's," "Oh nuts, oh nuts," "egocentric" seems acceptable. Such word play does not have a clear communicative intent or function. Describing one's own activity, however, does have a communicative intent, the intent of self-communication. The most realistic interpretation of the positive function of such descriptions of one's own activities would seem to be not full-fledged cognitive self-guidance but self-communication for self-awareness. This is a precursor to full-fledged self-guidance and seems to reflect the confusion of speech functions outlined by Vygotsky.

As we noted, Piaget does not discuss a function of self-awareness as explaining collective monologue. Such a function does follow from Vygotsky's and Mead's view, however. Collective monologue is a running stream of commentary on the self's activity to an auditor who is neither clearly the self nor clearly the other. Such commentary is "egocentric" or noncommunicative in the Piagetian sense because it conveys no information about the self to the listener not apparent to the listener from watching the child. From Mead's view, however, it is communicating the meaning or nature of the child's activity to the other and hence establishing some meaning to the activity from the perspective of another and the child can only take this perspective on himself by describing his activity to the other and so calling out in himself the implicit response of another to his description. The child does not start with an awareness of the meaning of his action to himself which he then endeavors to communicate to others. His awareness of the meaning of his action to himself arises in the process of communicating to the other. Consequently, the monologue represents processes of apparent communication to the other with primarily self-reflective functions.

We have discussed two forms of self-directed speech, "self-guidance," which clearly fits the Vygotsky interpretation, and "describing own activity," which may be an early form of self-directed speech for Vygotsky but is better explained in terms of a Meadian function of self-awareness through overt communication. Both forms of speech are understood best if they are viewed as part of a dialogue in which the self realizes the meaning of its actions and role through taking both sides of a dialogue. Mead described this dialogue structure of self-communication in the preschool child as follows:

> [The child] plays that he is, for instance, offering himself something, and he buys it; he gives a letter to himself and takes it away; he addresses himself as a parent, as a teacher; he arrests himself as a policeman. He has a set of stimuli which call out in himself the sort of response they call out in others. . . . A certain organized structure arises in him and in his other which replies to it, and these carry on the conversation of gestures between themselves. (pp. 150–151)

To illustrate the dialogic nature of self-directed speech, we shall quote more fully Episode 1 for David, from which extracts of self-guiding speech were taken.

David: Episode 1 (In solitary play with tinker-toys, observer across the room.)
The wheels go here, the wheels go here. Oh, we need to start it all over again. We need to close it up. See, it closes up. We're starting it all over again. Do you know why we wanted to do that? Because I needed it to go a different way. Isn't it going to be pretty clever, don't you think? But we have to cover up the motor just like a real car.

This example includes some use of Vygotsky's self-directed speech for cognitive guidance, "We need to start it all over again." It also includes some bare self-description for self-awareness, "See, it closes up." In addition to self-description and task self-guidance, the monologue focuses on evaluation and justification of the activity. Of most interest, however, is the fact that both self-description and self-guidance occur in a context in which the central theme is a dialogue with the self. This is indicated by the Kohlberg et al., category "Questions answered by the self," "Do you know why we wanted to do that? Because I needed it to do a different way." It is indicated by the "we" who spoke, a "we" who includes *both* two selves, the speaker self and the auditor self. Overall, this and other "collective monologues" are best conceived of as the self's realizing the meaning of its actions and role through taking both sides of a social dialogue as a social interaction.

Three basic forms of self-directed speech exist: (1) describing own activity, (2) self-dialogue (questions answered by the self), and (3) cognitive self-guidance. Mead's interpretation suggests that these three forms of self-directed speech should form a developmental hierarchy or sequence in a Vygotskian account of self-directed speech. It suggests that the child should: (1) first describe himself and his activity to present or semi-present others with his own response in the role of the other being implicit and unvocalized, (2) then carry on both parts of the dialogue, and finally (3) only vocalize the active directing or guiding response of the other to his own activity. It seems implicit in the Mead view that collective monologue describing one's own activity in nondialogue form is an earlier step in development than overt use of the dialogue form. The function of such speech was said to be the establishment of the meaning of the self's action to the self as an auditor. Some structural development of the self or an auditor is required before the self as auditor can talk back, reply, or elicit a dialogue. In part, the structural development of the self as auditor required by this step entails an increased differentiation of the listening self from a physically present other. Suppressing the question and supplying only the answer (cognitive self-guidance) involves an even clearer differentiation of the self as auditor from the external auditor.

Kohlberg et al. (1968) found age trends consistent with this assumed developmental order. Intercorrelations among these categories within an age group were also consistent with a Guttman simplex order implied by the developmental hierarchy assumption. Similar findings of a developmental order or hierarchy of these categories of private speech were obtained by Berner (1971). The major importance of the finding is its support for the notion that cognitive self-guiding speech and hence inner speech or verbal thought (found to be a later step in the developmental hierarchy) must develop out of a prior dialogue mode. The assumption of developmental order just stressed suggests a progressive differentiation of the self as auditor from an external auditor and an "internalization" of the auditor role prior to an internalization of the speaker role. Self-guiding speech presupposes an internalization of the auditor role, but not of the speaker role. This internalization precedes silent speech or internalization of the speaker role.

Berner (1971) investigated this hypothesis further by relating self-directed speech to: (1) the disposition to monitor one's own speech, and (2) cognitive capacity for social role-taking. The disposition to monitor or listen to one's own speech was measured by disruption in delayed auditory feedback. The speech of young children (under 4) is not disrupted when their own voice is being recorded and played back to them after a fraction of a second delay. In contrast, older children's speech is disrupted under this delayed auditory feedback condition.

Berner's first hypothesis was that the older child's language disruption, his attending to and monitoring his own speech, depended on, or was part of, a tendency "to take the role of the other," to take a social other's point of view on his own speech. To test this hypothesis, Berner administered the "guessing game" role-taking task presented in Chapters 6 and 13 to her subjects. To pass this task, the child must show awareness that in a "hide the penny in the hand" game, the other person is trying to get the child to guess wrong, to prevent the child from predicting the hand the penny is in. Berner found that this role-taking capacity was a necessary condition for monitoring one's own speech. All children who monitored their own speech passed the guessing game, though many children failed both tasks and some passed the guessing game without monitoring their own voices. Monitoring one's own voice requires "internalization" of the social auditor role. Such internalization also appears to be necessary for self-guiding speech, our Meadian assumption involved in making self-guiding speech the developmentally highest form of self-directed speech.

In the Berner study, children at each age (3, 4, and 5) who monitored their own voices were much more likely to engage in self-guiding speech than were children who did not. Presumably, the internalization of the auditor role required for self-guidance requires a differentiation of the self as auditor from external other as auditors. Our Meadian interpretation leads to a hypothesis proposed and tested by Vygotsky, with a slightly different rationale. Piaget had claimed that the child engaged in collective monologue because he did not differentiate himself as speaker from the external auditor in the room. The Meadian view of self-directed dialogue implies that the child engaging in self-directed speech makes a distinction between speaker and auditor, the two existing in complementary roles. The earlier forms of self-directed speech, however, do not imply a distinction between an external auditor and the auditor-self. Describing one's own activity in social settings should occur because of a confusion of the auditor's self with the external auditor.

Thus our interpretation views self-directed speech as a mechanism that encourages the differentiation and integration of social roles. This interpretation rests on the notion that speech provides unique opportunities for self-monitoring and dialogic interchange. To illustrate our claims, we will examine some segments of adult-child discourse in a problem-solving setting. Our purpose in examining this discourse is to demonstrate how the transition from interpsychological to intrapsychological functioning outlined by Vygotsky is made possible by the forms of dialogic communication proposed by Mead. That is, we will see how this transition is effected by coordinating and internalizing regulative roles that are initially external.

Our demonstration of these dialogic speaking and reasoning processes is based on social and self-directed speech data as well as on nonverbal behaviors that indicate the use of inner speech. The data examined come from a child's (and sometimes an adult's) behaviors in a problem-solving setting. In this setting a $2\frac{1}{2}$-year-old girl and her mother are working together on the task of inserting pieces in a "copy" puzzle such that they are arranged identically with pieces in a "model" puzzle. Our data come from three "episodes" of interaction. (In this task an episode is defined as the verbal and nonverbal interaction required to identify, select, and insert a piece in the copy puzzle.) In these three episodes the correct location of the piece in the copy puzzle could be determined only by consulting the model puzzle. In our present analysis we will be concerned with the initial phase of each episode. This phase included the strategic substep of consulting the model puzzle to determine where a piece should go in the copy puzzle.

The initial segment of the first episode between the mother (M) and the child (C) proceeded as follows:

(1) *C:* Oh. (C glances at the model puzzle, C looks at the pieces pile.) Oh, now where's this one go? (C picks up the black piece from the pieces pile, C looks at the copy puzzle, C looks at the pieces pile.)

(2)*M:* Where does it go on this other one? (C puts the black piece which is in her hand back down in the pieces pile, C looks at the pieces pile.)

(3)*M:* Look at the other truck and then you can tell. (C looks at the model puzzle, C glances at the pieces pile, C looks at the model puzzle, C glances at the pieces pile.)

(4) *C:* Well...(C looks at the copy puzzle, C looks at the model puzzle.)

(5) *C:* I look at it.

(6) *C:* Um, this other puzzle has a black one over there. (C points to the black piece in the model puzzle.)

Although it is true that the child glanced at the model puzzle at the very beginning of this episode, it does not appear that she did so at that point to determine where a piece should go in the copy puzzle. The first time she consulted the model for some clear purpose was in response to the mother's utterances (2) and (3). That is, it was part of an external social dialogue.

The initial segment of a subsequent episode between this mother and child proceeded as follows:

(7) *C:* (C glances at the pieces pile, C looks at the copy puzzle, C picks up the orange piece from the pieces pile.) Now where do you think the orange one goes?

(8)*M:* Where does it go on the other truck? (C looks at the model puzzle.)

(9) *C:* Right there. (C points to the orange piece in the model puzzle.) The orange one goes right there.

In this episode we see that the child's action of consulting the model puzzle again constituted a part of the social dialogue between herself and her mother.

The next episode between the mother and child began as follows:

(10) *C:* (C looks at the pieces pile, C picks up the yellow piece from the pieces pile, C looks at the copy puzzle.) Now how.... Now where.... Now (C looks at the model puzzle.)

(11) *C:* You...you...the yellow on that side goes.... One yellow one's right next there. (C points to the yellow piece in the model puzzle, C looks at the yellow piece she is holding in her hand.)

(12)*M:* Okay.

Comparisons among these three segments of interaction reveal some important trends in the verbal and nonverbal behaviors. Recall that the first two episodes began with the child's asking where a piece was to go [i.e., utterances (1) and (7)] and the mother's responding by directing the child's attention to the model puzzle [i.e., utterances (2), (3), and (8)]. In both these episodes, the child's original question led to a response by the mother which, in turn, led to the child's response of consulting the model. All these "moves" or "turns" were carried out through external social dialogue. The third episode began quite differently. First, the child did not produce a fully expanded question about where a piece should go [although it appears that she began to do so in utterance (10)]. Second, and more important, her gaze to the model puzzle after utterance (10) was not a response to an adult's directive in external social dialogue. Instead of relying on an adult to provide a regulative communication, she anticipated the moves that would have occurred in social dialogue and carried them out independently using egocentric and inner dialogue. Finally, the child's next utterance [i.e., (11)] in this third episode is strikingly similar to utterances (6) and (9) in the first and second episodes, respectively.

First episode

(6) *C:* Um, this other puzzle has a black one over there. (C points to the black piece in the model puzzle.)

Second Episode

(9) *C:* Right there. (C points to the orange piece in the model puzzle.) The orange one goes right there.

Third Episode

(11) *C:* You...you...the yellow on that side goes.... One yellow one's right next there. (C points to the yellow piece in the model puzzle, C looks at the yellow piece she is holding in her hand.)

In all three cases the verbal and nonverbal behaviors constitute a statement about the location of a particular piece in the model puzzle. In addition to the similarity in the structure and content of the utterances, an examination of the sequence of behaviors in the three episodes reveals that (6), (9), and (11) served the same function in the problem-solving strategy. In all three cases the statement advanced this strategy in the same way (i.e., they all were concerned with the strategic step of consulting the model to determine where a piece from the pieces pile was to go).

However, there is an important difference between (11) on the one hand and (6) and (9) on the other. Utterances (6) and (9) were moves in an external social dialogue. They were the child's responses to utterances by the adult. Utterance (11), on the other hand, was not a response to an adult utterance, that is, it was not part of an external social dialogue. We would argue that the reason for the striking similarity between (11) and other two is that (11) *also* is a response to a question. However, in this case, the question is one that the child had posed to herself. We wish to stress that utterance (11) was part of a dialogue—that in this case had been partially internalized. It obviously is not a speech act used to make a random, isolated observation about the location of the yellow piece. Rather, it is motivated by a self-addressed question and can be interpreted functionally only within the context of a dialogue.

The pattern of interaction seen in these excerpts is consistent with our Meadian extension of Vygotsky's account of self-directed and inner speech. Inner speech is best thought of as the internalization of a social dialogue, an internalization presupposing two parties in language transactions and presupposing the child's capacity to simultaneously take both parties' point of view on the language transaction. This interpretation is the exact opposite of Piaget's original hypothesis, which is that self-directed speech reflects a lack of role-taking ability. Instead, its presence is an indication of a certain level of differentiation between the perspective of self and other.

CONCLUSION

In this chapter we have outlined some of the issues that arise in developmental psychology in connection with the relationship between language and thought. We have seen that to compare approaches we must first identify what various approaches mean by language and what they mean by thought. In particular, we have seen that it is useful to distinguish between representation and communication when considering language and between unmediated and mediated psychological processes when considering thought. It is important to clarify the position of various theories on these issues before proceeding to further analyses.

Our review of Piaget's ideas revealed that his version of the distinction between unmediated and mediated psychological processes is the distinction between sensorimotor and representational intelligence. He viewed play and limitation as the mechanisms responsible for the emergence of representational intelligence. He recognized the role of language in representational intelligence, but he did not view its development as causing any qualitative change. It is simply one of several forms of representation. As we saw, Piaget's position has some impressive evidence to support it. Furth's studies of cognitive development in deaf children and Sinclair's language training study indicate that certain aspects of representational intelligence develop relatively independently of language. In this connection, however, it is important to recognize that when considering the influence of language on cognition these Piagetian researchers have focused on representation and have failed to address the issues of language as communication.

When we turn to Vygotsky's approach, we find that his version of the distinction between unmediated and mediated psychological processes is somewhat different. Instead of focusing on the difference between sensorimotor and representational intelligence, Vygotsky distinguished between elementary and higher mental functions. The crucial factor that gives rise to higher mental functions is not the representation used in symbolic play and imitation but in language. This is part of Vygotsky's broader claim that higher mental functions derive from social interaction. Thus Vygotsky's version of mediated psychological process is characterized by social origins and the necessity of linguistic mediation; Piaget's version is characterized by individual origins and general representational capacity (in which language is only one of several representational means).

We saw that Vygotsky's account of the linguistic mediation of higher mental processes focuses on two issues: the development of concepts and the development of self-directed and inner speech. In developing his ideas of the former he focused primarily on an aspect of language as representation (semantics), and when examining the latter he focused primarily on certain aspects of language as communication. In both cases, however, it is clear that his notion of language is based on an integrated picture of representation and communication. Thus he argued that the origins of the linguistic mediation of an individual's psychological processes are to be found in social interaction. Furthermore, in both cases he assumed that the linguistic mediation involved cannot be reduced to a general notion of representation such as that proposed by Piaget. In the case of concept development he noted that the relationships among word meanings and the hierarchical system of such relationships found in language are unique to language. In the case of self-directed speech we saw that the use of speech as its own context is an activity that imposes unique requirements on the child.

Overall, we see Piaget and Vygotsky as presenting approaches that complement one another. As we noted, Vygotsky's account of early ("elementary") mental function is quite unsophisticated. We view Piaget as providing a powerful account of this period of development. In addition to his brilliant analyses of sensorimotor intelligence, his account of early representational intelligence needs to be incorporated within a Vygotskian perspective. Conversely, we argue that Vygotsky recognized crucial aspects of linguistically mediated social (i.e., interpsychologial) and individual (i.e., intrapsychological) functioning that Piaget failed to recognize. In particular, Vygotsky's critique and reinterpretation of Piaget's claims about self-directed speech reveal unexplored and misunderstood aspects of Piaget's theory.

Finally, we view Mead's ideas on social communication and role-taking as an important extension of Vygotsky's ideas on language and thought. While Vygotsky seems to have recognized the dialogic nature of inner speech, he did not develop all the implications for self-monitoring and the coordination of perspectives that concerned Mead. The Meadian extension of Vygotsky's ideas continues to complement Piaget's approach in that it argues for the unique contribution of language to psychological processes; it assumes that the development of language introduces a qualitative change in thought. In this connection we identified Mead's distinction between unmediated and mediated psychological processes. In making his argument, Mead also sides with Vygotsky on the claim that individual psychological processes derive from social interaction. His account of the role of language in this argument reveals that he focused almost exclusively on communication and said almost nothing about representation.

In summary, we would argue that the issue of whether or not language and thought are related has neither a simple nor a definitive answer. During certain periods in ontogenesis the answer seems to be "Yes" and during other periods it seems to be "No"; for certain aspects of psychological functioning the answer seems to be "Yes" and for others "No"; and finally for certain definitions of language the answer seems to be "Yes" and for others "No." The only way to pose unambiguous questions about this relationship is to specify what is meant by language, what is meant by thought, and what ontogenetic period is being considered. The different answers provided by the three theorists we have examined are summarized in the accompanying table.

Does the approach	Piaget	Vygotsky	Mead
1. distinguish between unmediated and mediated psychological processes?	Yes*	Yes†	Yes
2. view the development of mediated psychological processes as occurring early in ontogenesis (i.e., before age 3)?	Yes	No	?
3. view mediated psychological processes as having social origins?	No	Yes	Yes
4. consider the development of language as causing a qualitative change in the development of thought?	No	Yes	Yes
5. consider language as representation?	Yes	Yes	No
6. consider language as communication?	No(?)	Yes	Yes

*Sensorimotor versus representational intelligence.
†Elementary versus higher mental functions.

REFERENCES

Berner, E. S. (1971). *Private speech and role-taking abilities in pre-school children.* Unpublished doctoral dissertation, Harvard University Press.

Bibler, V. S. (1975). *Myshlenie kak tvorchestvo* [Thinking as creation]. Moscow: Izdatel'stvo Politicheskoi Literatury.

Brown, R. (1973). *A first language.* Cambridge: Harvard University Press.

Bruner, J. S. (1962). Introduction to L. S. Vygotsky, *Thought and language*. Cambridge: MIT Press.

Buhler, K. (1930). *The mental development of the child*. New York: Harcourt Brace.

Chomsky, N. (1957). *Syntactic structures*. The Hague: Mouton.

Chomsky, N. (1965). *Aspects of the theory of syntax*. Cambridge: MIT Press.

Flavell, J., Botkin, P. T., Fry, C. L., Wright, J. W., & Jarvis, P. E. (1968). *The development of role-taking and communication skills in children*. New York: Wiley.

Furth, H. G. (1966). *Thinking without language: Psychological implications of deafness*. New York: The Free Press.

Furth, H. G. (1971). Linguistic deficiency and thinking: Research with deaf subjects 1964–1969. *Psychological Bulletin, 76*, 58–72.

Hood, L. (in press). Pragmatism and dialectical materialism in language development. In K. E. Nelson (Ed.), *Children's language*. Vol. 5. New York: Wiley.

Ivanov, V. V. (1976). *Ocherki po istoril semiotiki v SSSR* [Essays on the history of semiotics in the USSR]. Moscow: Izdatel'stvo Nauka.

Kohlberg, L., Yaeger, J., & Hjertholm, E. (1968). Private speech: Four studies and a review of theories. *Child Development, 39*, 691–736.

Kohler, W. (1925). *The mentality of apes*. New York: Harcourt Brace.

Levina, R. E. (1981). L. S. Vygotsky's ideas about the planning function of speech in children. In J. V. Wertsch (Ed.), *The concept of activity in Soviet psychology*. Armonk, NY: M. E. Sharpe.

Luria, A. R. (1959). The directive function of speech in development and dissolution. Part I: Development of the directive function of speech in early childhood. *Word, 15*, 341–351.

Luria, A. R. (1969). Speech development and the formation of mental processes. In M. Cole & I. Maltzman (Eds.), *A handbook of contemporary Soviet psychology*. New York: Basic Books.

Luria, A. R. (1976). *Cognitive development: Its cultural and social foundations*. Cambridge: Harvard University Press.

Meacham, J. (1979). The role of verbal activity in remembering the goals of actions. In G. Zivin (Ed.), *The development of self-regulation through speech*. New York: Wiley.

Mead, G. H. (1924–1925). The genesis of the self and social control. *International Journal of Ethnoscience, XXXV*, 251–277.

Mead, G. H. (1934). *Mind, self and society*. Chicago: University of Chicago Press.

Neisser, U. (1976). *Cognition and reality: Principles and implications of cognitive psychology*. San Francisco: Freeman.

Piaget, J. (1926). *The language and thought of the child*. New York: Harcourt Brace.

Piaget, J. (1952). *The origins of intelligence in children*. New York: International Universities Press.

Piaget, J. (1962). *Play, dreams and imiation in childhood*. New York: Norton.

Piaget, J. (1967). *Six psychological studies*. New York: Vintage.

Rubenshtein, S. L. (1957). *Bytie i soznanie* [Being and consciousness]. Moscow: Izdatel'stvo Nauk SSSR.

Rubenshtein, S. L. (1959). *Printsipy i puti razyitive psikhologii* [Principles and path of the development of psychology]. Moscow: Izdatel'stvo Nauk SSSR.

Scribner, S. (1977). Modes of thinking and ways of speaking. In P. N. Johnson-Laird &

P. C. Wason (Eds.), *Thinking: Readings in cognitive science*. New York: Cambridge University Press.

Sinclair, H. (1967). *Acquisition du langage et development de la pensee*. Paris: Dusod.

Sinclair, H. (1969). Developmental psycholinguistics. In D. Elkind & J. Flavell (Eds.), *Studies in cognitive development*. New York: Oxford University Press.

Sokolov, A. N. (1969). Studies of the speech mechanisms of thinking. In M. Cole & I. Maltzman (Eds.), *A handbook of contemporary Soviet psychology*. New York: Basic Books.

Tulviste, P. (1978). [On the origins of theoretic syllogistic reasoning in culture and in the child]. In *Problemy kommunikatsii i vosprivativa* [Problems of communication and perception]. Tartu: Izdatel'stvo Unversiteta Tartu.

Vygotsky, L. S. (1956). *Izbrannye psikhologicheskie issledovaniya* [Selected psychological investigations]. Moscow: Izdatel'stvo Nauk SSSR.

Vygotsky, L. S. (1960). *Razvitie vvsshykh psikhichaskikh funktii* [The development of higher mental functions]. Moscow: Izdatel'stvo Nauk SSSR.

Vygotsky, L. S. (1962). *Thought and language*. Cambridge: MIT Press.

Vygotsky, L. S. (1978). *Mind in society*. Cambridge: Harvard University Press.

Vygotsky, L. S. (1981a). The instrumental method in psychology. In J. V. Wertsch (Ed.), *The concept of activity in Soviet psychology*. Armonk, NY: M. E. Sharpe.

Vygotsky, L. S. (1981b). The genesis of the higher mental functions. In J. V. Wertsch (Ed.), *The concept of activity in Soviet psychology*. Armonk, NY: M. E. Sharpe.

Vygotsky, L. S. (1981c). The development of higher forms of attention in childhood. In J. V. Wertsch (Ed.), *The concept of activity in Soviet psychology*. Armonk, NY: M. E. Sharpe.

Wertsch, J. V. (1979a). From social interaction to higher psychological processes: A clarification and application of Vygotsky's theory. *Human Development, 22*(1), 1–22.

Wertsch, J. V. (1979b). The regulation of human action and the given-new organization of private speech. In G. Ziven (Ed.), *The development of self-regulation through private speech*. New York: Wiley.

Wertsch, J. V. (1980). The significance of dialogue in Vygotsky's account of social, egocentric and inner speech. *Contemporary Educational Psychology, 5*, 150–162.

Wertsch, J. V. (in press). A state of the art review of Soviet research in cognitive psychology. *Storia e critica della psicologia*.

Yakubinskil, L. P. (1923). *O dialogicheskoi rechi* [On dialogic speech]. Petrograd: Trudy Foneticheskogo Instituta Prakticheskogo Izucheniya Yazykov.

Chapter 6

The Developmental Social-Self Theories of James Mark Baldwin, George Herbert Mead, and Lev Semenovich Vygotsky

Daniel Hart, Lawrence Kohlberg, James V. Wertsch

James Mark Baldwin, George Herbert Mead, and Lev Semenovich Vygotsky have elaborated cognitive-developmental theories that offer challenging and profound insights into the development of self. Unfortunately, the value of their approaches has often been overlooked by mainstream developmental psychology, possibly because neither Baldwin nor Mead offer an observationally specified account of development. In this chapter, we explicate Baldwin's, Mead's, and Vygotsky's theories with the hope that contemporary developmental psychologists might find the theories as valuable as we have. We begin by briefly examining traditional cognitive developmental approaches to the self and social phenomena as exemplified in the works of Piaget (1927/1969, 1932/1965, 1971) and of Kegan (1982). The limitations of these approaches are then considered. Baldwin's imitation theory of self-development and Mead's symbolic interactionist theory of self-development are presented, and criticisms of the theories discussed. Finally, the implications of the theories for contemporary social developmental psychology are elabroated. Following that, Vygotsky's theory and its implications are examined.

PIAGET AND THE SELF

As noted in Chapter 1, although Piaget's original contributions to developmental psychology are innumerable and profound, his theory owes much to Baldwin. It was Baldwin who first propounded concepts such as assimilation, accommodation, circular reactions, adualisms, and genetic epistemology, concepts that gained widespread recognition in Piaget's work. Even though Piaget and Baldwin share many of the same basic assumptions (Kohlberg, 1969), Piaget's theory is quite different in regard to social and self-development.

In his theorizing, Piaget writes about the concept of egocentrism, which has many important implications for role-taking and self-development:

> In his manner of reasoning, equally, the child is only concerned with himself, and ignores more or less completely the point of view of others. But, in logic also, if the child sees everything from his own point of view, it is because he believes all the world to think like himself. He has not yet discovered the multiplicity of possible perspectives and remains blind to all but his own as if that were the only one possible. Also he states his views without proof since he feels no need to convince. The results of this are seen in play, make-believe, the tendency to believe without proof, the absence of deductive reasoning; in syncretism also which connects all things in terms of primitive subjective associations; in the absence of all relativity among ideas; and finally in "transductive" reasoning which, through the agency of syncretism, leads from one particular to another, heedless both of logical necessity and of general laws, because of a lack of feeling for the reciprocal nature of all relationship. (Piaget, 1927/1969, p. 167)

As seen in this citation, Piaget was primarily concerned with the child's seeming inability in many circumstances to take the perspective of others, especially on spatial tasks and in games. Two levels of egocentrism are described in Piaget's work (Shantz, 1983). Profound egocentrism is characterized by a complete fusion between self and world. The infant in the first seven months of life has no, or little, understanding that objects exist independent of the self. The beginning differentiation between self and non-self at approximately 12–18 months marks the end of the sensorimotor period in Piaget's scheme. At this age the child becomes aware that objects have an existence apart from the self's actions and perceptions, and are causal agents. Even though the child has some awareness of a self/non-self distinction, the tendency to fuse self and non-self continues into childhood. This later period of egocentrism is associated with the preoperatory level of cognitive development (age 18 months to 6 years) and has important consequences for social interaction.

> The social exchanges characteristic of the preoperatory level are precooperative; that is, at once social from the point of view of the subject and centered upon the child and his own activity from the point of view of the observer. This is precisely what one of us meant by "infantile egocentrism." (Piaget & Inhelder, 1969, p. 118)

This failure to take the role of others is manifested in several social activities mentioned by Piaget and Inhelder: marble-playing in which no rules govern the play of the participants, solitary work and an apparent lack of knowledge of ways to engage others in cooperative work, and egocentric speech or collective monologues in which children talk to themselves without listening to others.

The emergence of concrete operations, characterized by an understanding of the logic of reversible transformations, heralds the beginning of the truly sociable period of human life (Piaget & Inhelder, 1969, p. 117). It is not until the child grasps the logical consequences of reversible transformations that the last vestiges of egocentrism's influence on thought and social interaction fade.

The emphasis on the logical underpinnings of thought characteristic of Piaget's theory, and particularly his writing on egocentrism, has influenced a generation of investigation on role-taking. Researchers have analyzed specific tasks in terms of their logical demands (Flavel, Botkin, Fry, Wright, & Jarvis, 1968) or tried to relate role-taking performances to performances on Piaget's own logical tasks (Feffer & Gourevitch, 1960; Selman, 1980; Selman & Byrne, 1974). If the pre-operation child is asocial, the child's self prior to the age of concrete operation thought must also be asocial; in fact in Piaget's theory, the self is defined only as the "center of activity" (1970, p. 70) or the "epistemic subject" as opposed to a self-conscious or reflective self (1970, p. 139). The central function of the epistemic subject is to aid in the construction of new cognitive structures by role-taking:

> ...the subject's activity calls for a continual "de-centering" without which he cannot become free from his spontaneous intellectual egocentricity. This "de-centering" makes the subject enter upon, not so much an already available and therefore external universality, as an uninterrupted process of coordinating and setting in reciprocal relations. It is the latter process which is the true "generator" of structures. (Piaget, 1970, p. 139)

It is not until the period of concrete operations that role-taking and de-centering become truly characteristic. Since the Piagetian self is a function of cognitive structures, the individual's self-awareness or self-consciousness is irrelevant. The important characteristics of the subject are constituted by the cognitive structures of which the subject is mostly unaware, "cognitive structures do not belong to the subject's *consciousness* but to this *operational* behavior" (Piaget, 1970, p. 168). From Piaget's structuralist perspective, the self is an unconscious functional aspect related to role-taking and the consequent development of new mental structures, and not the phenomenologically evident organizer of experience found in the self theories of William James (1892) and other prominent self theorists.

Kegan (1982) has fully elaborated Piaget's preliminary thoughts into a theory of self-development that links the Piagetian emphasis on de-centering to an affective phenomenology. In Kegan's theory, self-development is a process in which the child increasingly differentiates the true self, the "I," from various characteristics of the self as object, or the "Me." As discussed in Chapter 8, the process of self-development occurs in a sequence of stages, which roughly parallels the cognitive stage sequence of Piaget and the moral stage sequence of Kohlberg (1969). Kegan describes the first development in the growth of self in the following passage:

> From a neo-Piagetian view, the transformation in the first eighteen months of life— giving birth to object relations—is only the first instance of that basic evolutionary activity taken as the fundamental ground of personality development. The infant's "moving and sensing," as the basic structure of its personal organization (the

reflexes), get "thrown from;" they become an object of attention, the "content" of a newly evolved structure. Rather than being my reflexes, I now have them, and "I" am something other. "I" am that which coordinates or mediates the reflexes; what we mean by "impulses" and "perceptions." (1982, p. 79)

Again, in Kegan's description of the first major development of the self, one can see the characteristically Piagetian emphasis on action, de-centering, and structure, with no apparent concern for the subject's knowledge of the self or social influences on the self.

As we suggested in the first paragraph, there are several problems with the Piagetian approach to social and self-development. Probably the most telling criticism to be leveled against Piaget's formulations is that they seem to lack empirical credibility.

It will be remembered that one characteristic of egocentrism was the "lacking in feeling for the reciprocal nature of all relationship" (Piaget, 1927, p. 167). Several studies lead us to question this view. Condon and Sander (1974) filmed infants in the first two days of life as they listened to works in English and Chinese, as well as to tapping noises and random consonants. Frame-by-frame analysis of the film, focusing on the microscopic behaviors such as finger movement and elbow extension, revealed that the infant's behavior was synchronized with the human speech, but not with the tapping noises or random consonants. Rosenthal (1982) observed infants up to three days old in feeding situations with the mother. She found that "the onset of the infant's vocalization is...responsive to antecedent maternal vocalization as early as the first three days of life" (p. 20). Finally, Trevarthen (1977) has examined films of 2-month-old infants playing with their mothers and has found that the infant can repeat behaviors or emit vocalization at the appropriate moment in a sequence of turn-taking. As Damon (1983) has pointed out, these types of findings must be interpreted cautiously. Although the child may be able to respond to adult-initiated interactions through vocalization, behavior, and turn-taking, it is unlikely that the child could initiate or sustain these interactions without the aid of attentive, skillful adults. Nonetheless, these studies do indicate that the young child is a social creature very early in life, with some capability to participate in reciprocal interactions.

In line with these findings, researchers have found evidence of role-taking long before operational thought emerges. Lempers, Flavell, and Flavell (reported in Hoffman, 1977) found evidence that children as young as 1 year old may have some spatial role-taking skills. Children of this age handed a picture will rarely "orient a picture so that only they can see it" (Hoffman, 1977, p. 126). Furthermore, the same authors reported that 2 year olds will turn the picture to orient it for a person who asks to see it. Borke (1973) has found that children as young as 3 years of age are able to infer the emotions of another child in an affect-eliciting situation.

BALDWIN

In sharp contrast to Piagetian-influenced theory, James Mark Baldwin (1902) posited a developmental self theory that emphasized the social nature of the young child. In this theory, the child's early social receptivity is the consequence of both evolution and mental development. Although we will be principally concerned with the aspects of Baldwin's theory that are concerned with the effects of cognitive or mental development on the evolving social competencies of the individual, a brief consideration of the evolutionary underpinnings of the child's social nature is informative, especially since Baldwin's musings on evolution have gained much recent attention from biologists.

Like his contemporaries G. Stanley Hall and Sigmund Freud, Baldwin was heavily influenced by the Darwinian evolutionary thesis (Sulloway, 1979). According to Darwin, two influences have importance for evolution: natural selection (the survival-of-the-fittest principle) and reproduction. These two influences work semiautonomously. For instance, a member of a species could have unique characteristics that will not be passed down to the next generation.

However, in contrast to many followers of Darwin who have claimed that only random mutations in the genetic code directly expressed in phenotypes are responsible for evolution, Baldwin believed that phenotypic or ontogenetic development could influence evolution. In Baldwin's theory the phenotypic or ontogenetic development that is of primary importance in controlling evolution is intelligence:

> We reach a point of view which gives to organic evolution a sort of intelligent direction after all; for all the variations tending in the direction of an adaptation, but inadequate to its complete performance, only those will be supplemented and kept alive which the intelligence ratifies and uses. (1896, p. 447)

This is the so-called Baldwin effect, and it has been revived by biologists such as Waddington (1969). Basically, what Baldwin is claiming is that only those genetic mutations useful to intelligence (which itself is primarily a nonprogrammed, phenotypic development) will provide either a survival or reproductive advantage and therefore be likely to appear in the succeeding generation's gene pool. In such instances, genotypes follow from, rather than determine, phenotypes: the 'Baldwin effect' "*secures by survival certain lines of determinate phylogenetic variation in the directions of the determinate ontogentic adaptations of the generation*" (1896, p. 447). Because one of the hallmarks of intelligence is a flexible approach to problem solving, Baldwin believed that genetic mutations that allowed intelligence more latitude and flexibility were more likely to be an advantage and therefore appear in the next generation. Furthermore, the development of intelligence, according to Baldwin, radically changes how natural selection affects the evolution of intelligent species:

It opens a new sphere for the application of the negative principle of natural selection
upon organisms, i.e., with reference to *what they can do*, rather than to what they are;
to the new use they make of their congenital functions other than to the mere
possession of the functions. A premium is set on congenital plasticity and adaptability
of function rather than on congenital fixity of function; and this adaptability reaches
its highest level in intelligence. (1896, p. 551)

Baldwin also believed that the social environment had an important effect on the
phylogenetic development of a species. First, by imitating adults, the young of a
species can learn adaptive behaviors or "functions which either are not yet, or
never do become, congenital at all" (1896, p. 537). The adaptations of preceding
generations, can, therefore, be transmitted to a present population in a nongenetic
fashion. Like the ontogenetic development of intelligence, the ontogenetic development of sociality (which proves to be of the adaptive value as described above)
aims human phylogenetic development in the direction of an increasingly social
nature. Baldwin believed that all but the most primitive organisms had an innate
social disposition, in addition to the self-preservative nature characteristic of
primitive and advanced species. The requirements of personal survival and fitting
into social groups throughout the phylogenetic history of the race have therefore
resulted in humans being both egoistic and social in nature.

Like Piaget (1970, p. 13), Baldwin partially endorsed the biogenetic law of
Haeckel which claims that much of the phylogenetic history of a species is mirrored
in ontogenesis (Voneche, 1982, has claimed that without such an assumption,
genetic epistemology would be impossible). The development of the child's social
nature mirrors the development of the species and therefore the child is at first
principally concerned with its own survival, because "attitudes for self-defense are
simpler and more direct than those for the defense of another" (Baldwin, 1902,
p. 300). Hence, the young infant acts apparently without concern for effects on
others. Although it is not as readily apparent as the egoistic, asocial nature of the
infant, Baldwin asserted that in the recapitulation of the development of humans in
personal ontogenesis, the infant must evidence a social dimension. At an early age,
the child's social nature is most clearly revealed in organic sympathy. Organic
sympathy is seen in young children when they oberve another in distress:

A certain subdued air is assumed throughout the entire muscular system, the corners
of the mouth droop even to the extent seen in weeping—to which, indeed, the
sympathetic feeling sometimes actually brings us—the movements take on a general
attitude as of proffering help to the individual toward whom the sympathy is directed,
and the voice reveals the peculiar quality characteristic of distress in man and of the
cries of suffering animals. (1902, p. 230)

It is in this period, the instinctive period usually associated with the first year of
life, that egoistic tendencies overshadow the child's social nature.

In the next period of social development, which also precedes the period in which cognitive developments are especially important, the child is more social than egoistic. This is what Baldwin called the "*spontaneous cooperation*" period:

> I find next a period of strong social tendency in the child, of toleration of strangers and liking for persons generally, in great contrast to the attitudes of organic distrust of the earlier period just mentioned. There seems to be in this a reaction against the instinct of...self-preservation characteristic of the earlier stage. (1902, p. 208)

Again, like the instinctive period, the period of spontaneous cooperation in the child mirrors the phylogenetic history of the race.

The last great epoch in the social development of the child is the reflective period. In this period cognitive and mental developments have their greatest influences on the social development of the child. It should not be surprising that Baldwin again believed the reflective period of development in the child echoes a similar development in the history of the race:

> So the race had to reconcile the instinctive tendencies which came down from the animals with the cooperative tendencies which social life prescribed; and *it was done by the race in the same way that it is done by the child: the race became reflective, intelligent, and so started on a career of social development in which two fundamental influences were to work together—the private selfish interest and the public social interest.* (1902, p. 228)

The child becomes reflective through the process of *imitation*, which is the underlying motor of virtually all development in the reflective period.

According to Baldwin, the demands of life in modern society are too great for an infant to master with recourse to and instruction from a sympathetic social environment. The individual in society must both learn from and teach others, since the human mind contains few wired-in survival competencies.

> Each one in turn has been born with none of these [survival] activities in any advanced state of development; but has depended—by the inflexible conditions of his organic make-up upon finding just this system of relationships [society] there beforehand, prepared to hail, embrace, and educate him. All were born helpless; all have been educated. Each has been taught; each is to become a teacher. Each learns new things by doing what he sees others do; and each improves on what the other does only by doing what he has already learned. Each teaches simply by doing and what he has already learned. Each teaches simply by doing and rules the other by his example. (1902, pp. 79–80)

The process of learning within Baldwin's theory is imitation. Imitation determines the process of self-development in two ways: (1) Imitation results in a particularly close relationship between self- and other-understanding, and (2) The developing ability to imitate in itself affects one's social interactions and one's thought of self. We will discuss these two consequences in turn.

There are four stages in the process of becoming a self, according to Baldwin. In the first, the *projective* stage, the child begins to distinguish people from other objects. This distinction is possible, in part, because from the child's perspective, people are more unpredictable: "A person stands for a group of experiences quite unstable in its prophetic as it is in its historical meaning" (1902, p. 13). At points in his discussion of the development of bashfulness, Baldwin also indicates that infants have some innate ability to distinguish people from objects: "The observation or organic bashfulness [in the first year of life]. . .confronts [us] with an element of organic equipment especially fitted to receive and respond to these peculiar objects, persons" (1902, p. 207). In the *subjective stage*, children become dissatisfied with their range of actions. Seeking to enlarge or improve the capabilities of the self, the child begins to imitate other people, because the others have demonstrated attractive action capabilities. In the course of imitation, the child comes to realize that there is a significant difference between his or her own actions and those of another:

> But it is only when a peculiar experience arises which we call effort that there comes that great line of cleavage in his experience which indicates the rise of volition, and which separates off the series now first really *subjective*. What has formerly been 'projective' now becomes 'subjective.' This we may call the *subjective* stage in the growth of the self-notion. It rapidly assimilates to itself all the other elements by which the child's own body differs in his experience from other active bodies—all in the passive inner series of pains, pleasures, strains, etc. (1902, p. 14)

During the subjective stage the child becomes self-aware; the differing experiences between observing another's actions and actually performing those actions heightens the child's awareness of the child's own body and its differences from the bodies of others.

Third, there is the *ejective stage* in which, "The subjective becomes *ejective*; that is, other people's bodies, says the child to himself, have experiences *in them* such as mine has. They are also me's; let them be assimilated to my me-copy" (1902, p. 14).

The fourth stage in which a sense of the social rules and regulations of the group become part of the self demarcates the truly socialized child and is one of the most important aspects of Baldwin's theory. The sense of the "socius," to use Baldwin's term, emerges from the child's dissatisfaction with his or her understanding of people that can be gained through the process of imitation and ejection which are the fundamental processes of the first three stages. As an imitator, the child is characterized "by a certain slavishness. . .in following all examples around him" (p. 23). The person being imitated by the child is perceived as knowledgeable, authoritative, inventive, bold, and commanding; the other with whom the self is interacting is viewed by the child as a follower, one who is subject to the child's commands. Unsurprisingly, younger children are usually the recipients of the ejective aspect of the child's self. The child understands interactions to be determined and controlled by the party that is the authoritative self (usually the adult), while the other party serves as little more than a recipient for the authoritative self's ejections. As intimated above, in the fourth stage of development, the child finds this conceptualization inadequate. The child begins to perceive that adult authoritative selves do not seem always to follow their own inclinations: the child notes that "there are extremes of indulgence. . .which even the grandmother does not permit; there are extremes of severity from which even the cruel father draws back" (1902, p. 42). The child cannot continue to view the ejective self as unrestricted and free to do as it will in light of the growing awareness of counterexamples. Instead, from these seemingly self-contradictory actions the child observes in others, he or she begins to discern "a circle of common interest, a family propriety, a mass of accepted tradition. . .[a] socius" (1902, p. 53). Through the process Baldwin called idealization "by which people construct ends which they know are not real, but nevertheless use to give coherence to their actions" (Lee, 1982, p. 171), the child develops an *ideal self*, an aspect of self that desires to be good and serve the "common interest" of society. The ideal self is not bipolar in the sense that the ejective and subjective selves are; in observing the parent's obedience to the rules of society, the parent's self is seen as simultaneously ejective (commanding the child) and subjective (obeying the rule). Thus imitating action and conforming are seen as both parts of the same self, a self-controlling self. This is a form of reciprocity, but a different form of reciprocity than that stressed by Piaget.

Such conformity to a third force might simply be perceived by the child as indicating that a third person dominates the parent as the parent dominates the child. However, the fact that such pressure to conform goes on in the absence of the third person or authority tends to give rise to the concept of a generally conforming self. In addition, the fact that the conformity is shared in the family or group gives rise to a sense of a common self that the child is to become.

Originally, such a general or ideal self is largely in the image of the parents. It is ideal to the child, it is what the child is to become, but it is largely realized in the child's parents. This does not mean that there is no differentiation of parents from the rule; the parents are seen as obeying the rule. It does mean that the image of a good, conforming self that obeys the rules is in the parent's image.

Baldwin characterizes the determinant of moral action as a "self," rather than as rules or as situational consequences, in an effort to account for the introspective phenomena connoted by *conscience*. Rules enter into moral decisions, not as habits, but in terms of a general rule-obeying self that is not certain in its decisions.

The concept of conscience implies some thinking process in which the mind exerts a strong force on the rest of the self to follow its behests, but which the self identifies with. That is, the compulsion is obeyed out of the self's strength and disobeyed out of the self's weakness, unlike neurotic or impulsive compulsions. It implies choosing in the "line of greatest resistance" as William James put it.

Concepts of conscience and duty imply a rather subtle mingling of feelings of freedom and constraint in action. They imply that I feel compelled to perform an act, but that this compelling force exists within the self or personality. I am "compelled" to do right in opposition to the remainder of the self, as opposed to impulse, fear, or self-interest. Thus, as opposed to the rest of the self, conscience is compelling. But, as opposed to outside forces, conscience is free. Just as it must override other forces within the self, it must override external forces. All this is implied in the phrase "ought to" as opposed to "want to" or "have to." When we define the "ought," when we see it as having a psychic locus, we call it conscience. In addition to its role in the development of morality, the growing awareness of the socius and the development of the ideal self acts "as a larger body of union to the different thoughts" (1902, p. 41) of self and other and provides a key to understanding the previously confusing actions of others. These points are clarified in Kohlberg (1969, 1982).

Throughout the development of the self, imitation and ejection are the essential processes:

> What he [any person] calls himself is in large measure an incorporation of elements that, at an earlier period of his thought of personality, he called someone else. The acts now possible to himself, were formerly only possible to the other; but by imitating that other he has brought them over to the opposite pole, and found them applicable, with a richer meaning and modified value, as true predicates of himself also. (1902, p. 133)

Since the evolution of self-understanding is interdependent with the understanding of the other, the two types of understanding are identical. What a person thinks of "another is—not stands for, or represents, or anything else than *is*—his thought of himself, until he adds to it a further interpretation; the further interpretation is in turn, first himself, then is—again nothing short of this *is*—his thought of the other" (1902, p. 89).

A consequence of Baldwin's imitative theory is that the development of self-understanding ought to be structurally identical with the development of an understanding of others, since the self imitates and ejects on others. Research that has investigated the development of both the understanding of self and others has generally confirmed Baldwin's thesis, although there do appear to be some differences (Lively & Bromley, 1973; Second & Peevers, 1974; Hart & Damon, 1983).

In addition to its function as the process by which other people's characteristics and abilities are incorporated as one's own, imitation in itself becomes a part of the child's thought of self and others. The developing child begins to become aware that he or she does imitate, and that imitation is the process by which one learns. An awareness of imitation brings with it a sense of volition because the child "begins to see that it is he who varies the copy by trying to reproduce it; that he turns out interesting combinations which are his own peculiar property" (1902, p. 113). According to Baldwin, the child is enamored with the dawning sense of personal volition, and between the ages of $1\frac{1}{2}$ and $2\frac{1}{2}$ he or she exercises volition through action. This is the subjective sense of agency stage because the child is content simply to "stop in wonder before his own doings" (1902, p. 113).

After the age of $2\frac{1}{2}$, however, the child is no longer content in merely his or her own subjective sense of agency. The child feels a need for social confirmation for both the competence and volition of the self. Imitative acts now must be demonstrated before the copied model in order for the act's accuracy to be checked and confirmed by the model. Age-developmental studies suggest that look-at-me attention seeking precedes the seeking of approval from others. It is clear that the child who shows off to the adult the act he has just learned from him will not seek the adult's approval. As the child matures, he recognizes that imitation of the act does not make him as competent as the model, and that performance of one competent act still leaves the adult a generally superior performer. As the child acquires a stable sense of the superiority of the older model, "look at me" after imitation becomes the request for approval, "did I do it right?" Baldwin's (1906) account suggests that much of the need for approval is born from the fact that most of the child's accomplishments are imitative. Almost everything young children strive to do or accomplish is something they see another person do first and which they learn, in part, imitatively. The young child's accomplishments, talking, walking, getting dressed, toileting, and so on, are all activities that the child sees others do and knows he or she can do. Because they are the models for activity, their approval of the child's performance counts. This point is elaborated in Kohlberg (1969, 1982).

Following Baldwin, we may propose that the motivational basis of social reinforcement is to be found in the child's imitative tendencies, those tendencies to engage in shared activities. The child's "look-at-me" behavior is not so much a search for adult response as it is a search for confirmation of social or imitative learning. Insofar as the desire for approval arises developmentally out of "look-at-me" behavior, it, too, is not a sign of some more concrete reward that the child seeks. The child's initial desires to perform competently, to succeed, rest on intrinsic competence motivation. The infant struggles to master a task without the least concern for adult reward for performing the task, and without the least concern for the adult's judgment as to whether or not he is doing it right. Social development up until age 6–7 is not a matter of internalizing "extrinsic" social reinforcement into intrinsic competence motivation; rather, it is a process of growing sensitivity to external social definers of standards of competence, and in that sense an increased sensitivity to "extrinsic" social reinforcement. This increased sensitivity, in turn, is the result of a growing sense of dependence on having a social model of performance. The tendency to imitate, to seek a model of performance, itself rests primarily on intrinsic competence motivation, on the "need" to act or function. The child's fundamental motive in imitation is expressed in the familiar cry, "What can I do?" Relying on models to do something interesting and effective, he comes to feel increasingly that he must rely also on them to tell him "how he is doing." In this view, competence motivation engenders imitation which engenders social dependency through an increased sense of discrepancy between the child's own activities and the norms embodied in the activities of the child's models. (This point is elaborated in Kohlberg, 1969, 1982). The imitative basis of social relations is supported by several studies indicating that imitation may be an attractive social characteristic. For instance, with first-grade children, Thelen, Dollinger, and Roberts (1975) found that "being imitated increased the subject's attraction toward the person who imitated him and increased the subject's subsequent imitation (reciprocal imitation) of the person who imitated him" (p. 471). Similarly, Bates (1975) discovered that adults in an experimental situation were more responsive to children who imitated than to those who did not. This finding is the converse of social-learning-theory-inspired studies that have found that children are more likely to imitate nurturant adults. As Yando, Seitz, and Zigler (1978) point out, results of these studies suggest that imitation, social development, and attachment are interdependent.

Furthermore, in addition to needing social confirmation of his or her competence, the child of this age must demonstrate the volitional power of the self to others, frequently in the course of play:

> The self, the playing self, is not content with being its own self, with asserting *itself*, with denying all sorts of foreign control: it goes further, saying "I will prove this to you by being, according as I will, some other self, by choosing that sort of self I will to be." (Baldwin, 1906, p. 128)

The child asserts the self's power by assuming the self of another and rejecting the child's own self, a most fundamental change even if it is done playfully.

The growing sense of self, alter, and socius also affects the child's social interactions. Knowledge of the self and the other can be used either socially or egoistically. Its most profound social consequences are to be found in sympathy and empathy, where one's knowledge of the self and other are so intimately bound that the emotions of another are in part the self's:

> As we have seen, the thought of the ego, and the thought of the alter, having the same presented content at bottom, excite the same emotion in kind; and so the emotion of suffering, appeal, joy, rebellion, etc., which one feels for himself must be aroused also when the same thought of personality comes up with the different term 'another' attached to it. (1902, p. 232)

(Evidence of the "empathy" of the young child is presented by Hoffman, 1977.) Although Baldwin did not describe in detail the psychological mechanism involved in this shared sense of self, Guillaume (1971), who was both a follower and critic of Baldwin, offered an interesting possibility:

> ...the perceptions the infant has of himself give only fragmentary elements of a mental image of his own person. The image is, in large part, an indirect consequence

of imitation, and can be constructed only with elements provided by the perception of the imitated models. If I no longer remember these models individually, *the image that I now form of my own activity, insofar as it is not only felt but pictured, externalized, still preserves features of the alter's image, to which it owes its origins.* (p. 136)

According to Guillaume, the actions of others that the young child imitates are known by the child in two aspects. First, the child is aware of his or her own kinesthetic feelings associated with the act. Second, the child has a visual image of his or her own act, but this image is in part composed of visual images of others performing this act. Thus, self-knowledge inevitably is partially knowledge of others; one literally cannot visualize one's self except in terms of other people.

On the other hand, the child can use the very same knowledge of the self and other in an egoistic manner, so as to "in a sense, to *victimize the alter*" (p. 277). The child is aware that certain stimuli cause the self to act in a certain way; by ejecting these same propensities into others, the child can act to control the other by presenting these same stimuli. For instance, the child knows that the crying of another makes him or her sad and sympathetic. The child can use this knowledge by willfully crying in situations in which the child wants sympathy.

The rise of the ethical or ideal self results in a child who has a true conscience. Prior to this age, egoism flourishes, with social and moral regulations wielding little influence. This is because the rules and regulations are believed to be exterior to the self, which only the punishments of various adults can enforce. But with the rise of the ideal self, in which the body of social regulations are distinguished from particular lawgivers and are seen to apply to all members of the family or group, social regulations are internalized. No longer does the motivation to follow social structures arise from the fear of punishment from others; the self, at first weakly, but with age more strongly, governs its own behavior so as to correspond to its ideal. Not only does the child act to conform actions to the dictates of the ideal self, but he or she comes to expect others to do so as well. The child demands that all siblings be held to the same law: "If the father makes an exception of one little being, he is quickly 'brought up' by the protests of other little beings" (p. 55).

Baldwin's contributions to developmental psychology have been long ignored— indeed, many of his most insightful contributions are just now being explored (Broughton & Moir, 1982; Fein & Kohlberg, this volume). There are, of course, some good reasons why Baldwin has failed to receive the attention he so richly deserves. His adherence to the discredited biogenetic law of Haeckel, his obscure terminology, his repetitive, labyrinthian writing style, and his propensity to reduce virtually all complex problems to the three stages of self-development have resulted in some of his readers rejecting all of his work (see Sewny, 1945, for a review of these problems in Baldwin's work).

In summary, Piaget and his successors in social cognition like Selman (1980) and Kegan (1982) trace a progression of differentiations and coordinates of the perspectives of self and others that are empirically accurate. They start, however, with the assumption of associated similarity between self and other as "an illogical" or egocentric projection of the self's attributes on the others, rather than with the postulate that the child makes a "realistic" assumption of a common self born in imitation and communication. The young child's sympathy is not basically born of a cognitive illusion but derives from the central reality of social life.

More sympathetic readers have always found something of value in Baldwin. For instance, Baldwin's work entitled *Mental development in the child and the race* led Sigmund Freud to wonder if there was anything he himself could contribute to the field of child psychology (Sulloway, 1979). Baldwin's imitative theory of self-development has sparked numerous attempts to improve on or replace it by theorists such as Cooley (1902), Piaget (1962), and Mead (1934). It is to the criticisms of these sympathetic readers of Baldwin that we now turn.

Perhaps that most profound criticisms of Baldwin's theory of self-development have focused on the prominent role he assigned to imitation in social development. Some have argued that although such imitation may be important, imitation itself is an acquired skill that rests on more basic cognitive processes. These critics maintain that Baldwin has left the central psychological problem—the development of imitation—unconsidered, and therefore that his theory reflects only a philosophy of social development. Other theorists have argued that the assignment of centrality in social development to imitation is an error because imitation cannot possibly do justice to the essence of self-development. We will consider each of these criticisms in turn.

In criticizing Baldwin for overlooking the psychology of imitation, Guillaume (1926) and Piaget (1962) have claimed that a careful analysis of imitation reveals that it is a complex, learned activity:

> That an infant be especially interested in people goes without saying; but that he *knows* how to imitate them is something that requires explanation. The regular perceptions that intervene in self-imitation are generally very different from those that operate in the contemplation of the objective movements of others. How can the latter possess the special motor efficiency of the former? (Guillaume, 1971, p. 82)

According to Piaget and Guillaume, the young infant cannot imitate others because the types of cues involved in acting and observing are so different. Thus, when one moves, one is largely guided by proprioceptive feedback. Observation, on the one hand, largely consists of visual percepts. Before the child can imitate others, he or she must coordinate the two types of cues. For Piaget (1962), this coordination is first achieved with body parts the child can see, especially the hand. When the infant watches his or her own hand move, proprioceptive feedback is coordinated with visual percepts. Piaget believed it is not until the eighth or ninth month of life that the child has good enough coordination between the two types of cues to coordinate the visual percepts of another person's movements with similar actions of the self, if the body parts of the self involved in the self's movement cannot be seen by the self. This coordination is made possible by the gradual coordination of action schemes, which, of course, Piaget believed to be the basis of all cognition. Thus, according to Piaget and Guillaume, Baldwin has superficially glossed over the key issue: What psychological mechanisms underlie imitation?

However, recent research by Meltzoff and Moore (1977) seems to confirm Baldwin's thesis that imitation is a fundamental, innate process that need not await other cognitive developments. In their study, with infants from 12 to 21 days of age, Meltzoff and Moore had an experimenter model three facial expressions: tongue protrusion, mouth opening, and lip protrusion. The babies' reactions were videotaped and then coded for the same facial expressions by scorers who were unaware of the order of the experimenter's presentations of the three expressions. Infants were found to imitate the experimenter's facial expression more often than exhibiting the other two expressions, even though they could not see their own faces. These results led the investigators to conclude that there is some innate ability to coordinate sense modalities that does not have to be learned in the fashion suggested by Guillaume and Piaget. Furthermore, in support of Baldwin's position, one might point out that imitation can be found from a very early age.

In an earlier work prior to his formulation of the epistemic subject, Piaget had another criticism of Baldwin's imitation theory of self-development:

> One can hardly deny, indeed, after reading our author's [Baldwin's] analyses, that the self can only know itself in reference to other selves. But imitation will never enable us to perceive in ourselves anything but what we have in common with others. In order to discover oneself as a particular individual, what is needed is a continuous comparison, the outcome of opposition, of discussion, and of mutual control; and indeed consciousness of the individual self appears far later than consciousness of the more general features in our psychological make-up. (1932, p. 393)

This criticism is clearly related to Piaget's construct of egocentrism; what he is claiming is that young children lack the ability to accurately eject their own self-thoughts into others. For instance, the child would be incorrect in assuming that because he or she wants a particular toy that others also want the same toy. Although the research reviewed earlier indicates that there is some ability to take the role of others, or to eject appropriate self-thoughts into others whose immediate context is different than the self's, Piaget's point is basically correct. Baldwin's imitative self-theory is incomplete to the degree to which it omits a consideration of the development of a sense of individuality. However, the central thrust of Baldwin's thought was to account for the construction and development of complex social phenomena such as sympathy, morality, and society, and not to elaborate on the theories of individuality that dominated his era and continue to influence ours.

One final criticism that we will consider is that of George Herbert Mead, whose own self-theory we will discuss shortly. Mead asserted that Baldwin's imitative theory of self- and other-understanding puts the cart before the horse; according to

Baldwin, the child first imitates people, and then comes to realize that the self and other are similar. From Mead's perspective, it would not make sense for the child to imitate another person without *first* knowing that the other is similar to the self. Mead believed that prior to the recognition of similarity between the self and other, the child might react to the action of another, but would not imitate that action.

> Young children...may be stimulated to many reactions which are like those which directly or indirectly are responsible for them without there being any justification for the assumption that the process is one of imitation—in any sense which is connoted by that term in our consciousness. When another self is present in consciousness doing something, then such a self may be imitated by the self that is conscious of him in conduct, but by what possible mechanism, short of a miracle, the conduct of one form should act as a stimulus to another to do, not what the situation calls for, but something like that which the first form is doing, is beyond ordinary comprehension. Imitation becomes comprehensible when there is a consciousness of other selves, and not before. (Mead, 1909, p. 405)

Mead denies that the child would be likely to imitate other people before the others are known as other people similar to the self, claiming that before this recognition arises the child is likely to produce an action that is a *re*action rather than a copy. In large part, Mead's objection to Baldwin's thesis stems from his different understanding of the ontogenesis of imitating other people. Baldwin, like Piaget (1962) and Guillaume (1971), believed that imitation of others is essentially self-imitation extended. Long before the infant begins to copy others, he or she repeats or copies previous actions of the self that the child finds interesting, which Baldwin described as a primary circular reaction. These primary circular reactions become well-established behavior schemes that may be stimulated by particular cues. For instance, an infant's handclapping may persist because the resulting sound reactivates the circular reaction. However, after the scheme is well established, it may be activated by an ojectively similar stimuli produced by another person; the father's handclapping may stimulate the child to do the same, as the child's own handclapping circular reaction is stimulated. This almost total assimilation of another person's actions gives way at the later stages of infancy to a more accommodative stance in Piaget's theory as the child comes to view the other as "the most interesting cognitive object, the most alive, the most unexpected, and at this level the most instructive one" (Piaget, 1954; quoted in Decarie, 1978, p. 196). From Baldwin's perspective, there is no reason to believe that recognition of the similarities between self and other necessarily precedes imitation because the behavioral similarities do not depend on conceptions of self. As we will see in the next section, however, Mead was not interested in the evolution of similar behaviors, but in the ontogenesis of communication through behaviors *with similar meanings*; he believed that the uninformed imitation of Baldwin, Guillaume, and Piaget could never lead to a common understanding.

GEORGE HERBERT MEAD

Like Baldwin, Mead was profoundly influenced by the Darwinian evolutionary thesis. Associated as he was with the Chicago school of functional pragmatism, it would have been difficult for him to avoid the influence of Darwin, since the earlier theoreticians of pragmatism (Pierce, James, and Dewey) were inspired by Darwin's doctrine (Wiener, 1949). A belief in the naturalness of man, faith in the value of the scientific method, and, most important for the purposes of this chapter, an assertion that the human organism is constantly adjusting itself and its environment to achieve temporary equilibria are the hallmarks of functional or evolutionary theory found in Mead's psychology which he called "social behaviorism." Unlike the behaviorisms of Watson (1925) and Skinner (1938), however, Mead's theory does not attempt to elucidate the nature of man solely by reference to principles applicable to organisms in general. As we will point out, Mead believed that humans have a number of unique interrelated qualities not found in animals.

Mead's conceptions of adaptation stresses the interaction between the individual and environment. According to Miller (1973), "for Mead, selection involves a living organism that is constantly making adjustments which require an environment, selection, and action" (p. 30). This emphasis generally aligns Mead with Baldwin's and Piaget's (1971) thesis regarding the interaction between phenome and genome while distinguishing him from the neo-Darwinian's fascination with interaction between the genesis of a species and the environment. Each "act" of the organism is intended to restore a never reached equilibrium through adaptation. Unique to humans, however, is the "act" that is interrupted by consideration: this break in the act during which an individual considers various possibilities arises from the human's hand that can manipulate objects, turning them so the organism can view the object from a variety of angles:

> The hand is responsible for what I term physical things, distinguishing the physical thing from what I call the consummation of the act. If we took our food as dogs do by the very organs by which we masticate it, we should not have any ground for distinguishing the food as a physical thing from the actual consummation of the act, the consumption of the food. . . such a thing comes in between the beginning of the act and its final consummation. It is in that sense a universal. (Mead, 1934, p. 184)

The pause in the act, in conjunction with significant symbols, which we will next discuss, constitutes the basis of intelligence and self-awareness.

Mead believed that only humans are capable of interacting by use of significant symbols. The interactions of animals are limited to conversations of gestures in which the gesture or movement of one animal causes another animal to react, which in turn stimulates the first to another movement. Mead offered as an example of conversation of gestures the dog-fight:

> The act of each dog becomes the stimulus of the other dog for his response. There is

then a relationship between these two; and as the act is responded to by the other dog, it, in turn, undergoes change. The very fact that the dog is ready to attack another becomes a stimulus to the other dog to change his own position or his own attitude. He has no sooner done this than the change in attitude in the second dog in turn causes the first dog to change his attitude. We have here a conversation of gestures. (1934, p. 43)

In contrast to the interactions of animals, humans are capable of exchanging significant symbols. Significant symbols differ from simple gestures in that "they implicitly arouse in an individual making them the same responses which they explicitly arouse, or are supposed to arouse, in other individuals, the individuals to whom they are addressed" (p. 47). If dogs were able to utilize significant symbols, then in the above example one dog might bare its teeth, knowing that baring the teeth implicitly arouses the tendency to run away, with the hope that the same gesture will cause the other dog to flee. Most usually in human interactions, significant symbols take the form of language. When an individual speaks to another, the gestures or words evoke in the other a meaning similar to that of the speaker. When a young child says "ball" and the parent picks up the ball, the meanings or implicit actions are the same.

Significant symbols and manipulation together are essential in the development of the intelligent, social human. The tendency of the hand to manipulate objects inserts a period of reflection between the initiation of the act and its consumma-tion, as well as allows the individual to view the object from a variety of perspectives. Significant symbols permit one individual to communicate his or her thoughts to another, or to exchange perspectives with another. However, neither significant symbols nor manipulation alone or together can produce an intelligent, social human; each individual must also have a self to be fully human. In the case of significant symbols, one cannot call out in the other by use of a gesture a response that is implicitly aroused in the self unless one is self-conscious. Similarly, without self-consciousness, manipulation of things can never result in an aware-ness of independent objects, since to have meaning the manipulations must have the self as a referent.

For Mead, the self was both a cognitive and social product. In sharp contrast to psychoanalytic and ego psychological positions (e.g., Ausubel et al., 1980; Mahler & Furer, 1968; Sullivan, 1953), Mead asserted that affective experiences are of secondary importance in self-formation: "Self-consciousness, rather than affective experience with its motor accompaniments, provides the core and primary structure of the self, which is thus essentially a cognitive rather than an emotional phenomenon" (1934, p. 173). Without self-consciousness, affective experience and kinesthetic feedback can have no personal meaning:

Until the rise of his self-consciousness in the process of social experience, the individual experiences his body—its feelings and sensations—merely as an immediate part of his environment, not as his own, not in terms of self-consciousness. The self and self-consciousness have first to arise, and then these experiences can be identified peculiarly with the self, or appropriated by the self; to enter, so to speak, into this heritage of experience, the self has first to develop within the social process in which this heritage is involved. (1934, p. 172)

The genesis of the self-concept must await the development of self-consciousness. According to Mead, self-consciousness arises from taking the perspective of the other toward the self; when an individual can regard the self as he or she could regard another, the individual becomes aware that both the self and the other have discrete boundaries and characteristic properties. The ability to take the perspective of another toward the self is contingent on the child's developing communicative competence: "The importance of what we term 'communication' lies in the fact that it provides a form of behavior in which the organism or the individual may become an object to himself" (1934, p. 138). Communication plays such a role, because communication involves the use of common or "significant" symbols. For Mead, the self is a cognitive, communicative, and social achievement.

Mead describes two levels of self-consciousness:

> At [the] first of these stages, the "play stage" the individual's self is constituted simply by an organization of the particular attitudes of other individuals toward himself and toward one another in the specific social acts in which he participates with them. But at the second stage in the "game stage" full development of the individual's self is constituted not only by an organization of these particular individual attitudes, but also by an organization of the social attitudes of the generalized other or the social group as a whole to which he belongs. (1934, p. 158) [The distinctions between Mead's "play" and "game" stages are elaborated in Chapter 9]

Self-consciousness constitutes the first of these stages. When the child comes to have a self-concept, as a result of self-consciousness, he or she can begin taking the other's view toward the self. With the self developed through self-consciousness serving as the referent of others' knowledge, the child may come to know that with the mother, the child is seen as polite and cute; with a peer, the child may know that the other thinks of him or her as a person with a nice house and lots of toys; and with a teacher, the child may know that the teacher regards the child as a good speller, but a poor reader. Since the self is constituted by the ability to take the perspective of the other, the child to some extent assumes these attitudes of these various others toward the self; thus, the child thinks of him or her self as a different sort of being depending on the context. At home, the child thinks of the self as polite and cute, and so on. Because early childhood self-consciousness is constituted through a process of assuming the attitude of a particular other (the mother, a peer, etc.), the self lacks stability. The self at this age varies according to which person's perspective the child assumes.

> The child is one thing at one time and another at another, and what he is at one

moment does not determine what he is at another. That is both the charm of childhood as well as its inadequacy. You cannot count on the child; you cannot assume that all the things he does are going to determine what he will do at any moment. He is not organized into a whole. The child has no definite character, no definite personality. (1934, p. 159)

Over the course of time, however, the child comes to organize and generalize the attitudes of single others to form a societal perspective, or a generalized other. In particular, those aspects of the other's attitudes that are social in nature are systematized.

The fundamental difference between the game and play is that in the latter the child must have the attitude of all the others involved in that game. The attitudes of the other players which the participant assumes organize into a sort of unity, and it is that organization which controls the response of the individual. The illustration used was of a person playing baseball. Each one of his own acts is determined by his assumption of the action of the others who are playing the game. . . . If one has the attitude of the person throwing the ball, he can also have the response of catching the ball. The two are related so that they further the purpose of the game itself. They are interrelated in a unitary, organic fashion. There is a definite unity, then, which is introduced into the organization of other selves when we reach such a stage as that of the game, as over against the situation of play where there is a simple succession of one role after another, a situation which is, of course, characteristic of the child's own personality. (Mead, 1934, pp. 153–158).

For Mead, the stability and organization of concepts of self and other are achieved only when the individual develops the ability to take the perspective to the "generalized other" toward the self and others.

Like Baldwin, Mead has often been criticized for his failure to seriously consider the subjective sense of individuality that each person has. As Flavell et al. point out, "his theoretical constructs (significant symbols and generalized others) are basically mechanisms for generating sameness, for creating interindividual homogeneity" (1968, p. 15). In Mead's view of society, role-taking is ubiquitous; communication, interaction, concepts of self and other exist only because of the possibility of role-taking. The thesis that the self is a cognitive construct of communicative origin is convincingly presented by Mead.

A BRIEF SUMMARY OF MEAD AND BALDWIN

There are a number of points of convergence between Baldwin and Mead; for one, they shared a common intellectual history, an era of scientific thought permeated by the promise of the Darwin-inspired evolutionism. Although we have pointed out the influences of evolutionism on each man's theory earlier in this chapter, the common intellectual heritage probably encouraged both to regard the self as an important aspect of human development. If each characteristic of a species persists over a period of time, even a characteristic such as self-awareness and self-consciousness, then from an evolutionary perspective one must assume that the quality in question has adaptive value. Baldwin's and Mead's assumption that self-awareness is an important development was lost for a long period of time because of the rise of empiricist behaviorism, a paradigm within which it was considered illogical and nonproductive to study ephemeral unobservable objects like the self (see Broughton, 1980, for further discussion of this point). The naturalism of the Darwinian revolution also encouraged both to reject the notion of transcendental selves that exist apart from society. Instead, Mead and Baldwin sought the origins of the self in the early social behavior of the infant and toddler; Baldwin by means of early imitation and Mead through reference to communication, primarily language. But more important for social developmental psychology are the points of agreement in their theories of selves. First, both men agreed that the self is a cognitive construct readily accessible to consciousness. Mead thought self-consciousness was the central attribute of the self. Baldwin went even further and claims that self-knowledge is crucial for social development: "Self-thoughts imitatively organized are, I contend, the essence of what is social" (1902, p. 595). This position is in sharp contrast to psychoanalytic writers and even Piaget who have claimed that an individual's self-knowledge is irrelevant or assumes a subsidiary role in a person's daily functioning.

Both Mead and Baldwin also agree that the self-concept is social in nature. For Mead, self-consciousness is the point of departure for the development of the self; self-consciousness can only develop in a social context in which significant symbols exist and are used by other members of a community. Baldwin claimed that the self and the self-concept are but one pole of the self-other dialectic. In this thesis, it would be impossible to have a thought of self, unless one had a thought of another.

A final point of accord between Mead and Baldwin is their common assertion that the last stage of self-concept development is characterized by the individual's recognition of the "generalized other" that emerges from a generalization of the common aspect of all the different perspectives or roles the child assumes in the course of social interactions. In Baldwin's theory, the child comes to recognize the socius in the limits he or she discerns in the behaviors of others. These limits are common to all, and the child imitating others identifies these common structures on behavior as an ideal, and seeks to align his or her behavior with them. These limits are the child's first realization of the socius, the common bond among all members of society.

Perhaps the most significant differences between the theories of Baldwin and Mead are their differing ideas regarding the process of self-development. Baldwin viewed similarity of self and other as directly striven for through imitation, whereas Mead viewed it as the indirect result of role-taking involved in communicative acts. The child's attitude, he thought, became like that of the other because both respond alike to a common symbol or gesture. Because the child has responded in the past to the other's gesture, when the child makes the gesture to the self, it calls out in the self implicitly the response that it calls out in the other. Mead further points out that much sociality, much mutual role-taking occurs through cooperative interaction in which each individual's role is different, in which roles are complementary rather than similar. Nevertheless, the study of infancy (e.g., Gardner & Gardner, 1970; Guillaume, 1927; Meltzoff & Moore, 1977; Piaget, 1962) indicates that similarity to others is directly striven for, and that such striving for imitation precedes, rather than follows, the development of linguistic communication. Accordingly, it seems to us that Mead's conceptions must be embedded in a broader developmental account of the self that includes early imitative behavior and the matrix of infant cognitive development out of which the self emerges.

IMPLICATIONS FOR SOCIAL DEVELOPMENT

These theories have, we think, a number of important perspectives to offer on social development. First, Baldwin and Mead are suggesting that much can be learned about social development in general and about the development of the self in particular through direct questioning of children and adults, since the self is essentially a cognitive construct that is available to conscious introspection. This kind of approach to empirical investigation is of course contrary to those methods advocated by psychoanalytic writers, in which the self or ego is studied through case analyses or by interpreting responses to ambiguous test materials such as ink blots. Direct questioning of children and adults about issues in social development, beginning with Piaget's (1932/1965) work on moral judgment, followed by Kohlberg and a number of others interested in social cognition, has proved immensely valuable. We believe that a similar approach to self-understanding could also be very productive, as partially evidenced by the little research that has used such a method (see Damon & Hart, 1982, for a review of such studies).

On a more theoretical plane, the theories of Baldwin and Mead suggest a fundamentally different view of human nature than that found in the psychoanalytic or the social learning paradigms in which people are totally egoistic in their concerns. Baldwin and Mead claim that to be human is to be innately social; infants do not trade some of their most cherished freedoms for the protection of society; nor do they come to be sympathetic and moral simply as the result of schedules of reinforcement, but rather infants desire and need true social interaction and involvement.

Two examples of phenomena in infancy and toddlerhood make the social nature of the child strikingly clear. The first is attachment. As Kohlberg (1982) has pointed out, attachment between infant and caretaker is a *social* relationship characterized by four qualities:

1. *Attachment involves similarity to the other.* Attachment is only to another person, not toward physical objects.

2. *Attachment involves love or altruism toward the other*, an attitude not felt toward bottles or cloth mothers. Altruism, of course, presupposes the "ejective" consciousness of the feelings and wishes of the other, i.e., empathy or sympathy for role taking in Mead's terminology.

3. *Attachment and altruism presuppose self-love.* The striving to satisfy another self presupposes the capacity or disposition to satisfy one's own self. Common sense assumes that the self (as a body and center of activity) is loved intrinsically, not instrumentally (i.e., not because the body or the body's activities are followed by reinforcement or drive reduction). It is this nucleus of self-love which is involved, also, in organizing attachment to others.

4. *Attachment presupposes the desire for esteem in the eyes of the other or for reciprocal attachment.* In other words, it presupposes self-esteem motivation and the need for social approval, again presupposing ejective consciousness (or role taking). (Kohlberg, 1982, pp. 321–322)

The truly social nature of the attachment bond between infant and caretaker is further demonstrated in a study by Cummings, Zahn-Waxler, and Radke-Yarrow (1981) in which sympathetic or empathic behavior in children was found as young as one year of age. In her observational study of preschool children, Murphy (1937) concluded that "experiencing distress when another is in distress seems primitive, naive, reasonably universal" (p. 295). To summarize, Baldwin and Mead conclude that the entire span of human development is truly social, involving relationships between selves.

The third point of convergence between the self theories of Mead and Baldwin, is their common assertion that the child's self undergoes an important transformation when the "socius" or "generalized other" is discerned in the course of interactions with others. Although both believed that this discovery by the child led to the stabilization of the child's character, Mead failed to consider any further implications of this development while Baldwin elaborated this aspect into a theory of moral development. The development of the ideal self, in Baldwin's theory, is the mechanism by which a conscience develops. In our view, Baldwin's ideal self provides an explanation of the moral phenomena of conscience or obligation that is superior to explanations found in psychoanalytic or Piagetian literature (Kohlberg, 1982). According to Freud (1923/1960) the sense of obligation or moral compulsion derives from the introjection of object cathexes (most prominently the opposite-sexed parent) and a corresponding identification with a more acceptable individual (most usually the same-sexed parent). As Kohlberg (1969) has pointed out, however, empirical research has consistently failed to find the expected correlation between parental moral values and attitudes and the child's moral values and attitudes that should exist if the Freudian account were true. Furthermore, a weakness of this explanation is that it fails to explain the sense of moral obligation that individuals who have rejected societal regulations as the essence of morality (post-conventional morality in Kohlberg's scheme) feel. Baldwin (1906) explicitly considered this problem, and concluded that it is possible to have an ideal self that supercedes current social regulations: "*in the ethical realm the individual may rule himself by rules which are in advance of those which society prescribes,* and also exact them" (p. 567). The ideal self can therefore prescribe obedience resulting in a sense of obligation in situations in which current societal norms are violated.

In the course of this chapter, we have presented the theories of Baldwin and Mead, shown how these theories are different from those of Piaget, and sketched some theoretical and empirical implications of their theories for social development. We believe the social-self-oriented theories of Baldwin and Mead, along with Vygotsky, whose work will be described next, can still offer insights as to where a social developmental theory should proceed in the future.

In contrast to Baldwin and Mead, Vygotsky did not make the notion of self a central part of his approach. However, he did produce a theoretical framework that is very suggestive of how one might approach the issues typically examined under the heading of self.

We begin our account of this theoretical framework and its implications for an account of self by examining briefly the unique sociocultural setting in which it emerged. By doing so, we can gain some insight into the reasons for the absence of an explicit account of self in Vygotsky's approach. Such an exercise also provides some insight into what Vygotsky would have proposed had he produced an account of self.

One could cite a number of reasons for the absence of the notion of self in Vygotsky's theoretical framework. The first is that there is no good equivalent term for self in the Russian language. Perhaps the closest word (which everyone agrees is by no means synonymous) is "lichnost." This, however, is usually translated as "personality," a term that is hardly equivalent to "self." Another possible Russian translation of self is "individ" (roughly equivalent to "individual" in English), but this again has its obvious problems.

The absence of a good Russian equivalent for self, however, does not explain Vygotsky's failure to include this notion in his approach. This becomes apparent when one considers that Vygotsky had access to this notion in other languages. In addition to Russian, he read or spoke German, French, English, and Hebrew. Furthermore, it is not the case that Vygotsky failed to incorporate an explicit notion of self into his theoretical framework because he was not familiar with relevant Western literature. Besides knowing the works of Baldwin and Freud, he was conversant with the writings of such figures as Jung, James, and Piaget. (There is no concrete evidence, however, that he read Mead.)

Hence, in order to understand why the notion of self never played a role in Vygotsky's approach, one must look beyond his linguistic skills and his acquaintance with others' writings. We would argue that the best place to look is in Russian culture and the concerns of Soviet psychology (especially developmental psychology) at the time Vygotsky was working. If one does this, it becomes apparent that a powerful underlying (though often implicit) concern of developmental psychologists was with the ways in which children are socialized into a collective setting. Rather than being concerned with self, individuation, self-assertion, and other such issues, Vygotsky's attention focused on ways in which children become productive members of school and other collectives. This does not mean that he was not concerned with mental processes of the individual (something that concerns any psychologist in one way or another); rather, it means that he approached such mental processes from the perspective of how they allow the individual to function in group activities and in broader sociocultural settings.

This is consistent with Vygotsky's implicit concern with "nation-building" as noted by Wertsch and Youniss (in press). An essential part of official Soviet policy after the Russian Revolution of 1917 was that the country had to construct a new socialist society in a relatively short time. One of the pillars of this policy was the national effort to create "the new Soviet man." The model for this type of person was highly educated and could function smoothly in collective settings such as those found in school and in the workplace.

In addition to the influence of official Soviet ideology, we would argue that a more deep-seated set of cultural beliefs and values was also behind Vygotsky's and other Soviet psychologists' focus on socialization into the collective, rather than on individual self, identity, and so forth. Specifically, it seems to us that the centuries-old Russian tendency to value collective functioning over individual functioning (at least by Western standards) was also behind his and others' approach to socialization.

If this sociohistorical and cultural setting provided the framework for Vygotsky's activities, what, specifically, was his approach? Not surprisingly, it was not simply another version of learning theory, pragmatism, or any other Western approach to development. While incorporating certain familiar constructs, it brought others to bear in an overall framework that is unique.

As Wertsch (1985) has noted, Vygotsky's general approach can be understood in terms of three general themes that run throughout his writings. These themes are: (a) a reliance on a genetic, or developmental, method; (b) the claim that social ("interpsychological") processes give rise to higher, uniquely human individual ("intrapsychological") processes; and (c) the claim that cultural tools, signs (especially human language), and other forms of mediation play a major role in human activity, both on the interpsychological and intrapsychological planes. In the chapter "Language and the Development of Thought" we touched on these issues, but in what follows we will present them in an integrated way in order to outline what a Vygotskian approach to self would involve.

Because they are part of an integrated theoretical framework, these three themes are thoroughly interrelated. For example, the relationship between interpsychological and intrapsychological processes mentioned in (b) is a developmental relationship. Vygotsky's version of genetic explanation, a method he viewed as fundamental for all psychology, led him to argue that one can understand higher mental functions such as reasoning, voluntary attention, and logical memory in the individual only by understanding their origins and the transformations they undergo. In his view, the key to understanding these origins, as well as several aspects of the transformations that lead up to intrapsychological functioning, is to be found in an analysis of interpsychological functioning. Hence, themes (a) and (b) are thoroughly intertwined.

Perhaps the best single statement from Vygotsky's writings in which this interconnection is manifested is his "general genetic law of cultural development" that we presented in Chapter 5. We repeat it here for the sake of convenience.

> Any function in the child's cultural development appears twice, or on two planes. First it appears on the social plane, and then on the psychological plane. First it appears between people as an interpsychological category, and then within the child as an intrapsychological category. This is equally true with regard to voluntary attention, logical memory, the formation of voluntary attention, logical memory, the formation of concepts, and the development of volition. (Vygotsky, 1981b, p. 163)

If one were to focus exclusively on themes (a) and (b) in Vygotsky's approach, his ideas, at least in their general outline, would appear to be quite similar to those of Baldwin, Mead, and, to some extent, Piaget. However, Vygotsky's account of tool and sign mediation provides a unique dimension to his approach. Furthermore, the fact that it is so thoroughly intertwined with the other two themes means that these other themes actually have a different interpretation than that found in the writings of Baldwin, Mead, or others. Indeed, as Wertsch (1985) has argued, Vygotsky gave this mediational theme an analytical priority in his approach. This means that both of the first two themes rest on the third for their interpretation. In the case of Vygotsky's genetic method the point is that developmental shifts in ontogenesis (as well as in other "genetic domains" such as phylogenesis and social history) are defined in terms of the appearance of new mediational means or the development of existing ones. In Vygotsky's claims about the transition from interpsychological to intrapsychological functioning in ontogenesis, the point is that mediational means are a critical component in defining both of these planes of functioning. Furthermore, he viewed the transition from interpsychological to intrapsychological functioning as being possible largely because of the connection made through semiotic mediational means. As noted in Chapter 5 his analysis of the semiotic means that facilitate this transition focuses on two major issues: the development of concepts and the transition from social to egocentric to inner speech.

Given this general theoretical framework, how would one go about formulating a Vygotskian account of self? We believe that the best answer to this lies in the way in which the three major themes in Vygotsky's work are worked out in his notion of "consciousness" (soznanie). For Vygotsky, consciousness is not primarily a phenomenon of levels of wakefulness or cortical activation (as in a physiological theory); nor is it a construct that contrasts with the unconscious, subconscious, or preconscious (as in psychodynamic theories). Rather, it is a term that applies to a wide range of mental phenomena concerning the ways in which humans can know and interact with the world; it is a term whose use reflects a general philosophical concern with the ways in which humans differ from animals in cognition and affect. In this sense consciousness was a part of several theories in Soviet psychology that took the writings of Marx as a critical part of their philosophical foundation.

As Wertsch (1985) has noted, one of the reasons the notion of consciousness played such a central role in Vygotsky's theoretical framework was that it provides a mechanism whereby he could overcome the fragmentation that he saw as endemic to existing schools of psychology. He invoked it in an attempt to create an account of mental functioning in which affect would not be separated from intellect, memory would not be separated from attention, attention would not be separated from perception, and so on. In his view it is naive, if not mistaken, to consider any aspect of consciousness in isolation. Indeed, he argued that one can understand any particular functional aspect of consciousness only by appreciating its interfunctional relationships with others.

At the most global level this means that Vygotsky objected to the isolation of affect and intellect. As Wertsch (1985) has noted, however, Vygotsky did not really deal with this problem in any comprehensive way. Instead, he devoted most of his efforts to providing an integrated account of the higher mental functions that are the components of the intellectual or cognitive side of consciousness. This means that Vygotsky was concerned with ways in which functions such as thinking, logical memory, and voluntary attention are interrelated. Furthermore, he was concerned with ways in which development consists of *changes* in these inter-connections. As Wertsch (1985) notes,

> Any discussion of Vygotsky's ideas on the organization properties of this "functional unity" of consciousness would be incomplete, if not misleading, if it did not make the point that his concern was with dynamic or dialectical, rather than static, organiza-tion. Just as important as the existence of interfunctional connections is the fact that these connections continually change.... [Vygotsky] argued that change in the interrelationships among higher mental functions rather than the development of the individual functions themselves was the primary cause of the development of consciousness. (pp. 190–191)

Vygotsky made this point by arguing that

> ...the psychological development of the child is not so much the development and perfection of separate functions as the change in interfunctional relationships.... The fate of each functional part in the development of consciousness depends on the change of the whole, and not vice versa. (1934, pp. 189–190)

Vygotsky used the following example to illustrate how various combinations or "mixtures" of higher mental functions characterize the activity of children at different stages of development.

The memory of older children is not only different from the memory of younger children; it also plays a different role in the older child's cognitive activity. Memory in early childhood is one of the central psychological functions upon which all the other functions are built. Our analyses suggest that thinking in the very young child is in many respects determined by his memory, and is certainly not the same thing as the thinking of the more mature child.... *For the young child, to think means to recall; but for the adolescent, to recall means to think.* (1978, pp. 50–51)

From this quotation, it is obvious that Vygotsky thought that it is possible to focus on one or another higher mental function in research. For example, he had no objection to conducting studies of memory or thinking. However, it is also clear that the very definition of any mental function changes in development as a result of its changing interrelationships with other mental functions. In the case outlined here, early forms of thinking or problem solving are viewed as consisting of some kind of relatively rigid calling up of existing images ("to think means to recall"); when confronted with a novel problem, the child in this phase of development is likely to try to impose an existing (often inappropriate) pattern of action on the setting. Furthermore, memory is viewed as being more eidetic (i.e., simply reproductive) than constructive. In contrast, for the older child memory is typically more constructive (i.e., it relies more heavily on reasoning or thinking) than had previously been the case. An analogous point has been made by Piaget (Heinz Werner lectures at Clark) in his analysis of the role of operative intelligence in memory.

For Vygotsky consciousness was a theoretical construct that recognizes the integrated, wholistic nature of human mental, especially cognitive, functioning. It is a construct that encourages investigators to remember that humans do not operate in an isolated memory, thinking, or other modes of cognitive activity. We have seen that Vygotsky did not object to studies that focus on reasoning, memory, attention, or some other higher mental function. However, the inclusion of consciousness as a construct in his theoretical approach means that an adequate account of any mental function can ultimately be arrived at only by examining how it is interrelated to other functions. Of course as a matter of common sense everyone knows that it is impossible to think without remembering, perceive without attending, and so on, but disciplinary fragmentation often creates subdisciplines and journals that seem to assume otherwise. It is exactly this kind of fragmentation that Vygotsky wished to combat.

We would argue that this integrated notion of consciousness is the construct in Vygotsky's theory most like a notion of self. In Vygotsky's approach it provides the integrating focus of various aspects of mental functioning that together result in the processes of the unified, active cognitive agent. To understand more of the specifics of this notion, one must consider the way in which the three general themes that run throughout Vygotsky's writings are manifested in it.

As noted above, the first of these general themes is a reliance on a genetic or developmental explanation. We have already touched on this issue somewhat in our comments on the dynamic or dialectical organizational properties of consciousness. Recall that the development of consciousness is posited to be more a matter of changing relationships among higher mental functions than the development of these functions in isolation.

A second way in which genetic explanation enters Vygotsky's account of consciousness is intertwined with the second theme in his general approach—the social origins and "quasi-social" nature of higher mental functioning in the individual. In this connection it is interesting to take note of a comment often made by A. N. Leont'ev, one of Vygotsky's major students and collaborators. Leont'ev (personal communication, 1976) related that Vygotksy loved to point out that in Russian the term for consciousness (soznanie) can be broken down into the prefix "so" (the rough equivalent of the prefix "co" in English) and the stem "znanie" (the equivalent of "knowledge"). Hence in Russian consciousness means "co-knowledge." That is, consciousness is an inherently social phenonenon.

The way this is manifested in ontogenesis is through Vygotsky's general genetic law of cultural development. This means that the functioning of consciousness first appears on the interpsychological, or social, plane and then is mastered and internalized to form the intrapsychological plane. For readers steeped in Western traditions of psychology it may seem strange to attribute a term like "consciousness" to the functioning of dyads or larger groups as well as individuals, but that is precisely what is entailed in the general genetic law of cultural development.* In formulating this law Vygotsky went on to write that

> We may consider this position as a law in full sense of the word. . . . Social relations or relations among people genetically underlie all higher functions and their relationships. (1981, p. 163)

In order to explicate the set of claims included in the general genetic law of cultural development, we will use a hypothetical, but very common and familiar example. In this example a child approaches an adult with a seemingly insoluble memory problem. For instance, consider the scenario in which a preschooler comes to his mother and reports that he cannot find his shoes "anywhere in the house." What is the likely course the adult will take to assist in the search? One option is that the mother herself may simply look for the shoes. Another option, and the one we wish to explore here, is for the mother to begin questioning the child about where the missing shoes were last seen, worn, and so forth. In such a case the dialogue might go something like the following (where M = mother and C = child):

---

*This does not mean that Vygotsky posited some notion of collective consciousness as outlined by Durkheim or the collective unconsciousness as proposed by Jung. In opposition to authors such as these, he was concerned with the coordinated social action of a dyad or other small group.

(1) C: I can't find my shoes.

(2)M: Oh no, not again.

(3) C: I've looked all over the house and they aren't anywhere.

(4)M: All right. Did you have them on when you came into the house?

(5) C: Yes. I just came back from the park then.

(6)M: What's the first thing you did when you came in?

(7) C: I went downstairs to feed the fish.

(8)M: Where did you go then?

(9) C: I went into my room to play.

(10)M: Where did you go then?

(11) C: I just came here.

(12)M: Did you look in your room?

(13) C: Yes, and they're not there.

(14)M: Did you look downstairs by the aquarium?

(15) C: No.

(16)M: Maybe you should look down there.

(17) C: Oh yeah.

When examining such adult-child dialogues, the question we wish to raise is: Who did the remembering? It turns out that one cannot answer this question by pointing to either of the participants in isolation. On the one hand, the child probably would not have approached the adult for help if he could have remembered where his shoes were; on the other hand, the adult did not have access to the information required in this memory task. To answer the question about who did the remembering, one must look elsewhere, namely, one must turn to Vygotsky's notion of consciousness as co-knowledge. From this perspective we see that the appropriate answer is that the *dyad* did the remembering. To say that a dyad, or group of any kind, remembers (or thinks, attends, and so forth) may once again strike many readers as a strange way to use the term, but that is precisely the usage implied by Vygotsky's claim that higher mental functions and consciousness in general first appear on the social or interpsychological plane. From this perspective, dyads *do* remember, think, attend, and so forth.

In our example we see that there is a division of responsibility between the mother and child such that the mother poses the questions and the child supplies the answers. In an important sense the mother is doing the thinking required in this memory task, and the child is doing the remembering (a very simple form of remembering, to be sure). The reason for the child's inability to "remember" is that he does not know the right sequence of questions. However, once those questions are posed, it turns out that the answers are relatively easy and are accessible to him. In the terminology of researchers such as Brown (1978) and Brown and DeLoache (1978), we might say that the dyad remembers "strategically," whereas the child at this stage and in this task setting does not.

In the case we have been reviewing, it becomes clear that something more than simple recall is being carried out by the dyad. Indeed, it illustrates that except for some kind of very primitive recognition memory, there may be no such thing as simple recall. Instead, memory often turns out to involve a complex mixture of mental processes along the lines found in Vygotsky's account of consciousness. This means that the very nature of higher mental functions such as memory typically changes with development. By becoming interrelated with thinking, what starts out as a form of simple recall is transformed into a more complex form of remembering.

Thus the interpsychological functioning in this example illustrates the kind of interpsychological functioning that Vygotsky seems to have had in mind when formulating the general genetic law of cultural development. In particular, it illustrates what he meant when he said that "Social relationships or relationships among people genetically underlie all higher functions and their relationships." In our example the relationship between the mother and the child underlies the relationship between thinking and memory that will eventually characterize the child's intrapsychological functioning.

Once we see how the unified, interfunctional operation of consciousness can occur on the interpsychological plane, the next question raised by Vygotsky's approach is: How does this interpsychological functioning give rise to strategic functioning on the intrapsychological plane? The answer is to be found in his claims about the mastery and internalization of mediational means used in social functioning. For Vygotsky, the essential point is that by mastering and internalizing dialogic patterns of language use such as the one outlined above, the child integrates previously distinct mental functions (in this case thinking and memory), and thereby transforms them into qualitatively new forms. This is precisely the kind of interfunctional reorganization that he specified as critical for the development of consciousness.

In talking about linguistic dialogue, we are invoking the third theme, concerned with semiotic mediation, in Vygotsky's approach. In examples such as the one above, this highlights how the child must master and internalize the language used in a pattern of dialogue. This is an essential aspect of Vygotsky's claims concerning the emergence of egocentric and inner speech as outlined in Chapter 5.

Vygotsky's claims about the mastery of dialogue have much in common with Mead's ideas as outlined in Chapter 5. However, there are important differences as well as similarities between Vygotsky and Mead on this point. The main way in which Vygotsky differs from Mead here, and perhaps in general, is to be found in his treatment of language and other semiotic phenomena. In this connection it is important to return to our example and witness the role that language plays in it. In a Vygotskian account the emphasis is on how language structure and language use determines the possibilities for people to regulate others and themselves. In the case we outlined above, one of the principle relevant phenomena is that language is used to represent objects and actions that are not present in the immediate speech situation. This was a major concern of Vygotsky and his colleagues (e.g., Levina, 1981) when analyzing social and self-regulative speech. The fact that objects and events not immediately present at the locus of the speech event are discussed in adult-child interaction such as that outlined above means that the child is confronted with "semiotic challenges" (Wertsch, 1985) to represent items that are essential for mature human mental processes. Vygotsky's focus on complex linguistic mechanisms* such as abstract categorization, meaning, reference (both indexical and symbolic), and contextualized sign functioning (cf. Wertsch, 1985) distinguish much of his analysis from that carried out by Mead. Among the many complex aspects to the formative power of language use as Vygotsky understood it are "emergent interactionism" and the differentiation of self-regulative, private speech from social speech as outlined in Chapter 5.

Further differences between Vygotsky on the one hand and Mead and Baldwin on the other appear when one conducts a detailed comparison of the latter authors' account of the self and Vygotsky's account of consciousness. As outlined earlier in this chapter, a major concern for Mead and Baldwin was role-taking. Just as he never addressed issues of self per se, Vygotsky never explicitly examined the notion of role-taking. It seems to us that there is nothing in principle that would have prevented him from doing so, but the fact that he did not is a reflection of a fundamental difference between him and other theorists covered here in the treatment of social phenomena. In the general genetic law of cultural development and throughout his work, Vygotsky stressed the notion that individual mental functioning emerges out of social functioning. In his first major presentation to psychologists in 1924 he argued that "the social dimension of consciousness is primary in time and fact. The individual dimension of consciousness is derivative and secondary, based on the social and construed exactly in its likeness" (1979, p. 30).

This notion of social phenomena contrasts somewhat with that found in Baldwin, Mead, or Piaget. Rather than being concerned with psychological mechanisms whereby one understands others' thoughts and feelings, it focuses on actual, concrete social interactional processes. That is, rather than presupposing psychological processes in the individual that allow him or her to take another's perspective, it poses what it views as the prior question: What are the origins of these psychological processes in the human individual?

Hence the fact that Vygotsky did not pay explicit attention to role-taking may be seen as a natural correlate to his primary concern with the social origins of individual mental processes. A concern with role-taking presupposes that one can begin by identifying an independent cognitive agent who takes others' perspectives

---

*Points similar to the ones raised here about a Vygotskian account of self have been made by Lee and Hickmann (1983). These authors have focused particularly on the role of semiotic phenomena in a Vygotskian analysis of self. For example, they touch on Vygotsky's notions of the multifunctionality of language, the functional differentiation of language into social and self-regulative forms, reflexive signs, and inner speech.

into account. Through this process of perspective-taking the individual is viewed as being socialized. Vygotsky's response to such approaches would have been to ask: "But what gave rise to the individual?"

Again, we would point out that there is nothing in principle that would have prevented Vygotsky from analyzing role-taking within his general theoretical framework. However, before one can examine such skills in the individual, his approach calls for the investigator to provide an account of the social interactional processes that gave rise to the individual. Among the consequences of such an approach is the expectation that the social interactional processes that produce intrapsychological functioning in different sociocultural settings may vary, thereby resulting in different skills and styles.

REFERENCES

Ausubel, D. P., et al. (1980). *Theory and problems of child development* (3rd ed.) (pp. 169–199). New York: Grune & Stratton.

Baldwin, J. M. (1896). A new factor in evolution. *American Naturalist, 30,* 441–451.

Baldwin, J. M. (1902). *Social and ethical intepretations in mental development.* New York: Macmillan.

Baldwin, J. M. (1906). *Thought and things or genetic logic. Vol. 1. Functional logic.* New York: Macmillan.

Bates, J. E. (1975). Effects of a child's imitation versus non-imitation on adult's verbal and nonverbal positivity. *Journal of Personality and Social Psychology, 31,* 840–851.

Borke, H. (1973). The development of empathy in Chinese and American children between 3 and 6 years of age: A cross-cultural study. *Developmental Psychology, 9,* 102–108.

Broughton, J. (1980). The divided self in adolesence. *Human Development, 24,* 13–32.

Broughton, J. M., & Freeman-Moir, D. J. (Eds.). (1982). *The cognitive developmental psychology of James Mark Baldwin: Current research in genetic epistemology.* Norwood, NJ: Ablex.

Brown, A. L. (1978). Knowing when, where, and how to remember: A problem of metacognition. In R. Glaser (Ed.), *Advances in intructional psychology.* Hillsdale, NJ: Erlbaum.

Brown, A. L., & DeLoache, J. S. (1978). Skills, plans and self-regulation. In R. Siegler (Ed.), *Children's thinking: What develops.* Hillsdale, NJ: Erlbaum.

Condon, W., & Sander, L. (1974). Synchrony demonstrated between movements of the neonate and adult speech. *Child Development, 45,* 456–462.

Cooley, C. H. (1902). *Human nature and the social order.* New York: Scribners.

Cummings, E., Zahn-Waxler, C., & Radke-Yarrow, M. (1981). Young children's responses to expressions of anger and affection by others in the family. *Child Development, 52,* 1274–1282.

Damon, W. (1983). *Social development from infancy through adulthood.* New York: Norton.

Damon, W. & Hart, D. (1982), The development of self-understanding from infancy through adolescence, *Child Development, 53,* 841–864.

Decarie, T. (1978). Affect development and cognition in a Piagetian context. In M. Lewis & L. Rosenblum (Eds.), *The development of affect.* New York: Plenum.

Feffer, M. J., & Gourevitch, U. (1960). Cognitive aspects of role-taking in children. *Journal of Personality, 28*, 383–396.

Flavell, J., Botkin, P., Fry, C., Wright, J., & Jarvis, P. (1968). *The development of role-taking and communication skills in children.* New York: Wiley.

Freud, S. (1923/1963). *The ego and the id.* New York: Norton.

Gardner, J., & Gardner, H. (1970). A note on selective imitation by a six-week-old infant. *Child development, 41*, 1209–1213.

Guillaume, P. (1926/1971). *Imitation in children.* Chicago: University of Chicago Press.

Hart, D., & Damon, W. (1983). Contrasts between the understanding of self and an understanding of others. In R. Leahy (Ed.), *The development of self.* New York: Academic.

Hoffman, M. (1977). Personality and social development. *Annual Review of Psychology, 28*, 259–321.

James, W. (1892/1961). *Psychology: The briefer course.* New York: Harper & Row.

Kegan, R. (1982). *The evolving self: Problem and process in human development.* Cambridge: Harvard University Press.

Kohlberg, L. (1969). Stage and sequence: The cognitive-developmental approach to socialization. In D. A. Goslin (Ed.), *Handbook of socialization theory and research.* Chicago: Rand McNally. Reprinted in L. Kohlberg (1984), *The psychology of moral development.*

Kohlberg, L. (1982). Moral development. In J. M. Broughton & D. J. Freeman-Moir (Eds.), *The cognitive developmental psychology of James Mark Baldwin: Current research in genetic epistemology.* Norwood, NJ: Ablex.

Kohlberg, L. (1984). *The psychology of moral development: Vol. II. Essays on moral development.* New York: Harper & Row.

Lee, B. (1982). Cognitive development and the self. In J. M. Broughton & D. J. Freeman-Moir (Eds.), *The cognitive developmental psychology of James Mark Baldwin: Current research in genetic epistemology.* Norwood, NJ: Ablex.

Lee, B., & Hickmann, M. (1983). Language, thought, and self: Vygotsky's developmental theory. In B. Lee & G. G. Noam (Eds.), *Developmental approaches to the self.* New York: Plenum.

Levina, R. E. (1981). L. S. Vygotsky's ideas about the planning function of speech in children. In J. V. Wertsch (Ed.), *The concept of activity in Soviet psychology.* Armonk, NY: M. E. Sharpe.

Livesly, W. J., & Bromley, D. B. (1973). *Person perception in childhood and adolescence.* New York: Wiley.

Mahler, M. S., & Furer, M. (1968). *On human symbiosis and the vicissitudes of individuation.* New York: International Universities Press.

Mead, G. H. (1909). Social psychology as counterpart to physiological psychology. *Psychological Bulletin, 6*, 401–408.

Mead, G. H. (1934). *Mind, self & society.* Chicago: University of Chicago Press.

Meltzoff, A. N., & Moore, M. K. (1977). Imitation and facial and manual gestures by human neonates. *Science, 198*, 75–78.

Miller, D. L. (1973). *George Herbert Mead.* Chicago: University of Chicago Press.

Murphy, L. B. (1937). *Social behavior and child personality.* New York: Columbia University, Press.

Piaget, J. (1927/1969). *The child's conception of the world.* Totowa, NJ: Littlefield.

Piaget, J. (1932/1965). *The moral judgment of the child* (Trans., M. Gabain). New York: Free Press.

Piaget, J. (1951/1962). *Play, dreams, and imitation in childhood.* New York: Norton.

Piaget, J. (1970). Piaget's theory. In P. Musson (Ed.), *Carmichael's manual of child · psychology,* New York: Wiley.

Piaget, J. (1971). *Biology and knowledge.* Chicago: University of Chicago Press.

Piaget, J. (1982). Reflections on Baldwin. In J. M. Broughton & D. J. Freeman-Moir (Eds.), *The cognitive developmental psychology of James Mark Baldwin: Current research in genetic epistemology.* Norwood, NJ: Ablex.

Piaget, J., & Inhelder, B. (1969). *The psychology of the child.* New York: Basic Books.

Rosenthal, M. (1982). Vocal dialogues in the neonatal period. *Developmental Psychology, 18,* 17–21.

Secord, P., & Peevers, B. (1974). The development and attribution of person concepts. In T. Mischel (Ed.), *Understanding other persons.* Oxford: Basil Blackwell.

Selman, R. (1980). *The growth of interpersonal understanding.* New York: Academic.

Selman, R., & Byrne, D. (1974). A structural-developmental analysis of role-taking in middle childhood. *Child Development, 45,* 803–806.

Sewny, V. D. (1945). *The social theory of James Mark Baldwin.* New York: King's Crown Press.

Skinner, B. F. (1938). *The behavior of organisms.* New York: Appleton-Century-Crofts.

Sullivan, H. S. (1953). *The interpersonal theory of psychiatry.* New York: Norton.

Sulloway, F. J. (1979). *Freud: Biologist of the mind.* New York: Basic Books.

Thelen, M. H., Dollinger, S. H., & Roberts, M. C. (1975). On being imitated: Its effects on attraction and reciprocal imitation. *Journal of Personality and Social Psychology, 31,* 467–472.

Trevarthen, C. (1977). Descriptive analyses of infant communicative behavior. In H. R. Schaffer (Ed.), *Studies in mother-infant interaction.* New York: Academic.

Voneche, J. (1982). Evolution, development, and the growth of knowledge. In J. M. Broughton & D. J. Freeman-Moir (Eds.), *The cognitive developmental psychology of James Mark Baldwin: Current research in genetic epistemology.* Norwood, NJ: Ablex.

Vygotsky, L. S. (1934). *Mysolenie i rech': Psiknologischeskie isslecovaniya* [Thinking and speech: Psychological research]. Moscow and Leningrad: Gosudarstvennoe Sotsial'no-Ekonomicheskie Izdatel'stvo [Abridged English translation: L. S. Vygotsky (1962). *Thought and language.* Cambridge: MIT Press; complete English translation: L. S. Vygotsky (in press). *Volume 2: Collected works.* New York: Plenum.]

Vygotsky, L. S. (1978). *Mind in society: The development of higher psychological processes.* Cambridge: Harvard University Press.

Vygotsky, L. S. (1979). Consciousness as a problem in the psychology of behavior. *Soviet Psychology, 17,* 3–35.

Vygotsky, L. S. (1981). The genesis of higher mental functions. In J. V. Wertsch (Ed.), *The concept of activity in Soviet psychology.* Armonk, NY: M. E. Sharpe.

Waddington, C. (1969). The theory of evolution today. In A. Koestler & J. R. Smythies (Eds.), *Beyond reductionism: New perspectives in the life sciences.* London: Hutchinson.

Watson, J. B. (1925). *Behaviorism.* New York: Norton.

Wertsch, J. V. (1985). *Vygotsky and the social formation of mind.* Cambridge: Harvard University Press.

Wertsch, J. V., & Youniss, J. (in press). Contextualizing the investigator: The case of developmental psychology. *British Journal of Social Psychology*.

Wiener, P. (1949). *Evolution and the founders of pragmatism*. Cambridge: Harvard University Press.

Yando, R., Seitz, V., & Zigler, E. (1978). *Imitation: A developmental perspective*. Hillsdale, NJ: Erlbaum.

Chapter 7

The Development of
Moral Judgment and Moral Action

Lawrence Kohlberg

MORAL DEVELOPMENT AS AN AIM OF EDUCATION

In our earlier chapters "The Child as a Philosopher" and "Development as the Aim of Education," we focused on cognitive and moral stages in defining the aims of education. We have argued John Dewey's (1895) view that

> The aim of education is growth, both intellectual and moral. Only ethical and psychological principles can elevate the school to a vital institution in the *greatest of all constructions—the building of a free and powerful character*. Only knowledge of the *order and connection of the stages in psychological development can insure the maturing of the psychical powers*. Education is the work of *supplying the conditions* which will enable the psychological functions to mature in the freest and fullest manner. (Dewey, 1895, 1964, p. 273) [italics added]

Dewey, like his great predecessors and successors in educational philosophy, thought cognitive and moral education were the core of education for development. He believed that an understanding of the stages of moral as well as cognitive development was the key to developmental education.

Piaget (1971) echoes Dewey and says:

> In the first place, every human being has the right to be placed in a scholastic environment during his formation which will enable him to build until completion the basic tools of adaptation which are the processes of logic. If logic itself is created rather than being inborn, it follows that the first task of education is to form reasoning. Second everyone would recognize the formative role of ethical education. The right of ethical education is second. This means the right to participate or to construct the rules and discipline that will obligate not only himself but the adults with whom he collaborates in forming discipline. (p. 14)

In this chapter, we will review the research findings on the development of moral judgment and moral character necessary for an informed concern for moral education. In addition to work on the stages of moral judgment of Piaget and ourselves, we will review findings on moral character and moral socialization based on other theories.

HISTORICAL SCHOOLS OF MORAL PSYCHOLOGY

The theme of moral stages or levels is as old as Plato in Western philosophy and is found equally in the Vedic and Buddhist philosophies of the East. Modern philosopher-psychologists like John Dewey (in Dewey & Tufts, 1932) and James Mark Baldwin (1906, 1906–11) have elaborated an ubiquitous triad of preconventional, conventional, and principled or postconventional morality.

Not all philosopher-psychologists have had an awareness of moral levels or stages, in particular the enlightenment philosophers of British "empiricist" utilitarianism, and the "rational apriorist" Kantian philosophers of the continent.

The British utilitarians (e.g., Hume, 1752/1930; Smith, 1759/1948; Mill, 1861/1957) assumed that moral values were the products of individual adults, possessed of language and intelligence, who judged the actions of other individual adults. The utilitarians suggested that actions by the self or by others whose consequences to the self are harmful (painful) are naturally deemed bad and arouse anger or punitive tendencies, and actions whose consequences are beneficial (pleasant) are naturally deemed good and arouse affection or approving tendencies. Because of natural tendencies of empathy, generalization, and the need for social agreement, acts are judged good (or bad) if their consequences to others are good (or bad), even if they do not help (or injure) the self. Logical tendencies lead these judgments of consequences to eventually take the form of judging that act right that does the greatest good for the greatest number.

I have argued (Grim, Kohlberg, & White, 1968; Kohlberg, 1964) that there is empirical evidence for the "British utilitarian" view of the development of moral reason as a natural extension of prudence or practical reason through a sentiment of sympathy or empathy. Moral behaviors, such as not cheating, seem to be less traits of moral conscience than a set of ego abilities corresponding to common-sense notions of prudence and will. In this view, moral action (action based on rational consideration of how one's action affects others) requires much the same capacities as does prudent action (action based on rational consideration of how it affects the self's long-range interests). Both require empathy (the ability to predict the reactions of others to actions), foresight (the ability to weigh alternatives and probabilities), and capacity to delay (delay of response and preference for the distant, greater gratification over the immediate, lesser gratification). In modern personality theory these factors are included with other aspects of decision making and emotional control in the concept of ego strength. Some ego abilities that have been found to correlate consistently with experimental and rating measures of children's honesty include the following: intelligence (IQ), delay of gratification (preference for a larger reward in the future over a smaller reward in the present), and attention (stability and persistence of attention in simple experimental tasks).

At the other extreme from the British utilitarian philosopher-psychologist were the followers of Kant (1785/1949). Kant held that there was an "apriori" or prior-to-experience intuition of rational conscience. He formulated the "categorical imperative" in two forms: "So act that the maximum of thy will may be universal law for all mankind" and "Treat every other rational being, not as a means only, but always as an end in himself." According to Kant, this intuition of rational conscience was inborn in all human beings in all cultures, and did not depend on experience for its development. Discontented with both the utilitarian view of moral development as a simple accumulation of external or empiricist associations strengthening prudence and sympathy and the Kantian view of an innate rational conscience, and inspired by both the Hegelian philosophy of stages and the Darwinian conception of evolution, at the end of the nineteenth century the philosopher-psychologists earlier mentioned, like Dewey, Baldwin and Mead, defined moral stages resulting from the social interaction between a structuring or *constructing* child and a socially *structured* world. This tradition, especially as empirically elaborated by Piaget, stands behind my own research and the viewpoint of this book.

Critical Theories

Before describing further this constructivist tradition and my elaboration of it, it is important to note that the development of theories of moral psychology guided by philsosopher-psychologists were sharply interrupted by the great "irrationalist" founders of modern sociology, anthropology, and depth psychology in the early portion of the twentieth century. For the sake of brevity we will cite only three towering figures, whose creative insight into previously ignored moral phenomena must be counterbalanced by the limits of the philosophic assumptions that lay behind their social-science moral theories: Karl Marx, Emile Durkheim, and Sigmund Freud. Marx, Freud, and Durkheim were "irrationalists" in the sense that they saw the essence of morality as grounded in emotional forces whose strength was independent of the cognitive or "rational" structures and justification of moral judgments. Both Durkheim and Freud were ethical and cultural relativists because they defined the domain and content of morality not in terms of some universal principles such as the utilitarian beneficence (concern for the welfare of others) or Kantian justice (respect for persons) but rather in terms of particular rules varying from culture to culture (or family to family) and serving rationally unjustified functions of maintaining a given system of authority, status, and order.

Habermas (1979/1983) makes a helpful distinction between the tasks that theorists of moral development have set themselves. The philosopher-psychologists mentioned have constructed theories that are *rational reconstructions of ontogenesis,* that is, they chart and explain movement toward the kind of morality persons striving toward rationality might agree on. Other "irrationalistic" theories, such as Freud and Marx's, may be seen as serving *critical and emancipatory functions,* one of helping the reflective individual to emancipate him or herself from elements of irrational moral ideologies serving hidden functions in justifying the societal or familial status quo and/or systems of authority and status in the family and the society. At the center of Marx and Freud's theories were the notions of moral values as "ideologies" based on "false consciousness." Marx, for instance, saw moral ideologies as "false consciousness." First, in the sense that epistemologically they were empirically untrue, and confused value statements with fact statements which were untrue. Second, they saw these ideologies as having a hidden function, the function of protecting the dominating interests of the elite class over the working class. Third, they regarded moral ideologies as "false consciousness" in that they originated from hidden motives when one examined their origin and genesis.

Having stated that a Marxist analysis views moral ideologies as "false consciousness" is not to deny the usefulness of such theories as liberating or emancipating. These theories, however, cannot be demonstrated by the usual "positivistic" notions of a social science conceived as devoted to predicting physical or sense-observations (like natural sciences), and used instrumentally to control nature. The same holds true for psychoanalytic theories of morality as false consciousness or as rationalization, reaction-formation, and other defenses against unconscious impulses or drives. Psychoanalytic theory has been, in my view, a failure as a source of positivistic empirical predictions about children's moral development (Kohlberg, 1963, 1964, 1984). This does not mean, however, that it cannot serve an emancipatory function for the individual analyzing, or being analyzed about, one's own personal moral ideology that may indeed conceal one's conflict and ambivalence about one's parents and one's "defensive" identifications with them.

To understand the usefulness of theories like those of Marx and Freud it is useful to frame them, not in the positivistic methodology that adopts an "objectivating" attitude toward persons as behaving things to be predicted, but by a "hermeneutic" methodology that adopts an interpretive stance toward the communications of other human beings as "texts," like the interpretations of philosophers and literary critics attempting to explicate the structure of Aristotle's *Ethics* or the novels of Henry James. I would argue that like good hermeneutic interpretors and critics, one should first exhaust the conscious or intended meaning of a subject before making hypotheses about unconscious meanings that are less easily verified.

The Rational Reconstruction of Ontogenesis

Once one adopts a hermeneutic or interpretive stance toward the developing person, the theorist, if not a critical unmasker, must undertake, as Piaget, myself, and my colleagues have done (as did Baldwin, Dewey, Mead, and Habermas), to construct a theory that is the "rational reconstruction of ontogenesis." To understand the child's meaning in an interview one must attribute a rational or "making sense" attitude to the child even though the child's attitude or rationality is very different from our own.

This, in turn, means taking not an "objectivating" mechanistic view of explanation but a "performative" dialogic and philosophic view of the growing rationality or adequacy of the child's structures or stages of thinking, and looking for universals in development across cultures, classes, and sexes.

Piaget, in the case of logic, and myself in the case of morality, attempt to define philosophically and to justify fully adequate structures along with steps on the way to these adequate structures, as well as assumptions thrown into question if the developmental data do not confirm these assumptions.

While working on defining developmental stages, I have been consciously trying to bootstrap in some progressive spiral between philosophic assumptions and empirical data. Empirical data, the "is" of psychology, cannot define or prove the "ought" of philosophy. However, the "is" of psychological research can cast doubt on philosophic assumptions and lead to their redefinition.

Durkheim's Theory

In contrast to both critical theories and the rational reconstructive theories of Piaget and other philosopher-psychologists is the "positivistic," "objectivating" attitude of a value-neutral prediction of behavior. This stance is that usually adopted by socialization and social learning theorists who view moral development as increasing internalized conformity to the norms of the culture, based on a value-neutral socially or culturally relative definition of morality.

Durkheim (1961), one of the most influential moral theorists partially wedded to a culturally relativistic stance, thought that a positivistic view of morality as a set of social facts could guide moral education in the most useful way. Durkheim most clearly stated the assumption that has guided much psychological as well as sociological thought: the problem of the origin of moral values is cultural or societal, and psychology's problem was to account for how moral values originating at the cultural level are transmitted to, or internalized by, the developing child through such cultural transmission methods as reinforcement learning or identification.

Durkheim's theory started as a critique of the utilitarian theories of Hume, Smith, and Mill as well as of Kantian theory. In his critique of the utilitarians, Durkheim pointed to the following four phenomena: (1) Morality is basically a matter of respect for fixed rules (and the authority behind those rules), not of rational calculation of benefit and harm in concrete cases; (2) morality seems universally to be associated with punitive sentiments toward rule-violators, sentiments incompatible with the notion that the right is a matter of human-welfare consequences; (3) from group to group there is wide variation as to the nature of the rules arousing moral respect, punitiveness, and the sense of duty; and (4) while modern Western societies divorce morality from religion, the basic moral rules and attitudes in many groups are those concerning relations to gods, not people, and hence do not center on human-welfare consequences (utilitarianism) or respect for human persons (Kantianism).

According to Durkheim, these facts in turn implied that the mere existence of an institutionalized rule endows it with moral sacredness, regardless of its human-welfare consequences. Accordingly, moral rules, attitudes, and a sense of obligation to them originates at the group, rather than the individual level. The psychological origin of moral attitudes lies in the individual's respect for authority figures who represent the group. The values most sacred to the individual are those that are most widely shared by, and most closely bind together, the group.

While Piaget and I make use of Durkheim's theory, we must, however, take account of certain philosophic criticisms of Durkheim's whole theory. The first is that the notion of a "group mind" is a useful fiction, not a psychological reality. Although individual children and adolescents quite consciously see norms as shared in the group, and this awareness of sharing makes these norms "stronger" for each individual who senses the norms as shared because he or she has a desire to belong to the group, individuals are also quite aware of their own individual moral judgments and are often willing and able to "stand up" to the group in the name of their own morality, of their own rights and those of others in or outside the group (Higgins, Power, & Kohlberg, 1984). Second, my theory rejects Durkheim's "social relativism", his philosophic tendency to think that moral norms are truly "moral" or "right" relative to the group that holds them. Durkheim himself did not accept total social relativism as do modern social learning theorists (as, for instance, Berkowitz, 1964, p. 4, who defines moral values as "evaluations of actions generally believed by members of a given society to be either 'right' or 'wrong'"). Unlike Berkowitz, Durkheim would not have held that the norms of Nazi Germany, or of the Mafia were "moral" because they were shared by groups or society. This, however, was because he believed that societies were developmental and that a given accepted norm might be wrong either (a) because it was a sign of "social pathology," that is, of "anomie" or societal lack of integration or (b) because the society was evolving to new and more adequate norms. Fundamental to modern societies was "the cult of personality," the norm of respect for individual persons. This norm—Kant's principle of treating each individual as an end, not a means—he did not justify on philosophic grounds, but instead because it represented an advance in social organization and culture from a hierarchical or status-based "mechanical solidarity" embodied at the extreme in tribal cultures to an "organic solidarity" based on contractual cooperation in societies with an advanced division of labor.

A third criticism of Durkheim's theory is that it is derived from a positivistic theory of the methods of social science. It dismissed the hermeneutic interpretation of the meanings of individual's thinking (or of the thinking of groups) in favor of using "objective" indicators of "social facts," like the rate of suicide in various social and religious groups as an indicator of "anomie." The domain of morality he defined in terms of an "objective indicator," the existence in a society of "diffuse repressive sanctions" that could be found objectively in law or custom, not in terms of a mental attitude or of philosophic considerations.

Although Durkheim's views of the "group mind" have been widely questioned, the essential implications of his position are widely accepted. Assumptions common to Durkheim and Freud underlie the research studies of moral internalization we will discuss. Unlike Durkheim, Freud (1923, 1930) derived moral sentiments and beliefs from respect for, and identification with, individual parents, rather than from respect for the group. Furthermore, Freud derived this respect and identification from instinctual attachments (and defenses against these attachments) and viewed the central rules of morality as deriving their strength and rigidity from the need to counter these instinctual forces. In spite of these differences, Freud and Durkheim agreed in viewing morality (superego) as fundamentally a matter of respect for concrete rules that are culturally variable or arbitrary, since these rules are a manifestation of social authority, and they agreed in viewing punitive or (self-punitive) sentiment toward deviation as the clearest and most characteristic expression of moral internalization or respect.

The research findings on individual moral judgments in a variety of cultures seem incompatible with the views just outlined. Moral judgments and decisions in all cultures are a mixture of judgments in terms of concrete utility consequences and categorical social rules. The utilitarian derivation of respect for rules from utilitarian consequences is as psychologically unfeasible as Durkheim's derivation of concern for individual welfare consequences from respect for social rules as such. Often *principled* moralities develop and function at a level of conscious opposition and transcendence of group authority, as the utilitarians implied, but this development itself presupposes the previous development of "conventional" respect for group authority discussed by Durkheim. This, at least, appears to be the implications of recent research oriented to the "developmentalist" concept of morality.

MODERN SOCIALIZATION THEORIES

During the 1950s and 1960s a general research paradigm flourished that was loosely inspired by the theories of Durkheim and Freud, a paradigm especially focused on child-reasoning parental practices and attitudes in relation to the "internalization" of moral norms. In addition to psychoanalytic theory, social learning theories suggested hypotheses for this type of study. The paradigm assumed that morality was the internalization of the norms of parents and cultures. Often called superego strength or "conscience strength," moral internalization was tapped either by behavioral measures of "resistance to temptation" or by projective measures of guilt in "temptation," situations using stories or doll play situations. "Resistance to temptation" was essentially measured by "honesty" tests, such as those developed by Hartshorne and May (1928–1930). In general, the two types of conscience measures, the behavioral and the guilt measures, did not correlate with one another, and as discussed later, were not very stable over time. The psychoanalytic hypothesis that moral behavior was motivated by anticipation of guilt was not supported by empirical research.

Correlations between child-rearing practices and children's moral behavior or guilty attitudes have not been replicable from one study to another (Kohlberg 1963, 1964, 1984). The centrality of parental discipline practices to moral character formation has again not been supported by empirical findings. A more recent review of parental practices and prosocial behavior [as distinct from "resistance to temptation" (Radke-Yarrow et al., 1983)] finds it equally difficult to derive general conclusions from studies correlating child-rearing attitudes and practices with moral behavior or affect. With regard to parental affection, Radke-Yarrow et al. say, "There have been many studies of nurturance in relation to children's prosocial development with many different indicators of nurturance. A review of the findings destroys a simple qualification of positive associations" (p. 504). Describing discipline techniques, these authors say, "Overall positive, negative and no associations have been found between power assertion techniques and prosocial behavior" (p. 508).

With the lack of success in finding stable and general relations between parental variables and assessments of guilt and moral behavior, the alliances between psychoanalytic and social learning models dissolved. Social learning theorists took to the laboratory and were able to demonstrate short-term situational learning through modeling and various reinforcement conditions. These short-term situational learnings were not meant, however, to demonstrate how a deep and stable moral character developed. Instead, social learning theorists tended to dispense with constructs of stable and general character and conscience in favor of a situationally variable social behavior as defining the nature of moral behavior (Mischel & Mischel, 1976).

The problems of the moral socialization research encountered must lead us to ask more basic questions, such as what moral development is, before causes for development can be found.

THE GENERALITY OF MORAL VIRTUES OR CHARACTER TRAITS

As used in psychological studies of the past fifty years, "moral character" has generally retained its common-sense meaning as the sum total of a set of virtues. Virtues or character traits are conceived of as "those traits of personality which are subject to the moral sanctions of society" (Havighurst & Taba, 1949). For Hartshorne and May (1928–1930) these traits included honesty, service or altruism (willingness to sacrifice something for a group or charitable goal), and self-control (persistence in assigned tasks). For Havighurst and Taba they included honesty, loyalty, responsibility, moral courage, and friendliness (which has doubtful status as a moral character trait). All these traits involve some notion of adhering to cultural norms of action, where such adherence involves effort, self-control, or sacrifice.

For a long time psychologists agreed with common opinion that moral character traits should be assessed from actions, rather than from judgments and feelings. In general, they followed Hartshorne and May's basic method of measuring honesty by adding together occurrences of obedience to rules in situations allowing cheating or stealing with no apparent risk of detection. The validity of these measurements was supported by the fact that they corresponded quite closely to the judgments of honesty made by peers and teachers. For the most part, teachers did not agree with one another in judging honesty but when they did agree, they also agreed with the Hartshorne and May experimental measurements.

Studies by Hartshorne and May (1928–1930) and other more recent studies of moral conduct in varying situations suggest that character traits are not general or consistent across situations (Mischel & Mischel, 1976).

These studies suggest that the most influential factors determining various "moral" behaviors are situational rather than fixed individual moral traits. The first finding leading to this conclusion is that of the low predictability of cheating in one situation for cheating in another. Correlations between cheating in one type of situation and in another ranged from .00 to .45 (Hartshorne & May, 1928–1930). Behaviors related to service, self-control, and sympathy have been found to be equally specific to the particular situation (Hartshorne & May, 1928–1930; Murphy, 1937).

A second related research finding is that children are not divisible into two groups: "cheaters" and "honest children." Children's cheating scores were distributed in bell-curve fashion around an average score of moderate cheating.

A third finding is the importance of the expediency aspect of the decision to cheat; that is, the tendency to cheat depends on the degree of risk of detection and the effort required to cheat. Chilren who cheated in more risky situations also cheated in less risky situations (Hartshorne & May, 1928–1930). Thus noncheaters appeared to be (possibly) more cautious than more honest in their conduct.

Other important aspects of the immediate situation were peer group approval and example, and respect for the teacher· or the moral atmosphere of the classroom. Some classrooms showed a high tendency to cheat, while other similarly composed classrooms in the same school showed little tendency to cheat.

These research findings on situational variation suggest that moral conduct is in large part the result of an *individual decision in a specific moral conflict situation*. This aspect of moral conduct tends to be ignored by common views of moral character as a set of general "good habits" or as a "strong conscience."

To some extent, however, Hartshorne and May's conclusion that moral conduct is specific to the situation must be qualified by the results of a factor analysis by

Burton (1963) of the Hartshorne and May data. This analysis indicated a small general factor in the various experimental tests of classroom cheating. Although most of the variation in cheating seems due to reactions to the individual situations, part is a product of stable individual differences in attitudes toward classroom cheating.

While it may be tempting to interpret this personality factor in cheating as a specific habit or trait of honesty, it may, however, simply represent differential cautiousness or sensitivity to possible punishment. Such an interpretation is suggested by the fact that Hartshorne and May were able to place children's cheating behavior on a scale of willingness to risk detection. Another and more basic interpretation is that the personality factor represents a character tendency more general than either a specific virtue or habit of honesty or a fear of being caught. The evidence for this is that Hartshorne and May found low positive correlations ($r = .21$ to .33) between their experimental measures of honesty and their measures of service and self-control (persistence and nondistractibility). These correlations were about as high as the correlations between various types of honesty and could not have been based on simple cautiousness because the risk covered a broad range.

These findings suggest a core of truth to common-sense notions of general character, and provide some justification for adding up measures of various aspects of moral conduct into a total assessment of moral character. Common sense seems to exaggerate this consistency, however, since, for example, the consistency found in teacher ratings of moral traits is much higher than the consistency found in experimental measures. Furthermore Grim, Kohlberg, and White (1968) found both teacher rating and experimental measures of honesty to be part of a general factor of ego-strength, of emotional and attitudinal stability measured by galvanic skin response and reaction-time measures of ego stability. Apparently the g or general factor in honest behavior was partly the "nonmoral" factor of ego-strength or attention-will, a general factor developing with age but not specifically related to moral training at home or in school (Grim, Kohlberg, & White, 1968; Mischel & Mischel, 1976).

AGE DEVELOPMENT OF MORAL TRAITS
AND THEIR STABILITY OVER TIME

Common-sense thinking about moral character traits or virtues like honesty imply that they develop with age, experience, and increased moral socialization. With regard to common-sense assumptions, psychoanalytic or neopsychoanalytic super-ego or "conscience-strength" theories of moralilty have tended to assume that the core of character develops and is stabilized in the first few years of life. As stated by Sears, Maccoby, and Levine:

So far as we can tell, there is a learning of internal control that goes on mainly in the years before puberty perhaps chiefly in the first six to ten years, determining the extent to which conscience will operate throughout all the rest of life. (1957, pp. 367–368)

Neither common-sense assumptions of gradual age increase in character or psychoanalytic assumptions of early formation of character are supported by research findings.

Experimental measures of resistance to cheating or stealing do not increase significantly or regularly with age in the whole period from nursery school to high school (Grinder, 1964; Hartshorne & May, 1928–1930). Ratings by adults of honesty, responsibility, or altruism also fail to show age increases during childhood (Hartshorne & May, 1928–1930). Kohlberg, 1963, 1964). While incidents of stealing and lying reported by parents decrease markedly after the years 6 to 8 (MacFarlane, Allen, & Honzik, 1954), stealing seems to increase again in adolescence insofar as can be judged by arrest statistics and self-report measures.

More basically, the results on age variation can be interpreted in light of the findings of situational specificity found by Hartshorne and May. These findings suggested that morally conforming conduct poorly represents underlying moral attitudes or "moral control." At younger ages, "moral" conduct may be based primarily on fear or lack of motivation to transgress (e.g., cheating motivated by desire to win) while at older ages it may be based more on moral beliefs, guilt, and ego factors. Age declines in fear-induced conformity may be counterbalanced by age increases in moral and ego-strength forces for moral conduct.

Longitudinal studies also provide inconsistent and problematic findings on stability of individual differences in moral conduct. Only a few longitudinal studies deal with this issue—that is, whether, for example, the "good" children at age 5 are the "good" children at age 15. Lack of stability is suggested by studies indicating that neither psychologists' ratings of aggressiveness nor parents' ratings of selfishness showed a substantial stability between age 6 and age 13 (MacFarlane, Allen, & Honzik, 1954; Kagan & Moss, 1962). My own conclusions from research is that there is little evidence for the common-sense and psychoanalytic hypothesis that character is formed in childhood and remains stable thereafter.

Only one study claims to find such results. Peck and Havighurst (1960) report considerable stability in moral character ratings by community informants of traits such as honesty and responsibility from the period of 10 to 17. The problem with their finding is that it may represent the stabilization of the child's reputation and role in a small city rather than "deeper" fixity of moral character. Revolutions in moral conduct and ideology occur when adolescents leave home and hometown to go to college or to work. Furthermore, the study's methodology is based on clinical ratings showing a suspect halo effect.

In contrast, an ego-strength or ego-development interpretation suggests moral character is a gradual product of development, since morally relevant ego-strength or ego-development variables increase regularly with age throughout early and middle childhood and throughout adolescence and youth (Loevinger, 1976; Chapter 9 of this volume).

Thus, the available evidence, based on studying individual moral traits, does not support the idea that moral character is fixed earlier and remains stable through late childhood and adolescence. Insofar as there are regularities in the age-development of moral conduct, it appears to be a stabilization of developing moral judgment and ego development or ego strength factors representing the core of moral character.

THE DOMAIN OF MORALITY

Since the times of Plato, the issue has been deliberated as to whether morality or virtue was unitary or multiple. Socrates and Plato thought that morality had to be cognitively guided to be virtue, since an apparent virtue like courage is foolhardiness unless it is cognitively steered toward a moral end. The central moral virtue for Plato was justice, which integrated the other virtue. Aristotle agreed that virtue had to be cognitively steered (while he believed moral cognition was not sufficient for virtuous action, he thought that virtue implied moral purpose which implies "reason and thought, it indicates previous deliberation"). Further, Aristotle, like Plato, thought that justice was the chief moral or "other-regarding" virtue (Kohlberg, 1984, ch. 7).

The Christian tradition introduced another central virtue, "charity" or agape, which for St. Paul was the greatest virtue. Recently, Gilligan (1982) has claimed that two distinct and opposed moral orientations exist, that of justice and that of "care." She has claimed further that there are sex differences, with males orienting more to justice and females to care, though both sexes basically use both orientations in constructing and resolving personal moral dilemmas (Lyons, 1983). Most reviews of studies of either moral judgment (Walker, 1984) or of moral behavior (Radke-Yarrow et al., 1983) do not find systematic sex differences in moral judgment or behavior. Regardless of the sex differences issue, the distinction between justice on the one hand and altruistic or prosocial behavior is enduring. In the most comprehensive research review, morality as cognitively guided justice and cooperation is assigned to one volume (Rest, 1983) and proscoial behavior to another (Radke-Yarrow et al., 1983).

In the literature of philosophic psychology reviewed above, the British utilitarian psychologist-philosophers like Hume, Smith, and Mill derive justice sentiments from prior sentiments of sympathy while the Kantian tradition derives morality directly from reason or cognitive considerations, ultimately grounded in respect for persons and for the equality and reciprocity between persons that that implies. As J. M. Baldwin long ago held ontogenetically, empathy and sympathy are to be found in infants, before a clear sense of justice arises (Radke-Yarrow et al., 1983). In my theory, grounded on Piaget and G. H. Mead (1934), an "empathic" "taking the role of the other" is a prerequisite for making judgments of justice, and in that sense is a developmental prerequisite to it.

Turning from the nature of virtue to the method of its study, we see that the statement that Hartshorne and May's behavioristic approach "failed" is not simply an empirical conclusion reached because of the very limited power they achieved in predicting behavior. It is, rather, in part a philosophic conclusion.

There are two central philosophic issues in defining moral or morally commendable action. The first involves the issue of relativity: Whose standard of rightness do we use in defining an action as moral: that of the actor, that of society, or that of some universal philosophic judgment of right action in light of moral principle? On both philosophic and psychological grounds, we argue that Hartshorne's use of generally accepted or majority-accepted norms, social relativism, is invalid. This is so, first, because it ignores the individual actor's own judgment, a necessary part of considering whether an action is moral or not. Hartshorne and May's judgment that it was right to deceive children to increase knowledge of character is a necessary part of judging their own "dishonest" action as moral. One part of a more adequate approach to defining moral conduct rests on studying the individual actor's own judgment, defining moral action as consistency between judgment and behavior. What, however, if the actor's own judgment of rightness is clearly wrong, for example, Lieutenant Calley's judgment that it was right to massacre civilians at My Lai? We argue that analysis of an action from the point of a moral principle like Kant's respect for persons or Mill's maximization of welfare helps in this discussion.

Aside from the issue of relativism, there is a second fundamental philosophic issue in defining moral action, that of whether the morality of an action is dictated by (a) the behavior itself as it conforms to a norm, (b) the intention, judgment, or principle guiding the act, or (c) the welfare consequences of the act, which depends on how the individual processes factual information about the situation and the interests and feelings of others and predicts outcomes to the action. These options are the focus of an article by Kleinberger (1982). Kleinberger notes that Hartshorne and May, as well as more recent social behaviorists, end up by adopting the view that it is the conformity of the behavior itself to a social norm like "Don't cheat" that defines moral action.

In contrast, Kant (1949) thought that a principle, or a universalizable and categorical or prescriptive judgment determining action, was both necessary and sufficient to define an action as worthy, regardless of the consequences. Other factors influencing action, he thought, were not strictly moral. An example is what in this chapter we will call self-control or ego strength. Of this factor Kant says, "Moderation in the passions, self-control and calm deliberation are not only good in many respects but even seem to constitute part of the intrinsic worth of a person; but they are far from deserving to be called good without qualification, although they have been unconditionally praised by the ancients. For without the principle of a good will, these qualities may become extremely bad. The coolness of a villain not only makes him far more dangerous, but immediately makes him more abominable in our eyes than he would have been without it."

Ego strength or will is an example of a factor closing the gap between moral judgment and moral action. Kant points out, however, that ego strength or attention-will is not in itself positively moral, it only "amplifies" moral judgment, making action based on moral judgment more moral and action based on unprincipled judgment more immoral. We will observe this in discussing the results of the Krebs and Kohlberg study showing that ego strength makes students high in moral judgment more "moral," that is, makes them cheat less, but makes students lower in moral stage cheat more.

For the Kantian reasons just given, Kleinberger attributes to us this Kantian philosophic presupposition about moral action.

> Why does the cognitive-developmental approach to moral education focus so heavily upon moral reasoning? Firstly because moral judgment is claimed to be the single most influential factor in moral behavior. But the main reason is that moral judgment is the only distinctively *moral* factor among all the factors which influence moral behavior. Therefore it is only by virtue of this factor that behavior may be considered genuinely moral. (Kleinberger, 1982, p. 154)

A distinctively moral judgment is a necessary component of an action judged moral, but it need not be sufficient for evaluating the morality of an action or actor. Other factors of knowledge and motivation that are not distinctively moral may be required for assuring a good outcome. Accordingly, it is only by starting theory and research in moral development with an examination of the necessary moral judgment component that one can move on to identifying other factors sufficient to complete the terms moral action or moral character.

COGNITIVE-DEVELOPMENTAL APPROACH
TO THE STUDY OF MORAL JUDGMENT

These comments on moral action and the criticism of a behavioristic approach to moral development imply that research must start by trying to understand the development of children's moral judgment or reasoning and go on to study the development of moral action in relation to moral judgments. This will be our strategy for the remainder of this chapter.

While moral behavior has not lent itself to age-developmental analysis, the study of moral judgment has readily suggested basic stages of development. Moral judgment has been primarily studied in the cognitive-developmental tradition as the child's use and interpretation of rules in conflict situations, and the child's reasons for moral action, rather than as correct knowledge of rules or conventional belief in them. Studies of "moral knowledge" and belief (Hartshorne & May, 1928–1930) at younger ages indicate that most children know the basic moral rules and conventions of our society by the first grade. Studies and tests of moral knowledge at older ages have not been especially enlightening. While showing relations to conduct, moral knowledge scores seem primarily to indicate intelligence, cultural background, and desire to make a good impression, rather than basic moral development.

An example of stage data on moral reasoning and judgment, as opposed to moral knowledge or belief, is provided by answers to hypothetical dilemmas such as to whether a boy should tell his father a confidence about a brother's misdeed. In reply, Danny, age 10, said: "In one way, it would be right to tell on his brother or his father might get mad at him and spank him. In another way, it would be right to keep quiet or his brother might beat him up." Obviously, whether Danny decides it is right to maintain authority or right to maintain peer "loyalty" is of little interest compared to the fact that his decision will be based on his anticipation of who can hit harder. This type of reasoning is an indication of a relatively low stage of moral judgment. Recalling our introduction of moral stages in Chapter 1, we see that this would be an example of a second of six stages of moral reasoning.

The stage approach to understanding responses characteristic of an age group like Danny's involves the analysis of their underlying thought structures and the comparison of such structures found in different age groups in order to define the general direction of development. Such "stages" are then used to understand developmental differences among children of a given age and to isolate major social and intellectual influences on development.

In Chapter 4, we clarified the sense in which intellectual or cognitive stages implied an interactional theory of why environments influence development. This is even more clearly the case for moral development.

It seems obvious that moral stages must primarily be the products of the child's interaction with others, rather than the direct unfolding of biological or neurological structures. The emphasis on social interaction does not mean, however, that stages of moral judgment directly represent the teaching of values by parents or of their direct "introjection" by the child. In the theories of moral stages of Piaget (1932), Mead (1934), and Baldwin (1906), parental training and discipline are viewed as influential only as a part of a world or social order perceived by the child. Children can internalize the moral values of parents and culture and make them their own only as they come to relate to a comprehended social order and to their own goals as social selves. In these stage theories, the fundamental factor causing such a structuring of a moral order is social participation and role-taking. In order to play a social role in the family, school, or society, the child must implicitly take the role of others toward himself and toward others in the group. Moral role-taking involves an emotional empathic or sympathetic component, but it also involves a *cognitive capacity* to define situations in terms of rights and duties, in terms of reciprocity and the perspectives of other selves. In Danny's reply just quoted, "role-taking" seems to be limited to a prediction about retaliation, which not only represents a limitation of empathic feelings but a primitive structuring of concepts of family rights and duties. In analyzing the bases of such role-taking, the theories mentioned have variously focused on the family (Baldwin), the peer group (Piaget), and the larger social institutions (Mead).

All, however, as cognitive-developmentalists, agree in stressing that role-taking opportunities are critical features of the social environment for moral judgment development. These implications for explaining the causes of moral development or its arrest will be clarified after presenting the stages themselves. Of special relevance to this chapter is Piaget's book (1932/1965) *The moral judgment of the child*, which was the first extensive empirical work on the development of moral reasoning.

In this book, Piaget did not try to define "true" stages, though he sketches a movement from premorality (no sense of obligation to rules and authority) to a heteronomous morality based on a belief in rigid adherence to rules and motivated by a sense of "heteronomous respect" to adult authorities (especially parents) toward whom the child felt a "sui generis" mixture of fear and affection, to an "autonomous morality" based on a rational concern for rules of cooperation and reciprocity with peers.

As elaborated in Piaget's developmental theory (1932/1965), the child first moves from an amoral stage to a stage of respect for sacred rules. Piaget believes that the cognitive limitations of children of 3 to 8 lead them to confuse moral rules with physical laws and to view rules as fixed eternal things, rather than as the instruments of human purposes and values. Piaget believed that children see rules as absolutes and confuse rules with things because of their "realism" (their inability to distinguish between subjective and objective aspects of their experience) and because of their "ego-centrism" (their inability to distinguish their own perspective on events from that of others). In addition to seeing rules as external absolutes, young children feel that their parents and other adults are all-knowing, perfect, and sacred. This affective attitude of unilateral respect toward adults, joined with children's cognitive "realism," is believed to lead them to view rules as sacred and unchangeable.

With growing age, Piaget believed that the morality of autonomy would gradually take predominance over a morality of heteronomy, at least in societies that were not strongly authoritatian or gerontocratic.

My own moral stages, presented shortly, reflect a shift in methodology between that used by the later Piaget and earlier Piaget, a methodology in defining stages. We follow the later Piaget, as described later in this chapter, by a methodology that defines "hard stages." This methodology sharply distinguishes (a) between the form or structure of reasoning from the content used in reasoning, (b) between the individual's level of competence and level of performance, and (c) assumes that stages are not in opposition to one another but that a higher stage is a transformation of a lower one.

Piaget's (1932/1965) early moral stages did not make these assumptions. They were instead ideal-type, a notion we will shortly elaborate. Central to Piaget's (1932/1965) "stages" were conceptions of two dichotomous types of social relationship, relationships based on hierarchical authority and those based on egalitarian cooperation.

Following Kant and in part Durkheim, Piaget sees morality as respect for rules and ultimately respect for the persons originating the rules. Piaget identifies two basic types of social relations in which this respect is grounded, corresponding to the two basic moral types or orientations. The first type of social relation is that of *unilateral respect* for parents or other authorities and the rules and laws they prescribe. This corresponds to the heteronomous type of morality, and is marked by a "sui generis mixture of affection and fear or awe" directed toward authority figures. The second type is that of *mutual respect* among peers and equals; it includes respect for the rules that guide the interaction of equals. Mutual respect corresponds to the autonomous type of morality; its underlying structure is that of fairness in the sense of reciprocity and equality (as opposed to conformity and obedience to authority and to authority-made rules that mark the underlying structure of the heteronomous type). As Piaget (1932/1965) argues, "Autonomy therefore appears only with reciprocity, when mutual respect is strong enough to make the individual feel from within the desire to treat others as he himself would wish to be treated" (p. 196).

The following passage provides a helpful overview of Piaget's (1932/1965) views on the two types of social relations that lead to the two types of morality:

> Our earlier studies led us to the conclusion that the norms of reason, and in particular the important norm of reciprocity, the source of the logic of relations, can only develop in and through cooperation. Whether cooperation is an effect or a cause of reason, or both, reason requires cooperation in so far as being rational consists in "situating oneself" so as to submit the individual to the universal. *Mutual respect* therefore appears to us as the necessary condition of *autonomy* under its double aspect, intellectual and moral. From the intellectual point of view, it frees the child from the opinions that have been imposed upon him while it favors inner consistency and reciprocal control. From the moral point of view, it replaces the norms of authority by that norm immanent in action and in consciousness themselves, the norm of reciprocity and sympathy.
>
> In short, whether one takes up the point of view of Durkheim or of M. Bovet, it is necessary, in order to grasp the situation, to take account of two groups of social and moral facts—*constraint* and *unilateral respect* on the one hand, *cooperation* and *mutual respect* on the other. Such is the guiding hypothesis which will serve us in the sequel and which will lead us in examining the moral judgments of children to dissociate from one another two systems of totally different origin. Whether we describe the facts in the terms of social morphology or from the point of view of consciousness (and the two languages are, we repeat, parallel and not contradictory) it is impossible to reduce the effects of cooperation to those of constraint and unilateral respect. (pp. 107–108)

Piaget (1932/1965) considers the domain of morality as justice to be the focus of his typology. He claims that the most fundamental form of justice is distributive justice. In the autonomous orientation distributive justice is reducible to equality and equity (equal distribution according to need)—both forms of reciprocity. In addition, Piaget examines corrective or retributive justice, which in the autonomous orientation is also directed to equality and reciprocity, that is, to restitution rather than expiation or retribution.

Piaget's method was twofold. In the first part of his book he observed children playing marbles and asked them in open-ended interview "method clinique" how they thought about the rules, their origin, changeability, and so on.

He identified three types of behavior in relation to rules and three corresponding types of rules. Briefly, the three types of rule-following behaviors are motor, egocentric, and cooperative. That is, the attitude of the baby and very young child toward rules is asocial, and the "rules" are individual motor rules (really rituals or habits whose regularity is based on intrigue with the action itself or its result) of which the child is not conscious and to which he or she feels no social obligation or external necessity to submit to. Strictly speaking, the rules of marbles are less in the domain of justice than they are in the domain of conventional social regulation, as we take up later in this chapter in connection with Turiel's (1983) work on the development of reasoning about conventions.

In contrast, and appearing somewhat later in relation to rules, is social behavior. The child learns (or tries to learn) other people's rules and submits to their authority, but practices rules according to egocentric assimilation—without realizing that his or her conception of the rule is different from that of those from whom the child "learned" it. In marbles, for example, Piaget found that young children may play without drawing a square, may sometimes keep the marbles they knock out and sometimes replace them in the square, and may take aim many times and even at the same time as the partner. They thus imitate the play of others in a global way that is schematically correct but incorrect in detail. Play is social only in a superficial sense. Although children play side by side, they do not unify their respective rules (often playing by different rules without realizing it or without caring). Nevertheless, egocentric rules are social in that the child accepts them as coming from a higher authority and therefore feels constrained to (try to) follow them. Piaget refers to this feeling of respect as unilateral respect (because the child submits to the higher authority) and this attitude to the rule as heteronomous (because the child follows it out of a feeling of necessity to obey the authority). Piaget terms young children's attitudes to adults and adult-created rules as heteronomous (as opposed to autonomous) since the child submits to regulation by others and by a rule whose reason is external to the child's understanding.

As children grow older, they are able to modify the rules of marbles through agreement. Rules are no longer seen as fixed or sacred but as functional to a cooperative and fair playing of the game.

Piaget believes that it is by means of experiences of role-taking in the peer group that the child gradually transforms the basis for moral judgment from authoritarian commands to internal principles. In essence, he views internal moral norms as logical principles of justice. Of these, he says:

In contrast to a given rule imposed upon the child from outside, the rule of justice is an immanent condition of social relationships or a law governing their equilibrium. The sense of justice is largely independent of adult precept and requires nothing more for its development than mutual respect and solidarity among children. (Piaget, 1932, p. 196)

By the sense of justice, Piaget means a concern for reciprocity and equality between individuals. Norms of justice are not simply matters of abstract logic, however; instead they are sentiments of sympathy, gratitude, and vengeance that have taken on logical form.

Piaget believes that an "autonomous" justice morality develops at about age 8 to 10 and eventually replaces the earlier "heteronomous" morality based on unquestioning respect for adult authority. He expects the autonomous justice morality to develop in all children, unless development is fixated by unusual coerciveness of parents or cultures or by deprivation of experiences of peer cooperation.

In the second part of Piaget's book, he asks children to choose one of two alternative solutions to a justice problem story. In the domain of distributive justice he asks whether each should get the same (equality and autonomy) or whether the authority should get more (heteronomy). In the domain of corrective justice, he asks whether a child should make restitution (autonomy) or be severely punished (heteronomy).

Subsequent research has shown that Piaget's story choice method mixes content and structure and does not define "true" or "hard" stages. Piaget himself did not think they did but represented developmental "ideal types."

Speaking of his empirical data on children's ideas of justice, he says,

A law of evolution emerges sufficiently clearly from all these answers. True we cannot speak of stages properly so called, because it is extremely doubtful whether every child passes successively through the four attitudes we have just described. It is greatly a question of the kind of education the child has received. (1932/1965, p. 284)

There are three reasons why Piaget does not believe his typology defines true or "hard" stages. First, his empirical observations mix content with structure as suggested by his statement that the type of response he gets may be influenced by the kind of education the child receives. Second, he sees the two moralities in opposition to one another, rather than the autonomous morality growing out of, and being a transformation of, the heteronomous morality. He says, "We find in the domain of justice that opposition of the two moralities to which we have so often drawn the reader's attention" (1932/1965, p. 324).

Even though Piaget does not conceive his typology as defining true stages, he does believe they are age-developmental. There are two reasons for this. First, as the child grows older he or she is more able to enter into peer relationships of mutual respect and solidarity that generate autonomous morality. Second, heteronomous morality is less equilibrated than autonomous morality. He says: "But what is certain is that the moral equilibrium achieved by the complementary conceptions of heteronomous duty and of punishment so called is an unstable equilibrium, owing to the fact that it does not allow the personality to grow and expand to its full extent" (1932/1965, p. 324).

According to Piaget, with age there is a gradual predominance of the autonomous type over the heteronomous type of morality rather than a qualitative transformation from one morality to the other. Stated in slightly different terms, Piaget does not think that there is an inner logic in terms of which developmental differentiation and integration lead heteronomous morality to be transformed into an autonomous morality that presupposes a prior stage of heteronomous morality.

Furthermore, according to Piaget, such a predominance of autonomous morality is dependent on the kind of social relations or society in which the child lives. Piaget expects that in traditional or geronotocratic societies, based on what Durkheim calls mechanical solidarity, heteronomous morality will extend into adulthood and that it is only societies based on "organic solidarity" or cooperation and on "egalitarian democracy" and the emancipation of one generation from another that render possible in children and adolescents the development he outlined (1932/1965, p. 325).

Research Based on Piaget's Theory

Subsequent research has demonstrated that Piaget's own investigations of justice using the story choice method yield two distinct clusters or dimensions. The first cluster or dimension is "moral realism" in which physical laws and consequences are confused with sociomoral laws and consequences, closely associated with egocentrism, the confusion of the self's perspective with that of "the others" or "the authority." The mature pole of moral realism and egocentrism is "moral subjectivism" or "moral perspectivism."

This cluster includes the following characteristics:

1. *Intentionality in judgment.* Young children tend to judge an act as bad mainly in terms of its actual physical consequences, whereas older children judge an act as bad in terms of the intent to do harm. As an example, children were asked who was worse—a child who broke five cups while helping his mother set the table or a boy who broke one cup while stealing some jam. Almost all 4 year olds say the child who committed the larger accidental damage was worse (as do about 60 percent of 6 year olds), whereas the majority of 9 year olds say the "thief" was worse (Kohlberg, 1964; Lickona, 1976).

2. *Relativism in judgment.* The young child views an act as either totally right or totally wrong, and thinks everyone views it in the same way. If the young child does recognize a conflict in views, he or she believes the adult's view is always the right one. In contrast, the older child is aware of possible diversity in views

of right and wrong. As an example, children were told a story in which a lazy pupil is forbidden by a teacher to receive any help in doing homework. A friendly classmate does help the pupil. The children were then asked whether the friendly classmate thinks he is right or wrong for helping, whether the lazy pupil would think he was right or wrong, what the teacher would think, and so on. The majority of 6 year olds expected only one judgment, on which everyone would agree; for example, they would say that the helping classmate would think he was wrong to help. By age 9, a majority of children recognized that there would be more than one perspective on moral value in the situation (Kohlberg, 1964).

3. *Naturalistic views of misfortune.* Six- to 7-year-old children have some tendency to view physical accidents and misfortunes occurring after misdeeds as punishments willed by God or by natural objects ("immanent justice"). Older children do not confuse natural misfortunes with punishment.
4. *Independence of physical sanctions.* The young child says an act is bad because it will elicit punishment; the older says an act is bad because it violates a rule, does harm to others, and so forth. For example, young children were asked to judge a helpful, obedient act (attentively watching a baby while the mother is away) followed by punishment (the mother returns and spanks the baby-sitting child). Many 4 year olds simply say the obedient boy was bad because he got punished, ignoring his act (Kohlberg, 1963).

    Again, this development indicates a movement from moral realism, a confusion of physical and psychological consequences of action to an awareness of this differentiation.

Extensive cross-cultural research indicates that the movement from moral realism to moral perspectivism is continuous with chronological age development from age 6 to 12 and is closely related to cognitive development in terms of both psychometric and Piagetian measure of "mental age" (Kohlberg, 1963, 1964).

In contrast, Piaget's assessments of "heteronomous justice" based on "unilateral respect" as opposed to "autonomous or cooperative justice" do not show cross-cultural regular development with either chronological age or with mental age. Heteronomous justice includes: (1) thinking obedience to adults is right (as opposed to obligations to peer), (2) ignoring considerations of reciprocal exchange in favor of obeying rules in either distributive or corrective justice, and (3) favoring differential reward for "virtue" or conformity to rules and authority rather than equality in distribution.

On these dimensions, periods of increase with age tend to be followed by periods of decrease; age increases are not found with all cultural or social class groups; and developmental trends vary depending on the story and situations used (Kohlberg, 1963; Kohlberg & Helkama, in press; Lickona, 1976).

In summary, further research has not demonstrated that Piaget defined two stages but rather defined developmental trends or dimensions. Furthermore, it has not been clearly demonstrated that all aspects of his moral types are developmental. The "moral realism" cluster of responses to his stories shows a decline with mental and chronological age in most cultures between the ages of 4 and 12. A developmental decline in heteronomous respect and justice has not been consistently found.

Advocates of Piaget's original theory of moral judgment such as Youniss (1980, 1981) and Wright (1982) elaborate the theory at the level of theory (Wright) or use quite different research methods (Youniss, 1980).

Wright stresses that Piaget's typology is an affective typology, based on two different sentiments of obligation rooted in actual social relationships, heteronomous respect, composed of fear, affection, and a sense of superior value and power felt toward parents and teachers, and autonomous respect, composed of mutual and reciprocal feelings toward equals, friends, or peers with whom the child cooperates. According to Wright, such sentiments of obligation are unlikely to be elicited by the "abstract," "cognitive" hypothetical dilemmas used by both Piaget (1932/1965) and myself (Kohlberg, 1958). Believing peer and adult relations to be quite distinct domains, Youniss (1980) collected data through interviews with children and young adolescents about their relations to parents and friends. He concludes that his data support the "two worlds" hypothesis of Piaget and of Harry Stack Sullivan (1953). "The goal of the present paper is to state and discuss a position within the structural framework which may provide some answers to critics. Throughout this paper, it is called *the two world perspective*, the two worlds being those the child shares with parents and with friends. The thesis is that parents and friends contribute equally but differently to the child's development" (p. 8).

For the first, the thesis begins with the premise that structures are built from *interpersonal interactions*. For the second, the thesis focuses on the *reciprocity* that is found to hold and recur across interactions. These are deceptively powerful starting points from which one can derive the two world viewpoint. Piaget, Sullivan, and others suggest that there is a common, recurring form to parents' interactions with children. They describe it through the concept of *reciprocity of complement*. The part parents play in interactions is that of leader or arbiter. This means that they tell the children what to do and not do by accepting or rejecting children's contributions to interactions. Children, in turn, have the part of learner or follower. Their role in interactions is to complete the part set forth by parents.

Parents have the right to step outside the ongoing flow of behavior to make a judgment on it. They need not do this all the time. The important element, however, is that they can do it, while children cannot. This gives the full meaning of arbiter which is found in its *unilaterality*. Were this not the case, the child would have the right to judge parents' actions.

More critically, when parent and child disagreed, neither would impose a resolution, but the two would enter into negotiation. Both would be willing to give up their respective viewpoints in adjustment to the other until a common view was rendered. This more apt description of interactions of peers follows the *reciprocity of symmetry.* In this form, each peer is free to act as the other has just acted, or is expected to act subsequently. Where one offers a toy, the other may offer candy. When one hits, the other may retaliate. When one asserts an opinion, "This is how we should play," the other is free to present a different opinion, "No, we should play like this." In the taking of turns in interactions, peers may duplicate each other's contributions, with neither being able to step outside and take charge. Should one of the peers try to do so, the other may do the same (Youniss, 1981, pp. 35–44).

Without accepting the two world hypothesis of Wright and Youniss, my colleagues and I have recently developed a method for defining heteronomous and autonomous "ideal types" that are developmental but not "true stages" (Kohlberg, 1984; Colby & Kohlberg, 1987).

In the ideal-typological approach a cluster of chosen content themes is assumed to hold together because of an underlying postulated but not observable structure that makes one element of content compatible with the others. After we had developed a "hard structural" manual for our stages, to be described shortly (Colby & Kohlberg, 1987), we saw the need independently to assess Piagetian heteronomous and autonomous types of moral judgment distinct from stages.

Our classification of an individual as Type B or "autonomous" was based on the criteria indicated in Table 7.1. Two out of three dilemmas must be scored Type B to classify a subject as Type B. Our longitudinal findings on type indicate that in the United States, Turkey, and Israel, there is an age developmental shift from Type A to Type B. Once a person moves from Type A to Type B they remain Type B even as they change from stage to stage.

In addition to the age developmental characteristics of the heteronomous-autonomous types, our types have been shown to fit a number of other expectations derived from Piaget's (1932/1965) theory. These include the following relations between Type B and the social environment: (1) Type B appears earlier in democratic and cooperative cultural and social settings than in more authoritarian or gerontocratic ones. The earliest and most frequent development to Type B, the autonomous type, was in the democratic and egalitarian Israeli kibbutz. Our American sample showed less early and frequent type change and the Turkish sample even less (though the differences between the American and Turkish sample were minor and not clearly statistically significant). (2) American subjects who are sociometrically chosen participants in the school peer group are more likely to be Type B (67 percent); subjects who are isolated from the peer group are more likely to be Type A (33 percent). (3) Students who attend democratic (alternative) schools are more likely to be Type B than those in traditional schools.

Finally, there are expectations from Piaget's theory that Type B subjects will act in a more fair and responsible (self-consistent) way than Type A subjects. This is because, following Piaget, the autonomous type is acting under norms that are

TABLE 7.1

"Piagetian" Criteria for Type B (Form A)

1. *Choice:* Chooses as right the action opposed to rules and authority and in line with human rights, welfare, and reciprocal justice.
2. *Autonomy:* The response to the dilemma must reflect an understanding that the actor in question is an autonomous moral agent, and hence must make moral judgments and decide on a moral course of action without determination by external sources of power or authority, using a rational and logical method of decision making.
3. *Mutual Respect:* This criterion reflects the understanding that the actors in the dilemma should have relations of mutual respect or solidarity with one another. As such, in Dilemma III, Heinz must be understood to have a relation of mutual respect or solidarity with his wife and friend and in Dilemma I, Joe and his father must have respect for each other.
4. *Reversibility:* The most important criterion from the Piagetian perspective (but also the most difficult one to indentify in an interview) is reversibility. It is understood to be present when the judgments made in response to the dilemma consider the interests and points of view of other actors involved, such that it is clear that the subject can view the problem from the perspective of other actors involved in the situation. The subject makes a decision with some awareness that he or she could logically trade places with other actors in the dilemma. As an example, in Dilemma I, a "good son" is not seen as having to obey the father, since the expectations of the father are not those which a "good father" would have, that is, the role of "good father" is defined by the respondent putting himself in the father's place and expecting the father to be able to put himself in the son's place. Reversibility is a mutual perspective taking or mutual use of the Golden Rule. For Piaget, *logical* operations are equilibrated when they are reversible; hence, a formal criterion for equilibrated *moral* judgments, that is, type B judgments, must be a correlative form of reversibility.
5. *Constructivism:* This criterion reflects the subject's awareness that the rules, laws, and role-prescriptions used to guide and frame moral decision making are *actively constructed* by human beings, in the context of a social system of cooperation for human welfare and justice. In other words, all of society (however "society" is interpreted by the subject), including its institutions, rules, and laws, is understood to be derived from communication and cooperation between and among persons. (Note: This notion of constructivism is understood to refer only to the subject's *normative ethical judgments*, and not to his or her *metaethical judgments*.)

Source: Kohlberg, 1984, p. 665.

autonomously or cooperatively constructed and intrinsically respected whereas the heteronomous type is constrained by rules that are not experienced as intrinsically obligating. These relationships were found in the Berkeley Free Speech movement study, the Milgram study of obedience, and the McNamee studies described later as examples of judgment action relations (and elaborated in Kohlberg 1984, Ch. 7).

Three Major Levels—Their Nature and Description

Piaget's research and theory inspired my own investigations leading to the conclusion that Piaget was incorrect in asserting that clear structural stages in the emergence of moral judgment cannot be identified. We need now to present the theoretical definitions of our moral stages and to report some of the research supporting the idea that they do represent genuine moral stages.

Table 7.2 presents a summary description of the six moral stages grouped into three major levels, the preconventional (Stages 1 and 2), the conventional (Stages 3 and 4), and the postconventional (Stages 5 and 6).

To understand the stages, it is best to start by understanding the three moral levels. The term conventional means conforming to and upholding the rules and expectations and conventions of society or authority just because they are society's rules, expectations, or conventions. The individual at the postconventional level understands and basically accepts society's rules, but this acceptance is derived from formulating and accepting the general moral principles that underlie these rules. These principles in some cases come into conflict with society's rules, in which case the postconventional individual judges by principle rather than by convention. The preconventional moral level is that of most children under 9, some adolescents, and many adolescent and adult criminal offenders. The conventional level is the level of most adolescents and adults in our society and in other societies. The postconventional level is reached by a minority of adults and is usually attained only after the age of 20.

One way of understanding the three levels is to think of them as three different types of relationships between the self and society's rules and expectations. From this point of view, the Level I preconventional person is one for whom rules and social expectations are something external to the self. The Level III postconventional person is one who has differentiated his or her values from the rules and expectations of others and defines these values in terms that may sometimes conflict with those of society.

Within each of the three moral levels, two stages exist. The second stage is a more advanced and organized form of the general perspective of each major level. Table 7.2 defines the six stages in terms of: (1) what is right, (2) the reason for upholding the right, and (3) the social perspective behind each stage. This social perspective is a central concept in our definition of moral reasoning, and the discussion now turns to its elaboration.

Social Perspective as Unifying Concept

In order to characterize the development of moral reasoning structually, we seek a single unifying construct that will generate the major structural features of each stage. Selman (1980) offers a point of departure in the search for such a unifying construct. He has defined levels of role-taking that parallel our moral stages and

TABLE 7.2
The Six Moral Stages

Level and Stage	Content of Stage		Social Perspective of Stage
	What Is Right	Reasons for Doing Right	
Level I: Preconventional Stage 1—Heteronomous Morality	To avoid breaking rules backed by punishment, obedience for its own sake, and avoiding physical damage to persons and property.	Avoidance of punishment, and the superior power of authorities.	*Egocentric point of view.* Doesn't consider the interests of others or recognize that they differ from the actor's; doesn't relate two points of view. Actions are considered physically rather than in terms of psychological interests of others. Confusion of authority's perspective with one's own.
Stage 2—Individualism, Instrumental Purpose, and Exchange	Following rules only when it is to someone's immediate interest; acting to meet one's own interests and needs and letting others do the same. Right is also what's fair, what's an equal exchange, a deal, an agreement.	To serve one's own needs or interests in a world where you have to recognize that other people have their interests, too	*Concrete individualistic perspective.* Aware that everybody has his own interest to pursue and these conflict, so that right is relative (in the concrete individualistic sense).
Level II: Conventional Stage 3—Mutual Interpersonal Expectations, Relationships, and Interpersonal Conformity	Living up to what is expected by people close to you or what people generally expect of people in your role as son, brother, friend, etc. "Being good" is important and means having good motives, showing concern about others. It also means keeping mutual relationships, such as trust, loyalty, respect, and gratitude.	The need to be a good person in your own eyes and those of others. Your caring for others. Belief in the Golden Rule. Desire to maintain rules and authority which support stereotypical good behavior.	*Perspective of the individual in relationships with other individuals.* Aware of shared feelings, agreements, and expectations which take primacy over individual interests. Relates points of view through the concrete Golden Rule, putting yourself in the other person's shoes. Does not yet consider generalized system perspective.

| Stage 4—Social System and Conscience | Fulfilling the actual duties to which you have agreed. Laws are to be upheld except in extreme cases where they conflict with other fixed social duties. Right is also contributing to society, the group, or institution. | To keep the institution going as a whole, to avoid the breakdown in the system "if everyone did it," or the imperative of conscience to meet one's defined obligations. (Easily confused with Stage 3 belief in rules and authority: see text.) | *Differentiates societal point of view from interpersonal agreement or motives.* Takes the point of view of the system that defines roles and rules. Considers individual relations in terms of place in the system. |
| *Level III: Postconventional, or Principled* Stage 5—Social Contract or Utility and Individual Rights | Being aware that people hold a variety of values and opinions, that most values and rules are relative to your group. These relative rules should usually be upheld, however, in the interest of impartiality and because they are the social contract. Some nonrelative values and rights like *life* and *liberty*, however, must be upheld in any society and regardless of majority opinion. | A sense of obligation to law because of one's social contract to make and abide by laws for the welfare of all and for the protection of all people's rights. A feeling of contractual commitment, freely entered upon, to family, friendship, trust, and work obligations. Concern that laws and duties be based on rational calculation of overall utility, "the greatest good for the greatest number." | *Prior-to-society perspective* Perspective of a rational individual aware of values and rights prior to social attachments and contracts. Integrates perspectives by formal mechanisms of agreement, contract, objective impartiality, and due process. Considers moral and legal points of view; recognizes that they sometimes conflict and finds it difficult to integrate them. |

285

TABLE 7.2—Continued

	Content of Stage		
Level and Stage	What Is Right	Reasons for Doing Right	Social Perspective of Stage
Stage 6—Universal Ethical Principles	Following self-chosen ethical principles. Particular laws or social agreements are usually valid because they rest on such principles. When laws violate these principles, one acts in accordance with the principle. Principles are universal principles of justice: the equality of human rights and repect for the dignity of human beings as individual persons.	The belief as a rational person in the validity of universal moral principles, and a sense of personal commitment to them.	*Perspective of a moral point of view* from which social arrangements derive. Perspective is that of any rational individual recognizing the nature of morality or the fact that persons are ends in themselves and must be treated as such.

Source: Kohlberg, 1984, pp. 174–177.

286

form a cognitive-structural hierarchy. Selman defines role-taking primarily in terms of the way the individual differentiates his or her perspective from other perspectives, and the way one relates these perspectives to one another. Focusing on justice and morality, there is a more general construct that underlies role-taking and moral judgment, the concept of *sociomoral perspective*, which refers to the point of view the individual takes in explaining sociomoral values, or "oughts." Corresponding to the three major levels of moral judgment postulated are the three major levels of social perspective as follows:

Moral judgment	*Social perspective*
I. Preconventional perspective	Personal individual
II. Conventional	Member-of-society perspective
III. Postconventional, or principled	Prior-to-society perspective

The conventional level of moral reasoning is different from the preconventional in that it is characterized by the following kinds of concerns: (1) concern about social approval; (2) concern about loyalty to persons, groups, and authority; and (3) concern about the welfare of others and society. We need to ask what underlies these characteristics of reasoning and holds them together. What fundamentally defines and unifies the characteristics of the conventional level is its particular *social perspective*, this notion of a viewpoint shared by the participants in a relationship or group. The conventional individual views the needs of the single individual as subordinate to the viewpoint and needs of the group or the shared relationship. To illustrate the conventional social perspective, here is 17-year-old Joe's response to the following question:

Why shouldn't you steal from a store?
It's a matter of law. It's one of our rules that we're trying to help protect everyone, protect property, not just to protect a store. It's something that's needed in our society. If we didn't have these laws people would steal, they wouldn't have to work for a living and our whole society would get out of kilter.

Joe is concerned about *keeping the law*, and his reason for being concerned is the *good of society as a whole*. Clearly, he is speaking as a member of society—"It's one of *our* rules to protect everyone in *our* society." This concern for the good of society arises from his taking the point of view of "we members of society," which goes beyond the point of view of Joe as a concrete, individual self.

This *conventional member-of-society perspective* is in contrast to the *preconventional concrete individual perspective*. This point of view involves the individual actor in the situation thinking about his interests and those of other individuals he may care about. Seven years earlier, at age 10, Joe illustrated the concrete individual perspective in response to the same question.

Why shouldn't you steal from a store?
It's not good to steal from the store. It's against the law. Someone could see you and call the police.

It is clear that the idea of something being "against the law" means something very different at the two levels. At Level II, the law is made by and for "everyone," as Joe indicates at age 17. At Level I, it is just something enforced by the police and, accordingly, the reason for obeying the law is to avoid punishment. This reasoning derives from the limits of a Level I perspective, the perspective of an individual considering his or her own interests and those of other isolated individuals.

Let us now examine the perspective of the *postconventional level*. It is like the preconventional perspective in that it returns to the standpoint of the individual rather than taking the point of view of "we members of society." However, the individual point of view taken at the postconventional level can be universal in that it is that of *any rational moral individual*. Aware of the member-of-society perspective, the postconventional person questions and redefines it in terms of an individual moral perspective, so that social obligations are defined in ways that can be justified to any moral individual. An individual's commitment to basic morality or moral principles is seen as preceding, or being necessary for, that person's taking society's perspective or accepting society's laws and values. Society's laws and values, in turn, should be ones any reasonable person could commit to whatever one's place in society and whatever society one belongs to. The postconventional perspective is *prior to society* in the sense that it is the perspective of an *individual who has made the moral commitments or holds the standards on which a good or just society must be based*. This is a perspective by which (1) a particular society or set of social practices may be judged and (2) a person may rationally commit himself to a society.

Joe may again be an example, interviewed at age 24:

Why shouldn't someone steal from a store?
It's violating another person's rights, in this case to property.
Does the law enter in?
Well, the law in most cases is based on what is morally right so it's not a separate subject, it's a consideration.
What does "morally right" mean to you?
Recognizing the rights of other individuals, first to life and then to do as he pleases as long as it doesn't interfere with somebody else's rights.

From Joe's postconventional perspective, the wrongness of stealing is that it violates the moral rights of individuals, which are prior to law and society. Property rights follow from more universal human rights (such as freedoms, which do not interfere with the like freedom of others). The demands of law and society derive from universal moral rights, rather than vice versa.

It should be noted that use of the words *rights* or *morally right* or *conscience* does not necessarily distinguish conventional from postconventional morality. Orienting to the morally right thing, or following conscience as against following the law, need not indicate the postconventional perspective of the rational moral individual. The terms morality and conscience may simply be used to refer to group rules and values in conflict with civil laws or the rules of the majority group. For example, to a Jehovah's Witness who has gone to jail for "conscience," conscience may mean God's law as interpreted by his religious sect or group rather than the standpoint of any individual oriented to universal moral principles or values. To be postconventional, such ideas or terms must clearly reflect a foundation for a rational or moral individual underlying commitment to any group or society or its morality. Trust, for example, is a basic value at both the conventional and the postconventional levels. However, at the conventional level, trustworthiness is something you expect of others in your society while at the postconventional level it is considered a necessary ingredient in any functioning society or relationship. Joe expresses a conventional view as follows at age 17:

Why should a promise be kept, anyway?
Friendship is based on trust. If you can't trust a person, there's little grounds to deal with him. You should try to be as reliable as possible because people remember you by this. You're more respected if you can be depended upon.

At the conventional level, Joe views trust as a truster, as well as someone who could break a trust. He sees that the individual needs to be trustworthy not only to secure respect and maintain social relationships with others, but also because as a member of society he expects trust of others in general.

At the postconventional level, the individual has taken a further step. He does not automatically assume that he is in a society in which he needs the friendship and respect of other individuals. Instead he considers why any society or social relationship presupposes trust, and why the individual, if he is to contract into society, must be trustworthy. At age 24, Joe is postconventional in his explanation of why a promise should be kept:

I think human relationships in general are based on trust, on believing in other individuals. If you have no way of believing in someone else, you can't deal with anyone else and it becomes every man for himself. Everything you do in a day's time is related to somebody else and if you can't deal on a fair basis, you have chaos.

We have defined a postconventional moral perspective in terms of the individual's reasons *why* something is right or wrong. Now this perspective will be illustrated as it enters into making an actual decision or defining what is right. In making such a decision, the postconventional person considers the moral point of view that each individual in a moral conflict situation ought to adopt. Rather than defining expectations and obligations from the standpoint of societal roles, as someone at the conventional level would, the postconventional individual holds that persons in these roles should orient to a "moral point of view." While the postconventional moral viewpoint includes recognition of fixed legal-social obligations, recognition of moral obligations takes priority when moral and legal viewpoints conflict.

At age 24 Joe reflects the postconventional moral point of view as a decision-making perspective in response to Heinz's dilemma about stealing a drug to save his wife.

It is the husband's duty to save his wife. The fact that her life is in danger transcends every other standard you might use to judge his action. Life is more important than property.
Suppose it were a friend, not his wife?
I don't think that would be much different from a moral point of view. It's still a human being in danger.
Suppose it were a stranger?
To be consistent, yes, from a moral standpoint.
What is this moral standpoint?
I think every individual has a right to live and if there is a way of saving an individual, he should be saved.
Should the judge punish the husband?
Usually the moral and the legal standpoints coincide. Here they conflict. The judge should weigh the moral standpoint more heavily.

Kohlberg's Six Moral Stages—Description

This section focuses on the social perspective differences between the two moral stages, within each of the three levels, showing how the second stage in each level completes the development of the social perspective entered at the first stage of the level.

The clearest differences are those distinguishing Stages 3 and 4 that constitute the conventional level. Stage 4 reasoning was expressed in the preceding section by Joe's full-fledged member-of-society perspective at age 17. His statements about the importance of trust in dealing with others clearly reflect the perspective of someone taking the point of view of the social system. The social perspective at Stage 3 does not include awareness of society's point of view, or of the good of the whole of society, but is limited to the perspective of individuals in a personal relationship. As an example of Stage 3, let us consider the following response of Andy to a dilemma about whether an older brother should tell the father about a younger brother's disobedience revealed in confidence.

He should think of his brother, but it's more important to be a good son. Your father has done so much for you. I'd have a conscience if I didn't tell, more than to my brother, because my father couldn't trust me. My brother would understand; our father has done so much for him, too.

Andy's perspective takes into account particular personal relationships that are not viewed as constituting a system of mutually reciprocal relational obligations to be fulfilled for optimal functioning of the family. The son-father relationship supercedes the brother relationship on the basis of personal loyalty or for how much the father has done for the sons. The importance of maintaining trustworthiness is considered in relation to the father, but not in relation to the brother. Andy fails to take account of the brother's possible loss of trust in reaction to betrayal, and expects the brother to share his feeling of obligation to the father.

Being a good son is said to be more important not because it is a more important role in the eyes of, or in terms of, society as a whole or even in terms of the family as a system. The Stage 3 member-of-a-group perspective is that of the average good person, to that of society or an institution as a whole. The Stage 3 perspective sees things from the point of view of shared relationships between two or more individuals—relations of caring, trust, respect, and so on—rather than from the viewpoint of institutional wholes. In summary, whereas the Stage 4 member-of-society perspective is a "system" perspective, the Stage 3 perspective is that of a participant in a shared relationship or shared group. It may be added that in this and other dilemmas Andy was Type A or heteronomous in focusing on unilateral obligations to the father.

Let us turn to the preconventional level. Whereas Stage 1 involves only the point of view of the individual in question, Stage 2 includes awareness of a number of other individuals, each having other points of view. At Stage 2, in serving my interests I anticipate the other guy's reaction, negative or positive, and he anticipates mine. Unless we make a deal, each will put his own interests first. If we make a deal, each of us will do something for the other.

An example of the shift from Stage 1 to Stage 2 is shown by the following change in another subject's response between age 10 and age 13 to the question about whether a boy should tell his father about his brother's misdeed. At 10, the subject gives a Stage 1 answer:

In one way it was right to tell because his father might beat him up. In another way it's wrong because his brother will beat him up if he tells.

At age 13, he has moved to Stage 2:

The brother should not tell or he'll get his brother in trouble. If he wants his brother to keep quiet for him sometime, he'd better not squeal now.

In the second response, there is an extension of concern to the brother's welfare but as it affects the subject's own interest through anticipated exchange. There is a much clearer picture of the brother's point of view and its relationship to his own than at Stage 1.

Turning to the postconventional level, a typical Stage 5 orientation reflects a distinction between a moral point of view and a legal point of view, but also a difficulty in defining a moral perspective independently of the perspective behind contractual-legal rights. Joe, at an advanced Stage 5, says with regard to Heinz's dilemma of whether to steal the drug to save his wife:

Usually the moral and the legal standpoints coincide. Here they conflict. The judge should weigh the moral standpoint more.

For Joe, the moral point of view is not yet something prior to the legal point of view. Both law and morality for Joe derive from individual rights and values, and both are more or less on an equal plane. At Stage 6, obligation is defined in terms of an ethically principled respect for persons, Kant's categorical imperative to treat each person as an end, not a mere means. Here is a Stage 6 response to Heinz's dilemma:

It is wrong legally but right morally. Systems of law are valid only insofar as they reflect the sort of moral law all rational people can accept. One must consider the personal justice involved, which is the root of the social contract. The ground of creating a society is individual justice, the right of every person to an equal consideration of his claims in every situation, not just those which can be codified in law. Personal justice means, "Treat each person as an end, not a means."

This response indicates a very clear awareness of moral point of view based on a principle ("Treat each person as an end, not a means") which is more basic than, and from which one can derive, the sociolegal point of view.

In What Sense Is a Higher Stage a Better Stage?

An understanding of our stages may be helped by clarifying why we think a higher stage is a more adequate or morally better stage. In saying this, we do not mean that someone giving a higher stage response is morally more worthy than someone giving a lower stage response. Worthiness is related to actual moral action, not verbal judgments, and we have no philosophic theory that tells us how to judge a person's moral worth except for our Stage 6 theory or principle that each human being is worthy of equal dignity and respect.

Nevertheless, holding development as the central aim of education, we do argue that a higher moral stage is a better stage in solving moral problems as problems of conflicting interests and claims, especially justice claims on which we and Piaget have focused.

Because of differing conceptions of the nature and scope of the moral domain, we will denote the most inclusive conception of the good and the right as the ethical. Such a conception includes Erikson's scheme of ego strengths and virtues as well as the varying orientations and domains of judgment and reasoning of justice, personal care, ideals of the good life, and religious orientations. All these are included in classic books called "Ethics" like those of Aristotle and Spinoza, which include views of human nature and the wider social and natural (or supernatural) order.

Although this chapter focuses on the broader ethical dimensions of human development, its central focus is on moral justice stages. Justice as a central focus of a theory of moral development makes sense for a number of reasons. First, posing situations requiring a choice between conflicting norms or rights elicits generalized reasons or reasoning whose structure can be analyzed and used to define "structural stages." Whether some other forms of morality can be defined in terms of structural stages is still an open question.

We have argued extensively that our notion of adequacy must be justified philosophically (Kohlberg, 1981, 1984). Western philosophers from Plato and Aristotle to Kant, Mill, and Hume have seen justice as the first or central moral or other-regarding virtue of individuals and societies, and their moral theories have been primarily theories of justice. In addition, all have held that justice is in some sense rational, that good and compelling reasons may be given for one or another principle of justice. Central to post-Medieval philosophies of justice are the principles of liberty, equality, and equity (or equality compensating for unequal need, opportunity, etc.). Our theory stresses that a single attitude or principle may be seen as underlying each of these principles, the principle or attitude of respect for persons (Kant's categorical imperative to treat each person as an end, not solely as a means). This attitude or principle especially central to Stage 6 justice may be seen as including active sympathy for others and the principle of beneficence. Other theories, like utilitarianism, view beneficence as giving rise to justice principles like liberty, as it does for J. S. Mill. These differences in philosophic theory need not disturb our philosophic assumption that a principled judgment of justice is the end point of development in this domain.

The need for rational principles of justice, or some agreement on justice, as compared to agreements about ideals of the good life, arises from the fact that reasoning about justice is required to resolve the basic conflicts between persons in society. Each of us may have his or her own ideal of the good life or of special relations of care and friendship, yet social life requires some consensus about justice. We believe that the ideal toward which justice reasoning moves is that of universal agreement of all those potentially involved in a justice conflict. Justice reasoning aims at a dialogue on which all concerned parties could agree through discussion and common principles, rather than through settling conflicts through authority, manipulation, or coercion. This involves taking what philosophers call a "moral point of view."

> The "moral point of view" stresses attributes of reversibility, impartiality, univer-
> salizability, and the effort and willingness to come to agreement or consensus with
> other human beings in general about what is right. (Baier, 1965; Frankena, 1973)

In addition to a willingness to engage in open dialogue, and to strive for impartiality or fairness in arriving at a decision, we have stressed (Kohlberg, 1981) the centrality of the Golden Rule, of ideal or reversible role-taking as an attribute of the moral point of view. Found first at Stage 3 in judging in terms of the point of view of another person, that view at the highest moral stage as "moral musical chairs" involves willingness to engage in dialogue or imaginatively reverse roles with any or all of the possible persons affected by a decision. A particularly vivid portrayal of the moral point of view as including reversibility is suggested by John Rawls' (1971) *Theory of justice*. According to Rawls, the principles of justice that should be agreed to in any society are those that would be picked in "an original position" under a "veil of ignorance" as to what role or circumstances one might turn out to have in the society, rich or poor, black or white, intelligent or retarded, male or female. Following a long, careful but controversial argument, the principles so chosen would be, first, the maximum liberty compatible with the like liberty of others, and, second, the elimination of all inequalities in income and respect not justifiable from the point of view of the worst-off members of the society.

Another related portrayal of the moral point of view is provided by Habermas (1979). Habermas characterizes the moral point of view in terms of an "ideal communication situation" in which justice relations or claims are open to dialogue and argumentation, a situation presupposing the freedom, equality, and openness to reason and questioning of all the participants. In this view, autonomy or commitment to moral principles is not an individualistic self-enclosed commitment to principles indifferent to the view of others but a commitment to seeking ideal social consensus. Where consensus cannot be found, the moral individual must stand firm in acting in terms of principles of respect for persons and their rights and in terms of beneficence or the welfare of others, but such firmness must be consensus-seeking as in principled civil disobedience. The notion that a later stage of justice judgment and reasoning is more adequate than an earlier stage is implied by the idea of moral development itself. The study of moral development implies some increased adequacy in the notion of development itself as does the study of intellectual development. The study of moral development cannot be carried on in a totally value-neutral way in which any age change would constitute development including age change in Nazi Germany to the storm-troopers' mode of judgment and reasoning. Instead, it must be guided by philosophic ideals of morality and its adequacy. Of course, a logical and philosophic construction of moral development could be empirically wrong, a logically and philosophically plausible construction of a set of steps toward a more adequate morality could be discrepant with the facts of the development of reasoning. In fact, some factual discrepancies between our initial formulation of stages were found in our longitudinal studies, but the anomalies led to some revisions of our stage definition, using the same general logic (Kohlberg, 1984).

These revisions were then tested by new longitudinal sequence data, with no anomalies not attributable to measurement error. In our view, the tasks of the moral philosopher and the moral psychologist in the study of moral development are complementary.

The developmental psychologist's assumption that development is moving forward presupposes some philosophic notions of greater moral adequacy. The psychologist's account of why the person moved from stage to stage in the past rests on philosophic arguments and analyses as to the problems faced by a lower stage and solved by a higher one. If the facts of development do not support these philosophic arguments, they cast doubt on them. Thus psychology can aid philosophy while philosophy must be evoked by psychologists of development. This is apparent if they want their findings to be of use to education and if development is to be an aim of education as John Dewey and his followers (myself included) have claimed.

As our discussion has suggested, we see each higher stage as coming closer to a fully moral point of view, that is, being (a) more inclusive and (b) more reversible than the prior stage. We have partially described each as having a more inclusive sociomoral perspective, considering all perspectives involved in a problem. At the preconventional level (Stages 1 and 2) the child takes only the perspective of a given individual obeying, rejecting, or dealing with another individual in the society. At the conventional level (Stages 3 and 4) the person takes the shared point of view of "we, the members of the family or peer group" (Stage 3) or "we, the members of society" (Stage 4). At the principled level, the individual takes the perspective of any rational individual potentially in any society with rights prior to society "contracting" into society.

Each stage may also be seen as being more integrated or reversible in terms of the justice operations it uses (Kohlberg, 1984). At Stage 1, the child can see distributive justice as dividing goods equally. The child can also see as a justice of reciprocity returning bad with punishment, good with reward. He does not see the two as integrated however. At Stage 2, the child regards individuals as potentially equal in their right to achieve their goals or needs with obligations to give up goals and needs based on concrete reciprocity. These two operations are integrated at Stage 2 but not so as to achieve a more ideal equity. At Stage 2, the Golden Rule means do back to the other what he does to you. At Stage 3, reciprocity is ideal; the reciprocal is integrated with the inverse so that it means acting toward others as you would like to be treated, not as you are treated. At Stage 4, equality is integrated with Stage 3 ideal reciprocity, fairness in treating any person equally before the law, civil or religious. At Stage 5, equality is integrated with other operations to a conception of equality as fair distribution in terms of rights or welfare prior to particular social roles, rights to freedom of choice and rights of equal opportunity. Stage 6, still poorly defined empirically, bases action on a universal and general principle on which all persons taking the moral point of view could agree, on equal respect for persons and the condition of moral perspective-taking and dialogue itself. From the point of view of achieving free consensus about justice conflicts, Stage 3 can lead to consensus as a particular small group, Stage 4 in a particular society or institution, Stage 5 to some consensus on universal human and civil rights, and Stage 6 to some consensus on principles of human obligations. As noted, the empirical nature and philosophic claims to validity of a sixth stage are still open and require much further work.

Leaving Stage 6 and the claim of greater adequacy, there is a philosophic premise built into the stages themselves, a premise acceptable from a number of particular moral philosophies. Empirically, it could have been the case that individual egocentrism followed social or principled morality. The fact that a philosophic argument for the greater adequacy of each higher stage runs consistent with the empirical evidence on the sequence of stage movement, as well as the reasons for movement from stage to stage, is extremely important for the educator.

MEASUREMENT OF THE KOHLBERG STAGES

Stages in development were emphasized in earlier chapters as central to the cognitive-developmental view. We reviewed in Chapter 6 logical and empirical criteria of stages along with evidence bearing on the validation of stages in cognitive development. Although Piaget's view of the development of moral judgment is a cognitive one, he did not identify clear-cut stages. Rather, he concluded that heteronomous morality and a morality of subjective responsibility are broad, overlapping divisions in development. In contrast, the Kohlberg stages are defined as structural stages. In this section, the method of defining these stages is described, and evidence bearing on their validity is reviewed.

Kohlberg stages emerged from a 20-year longitudinal study of American males commencing in 1956. Seventy-two boys aged 10 to 16, were reinterviewed every three or four years on nine hypothetical dilemmas, and their responses constitute the study of changes in the moral reasoning of these subjects as they grew older and led to changes in the conceptualization of moral stages. These changes are reflected in revisions in scoring systems used to organize these data. Originally, the data were scored using a rough sentence-coding and story-rating guide oriented to 25 "aspects" of moral judgment (Kohlberg, 1958). Scoring by this method yielded some challenging deviations from expectations derived from the stage hypotheses (Kohlberg & Kramer, 1969). That is, some subjects seemed to regress or skip stages. The most outstanding inversion of sequence was an apparent shift from a Stage 4 society-orientation to a Stage 2 relativistic hedonism in some subjects who became "liberated" and "relativized" in their college years. Based on the fact that these subjects eventually moved on to Stage 5 principled thinking, we eventually concluded that this relativistic egoism was a transitional phase, a "Stage $4\frac{1}{2}$"—a no-man's land between rejection of conventional morality and the formulation of nonconventional or universal moral principles. The social perspective of the $4\frac{1}{2}$ was clearly different from that of naive Stage 2. The $4\frac{1}{2}$ questioned society and viewed himself and the rules from an "outside of society" perspective, whereas the Stage 2 saw things as a particular individual relating to other individuals through concrete reciprocity, exchange, and utility (Kohlberg, 1984; Turiel, 1974).

A second inversion of sequence was found in a small proportion of individuals who "regressed" from Stage 4 to Stage 3, or skipped from Stage 3 to Stage 5. These inversions, in turn, could be seen as resulting from an inadequate definition of Stage 4, a definition that equated "law and order" ideas (content) with taking a social system perspective (stage structure). As a result, we redefined as Stage 3 any "law and order" thinking (such as that of Archie Bunker) that did not display a social-system perspective.

These changes in conceptions of the stages reflected a growing clarity regarding the distinction between structure and content that led us to abandon aspect-scoring. Our 1958 aspect scoring was based not on "structure" but on certain statistical or probabilistic associations between structure and content. For example, a social-system perspective tends to yield moral judgments whose content is law and order. One can, however, have much of this content at Stage 3 without the social-system perspective, or one can have the social-system perspective without this content. Accordingly, we generated a new, more structural scoring method, which we called Standardized Issue Scoring (Colby & Kohlberg, 1986).

To develop a more structural scoring system, the first step involved analyzing and standardizing types of content used to score each stage. Stage differences, of course, must be defined in terms of common issues or values. These types of content represent *what* the individual is valuing, judging, or appealing to rather than the mode of reasoning about the issue. Accordingly, we developed the following list of moral issues, values, or norms found in every society or culture.

Laws and rules

Conscience

Personal roles of affection

Authority

Civil rights

Contract, trust and justice in exchange

Punishment and justice in punishment

The value of life

Property rights and values

Truth

Sex and sexual love

This most recent manual provides scoring criteria for a standardized interview that probes only two issues on each of three stories. One standard form, Form A, contains three stories covering six issues as follows:

Story III. Heinz steals the drug—*Life* and *Law*.
Story III'. Should Heinz be legally punished for stealing?—*Conscience* and *Punishment*.
Story I. The father breaks a promise to his son—*Contract* and *Personal relationship*.

A second and third form, for retest purposes, Form B and Form C, contain different stories covering the same issues. Each of the six issues is assigned a stage score according to criteria in the manual, and a single global score is given to each subject based on the average of the issue scores. Most subjects display two stages in their thinking: the stage they are moving out of and the stage they are moving into. The mean usage of the individual's chosen or modal stage is 2/3 or 67 percent. The remaining thinking is at the individual's secondary stage, with very few subjects choosing usage of more than two stages of reasoning. Major and minor stages are always found to be adjacent. Accordingly, subjects are assigned a qualitative stage score, for example, mixed (2/3), meaning that most thinking is Stage 2 but that 25 percent or more is Stage 3 or pure (3). In addition, a subject is assigned a continuous weighted average score representing the percentage of each stage used multiplied by the ordinal scale value of the stage, for example, 233 if the subject showed 67 percent Stage 2 reasoning and 33 percent Stage 3 reasoning.

The manual for standardized issue scoring presents "criterion judgments" defining each stage on each issue for each story. A criterion judgment is a pattern of reasoning that is most distinctive for a given stage. Theoretically, such reasoning follows from the structural definition of the stage. Empirically, it is used by a substantial number of subjects at that stage (as defined by their average stage on all stories) and not used by subjects at other stages.

An example of a criterion judgment from the standardized manual is presented in Table 7.3. The dilemma to which it refers involves euthanasia: Should a doctor give a drug that will relieve a patient's pain but cause the patient to die sooner, if the terminally ill person rationally requests it?

Scoring the stage of an idea on the given story begins with its classification by issue and then proceeds to smaller units called Norms (the same 10 issues listed above) and Elements (17 types of value given to a norm). The norms and elements are listed in Table 7.4.

The aim of the scorer is to arrive at stage structure, to discern the structure underlying responses. To do this, successive classifications are made with regard to the content of the responses. The first classification involves a determination of the issue (or norm) reflected by two conflicting values in a response; in Table 7.3, the chosen issue is law. Classification of content is the first step because law obedience may be valued at any stage. These reasons, called *elements of value*, take us closer to structure for valuing law obedience. The elements of value are derived from the efforts of moral philosophers to classify types of moral value (listed in Table 7.4). Note that the example from the manual in Table 7.3 falls under Element 7, *avoiding punishment*. While it might seem that this classification would place the response at Stage 1, further discrimination is necessary. Stage 1 obedience is not unequivocally indicated by a response showing the valuing of the element of punishment avoidance because it can also indicate Stage 2 instrumentalism. To aid the scorer in making this discrimination, the manual provides a theoretical statement of the structure for the stage, issue, and element in question. In Table 7.3, under "Stage Structure," the scorer finds that a response including consideration of risk rather than certainty of punishment indicates a Stage 2 structure.

A second, and complementary, tool for arriving at stage structure is presented in the paragraph designated *Critical Indicators*. This category comprises those indicators reflecting whether a certain kind of set (here, a Stage 2 egoistically pragmatic set) is involved in thinking about punishment.

TABLE 7.3
Example of Moral Judgment Manual Item

Criterion Judgment #7

Dilemma: IV
Issue: Law
Norm: Law
Element: Seeking reward (avoiding punishment), 11.7
Stage: 2

Criterion Judgment

[The doctor should not give the woman the drug] because he would risk losing his job or going to jail.
[Note: Do not match score this point if it is a response to the general question "Why is it important to obey the law?" unless the response refers to the doctor in this mercy-killing situation.]

Stage Structure

Not killing the woman is justified because it involves a risk (rather than certainty) of punishment. Punishment is seen as something to be instrumentally avoided. The risk of punishment overrides the recognition of the pragmatic reasonableness from the woman's point of view of giving her the drug.

Critical Indicators

One of the following must be used as the central justification for not killing the woman: (*a*) punishment as possible or probable, a risk to be weighed in the decision; *or* (*b*) other disadvantageous consequences to the doctor (he might lose his job, etc.).

Match Examples

1. Should the doctor give her the drug that would make her die? Why? No, the doctor could be charged with killing her. He should give something to calm her. [Why?] He would lose his career and go to prison. He should protect himself first and not kill her.
2. Should the doctor give her the drug that would make her die? Why? No. He would be blamed for killing her. She could take her own overdose. If he did, he could lose his license and be out of a job.

Guess Example

[Note: Guess scored only if no other scored material on the issue and weighted $\frac{1}{2}$ match. Otherwise, material is a nonmatch.]
1. Should the doctor do what she asks and give her the drug? No, I don't think so. I think it's asking too much of a doctor for one thing, that she should ask this even though she is in great pain. A doctor isn't supposed to do this. [Why?] I believe it's in their code that you shouldn't give a drug to any person to help them die sooner or to put them to death

TABLE 7.3—Continued

Guess Example

---

right away. *If he were found out to have given her this drug, he'd probably be kicked out of his profession and he might not be able to get into something else.*
[Note: This refers to the likelihood that the doctor will lose his job as required by critical indicator (b), but the risk of undesirable consequences is not used as the central argument against mercy killing as the critical indicators specify.]

Source: Kohlberg, 1984, pp. 403–404.

The responses for each subject on each of the six issues are assigned a stage score. These are then averaged to give a single stage score for each issue on each dilemma. These are averaged or summed across dilemmas to give the individual a stage score Pure (Stage 3) or Mixed (Stage 3/4).

Validation of Moral Stages

Two broad issues addressed now are the validity of moral stage assessment and the validity of stage theory. We should also mention that reliability studies indicate that the Kohlberg stages can be objectively measured, and that individual assessments are valid. Interscorer reliability test-retest and alternate-forms correlations are in the 90s, with over 80 percent exact agreement on classification of individuals by either a single stage or a mixture of two adjacent stages (Colby et al., 1983; Colby & Kohlberg, 1987).

The most important validity criterion of a stage test is evidence for its meeting the criterion of invariant sequence. This means, first, that change over time is always forward, that there are no regressive changes. To investigate this, we looked at all comparisons between stage at one time of testing and stage at the next time of testing. In only 7 percent of these comparisons did a downward shift of stage exist. There was more than twice as large a percentage of downward shifts in our test-retest reliability study, so that the regressions are less than what would be expected on the basis of measurement error.

The invariant-sequence criterion means, second, that there is no stage-skipping. There were no cases in our longitudinal data falling into the stage-skipping category. Longitudinal data from a Turkish village and an Israeli kibbutz, scored blind, yielded results equally supportive of the stage model providing some evidence that the longitudinal sequence finding is cross-cultural (Kohlberg, 1984, ch. 7, ch. 8).

Over forty cross-cultural studies have been conducted showing the expected age order to the stages, as discussed shortly (reviewed by John Snarey, 1985).

After sequence, the most important issue of validity of the stage construct is its success in meeting the criterion of "structured wholeness." In our chapter on intelligence we discussed this criterion at length, and the use of factor analysis to

TABLE 7.4

The Elements and Norms for Classifying Content

The Elements

I. *Modal Elements*
    1. Obeying (consulting) persons or deity. Should obey, get consent (should consult, persuade).
    2. Blaming (approving). Should be blamed for, disapproved (should be approved).
    3. Retributing (exonerating). Should retribute against (should exonerate).
    4. Having a right (having no right).
    5. Having a duty (having no duty).

II. *Value Elements*
  A. *Egoistic Consequences*
    6. Good reputation (bad reputation).
    7. Seeking reward (avoiding punishment).

  B. *Utilitarian Consequences*
    8. Good individual consequences (bad individual consequences).
    9. Good group consequences (bad group consequences).

  C. *Ideal or Harmony-Serving Consequences*
    10. Upholding character.
    11. Upholding self-respect.
    12. Serving social ideal or harmony.
    13. Serving human dignity and autonomy.

  D. *Fairness*
    14. Balancing perspectives or role taking.
    15. Reciprocity or positive desert.
    16. Maintaining equity and procedural fairness.
    17. Maintaining social contract or freely agreeing.

The Norms

1.	Life	6.	Authority
	a. Preservation	7.	Law
	b. Quality/quantity	8.	Contract
2.	Property	(9.	Civil Rights)
3.	Truth	(10.	Religion)
4.	Affiliation	11.	Conscience
(5.	Erotic Love and Sex)		

Source: Kohlberg, 1984, p. 406.

support it. Factor analyses indicated that there was a single general stage factor cutting across dilemmas and norms or issues (Colby, et al., 1983; Colby & Kohlberg, 1987).

Now it should be noted that these results were achieved with a bootstrapping approach. Both stage definitions and measurement methods were revised when the sequence criteria broke down in some cases (Kohlberg & Kramer, 1969). The methodological approach we have taken is that described by Lakatos (1978) as a "progressive research program." Some psychologists have viewed stage theory as a fixed theoretical construct to be tested by predictors from the theory. Others have viewed stages as inductive from age developmental data. Lakatos suggests that theories have a "hard core" of assumptions, which in our case include the invariant sequence assumption, and a "protective belt" of other propositions and measurement operations that are revisable in the face of new data. For these revisions to be "progressive" they must however be "content" or information enhancing. As an example, the finding of "regression" in college led us to develop a system of heteronomous and autonomous moral types to account for our supposedly principled (Stage 5 or 6) high school students. This in turn led to the findings described for the moral types including their relationship to action. We and others believe these revisions and expansions to be information enhancing, representing a "progressive" rather than a "degenerating" research program in Lakatos' (1978) terms (Lapsley & Serlin, 1984).

Cross-Cultural Validation of the Moral Stages

My colleagues and I have engaged in two long-term cross-cultural longitudinal studies. The first by Nisan, Turiel, and myself (Nisan & Kohlberg, 1982; Kohlberg, 1984) was a study of village and city males in Turkey. In the city sample, sequential progressive movement through all the stages (including Stage 5 for a few) was found. In the village, development was slower and most youths stabilized at Stage 3 with one or two reaching Stage 4.

The second study by Snarey, Reimer, and myself was a 10-year study of kibbutz-born and city-born adolescents living in an Israeli kibbutz residential school (Kohlberg, 1984, ch. 9). As in the Turkish study, invariant sequence was found within the limits of measurement (test-retest) error up to Stage 5.

The Israeli adolescents moved somewhat faster than our American subjects and were somewhat more likely to reach Stage 5 than their American counterparts. As we discuss later, we attribute this to the democratic and cooperative nature of the kibbutz, which provides adolescents with extensive role-taking opportunities.

Snarey (1985) reviews 45 cross-sectional studies of moral reasoning development in a wide variety of cultures, including India, Taiwan, Kenya, Indonesia, Japan, and other non-Western cultures. In all urbanized cultures with systems of higher education all five stages are found in the expected age order. As in the Turkish village study, most village cultures show development to Stage 4 but not to Stage 5.

Snarey summarizes his conclusions as follows:

Over the past 15 years children and adults around the world have been asked if Heinz should steal a drug to save his dying wife, if Njoroge should disobey the rules to help a lost child, or some other similar moral dilemma. These cross-cultural studies have been undertaken to test Lawrence Kohlberg's theory, which posits a universal model of moral development. This review identifies the major empirical assumptions underlying Kohlberg's claim for cross-cultural universality, including culturally diverse samplings, universal moral questions, invariant stage sequence, full range of stages, and general applicability of the stages. It then reviews the cross-cultural research literature, much of which has not been previously published, and evaluates the support for each assumption. In addition to providing striking support for the underlying assumptions, the 45 studies examined here also identify some major caveats regarding the range and general applicability of the stages across cultures. In particular, biases in favor of complex urban societies and middle-class populations are identified. Based on these findings, the conclusion presents an alternative to Kohlberg's perspective on the relation between culture and moral development. (Snarey, 1985, p. 202)

Snarey interprets the absence of Stage 5, the current terminal stage in our American sample, as indicating a cultural bias in this stage. I theoretically predicted that not all societies would show Stage 5 (Kohlberg, 1971) if the conditions for post-conventional moral development were not present. These center on experience of conflicting value systems, which require movement to a "prior to society" or "universal across society" perspective identifying universal human rights or human value present at Stage 5. In village cultures, there is, we believe, much greater consensus on interpersonal relations and on rules of a civic or religious order, so that problems or cognitive-moral conflicts leading to movement to Stage 5 do not exist. In contrast, complex literate and Eastern urban cultures or civilizations such as China and India as well as Western cultures going back to Greece and Israel have elaborated universalistic ethics since around 1000 B.C. Snarey points out correctly that our standard scoring manual does not exhaust the concerns or "criterion judgments" of Stage 5 as it exists in Eastern cultures, or even in more collectivistic cultures like the kibbutz, but researchers with knowledge of the stage theory have little difficulty identifying as "guess scorers" Stage 5 thinking in cultures less oriented to "liberal" notions of rights and social contract. He recommends—and we agree with him—that our manual should be extended to include this material. It should be noted, however, that so far no research has elaborated a postconventional or Stage 5 mode of moral judgment that is radically different from our own. India, for instance, may extend the priority of life over property typical in the Heinz dilemma to animals as well as human life, but so do philosophic Western vegetarians.

Snarey's second criticism, that middle-class and educated persons are more likely to reach the higher stages than working class persons, is also in accord with our theory. I have claimed that individuals denied full participation in a social system are less likely to take the point of view of the system or "the generalized other" than those who are in a position of greater participation as we discuss later.

Finally, we should note that a criticism of "cultural bias" should not be based on the assumption that our stages are meant to evaluate one culture as "morally better" than another (Kohlberg, 1981, ch. 4). As we have pointed out, the claim that a higher stage reasoning more adequately solves justice problems than a lower stage does not mean that an individual scored as higher on a moral judgment interview is a morally worthier person than someone scoring at a lower stage. Besides the fact that moral action, not reasoning, enters into a judgment of worth, judgments of relative worth of persons (aretaic judgments) are not contained in our theory. American culture, riddled with crime, violence, and privatistic self-concern, containing persons who reason at Stage 2 as well as Stage 5, is not to be judged as a morally better culture than a peaceful and cooperative village in which individuals reason at Stage 3 or Stage 4.

In summary, research looking at cultural differences as well as cultural universality in moral reasoning is needed, but the basic claim to a culturally invariant stage sequence is supported by the data.

Gender Differences

Carol Gilligan (1982) has written an interesting book centering on her ideas of gender differences in morality. Her book suggests, though it does not directly claim, that my moral stages have a gender bias since the original longitudinal work was carried out on an all-male American sample. This limitation came because of the complex design of my cross-sectional doctoral study, which led me to control for many variables, including gender. In the next longitudinal study conducted, the Snarey, Reimer, and Kohlberg study of an Israeli kibbutz (Kohlberg, 1984, ch. 9), females were equally represented in the sample. This study indicated that there were no more anomalies for females than males in the sample, and no differences in stage on moral maturity between males and females. A recent comprehensive view and meta-analysis by Walker (1984) indicates no significant sex differences in moral stage in a large number of cross-sectional studies. The only studies suggesting sex differences were those with adults, in samples where males had higher education than females. Higher education is moderately related to stage or average moral reasoning scores in both males and females. When the factor is controlled, sex differences in adulthood disappear in most studies.

A more important and interesting claim made by Gilligan than that of test bias is that when asked to report moral dilemmas they have experienced, females are more likely to focus on issues of care than males, while males are more likely to focus on issues of justice. According to Gilligan (1982), the moral "voice" or "orientation" of women is predominantly of care; for males, it is justice. Research by Lyons (1983) using a complex coding scheme suggests that while both sexes use both orientations, males focus more on justice, females on care. These findings are not inconsistent with findings of no sex difference in stage in our justice dilemmas.

With regard to gender differences in care, Radke-Yarrow et al. (1983, pp. 518–522) summarize the sex differences situations on care-giving, empathy, and sharing and find no consistent sex differences in these variables. Nevertheless, Gilligan's thesis that there are two tracks of development, one of justice and one of care, represents a distinction between love and justice with intuitive appeal. Furthermore, my moral reasoning dilemmas can be most easily seen as justice dilemmas since they require deciding between two conflicting norms (e.g., a wife's right to life and a druggist's right to property). Morality as justice centers on a moral point of view that is impartial and universalizable. Situations or dilemmas of care more typically center on the special responsibilities of parents for their children, friends, for one another—responsibilities that do not and cannot be really seen as springing from an impartial and universalizable point of view. It remains a task for future research by Gilligan and her colleagues to determine whether there is stage-type development in dilemmas of care, and whether stage development in such dilemmas is synchronous with stage development in justice reasoning or whether they are radically asynchronous. Eisenberg-Berg (1986) has described stage-like development in prosocial reasoning but her studies indicate no sex differences in development of this reasoning and a moderately positive correlation with our own stages of "justice reasoning." My own view is that judgments of justice presuppose "caring" and "sympathy"; only if the individual sympathizes with the good of others can the justice problem of how the good should be distributed become a problem for moral reasoning. Stated in different terms, justice (at the higher stages) centers on equal respect for human persons, treating others as ends not merely as means. To treat others as ends means actively to sympathize with their interests and concerns as well as to respect them as persons with rights.

Moral Stage and Action

We do not view the relation of moral judgment to action as one of the simple validity of the moral stages, that is, stage assessment is not a test to be validated by its prediction of action. Instead we view the relation between the two as raising theoretical questions requiring research for these answers. This research is still in progress but I summarize here my conclusions on the extensive research conducted to date, conclusions elaborated in Kohlberg, 1984 (ch. 7).

In the late 1960s and early 1970s my theoretical articles called attention to a number of studies that reported correlations between higher stages of moral judgment and "moral action." My interpretation of the results of these studies stressed that moral stages formed a lens or screen (a) through which a moral situation and the emotions it aroused were perceived and (b) through which the alternative courses of action available to the subject were formulated. In 1980, Blasi wrote an exhaustive review of the literature and concluded that the majority of studies using the Kohlberg stage measure reported correlations between relatively high stage moral judgment and what is commonly called moral behavior, including such dimensions as honesty, resistance to temptation, and altruistic or prosocial behavior. Despite these correlations however, Blasi concluded that the studies cast almost no theoretical light on the problem of relating judgment to action. Blasi went on to suggest that one theoretical bridge between moral judgment and moral action might be found by focusing on judgments of responsibility to act in a "morally right" manner.

Blasi's (1980) review and the studies by Kohlberg and Candee (Kohlberg, 1984, ch. 7) indicate that the relationship of moral stage to action is a monotonic one. In other words, the higher the stage reasoning, the more likely action will be consistent with the moral choice made on a dilemma. This monotonic relationship has been observed even in situations where the content factor of moral choice is consistent across stage. For example, McNamee (1978) found that a large majority of Stage 3 and Stage 4 subjects in her sample thought it was right to help an apparently drugged stooge who was appealing for help. Even with this agreement on deontic choice, however, Stage 4 subjects were still more likely actually to help the stooge than were Stage 3 subjects, and Stage 5 subjects more likely than Stage 4. Results similar to McNamee's are reported in both the Candee and Kohlberg reanalysis of the Berkeley Free Speech Movement data of Haan, Smith, and Block (1968), and in the Candee and Kohlberg reanalysis of the Milgram (1963) data, in which a subject is ordered by an experimenter to give electric shocks to a stooge victim as part of a supposed study of measuring learning through punishment.

Based upon Blasi's (1980) review as well as work by Rest (1983a, 1983b), Candee and I explain the monotonic relationship between moral stage and action reported in the literature by hypothesizing that moral action results from a four-step process following Rest (1983). The first step is sensitizing to the existence of a moral problem, primarily a matter of role-taking. The second step is the making of a deontic judgment of rightness or justice in the situation. The third step is the making of a judgment that the self is responsible or accountable for carrying out this deontic judgment in the moral situation. The fourth step is carrying it out, execution. Moral stage enters into the first step through its role-taking prerequisite, in the second step through deontic judgments of rightness or obligation. In the third step, responsibility judgment, there is a monotonic increase in consistency by stage between the deontic judgment made and a judgment of the self's responsibility to carry out the judgment in action.

This hypothesized monotonic increase in consistency by stage between deontic judgments and judgments of responsibility has been observed by Helkama (1979) on responses to hypothetical dilemmas. Helkama found, for instance, that at Stages 3 and 4 about 50 percent of subjects said that Heinz should steal the drug, but only 28 percent of that 50 percent believed that Heinz would be responsible if his wife died because he did not steal for her. At Stage 5 (and 4/5), however, over 50 percent of the subjects felt Heinz would be responsible if his wife died. Thus, there was almost twice the consistency between a deontic judgment of rightness and a judgment of responsibility at Stage 5 as observed at the conventional stages.

Thus, judgments of responsibility to act become increasingly consistent with both hypothetical and real-life deontic judgments as one moves up the Kohlberg stage hierarchy. This increased consistency is what one would expect on the basis of my claim (Kohlberg, 1981, ch. 4) that each higher stage is more prescriptive in the sense that it more successfully differentiates moral obligation and responsibility from nonmoral considerations. For example, at the conventional stages subjects may think it is right or just to help a victim or to refuse to shock a victim (Kohlberg, 1984, ch. 7) and yet at the same time feel that they do not have the moral responsibility to carry out these actions because for them it is the experimenter who has the authority or responsibility to make final decisions in the situation. However, for Stage 5 reasoners (and very often lower Stage Type B or autonomous reasoners), taking the responsibility to act in a manner consistent with their autonomous deontic choice is considered necessary. Excuses for not taking the responsibility to act, such as an appeal to the experimenter's authority or a concern for his or her approval, are considered illegitimate by such reasoners.

Thus, we suggest that moral stage influences both deontic choice and judgments of responsibility. Where situations are controversial, we may expect to find differences in deontic choice with subjects at each higher stage more likely to agree on the choice as determined by moral principles. In situations where there is general agreement on the deontic choice (e.g., in the McNamee, 1978, study), we still expect to find a monotonic relationship between stage and action because of increases in consistency, by stage, between deontic choice and a judgment of responsibility.

The notion that judgments of responsibility are more consistent with deontic judgments at the postconventional level allows us to avoid certain philosophic issues about what is really morally right or what "moral" action is. This notion also helps us avoid the problem of finding some "objective" standard for making a judgment of the moral worthiness of an action or actor. Instead, we rely on the subject's own response to define what is right and understand the increased consistency between moral judgment and moral action as a phenomenon related to moral stage growth. However, in addition to defining moral action as relative to the subject's own judgment and as a function of consistency between action and judgment, we also explore a more universal approach to defining moral action. In doing this, we examine whether principled subjects (i.e., subjects using Stage 5 or 6 reasoning) reach consensus in their judgment of a particular dilemma situation. In cultures where we have studied the relation between structure and deontic choice (e.g., in the United States, Finland, and Israel) we find that Stage 5 or Stage 6 subjects reach consensus that Heinz is right to steal and show consensus on seven of our nine dilemmas. Both the philosophers and the lay subjects we have studied at Stage 5 use Kantian or deonotological principles of respect for the life or personhood of another to make their deontic choice. The druggist claims the right to property in the story, and this claim shows no recognition of the wife's right to life, which, in the Stage 5 view, takes precedence over property rights. We also note that the use of the utilitarian principle of obtaining the greatest welfare for all involved in the dilemma also leads to the same choice to steal.

Our philosophic considerations leave us with the view that a *moral* action is an action (1) that is "objectively right" in the sense that the use of philosophic principles by Stage 5 or Stage 6 reasoners leads to agreement on what constitues "right" action, and (2) that is "subjectively right" if it is both guided by a moral judgment or reason that is "right" in the form of, and consistent with, the objectively right choice.

This approach to moral action is controversial and for many purposes it is sufficient to define moral actions as action consistent with the actor's judgment. Further, it is not only principled subjects who seem to act in a morally consistent manner. So, too, do the autonomous or Type B conventional (Stage 3 and 4) subjects in the limited number of studies assessing this variable. For instance, in the analysis by Candee and myself (Kohlberg, 1984, ch. 7) of the Milgram situation with college students, all subjects were Stage 3, 3/4, or 4. Of the classified Type B or autonomous, 86 percent quit or refused to continue shocking the stooge victim, whereas more of the Type A subjects quit. Most subjects expressed the idea that they should stop, but only the Type B's acted consistently with the idea of what they should do. In the experiment, the experimenter said he would take the responsibility for shocking. Those who quit asserted that the responsibility lay in themselves.

We have so far talked about three phases of moral action, a problem-sensitizing phase, a second phase of deontic judgment of justice, and a third phase of a judgment of responsibility to act consistently. A fourth phase of action (Rest, 1984) is execution of the judgment in the face of distraction or temptation. This seems to involve a set of ego controls somewhat independent of the development of moral judgment. As an example noted earlier, subjects high in attention were less likely to cheat than distractable children (Grim, Kohlberg, & White, 1968). This increase in resistance to cheating, however, was dependent on conventional (Stage 3 or 4) moral judgment. High school students at the preconventional level high in attention were more, rather than less likely to cheat, presumably because they had the strength to carry out their preconventional moral judgments (Krebs, 1967; Krebs & Kohlberg, 1986). Finally, as we noted in discussing Hartshorne and May, situational factors are extremely important in moral action. In many cases peer group and institutional shared norms may be moral or nonmoral in their content. A focus on these is central to the writer's approach to moral education directed to making the classroom or the school a more just community (DeVries & Kohlberg, 1987; Power et al., 1986).

THE PLACE OF MORAL JUDGMENT IN THE TOTAL PERSONALITY

To understand moral stage, it is helpful to locate it in a sequence of development of personality. We know that individuals pass through the moral stages one step at a time as they progress from the bottom (Stage 1) toward the top (Stage 6). Individuals must also go through other stages, perhaps the most basic of which are the stages of logical reasoning or intelligence studied by Piaget and discussed in Chapter 6. Moral stage theory (Kohlberg, 1984) postulates parallelisms between cognitive stages and moral stages, and that attainment of a given cognitive stage is necessary but not sufficient for the attainment of the parallel moral stage. For instance, around age 7 concrete operations are attained with the ability to use logical operations of equality, reciprocity, and transitivity on concrete objects, and to coordinate these with one another. Possession of concrete operations is necessary but not sufficient for the second moral stage, in which the child sees fairness as equality and concrete reciprocity in exchanges of value. Around age 10, the child develops what we call "early formal operations" marked by the capacity to coordinate the inverse (the negation of classes) and the reciprocal (the reversal of relationships) (Colby & Kohlberg, 1974). Early formal operations may be defined in two ways. First, they involve coordination of the inverse and the reciprocal. Simple reciprocity entails concrete exchange. Asked, "If someone comes up and hits you, what does the Golden Rule say to do?," Stage 1 and 2 children (or preformal children) say, "Hit him back, do to him what he does to you." They do not coordinate the reciprocal with the inverse, which would negate hitting the other back. Beginning formal operations are embodied in tasks like verbal seriation, for example,

Edith is fairer than Suzanne, Suzanne is darker than Edith. Who is the darkest?

It is also involved in seeing the absurdity of a sentence like "The judge told the prisoner you are going to be hanged and I hope it will be a lesson to you." Both involve the construction of the inverse (i.e., hanged means you can't be alive to learn a lesson), and its coordination with the reciprocal. Inhelder and Piaget (1958) have not stressed this early level and instead have focused on two later levels of formal operations: basic formal operation and consolidated formal operation. Basic formal operations involve considering all possibilities, for example, all combinations of four chemicals. Consolidated formal operations involve the ability to hypothetico-deductively examine and isolate variables. For example, to determine that the period of a pendulum is caused by its length and not by other variables such as weight, force, etc., which the adolescent manipulates systematically to isolate the length factor. Basic formal operations are required for Stage 4 reasoning, which necessitates considering society as a system of relationships. Walker and Richards (1979) tested a group of female adolescents on basic formal operations who were all Stage 3 in moral judgment. They then used a short training situation (conflicting advice at Stage 4). Only subjects who showed basic formal operations moved to Stage 4.

In another study, Walker (1980) exposed Stage 2 children to a role-playing training session with conflicting advice at Stage 3. Only children who shared beginning formal operations displayed change to Stage 3. Although logical development is a necessary condition for moral development, it is not sufficient. Many individuals are at a higher cognitive, logical stage than the parallel moral stage, but essentially none are at a higher moral stage than their logical stage.

Next, after stages of logical development, come stages of social perception or social perspective- or role-taking (see Selman, 1980). We partially describe these stages when we define the way the person sees other people, interprets their thoughts and feelings, and views their role or place in society. These stages are very closely related to moral stages, but are more general since they do not make a judgment of fairness at a given level. It is more difficult to make a judgment of fairness at a social perspective level than to simply see the world at that level. So, just as for logic, development of a stage's social perception precedes, or is easier than, development of the parallel stage of moral judgment. Just as there is a vertical sequence of steps in movement up from moral Stage 1 to moral Stage 2 to moral Stage 3, so there is a horizontal sequence of steps in movement from logic to social perception to moral judgment. First, individuals attain a logical stage, say, partial formal operations, which allows them to see "systems" in the world, to regard a set of related variables as a system; next they attain a level of social perception or role-taking where they see other people understanding one another in terms of the place of each in the system. Finally, they attain Stage 4 of moral judgment, where the welfare and order of the total social system or society is the focus of justice operations.

As a further example, the role-taking advance necessary for Stage 2 moral reasoning is awareness that each person in a situation can or does consider the intention or point of view of every other individual in the situation. A child may attain this role-taking advance necessary for Stage 2 moral reasoning (awareness that each person in a situation can or does consider the intention or point of view of every other individual in the situation) and still hold the Stage 1 notion that right or justice is adherence to fixed rules that must be automatically followed. But if the child is to see rightness or justice as a balance or exchange between the interests of individual actors (Stage 2), the child must have reached the requisite level of role-taking.

As discussed at more length in the next chapter, this has been confirmed experimentally by Walker (1980) who found that *only* children with both the logical and social perspective-taking prerequisites were stimulated to move from Stage 2 to Stage 3 through role-playing exposure to the next stage up.

It is tempting to think that there might be a further progression in which moral stage was necessary but not sufficient for a moral self-conception at that level, but current studies of the relation of moral stage to ego stage (as discussed in the next chapter) do not clearly support such a conclusion (Lee & Snarey, 1986).

FACTORS INFLUENCING MORAL DEVELOPMENT—SOCIALIZATION THEORY AND COGNITIVE DEVELOPMENTAL THEORY

We earlier critiqued socialization theories because their dependent variables, "resistance to temptation," guilt, and "prosocial behavior" were not age-developmental, were not stable or consistent over time, and did not represent a philosophically justified conception of moral development and were instead relativistic in their effort to be value neutral. Focusing now on moral development, we still need to consider the factors stressed by socialization theories as well as those emphasized by cognitive developmental theories in relation to moral development. Having stressed the formal or structural-stage properties of moral development, we must also note that there are content features of morality as well as formal or structural features (Nisan, 1984).

Through socialization processes the child may learn strong normative contents (e.g., don't steal or don't lie), which may be only partly consistent with the child's reasoning structure. Indeed, if children and adolescents are asked first for an immediate choice and only later asked to reason about the choice, they will often give choices based on a "socialized" cultural norm and later reverse it after being asked to reason about it. As an example, children may first respond to the Heinz dilemma by saying "Don't steal" and only under conditions of asking for reasons come up with the decision that the husband should steal to save his wife's life (Nisan, 1984). The basic views of socialization and cognitive-developmental theories may be contrasted as follows.

Cognitive development views	*Social learning and psychoanalytic views*
1. Moral development involves sequential stages in qualitative reorganization of judgment and reasoning.	1. Moral development involves behavioral and affective conformity to moral rules.
2. Stages in forms of moral judgment are culturally universal.	2. Content of moral judgment is culturally relative.
3. Moral norms and principles are structured through interactional experiences of the individual with the social environment.	3. External societal rules are internalized through manipulation of reward, punishment, prohibitions, modeling.

4. The basic motivation for morality is rooted in a generalized motivation for acceptance, competence, self-esteem, or self-realization.

4. The basic motivation for morality is rooted in biological needs or motives for reward and avoidance of punishment.

These contrasting positions will serve as a reference in the discussion below of various forms of moral experience that have been proposed as important factors in moral development.

Forms of Moral Experience

If differences in moral stage are primarily differences in the form rather than in the content of moral reasoning, the characteristics of group membership that should influence moral stage should be differences in *forms* of moral experience related to group membership rather than the *content* of moral belief upheld by the particular group. Forms of moral experience we will consider are role-taking opportunities, cognitive-moral conflict, general moral atmosphere, parental discipline, and identification.

Socialization theories have typically focused on cultural, subcultural, and family differences in moral content. Cognitive-developmental theories have usually emphasized universals of development. Eventually, there must be an integration between the two types of theories but first we need briefly to clarify these differences.

Role-Taking Opportunities and Moral Development

We have already partially discussed role-taking experiences in terms of Selman's levels of perspective-taking. When the emotional side of role-taking is stressed, it is typically termed empathy (or sympathy). The term role-taking, coined by G. H. Mead (1934), is preferable, however, because it: (1) emphasizes the cognitive as well as the affective side; (2) involves an organized structural relationship between self and others; (3) stresses that the process involves understanding and relating to all the roles in the society of which one is a part; and (4) emphasizes that role-taking goes on in *all* social interactions and communication situations, not merely in ones that arouse strong emotions of sympathy or empathy. Theorists of empathy like Hoffman (1976; 1979) interpret empathy as going through cognitive-developmental stages, stages earlier than those described by Selman (1980). According to Hoffman, in the first year distress in another may cause distress in the self (by "contagion"). In the second year, awareness of the other as separate and different from the self may lead to comforting actions. With the beginning of Selman's perspective-taking level at around age 3 or 4, the child can empathize with needs and feelings different from the child's own in the other's situation.

Hoffman and I would agree that levels of empathy or sympathy or role-taking are presupposed by a level of justice or of moral reasoning. One may react to the plight of a victim or one disadvantaged with both profound sympathy and with a sense of outrage or injustice. After an empathizing or role-taking process in moral conflict situations, moral judgment has the added justice problem of deciding whose perspective to take, to adjudicate. But role-taking opportunities may be seen as including both experiences promoting sympathetic or "prosocial" behavior and justice-seeking behavior. In understanding moral development, we must then consider the environment's provision of role-taking opportunities to the child. Clearly, variations in role-taking opportunities exist in terms of the child's relation to family, peer group, school, and social status vis-à-vis the larger economic and political structure of the society.

With regard to the family, the disposition of parents to allow or encourage dialogue on value issues is one of the clearest determinants of moral stage advance in children (Holstein, 1972; Parikh, 1980). In these studies both parents and an adolescent child were asked to discuss disagreements about our hypothetical dilemmas, previously administered individually to them. Parental behavior in the discussion, encouraging the child to express an opinion, was significantly correlated with the adolescent's moral stage. Such an exchange of viewpoints and attitudes is part of what we term "role-taking opportunities." With regard to peer groups, children high in peer participation are more advanced in moral stage than those who are low (Colby et al., 1983). We have noted that socioeconomic status is correlated with moral development in various cultures (Snarey, 1985). This, we believe, is because middle-class children have more opportunity to take the point of view of the more distant, impersonal, and influential roles in society's basic institutions (law, economy, government, economics) than lower-class children. In general, the higher an individual child's participation in a social group or institution, the more opportunities the child has to take the social perspectives of others. From this point of view, participation in any particular group is not essential to moral development, but active participation in some group is. Not only is participation necessary, but mutuality of role-taking is also necessary. If, for instance, adults do not consider the child's point of view, the child may not communicate or take the adult's point of view.

To illustrate environments at opposite extremes in role-taking opportunities, we may cite studies of an American orphanage and an Israeli kibbutz. Of all environments we have studied, only the American orphanage had children at the lowest level, Stages 1 and 2, even through adolescence (Thrower, 1972). Of all environments studied, an Israeli kibbutz had the highest percentage who had attained conventional morality by the end of high school, and the highest percentage of post-conventional subjects in their twenties (Kohlberg, 1984, ch. 9). These included adolescents living on the kibbutz with little contact with their city parents.

Both orphanage and kibbutz environments involved relatively low interaction with parents (for the city-born) but were dramatically different in other ways. The American orphanages not only lacked parental interaction but involved very little communication and role-taking between staff adults and children. Relations among the children themselves were fragmentary, with very little communication and no stimulation or supervision of peer interaction by the staff. In contrast, children in the kibbutz engaged in intense peer interaction supervised by a group leader who was concerned about bringing the young people into the kibbutz community as active dedicated participants. Discussing, reasoning, communicating feelings, and making group decisions were central everyday activities.

In both social class and peer group comparisons, the children involved in more extensive social participation or responsibilities (the middle-class children and the popular children) were on the whole more mature in moral judgment. This was not because the middle-class children (or the popular children) heavily favored some one type of thought, which could be seen as corresponding to the prevailing middle-class pattern (or the prevailing youth culture pattern). Instead, middle-class and working-class children seemed to move through the same sequences, but the middle-class children appeared to go faster and farther.

These findings contrast with many sociological notions as to how group memberships determine moral development. It is often thought that children get some of their basic moral values from their families, some from their peer groups, and others from the wider society, and that these basic values tend to conflict with one another. Instead of participation in various groups causing conflicting developmental trends in morality, it appears that participation in various groups converges in stimulating the development of structures of moral reasoning, which are not transmitted by one particular group as opposed to another. The child lives in a total social world in which perceptions of the law, of the peer group, and of parental teachings all influence one another. Various people and groups may make conflicting immediate demands on the child. In the course of "normal" development, however, the conflicts between demands of groups and individuals constitute conditions of cognitive-moral conflict that stimulate the development of structures or stages of moral judgment.

The institutions with moral authority (law, government, family, the work order) and the basic moral rules are the same regardless of the individual's particular position in society. The child's position in society does to a large extent, however, determine the interpretation of these institutions and rules. Law and the government are perceived quite differently by the child if the child feels a sense of potential participation in the social order than if he or she does not. The effect of such a sense of participation on development of moral judgments related to the law is suggested by the following responses of 16 year olds to the question, "Should someone obey a law if he doesn't think it is a good law?" A lower-class boy replies, "Yes, a law is a law and you can't do nothing about it. You have to obey it, you should. That's what it's there for." (For him the law is simply a constraining thing that is there.

The very fact that he has no hand in it, that "you can't do nothing about it," means that it should be obeyed.)

A lower-middle-class boy replies, "Laws are made for people to obey and if everyone would start breaking them. . . . Well, if you owned a store and there were no laws, everybody would just come in and not have to pay." (Here laws are seen not as arbitrary commands but as a unitary system, as the basis of the social order. The role or perspective taken is that of a storekeeper, of someone with a stake in the order.)

An upper-middle-class boy replies, "The law's the law but I think people themselves can tell what's right or wrong. I suppose the laws are made by different groups of people with different ideas. But if you don't believe in a law, you should try to get it changed, you shouldn't disobey it." (Here the laws are seen as the product of various legitimate ideological and interest groups varying in their beliefs as to the best decision in policy matters. The role of law-obeyer is seen from the perspective of the democratic policy-maker.)

Although class differences in perspective are especially pronounced with regard to law and generalized social authority, they are also evident in the areas of family and friendship relationships. Peer-group participation differences are similar to class differences in societal participation but somewhat more pronounced in the family and friendship areas. Thus neither the view that the child gets some values from family and some from peers should obscure the elements of stimulation of moral development that appear common to them all.

The general conception of role-taking opportunities may be divided into the following conditions for moral growth:

1. A perception that the environment is concerned about *fairness* and that its rules are fair.
2. A perception that there is opportunity for *discussion* and exchange about rules and fairness.
3. A sense that each participant has some *responsibility* for the group's goals and rules and the welfare of its members.

The presence of these conditions in an institution or group was assessed by an "ethnographic" moral atmosphere interview asked of adolescents and differentiated group homes in which moral change occurred over a year and those in which it did not (Jennings, Kilkenny, & Kohlberg, 1983). As with our contrast between the orphanage and the kibbutz, this study indicates that nonfamilial settings may stimulate social development given the provision of role-taking opportunities.

Cognitive-Moral Conflict

We have discussed at length role-taking opportunities as a stimulus to moral judgment development. A second principle has more ambiguous theoretical status.

This is the principle of exposure to the next stage up. Turiel (1966) experimentally exposed students to reasoning pro and con. Some were exposed to reasoning one stage above their own (+1), some to reasoning two stages above their own (+2), some to reasoning at a stage one below their own (−1). The greatest change occurred in the +1 condition, a change of increase in reasoning to the next stage. Presumably, students failed to comprehend +2 reasoning and rejected −1 reasoning. Studies by Rest, Turiel, and Kohlberg (1969) and by Rest (1973) confirmed this interpretation. In the best designed study, that of Rest (1973), students were exposed to reasoning at all stages besides their own. Students comprehended (could paraphrase correctly) all stages at or below their own stage of reasoning and usually the next stage up, if they showed some usage of that stage in spontaneous production. Comprehension formed a Guttman scaled hierarchy demonstrating this fact. Students tended to prefer higher stage reasoning, often without comprehending it. Change after exposure to the various stages was to the next stage up (+1). A series of classroom discussion studies, commencing with that of Blatt and Kohlberg (1975), demonstrated that free discussion and argumentation about moral dilemmas with classes of students at several stages led to about a one-half stage upward movement, with no change in control classes without such dilemma discussion. Movement in these classes was always to the next stage up; there was no stage slipping or regression (Blatt & Kohlberg 1975). While demonstrating the hierarchy of moral stages, these studies are ambiguous as to the mechanism of upward change. One explanation would combine principles of content learning like the principles of observational learning of social-learning theory with the nature of stage structure. In this interpretation, movement to the next stage up represents "passive learning" moderated by factors of comprehension and preference based on stage-structural considerations. An alternative explanation more aligned to Piaget's theory sees cognitive-moral conflict and reintegration at the next stage up as the key principle of such development. In this explanation, exposure to moral dilemmas indicates conflict because the student recognizes that his or her stage structure or operative moral norms are in potential conflict. Faced with the Heinz dilemma, a Stage 3 subject recognizes that the norm of affection for one's wife or valuing of life is in conflict with the norm of obligation to law. Faced with the conflict, the individual is motivated for a solution that will overcome the relativity or disequilibrium of operating Stage 3 structures, a solution recognizing what is right for anyone to do (Stage 4). This conflict is intensified when the student is faced with arguments opposing his or her own choice or systematically showing how "good" reasons can lead to opposite conclusions and be opposed to one another. More recent research by Walker (1986) seems to favor the "cognitive conflict" model. Walker found that exposure to conflicting arguments led to movement to the next stage up whether those arguments were at the student's own stage (0), the next stage up (+1), or two stages up (+2). Exposure to models of conflicting reasoning whether at 0, +1, or + 2 led to roughly similar amounts of stage change and always to the next stage up (+ 1).

Ongoing work on the conditions of dialogue in pairs and small groups of students at different stages leading to stage change will help elaborate the cognitive-conflict model (Berkowitz & Gibbs, 1983).

It should be noted that cognitive-moral conflict is a mechanism not only for change in moral judgment but in moral action. In "just community" schools, students who violate rules that they have democratically endorsed are publicly confronted with discrepancies between their public judgments and their actual actions. This appears to be a mechanism not only promoting greater judgment action consistency but upward moral change.

A central question in moral development research is to integrate a greater understanding of the learning and acceptance of the content of moral norms (e.g., the values of trust or contract, property rights, truthfulness) with a greater understanding of stage-structured change. This is the focus of a research program starting in 1974 on democratic or "just community schools" (Power, Higgins, Kohlberg, & Reimer, 1987).

The research we have described, based on Kohlberg's model, has been carried out primarily on subjects over age 10. We have reviewed Piaget's research on younger children. Another look at younger children's morality somewhat different from that of Piaget or this writer has been provided by Damon (1977).

DAMON'S DESCRIPTION OF MORAL STAGES IN EARLIER CHILDHOOD

In Chapter 1 we discussed a "Stage 0" coming earlier than our Stage 1, which is typically attained before age 7. A more intensive treatment of early moral stages is provided by Damon's (1977) important book, *The social world of the child.* Damon starts by questioning the appropriateness of our hypothetical dilemma methodology for studying young children. Selman and I had similar but less serious questions and developed sound filmstrip dilemmas for children aged 4 to 8, dilemmas described in Chapter 9 on programs of early moral education. These dilemmas, like our dilemma for adolescents, pit one issue of value against another. Our Heinz dilemma pits the value of a woman's life against obedience to the law. Our childhood parallel pits a kitten's life against obedience to a father's directive.

Damon, however, questions even these adaptations as getting at the issues of significance to young children. He says:

> Kohlberg's methodology is a first methodology for studying children's morality. Whatever else may be said about the Kohlberg dilemmas, they are clearly foreign to the lives of young children since a child has no experience of live-saving drugs; euthanasia; etc. For a deeper sense even the basic moral issues incorporated in these

dilemmas are probably unfamiliar to children. How often does a child wrestle with the value of a life or the responsibilities of a husband or a father? There is at least a reasonable doubt that children's versions of an adult's knowledge really represents the early form of the adult's knowledge. In the genesis of adult morality we may have doubts that children's responses to adult dilemmas are the earliest steps of adult answers to these questions. Other childhood behaviors may have a more direct genetic connection to adult morality. One likely choice may be the rules by which children regulate their own patterns of social behaviors in childhood activities. Like play and games or like sharing, Piaget's (1932) investigation into early morality is an example of his second "worm's eye" view approach into early morality and provides us with a good contrast to Kohlberg's methodology. Piaget studies the rules children construct and use in their own games, like marbles, rather than their responses to adult laws and rules. We have chosen this second "worm's eye" approach and attempted to use methods of investigation that engage children in tasks or activities that are in their eyes interesting, comprehensible and representative of concerns or problems that morally engage them in their social lives. (1977, p. 38)

Damon's problem for children rests on the "worm's eye view" method of posing childhood problems to children. Second, it focuses on getting problems that can be made into situations in which the child's behavior can be observed and questioned as well as presenting these problems in verbal hypothetical dilemma form.

An example of such a problem from Damon is the following:

Four children at a time are brought into a room with two adults. Three children are of the same age, and one child is a year or two younger than the others (one year for the youngest groups, two years for the older ones). In the room is a table with an array of beads and strings on it, and six small chairs are set around the table. The children are told by one of the adults that he loves bracelets made by little children. He asks the children if they will make some for him.

The four children work for about twenty minutes making bracelets. The two adults help the children string and tie up the bracelets upon request. At the end of about twenty minutes—or when the group has made an assortment of bracelets—the adults stop the bracelet making and lead the children from the room. The children are separated, and the younger child is thanked for his efforts and taken home. (The younger child has almost invariably made the fewest bracelets.)

The remaining three children are brought back into the room, and each is asked to place the bracelets he has made in front of himself. One child has invariably made the most bracelets, since the experimenters are instructed not to stop the bracelet making until one child is ahead of the others in number made. This child is now congratulated and told that the experimenter also considers his bracelets the prettiest. The child's name is then written on a board next to the words *Prettiest and Most*. A second child is then picked out as either the biggest boy or biggest girl present (whichever is appropriate). This child's name is then written on the board next to the words *Biggest Boy* (or *Biggest Girl*). The third child is also thanked and told that his bracelets were very nice too. His name is written on the board next to the word *Nice*.

The three children are then taken from the room again and brought back one at a time. As each is brought back, he is told that the experimenter is very grateful for the bracelets that the children have made for him. For a reward, he says, the group is to receive ten candy bars. But the children themselves must decide how to split them up between them. Each child is asked for a decision and interviewed about that decision. The three children are then brought back as a group and asked to reconcile their individual decisions. They are asked to reach a group decision both in the presence and in the absence of an adult. All actions and reasoning of all children are recorded, both in the individual session and in the group sessions. While interviewing the children, the experimenter points out the possible claims that each child might have (the child who made the most and the prettiest, the biggest, the absent younger child who made the fewest bracelets, the child who made the nice ones, and so on). (1977, p. 62)

Based on observations of this and similar problems in both "real" and hypothetical form, Damon defined the stages described in Table 7.5. Where there were discrepancies between level on the hypothetical dilemma and on the experimental or real one, the differences tended to favor the hypothetical dilemmas as the area eliciting the higher level of reasoning.

An example of reasoning at Level 0-B is the following interchange of three 4 year olds.

Experimenter: OK, here are the ten candy bars, and we want to ask you as a group how to split them up. Any ideas?

Sean: I want seven. Then one for you, one for you and one for her [Tina, not present].

Experimenter: And you are going to take seven and put them in your bag.

Sean: Yeah, 'cause I have seven friends at home.

Experimenter: What do you guys think?

Sean: And some of the kids want some of these.

Jason: That wouldn't be fair.

Experimenter: How should it be different?

Jason: It should be different like that [gives himself four, Sean three, Bonnie two, and Tina one]. I'm gonna' get four.

Bonnie: [Picks up candy and gives everyone two, with two left over.]

Jason: No! I get four. [Takes two extra bars for himself.] Look how they cheat.

Bonnie: Put them back.

Jason: I get four because I'm four and you're only two.

Bonnie: I'm four too.

Jason: She's [Tina] only one.

Bonnie: No she's not, she's three.

Jason: One.

Bonnie: Three.

TABLE 7.5
Brief Descriptions of Early Positive Justice Levels

Level 0-A

Positive justice choices derive from S's wish that an act occur. Reasons simply assert the choices rather than attempting to justify them (i.e., I should get it because I want to have it).

Level 0-B

Choices still reflect S's desires but are now justified on the basis of external, observable realities such as size, sex, or other physical characteristics of persons (i.e., We should get the most because we're girls). Such justifications, however, are invoked in a fluctuating, *a posteriori* manner, and are self-serving in the end.

Level 1-A

Positive justice choices derive from notions of strict equality in actions (that is, that everyone should get the same). Justifications are consistent with this principle but are unilateral and inflexible.

Level 1-B

Positive justice choices derive from a notion of reciprocity in actions: that persons should be paid back in kind for doing good or bad things. Notions of merit and deserving emerge. Justifications are unilateral and inflexible.

Level 2-A

A moral relativity develops out of the understanding that different persons can have different, yet equally valid, justifications for their claims to justice. The claims of persons with special needs (i.e., the poor) are weighed heavily. Choices attempt quantitative compromises between competing claims (e.g., He should get the most, but she should get some too).

Level 2-B

S coordinates considerations of equality and reciprocity, so that S's positive justice choices take into account the claims of various persons and the demands of the specific situation. Choices are firm and clearcut, yet justifications reflect the recognition that all persons should be given their due (though, in many situations, this does not mean equal treatment).

Source: Damon, 1977, p. 60.

Jason:	One.
Sean:	I want to get seven for my seven bosses at home.
Experimenter:	Do you think you should?
Sean:	Yeah, 'cause my bosses want some of these.
Experimenter:	What do you mean, bosses?

Sean: 'Cause I like them.

Bonnie: I want three.

Sean: But I want seven.

Bonnie: Well, I'm going to take three. [Takes three, gives Sean three, Jason two, and Tina two.]

Sean: [Grabs one of Tina's.]

Bonnie: No! That one's for Tina.

Experimenter: Why are those two for Tina, Bonnie?

Bonnie: 'Cause she's the littlest.

Sean: She just wants one.

Experimenter: How do you know she just wants one?

Sean: 'Cause I know she says she wants one. She needs one. She says she wants one.

Bonnie: She wants two.

Sean: No! If you do that, I'm going to punch you out of the room.

Jason: Well, then we'll all agree on this.

Experimenter: What do you mean, Jason?

Jason: We'll just talk about the candy bars.

Sean: Yeah, 'cause I want seven.

Jason: Well, I'll just take two. [Takes two.]

Bonnie: Well, I'll just take one more. [Takes three in all.]

Sean: But that one's Tina's. [Takes all of the remaining five and holds them in front of himself.]

Bonnie: No, you've got Tina's.

Sean: [Goes to other end of room with his five.] No, I need five 'cause my mother needs five. And I need five for all my bosses.

[The discussion continues in this manner until the experimenter is forced to arrange a compromise.] (Damon, 1977, p. 65)

An example of reasoning at Levels 1A and 1B is the following interchange of three 6 year olds.

Experimenter: So what Jay said is he put them out, three for him and three for Juan, two for Susan and two for Jennifer [not present]. And Susan said that's OK too. That's the way she did it.

Jay: [To Juan] You should think that's fair too. You have three, and I have three, and they have two.

Juan: I don't think that's fair.

Jay: Why?

Juan: We shouldn't give the boys more than the girls. We should break them in half and give the girls two, the boys two, then . . .

Jay: No, No, No. I said ours were the prettiest, that's why we should get more.... See, we made the prettiest. I say we made the prettiest. Do you think that's a nice one? And you made nice ones, and we made the prettiest. I think that's fair because we made the prettiest.

Juan: We should break them in half, and then that would be really fair.

Experimenter: What do you think, Susan? Didn't you at one point say you thought we should split them in half?

Susan: That's what I said. Now I say...[Susan gives them out three, three, two, two, as Jay wishes.]

Experimenter: What? This way?

Jay: Yeah. Because she thinks that we made the prettiest.

Juan: She got some in her lunch box. Do you have candy?

Jay: Do you have a Hershey bar? She's got some Nestles or a Hershey bar.

Experimenter: Susan says it's OK. How about Jennifer?

Jay: I think she would say it's OK.

Juan: If she didn't leave, I think it wouldn't be OK.

Experimenter: So what are you going to do?

Jay: I think that this is the way to do it, because me and Juan made the prettiest.

Juan: She [Jennifer] made pretty, and she made the same.

Jay: No, No, No. What I mean, Juan—see how yours in pretty, and see how pretty this is too. I think these two are pretty, right. And all of these are pretty. And I think hers too and these are nice too. But I think these are pretty.

Juan: They're all the same, they're all pretty.

Jay: I know, but I think these are the prettiest.

Juan: They all are.

Jay: No, No.

Experimenter: So what about now? What do you guys want to do?

Jay: Juan, that's fair!

Juan: She has one in her lunch, but I don't know about Jennifer.

Jay: Think that would be fair! She would have three, and we would all have three.

Experimenter: We don't have eleven, we have ten.

Jay: But she only made one, and it's not pretty.

Juan: It's good. She's only in kindergarten. She would think it's fair, I think. Yeah, she would.

Experimenter: What are you guys going to do?

Jay: If you think it's fair, and Susan thinks it's fair, and I think it's fair, she [Jennifer] might think it's fair.

Experimenter: Well, let's see what Juan thinks. What do you suggest, Juan? What's the best way? What's the best thing to do with the candy bars?

TABLE 7.6
Brief Descriptions of Early Authority Levels

Level 0-A

Authority is legitimized by attributes that link the authority figure with the self, either by establishing affectional bonds between authority figure and self or by establishing identification between authority figure and self. The basis for obedience is a primitive association between authority's commands and the self's desires.

Level 0-B

Authority is legitimized by physical attributes of persons—size, sex, dress, and so on. The specific attributes selected are those the subject considers to be descriptive of persons in command. These legitimizing attributes may be used in a fluctuating manner, since they are not linked logically to the functioning of authority. The subject recognizes the potential conflict between authority's commands and the self's wishes, and thinks about obedience in a pragmatic fashion: commands are followed as a means of achieving desires, or to avoid actions contrary to desires.

Level 1-A

Authority is legitimized by attributes that enable authority figure to enforce commands (physical strength, social or physical power, and so on). Obedience is based on subject's respect for authority figure's social or physical power, which is invested with an aura of omnipotence and omniscience.

Level 1-B

Authority is legitimized by attributes that reflect special talent or ability, and that make the authority figure a superior person in the eyes of the subject. This special talent or ability is no longer associated simply with power, but is rather indicative of the authority figure's ability to accomplish changes that subordinates cannot. Obedience is based on reciprocal exchange; one obeys because authority figure takes care of one, because authority figure has helped in the past, or because authority figure otherwise "deserves" one's obedience.

Level 2-A

Authority is legitimized by prior training or experience related to the process of commanding. Authority figure therefore is seen as a person who is able to lead and command better than subordinates. Obedience is based on subject's respect for this specific leadership ability and on the belief that this superior leadership ability implies a concern for the welfare and the rights of subordinates.

Level 2-B

Authority is legitimized by the coordination of a variety of attributes with specific situational factors. Subject believes that a person might possess attributes that enable him or her to command well in one situation but not in another. Authority, therefore, is seen as a shared, consensual relation between parties, adopted temporarily by one person for the welfare of all. Obedience is seen as a cooperative effort that is situation-specific rather than a general response to a superior person.

Source: Damon, 1977, p. 98.

Juan: I think that's [three, three, two, two] the best way, if she's only in kindergarten. (Damon, 1977, p. 69)

Damon's levels of distributive justice sound rather advanced in light of our characterization of young children's response to problems of authority and the resulting levels he found sound very similar to Kohlberg's stages. Damon's levels of authority are summarized in Table 7.6.

Damon does not, as I did, attempt to define general stages across the various issues like positive justice and authority. Kohlberg's dilemmas pit one issue against another (e.g., authority versus life or authority versus distributive justice). When such dilemmas are presented to young children they tend to focus on authority as the key issue, and therefore sound more like examples of Damon's stages of authority than of his stages of justice. Instead of leading to radical revision of Kohlberg's stage descriptions for young children, Damon's work seems to reinforce Piaget's claim that the young child has two moralities, a heteronomous morality in relation to adult authority and rules, and a more autonomous morality of justice in relation to peers. Piaget's (1932) work and my own (Kohlberg, 1958) suggests that the heteronomous morality predominates for the young child and defines the major features of a Stage 1 of morality. Damon's work shows, however, that an "autonomous" morality exists at the same time and can be found in peer justice problems. This morality continues to develop until it becomes a predominant Stage 2 morality in later childhood.

REFERENCES

Baier, K. (1965). *The moral point of view: A rational basis of ethics.* New York: Randon House.

Baldwin, J. M. (1906). *Social and ethical intepretations in mental development* (4th ed.). New York: Macmillan.

Baldwin, J. M. (1906–1911). *Thoughts and things or genetic logic*, 3 Vols. New York: Macmillan.

Berkowitz, L. (1964). *Development of motives and values in a child.* New York: Basic Books.

Berkowitz, M. W., & Gibbs, J. C. (1983). Measuring the developmental features of moral discussion, *Merrill-Palmer Quarterly, 29,* 399–410.

Blasi, A. (1980). Bridging moral cognition and moral action: A critical review of the literature. *Psychological Bulletin, 88,* 324–336.

Blatt, M., & Kohlberg, L. (1975). The effects of classroom moral discussion upon children's moral judgment. *Journal of Moral Education, 4,* 129–161.

Burton, R. V. (1963). Generality of honesty reconsidered. *Psychological Review, 70,* 481–499.

Colby, A., & Kohlberg, L. (1974). Relations between logical and moral reasoning. Unpublished manuscript. Cambridge, MA: Harvard Center for Moral Education.

Colby, A., & Kohlberg, L. (1987). *The measurement of moral judgment.* New York: Cambridge University Press.

Colby, A., Kohlberg, L., Gibbs, J., & Lieberman, M. (1983). A longitudinal study of moral judgment. *Society for Research in Child Development: Monograph Series, 48.*

Damon, W. (1977). *The social world of the child.* San Francisco: Jossey-Bass.

DeVries, R., with Kohlberg, L. (1987). Programs of early education: A cognitive-developmental view. White Plains, NY: Longman.

Dewey, J. (1895/1964). In R. D. Archambault (Ed.), *On education: Selected writings.* New York: The Modern Library.

Dewey, J., & Tufts, J. H. (1932). *Ethics.* New York: Henry Holt & Co.

Durkheim, E. (1961). *Moral education: A study in the theory and application of the sociology of education.* New York: Free Press.

Eisenberg-Berg, N. (1986). *The development of prosocial reasoning and behavior.* New York: Academic.

Freud, S. (1923/1960). *The ego and the id* (J. Riviere, Trans.). New York: Norton.

Frankena, W. K. (1973). *Ethics.* Englewood, N.J.: Prentice-Hall.

Freud, S. (1930/1961). *Civilization and its discontents* (J. Strachey, Trans.). New York: Norton.

Gilligan, C. (1982). *In a different voice.* Cambridge: Harvard University Press.

Grim, P., Kohlberg, L., & White, S. (1968). Some relationships between conscience and attentional processes. *Journal of Personality and Social Psychology, 8,* 239–253.

Grinder, R. E. (1964). Relations between behavioral and cognitive dimensions of conscience in middle childhood. *Child Development, 35,* 881–893.

Haan, N., Smith, B., & Block, J. (1968). Moral reasoning in young adults. *Journal of Personality and Social Psychology, 10,* 193–201.

Habermas, J. (1979). *Communication and the evolution of society* (T. McCarthy, Trans.). Boston: Beacon Press.

Habermas, J. (1983). Interpretive social science vs. hermeneuticism. In N. Haan, R. N. Bellah, P. Rabinow, & W. Sullivan (Eds.), *Social science as moral inquiry.* New York: Columbia University Press.

Hartshorne, H., & May, M. (1928–1930). *Studies in the nature of character,* Columbia University, Teachers College. *Vol. 1. Studies of deceit; Vol. 2. Studies in service and self-control; Vol. 3. Studies in organization and character.* New York: Macmillan.

Havighurst, R. J., & Taba, H. (1949). Adolescent character and personality. New York: Wiley.

Higgins, A. (1980). Research and measurement issues in moral education interventions. In R. L. Mosher (Ed.), *Moral education: A first generation of research and development.* New York: Praeger.

Higgins, A., Power, C., & Kohlberg, L. (1984). Student judgments of responsibility and the moral atmosphere of high schools: A comparative study. In W. Kurtines & J. Gewirtz (Eds.), *Morality, moral behavior, and moral development.* New York: Wiley Interscience.

Helkama, K. (1979). *The development of the attribution of responsibility. Research Reports of the Department of Social Psychology, 3,* University of Helsinki.

Hoffman, M. L. (1976). Empathy, role-taking, guilt, and development of altruistic motives. In T. Lickona (Ed.), *Moral development and behavior: Theory, research, and social issues.* New York: Holt, Rinehart.

Hoffman, M. L. (1979). Development of moral thought, feeling and behavior. *American Psychologist, 34,* 958–966.

Holstein, C. (1972). The relation of children's moral judgment level to that of their parents and to communication patterns in the family. In R. C. Smart & M. S. Smart (Eds.), *Readings in child development*. New York: Macmillan.

Hume, D. (1752/1930). *An enquiry into the principles of morals*. Chicago: Open Court.

Inhelder, B., & Piaget, J. (1958). The growth of logical thinking from childhood to adolescence. New York: Basic Books.

Jennings, W. S., Kilkenny, R., & Kohlberg, L. (1983). Moral-development theory and practice for youthful and adult offenders. In W. S. Laufer & J. M. Day (Eds.), *Personality theory, moral development & criminal behavior*. Leyington, MA: Lexington Books.

Kagan, J., & Moss, H. (1962). *Birth to maturity*. New York: Wiley.

Kant, I. (1785/1949). *Fundamental principles of the metaphysics of morals*. New York: Liberal Arts Press.

Kleinberger, A. F. (1982). The proper object of moral judgment and of moral education. *Journal of Moral Education, 11*, 147–158.

Kohlberg, L. (1958). *The development of modes of moral thinking and choice in the years ten to sixteen*. Unpublished doctoral dissertation, University of Chicago.

Kohlberg, L. (1963). The development of children's orientations toward a moral order: Sequence in the development of moral thought. *Vita Humana, 6*, 11–33.

Kohlberg, L. (1964). Development of moral character and ideology. In M. L. Hoffman (Ed.), *Review of child development research*, Vol. 1. New York: Russell Sage Foundation.

Kohlberg, L. (1971). Cognitive-developmental theory and the practice of collective moral education. In W. Wolins & M. Gottesman (Eds.), *Group care: An Israeli approach*. New York: Gordon & Breach.

Kohlberg, L. (1981). *Essays in moral development. Volume I: The philosophy of moral development*. San Francisco: Harper & Row.

Kohlberg, L. (1984). *Essays in moral development. Volume II: The psychology of moral development*. San Francisco: Harper & Row.

Kohlberg, L., & Helkama (in preparation). Research on Piaget's theory of moral judgment. In L. Kohlberg, D. Candee, & A. Colby (Eds.), *Research in moral development*. Cambridge: Harvard University Press.

Kohlberg, L., & Kramer, R. (1969). Continuities and discontinuities in childhood and adult moral development. *Human Development, 12*, 93–120.

Krebs, R. (1967). *Some relationships between moral judgment, attention, and resistance to temptation*. Unpublished doctoral dissertation, University of Chicago.

Krebs, R., & Kohlberg, L. (in preparation). Moral judgments and ego controls as determinants of resistance to cheating. In L. Kohlberg, D. Candee, & A. Colby (Eds.), *Research in moral development*. Cambridge: Harvard University Press.

Lakatos, I. (1978). Falsification and the methodology of scientific research programs. In J. Worrall & G. Currie (Eds.), *The methodology of scientific research programs*. Cambridge: Cambridge University Press.

Lapsley, D. K., & Serlin, R. C. (1984). On the alleged degeneration of the Kohlbergian research program. *Educational Theory, 34*, 157–269.

Lee, B., & Snarey, J. (1986). *Relationships between moral and ego stages*. Unpublished manuscript, Harvard University.

Leming, J. S. (1981). Curricular effectiveness in moral/values education: A review of the research. *Journal of Moral Education, 10*, 147–164.

Lickona, T. (Ed.). (1976). *Moral development and behavior: Theory, research, and social issues*. New York: Holt, Rinehart.

Lockwood, A. (1978). The effect of values clarification and moral development curricula on school-age subjects: A critical review of the recent research. *Review of Educational Research, 48,* 325–364.

Loevinger, J., with Blasi, A. (1976). *Eqo development: Conceptions and theories.* San Francisco: Jossey-Bass.

Lyons, N. (1983). Two perspectives: On self, relationships, and morality. *Harvard Educational Review, 53,* 125–145.

MacFarlane, J., Allen, L., & Honzik, N. (1954). *A developmental study of behavior problems of normal children between 21 months and four years.* Berkeley: University of California Press.

McNamee, S. (1978). Moral behavior, moral development, and motivation. *Journal of Moral Education, 7,* 27–31.

Mead, G. H. (1934). *Mind, self, and society.* Chicago: University of Chicago Press.

Milgram, S. (1963). Behavioral study of obedience. *Journal of Abnormal and Social Psychology, 67,* 371–378.

Mill, J. S. (1861/1957). *Utilitarianism.* Indianapolis: Bobbs-Merrill.

Mischel, W., & Mischel, H. (1976). A cognitive social-learning approach to morality and self-regulation. In T. Lickona (Ed.), *Moral development and behavior: Theory, research, and social issues.* New York: Holt, Rinehart.

Murphy, L. B. (1937). *Social behavior and child personality.* New York: Columbia University Press.

Nisan, M. (1984). Social norms and moral judgment. In W. Kutines & J. Gewirtz (Eds.), *Morality, and moral development* (pp. 208–224). New York: Wiley.

Nisan, M., & Kohlberg, L. (1982). Universality and cross-cultural variation in moral development: A longitudinal and cross-sectional study in Turkey. *Child Development, 53,* 865–876.

Parikh, B. (1980). Moral judgment development and its relation to family environmental factors in Indian and American families. *Child Development, 51,* 1030–1039.

Peck, R. F., & Havighurst, R. J. (1960). *The psychology of character development.* New York: Wiley.

Piaget, J. (1932/1965). *The moral judgment of the child* (M. Gabain, Trans.). New York: Free Press.

Piaget, J. (1971). *Science of education and the psychology of the child.* New York: Viking.

Power, C., Higgins, A., Kohlberg, L., & Reimer, J. (1987). *Moral education, justice and community.* New York: Columbia University Press.

Radke-Yarrow et al. Prosocial behavior. In M. Hetherington (Ed.), *Manual of child psychology* (4th ed.): *Vol. 4. Socialization.* New York: Wiley.

Rawls, J. (1971). *A theory of justice.* Cambridge: Harvard University Press.

Rest, J. R. (1973). The hierarchical nature of moral judgment: A study of patterns of comprehension and preference of moral stages. *Journal of Personality, 41,* 86–109.

Rest, J. (1983). Morality. In J. H. Flavell & E. Markman (Eds.), *Manual of child psychology* (4th ed.), Vol. 3: *Cognitive Development.* New York: Wiley.

Rest, J. (1984). Major component processes in the production of moral behavior. In W. Kurtines & J. Gewirtz (Eds.), *Morality, moral behavior, and moral development* (pp. 24–38). New York: Wiley Interscience.

Rest, J., Turiel, E., Kohlberg, L. (1969). Level of moral development as a determinant of preference and comprehension of moral judgments made by others. *Journal of Personality, 37,* 225–252.

Turiel, E. (1974). Conflict and transition in adolescent moral development. *Child Development, 45*, 14–18.

Thrower, J. (1972). *Moral judgment of orphanage and family-raised children.* Unpublished dissertation, Harvard University, Cambridge, MA.

Sears, R. R., Maccoby, E. E., & Levine, H. (1957). *Patterns of child rearing.* Evanston, IL: Row, Peterson.

Selman, R. L. (1980). *The growth of interpersonal understanding.* New York: Academic.

Smith, A. (1759/1948). Theory of moral sentiments. In *Smith's moral and political philosophy.* New York: Hafner.

Snarey, J. R. (1985). Cross-cultural universality of social-moral development: A critical review of Kohlbergian research. *Psychological Bulletin, 97*, 202–232.

Sullivan, H. S. (1953). *An interpersonal theory of psychiatry.* New York: Norton.

Turiel, E. (1966). An experimental test of the sequentiality of developmental stages in the child's moral judgment. *Journal of Personality and Social Psychology, 3*, 611–618.

Turiel, E. (1983). *The development of social knowledge, morality, and convention.* New York: Cambridge University Press.

Walker, L. (1980). Cognitive and perspective-taking prerequisites for moral development. *Child Development, 51*, 131–140.

Walker, L. (1984). Sex differences in the development of moral reasoning: A critical review. *Child Development, 55*, 677–691.

Walker, L. (in preparation). The validity of stage of moral reasoning. In L. Kohlberg & D. Candee (Eds.), *Research in moral development.* Cambridge: Harvard University Press.

Walker, L., & Richards, B. S. (1979). Stimulating transitions in moral reasoning as a function of stage of cognitive development. *Developmental Psychology, 15*, 95–103.

Wright, D. (1982). Piaget's theory of moral development. In S. Modgill and C. Modgill (Eds.). *Jean Piaget consensus and Controversy.* New York: Praeger.

Youniss, J. (1980). *Parents and peers in social development: A Sullivan–Piaget perspective* Chicago: University of Chicago Press.

Youniss, J. (1981). Friendship and development. *Social Thought, 7*, 35–46.

Chapter 8

Ego Development and Education:
A Structural Perspective

John Snarey, Lawrence Kohlberg, Gil Noam

Ego development, we suggest, is one of the most important current areas of research in developmental psychology. We would also claim that ego development should be the larger aim of education. In this chapter we present a *structural stage* approach to ego development and distinguish it from two other approaches, which we term *functional phases* and *cultural ages* of ego development. We also distinguish two subtypes within a structural stage theory of ego development—a monodomain approach and a multisubdomain approach—and argue for the latter. The three general approaches mentioned above are then used to critique several prominent competing theories of ego development—those of Robert Selman, Robert Kegan, Jane Loevinger, and Erik Erikson. In this process of bringing these theories together we will clarify the important similarities and critical differences between them and also use the theories to offer some light on what it means to say that ego development should be the aim of education.

EGO DEVELOPMENT AS THE AIM OF EDUCATION

John Dewey viewed the aim of education as the "building of a free and powerful character" (Dewey & McLellan, 1895, p. 202). In Chapter 3 we interpreted this developmental aim as the eventual attainment of a high stage of moral judgment and the concordance of moral action with such moral judgment (1972). We now wish to go beyond that previous formulation, however, and argue that Dewey's vision of character development was more comprehensive than moral development. While moral development broadens the aim of developmental education beyond the purely cognitive, there is still a more inclusive unity, called ego development, of which both cognitive and moral development are part. Thus, education for general cognitive development and for moral development must be

329

judged by its contribution to a more general concept of ego development—the awareness of new meanings in life.

Nearly all social scientists presently concerned with human development have acknowledged the crucial importance of the formation of the ego during childhood, adolescence, and adulthood. Developmental educators in particular feel the need for a more holistic conception of growth—what we have called stages of ego development. Just as only about half of the adult population in the United States reaches the cognitive stage of full formal operations, and approximately 80 percent never go beyond the conventional level of moral reasoning, many persons remain at less than the highest levels of ego development (cf. Loevinger, 1976). Since diverse research has shown that self-concept and ego development predict many kinds of success, including success in the classroom, individuals who are functioning at relatively low levels of ego development stand at a disadvantage in achieving their educational potential (Braun, 1976; Duke, 1978; Glasser, 1969; Loevinger, 1978b; Shavelson, Hubner, & Stanton, 1976; Wattenberg & Clifford, 1962). The aim of developmental educators, of course, is not to accelerate artificially the natural development of the person, but rather to support his or her passage to the succeeding stage of development and thus help the individual avoid being arrested at levels of development that are below his or her potential at that point in time.

Barbara Biber and her colleagues at Bank Street have articulated the need to ground their philosophy of early education in a concept of ego development (Biber et al., 1963, 1971; Shapiro & Biber, 1972). Bank Street has been based on two theoretical sources, the cognitive-developmental theories of John Dewey, Jean Piaget, and Heinz Werner, and the neo-Freudian theories of autonomous ego development propounded by Heinz Hartman, Robert W. White, and Erik Erikson. Biber and her colleague Edna Shapiro suggest that ego development and ego strength should be the aims of education. Defining educational aims in terms of ego development, they feel, adds psychosocial goals and puts cognitive development in a larger framework. They suggest:

> [The school's] central responsibility is fostering the development of ego strength, the individual's ability to deal effectively with the environment. Competence is central to the idea of ego strength, though to have ego strength the individual must perceive his competence as valid. . . . [Similarly,] the school is also responsible for contributing to the child's autonomy. (1972, p. 61)

Shapiro and Biber relate ego development to cognitive development as follows:

> The growth of cognitive functions—ordering information, judging, reasoning, problem-solving, symbol use—cannot be separated from the growth of personal and interpersonal processes—the development of self-esteem and a sense of identity, internalization of impulse control, capacity for autonomous response. (1972, p. 61)

Ego development as the aim of education is quite consistent with the general constructivist implications of Dewey's philosophy and Piaget's research. That is, teachers should promote children's autonomy by structuring the learning environment in such a way that they will be encouraged to act based on their own choices.

Similarly, the perspective of ego development as the aim of education underlies the application of Piaget's theory to childhood education by Constance Kamii and Rheta DeVries (Kamii & DeVries, 1977). They emphasize that the most fundamental principle of teaching they have gleaned from Piaget's constructivism is to accept the child's efforts to make sense of things and to promote the child's autonomy by taking his or her questions and convictions seriously.

APPROACHES TO THE EGO AND EGO DEVELOPMENT

Ego, according to Erik Erikson, is "an age-old term which in scholastics stood for the *unity* of body and soul, and in philosophy in general of the *permanency* of conscious experience" (1964, p. 147). The history of the term, thus, does not begin with Freud. His use of the term, however, evolved in important ways over time, leading to a conception of the ego, the id, and the superego as the parts of a tripartite mind (cf. Gedo & Goldberg, 1973). This model defined the ego as an organizing structure with cognitive functions—thought, memory, language—that establishes contact with the outside world and adapts the individual's instinctual drives to the requirements of the environment or "reality." Anna Freud extended the theory by specifying the ego's defense mechanisms and their development.

Heinz Hartman modified the Freudian conception of the ego by applying it to normal functioning and to autonomous ego adaptation (1939). Other psychoanalytic ego psychologists have also modified Freud's conception by adapting the concept of the ego to that of a supraordinate regulatory system with synthetic functions that serve to maintain various parts of the personality in equilibrium with each other (Redl, 1951; Klein, 1968). Erik Erikson outlined ego development through the life cycle and introduced the term *ego identity* to describe mature ego development during later adolescence. These modifications of Freud's concept, in addition to creating some confusion over the term's psychoanalytic meaning, also illustrate that the use of the term *ego* need not imply acceptance of the Freudian notion of the ego as a separate organ or part of the personality. For instance, Ausubel and Sullivan have defined "ego" and related concepts as follows:

> The *self* is a constellation of individual perceptions and memories consisting of the visual image of the appearance of one's body, the auditory image of the sound of one's name, images of kinesthetic sensations and visceral tension, memories of personal events, and so forth. The *self-concept*, on the other hand, is an abstraction of the essential and distinguishing characteristics of the self that differentiate an individual's "selfhood" from the environment and from other selves. In the course of development, various...attitudes, values, aspirations, motives, and obligations become associated with the self concept. The organized system of interrelated self-

attitudes, self-motives, and self-values that results may be called the *ego*. (1980, pp. 169–170)

Although the position we will develop in this chapter is different from Ausubel's, we do agree that the minimal requirement for a concept of the ego is simply a system of activity or functioning related to a holistic concept of the self.

It is now within structural psychology, we suggest, that ego development theory seems to have the greatest potential for further development; for here the search for a more inclusive understanding of the overall unity of the developing person has found recent expression in *structurally defined stages* of ego development. As an approach to development, structural stages are quite distinct from two other approaches that we distinguish: *culturally defined ages* and *functionally defined phases* of ego development. Stage and age-period approaches to human development were developed within two different disciplines, developmental psychology and psychological anthropology, and the functional phase approach has drawn elements from both of these two disciplines. Unfortunately, developmental psychologists and educators have often used the terms *stages*, *phases*, and *ages* of development confusingly, as if they were more or less synonymous. In this section we will differentiate these three different approaches and give each a precise meaning. With these distinctions in mind, the subsequent sections of this chapter will present the most important and promising theories of ego development and critique them from a structural perspective. Our discussion will also clarify the important contributions that all three approaches can make to a fuller understanding of development.

Structurally Defined Stages of Development

Piaget's concept of structurally defined cognitive stages refers to the transformations that take place as an individual moves from one structure or form of thinking to a qualitatively new structure of thinking. We suggest that the concept of *ego*, from a Piagetian structural perspective, refers to a fundamental structural unity of personality organization and the concept of a *developing ego* refers to the progressive redefinition or reorganization of the self in relation to the nonself—both nonpersons and other persons. Ego stage development comes about from neither nature nor nurture alone, but from the interaction of the two. The actual interaction of the ego with its environment can be described in terms of the same processes—assimilation and accommodation—that Piaget believed characterize biological and intellectual functioning. "Both are evident in the ego's ceaseless work of absorbing and integrating ongoing experiences to already existing constructions (assimilation) and of constructing particular reactions and responses (accommodation) to these experiences" (Haan, 1977, p. 48). Ego development, then, may be understood as the overall unity of the ego as it progressively reconstructs itself through a dialectical process in which the ego "makes sense" of its evolving relationship with others, the world, and life as a whole. Ego development thus includes the continuous redefinition of what is subjective and what is objective; on the subject side is an evolving self and on the object side is an evolving differentiation of one's natural, social, and ultimate environments. In this conceptualization we are presupposing that encompassing the human striving for logical consistency and the striving for moral consistency, individuals strive for a more general sense of self-consistency. Following William James (1890), our approach also makes a distinction between ego development and will or ego strength. The more sophisticated ego is not *necessarily* the strongest ego. Persons with internal self-chosen values and complex awareness do not necessarily have the greatest strength of will, the largest amount of resistance to stress and pressure, or the sturdiest self-esteem. Thus the concept of ego strength adds a quantitative dimension to the qualitative stages of ego development.

One strength of such a Piagetian structural stage approach to ego development, we believe, is that it is capable of bringing together the current proliferation of individual stage theories about various dimensions of the developing person, such as Piaget's scheme of cognitive development, Kohlberg's theory of moral development, and Selman's theory of social cognition. Each of these stage theories, at least in part, grew out of a desire for a more complete understanding of the various dimensions of the person as a whole—the developing ego—and each theorist has attempted to fill the theoretical gap that most concerned him. To date, the two most inclusive structural ego stage theories have been put forth by Jane Loevinger and Robert Kegan. Both theories can account for stage-related similarities between individuals at the same point of development and for differences between individuals at different points of development, regardless of sociocultural setting. They cannot, however, account for cultural differences between individuals in different societies, except by referring to variations in the rate of speed a person goes through the stages (cf. Piaget, 1972).

Culturally Defined Ages of Development

The polar opposite of universal stages is culturally relative ages or age-periods of development. Culturally defined ages are successive age-periods in the life cycle of socially recognized adjustment as defined by a particular culture. Every society has its "recognized division of the life of the individual as he passes from infancy to old age" (Radcliffe-Brown, 1929, p. 21). Thus, "anthropologists long ago recognized that development in the life cycle was a potential basis for cross-cultural comparison," and the earliest ethnographies often included data on the culturally recognized age-periods in the course of a person's development (LeVine, 1973, p. 240; cf. Van Gennep, 1908, M. Mead, 1928). Periods of development, from this perspective, are defined primarily by shifts in culturally defined roles (social obligations and expectations) and status (social privileges and rights) as they have impact on the emerging or established maturational capacities and acquired response patterns of the individual. Thus, cultural ages of development can theoretically be conceived of as a combination of social learning and biological maturation whereby the individual acquires, in an orderly sequence, the social knowledge and role-defined tasks considered culturally appropriate for the person's age. Cultural ages are therefore not synonomous with chronological ages even though cultural age-periods and chronological age are highly correlated. For instance, the culturally defined periods of development for an Israeli kibbutznik have rough age boundaries even though the contents of those periods are primarily defined by the cultural fact that kibbutzniks are raised as members of peer groups within a communal child rearing system: at 4 days of age the kibbutz infant joins the communal infants' house where he lives for 1½ years and is visited by his parents. Then he and his peer group become residents of a communal toddlers' house until age 4; kindergarten until age 7; and the children's house until age 12. From ages 12 to 18 the kibbutznik is a member of the senior children's society; service in Israel's defense force follows, at which time his or her life cycle parallels that of nonkibbutz Israelis. We would argue that there is a sense in which, just as stages of cognitive operations represent internal personal developments growing out of the interaction between the organism and the social environment, age-periods of social cooperations represent external cultural developments which historically evolved out of the same interaction. One must be careful, however, not to "conceive of [such] age level roles in a reified sense, as an ordered sequence of socially stylized masks and robes racked up in a cultural prop room all ready to don as the player moves across the stage of life." Rather, as David Ausubel continues, "It is necessary to insist explicitly on the fact that biosocial status is, for the most part, an *individual achievement*," within a cultural setting (Ausubel et al., 1980, p. 173).

The concept of cultural age-periods can be used to account for differences in beliefs, values, and roles between individuals of the same chronological age living in different sociocultural settings and for age-typical personality changes within a particular culture as individuals adapt to new social tasks. It cannot, however, account for cross-cultural individual similarities, such as universals in cognitive development, except by alluding to biological maturation, nor can it account for inward patterns of developmental change that are not age-specific.

Functionally Defined Phases of Development

The concept of functionally defined phases of development is quite distinct from both structural stages and cultural age-periods, even though it also can be said to be based on the synchronization of stages and ages. A functional analysis of development looks at a particular behavior or mental process in terms of its function for the person rather than simply, on the one hand, at its structural level or, on the other hand, at its cultural content. As an intermediate model between stages and ages, functional phases address the interaction and synchronization of stages and ages through the life cycle. Functional phases of human ontogeny are based on the availability of new stages of cognitive structures that enable the individual to make sense of as well as to perform new social roles that are simultaneously required during the parallel cultural age-period. An age-period change reflects in part that particular society's response to a universal structural stage change that generally occurs within a certain parallel age range; at the same time, a structural stage change may be precipitated by an age-period change, which means the necessary environmental support and impetus for structural stage development are available (cf. Inhelder & Piaget, 1955, pp. 157, 338; Kuhn & Angeleu, 1976, p. 704). Functional phases are defined by the products of this interaction—new psychosocial developmental tasks that take on dominant importance to the ego.

This general process of structural stage and cultural age synchronization on which functional phases are based can be illustrated by the research of Barbara Rogoff and colleagues who analyzed the ethnographies from a global sample of 50 cultures in which anthropologists had included extensive information about childhood (Rogoff et al., 1975). The cultures were rated for the age at which children were considered by that society to be responsible enough to assume any one of 27 different types of activities. The results indicate that for most cultures 16 of the 27 categories of social roles and responsibilities were assigned during the 5 to 7-year age range (e.g., household chores, running errands, adult sleeping habits, care of siblings, considered sexual, considered to have common sense, teaching of social rules). Four of the remaining eleven were commonly assigned at puberty (e.g., adoption of adult clothing, independence from family, being considered sexually attractive). These findings illustrate that in many of the world's cultures children join up with society around ages 5 to 7 (e.g., in the United States they begin elementary school). During this period they also, of course, develop concrete operations. The synchronization and interaction of these cultural ages and structural stages of development gives rise to the child's ego-functioning task, which is to become socially productive and to derive a sense of competence from the achievement. The functional synchronization of developing cognitive structures with changes in the way people are linked to the social structure of their culture is also evident during adolescence. The formal ability to think about infinite hypothetical possibilities and the social requirement of learning to fill specific adult roles are synchronized in the American adolescent's functional task of identity achievement and working out what one should do with one's life.

A detailed summary of the contrasting characteristics and assumptions of stages, ages, and phases is presented in Table 8.1.

Structural Subdomains of Ego Development

We have distinguished structural stages, functional phases, and cultural ages of ego development. There are, however, competing interpretations of ego develop-

TABLE 8.1

Contrasting Characteristics of Structural Stage, Cultural Age, and Functional Phase Conceptions of Human Development

Structural Stages	Functional Phases	Cultural Ages
1. Process versus Content		
Stages are based on transformations in cognitive structures—in the way the mind processes the content about which it is thinking. These patterned processes of thinking are an integrated set of mental operations that account for how the individual makes sense of, or performs operations on the contents of his or her world.	Phases illuminate how both structural processes and cultural contents function together to give rise to new functional tasks in the individual's development. For instance, Kohlberg's stages define how moral issues will be processed at a particular stage.	Cultural periods are tied more directly to the content of reasoning rather than to the process. New cultural contents or knowledge are introduced in each age-period.
2. Development versus Aging		
Stages are not based on particular ages, although it is generally possible to give modal age ranges for each stage. Chronological age does not guarantee a corresponding stage of development; some adults are fixated at stages typical of children and a precocious child may be more mature than age would predict.	Phases are based on the synchronization of structural development (stage change) and cultural aging (aging in the context of cultural expectations). Similar to ages, they are somewhat inevitable; the next phase comes in a maturational sequence. Similar to stages, the successful resolution of later tasks is partially dependent on the resolution of prior developmental crises.	Periods, as times of stability and transition in the life cycle, are critically linked to age. All societies divide their membership into age categories (e.g., infant, lap child, yard child . . elder). These function as taxonomic devices to organize the process of status and role changes within the life cycle and to establish the person's participation in society in a way that takes into consideration maturation, physical energy, and needs.

Stages represent distinct qualitative structural differences in thinking about and orienting one's self to the world. A child's developmental stage is not simply an immature version of adult meaning-making, but is a general organizing tendency that is truly different from adults. Stages are total ways of thinking, qualitatively consistent from one task to the next and qualitatively different from other stage approaches to the same task.	*3. Qualitative versus Quantitative* Phases involve both qualitative and quantitative change. For instance, as a result of qualitative changes in cognitive structures and quantitative changes in social status, the individual is faced with a new developmental task in ego functioning.	Culturally defined periods put much greater emphasis on quantitative changes in age, mastery, performance, knowledge, rights, and responsibilities. Puberty rites, for instance, often involve exposure to greater quantities of stress and knowledge than a younger person is permitted to experience.
Stages are not simply the result of internal factors (inherited maturation) or external factors (nurturing environment); they are forms of equilibrium constructed out of the interaction between an individual and milieu. Within this interactive exchange, however, stages tend to stress the activity of the internal organism on the external environment. Activity is typically portrayed as taking place within the mind and cognitive operations are defined as interiorized generalizable actions.	*4. Active Individual versus Active Society* Phases are characterized by new psychosocial tasks that grow out of the interaction of individual and social action. The paradox of how new culturally programmed roles are fully self-chosen individual achievements is illuminated in part by the functional phase synchronization of individual and social action.	Age-periods emphasize the active instructional function of the external social setting—the individual is acted on by society. Whereas stages emphasize cognitive operations, periods emphasize cultural cooperations. Social roles are the primary mechanism by which the needs of the individual are met in the process of meeting the needs of society. Rites of passage between periods foster separation of an individual from a previous social sphere and incorporate the person into a new social role.

TABLE 8.1—Continued

5. Unconscious versus Conscious

Stages are unconscious cognitive structures. In the manner of a child who speaks grammatically but does so without being consciously aware of the grammatical structures, the ego is not consciously aware of the structures on which the ability to construct meaning depend, although an adult's ability to think about his own thinking does bring a general awareness of thought structures. Developmental change and the stability of a new stage are also not the result of conscious choice.	Phases are characterized by new psychosocial tasks that grow out of the interaction of individual and social action. The paradox of how new culturally programmed roles are also fully self-chosen individual achievements is illuminated in part by the functional phase synchronization of individual and social action.	Age-periods are based on the conscious passage of time, consciously observable events, and consciously acquired cultural knowledge and skills. The person is consciously aware of the contents of his or her thoughts. Periods are thus highly conscious in most cultures and fairly conscious in all. Even in U.S. society, where adult periods of the life cycle are inadequately objectified, they can be brought into public consciousness fairly easily (e.g, Sheehy, Levinson).

6. Hierarchical versus Nonhierarchical

Stage sequences are hierarchical. A higher stage is constructed on the previous stage, reintegrating it into a more highly differentiated, flexible, and complex stage. Later stages are more adequate than earlier stages since they include earlier stage patterns, resolve the same problems better, and are more justifiable in terms of the universal inclusiveness of their ordering of experience.	Later phases are more adequate than earlier phases, not necessarily in terms of complexity, but in terms of their ability to give order to or make sense of one's life in a form that is stable and meaningful.	Age-periods are relatively nonhierarchical. It is difficult to say that a later period is more adequate than an earlier one because attainment of and the adequacy of performance at a particular age-period are distinct. Furthermore, the period that society defines as life's best time varies from culture to culture.

7. Invariance versus Variation

Stages are invariant; each stage develops out of the previous one and a person must progress up the hierarchy one step at a time, without skipping or reversing any of the stages. Although an individual may become fixated at a particular stage, or even regress, all forward progress requires an invariant sequence of development in accord with the stage hierarchy. Environmental factors and innate capabilities may help one person reach a given stage of development earlier than another, but all people go though the same stage sequence.	The achievement of earlier phases or the resolution of previous crises serves as a foundation for new phases. Later phases subsume earlier phases. The successful achievement of later tasks is partially but not completely dependent on the successful achievement of earlier tasks. The specific sequence of adjoining phases may be reversed or difficult to distinguish among some individuals in our culture and many individuals in some other cultures.	Cultural ages vary in sequence between cultures and between subcultures within a particular culture. The accepted sequence in one sociocultural system may be reversed or absent in another. Even such generally defined periods as adolescence or the elderly can be absent where the culturally defined life cycle takes a person directly from late childhood into adulthood or where a person does not reach full adulthood until very late in life.

8. Universal versus Relative

Stages are structurally universal phenomena. Stage theories form an international road map predicting the sequential development of the ability to structure or make sense of the world. All persons, regardless of their sociocultural setting, can be expected to go though the same stages. The order of forward movement is universal, although individuals raised in different environments will no doubt progress through the stages at varying rates.	Phases are neither as universal as stages nor as relative as cultural ages. More plastic than the former and firmer than the latter, phases address both the commonality and uniqueness of personal experience and developmental conflicts.	Cultural age-periods are local road maps that predict the contents one will be concerned with during various ages of life in that particular culture. Periods cannot be universal since they vary tremendously from one culture to another. The relativity of age-periods between cultures, however, also implies a general uniformity within a culture or subculture.

Source: Snarey, 1982.

ment within structural psychology. The primary contrast lies between two different conceptions of ego domains. Some structural theorists have postulated an indivisible monodomain ego simultaneously engaged in different types of structuring activities—logical, moral, interpersonal, metaphysical. Jane Loevinger, who takes this approach, states that "there is but one major source for all of the conceptions of moral and ego development, one thread of reality to which all of the conceptions give varying access" (1976, p. 441). This viewpoint argues that cognitive and moral development, for instance, cannot really be distinguished within the one unified structure of the developing ego. To support this interpretation, research is cited that has used Loevinger's measure which, after a statistical analysis of the parts of her instrument, has not been able to separate out subdomains or strands of ego development (e.g., Lambert, 1972). Those who hold this position, however, readily acknowledge that this research is "not conclusive evidence against...dimensions" within a unifying ego (Loevinger, 1976, p. 188).

In contrast, our position is that there are several related but differentiated lines of development within a unified but multi-faceted ego. This view suggests that the ego comprises relatively circumscribed subdomains that stand in asymmetrical relation to each other. Each domain is characterized by a relatively distinct substructure that is included within the more holistic superstructure of the unifying ego. Most important, this approach utilizes Piaget's concept of ordered decalage to allow the various strands of ego development to be separated out. This means that development in a logically prior domain is necessary but not sufficient for the parallel level of development in another domain. On the basis of Piagetian theory, as modified under the impact of empirical findings which we will discuss in a later section, we assume that cognitive structures are embodied in more general and inclusive ego structures. For instance, cognitive development is a necessary part but not a sufficient condition for ego development. There would thus occur structural parallels or corresponding stages between each subdomain of ego development, and the attainment of a stage in any one domain is dependent on the prior attainment of the parallel stage in other, more fundamental domains. This approach, of course, raises the questions of what are the subdomains and how many are there? In the last chapter we suggested an order of cognitive level, social perspective level, and moral level as subdomains of what we here call ego development.

The distinctions we have drawn will now be used as lenses through which to consider four prominent theories of ego development (see Table 8.2). The first to be presented is Robert Selman's theory of social cognition, an example of a structural approach to the social epistemology subdomain of ego development; the second is Robert Kegan's holistic structural approach to the evolving ego; and the third is Jane Loevinger's quasi-structural theory of ego stages. We will finally consider Erik Erikson's functional model of ego development—an intermediate approach because it includes both structural and cultural elements. Our discussion,

TABLE 8.2

Continuum of Theoretical Approaches to Ego Development

Structural Developmental Stages		Functional Developmental Phases		Cultural Developmental Ages
Selman Kegan	Loevinger	Erikson	Freud	Levinson

however, will not include a particular age-period model. It would, in fact, be somewhat of a contradiction in terms to present a general theory of developmental cultural ages since there are as many age-period models of human development as there are peoples and cultures of the world. Some psychologists, to be sure, have tried to clarify or abstract the ages of development within a particular culture but they risk the trap of trying to universalize that which is primarily culturally relative (Levinson, 1978). Rather, we will use the cultural age-period approach to clarify the unique elements within Erikson's more functional approach.

ROBERT SELMAN'S THEORY

Robert Selman, along with his colleagues at Harvard University and the Judge Baker Guidance Center, has constructed a stage theory of social cognition based on perspective-taking levels that focus on the development of epistemological reasoning about the social environment. His approach is strongly structural-developmental in its concern with satisfying the Piagetian stage criteria of structured wholeness, invariant developmental sequence, and universality. As Selman states, "the term *stage* is viewed as a construct implying stronger claims of formal characteristics. For example...the criterion of structured wholeness must be demonstrated across many contexts or modes of functioning for stages" (Selman, 1980, p. 80). That is, stronger than the constructs of functional phases or cultural ages which only require a general sequence in the trajectory of development. Building on the work of Piaget and Kohlberg, Selman has abstracted a developmental structuring process that is more general or fundamental than Kohlberg's theory but less so than Piaget's stages. In essence, he has explicated the structural basis for a child's social knowledge. We consider Selman's domain to be an important strand or line of development within the more holistic and unifying developing ego. Selman himself suggests that social cognition must be "understood within the context of a theory of ego development" or "ego-development matrix" if it is to be helpful to teachers in understanding the student's total development and what is needed in terms of educational and clinical intervention (Selman, 1976, pp. 299, 316).

Selman's stages have been empirically verified through interviews with a large

TABLE 8.3
Selman's Stages of Social Cognition

Stage 0: Undifferentiated and Egocentric Perspective Taking (about Ages 3 to 6)*

Concepts of Persons: Undifferentiated. At this level, young children do not clearly differentiate physical and psychological characteristics of persons. Feelings and thoughts can be observed and recognized, but the confusion between the subjective-psychological and the objective-physical leads to confusion between acts and feelings or between intentional and unintentional behavior.

Concepts of Relations: Egocentric. Selves and others are clearly differentiated only as physical entities, not psychological entities. Thus subjective perspectives are undifferentiated and that another may interpret the same situation differently is not recognized. Concepts of relations of perspectives are limited by inability to differentiate clearly and by concomitant reduction of differences in perspectives to merely differences in *perceptual* perspectives.

Stage 1: Differentiated and Subjective Perspective Taking (about Ages 5 to 9)

Concepts of Persons: Differentiated. At Level 1, the key conceptual advance is the clear differentiation of physical and psychological characteristics of persons. As a result, intentional and unintentional acts are differentiated and a new awareness is generated that each person has a unique subjective covert psychological life. Thought, opinion, or feeling states within an individual, however, as seen as unitary, not mixed.

Concepts of Relations: Subjective. The subjective perspectives of self and other are clearly differentiated and recognized as potentially different. However, another's subjective state is still thought to be legible by simple physical observation. Relating of perspectives is conceived of in one-way, unilateral terms, in terms of the perspective of and impact on one actor.

Stage 2: Self-reflective/Second-person and Reciprocal Perspective Taking
(about Ages 7 to 12)

Concepts of Persons: Self-reflective/Second-person. Key conceptual advances at Level 2 are the growing child's ability to step mentally outside himself or herself and take a self-reflective or second-person perspective on his or her own thoughts and actions *and* on the realization that others can do so as well. Persons' thought or feeling states are seen as potentially multiple, for example, curious, frightened, and happy, but still as groupings of mutually isolated and sequential or weighted aspects, for example, mostly curious and happy and a little scared. Both selves and others are thereby understood to be capable of doing things (overt actions) they may not want (intend) to do. And persons are understood to have a dual, layered social orientation: visible appearance, possibly put on for show, and the *truer* hidden reality.

Concepts of Relations: Reciprocal. Differences among perspectives are seen relativistically because of the Level 2 child's recognition of the uniqueness of each person's ordered set of values and purposes. A new two-way reciprocity is the hallmark of Level 2 concepts of relations. It is a reciprocity of thoughts and feelings, not merely actions. The child puts himself or herself in another's shoes and realizes the other will do the same. In strictly

TABLE 8.3—Continued

mechanical-logical terms, the child now sees the infinite regress possibility of perspective taking (I know that she knows that I know that she knows...etc.).

Stage 3: Third-person and Mutual Perspective Taking (about Ages 10 to 15)

Concepts of Persons: Third-person. Persons are seen by the young adolescent thinking at Level 3 as systems of attitudes and values fairly consistent over the long haul, as opposed to randomly changeable assortments of states as at Level 2. The critical conceptual advance is toward ability to take a true third-person perspective, to step outside not only one's own immediate perspective, but outside the self as a system, a totality. There are generated notions of what we might call an "observing ego," such that adolescents do (and perceive other persons to) simultaneously see themselves as both actors and objects, simultaneously acting and reflecting upon the effects of action on themselves, reflecting upon the self in interaction with the self.

Concepts of Relations: Mutual. The third-person perspective permits more than the taking of another's perspective on the self; the truly third-person perspective on relations which is characteristic of Level 3 *simultaneously* includes and coordinates the perspectives of self and other(s), and thus the system or situation and all parties are seen from the third-person or generalized other perspective. Whereas at Level 2, the logic of infinite regress, chaining back and forth, was indeed apparent, its implications were not. At Level 3, the limitations and ultimate futility of attempts to understand interactions on the basis of the infinite regress model become apparent and the third-person perspective of this level allows the adolescent to abstractly step outside an interpersonal interaction and simultaneously and mutually coordinate and consider the perspectives (and their interactions) of self and other.

Stage 4: In-depth and Societal-Symbolic Perspective Taking (about Ages 12 to Adult)

Concepts of Persons: In-depth. Two new notions are characteristic of Level 4 conceptions of persons. First, actions, thoughts, motives, or feelings are understood to be psychologically determined, but *not necessarily* self-reflectively understood. In this view, there are more complicated interactions *within* a person that cannot always be comprehended by the "observing ego" of Level 3. Thus, we see, whether or not it is so named, the generation of a notion of the unconscious in individuals. Persons are thereby seen to be capable of doing things not that they "don't want" to do, as at Level 2, but that they don't understand why they don't. Second, there emerges at Level 4 a new notion of personality as a product of traits, beliefs, values, and attitudes, a system with its own developmental history.

Concepts of Relations: Societal-Symbolic. The individual now conceptualizes subjective perspectives of persons toward each other (mutuality) as existing not only on the plane of common expectations or awareness, but also simultaneously at multidimensional or deeper levels of communication. For example, in a dyad, perspectives can be shared at the level of superficial information, of common interests, or of deeper unverbalized feelings and communication.

*All age-norms are approximate and were obtained from verbal responses to hypothetical dilemmas in reflective interviews.

Source: Adapted from Selman, 1980, pp. 37–40.

number of subjects who represent a range of ages from 4 to 30 (1980). His basic research instrument is a set of interpersonal story-dilemmas that focus on the social relations between the actors. A filmstrip is often used to present the dilemma audiovisually (Selman & Kohlberg, 1972; Selman, Bryne, & Kohlberg, 1975, 1976). The story-dilemma is followed with a series of semi-clinical probe questions that focus on the relationships between perspectives and conflicts within a particular point of view. This research procedure has also been used as an intervention, similar to the manner in which Kohlberg's dilemmas have been used in classroom discussions, in order to facilitate the development of more mature social cognition. The five stages of social cognition, which Selman has abstracted from the various responses to his interview stories, are summarized on an abstract structural level in Table 8.3

We will now briefly describe, on a less abstract level, the stages in Selman's model with reference to four social content areas—conceptions of individuals, friendships, peer groups, and parent-child relations. We will also illustrate each stage with concrete examples from interviews. Unless otherwise indicated, all interview excerpts are taken from Selman's book, *The growth of interpersonal understanding* (1980, pp. 132–151).

Stage 0, *undifferentiated and egocentric perspective taking*, is typical of pre-schoolers. The child does not differentiate between his social perspective and that of another. He or she conceives of individuals as physical or material entities and close friendships as momentary physical or geographical associations. The peer group is also a temporary physical connection and the parent-child relationship is that of a boss and servant.

I am a good boy. *Why?* Because I am big.

Who is your best friend? Eric.
Do you trust him? Yes.
What does it mean to trust Eric?
If I give him a toy I know he won't break it.
How do you know?
He isn't strong enough.

What kind of person makes a good friend?
Boys play with boys, trucks play with trucks, dogs play with dogs.
Why does that make them good friends?
Because they do the same things.

Stage 1, *differentiated and subjective perspective taking*, is typically found among early elementary school children. The child has an increased ability to differentiate between an individual's psychological motives and physical causality, but understands friendship as an "uneven handed" or one-way assistance since he or she cannot yet see the reciprocity between perspectives. The child conceives of the peer group as a series of unilateral physical relations and the parent-child relation as the parental caretakers with their child helper.

[*Why are friends important?*]
You need a friend because you want to play some games and you have to get someone who will play the way you want him to.

What causes fights between friends?
If she calls you a name or something like that.
How can you get to be friends again?
Make her take it back; make her say she was lying.

Stage 2, *self-reflective second-person reciprocal perspective*, is typical of later elementary school children who conceive of individuals as introspective selves and see friendships as "fair-weather," but even handed, cooperation in the reciprocal interest of both parties. Each must respond to the needs or desires of the other. Friendship is subjective; one person may like or dislike the other because of certain traits; liking is not automatically associated with playing together. The child at Stage 2 understands the peer group as a chain of bilateral partnerships between people who like each other and, in the parent-child relationship, sees the parent as a guidance counselor but also realizes that the child himself satisfies psychological needs of the parents, such as the pleasure of seeing the child grow.

Who is your best friend?
Don.
Why?
We hang around together. . . .
Because I buy him stuff and he buys me stuff.
Complete this sentence. A friend is someone who:
Helps you and someone you can trust.
How do you know when you can trust someone?
If they did a lot for you, and you did a lot for them, and they didn't do anything bad, then you could trust them. (Damon, 1979, p. 159)

We like each other.
Why is it important that group members all like each other?
Everyone has to like each other, or it wouldn't be a group.

You have to like the same things, because if one guy wants to play baseball and another guy wants to play football, they would get bored.

Stage 3, *third-person and mutual perspective-taking*, may emerge during late childhood and is common during the early adolescent years. The child now views individuals as stable personalities who have, rather than are, their mixed thoughts and feelings and understands the self as organizing this inner psychological life. He or she thinks of friendships as intimate and mutual sharing between two personalities; friends are persons who have taken each other into their confidence and who understand one another's inner thoughts and feelings. Friends are selected according to compatability of mutual interests; friendship involves long-term relationships and includes the possibility of helping each other with psychological problems. Peer groups are now homogeneous communities or social wholes of which the person is or is not a member; the peer group must work together and stick together. The person can now understand, from a third person perspective, that parents may want their children to be an extension of themselves. Ideal parents show tolerance and support their children's development, whereas the ideal child is respectful of his parents and sensitive to their psychological needs.

Who is your best friend? Carol, but she lives far away.
Why is Carol your best friend?
She's not snobby or bratty, so we like to play together....
What is a good friend like?
...Someone who does what both of you want to do.
[She] is good to talk to....
What do you do to be nice [to a friend]?
If she has a problem like if she was in a fight I'd try to straighten it out between them and make them not fight, like helping them figure things out so they're not mad any more. (Damon, 1979, p. 162)

[What about parents?]
The problem with most parents is that they don't remember what it is like to be kids.... [They] need to be more understanding of what the child is going through. The father should try to treat him as an equal, but the father and mother would have to be the final arbiter. (Colby et al., 1979, p. 362)

This third stage of perspective-taking evokes the conformity of early adolescents who realize that the self and the other can be simultaneously viewed or mutually known by each other. They thus proceed to evaluate their self from the perspective of others, making the false assumption that everyone else is as concerned with their self and appearance as they are. This increased interpersonal sensitivity, however, also allows them to construct concepts of tolerance and mutual respect as the characteristics of an ideal parent-child relationship.

Stage 4, *in-depth and societal-symbolic perspective-taking*, is the final stage in Selman's scheme. Although it might occur in some precocious individuals as young as 12, it is most commonly found from late adolescence through adulthood. Thus, its relevance for teachers is in understanding their own stage of development as well as enabling them to foresee where students ideally are headed. According to Selman, the critical realization of Stage 4 is "that no matter how vigilant the conscious mind is, no matter how hard the mind works, there are still internal experiences not readily available" (1980, p. 105). At Stage 3 this may be seen but it is explained as due to a failure of the person's will. Stage 4 goes beyond the Stage 3 notion of an "observing ego" that can see one's self as both acting and reflecting upon one's actions to the discovery of two unique characteristics. "First, there is the discovery of the concept of the unconscious and of unconscious psychological causes of behavior, that is, that below inner reality there may be an even deeper reality, and this affects feelings and behavior. Second, there is a natural conceptualization of the existence of unconscious *processes*—the focus here being on the child's own growing natural theory of psychic phenomena such as coping and defending as autonomic processes" (1980, p. 105). The concept of friendship, at Stage 4, includes a "partial rejection of [Stage 3] mutuality when it precludes autonomous growth and development." This view is "tempered by the belief that total independence is as futile as total dependence" (1980, p. 113). Interpersonal conflicts are now understood as being amenable to resolution or repair through symbolic action (e.g., nonverbal communication). The peer group is understood as a complex and pluralistic organized system. The obligations and rights of a leadership role are now distinguished from the individuals filling those roles. These positions of leadership are further differentiated in terms of several different abstract functions, such as task leadership and social-emotional leadership. This social systems perspective is also applied to the parent-child relationship which is conceived of as an evolving system in which autonomy and dependency are established and also fluctuate predictably throughout the course of the life cycle. The concept of punishment, for instance, includes an understanding that it may function "as an unconscious attempt to maintain psychological control or fusion" on the part of parents or teachers (1980, p. 129). "This ability to acknowledge the double-edged functions of parenting [and teaching], (parenting for the parent's sake as well as for the child's) and to see the potential for unawareness of these multiple functions on the part of the parent has its complement in the understanding of punishment-eliciting behavior of children." In other words, "children are not merely passive victims of parental anger or targets for their parents' need for punishment, but that some children, some of the time, have a need for punishment, insofar as punishment symbolizes for them that their parents care about them" (1980, p. 130). We will again illustrate this stage with interview excerpts.

[How can a person repair a friendship in trouble?]
One good way to straighten things out between friends is to understand how the problem may relate to problems the person has in general. For example, lots of people have problems with authority. If they start to see the friendship as an authority relation, there might be trouble. But to solve it they have to sort out their own feelings.

Is there more than one kind of leadership in a group?
Well, there is the person who takes charge in making sure that the group's task is accomplished, and there is the person who smooths the rough edges that arise when the task is being carried out, either by supplying comic relief or emotional support.

Why do you think a group needs these different kinds of leadership?
When the group is carrying out its task, many times it creates friction among group members who have different points of view on interests. The group action which involves compromise would leave some members disenchanted. The task of the leader is to see that the task is reached, and the person providing the emotional support is there to see that

group members are not so disenchanted with the group that they would leave. . . . I can think of the leadership role of both types being shared by a number of individuals.

Having summarized and illustrated Selman's stages, we will now discuss the relationship between social cognition and other subdomains of ego development. Selman's own perspective has some parallels to our domain approach, but his position is somewhat different in that he prefers to stress that models of ego development are at a deeper level of analysis while forms of cognition, including his own theory, are somewhat more influenced by context even though they are also fundamentally developmental.

> Interpersonal reasoning or understanding is just one part or process in the ego-stage construct. In this sense, ego stages reflect a greater level of theoretical abstraction than do interpersonal understanding stages. Ego stages do not describe a formal or structural cognitive function, but a further abstraction, one which nevertheless is dependent on the level of competence that each social-cognitive structure provides. In other words, developmental ego stages are an inferential step further removed from observed action than reasoning stage; inferences about ego stages must rely in part on inferences about social-cognitive stages. (Selman, 1980, p. 307)

Fully consistent with our perspective, however, he also suggests that the equivalent Piagetian stage of physical cognition is a necessary prior achievement but is not sufficient to ensure attainment of the parallel level of social cognition, and that both of these, in turn, are necessary but not sufficient for attainment of the parallel level of ego development. In this sense, Selman's domain of social cognition is a crucial link in our structural subdomain theory of ego development.

This general understanding of stage-by-stage parallels between social cognition and other domains has received support from several studies. Selman has demonstrated logical parallels between his stages and Loevinger's ego stages (1980, pp. 304–307). Positive correlations between the development of social cognition and social moral reasoning have also been demonstrated—no children who had attained conventional morality failed the equivalent level of social perspective-taking (Moir, 1974; Selman, 1971; Selman & Damon, 1975). Going beyond empirical correlations between measures, Lawrence Walker conducted an experimental study in which he documents the proposition that both Piagetian early formal operations and Selman's third stage of mutual role-taking are prerequisite to attainment of Kohlberg's third stage. Walker assessed the stage of development in each domain for 72 fourth through seventh grade children, 36 assigned to the experimental group and 36 to the control group. This pretest portion of the research was followed by a treatment in which the children were exposed to moral Stage 3 reasoning in a role-playing situation. This was followed by a moral reasoning post-test and a follow-up. The results indicate that a transition to moral Stage 3 occurred only for those children in the experimental group who had attained the hypothesized prerequisite level of formal operations and social perspective-taking (Walker, 1980).

We have presented Selman's work as an example of a structural subdomain approach to ego development. We will now consider a more holistic structural model of the developing ego by Robert Kegan.

ROBERT KEGAN'S THEORY

Robert Kegan has offered a coherent structural logic for a hierarchical model of ego development—a description of the different meanings of experience that are constructed from similar life experiences by individuals at different stages of ego development (1977, 1979a, 1979b, 1980a, 1980b, 1982). But "stages" for Kegan are primarily resting points or temporary truces along the way. His structural-developmental theory of ego development defines the overall unity of the self that springs from and has consequences for the dialectical process in which the ego dynamically constructs itself. "Persons are not their stage of development; persons are. . .a creative motion" (1980b, p. 407). Adapting the frameworks of Piaget and Kohlberg to the study of the self in transformation, he addresses "meaning-making" activity over the lifespan; meaning-making *is* development for Kegan. He seeks to unify an understanding of the ego's total constitutive activities by defining an underlying "psychologic" of self-other differentiation. The subject-object relation, according to Kegan, is the common ground or larger context of which all other Piagetian theories can be seen as parts. "The person's construction of the physical (Piaget), moral (Kohlberg), interpersonal (Selman), self-reflective (Perry), [and] theological (Fowler) worlds" are strands within this more basic activity (1979a, p. 9; 1977). Kegan's self-other differentiation refers not only to the re-lationship between a person and other persons, but to ways the self understands and deals with itself and deals with the meaning of its actual relationships in the real world. Thus, his theory addresses: (1) a perspective of a self "about itself," (2) a perspective of important others that have been taken in and are part of an inner dialogue or of inner voices of a person, and (3) a perspective of real others with whom the person is interacting.

Similar to the way Kohlberg describes the underlying social perspective for each stage of moral development, Kegan describes the social perspectives underlying stages of ego development. Where psychoanalysis has looked at how people internalize objects—the process of taking in important others into the self and relating it to childhood—Kegan describes a number of internalizations—how we construct, view, and are influenced by others over the lifespan. He does so by focusing on the nature of the balance in the relationship between the self and an object. In his model of the subject-object balance, the term object refers to those feelings, thoughts, and relationships that we have consciously, that we can observe, and that are thus available for coordination and mediation. The subject side of this balance refers to those aspects of the ego of which a self-observing person is not yet aware—that which the person is embedded in and has no distance from. Kegan's distinction between subject and object is similar to the distinction between "being" and "having," two concepts that have been a long preoccupation in philosophy and psychology (Fromm, 1976). "Being" refers to that part of the self that is lived out without being reflected upon. For instance, at Kegan's interpersonal stage identity derives from being the dyad that one is a part of—"I am my relationships." As soon as a person has moved beyond that stage, what was subject moves to the object side. Now one *has* relationships in the sense that ones identity is no longer derived from relationships. The move from subject to object is a process of disembedding and of re-embedding. Kegan's stages of ego development are summarized in Table 8.4. We will now trace these subject-object or self-other differentiations through each of his stages.

Stage 0, *the incorporative ego*, corresponds to the beginnings of life, in which the infant is embedded in his reflexes and has no consciousness of them. All developmental theories consider the infant to be "undifferentiated," the essence of which is actually the absence of any self-other boundary—hence stage zero rather than stage one. The infant is considered to take all of the phenomena it experiences as extensions of itself. Thus, the incorporative ego consists of total subject, the mother-infant symbiosis, an objectless incorporative embeddedness. The most widely researched but rarely related phenomena of infancy are *object permanence*—the gradual ability to hold an object in memory and recognize that it still exists when absent—and *separation anxiety*—the protest of the infant upon separation from the primary caretaker. These, according to Kegan, are the cognitive and affective expressions of a single "motion" in personality development. The transition from Stage 0 to Stage 1 is a process in which the young child practices separation while having to be assured of the presence of the caretaker. The negativistic protestations of the 2 year old, the "no" of Freud's anal phase, represent an affirmation of an emerging separate identity. Once others can be seen as others, the child stops protesting.

At Stage 1, *the impulsive ego*, the reflexes move to the object side and thus become manageable. The new subject into which the child of approximately 2 to 5 years of age is embedded consists of impulses and perceptions. The child is not free of his or her reflexes but has begun to look at them objectively from the outside. The child *is* its impulses, but *has* reflexes. Since the preschooler lacks impulse control, or rather since he is those impulses, "their non-expression raises an *ultimate* threat; they risk who I am" (Kegan, 1979b, p. 22). The child's very organization rather than just an element of his organization is frustrated. Just as the preschooler cannot hold and compare two aspects of reality at once—such as height and width, necessary for recognizing volume constancy—so two emotions also cannot be held. As Kegan states,

> This...suggests why the preschooler lacks the capacity for ambivalence, and it understands the tantrum—the classical expression of distress in this stage—as an example of a system overwhelmed by internal conflict because there is no self yet which can serve as a context upon which the competing impulses can play themselves out; the impulses *are* the self, are themselves the context. (1979b, pp. 22–23)

TABLE 8.4
Kegan's Stages of Ego Development

Stages: The Evolving "I"	Subject-Object Relation		Parallels with		
	(Self)	(Other)	Piaget	Kohlberg	Loevinger
Stage 0: The Incorporative "I"	sensing, moving, reflexes ↗	none	Sensorimotor		Presocial
Stage 1: The Imuplsive "I"	impulses, perceptions ↗	sensing, moving	Pre-operations	Punishment and obedience orientation	Impulsive
Stage 2: The Imperial "I"	needs, interests, wishes ↗	impulses, perceptions	Concrete operations	Instrumental orientation	Opportunistic
Stage 3: The Interpersonal "I"	interpersonal, mutuality, shared contexts ↗	needs, interests, wishes	Early formal operations	Interpersonal concordance orientation	Conformist
Stage 4: The Institutional "I"	authorship, ideology, psychic institution, self-system identity ↗	interpersonal, mutuality, shared contexts	Full formal operations	Societal orientation	Conscientious
Stage 5: The interindividual "I"	individuality, interpenetrability of self-systems	authorship, ideology, psychic institution	Post formal operations, Dialectical?	Principled orientation	Autonomous

Source: Adapted from Kegan, 1979, 1980a, 1980b.

The transition out of this embeddedness in a world of impulses and reflexes to the world of Stage 2 typically occurs between ages 5 and 7. This is the transition from fantasy to reality—from fantasy about the fantastic (e.g., being Spiderman) to a fantasy life about things that actually could be (e.g., being a doctor).

Stage 2, *the imperial ego*, is marked by a shift from *being* impulses and perceptions to *having* them. As children get ready to attend school, they begin to deal with their impulses by themselves and the impulses thus move to the object side. The child can now experience and see the effects and representations of the impulses and can begin to manipulate them and to set limits on them. Now the child *has* impulses while *being* his or her needs. Stage 2 includes a new social cognitive capacity that enables the child to acknowledge that others exist separately—rather than depending on or revolving around himself or herself. Kegan observes,

> A distinguishing feature of this new subject-object relation is that the child seems to "seal up" in a sense; there is a self-containment that was not there before; the adult no longer finds himself engaged in the middle of conversations the child has begun all by himself; the child no longer lives with the sense that the parent can read his private feelings. He has a private world which he did not have before. (1979b, p. 30)

At Stage 2 the child comes to see that persons have an individual distinctiveness which makes unrealistic the notion that another person can be perfectly attuned to, invested in, or coincident with one's personal experience of the world. In addition to the signs that go up on the bedroom door, "Adults Keep Out," other manifestations of a transition in the social cognitive domain include the increasing orientation to "reality," the separation of appearance from reality, the recognition of subterfuge, and the stereotyping of drawings. The cognitive and affective expressions of this new organization can be said to parallel Piaget's concrete operations and Freud's latency period, respectively. When the impulses become object, the new system can coordinate an impulse at one moment with an impulse at another. This brings into being what Kegan calls the enduring disposition, a "way I tend to feel" over time, as opposed to the moment-by-moment lability of the earlier organization. With the coordination of the perceptions comes the ability to conserve or hold constant any object, despite changing appearances. Among those objects that are conserved, none is as important as the self. During these years, roughly ages 7 to the early teens, the child begins to construct a self-image or way of being—"I am one of the smart kids; a Catholic; a poor kid; a kid whose parents are divorced." What the child at Stage 2 cannot do is genuinely consider both his or her own needs and the needs and wishes of others at the same time. The person cannot take the system of needs as an object or element of a larger system. It is in the transition to the next stage that the individual emerges from this embeddedness and can coordinate the interests of others.

At Stage 3, which Kegan calls *the interpersonal and mutual ego*, a person *has* needs but *becomes* an interpersonal and intrapsychic coordinator between need perspectives. This stage allows for the construction of reciprocal relations based on mutual obligations and expectation. It allows the individual to move back and forth, intrapsychically, between different need perspectives. This self-reflectiveness creates feelings of subjectivity that are experienced as one's own internal feelings rather than as social negotiations. The self has now become interpersonal; it is located in the shared reality of coordinated points of view. Its strength lies in its capacity to create the shared reality; its limit lies in its inability to consult itself about the shared reality. It cannot because it *is* that shared reality. It lacks a separate identity; the person is derived from and embedded in others and their expectations. The person is interwoven into the group and the interpersonal context. At Stage 3, therefore, personal conflicts are often not really conflicts between what one wants and what someone else wants. When scrutinized, they regularly turn out to be conflicts between what one wants to do as a part of one shared reality and what one wants to do as part of another shared reality. Assertiveness and the expression of anger are therefore often experienced as threatening at this stage because these thoughts and feelings interfere with the process of relating that defines the self. Anger acknowledged and expressed is a risk to the interpersonal fabric. Getting angry amounts to a declaration of a sense of self separate from the relational context. To ask someone in this evolutionary balance to resolve such a conflict by bringing both shared realities before itself is to name precisely the limits of this way of making meaning. The transition out of Stage 3 to Stage 4 is a development that usually occurs during late adolescence or adulthood.

At Stage 4, *the institutional ego*, an internal agency emerges that asserts autonomy, self-ownership, self-dependence, thus leading to the achievement of identity. In moving from "I *am* my relationships" to "I *have* relationships," Kegan indicates that "there is now somebody who is *doing* this having, the new I, who, in coordinating or reflecting upon mutuality, brings into being a kind of psychic institution" (1979b, pp. 31–32). At Stage 3 the person needed the dyadic embed-dedness to define the self but now the new psychic institution allows for the having of relationships without making them the central definers of the self. This psychic institution "constructs the self itself as a system, and makes ultimate (as does every balance) the maintenance of its integrity" (1979b, p. 32). This makes emotional life at Stage 4 a matter of holding both sides of a feeling simultaneously, whereas at Stage 3 one experiences ambivalence one side at a time. There is also an interior change in the way feelings are regulated in that the emotions that arise out of interpersonal relations do not reflect the very structure of one's "psychologic" but are rather reflected upon by that structure. Feelings that depend on mutuality for their origin and their renewal remain important but are relativized by that context which is now considered ultimate, the psychic *system*. That is, the institutional self constructs systems—ideological, philosophical, religious—to coordinate and unify all the varying relationships that previously defined the self differently in each important life-context. Feelings related to personal competence, achievement, psychological autonomy, and future direction are now more central. A person at Stage 4 holds such feelings together by making them consistent with this ideological system. The institutional self's decisions are thus embedded in its meanings, purposes, and decisions, which are the source of the self. This stage's conception of the self, as an organized system with an executive function, is thus remarkably similar to Freud's general conception of the ego. The cognitive domain of this institutional ego is Piaget's full formal operations. The sociomoral domain involves the constructing of the legal, societal, normative systems characteristic of Kohlberg's fourth stage. In the sense that Kegan's fourth stage is inevitably ideological (though not necessarily a publically shared or recognized ideology), it also parallels Erikson's discussion of identity versus identity confusion.

Stage 5, which Kegan calls *the inter-individual ego*, may be viewed as an embeddedness in a new form of individuality, where ideology and other aspects of the previous balance are questioned. The person "re-cognizes" the "person-ality" prior to the institutional self. This new self brings about a revolution in Freud's favorite concerns, love and work. For instance, one now *has* a career; one no longer *is* a career. The self is no longer so vulnerable to the kind of ultimate humiliation that the threat of performance-failure holds out, for the performance is no longer ultimate. Similarly, the mature quality of interpersonal relations and intimacy at this stage is due to the self's surrender of its counter-dependent independence for an *interdependence*. Where a relationship is between partners making deals together in Stage 2, a fusion in Stage 3, and an interaction between compatriots or loyalists in Stage 4, at Stage 5, persons are individuals—separate identity is not lost, but securely experienced and compared. One interprets the other psyche, while both are interactive. This sharing of the self at the level of imtimacy permits the emotions and impulses to live in the intersection of systems, to be resolved between one self-system and another. Rather than the attempt to be closed, interindividuality permits one to "give oneself up" to another. Erikson's concepts of the "counterpointing of identities" and "intimacy versus isolation" parallel Kegan's definition of Stage 5 intimacy in that the boundaries of the self are secured so that the opening toward another self does not represent an ultimate threat of loss of identity.

In general, the logics and processes of self-other relations suggested by Kegan's theory might be best represented by a helix in which personality swings back and forth, between either side of an enduring developmental tension, between individuation and separation, between differentiation and integration. (See Table 8.5.) The helix also suggests that each stage is a relative balance in the lifespan, a temporary resolution to the lifelong yearning for inclusion or affiliation and for autonomy or separateness. This notion that ego development is the setting and resetting of the boundaries between self and other is quite fundamental, as we see it, in that it provides a more inclusive context for integrating the various subdomains of development that structural-developmental researchers have discovered. Thus, Kegan's work subsumes Kohlberg's stages of moral development in

TABLE 8.5
Kegan's Helix of Self-Other Relations

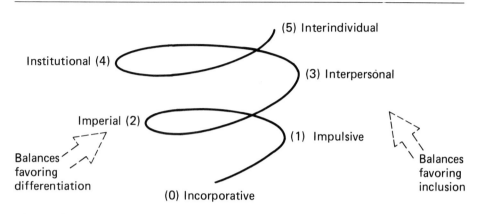

terms of people's understanding of rules, norms, and social obligations. With Selman's model he shares a focus on the process of social perspective-taking; each stage of ego development includes a more differentiated and complex social perspective. For instance, a systematic social perspective, which in moral development leads to an understanding of a social system that is regulated by laws and social obligations, also underlies in terms of ego development a systematic understanding of a self that is able to self-regulate an ideological system's consistency regarding identity.

Kegan's underlying ego structures are harder to capture than social-epistemological or social-moral structures, however. Although the parallels between the stage models are clear, Kegan's orientation toward a hierarchy of biological and social organizing principles, such as reflexes, impulses, needs, and interpersonality, raises important questions. Are these constructs truly structural and developmental? Do impulses transform into needs, for example, or are they parallel processes? Kegan also seems to give up the important Piagetian boundary between judgment and action. In turn, however, he gains a concept of the ego that includes thinking, feeling, and acting; to think, to feel, is to construe reality or act. These structures can thus be characterized and estimated both through verbal behavior (e.g., responses to interview questions) and by observation of nonverbal behavior (e.g., the temper tantrum of children at Stage 1).

Kegan has demontrated the power of his framework by applying it to the study of counseling and the understanding of psychological and educational problems in general. For instance, in an exploratory study of 39 persons during their stay on a psychiatric ward, Kegan analyzed forms of depression and related it to stages of moral reasoning which he used as a bench mark for stage of ego development (1977, 1979a). Focusing on the transition points in development, as periods of disequilibrium, he postulated that psychopathology is strongly related to those times in the life cycle when an old balance of knowing has fallen apart and a new one has not yet been established. He identified three types of depression: the "self-sacrificing depression," the "dependent depression," and the "guilty depression." The comparison between types of depression and scores on Kohlberg's moral interview revealed clear parallels. Self-sacrificing depression occurs primarily during the transition from Stage 2 to 3, the dependent depression occurs at Stage 3 or 3/4, and the guilty depression at Stage 4 or 4/5. More than half of his psychiatric sample was scored as in transition. The Stage 2 or 2/3 self-sacrificing depression was characterized by acting-out behavior, lack of internal reflection, and a sense of "being the victim." Problems were typically defined as outside the self, in terms of the demands of others which frustrated the needs of the self. The dependent depression typically involved the loss of relationships, the feeling of dependency and helplessness, loneliness, the fear of abandonment, and the fear of making others feel angry or of hurting others. The loss of the other was experienced as the loss of self. Kegan relates the third type, guilty depression, to problems of not meeting standards or goals set by the self. Feelings of guilt, meaningless-ness, inferiority, the fear that others and the self are criticized harshly were predominant.

Kegan's analysis also emphasizes the role of the "holding environment" or institutional setting. He describes problems arising from a mismatch of the self and the holding environment—family, school, interpersonal relationships—at any given stage. For him, therapeutic endeavors include more than traditional patient-therapist relationships. Kegan defines "natural therapists" as people and insti-tutions that support development. The natural therapists thus include teachers who are critical in the creation of the child's holding environment outside the family. The clinical applications of Kegan's theory suggest, for instance, that one of the important tasks of the teacher is to support the development of more mature coping patterns. Further research on the relationship of ego development and pathology, education, and therapy is currently in progress, (Noam & Kegan, in press; Quinlan & Rogers, 1981).

While Kegan's theory is well developed, his research procedure is still somewhat exploratory or dependent on the measures of others. In contrast, Jane Loevinger's measure of ego development is well established but her theoretical underpinnings remain elusive. We will now turn to Loevinger's work.

JANE LOEVINGER'S THEORY

Jane Loevinger presents ego development "as the master trait in personality, as the frame that provides more specific traits with their meaning and around which the whole edifice of personality is constructed." Personalities are structures. "That human beings, developing, go through an ordered sequence of such structures is the premise" of Loevinger's theory of ego development (Blasi, 1976, pp. 41, 45).

This development is characterized by qualitative changes in complexity as the developing ego passes through an invariant hierarchical sequence of structural stages and integrates various "strands" of personality development (e.g., cognitive, social, moral). The essence of ego development, states Loevinger, "is the search for coherent meanings in experience" (Loevinger & Wessler, 1970, p. 8). Ego development, to Loevinger, represents a development of a central unity of ego "functions." It also represents the development of "structures" in the cognitive-developmental sense of "an inner logic to the stages and their progression" (1976, p. 11). Thus her model can be understood as a member of the structural family of developmental theories, but not purely so since her theory also includes elements that we have suggested characterize functional phase approaches. These elements will become more clear as we summarize and critique her work. An outline description of Loevinger's ego stages is presented in Table 8.6.

In the *presocial stage* (I–0), the child lives in an egocentric world where the self is not distinguished from the nonself. "The baby at birth cannot be said to have an ego. His first task is to learn to differentiate himself from his surroundings." The child who remains at this stage "long past its appropriate time is referred to as autistic" (1976, p. 15). The *symbiotic stage* (I–1) differentiates the self-mother unit from the external world and the beginning of the differentiation of self from mother. The *impulsive stage* (I–2) shows a basic awareness of the external world, but a simplicity of cognition is manifested in stereotyping, preoccupation with bodily feelings, and impulsivity. "The child's own impulses help him to affirm his separate identity. The emphatic 'no!' and the later 'Do it by self' are evidences." Older children at this stage tend to characterize their emotions in limited terms such as "mad, upset, sick, high, turned on, and hot" (1976, p. 16). Adults tend to characterize a child who remains at this stage too long as being incorrigible or uncontrollable. The *self-protective* stage (Delta) contains "the first step towards self-control of impulses...taken when the child learns to anticipate immediate, short-term rewards and punishments.... The child at this stage understands that there are rules.... His main rule is, however, 'Don't get caught.'" Older children and adults functioning at this stage tend to be "opportunistic, deceptive, and preoccupied with control and advantage in (their) relations with other people." (1976, p. 17). In the *conformist stage* (I–3), the child internalizes social standards. "The child starts to identify his own welfare with that of the group, usually his family for the small child and the peer group for an older child" (1976, p. 17). The person at this stage tries to belong and help; to be nice, acceptable; and worries about appearance and behavior. Morality is expressed as guilt for breaking rules, which are understood in a singular manner. Responses to questions are characterized by "concreteness, externality, and cliché-like quality" (Loevinger, 1978a, p. 14). A person in transition following the conformist stage (I–3/4), capable of seeing multiple possibilities and alternatives, recognizes individual differences that do not meet conformist standards and stereotypes. This recognition marks the onset of individualized standards and an increased genuine interest in people and relationships.

TABLE 8.6

Loevinger's Stages of Ego Development

Stage	Code	Impulse Control, Character Development	Interpersonal Style	Conscious Preoccupations	Cognitive Style
Presocial Symbiotic	I-1		Autistic Symbiotic	Self vs. non-self	
Impulsive	I-2	Impulsive, fear of retaliation	Receiving, dependent, exploitative	Bodily feelings, especially sexual and aggressive	Stereotyping, conceptual confusion
Self-Protective	Δ	Fear of being caught, externalizing blame, opportunistic	Wary, manipulative, exploitative	Self-protection, trouble, wishes, things, advantage, control	
Conformist	I-3	Conformity to external rules, shame, guilt for breaking rules	Belonging, superficial niceness	Appearance, social acceptability, banal feelings, behavior	Conceptual simplicity, stereotypes, cliches
Conscientious-Conformist	I-3/4	Differentiation of norms, goals	Aware of self in relation to group, helping	Adjustment, problems, reasons, opportunities (vague)	Multiplicity
Conscientious	I-4	Self-evaluated standards, self-criticism, guilt for consequences, long-term goals and ideals	Intensive, responsible, mutual, concern for communication	Differentiated feelings, motives for behavior, self-respect, achievements, traits, expression	Conceptual complexity, idea of patterning
Individualistic	I-4/5	*Add:* Respect for individuality	*Add:* Dependence as an emotional problem	*Add:* Development, social problems, differentiation of inner life from outer	*Add:* Distinction of process and outcome

Autonomous	I-5	*Add:* Coping with conflicting inner needs, toleration	*Add:* Respect for autonomy, interdependence	Vividly conveyed feelings, integration of physiological and psychological, psychological causation of behavior, role conception, self-fulfillment, self in social context *Add:* Indentity	Increased conceptual complexity, complex patterns, toleration for ambiguity, broad scope, objectivity
Integrated	I-6	*Add:* Reconciling inner conflicts, renunciation of unattainable	*Add:* Cherishing of individuality		

Note: "*Add*" means in addition to the description applying to the previous level.

Source: Loevinger, 1976, pp. 24–25.

Subsequent stages are not found during childhood, but they are relevant for the children's teachers. At Stage 4, *conscientious*, the shift is complete and "there is a sense of behavior having patterns, hence of people having traits" such as outspokenness. There is the realization of people "being rather than doing something" (Loevinger, 1978a, p. 14). A typical conscientious teacher may also feel obligated to prevent a student from making errors. The person in the I–4/5 transition, called the *individualistic* stage, develops a concern for emotional independence and a sense of respect for the individuality of others and one's self. "Where the conscientious person has an understanding of individual differences in traits, the person at this level is concerned about tolerance" (Loevinger, 1978a, p. 19). The last stage that has clear empirical support is the *autonomous* (I–5). Here the person has a new ability to acknowledge and cope with inner conflict in a way that contributes to self-fulfillment—a major goal of this stage. Here we also see a heightened respect for the autonomy of others and a freeing of the self from the "oppressive demands of the conscience in the previous stage" (Loevinger, 1976, p. 23). In contrast to the conscientious teacher, for instance, the autonomous one recognizes a student's need to learn from his or her own mistakes if he or she is to develop and achieve self-understanding.

In sum, then, Loevinger is charting ego development from *pre-conformist* (self-interest, fear, impulsivity, stereotyping, exploitation, and anticipation) to *conformist* (genuine interest in others, awareness of social standards, awareness of self in relation to others, helpfulness, multiplicity, mutuality) to *post-conformist* stages (which add intrapsychic insight to coping, creative resolution of conflicts, respect for autonomy, inter-dependence, conceptual complexity, and integration of identity). This model is applicable to all ages—children, adolescents, adults—although her research has focused on development during adulthood. The research instrument used to measure her conception of ego development is a sentence completion test consisting of thirty-six incomplete sentence stems; there are different versions for adults and children, males and females. Subjects are simply directed to "Complete the following sentences." Typical sentence stems include, "When I am nervous, I . . . ," "A woman's body . . . ," and "Education. . . ." With the use of a scoring manual, the responses to those stems are rated for level of ego development. Examples of responses to the "Education . . ." stem are summarized in Table 8.7.

Loevinger's sentence completion test has been shown to have an acceptable degree of reliability and construct validity (Hauser, 1976; Loevinger, 1979). Interjudge agreement of raters, test-retest correlations of total protocol ratings, and split-half reliability are all quite admirable. Furthermore, although Loevinger has not claimed that her model and method have universal or cross-cultural validity, we suggest that it probably has in light of the support received from research in Cuaracao, Israel, Germany, French-speaking Quebec, and Japan (Kusatsu, 1978; Lasker et al., 1974a, 1974b; Lasker, 1977; Limoges, 1978; Snarey, 1982; Snarey & Blasi, 1980; Vetter, 1978).

TABLE 8.7

Stage-Related Responses to the "Education..." Sentence Stem

Ego Stages	"Education..." Sentence Stem Completions*
I-2 Impulsive	...is fun; is no fun; is hard ...is good for you ...helps you learn; helps in school
Delta Self-protective	...is good, nice, fine; is good to have ...is good for getting a job ...is boring; is for the birds; is not good ...is needed but I don't like it
I-3 Conformist	...is important, important nowadays, in the world today ...is necessary, good for everyone, for special groups ...is essential, something everyone should have ...is wonderful, desirable, great
I-3/4 Conscientious/conformist	...is an important part of life; is necessary for success ...is worthwhile; is worth it; an asset; is a goal ...can't be taken away ...everyone should have as much as possible
I-4 Conscientious	...is important for social goals ...should be improved ...is more than book learning; gained in different ways ...should be available to all; an opportunity ...is satisfying, stimulating, enriching ...leads to growth, improvement, prepares one for life ...is a way of solving problems; opens doors ...is not an end in itself; is not enough
I-4/5 Individualistic	...should never end; continues throughout life ...is essential for a full life; for enjoyment of life ...is not always what it seems to be
I-5 Autonomous	...is intrinsically valuable, admirable ...is important socially and in individual lives ...helps you cope with life (original, elaborated) ...leads to self-fulfillment, self-understanding, new values

*These are summaries only.
Source: Adapted from Loevinger, Wessler, and Redmore, 1970, Vol. II, pp. 97–107.

To understand Loevinger's stages, it is important to grasp how her approach differs from psychoanalytic approaches as well as from more uniformly structural approaches, such as those of Kegan and Kohlberg. Loevinger makes it clear that her conception of ego development, both as a sequence of character development and as a dimension of individual differences, differs from the psychoanalytic conception where the term ego development is usually restricted to the birth of the ego in the early years and is understood to refer to a collection of functions and skills (cf. Bellak et al., 1973; Haan, Stroud, & Holstein, 1973). Stuart Hauser, in a review of Loevinger's work, summarizes the difference as follows:

> In psychoanalytic theory, the orientation is often toward…the conception of ego…in terms of it as a collection, an "inventory" of related processes whose overall function is "task solving" or "attempted solution" as contrasted with instinctual expression. In this framwork, ego development refers either to the development of multiple processes, cognitive functions, defenses, and interpersonal skills or to early infancy when ego processes are thought to emerge…. We see a striking shift of meaning when we turn to Loevinger's description of ego development…. Loevinger's approach is best characterized as one which takes account of the individual's integrative processes and overall frame of reference. Her conception of ego development assumes that each is a continuum of development along which these frames can be analyzed. (1976, p. 928)

Loevinger herself states that "there are at least four meanings given to ego development in psychoanalysis, of which only one, Erikson's chronicle of psychosocial development, is at all compatable with its use in this book" (1976, p. 4). Loevinger's model differs from Erikson's, however, in that her schema is a model of individual differences within age cohorts while Erikson's is not. Loevinger assumes that the ego is a unitary system of functions; Erikson does not necessarily assume this unity.

We will further compare views of Loevinger's ego stages with what we would understand as a more consistent structural approach. We will begin with an examination of their shared assumptions, the most basic of which is the concept of *ego*. Both Loevinger and our structural perspective agree that there is a relative unity to personality—the ego—that reasons, judges, evaluates, and generally functions to make sense of the world. Second, both accept the applicability of Piaget's hierarchical stage model to the characterization of ego development. These stages form: (a) an invariant sequence of (b) hierarchical transformations, which are (c) structured wholes. In addition, both accept the idea that moral judgment and character are major aspects or dimensions of ego development, relating to a more general ego stage. A third area of agreement between Loevinger and our structural perspective concerns test construction and test scoring. Both Loevinger, who comes from a psychometric background, and structuralists, who have been governed by Piagetian assumptions, move away from traditional psychometric procedures and construct tests that attempt to tap underlying structures. Loevinger is consistent with structuralism in that she agrees that the test constructor finds developmental structures, not by the inductive method, but by an "abductive" method, a sort of mutual bootstrapping that involves a working back and forth between theoretical reflections and the responses subjects actually give.

Fourth and finally, there are striking conceptual parallels in the stage descriptions that emerge from a comparison of Loevinger's and other stage descriptions, such as Kohlberg's (Erickson, 1977c). This parallelism is empirically supported, even when researchers control for age and IQ. A study that presents one of the first major comparisons of Loevinger's theory of ego development and Kohlberg's theory of moral development is that of Howard Lambert (1972). His 107 subjects ranged in age from 11 to 60 and included both men and women. The results of a cross-tabulation of his data on ego stages and moral stages yielded an overall correlation coefficient of .80 which decreased to .60 when controlled for age. Lambert discussed his findings as follows:

> A striking aspect [of this contingency table analysis] is the extent of correspondence between the Loevinger pure stages. If we temporarily disregard the five subjects who received scores of delta on the Loevinger Sentence Completion Test and stage 1 on the Kohlberg Moral Development Test, there are clear parallels between the two series of stages. They are: ego stage 2 with moral stage 2; ego stage delta with moral stage 3; 3 with 4, 4 with 5; and 5 with 6. Some of these pairings would be predicted from the general theories (e.g., I–4 with M–5) and others would not (e.g., I–Delta with M–3). (1972, pp. 48–49)

The Lambert effect was true for both men and women in his sample and provides general empirical support for our theoretical position that moral development is necessary but not sufficient for the parallel level of ego functioning in that an individual's moral development score was generally the same as or higher than his ego development score. Lambert's research must be interpreted cautiously, however, since there have been significant changes and refinements in Kohlberg's scoring since his research was completed. There have been three recent studies, however, that have made use of the revised moral development scoring manual.

In the first one, Kohlberg's 20-year longitudinal study of moral development, the male subjects completed Loevinger's ego development test during the last three interview times in addition to Kohlberg's measure. Although these data are still being analyzed, it has been found that moral and ego development scores are significantly correlated and that the stage of moral development is generally the same or more advanced than that of ego development, for example, moral Stage 5 (M–5) predicts ego Stage 5 or 4 (I–5 or I–4), M–4 predicts I–4 or I–3 (Kohlberg, 1981). In the second one, a cross-sectional cross-cultural study of the moral and ego development of 60 kibbutz founders, equally divided between men and women, John Snarey found that the moral and ego stages were significantly correlated (1981). In sum, he found that 48 percent received the exact same score on both measures; 38.5 percent received a moral score one-half or one full stage higher than their ego score; and only 3.5 percent registered a full stage higher in ego development than moral development. Thus, 86.5 percent of the cases fitted the hypothesized pattern of décalage and of those that deviated, only 3.5 percent did so by a full stage, a finding that can be attributed to scoring error. A third study by Lois Erickson, however, appears to suggest a different relationship between ego and moral development stages. She conducted a 5-year longitudinal study of moral and ego development among 23 females (aged 15 at time one) and found that the ego development scores were one-half to one full stage higher than the moral development scores for 76 percent of the subjects at time one and for 81 percent of them at time five. In the remaining cases, moral and ego stages were identical (1977a, 1977b, 1980). Erickson's findings could be interpreted as suggesting that our hypothesis of the décalage relationship between moral and ego development is reversed for women or that while Kohlberg's measure, originally based on an all-male sample, is biased toward men, Loevinger's measure, orginally based on an all-female sample, is biased toward women. This interpretation is possible but, unlike the Erickson study, the Lambert and Snarey studies included both men and women in their samples and no sex differences were found. Another possible interpretation for the difference between Erickson's findings and those of the other three studies may be due to the unconventional methodology used in her study. Erickson's subjects completed both tests in written form, either in a group setting or individually through the mail. While Loevinger's test was designed to be completed in writing, Kohlberg's test was specifically designed for use as an oral interview where individuals would be probed for their best reasons "why" they prefer a particular moral choice. Written interviews, where of course no probing is possible, have proven to be less reliable. In a longitudinal intervention study or in a study that addresses the relationship between moral development and another domain, the written interview is particularly inadequate. This methodological critique is supported by an examination of the Erickson data which revealed that the responses to the moral interview questions were quite brief. On the other hand, a possible response to our critique might be that Erickson's subjects were all ages 15 to 19 while the other studies included adults. Thus there may be something unique about the relationship between moral and ego development during adolescence. Lambert's study, which also included adolescents, would not support this interpretation but, as we have indicated, his data ideally should be rescored. In sum, then, the research tentatively supports the hypothesis that moral and ego development are empirically, as well as theoretically, parallel and that moral development is generally necessary but not sufficient for the equivalent level of ego development. More research, of course, is needed, particularly since correlational studies do not conclusively define a causal relationship between moral and ego development.

Leaving the shared theoretical assumptions and the empirical parallels, we will now turn to divergences between the theories. To begin, Loevinger's orientation draws from neopsychoanalytic conceptions of the ego, even though she has consciously departed from her initial psychoanalytic moorings and from a Piagetian conception of hierarchical stages (cf. 1976, pp. 314–395; 1978a, pp. 25–55). In contradistinction, Kohlberg's, Selman's, and Kegan's orientation is not to psychodynamic theory, but only to the cognitive-developmental theories of

Piaget (1932) and of the American forerunners of Piaget (Baldwin, 1902; Dewey, 1908; Mead, 1934). This difference in theoretical orientation leads to at least four differences in the nature of the development that Loevinger and structuralists seek to define and measure.

First, there are differences of how to articulate the inner logic of ego stages. Loevinger defines her stages partly in terms of structures, but also partly in terms of *functions and motives* pertaining to self-enhancement and defense. The self-protective stage, for instance, is characterized primarily by an interpersonal style that functions to defend the self and less by the structures that that stage uses to make sense of the world. Thus Loevinger has been criticized for a lack of an underlying logic guiding her developmental sequence (Broughton & Zahaykevich, 1977; Habermas, 1975). What makes a higher stage better? What is the structure underlying each stage? Piaget, Kegan, Kohlberg, and other structuralists have defined stages solely in terms of cognitive structures or ways of thinking in contrast to Loevinger who has not spelled out the theoretical inner structural logic of each stage or the logic of the sequence from one stage to the next. Both Kegan and Loevinger have an "impulsive" stage, for instance, but Kegan defines it structurally as a way of the self "cognizing" or making meaning, while Loevinger presents it as an ideal-type characterlogical portrait. Such an ideal-type characterization, following Max Weber's (1949) conception of the term, is a profile of traits that have some logic for cohering or going together and which are described by appeal to a "pure" or extreme case. Specific cases are seldom found to fit such pure or extreme case descriptions, but they form the conceptual anchor for concrete description and classification. Piagetian stages, in contrast, do not lend themselves to ideal-type character portrayals. The stage of concrete operations, for instance, is not characterized by a typological characterization of an adult character fixated at the concrete operational level, or by a portrait of a typical child at that stage.

Second, there are differences in dividing the domain of ego development. Loevinger posits an indivisible ego simultaneously engaged in what she calls impulse control, interpersonal style, conscious preoccupations, and cognitive functioning. From Loevinger's point of view, there is no need to divide the ego domain. From our perspective, the unitary ego includes subdomains, each possessed of a distinct structure and each capable of empirical separation. Whereas Loevinger seeks to capture within her stages the interpenetration of cognitive style, self-concerns, and moral character, we consider these to be governed by separate substructures within the inclusive ego. Our approach accounts for the research findings previously reviewed regarding the décalage relationship between sub-domains while Loevinger's approach cannot do so. What Loevinger calls the "cognitive style" facet of ego development for us points to the subdomain defined by Piaget's stages of cognitive or logical operations. "Interpersonal style and self-concerns" indicates for us the subdomain studied by Selman in his attempt to delineate stages of social cognition; "impulse control and character," the domain of structure called moral judgment. In sum, this difference has led Loevinger to hypothesize an ego system of which subdomains are actually artificial distinctions or indistinguishable, while it has led us to hypothesize a necessary-but-insufficient relationship between subdomains within a more holistic underlying, unifying ego.

Third, building on the first two differences, there are contrasts between what Loevinger and other structuralists are trying to measure. Although her test has been used for educational and experimental change studies, this was not her goal in constructing the test. Kohlberg, on the other hand, wanted to construct a test that would not only assess the current stage of moral functioning but would also reflect his concern with educational goals and his belief that a higher stage is a better stage. This normative concern has led Kohlberg to rely on philosophical as well as psychological theory in defining what is being studied and to give a philosophical theory in defining what is being studied and to give a philosophical rationale for why a higher stage is a better stage. This philosophical conception of moral judgment is based on principles of justice and is dependent on the theories of Kant and Rawls. Loevinger has not attempted a similar normative justification as to why a higher ego stage is a better stage, or why ego development might be an aim of education. She makes no claim that a higher ego stage is a more healthy stage. Nevertheless, in secondary school educational and guidance practice, attainment of a higher Loevinger stage has been taken as an aim—as a mark of success of programs of "deliberate psychological education" (Miller, 1977). This educational use suggests that, even if Loevinger is reluctant to acknowledge it, there may actually be norms or standards defining the sense in which a higher Loevinger ego stage is a better stage. The underlying norm is the norm of psychology itself, that is, the norm of *adequacy* of the implicit psychological theory used by individuals. Behind the perceptions of self and of others by an individual at Loevinger's self-protective stage (Delta) is an implicit psychological theory. If this theory were formalized it would sound something like Skinner's theory of operant learning. It would say that behavior is instrumentally motivated to get rewards or payoffs and that ordinarily each individual is oriented to his own set of payoffs. The theory of operant learning is, of course, much more complex and sophisticated but, like Skinner's theory, the psychology of the self-protective stage must reduce shared sociomoral interests to individual instrumental interests. Loevinger's next I-3 conformist stage, while naive in its stereotyping, is a more adequate psychological theory than the self-protective's psychology because it postulates trust and socially altruistic motives as given in explaining social behavior. By the standards of adequacy of psychology, rather than of moral philosophy, then, one might claim that a higher Loevinger stage is a better stage.

The fourth and final area of disagreement is that Loevinger diverges from a structural approach to test scoring. Briefly: (a) Loevinger does not clearly differentiate between content and structure; (b) Loevinger constructs and scores test items so as to be able to infer to a hypothetical entity, a kind of underlying structure akin to the psychoanalytic ego, rather than to the ego's structure, form, or quality; (c) Loevinger makes use of a psychometric "sign approach," one that combines empirical probabilities with theoretical considerations in a process she calls "saving circularity." Piagetian structuralists have rejected the sign approach and have required each item in a scoring manual to reflect clearly the structure of the stage to which it is keyed. Loevinger's scoring manual, in contrast, does not include interpretive statements that explicate the structure of manual items, tying them to the overall structure of the stages they represent. A comparison of an item in Loevinger's scoring manual (Delta stage) with the parallel level from Kohlberg's scoring manual (Stage 2) illustrates this contrast. (Compare Table 8.8 and Table 8.9.) For instance, with reference to the sentence stem, "My conscience bothers me if...," the response "...I steal" is classified as a self-protective Delta stage response. The Loevinger manual notes that stealing is a more concrete content of moral valuing than lying or cheating. But, in our terms, it is clearly content, a statement of what *is* wrong or right, not a direct expression of structure or form of reasoning about *why* something is wrong or right. The response "...I steal" has no clear face validity as reflecting a self-protective stage. Loevinger has placed it as an example of the self-protective stage based on statistical item analysis that indicated it is associated with the clinical assignment of the total protocol to that stage. Clinical inference of that stem alone, however, could just as easily place it at the conformist stage. Because Loevinger sees her test items as signs that are probabilistic indicators of an underlying personality organization, she sees little need to distinguish clearly between content and structure or for her stage definitions or scoring categories to be structurally defined.

Loevinger, of course, does see the ideal approach as one that is both empirically verifiable and logically satisfying but, since she also sees empirical data as the only court of last resort, she has focused on it almost exclusively. Her approach has been a tradeoff between significant empirical gains and obvious philosophical shortcomings. In contrast, a more consistent structural approach attempts to focus on a method that "unites philosophic and psychological considerations" by "being based on the psychological and sociological facts" of development and by "being based on a philosophically defensible concept" of development (Kohlberg, 1971, p. 25). In sum, in terms of the three types of approaches to ego development with which we began, Loevinger's work is a quasi-structural model that can be understood as located on a continuum between a structural stage and a functional phase approach. We will now consider a clearer example of a functional approach to ego development—Erik Erikson's theory of psychosocial development.

ERIK ERIKSON'S THEORY

Erik Erikson is perhaps the most important psychological heir of Sigmund Freud and Anna Freud, his mentor and analyst, respectively. His epigenetic theory of human development, to a considerable extent, derives age-typical contents of concern from Freudian psychosexual age-periods, which are defined by the biological-maturational activation of a new organ or locus of pleasure (oral, anal,

TABLE 8.8

Example of an Item from Ego Development Scoring Manual

Delta

Characteristic Delta reactions displayed on this item are callousness ("I let it") and willful demanding ("always do what I want to do"). "I have to lie to someone who trusts me" displays also denial of responsibility for one's actions. "I can't have my own way" is illogical as an answer but clear as an expression of willfulness. Answers based on not succeeding or on being talked about indicate a lack of conscience almost as clearly as saying one does not have one. The one category here that names transgression of a rule refers to stealing; one may surmise that it is the concrete character of this transgression that impresses it on people earlier in development than lying or cheating.

My Conscience Bothers Me If—

1. —I steal
    If I take his money
    I take something that is not mine
2. —I don't have a conscience; my conscience never bothers me
    none

    it doesn't
    I don't have any bothers
    always do what I want to
3. —I let it
    I realize it
4. —I am being talked about, suspected
    my mother is suspicious of what I have been doing
    I feel that someone is watching me
5. —I happen, have to lie, cheat, etc. (I–3, 1)
    I have to lie to someone who trusts me
    I happen to lie about something
    I am forced into a white lie
6. —I don't succeed in what I want to do (I–3, 13; I–3/4, 14)
    I can't have my own way
    I'm unconsiderate & don't succeed in making a fool out of Jan
    do something stupid
Unclassified
    I waste precious time taking tests like this

Source: Loevinger, Wessler, Redmore, 1970, pp. 432–433.

phallic, genital). Erikson's model was presented in his first book, *Childhood and Society* (1950a), which combined the methods of psychoanalysis and social anthropology. In the years following this pioneer work, he has elaborated on each

TABLE 8.9
Example of Moral Judgment Scoring Manual Item

Criterion Judgment # 7	
Dilemma: IV, Mercy Killing	Stage and Substage: 2A
Issue: Law Norm: Law	Element: Seeking reward (avoiding punishment)

Criterion Judgment

[The doctor should not give the woman the drug because he would risk losing his job or going to jail.] . . .

Stage Structure

Not killing the woman is justified because it involves a risk (rather than certainty) of punishment. Punishment is seen as something to be instrumentally avoided. The risk of punishment overrides the recognition of the pragmatic reasonableness from the woman's point of view of giving her the drug.

Critical Indicators

One of the following must be used as the central justification for not killing the woman: (a) punishment as possible or probable, a risk to be weighed in the decision; or (b) other possible disadvantageous consequences to the doctor (he might lose his job, etc.)

Distinctions—Other Stages

This Stage 2 treatment of sanctions as a factor to be included among one's pragmatic or instrumental considerations should be distinguished from the Stage 1 view of sanction as automatically defining the wrongness of an act (Criterion Judgment 2) and from the Stage 1/2 focus on the *likelihood* of punishment as a reason not to mercy kill. In Stage 1/2 judgments, it is ambiguous as to whether punishment automatically defines the act as wrong or whether it is seen as a pragmatic consideration. At Stage 2, the pragmatic quality of the concern is clear.

Do not score as matches the statements that it is unfair of the woman to expect the doctor to risk punishment, that the doctor is not *obligated* to kill her if he will be risking punishment or loss of license, that he has the right to consider consequences to himself, or that he should not do it if it will mean loss of the right to practice medicine, destruction of his career, etc. (Criterion Judgment 22, Stage 4)

Match Examples

1. *Should the doctor give her the drug that would make her die? Why?*
   No, the doctor could be charged with killing her. He should give something to calm her. [*Why?*] He would lose his career and go to prison. He should protect himself first and not kill her.
2. *Should the doctor give her the drug that would make her die? Why?*
   No. He would be blamed for killing her. She could take her own overdose. If he did, he could lose his license and be out of a job.

TABLE 8.9—Continued

3. Oh, well by, like I said before, there might be another patient and he'll do it, and society will be pretty mad at him and stuff, and he'll lose all his patients and stuff.
4. Like on one side, you'd have to think about, she'd be suffering and in pain a lot and stuff, you know and if he didn't give it to her, she'd really be groaning a lot and (inaudible) stuff. And if he did give it to her, that he'd lose his job and stuff. He might get the death sentence or lose a lot of people as his customers and his reputation.

Source: Colby et al., 1979, pp. 90–91.

of the eight phases in his theory of ego development (1950b, 1956, 1959, 1961a, 1965, 1968a, 1968b, 1969, 1970a, 1970b, 1974a, 1974b, 1975, 1977, 1980).

The focus of each phase in Erikson's model is on the maturing person as the person experiences new sociocultural spheres and roles. The child's self, competence, and position in the world is constantly changing. During each new phase the ego must reestablish itself. Erikson characterizes these changes around a sequence of psychosocial changes in ego strength and integrated identity. As he states:

> The sense of ego identity...is the accrued confidence that one's ability to maintain inner sameness and continuity...is matched by the sameness and continuity of one's meaning for others. Thus, self-esteem, confirmed at the end of each major crisis, grows to be a conviction that one is learning effective steps toward a tangible future, that one is developing a defined personality with a social reality that one understands. The growing child must, at every step, derive a vitalizing sense of reality from the awareness that his individual way of mastering experience is a successful variant of the way other people around him master experience and recognize such mastery. (1956, p. 89)

These changes are defined as age-specific "crises" involving particular tasks or concerns in psychosocial development. Each crisis represents the intersection of psychomotor, cognitive, psychosexual, and interpersonal development, which intersect at a given age to challenge the self with a particular task in its interaction with its environment. These developmental tasks with which the self is sequentially preoccupied are biologically embedded in the life cycle and in the society's role expectations that evolution has synchronized with human maturation. According to Erikson's epigenetic principle, however, each task is also present throughout the entire life cycle; "earlier stages are not replaced, but...are absorbed into a hierarchic system of increasing differentiation" (1974, p. 206). That is, each of the eight concerns is present throughout the entire life cycle, but each concern intensifies to a crisis level in an ordered sequence. Thus, ego identity is a constant activity during each phase, even though it is not until adolescence that it becomes an overwhelming preoccupation. The achievement of a "favorable ratio" or successful resolution of each phase's developmental crisis also results in a unique psychosocial virtue or ego strength. Table 8.10 summarizes Erikson's ego develop-ment "stages," the term he generally uses to refer to segments of the life cycle. The ego strength for each phase, to use our term, is indicated in parentheses.

Erikson relates identity formation during the first year of life, which is parallel to Freud's oral period, to the infant's psychosocial task of developing a favorable ratio of basic *trust over mistrust*.

> The infant's first social achievement, then, is his willingness to let the mother out of sight without undue anxiety or rage, because she has become an inner certainty as well as an outer predictability. Such consistency, continuity, and sameness of experience provide a rudimentary sense of ego identity. . . . Mothers create a sense of trust in their children by that kind of administration which in its quality combines sensitive care of the baby's individual needs and a firm sense of personal trustworthiness with-in the trusted framework of their culture's life style. This forms the basis in the child for a sense of identity which will later combine a sense of being "all right," of being oneself, and of becoming what other people trust one will become." (1950, pp. 247, 249)

There is a parallelism here between the oral consumption question, "Will I be nursed again?," and the interpersonal question, "Will I trust again?" The successful resolution of this first ego crisis assures that *hope* will become a fundamental quality of all later phases in the life cycle. "Hope is the enduring belief in the attainability of fervent wishes, in spite of the dark urges and rages which mark the beginning of existence. Hope is the ontogenetic basis of faith, and is nourished by the adult faith which pervades patterns of care" (1964, p. 118).

Beginning around the second year of life, the toddler's cognitive differentiation of self and other as agents, his growing motor control, anal interests and parental toilet training, and cleanliness and order concerns all combine to focus on doing it by oneself by free choice—the crisis of *autonomy versus shame and doubt*.

> Firmness must protect [the child] against potential anarchy of his as yet untrained sense of discrimination, his inability to hold on and to let go with discretion. As his environment encourages him to "stand on his own feet," it must protect him against meaninglessness and arbitrary experiences of shame and of early doubt. (1950, p. 252)

The child's caretakers, Erikson suggests, must both encourage autonomy and protect the child from overwhelming defeat. The ego's achievement of a favorable ratio of autonomy over shame at this phase becomes decisive for the development of the ego strength that Erikson calls *willpower*. "Will. . .is the unbroken deter-mination to exercise free choice as well as self-restraint, in spite of the unavoidable experience of shame and doubt in infancy" (1964, p. 119).

The third phase in Erikson's scheme, *initiative versus guilt*, is parallel to the phallic and Oedipal sexuality of Freud's model. This phase is marked by an extension of concerns into related interpersonal modalities—qualities of "intru-

TABLE 8.10

Parallels between Ego Development Theories and Subdomains of Ego Development

	Ego Development			Epistemological Reasoning		
				Natural Environment Piaget	Social Environment Selman	Social & Ultimate Perry
	Erikson	Loevinger	Kegan			
Infancy (0–2)*	1. Trust vs. Mistrust (Hope) 2. Autonomy vs. Doubt (Will)	0. Presocial, Autistic	0. Incorporative	0. Sensori-motor		
Early Childhood (2–6)	3. Initiative vs. Guilt (Purpose)	1. Symbiotic	1. Impulsive	1. Preoperational	0. Egocentric	
Middle Childhood (6–9)	4. Industry vs. Inferiority (Competence)	2. Impulsive	2. Imperial	2. Concrete Operations Substage A	1. Subjective Perspective	1. Simple Dualism
Late Childhood (8–12)		Δ Delta or Self-Protective		Concrete Operations Substage B	2. Self-Reflective Perspective	2. Dualism
Early Adolescence (11–)	5. Identity versus Identity Confusion (Fidelity)	3. Conformist	3. Inter-personal	3. Formal Operations Substage A	3. Mutual Perspective-Taking	3. Subordinate Multiplicity
Later Adolescence (15–)		4. Conscientious	4. Institutional	Formal Operations Substage B	4. Systems Perspective-Taking	4. Multiplicity 5. Relativism
Early Adulthood (21–)	6. Intimacy versus Isolation (Love)	5. Autonomous	5. Inter-individual	Formal Operations Substage C	5. Symbolic Interaction Perspective	6. Commitment Foreseen
Middle Adulthood (31–)	7. Generativity vs. Self-Absorption (Care)	6. Integrated				7. Initial Commitment
Maturity (51–)	8. Integrity vs. Despair (Wisdom)					8–9. Developing Commitments

*Note: The suggested age ranges represent only average expectations in the United States.

Moral Reasoning			Metaphysical Reasoning	
Natural Environment Snarey	Social Environment Kohlberg	Ultimate Environment Oser	Natural & Social Broughton	Ultimate Environment Fowler
0. Amoral Protoplasmic	0. Amoral Egocentrism		0. Undifferentiated	0. Primal
1. Animal Attraction and Avoidance	1. Obedience-Punishment	1. Complete Determinism	1. Objective	1. Intuitive-Projective
2. Natural Reciprocity	2. Hedonism, Concrete Reciprocity	2. Instrumental Reciprocity with Deity	2. Individual	2. Mythic-Literal
3. Animal Lover or Friend of Animals	3. Interpersonal Accord, Conformity	3. Voluntarism	3. Divided	3. Conventional
4. The Natural System, Ecological Perspective	4. Social Accord & System Maintenance	4. Divine Plan	4. Dualist	4. Individuating and Reflexive
5. Animal Rights	5. Social Contract	5. Inter-subjectivity, God as Liberator	5. Subjective	
			6. Rational	5. Paradoxical-Consolidative
6. Universal Oneness with Nature	6. Universal Ethical Principles	6. Universal Communion	7. Dialectical Materialist	6. Universalizing

sion into" and "making" others. Erikson's phase of "initiative" is characterized by the child's increased curiosity and ability to explore his world physically and intellectually (running fast, riding a tricycle, game activities, play, questions about how things work or are made). During this phase, according to Erikson,

> [The child] is in free possession of a surplus of energy which permits him to forget failures quickly and to approach what seems desirable (even if it also seems uncertain and even dangerous) with undiminished and more accurate direction. Initiative adds to autonomy the quality of undertaking, planning and attacking a task for the sake of being active and on the move.... The danger of this stage is a sense of guilt over the goals contemplated and the acts initiated in one's exuberant enjoyment of new locomotor and mental power: acts of aggressive manipulation and coercion which soon go far beyond the executive capacity of organism and mind. (1955, p. 255)

If the child completes this phase with a sense of initiative outweighing his sense of guilt, *purpose* will be an enduring ego strength. Purposefulness, limited but not inhibited by guilt, "is the courage to envisage and pursue valued goals uninhibited by the defeat of infantile fantasies, by guilt and by the foiling fear of punishment" (1964, p. 122).

The elementary grade child is generally in the fourth phase of Erikson's model, *industry versus inferiority*. Whereas in the previous phase, the child enjoyed the process of play, he or she now becomes occupied with the end product of the process. A sense of *competence* develops as the child earns social recognition for making things. An unfavorable ratio of inferiority and inadequacy results, however, to the extent that the child perceives itself as not measuring up to expected standards or if her efforts are not recognized or are deprecated. This phase parallels the Freudian latency period that precedes puberty, "a period of delay which permits the future mate and parent first to 'go to school' (i.e., to undergo whatever schooling is provided for in his technology) and to learn the technical and social rudiments of a work situation" (1956, p. 111). There is, thus, a functional synchronization between the child's readiness to work and to learn and the beginning of the schooling period in the culture's socialization process.

Adolescence brings a conclusion to the way of thinking known during childhood and brings a responsibility to begin preparing career roles that will not be known fully until adulthood. The synchronization of qualitative changes in cognitive structures and quantitative changes in social status thrust upon the individual a need to achieve identity. Erikson describes this fifth phase, *identity formation versus identity confusion*, as follows:

> The growing and developing youths, faced with [a] physiological revolution within them and with tangible adult tasks ahead of them, are now primarily concerned with what they appear to be in the eyes of others as compared with what they feel they are.... In their search for a new sense of continuity and sameness, adolescents have to refight many of the battles of earlier years.... The integration now taking place in the form of ego identity is...[however] more than the sum of the childhood

identifications. It is the accrued experience of the ego's ability to integrate all identifications with the vicissitudes of the libido, with the aptitudes developed out of endowment, and with the opportunities offered in social roles. The sense of ego identity, then, is the accrued confidence that the inner sameness and continuity prepared in the past are matched by the sameness and continuity of one's meaning for others, as evidenced in the tangible promise of a "career." (Erikson, 1950, pp. 261–262)

This process of forming an adult identity often takes the form of a political, religious, or moral ideological search after an inner coherence based on a durable set of values (Erikson, 1959). The failure of such an attempt to restructure or integrate "previous identifications in light of an anticipated future" will result in role confusion rather than identity formation (1969, p. 36). This confusion is particularly evident in the areas of love and work, that is, doubt about one's sexual and occupational roles. If the adolescent is able to maintain a sense of ego identity and inner coherence behind his various roles, however, the ego strength of *fidelity* emerges. The quality of fidelity refers to "the ability to sustain loyalties freely pledged in spite of the inevitable contradictions of value systems." Receiving "inspiration from confirming ideologies and affirming companions," fidelity involves the courage to make adult commitments in spite of a relativistic and contradictory world (Erikson, 1964, p. 125).

Erikson states clearly that, while adolescence is a time of overt concern with identity,

> ... identity *formation* neither begins nor ends with adolescence: it is a lifelong development largely unconscious to the individual and to his society. Its roots go back all the way to the first self-recognition: in the baby's earliest exchange of smiles there is something of a self-realization coupled with a mutual recognition. (Erikson, 1956, p. 114)

Critical to identity formation throughout the life cycle is the resolution of the particular polar tension that characterizes each phase—in early childhood there is the bipolar tension between self-other identification and the danger of autism, in later childhood there is the tension between work identification and identity foreclosure. Similarly, after adolescence, identity formation is at the heart of the early adulthood phase of intimacy, which we will now consider.

The sixth phase in Erikson's scheme, *intimacy fusion versus isolation*, is characterized by the psychosocial task of identity fusion. This requires "the capacity to commit [oneself] to concrete affiliations and partnerships and to develop the ethical strength to abide by such commitments, even though they may call for significant sacrifices and compromises" (Erikson, 1950, p. 263). The successful "ability to fuse your identity with somebody else's without fear that you're going to lose something yourself" gives rise to the ego strength of *love* (Evans, 1969, p. 48). Based on the prior achievement of personal identity, the structural ability to see the limits of a logic that can generate infinite possible relationships, society's need to survive through culturally defined roles of spouse and parent combine to contribute the new developmental crisis of intimacy—a special commitment made to one other, in spite of many possible others, and in preparation for the next phase of creating a new other.

The next ego development crisis, Erikson's seventh of full-adulthood, is that of *generativity versus self-absorption.* "Generativity is primarily the interest in establishing and guiding the next generation," whether they be one's own off-spring, students, mentees, or whomever" (Erikson, 1950, p. 267). Those unable to do this become self-absorbed while those who are able to be generative develop the ego strength of *care.* Care, according to Erikson, "is the widening concern for what has been generated by love, necessity, or accident; it overcomes the ambivalence adhering to irreversible obligation" (1964, p. 131). Obviously, the task of guiding the next generation with care is at the heart of effective teaching. On the other hand, schools should also provide support for the teacher's own developmental needs for generativity just as educators aim to support the school age child's striving for industry. When teachers fail to become generative, however, they begin to feel personal stagnation. Without interpersonal and institutional support, self-absorption may follow in which they may "begin to indulge them-selves as if they were their own...one and only child" (1950, p. 267).

Finally, as a person approaches old age, *integrity versus despair* becomes the major issue of ego development and retirement. For those who had been the generators of ideas and mentors of others' development, integrity will usually "ripen." Integrity is "a post-narcissistic love of the human ego...as an experience which conveys some world order and spiritual sense, no matter how dearly paid for. It is the acceptance of one's one and only life cycle as something that had to be and that, by necessity, permitted no substitutions." (1950, p. 268) On the other hand, "Despair expresses that feeling that time is now short, too short to attempt to start another life and to try out alternative roads to integrity" (1950, p. 269). The victory of integrity over despair gives rise to the ego strength of *wisdom,* "a detached concern with life itself, in the face of death itself" (1964, p. 133).

Erikson claims that his sequence is universal in the sense that "whether school is field or jungle or classroom...in all cultures," during the phase of industry versus inferiority, "children receive some systematic instruction" (1950, pp. 258–259):

> All cultures, therefore, meet this [fourth] stage with the offer of instruction in per-fectible skills leading to practical uses and durable achievements. All cultures ...have their logic and their "truths" which can be learned, by exercise, usage, and ritual. (1964, pp. 123–124)

Even though Erikson tends to present his theory as culturally and historically universal, we suggest that his theory is a functional phase approach that thus actually includes some of the characteristics of both universal structural stages and relative cultural ages. This dual nature is reflected, for instance, in the fact that he originally referred to his work as a "psychosexual" theory of ego psychology, latterly he consistently calls his contribution "psychosocial." His theory can also be classified as an intermediate functional model in that it slides over the distinctions between structure and content, competence and performance, self and society, and quality and quantity of development.

Let us first describe the cultural-age elements within Erikson's functional approach. Regarding the conscious versus unconscious distinction, for instance, his theory tends to describe the person as more or less conscious of his or her developmental phase. An adolescent in turmoil is more or less aware that he is in a time of identity crisis even though he is basically unconscious of the overall course of ego development, just as he does not know that he is also moving to the second substage of formal operations. The sources of these age-period elements in Erikson's model are in both psychoanalysis and cultural anthropology. Psychoanalytic research has been totally unable to establish empirically the universality of Freud's psychosexual periods, originally developed in Viennese society; it is very difficult even to apply them within North America (Friedan, 1962). On the other hand, cultural anthropology has been able to establish overwhelmingly the relativity of culturally defined periods of the life cycle. The price Erikson pays for his vague differentiations and cultural elements is that he is not able to verify empirically that his phases of the life cycle represent a universal invariant sequence. There are also certain benefits to his approach, however. One is that he illuminates developmental stress and anxiety. Because developmental tasks are basically conscious, the individuals are aware of discrepancies between the culturally ideal life cycle and where they see themselves in relation to it. In many cultures anxiety results over the perceived gap between the ideal and the real since individuals tend to feel that they are personally responsible for their inability to resolve the developmental task that is preoccupying them at that period in their life. Another benefit of Erikson's approach is that human development is not starkly abstracted from concrete life histories, that is, his analyses read like biographies. Erikson's emphasis on both the self and the society in which the self is embedded helps one not to lose sight of how each fulfills the other, that is, "the very processes of growth provide new energy even as a society offers new and specific opportunities according to its dominant conception of the phases of life." Thus, "it is the joint development of cognitive and emotional powers paired with appropriate social learning which enables the individual to realize the potentialities" of each phase of development (1968, p. 163; 1964, p. 225). Of course, as Erikson suggests, the ideal of coordinated interdependence and optimum mutual activation between cognition and culture within each developmental phase is never perfectly achieved. It follows that phases of ego functioning can be supported, fixated, or retarded as a result of sociocultural conditions.

Erikson's approach is also nonstructural or at least difficult to integrate with structural-developmental approaches in that he does not assume the ego originates only from autonomous motivation for competence and adaptation to the world. Rather he also retains aspects of the classical Freudian view that the ego originates from libidinal drives and eventually mediates between the id, the superego, and external reality (1950, pp. 142–143). Moral development for Erikson, at least in his early writings, is also not originally or primarily a function of ego development, as it is for Loevinger, but it is rather a superego function:

> The other inner institution recognized and designated by Freud is the "super-ego," a kind of automatic governor which limits the expression of the id by opposing to it the demands of conscience. Here, too, the emphasis was at first on the foreign burden imposed on the ego by its super-ego. For this superimposed, this superior ego was the (internalized) sum of all the restrictions to which the ego must bow. But conscience, too, contains traces of the cruel forces of suppression in human history—i.e., the threat of mutilation or isolation. In moments of self-reproach and depression the super-ego uses against the ego methods so archaic and so barbaric that they become analogous to those of the blindly impulsive id. (1950, p. 193)

For Erikson, ego phases develop out of the ego's efforts to cope with all the forces implied by the three agencies of id, superego, and ego. The id or the libido was thought by Freud to develop as an individual matures, and since his account is accepted by Erikson, an embryological model is appropriate.

> Embryology now understands epigenetic development, the step-by-step growth of the fetal organs. I think that the Freudian laws of psychosexual growth in infancy can best be understood through an analogy with physiological development *in utero*. In this sequence of development each organ has its time of orgin. This time factor is as important as the place of origin. If the eye, for example, does not arise at the appointed time, "it will never be able to express itself fully, since the moment for the rapid outgrowth of some other part will have arrived, and this will tend to dominate the less active region and suppress the belated tendency for eye expression." (Erikson, 1950, p. 65)

Just as periods of libido are embryological for Freud, ego phases are tied to maturation for Erikson. Each ego phase develops out of the tasks facing the ego as it copes with the id, the superego, and the social environment.

Let us now consider the structural elements contained within Erikson's own theory. Erikson's phases of development, as forms of will and forms of self-esteem, can be said to represent a logical sequence in the sense that each higher form presupposes the lower and represents a differentiation of it. The model can be seen as a sequence in which each virtue logically presupposes the earlier virtue in the sequence and logically anticipates the next virtue. Trust and hope are qualities that do not differentiate what the self can do or what is positive in the self from what the parent or the world can do. A later sense of autonomy or will makes this distinction, but does not distinguish the goal of an activity from the activity itself. A sense of purpose or initiative is a positive valuing of goals, which presupposes this distinction. Competence or industry implies or takes for granted a positive goal and concentrates on "confidence" in the self's generalized means (skills and tools) to obtain these goals. Erikson himself is perhaps not very interested in the fact that he defines an abstract logical succession of forms of competence and self-esteem somewhat apart from his detailed psychosocial theory. From a structural point of view, however, focusing on this logical sequence helps to relate his functional description of ego development to the universals of cognitive, moral, and ego structures without necessarily accepting his psychosexual theory.

The element of Erikson's approach that has perhaps the greatest potential for integration with structural approaches is his types of vital virtues or ego strengths that emerge with the resolution of each developmental crisis (cf. Smith, 1975). Erikson's familiar succession of virtues (hope, will, purpose, skill, fidelity, love, care, wisdom) are primarily defined functionally, but also somewhat structurally. They offer a perspective on the way in which an ego "uses" cognitive and affective processes and experiences and the way in which an ego makes choices. There is first the structure of a psychological process as it is experienced within a particular sociocultural setting and then there is its function or meaning and use to an integrating and choosing ego. From a structural point of view, it is possible to abstract a simplified picture of Erikson's developmental phases and their related accruals of ego strength, a picture which stresses the universal ego domains of cognitive and moral levels. From this point of view, the psychosexual content of an Eriksonian stage is less decisive than the form of the developmental task and its resulting strength or weakness. Each phase in the Erikson hierarchy leads to a form of virtue which, Erikson believes, represents a certain type of active competence or ego strength. At its intuitive roots, his concepts of ego strength seem to denote qualities of moral will as well as self-esteem. Erikson specifically labeled the second phase's virtue "will," and uses it to refer to the sense of freedom in willing or acting. "Purpose" is clearly another strength of will as is "competence," the free exercise of intelligence in the completion of tasks. From a qualitative and developmental point of view, then, Erikson's virtues can be understood as stages of moral courage, a strand within the developing ego. For instance, the sense of "hope" and "will," which emerges with the successful *resolution* of the concerns of Erikson's first two phases, parallels the emergence of Kohlberg's first stage of moral reasoning, the hope for reward and the fear of punishment. The child's sense of "purpose," a courage to pursue valued goals, which emerges at the *end* of Erikson's third period, parallels the child in Kohlberg's second stage being able to pursue valued goals through concrete reciprocity. The moral flavor of all the childhood phases, in fact, can be seen in their negative poles that characterize negative moral will (shame, guilt, inferiority). As higher levels are reached, the Eriksonian virtues become more and more matters of moral will. Adolescent "fidelity," young adulthood "love," and adulthood "caring" represent successive capacities for ethicality, for sociomoral commitments that are freely made, but ethically binding.

Some might argue that the presence of such structural elements in Erikson's theory is accounted for by his roots in Freudian theory which, they would suggest, has many structural characteristics in common with Piaget's work (cf. Coblener,

1967; Greenspan, 1979; Odler, 1956; Rapaport, 1960; Wolff, 1960). We would argue, however, that this approach ignores basic epistemological differences between the theories (cf. Kegan, 1977, p. 35) and would suggest rather that it is Erikson's own expansion and modification of Freud's work to include life-span phases of healthy personality development that has far more in common with structuralism (cf. Erikson, 1977, p. 35; Noam, Higgins, & Goethals, 1983). Erikson himself has stated his general acceptance of the Piagetian and Kohlbergian models as "strands of development" that describe the structural basis of the person's functional unity at each stage (1974, pp. 204–206; 1964, pp. 136–141, 171–172). Similarly, Piaget and Kohlberg have alluded to or argued for logical parallels between their theories and Erikson's model (Kohlberg, 1973b; Kohlberg & Gilligan, 1971; Kohlberg & Kramer, 1969; Piaget, 1973). Both Erikson and structuralists assume that the prior potential for a particular course of human development is intrinsic in the human condition, both stress to varying degrees the interaction of the organism with its environment, and both see successive stages of development to be characterized by greater degrees of self-differentiation and self-transcendence. There are also several specific theoretical parallels, for example, an infant's attachment to his mother with the achievement of object permanence; the development of formal operations and the questioning of conventional morality with the questioning of one's own identity; the problems of narcissism with the limitations of egocentrism. Thus it is not surprising that *empirical* parallels between stages of moral judgment and Eriksonian identity development, as measured by Marcia's clinical interview procedure and Stewart's TAT rating system, have been demonstrated (Boyd, 1973; Marcia, 1966; Podd, 1972; Stewart, 1974).

The interaction of both structural and cultural elements within Erikson's functional approach raises the question of the model's universality. Although Erikson's scheme is culturally relative, compared to structurally defined stage models, it is also more universal than purely culturally defined ages of development. In addition to its penetrating relevance to Euro-Americans, it has been successfully applied to the life cycle in other cultures, including the Sioux and Yourok Indians (Erikson, 1950) and adult development in India (Erikson, 1969). It can be argued, for instance, that the very fact that a culture has provided such an effective solution to an adolescent's identity crisis so that the young person experiences little sense of turmoil does not necessarily mean that this developmental phase is culturally relative, but rather that there are relative levels of effectiveness with which different societies handle this near universal phase of human development. Functional phases of development appear to be facilitated by the optimal interaction or matching of structural stage abilities and cultural age responsibilities.

This interaction of structural and cultural elements can possibly be illustrated by an example from common educational practice in the U.S. school culture. Students ideally matriculate into algebra and other academic subjects at a time that corresponds to the acquisition of formal structures in cognitive development. The ability to do well in a first year algebra course, thus, is often used as evidence that the individual should be put in the academic track. But, in fact, many bright students do not acquire formal operations until later in high school, yet they have already been given the identity of commercial or vocational track students. This premature foreclosure of other identifications can create feelings of personal inferiority or second class citizenship within the school and it may also spawn feelings of antagonism against education in general when the student realizes that he or she is actually quite bright but was prematurely placed on the nonacademic track, a position that also unfairly limits their future career options. Since middle-class students, with the support of well-educated parents and middle-class teachers, generally reach formal operations somewhat sooner than working-class adolescents, this mismatch between structural stage and cultural age places the burden of functional phase turmoil on working-class students and also functions to maintain the status quo of the class system. Greater attention to the synchronization of structural stage and cultural age for each individual student and for each subculture represented in a school system would provide greater support for a more adequate resolution of the functional crisis of identity formation. In this sense, then, the real genius and major advantage of Erikson's functional approach is that it draws from both cultural and structural models to construct phases of ego functioning that are both abstract in regard to universal structures and concrete in regard to the sociocultural context of development.

CONCLUSION

We have taken a number of positions in this chapter: that an inclusive structural stage theory of ego development is useful in providing coherence to the proliferation of structural subdomain theories of human development; that a structural stage approach is distinct from but complementary with what we have termed functional phases and cultural ages of development; and that these theories together clarify the importance of the claim that ego development should be the broad aim of education. The ego psychologists we have discussed have all suggested, to a greater or lesser degree, parallels between their own theory and the theories of others. In Table 8.11 we summarized an integration of these theories within a holistic concept of the developing ego. Such a conception is imperative if education is to encompass the total development of individuals. Throughout our discussion we have noted examples of the relevance of developmental psychology for educational pedagogy. We would like to conclude by offering three suggestions and one principle regarding the implications of ego development theory for educational practice.

The *first* suggestion is simply that education must address multi-domains of development—cognitive, moral, and metaphysical orientations to our social, natural, and ultimate environments—if education is to facilitate maximally the overall aim of ego development. For instance, using opportunities to discuss social moral dilemmas in a U.S. history class or ecological moral dilemmas in a science class can contribute to ego development since moral reasoning is tied into one's concept of one's self and others.

Second, we wish to echo Anna Freud's seminal suggestion that educators must take a life-span perspective on their students since many stages are not reached until after childhood and adolescence. She made the point this way:

> It is not a good practice for teachers to be confined to one age group because this encourages them to disregard the fact that any given age is merely a transitional stage within the whole process of childhood. It is important for the school teacher to have knowledge of children of all ages. The good teacher and child psychologist see every phase of childhood in terms of what has gone before and what will come afterwards. (1952, p. 72)

Such a perspective will not only help us keep in mind the qualitatively different systems of meaning-making typical of childhood, but, as James Fowler has also argued, it will help us to "avoid viewing the stages as constituting an achievement scale or a program by which to rush people to the next stage. The potential fullness of each stage needs to be recognized and realized. Each stage has a potential wholeness, grace, and integrity" (Fowler, 1980, p. 82).

A *third* suggestion regarding the implications of ego development theory is that psychology and pedagogy engage in "a very intense cooperation" in order to create a developmental-based education (cf. Werner, 1937, p. 43). It is simply not possible to derive an ideal system of developmental education directly from ego development theory. Effective education grows out of a dialectical interpenetration of psychological theory and classroom practice; this interplay is as important for achieving a comprehensive developmental theory as it is for achieving an effective application of it (cf. Kuhn, 1979). Fortunately some of the beginning steps have been taken in the sense that ego development theories—especially Selman's on the elementary school level and Loevinger's on the junior and senior high school level—have influenced and been influenced by educational practice. For instance, on the elementary school level, Robert Enright has used a cross-age teaching approach (sixth graders tutoring first graders) to promote social cognitive maturity (Enright, 1977; Enright et al., 1977). Several other studies have similarly been successful in promoting the development of school children (Cooney, 1977; Darrigrand & Gum, 1973; Pardew & Schilson, 1973; Selman & Liberman, 1975) including the work at Bank Street to which we referred in the beginning (Biber, 1974). On the junior and senior high school level, Kenneth Nichols and his colleagues have designed a curriculum to promote the psychological growth of 7th, 8th, and 9th graders (1977); Lois Erickson has developed a structural-developmental curriculum model that has successfully promoted ego maturity among young women (1977a, 1977b, 1980); Anna Miller-Tiedman has applied Jane Loevinger's theory to facilitate ego maturity through the teaching of English literature (1977a, 1977b). Andrew Garrod has used literary works as a vehicle for fostering moral and ego development (Garrod & Bramble, 1977; Garrod, 1981); and Thomas Landenburg has integrated developmental concerns into the teaching of history (1977a, 1977b). Several other projects have also used developmental theory in intentional psychological programs with college students (Exum, 1977; Goldsmith, 1977; Mosher & Sprinthall, 1971; Touchton et al., 1977; Tucker, 1977; Wasserman, 1977; Whiteley, 1980).

We must conclude by highlighting a principle underlying this chapter. Our discussion of structural, functional, and cultural approaches may have functioned in part to underscore the unique importance of our structural perspective. This was not intended to suggest, however, that these three approaches are mutually exclusive. They are in fact complementary. Kluckhohn and Murray's well-known aphorism may be helpful here (1948, p. 53): "Every man is in certain respects: a. like all other men, b. like some other men, c. like no other man." If we can overlook their sexist language for the moment, we would translate their statement into the aim of education as follows: By attempting to understand how an individual's ego development is structurally like that of all other people, functionally like that of most other people, and culturally like that of only some other people, we may also contribute to understanding how the ontogeny of a particular person is like that of no other person and how this unique course of development can be facilitated so that the person may fully become all that he or she has the potential to be.

REFERENCES

Ausubel, D. et al. (1980). *Theories and problems of child development.* New York: Grune and Stratton.

Baldwin, J. M. (1902). *Social and ethical interpretations in mental development.* New York: Macmillan.

Beilin, H. (1971). Developmental stages and developmental processes. In D. R. Green et al. (Eds.), *Measurement and Piaget.* New York: McGraw-Hill.

Bellak, L. et al. (1973). *Ego functions in schizophrenics, neurotics, and normals.* New York: Wiley.

Biber, B. et al. (1963). *Perspectives on learning and teaching.* New York: Bank Street College.

Biber, B., E. Shapiro, & D. Wickens. (1971). *Promoting cognitive growth: A developmental-interaction point of view.* Washington, D.C.: National Association for the Education of Young Children.

Blasi, A. (1976). Concept of development in personality theory. In J. Loevinger, *Ego development: Conceptions and theories.* San Francisco: Jossey-Bass.

Boyd, D. (1973). *From conventional to principled morality.* Unpublished manuscript, Center for Moral Education, Harvard University.

Garrod, A. C., & Bramble, G. A. (1977). Moral development & literature. *Theory into Practice, 16*(2), 105–111.

Braun, C. (1976). Teacher expectation: Sociopsychological dynamics. *Review of Educational Research, 46,* 185–213.

Broughton, J. M. (1980). Genetic metaphysics: The developmental psychology of mind/body concepts. In R. W. Rieber (Ed.), *Mind and body*. New York: Academic.

Broughton, J., & Zahaykevich, M. (1977). Review of of J. Loevinger's Ego development: Conceptions and theories. *Telos, 32,* 246–253.

Chickering, A. W. (1976). Developmental change as a major outcome. In M. Keeton (Ed.), *Experiential learning: Rationale, characteristics, and assessment.* San Francisco: Jossey-Bass, pp. 62–90.

Cobliner, W. (1967). Psychoanalysis and the Geneva school of genetic psychology: Parallels and counterparts. *International Journal of Psychiatry, 3*(2), 82–129.

Colby, A., Gibbs, J., Kohlberg, L., Speicher-Dubin, B., & Candee, D. (1979). *Standard form scoring manual.* Cambridge: Harvard University, Center for Moral Education, 1979. (New York: Cambridge University Press, in press.)

Cooney, E. W. (1977). Social-cognitive development: Applications to intervention and evaluation in the elementary grades. *The Counseling Psychologist, 6*(4), 6–9.

Damon, W. (1979). *The social world of the child.* San Francisco: Jossey-Bass.

Darrigrand, G., & Gum, M. (1973). A comparison of the effects of two methods of developmental guidance on the self-concept, peer relationships, and school attitudes of second grade children. In G. D. Miller (Ed.), *Additional studies in elementary school guidance.* St. Paul: Minnesota Department of Education.

Dewey, J. (1909/1959). *Moral principles in education.* New York: Philosophical Library. (Originally published 1909.)

Dewey, J., & McLellan, J. (1895/1964). The psychology of number. In R. Archambault (Ed.), *John Dewey on education: Selected writings.* New York: Random House, 1964. (Originally published 1895.)

Duke, D. L. (1978). The etiology of student misbehavior and the depersonalization of blame. *Review of Educational Research, 48,* 415–437.

Enright, R. (1977). A cross-age interventional in interpersonal conceptions: A curriculum for intermediate school-age children. *Pupil Personnel Services Journal, 6*(1), 85–92.

Enright, R., Colby, S., & McMullin, I. (1977). A social cognitive developmental intervention with sixth and first graders. *The Counseling Psychologist, 6*(4), 10–12.

Erikson, E. H. (1950a/1963). *Childhood and society.* New York: Norton. (Originally published 1950a.)

Erikson, E. H. (1950b/1959). Growth and crises of the healthy personality. *Psychological Issues, 1*(1), 50–100. (Originally published 1950.)

Erikson, E. H. (1956/1959). The problem of ego identity. *Psychological Issues, 1,* 101–171. (Originally published 1956.)

Erikson, E. H. (1959). Identity and the life cycle. *Psychological Issues, Monograph 1.* New York: International Universities Press.

Erikson, E. H. (Ed.). (1961a/1963). *The challenge of youth.* Garden City, NY: Anchor Books. (Originally published as *Youth, change and challenge.* New York: Basic Books, 1961a.)

Erikson, E. H. (1961b). Youth: Fidelity and diversity. In E. Erikson (Ed.), *The challenge of youth.* Garden City, NY: Doubleday, pp. 1–28.

Erikson, E. H. (1964). *Insight and responsibility: Lectures on the ethical implications of psychoanalytic insight.* New York: Norton.

Erikson, E. H. (1968a). *Identity: Youth and crisis.* New York: Norton.

Erikson, E. H. (1968b). Life cycle. In *International encyclopedia of the social sciences*. New York: Macmillan, pp. 286–292.

Erikson, E. H. (1969). *Gandhi's truth: On the origins of militant nonviolence*. New York: Norton.

Erikson, E. H. (1970a). Autobiographic notes on the identity crisis. *The making of modern science: Biographic studies, Daedalus, 99*(4), 730–759.

Erikson, E. H. (1970b). Reflections on the dissent of contemporary youth. *Daedalus*, Winter, *99*, 154–176.

Erikson, E. H. (1974a). *Dimensions of a new identity*. New York: Norton.

Erikson, E. H. (1974b). Womanhood and the inner space. Once more the inner space. In J. Strouse (Ed.), *Women and analysis*. New York: Grossman, pp. 291–340.

Erikson, E. H. (1975). *Life history and the historical moment*. New York: Norton.

Erikson, E. H. (1977). *Toys and reason: Stages in the revitalization of experience*. New York: Norton.

Erikson, E. H. (1980). Themes of adulthood in the Freud-Jung correspondence. In N. Smelser and E. Erikson (Eds.), *Themes of work and love in adulthood*. Cambridge: Havard University Press.

Erickson, V. L. (1977a). Deliberate psychological education for women: A curriculum follow-up study. *The Counseling Psychologist, 6*(4), 25–29.

Erickson, V. L. (1977b). Beyond Cinderella: Ego maturity and attitudes toward the rights and roles of women. *The Counseling Psychologist, 7*(1), 83–88.

Erickson, V. L. (1977c). The domains of ego and moral development. *Moral Education Forum, 2*(4), 1–4.

Erickson, V. L. (1980). The case study method in the evaluation of developmental programs. In L. Kuhmerker, M. Mentkowski, & L. Erickson (Eds.), *Evaluating moral development*, Schenectady, NY: Character Research Press.

Evans, R. (1969). *Dialogue with Erik Erikson*. New York: Dutton.

Exum, H. (1977). Deliberate psychological education: Facilitation of psychological maturity at the junior college level. *Pupil Personnel Services Journal, 6*(1), 197–224.

Fowler, J. W. (1973). Agenda toward a new coalition. *Engage/Social Action, 1*(5), 45–63.

Fowler, J. W. (1980). Faith and the structuring of meaning. In Fowler et al. (Eds.), *Toward moral and religious maturity*. Morristown, NJ: Silver Burdett.

Fowler, J. W. (1981). *Faith and human development*. New York: Harper & Row.

Freud, A. (1952/1981). The role of the teacher. In J. Snarey et al. (Eds.), *Conflict and continuity: A history of ideas on social equality and human development*. Cambridge: Harvard Educational Review, pp. 72–76. (Originally published 1952.)

Friedan, B. (1962). *The feminine mystique*. New York: Dell Books.

Fromm, E. (1976). To have or to be. *World Perspective, 50*, 14–32.

Garrod, A. (1981). *Experimental curriculum in moral development which uses literary works as vehicles for moral discussion*. Doctoral qualifying paper, Harvard University, Graduate School of Education.

Garrod, A., & Bramble, G. (1977). Moral development through English literature. *Theory into Practice, 16*(2), 105–111.

Gedo, J., & Goldberg, A. (1973). *Models of the mind: A psychoanalytic theory*. Chicago: University of Chicago Press.

Glasser, W. (1969). *Schools without failure*. New York: Harper & Row.

Goldsmith, S. (1977). Application of Perry's schema in a college course on human identity. *Pupil Personel Services Journal, 6*(1), 185–196.

Greenspan, S. I. (1979). Intelligence and adaptation: An integration of psychoanalytic and Piagetian developmental psychology. *Psychological Issues Monographs.* New York: International Universities Press.

Haan, N. (1977). *Coping and defending: Processes of self-environment organization.* New York: Academic.

Haan, N., Stroud, J., & Holstein, C. (1973). Moral and ego stages in relationship to ego processes: a study of "hippies." *Journal of Personality, 41,* 596–612.

Habermas, J. (1975). Moral development and ego identity (George Ellard, Trans.). *Telos, 24,* 41–55.

Hartman, H. (1939). *Ego psychology and the problem of adaptation.* New York: International Universities Press.

Hauser, S. T. (1976). Loevinger's model and measure of ego development: A critical review. *Psychological Bulletin, 83*(5), 928–955.

Inhelder, B., & Piaget, J. (1955/1958). *The growth of logical thinking from childhood to adolescence* (A. Parsons and S. Milgram, Trans.). New York: Basic Books. (Originally published, 1955.)

James, W. *Principles of psychology.* (1890). New York: Holt, Rinehart.

Kamii, C., & DeVries, R. (1977). Piaget for early education. In M. C. Day & R. K. Parker, (Eds.), *The preschool in action* (2nd ed.). Boston: Allyn and Bacon.

Kegan, R. (1977). *Ego and truth: Personality and the Piaget paradigm.* Unpublished doctoral dissertation, Harvard University.

Kegan, R. (1979a) The evolving self: A process conception of ego psychology. *The Counseling Psychologist, 8*(2), 5–34.

Kegan, R. (1979b). *A neo-Piagetian approach to object relations.* Paper presented at the conference on New Approaches to the Self, Center for Psychosocial Studies, Chicago. (New York: Plenum Press, in press.)

Kegan, R. (1980a). Making meaning: The constructivist-developmental approach to persons and practice. *Journal of Personnel and Guidance, 58*(5), 373–380.

Kegan, R. (1980b). There the dance is: Religious dimensions of a developmental framework. In J. Fowler & A. Vergote (Eds.), *Toward moral and religious maturity.* Morristown, NJ: Silver Burdett, pp. 403–440.

Kegan, R. (1982). *The evolving self.* Cambridge: Harvard University Press.

Kierkegaard, S. (1941). *Fear and trembling and the sickness unto death.* Princeton, NJ: Princeton University Press.

Klein, G. (1968). Psychoanalysis: ego psychology. In *International encyclopedia of the social sciences.* New York: Macmillan, pp. 11–31.

Kluckhohn, C., & Murray, H. (1948). *Personality in nature, society, and culture.* New York: Knopf.

Kohlberg, L. (1958). *The development of modes of thinking and choices in years 10 to 16.* Unpublished doctoral dissertation, University of Chicago.

Kohlberg, L. (1969). Stage and sequence: The cognitive developmental approach to socialization. In D. Goslin (Ed.), *Handbook of socialization theory and research.* New York: Rand McNally.

Kohlberg, L. (1971). Stages of moral development as a basis for moral education. In C. M.

Beck et al. (Eds.), *Moral education: Interdisciplinary approaches*. Toronto: University of Toronto Press, pp. 23–92.

Kohlberg, L. (1972). The concepts of developmental psychology as the central guide to education. In M. C. Reynolds (Ed.), *Psychology and the process of schooling in the next decade: alternative conceptions*. Minneapolis: University of Minnesota Press.

Kohlberg, L. (1973a). The claim to moral adequacy of a higher stage or moral judgment. *Journal of Philosophy*, *77*(18), 630–646.

Kohlberg, L. (1973b). Continuities and discontinuities in childhood and adult moral development: revisited. In P. B. Baltes & K. W. Schaie (Eds.), *Life span developmental psychology: Personality and socialization*. New York: Academic.

Kohlberg, L., & Gilligan, C. (1971). Adolescent as philosopher: the discovery of the self in a post-conventional world. *Daedalus*, *100*(4), 1051–1086.

Kohlberg, L., & Kramer, R. (1969). Continuities and discontinuities in childhood and adult moral development. *Human Development*, *12*, 93–120.

Kohlberg, L., & R. Mayer. (1972). Development as the aim of education. *Harvard Educational Review*, *42*(2), 449–496.

Kuhn, D. (1979). The application of Piaget's theory of cognitive development to education. *Harvard Educational Review*, *49*(3), 340–360.

Kuhn, D., & Angeleu, J. (1976). An experimental study of the development of formal operational thought. *Child Development*, *47*, 697–706.

Kusatsu, O. (1973). Ego development and socio-cultural process in Japan. *J. Economics* (Asia University, Tokyo, Japan), *3*, 41–128.

Lambert, H. V. (1972). *A comparison of Jane Loevinger's theory of ego development and Lawrence Kohlberg's theory of moral development*. Unpublished doctoral dissertation, The University of Chicago.

Landenburg, T. J. (1977a). Cognitive development and moral reasoning in the teaching of history. *History Teacher*, *10*(2), 113–125.

Landenburg, T. J. (1977b). Moral reasoning and social studies. *Theory into Practice*, April, 112–117.

Lasker, H. M. (1977). *Interim summative evaluation report: An initial assessment of the Shell/Humanas OD program*. Cambridge: Harvard University.

Lasker, H. M., et al. (1974a). Stage specific reactions to ego development training. In *Formative research in ego stage change: Study no. 3*. Willemstad, Curacao: Humanas Foundation.

Lasker, H. M. et al. (1974b). Self-reported change manual. In *Formative research in ego stage change: Study no. 4*. Willemstad, Curacao: Humanas Foundation.

Levinson, D. J. (1978). *The seasons of a man's life*. New York: Ballantine Books.

LeVine, R. A. (1973). *Culture, behavior and personality*. Chicago: Aldine.

Limoges, J. (1978). *French translation of the sentence completion test*. Unpublished manuscript, University de Sherbrooke, Sherbrooke, Quebec, Canada.

Loevinger, J., with Blasi, A. (1976). *Ego development: Conceptions and theories*. San Francisco: Jossey-Bass.

Loevinger, J. (1978a). *Scientific ways in the study of ego development*. Worcester, MA: Clark University Press, Heinz Warner Lecture Series, Volume XII.

Loevinger, J. (1978b). *Recent research on ego development*. Paper presented at the Harvard Graduate School of Education, April 5.

Loevinger, J. (1979). Construct validity of the sentence completion test of ego development. *Applied Psychological Measurement*, *3*(3), 281–311.

Loevinger, J., & Wessler, R. (1970). *Measuring ego development I: Construction and use of a sentence completion test.* San Francisco: Jossey-Bass.

Loevinger, J., Wessler, R., & Redmore, C. (1970). *Measuring ego development II: Scoring manual for women and girls.* San Francisco: Jossey-Bass.

Looft, W. R. (1973). Socialization and personality throughout the life span: An examination of contemporary psychological approaches. In P. Baltes & K. W. Schaie, *Life-span developmental psychology, personality, and socialization.* New York: Academic, pp. 25–52.

Marcia, J. E. (1966). Development and validation of ego identity status. *Journal of Personality and Social Psychology*, *3*, 551–558.

Mead, G. H. (1934). *Mind, self and society.* Chicago: University of Chicago Press.

Mead, M. (1928). *Coming of age in Samoa.* New York: Mentor Books.

Meyer, P. (1977). Intellectual development: Analysis of religious content. *Counseling Psychologist*, *6*(4), 47–50.

Miller, G. D. (Ed.). (1977). *Developmental theory and its application to guidance programs.* St. Paul, MN: Pupil Personnel Service Section, Department of Education.

Miller-Tiedeman, A., & Niemi, M. (1977a). Structuring responsibility in adolescents: Actualizing 'I' power through curriculum. *Pupil Personnel Services Journal.* St. Paul: Minnesota Department of Education, *6*(1), 123–166.

Miller-Tiedeman, A., & Tiedman, D. (1977b). An 'I' power primer: Structure and its enablement of intuition. *Focus on Guidance*, March, 79–88.

Moir, D. J. (1974). Egocentrism and the emergence of conventional morality in preadolescent girls. *Child Development*, *45*, 299–304.

Mosher, R., & Sprinthall, N. (1971). Deliberate psychological education. *Counseling Psychologist*, *2*(4), 3–80.

Nichols, K., Isham, M., & Austad, E. (1977). A junior high school curriculum to promote psychological growth and moral reasoning. *Pupil Personnel Services Journal*, Minnesota Department of Education, *6*(1), 93–102.

Noam, G. (1985). Stage, phase and style: The developmental dynamics of the self. In M. Berkowitz and F. Oser (Eds.), *Moral education: Theory and application.* Hillsdale, NJ: Erlbaum.

Noam, G., Higgins, R. & Goethals, G. (1983). Psychoanalytic approaches to developmental psychology. In B. Wolman (Ed.), *Handbook of developmental psychology*, Englewood Cliffs, NJ: Prentice-Hall.

Noam, G., & Kegan, R. (1983). Social cognition and psychodynamics: Towards a clinical-developmental psychology. In W. Edelstein (Ed.), *Soziale kognition.* Frankfurt: Suhokamp Verlag.

Odler, C. (1956). *Anxiety and magical thinking.* New York: International Universities Press.

Oser, F., Power, C., Gmuender, P., Fritzsche, U., & Widmer, K. (1980). Stages of religious judgment. In J. Fowler (Ed.), *Toward moral and religious maturity.* Morristown, NJ: Silver Burdett, pp. 278–315.

Pardew, E., & Schilson, E. (1973). Self-concept change: The effect of a self-concept enhancement program on preschool children. In G. P. Miller (Ed.), *Additional studies in elementary activities evaluation.* St. Paul: Minnesota Department of Education, pp. 1–62.

Perry, W. G. (1968). *Forms of intellectual and ethical development in the college years: A scheme.* New York: Holt, Rinehart.

Piaget, J. (1929), *The child's conception of the world.* London: Routledge & Kegan Paul.

Piaget, J. (1932/1965). *The moral judgment of the child* (M. Gabain, Trans.). New York: The Free Press. (Originally published 1932.)

Piaget, J. (1936/1963). *The origins of intelligence in the child* (M. Cook, Trans.). New York: Norton. (Originally published 1936.)

Piaget, J. (1937/1971). *The construction of reality in the child* (M. Cook, Trans.). New York: Ballantine. (Originally published 1937.)

Piaget, J. (1968/1970). *Structuralism* (C. Maschler, Trans.). New York: Harper & Row. (Originally published 1968.)

Piaget, J. (1972). Intellectual evolution from adolescence to adulthood. *Human Development, 15,* 1–12.

Piaget, J. (1973). *The Child and Reality.* New York: Grossman Publishers.

Podd, M. (1972). Ego identity status and morality: The relationship between two developmental constructs. *Developmental Psychology, 6*(3), 447–507.

Prelinger, E., & Zimet, C. (1964). *An ego psychological approach to character assessment.* Glencoe, Ill.: Free Press.

Quinlan, D., & Rogers, L. (1981). *Moral development and psychiatric symptoms.* Unpublished manuscript, Yale University Medical School.

Radcliffe-Brown, A. R. (1929). Age organization terminology. *Man, 13,* 21.

Rapaport, D. (1960). The structure of psychoanalytic theory: A systematizing attempt. *Psychological Issues, 2*(2).

Redl, F. (1957). *Children who hate.* Glencoe, Ill: Free Press.

Rogoff, B. et al. (1975). Age of assignment of roles and responsibilities to children: A cross-cultural survey. *Human Development, 18,* 353–369.

Selman, R. (1971). The relation of role-taking to the development of moral judgment in children. *Child Development, 42,* 79–91.

Selman, R. (1975a). A developmental approach to interpersonal and moral awareness in young children: some theoretical and educational implications of levels of social perspective taking. *Values Education,* 127–139.

Selman, R. (1975b) Level of social perspective taking and the development of empathy in children: Speculations from a social-cognitive viewpoint. *Journal of Moral Education, 5*(1), 35–43.

Selman, R. (1976). Social-cognitive understanding: A guide to educational and clinical practice. In T. Lickona (Ed.), *Moral development and behavior: theory, research, and social issues.* New York: Holt, Rinehart, pp. 299–316.

Selman, R. (1977a). A structural-developmental analysis of interpersonal conceptions in poorly adjusted and well adjusted preadolescents. In A. Pick (Ed.), *Tenth annual symposium on child development.* Minneapolis: University of Minnesota Press.

Selman, R. (1977b). A structural-developmental model of social congition: Implications for intervention research. *Counseling Psychologist, 6*(4), 3–6.

Selman, R. (1980). *The growth of interpersonal understanding developmental and clinical studies.* New York: Academic.

Selman, R., & Damon, W. (1975). The necessity, but insufficiency, of social perspective taking for conceptions of justice at three early levels. In D. DePalama & J. Foley (Eds.), *Contemporary issues in moral development.* Hillsdale, NJ: Erlbaum.

Selman, R., & Kohlberg, L. (1972). *First things: Values.* New York: Guidance Associates Filmstrips.

Selman, R., & Kohlberg, L. (1975). *First things: Social reasoning.* New York: Guidance Associates Filmstrips.

Selman, R., & Kohlberg, L. (1976). *Relationships and values.* New York: Guidance Associates Filmstrips.

Selman, R., & Liberman, M. (1975). Moral education in the primary grades: an evaluation of a developmental curriculum, *Journal of Educational Psychology, 67*(5), 712–716.

Shapiro, E., & Biber, B. (1972). The education of young children: a developmental-interaction approach. *Teachers College Record, 74*(1), 55–80.

Shavelson, R. J., Hubner, J. J., & Stanton, G. C. (1976). Self-concept: Validation of construct interpretations. *Review of Educational Research, 46,* 407–441.

Smith, J. (1975). *The role of ego virtues in moral development: A theory of moral stage transition.* Unpublished paper, Harvard University, Center for Moral Education.

Snarey, J. (1981). *The development of moral reasoning about animal life and the natural environment.* Unpublished manuscript, Harvard University, Center for Moral Education.

Snarey, J. (1982). *The moral development of kibbutz founders and sabras: a cross-sectional and ten-year longitudinal study.* Doctoral dissertation, Harvard University, Graduate School of Education.

Snarey, J., & Blasi, J. (1980). Ego development among adult kibbutzniks: A cross-cultural application of Loevinger's theory. *Genetic Psychology Monographs, 102,* 117–157.

Sprinthall, N. A. (1976). Learning psychology by doing psychology: A high school curriculum in the psychology of counseling. In D. G. Miller (Ed.), *Developmental education.* St. Paul: Minnesota Department of Education, pp. 23–43.

Stewart, J. S. (1974). *Toward a theory for values development education.* Unpublished doctoral dissertation, Michigan State University.

Sullivan, P. J. (1975). *A curriculum for stimulating moral reasoning and ego development in adolescents.* Unpublished doctoral dissertation, Boston University, School of Education.

Tillich, P. (1952/1975). *The courage to be.* New Haven, Conn.: Yale University Press. (Originally published 1952).

Touchton, J. G., Wertheimer, L. G., Cornfels, L., & Harrison, K. H. (1977). Career planning and decision-making: A developmental approach to the classroom. *The Counseling Psychologist, 6*(4), 42–47.

Tucker, A. (1977). Psychological growth in a liberal arts course: A cross-cultural experience. *Pupil Personnel Services Journal, 6*(1), 225–250.

Van Gennep, A. (1908). *The rites of passage.* Chicago: University of Chicago Press.

Vetter, M. (1978). *Dimensionen des Selbskonzeptes und Ich-Entwicklung.* Unpublished master's thesis, Johannes-Gutenberg Universitat, Mainz, Germany.

Walker, L. (1980). Prerequisites for moral reasoning development. *Child Development, 51,* 131–139.

Wasserman, E. R. (1977). *The development of an alternative high school based on Kohlberg's just community approach to education.* Doctoral dissertation, Boston University.

Wattenberg, W. W., & Clifford, C. (1962). *Relationship of self-concept to beginning achievement in reading.* U.S. Office of Education Cooperative Research Project, No. 733. Detroit: Wayne State University.

Weber, M. (1949). *The methodology of the social sciences.* Glencoe, Ill.: Free Press.

Werner, H. (1937/1981). Process and achievement: a basic problem of education and developmental psychology. In J. Snarey et al. (Eds.), *Conflict and continuity: A history of ideas on social equality and human development*. Cambridge: Harvard Educational Review, 31–45. (Originally published 1937.)

Whiteley, J. (1980). Evaluation of character development in an undergraduate residential community. In L. Kuhmerker et al. (Eds.), *Evaluating moral development*. Schenectady, NY: Character Research Press, pp. 63–74.

Wolff, P. H. (1960). The developmental psychologies of Jean Piaget and psychoanalysis. *Psychological Issues Monographs*. New York: International Universities Press.

Chapter 9

Play and Constructive Work
as Contributors to Development

Lawrence Kohlberg, Greta G. Fein

In both cognitive-developmental and neopsychoanalytic theories, the central characteristic of young children is their active and constructive nature. Accordingly, the educator's interest in the young child must take this active nature into account. Developmental educators have thus advocated play as the best vehicle by which to promote learning and development. By play, we refer to activity engaged in for its own sake, motivated by the pleasure experienced in the activity itself. In this form, play and work are not opposed, since for young children work means constructive activity primarily engaged in for its own sake and not simply for the enjoyment and use of the thing constructed. The opposite of play is not work but labor, engagement in an activity for the sake of an external reward or out of coercion.

As noted, both the cognitive-developmental and the neopsychoanalytic approaches to early education see play as a central educational activity in early education. In this chapter, we survey the meaning of play in these theories, and the reasons play is seen as educational: that is, as experience stimulating development. Such an understanding of play is critical if early education is to regard the opportunities for play and the guidance of play as its central focus.

Our starting point in understanding play will be Piaget's analysis of play as an extension of the autonomously motivated activities of mastery and cognitive exploration of the young child. Contemporary interest in play started not with this view but with the classical Freudian view of play as the symbolic expression of the child's sexual and aggressive drives and of the anxieties and reactions these drives aroused in the child. Such a view of play has validity both theoretically and practically in the constructive use of play in therapy. From our point of view, however, such interpretations of play are special cases and the more general case for the educator is play as a form of mastery over real objects of adaptive significance to the child.

This point of view is developed in Piaget's (1962) volume, *Play, dreams and imitation in young childhood*, from a cognitive-developmental perspective that acknowledges the Freudian view. It is also developed in E. Erikson's (1977) *Toys and reasons* from a neopsychoanalytic view. This chapter reviews not only Piaget's and Erikson's theories of play, but the important cognitive-developmental theories of play of Baldwin (1906), of Mead (1934), and of Vygotsky (1978). The chapter draws heavily on recent research reviews of the area by Fein (e.g., Fein, 1979a; 1981a).

PLAY AS INTRINSICALLY MOTIVATED BEHAVIOR

Play has been difficult to define precisely even though most people know what the term means. For theorists such as Erikson, the meaning of play is best captured in metaphor. Erikson says:

> The sunlight playing on the waves qualifies for the attribute "playful" because it faithfully remains within the rules of the game. It does not really interfere with the chemical world of the waves. It insists only on an intermingling of appearances. These patterns change with effortless rapidity and with a repetitiveness which promises pleasing phenomena within a predictable range without ever creating the same configuration twice.... When man plays he must intermingle with things and people in a similarly uninvolved and light fashion. He must do something which he has chosen to do without being compelled by urgent interest or impelled by strong passion; he must feel free. (1963, p. 212)

Most theorists would agree with Erikson that whether a behavior is play depends on the feelings and circumstances under which it occurs. Implied in the idea of freedom—freedom of choice without compulsion or impulsion—are issues concerning the motivation of play, the relation between the player and the environment, and the player's goals or purposes. In this vein, play can be viewed as *intrinsically* rather than extrinsically motivated behavior.

Extrinsic motivation is governed by appetitive drives, or by social demands or inducements external to the behavior. By contrast, intrinsic motivation derives from the behavior itself. Exploration, self-initiated mastery learning, and play are examples of intrinsically motivated behavior.

According to some theorists, people become uncomfortable or restless when they do not understand something (Berlyne, 1966). Curiosity is the name given to the feeling of uncertainty that motivates efforts to explore a novel object or to figure out a puzzling event. In this sense, the exploratory behavior of children as well as the experiments of scientists are intrinsically motivated by a desire to make sense out of the world.

In Piaget's theory, intrinsic motivation is not simply activity in response to an uncertain situation. Rather, the general direction of the child's activity is toward mastery over or adaptation to some part of the world. The child is inherently active—a seeker of things to do, primed to detect events that are interesting, puzzling, or curious and then to relate these events to its own activity.

This motivation is best described as what Robert White (1963) calls "effectance motivation" or "primary competence motivation." In this view, the infant kicking to make a mobile turn, the toddler going down a slide, the preschooler building a tower of blocks, and the school age child trying to solve the Rubic cube are each motivated by a desire for effectiveness, mastery, and competence. An adult might climb a mountain, look at it, paint it, or study it—simply because it presents a physical, aesthetic, or intellectual challenge. Of course, extrinsic rewards in the form of prizes, praise, or fame might be added as well. But the evidence indicates that under these circumstances, intrinsic motivation is the more fragile of the two. As Erikson astutely observed, intrinsically motivated behavior is "the undisputed master of only a slim margin of existence." An illustration of the slimness of the margin comes from a study by Lepper, Greene, and Nisbett, cited by Fein (1981). In the study, children were first observed in a preschool classroom in which they were free to do what they wished. The investigators identified a group of children who spontaneously preferred drawing, painting, and other expressive activities. Then, in the experimental part of the study, whenever these children engaged in an expressive activity, the adults dispensed external rewards (e.g., praise or prizes). Rather than increasing the frequency of these activities or improving the quality of the art work, the opposite effect occurred. When extrinsic rewards were superimposed on an intrinsically motivated activity, the children shifted to other activities and when they did draw, the quality was degraded. The study makes two important points. First, children know whether an activity is undertaken to please themselves or to please the teacher. Second, adults need to respect and protect children's natural curiosity or desire for mastery. Although there may be ways of cultivating and strengthening this motivational source, providing external rewards is not one of them.

PIAGET: PLAY AS ASSIMILATION

Although play is intrinsically motivated, not all forms of intrinsically motivated behavior are play. Piaget's theory provides a useful way of distinguishing play from other activities in which the child's aim is to explore the environment, master a skill, or solve a problem.

In Piaget's theory, the child's natural tendency toward mastery over or adaptation to some part of the world has two sides. Piaget calls the more initiatory side of this tendency assimilation and the less initiatory accommodation. Assimilation is the disposition to act toward a stimulus or object in such a way as to incorporate it, or relate it to one's own pattern of activity, one's own schemata, concepts, or self-concept. Such motivation is intrinsic in the sense that it does not depend on deficit or drive states to be alleviated. It is also intrinsic in that the events in the world that the child is seeking are not fixed rewards but feedback—

events whose meaning depends on their relations to the child's own activity. When children explore, they are seeking feedback from the environment but this feedback is not a reward or reinforced in the sense of fixed reactions under the control of others. Rather, the reinforcer is information about the consequences of activity. Once children know what feedback will occur and how it relates to their activity, the feedback loses its value. In exploring a novel object, or in mastering a new pattern of activity, the child's relation to object and activity changes; what is novel or challenging today is familiar or mastered tomorrow. An example is a young infant's kicking to make the toy birds suspended over the crib move. The infant does this initially to control or influence their movement. She wants to assimilate the movement of the birds to her own pattern of activity. If the baby has a sense of causality, she wants to "cause" this movement. The movement of the birds is not an extrinsic reward for activity. If it were, the bird's movement would make the baby stop her kicking, as a pellet temporarily stops bar pressing. In fact, the opposite occurs. If one starts the birds swinging, the infant starts to kick. Something is going on that she must relate her activity to, that she must master. Like the motivation of most of the child's activity, the infant's desire to get the birds to move is not fixed and repetitive—it is not for a fixed goal. Once the child has mastered the movement of the birds, she either loses interest and turns to other things to relate to, or she begins to play.

We have used as an example of intrinsically motivated behavior an infant's kicking to make the birds above her move. This behavior illustrates exploratory behavior, not play. Often in the literature, a clear distinction between play and exploratory behavior is not made. Sometimes play is subsumed under exploratory behavior, sometimes exploratory behavior is subsumed under the broader category of play. In Piaget's world, however, a clear distinction is made between play and exploratory behavior.

For example, when children explore a new environment, they investigate one object after another until they become familiar with what is available. Or, if presented a novel object with buttons, switches, bells, and lights, children will investigate it until they have discovered its features (Hutt, 1979). This behavior is dominated by physical aspects of the environment, as if the child is asking, "What is this object and what can it do?" According to theorists such as Hutt (1979), play is dominated by the interests and intentions of the child, and so the question becomes, "What can *I* do with this object?" In Piaget's theory, the child not only asks the question, but then answers it. In play, the child's answer is "Anything I wish."

For Piaget, the child's question and answer are due to the fact that play is more or less dominated by the "pure" tendency toward assimilation of the world. In cognitive exploration and in task solution, the child is accommodating to or adjusting his or her pattern of action to the object as well as simply assimilating it into the child's own pattern of action. In play, says Piaget, children impose their own organization on the object. Play is dominated by assimilation, by behaviors for the joy of exercising mastery independent of accommodation to the object. The opposite of play as pure assimilation is pure "accommodation" to the object by the passive reproductive copying or imitation of it. Most activity is neither primarily assimilative or accommodative; it is the balance of the two that, according to Piaget, is active intelligence.

> Play in its initial stages is merely the pole of behavior defined by assimilation. Almost all the behaviors we structure in relation to intelligence are susceptible of becoming play as soon as they are repeated for assimilation, i.e., for functional pleasure.
>
> In this regard, play is the converse and complement of accommodation or imitation. Imitation is a kind of hyperadaptation through accommodation to models which are virtually though not actually useable. Play, on the contrary, proceeds by the relaxation of the effort at adaptation and by the exercise of activities for the mere pleasure of master, offering thereby a feeling of virtuosity or power. (Piaget, 1962, p. 89)

In viewing play as "pure" assimilation, Piaget extended the idea that play is intrinsically motivated and person dominated by adding the idea that in play, the *goals* of an activity are self-imposed, and therefore under the control of the player. These goals can therefore vary and change according to the mood or wishes of the child. A child may decide to build a block tower, a goal that may recede as different ways of stacking blocks become more important than building a standing structure. A simple activity of going down a slide may become deliberately complicated by new and varied ways of getting to the bottom. As Miller (1973) puts it, play is characterized by "gallumphing." Freed of the straitjacket of means-ends considerations, the child is able to dismantle established instrumental behavioral sequences and reassemble them in new ways. This characteristic helps distinguish play from intrinsically motivated activities directed to the attainment of specific goals (skill learning, enjoyable work). In Piaget's theory, play occurs *after* a skill or means-end relation has been mastered.

Consider, for example, the 18 month old who goes down a slide for the first time. The child climbs the stairs willingly enough, but once at the top, there is a pause. The child's face becomes tense, her eyes widen, and her body stiffens. She scans the ground, looks pleadingly at the adult who offers reassurance—"It's OK, I'm here; let go." The child lets go cautiously but just for a short distance. With the adult's continued reassurance, the child makes it to the bottom. The next trip goes more easily, but the child's expression is still one of intense concentration. The next turn is easier, and the next even easier; with each trip, the child's expression and posture relaxes. This sequence describes the child's acquisition of a new skill— traversing an inclined plane. The skill involves numerous aspects—sensorimotor coordination of the child's body with respect to object, space, and movement, and control over mixed feelings of apprehension and pleasure. Mastering the skill is a challenge—a little scary, but not impossible—and the child willingly undertakes it. This desire for mastery is "effectance motivation" or "primary competence motivation."

A different process begins when the skill is mastered. When the core sensori-motor coordinations have been acquired, the child luxuriates in the exercise of a newly acquired skill. In play, the child repeats an action for the sake of "showing off to himself his own power of subduing reality" (1962, p. 89). Now the child goes down the slide again and again. But soon, variations are added—no hands, kicking, singing, fast and slow—and the activity becomes "galumphing."

Sensorimotor Play

In infancy, different types of *practice play* emerge with the sequential development of primary, secondary, and tertiary circular reactions. But, since play is nonadap-tive (as adaptation is defined in the theory), play as assimilation becomes the repetition of already acquired modes of behavior detached from the functional focus under which the behavior was initially acquired. When Piaget's infant son Laurent discovers that he can see a toy by throwing his head back and then repeats the movement for its own sake, the behavior becomes play, that is, the exercise of an acquired schema detached from its initial adaptive purpose of bringing an interesting object into view. Play at the level of secondary circular reactions is illustrated by a child continuing to pull the string that makes a toy parrot move without seeming to be involved in the consequence as much as in the pulling. And, with relentless consistency, Piaget describes play at the level of tertiary circular reactions as the combination and repetition of different behaviors, again, without attention to the impact of these variations on the environment. Rather, the child's attention is focused on combining for the sake of combining, on the production of "deliberate complications" that put obstacles in the way of accomplishing goals that may intially have served to organize the behavior. According to Piaget, the pleasure of practice play comes from the child's sense of control over self and environment. The skill was difficult to master, the problem was difficult to solve. But once mastered or solved, the child luxuriates in the feeling of competence and confidence arising when control is repeatedly demonstrated.

One psychological result of the practice is that the acquired skills become "consolidated." First, the repetition is not mechanically exact; skills or problem solutions permit variations that might be less than optimally efficient but nonetheless represent different ways of doing the same thing. For example, a child can go down a slide in numerous ways that do not alter substantially the central physical-spatial relations of a body navigating an inclined plane. The slide can be navigated while rocking, kicking, singing, or waving hands; by sitting, standing, laying, head first or feet first. These variations indicate how in play a core set of physical-spatial relations might be varied and yet preserved. Piaget's point is that this behavior differs from the intense, concentrated, and tentative behavior shown when the child first learned how to use the slide. The exercise of a skill is play; but the exercise serves to consolidate the initial learning by incorporating old skills (rocking, kicking, singing) into the new one, by smoothing out the new performance, or, perhaps, by separating out the essential core of a skill from nonessential, elaborative variations.

Symbolic or Pretend Play

Sensorimotor (or practice) play is the form of play that appears in infancy. But between the years of 1 and 2, a profound change occurs in the play of children. Prior to this period, the baby sleeps when tired and eats when hungry; objects are banged, waved, or pushed; a spoon might be put into a cup, a top on a jar, but even these gestures of relatedness are brief and tentative. Then, quite suddenly, a new element appears. Piaget's classical observation vividly illustrates the nature of this new element:

> In the case of J., the true ludic symbol with every appearance of "make-believe" first appeared at 1:3 (12) in the following circumstances. She saw a cloth whose fringed edges vaguely recalled those of her pillow: she seized it, held a fold of it in her right hand, sucked the thumb of the same hand and lay down on her side laughing hard. She kept her eyes open, but blinked from time to time as if she were alluding to closed eyes. Finally, laughing more and more, she cried "nene" (nono). The same cloth started the same game on the following days. At 1:3 (13) she treated the collar of her mother's coat in the same way. At 1:3 (30) it was the tail of her rubber donkey which represented the pillow. And from 1:5 onwards she made her animals, a bean and a plush dog, also do "nono." (1962/1945, pp. 96–97)

Piaget's interpretation of this behavior is also worth noting.

> As for symbols, they appear towards the end of the first year. . . . For the habit of repeating a given gesture ritually gradually leads to the consciousness of "pretending." The ritual of going to bed. . . is sooner or later utilized "in the void," and the smile of the child as it shuts its eyes in carrying out this rite is enough to show that it is perfectly conscious of "pretending" to go to sleep. (1965/1932, p. 32)

In the Piagetian framework, the onset of pretend play coincides with other milestones of cognitive development and so warrants detailed attention. The precursors of pretend play appear during the fifth stage of sensorimotor development. The child indicates an understanding of object use or object relations by brief gestures of recognition; the child touches a comb to his or her hair, a spoon to the mouth, puts a spoon in a bowl, a top on a jar, or rubs a pencil along a surface.

Pretend play first appears as fleeting gestures. The child produces the motions of sleeping without intending to sleep or the motions of eating without intending to eat. These activities seem to take place outside their customary functions of rest and nourishment.

Then, over the next year and a half, these ephemeral gestures become elaborated and enriched in a sequence of changes described in Table 9.1. At first a doll is simply an object to be touched, moved, banged. Somewhat later, the doll (rather than the child) is used as the recipient of food and eventually is made the recipient of a complex array of caregiving activities: it is put to bed, dressed, patted, and spanked. The child's voice quality might change to sound like a parent; gestures, clothing, and other elements might combine to indicate that a role enactment is occuring (Fein, 1979(a & b); Piaget, 1962).

At first, the objects used in pretense tend to be similar to the things used in the real-life situations that pretend activities mimic (babylike dolls, cuplike cups). Gradually, the need for verisimilitude weakens and assorted objects (sticks and shells) can be used as substitutes in pretend enactments. Eventually, the child can create the semblance of an object (cupped hand; molded clay) or use pantomime gestures in the absence of a physical entity (hand holding absent cup or arms rocking absent doll).

Sociodramatic Play

For Piaget, pretense begins as a solitary activity. During the second and third years of life, the child masters the ability to represent people and things. On the people side, the child can think about herself as someone other than she really is. On the thing side, she can think about immediate objects as if they were something else. A schematic outline of these transformations is shown in Figure 9.1. Early role-taking appears as the child feeds the doll as if it were a baby and the child were a mother. Gradually, less realistic objects are used in these games.

Soon, pretense becomes a social activity and other children play the roles of mother, father, sister, or baby. Pretend play becomes a group activity (i.e., sociodramatic play). In addition to thinking about roles in relation to inanimate

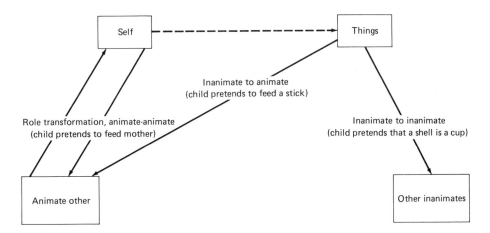

Figure 9.1 Transformation categories in role-related pretends. (*Source:* Fein, 1975, p. 292)

TABLE 9.1
Sequence of Symbolic Levels

	Scheme	Examples
Prior to Stage VI	*Presymbolic schemes:* The child shows understanding of object use or meaning by brief recognitory gestures. No pretending. Properties of present object are the stimulus. Child appears serious rather than playful.	*The child picks up a comb, touches it to his hair, drops it. *The child picks up the telephone receiver, puts it into ritual conversation position, sets it aside. *The child gives the mop a swish on the floor.
Stage VI	*Autosymbolic schemes:* The child pretends at self-related activities. Pretending. Symbolism is directly involved with the child's body. Child appears playful, seems aware of pretending.	*The child simulates drinking from a toy baby bottle. *The child eats from any empty spoon. *The child closes his eyes, pretending to sleep.
Type 1A: Assimilative	*Symbolic schemes:* 1. Symbolic projection A. Child extends symbolic schemes to new objects, actors or receivers of action.	A. J. said "cry, cry" to her dog and imitated sound of crying (Stage V). On following days she made her bear, a duck, her hat, cry.
Type 1B: Imitative	B. Child extends imitative schemes to new objects. Pretending at activities of other people or objects such as dogs, trucks, adults, etc.	B. J. pretended to be telephoning, then made her doll telephone. She telephoned with all sorts of things: a leaf instead of a receiver.

400

Type IIA	*Symbolic identification:* A. Identification of one object as another.	A. Child picks up play screwdriver, says "toothbrush," and makes the motions of toothbrushing.
Type IIB	B. Identification of the child's body with some other person or object; pretending to be other person or object.	B. She crawled into my room on all fours saying "miaow."
Type III	*Symbolic combinations:* Combinations with planned elements. These are constructed of activities from other levels, but always include some planned element. They tend toward realistic scenes.	*Child puts play foods in a pot, stirs them. Then says "soup" or "mommy" before feeding the mother. She waits then says "more?" offering the spoon to the mother.
Type IV	*Collective symbolism*	*Sociodramatic play: Jule finds a dirty popsicle stick and gives it to Teddy. "This is your spoon baby." Teddy pretends to eat like a baby.

Source: Adapted from Piaget (1962), Nicolich (1977), and Fein (1979b).

objects, the child must coordinate her thinking with the thinking of others. For sociodramatic play to occur, representations must be collective or shared by others. However, in Piaget's theory, the implications of role play for social development have not been elaborated. In later sections we discuss the theories of J. M. Baldwin and G. H. Mead for whom the development of self is a central issue.

Piaget, more so than any other theorist, stresses the evolving forms and organizations of play over a long sweep of developmental time. For psychological researchers, Piaget provides valuable insights into *what* develops. For teachers and parents, these insights provide a basis for appreciating the developmental richness of the young child's behavior.

PLAY AS IMAGINATION: THE CONTRIBUTIONS
OF BALDWIN AND VYGOTSKY

Piaget's approach to play largely defines it in relationship to cognitive activity and cognitive development, including the development of symbolism as a cognitive activity. If Piaget saw a broader or more enduring function for symbolic play, he offered it in a cryptic comment:

> The minds which are best able to control abstractions are those which succeed in embodying them in concrete examples or schemes which then serve as symbolic springboards without introducing any limitations. (Piaget & Inhelder, 1971, p. 11)

A richer view of play and its contribution to later development comes from seeing play as imaginative activity, with an awareness that imagination has functions and values that go beyond the cognitive, with a view of the child as artist, or mythmaker, not only as reasoning philosopher. Sutton-Smith (1971), for instance, faults Piaget for not recognizing that pretend play is the foundation of later creative or divergent thinking. At a deeper level, the cognitive-developmental theories of G. H. Mead, J. M. Baldwin, and Lev Vygotsky view pretend play as basic for the development of the self. Because Piaget has no theory of the self and because he emphasizes the pure cognitive or epistemic subject, he does not focus on the functions of play for the development of the ego or self. For all three theoreticians (Baldwin, Mead, Vygotsky) it is in play that the child chooses the experiences and roles that constitute the self. One self theory related to play is that of J. M. Baldwin (1906) discussed in Chapter 6.

Baldwin's Theory

The major step in ego development in the years 4 to 8 in the Baldwin scheme is the growth of the differentiation of the self as mental from the self as physical. According to Baldwin, this differentiation arises largely in play.

Play makes possible the determination of the great dualism of *Mind and Body*, a dualism developing out of that of *Inner and Outer*, but not possible in the mode of fantasy and memory. (1906, p. 16)

Baldwin was impressed by the role of imagination and the "let's pretend" attitude in all adult experience, not only in aesthetic creation and experience, but in the construction of scientific hypotheses and of sociomoral ideals. In talking of childhood play as the origin of later imaginative activity, Baldwin points to the paradoxical quality of childhood play, the paradox that in play the child both does and doesn't believe in the reality of what he is doing or making or saying. In Chapter 2 we cited as an example the author's son, asked when in a dog costume whether he was a dog or not. He responded by saying "I'm a real doggie," getting a dog biscuit, and pretending to eat it. "Being" a dog is acting like a dog and being treated like one—the adult question is irrelevant to the play mode of the child. The reality of the play experience is neither completely asserted nor denied, the distinctive quality of play is the child's sense that its reality value is under his own control. It is a sense of "I believe it but I don't have to believe it." While symbolic and sociodramatic play involve representation, the effort to literally represent another reality cannot be the child's intention, or the activity would cease to be play. Play involves the inner freedom to represent reality tentatively, but deliberately. According to Baldwin, this "let's pretend" attitude of representing reality without being dominated by it symbolizes the roots of later aesthetic production and later scientific hypothesis making. The young child's statement "If I were a dog, then..." is structurally comparable to the scientist's statement "If the earth were round, then...." Symbolic play offers the first indication that representation is not "given" in the material world, but rather, is a deliberate mental act, controlled by the person, and free to transcend the boundaries of physical and social experience. Piaget's "symbolic springboard without... limitations" occupies a central place in Baldwin's theory. In coming to appreciate the mental nature of representation, the child arrives at a major insight concerning the relation of mind to experience.

According to Baldwin, the "let's pretend" attitude also gives the child a sense of himself and his mind as a source of inner freedom distinct from his body and the external material world. Before the play experience, the child is at the first stage in his self-experience, the stage in which the self's physical and mental processes are either copies of external realities or are fantasies with no validity except as bodily impulses. Play provides a new set of experiences of mind and self for the child. Play ideas and purposes are not literal copies of reality; they are the child's own inventions and ideas. At the same time, play inventions are not mere fantasies— pseudo-memories of bodily impulses, they are freely held. The child assimilates his experience into a self by constructing the experience in play as something the mind or self chooses and controls. At an earlier point, the child has memories and wishes that, when reproduced in external reality, cease to exist as mental. In contrast, in the play attitude the child sets up his intentions in a separate realm, a play sphere, and while in one sense he is realizing his intention in external reality, in another sense he is keeping his intentions and plans as his own. In this sense, he is building up a sphere of mind and self distinct from his body, using his body to realize this sphere, but keeping it as subjective and as his own. Consequently, play involves "playing with" the appearance-reality, subjective-objective differentiation and is a vehicle for the further development of the distinction. Symbolic play as exercises in meta-representation thus promotes the progressive differentiation and organization of a sense of self as a coherent, psychological entity.

We have suggested the way in which Baldwin's theory makes early childhood play the basis of a fundamental aspect of self-linked cognitive development, the differentiation of mind as mental and body as physical. Differentiating the mental from the physical, the child then defines the sphere of the mental as the sphere of the free. The child can then control his own mind, even if he cannot always control his own body or the other physical objects in the world of which his body is one.

Vygotsky's Theory

Vygotsky, in an analysis of play that parallels Baldwin in important ways, starts also with the observation that play is the realm in which the child differentiates the mental from the perceptual-physical and the birth of imaginative play for the young child is the genesis of the realm of freedom. For rough purposes, Vygotsky sets the age of appearance of this play as about age 3. He says:

> Play in an imaginary situation is essentially impossible for a child under three. It is impossible for the child before this age to engage in that novel form of behavior called imaginative play which liberates him from the constraints of the situation. Before the age of play, the infant and the very small child is bound by the perceptual situation.... A door demands to be opened or closed, a staircase to be climbed, a bell to be rung.
>
> In play, however, *things* lose their determining force. A condition is reached in which the child begins to act independently of what he sees. In the play situation, the meanings of words and thoughts are separated from objects, and *actions arise from thoughts rather than from things*; a piece of wood becomes a doll, a stick becomes a horse. Action according to rules begins to be determined by ideas and not by objects themselves. Play provides a transitional stage in this direction whenever an object (for example, a stick) becomes a pivot for separating the meaning of horse from a real horse. (1967, p. 8)

Vygotsky discusses not only pretend play, but its evolution into games with rules and the functional value of game rules for development.

> In addition to freedom from the constraint of the situation, play creates demands on the child to act against immediate impulses and to act in accordance with the rules of the game.... In play, renunciation of action on immediate impulse is in the service of

maximum pleasure. To carry out the rule is a source of pleasure and the rule wins because it is the strongest impulse—it is a rule of self-restraint and self-determination, not a rule a child obeys like a physical law. (1967, p. 8)

Vygotsky stresses the role of play in developing that form of ego-strength we have defined as "delay of gratification." He says:

A young child tends to gratify his desires immediately. However, at the preschool age of three to six, a great many unrealizable desires emerge. If this did not occur, there would be no play, because play seems to be invented at the point when the child begins to experience unrealizable tendencies. Suppose a two year old child wants to occupy her mother's role. She wants it at once, and if she cannot have it, she throws a temper-tantrum. Toward the beginning of the preschool age (3) when desires that cannot immediately be realized make their appearance, the child's behavior changes. To relieve the tension the preschool child enters an imaginary illusory world in which the unrealizable conditions can be realized, and this world we call play. Imagination is a new psychological process for the child. Like all functions imagination originally arises in action. The old adage that play is imagination in action must be reversed, imagination in adolescents and school children is play without action. The imaginary situation is the defining characteristic of play in general. (Vygotsky, 1967, p. 7)

For Vygotsky, egocentric speech "goes underground" as internalized thought (cf. Chapter 7). In a similar fashion, play "goes underground" as internalized imagination with development.

Comparison of Piaget and Vygotsky

There are close relations between the contrasting views Piaget and Vygotsky take on private speech and the views each take on play. We can focus the contrasts around the question of origin and endpoint. Why does full-blown pretend play appear around the third year and why does it decline or disappear around the sixth year? The age curve of the two functions of private speech and pretend play are quite similar. For Vygotsky, private speech goes underground as internal thought at around age 6 and symbolic play goes underground as internal imagination. For Piaget, as the child gives up preoperational egocentrism for operational and socialized thought, both private speech and pretend play disappear.

Two major differences exist in the general theories of Piaget and Vygotsky. First, Piaget is a structuralist who explains age-developmental phenomena in terms of change in thought-structures. In contrast, Vygotsky focuses on functional explanations of age development. Second, they differ in the relative weights they assign to biological and cultural factors. For Vygotsky, the influence of culture on mind is decisive; it appears early in development, mediated through the first words acquired by the child. For Piaget, the influence of biological predispositions is primary; the influence of culture appears later mediated through the language of propositional logic. Vygotsky's child is inherently social, whereas Piaget's child is inherently egocentric. For Vygotsky, development is a process of individualization; for Piaget, development is a process of socialization. These differences influence the way these theorists approach play. According to Vygotsky, play provides a means of tension reduction, a way of accommodating to the conflicts and frustrations of real life. Vygotsky thus subscribes to a cathartic theory of play in which symbolization originates in a need for reality substitutes.

By contrast, Piaget views play as an "infinitely varied symbolic system" that provides the child with a means of assimilation needed "in order to rethink past experience." Symbolic games

> either reproduce what has struck the child, evoke what has pleased him or enable him to be more fully part of his environment. In a word they form a vast network of divides which allow the ego to assimilate the whole of reality, i.e., to integrate it in order to relive it, to dominate it or compensate for it. (Piaget, 1962, p. 154)

Conflicts and frustrations may be rendered in play, but for Piaget, other aspects of reality appear as well. Most especially, behavior in the process of being acquired is consolidated by the functional assimilation of play. Piaget thus views symbolization in play as an aspect of mental development in which past experiences are comprehended by symbolic means; but in the process, symbols may be charged with emotional meaning.

If for Vygotsky the origin of symbolic play is emotional, for Piaget it is intellectual. And yet, in developing their positions, these theorists switch sides. What for Vygotsky is created by unrealizable desires becomes an occasion for the organization of meaning in language and thought. What for Piaget is created by the functioning of intelligence becomes a medium for the expression of personal concerns.

Vygotsky stresses the homologies of play and language, claiming that

> children's symbolic play can be understood as a very complex system of "speech" through gestures that communicate and indicate the meaning of play things. (Vygotsky, 1978, p. 108)

In speaking of advanced symbolic play, Vygotsky singles out the phenomenon of substitution:

> some objects can readily denote others, replacing them and becoming signs for them, and the degree of similarity unimportant. What is most important is the...possibility of executing a representational gesture with it...The child's self-motion, his own gestures, are what assign the function of sign to the object and give it meaning. (1978, p. 108)

According to Vygotsky, when children first begin to use words, the word is perceived as a property of the object rather than a symbol of it. The child grasps the external structure of word-object earlier than the internal, symbolic structure of sign-referent. (Vygotsky, 1962, pp. 27–28). To understand the importance of this discrepancy, it is necessary to consider Vygotsky's theoretical frame of reference. For Vygotsky, language plays a central role in the development of thinking. As inner speech, language serves an open-ended, organizing, planning, self-controlling function in the analysis and solution of practical problems. This mediating system appears in the course of development when social speech and inner speech become separated and begin to acquire different structures and functions (Vygotsky, 1962, 1978). Prior to this time, the behavior of the child is dominated by stimuli in the immediate perceptual field; the infant perceives an object and reacts to it. Meaning is dominated by the perceived object and by the behaviors it promotes. By contrast, the older child is able to generate a thought (or word) and act on the perceptual field accordingly. Language and symbolic play are expressions of a mediating system in which internal events (whether images or words) serve to orient and direct behavior. But Vygotsky (1967) goes further. Symbolic play is the behavioral mechanism that precipitates the transition from "things as objects of action" to "things as objects of thought." According to Vygotsky,

> Play is a transitional stage. . . . At the critical moment when a stick—i.e. an object— becomes a pivot for severing the meaning of horse from a real horse, one of the basic psychological structures determining the child's relationship to reality is altered. . . . To a certain extent, meaning is emancipated from the object with which it had been directly fused before. (1967, pp. 12–13)

The central event in symbolic play is the child's use of a substitute object. This event is viewed by Vygotsky as the first step in the detachment of meaning (the concept of horse) from the actual object (a real horse). The substitute object serves as a "pivot" and, in a sense, precipitates the detachment. In grasping the notion that a dissimilar object can be given the meaning "horse," the child has taken a critical step in grasping the notion that a word can be given the same meaning. Vygotsky's insight is that pretend substitutions serve a designative function and prepare the child to understand that words, too, can have such a function. Of course, Baldwin offered a similar insight. To play with representatives of reality (as distinct from the derivation or use of representations) reflects at a *metasemantic level* the child's knowledge of cognitive-linguistic relations.

In contrast, for Piaget, deferred imitation marks the beginnings of the semiotic function and the differentiation of signifier from signified. When deferred imitations are internalized, the results are images. In a sense, accommodative deferred imitations are images in action prior to being images in thought. These images are not produced by assimilating play, rather they are used in play to give personal meanings to objects and events. And language, as a uniform system of signs designating socially shared concepts, has little to do with the symbols of play. For Piaget, play (as assimilation) is an expressive activity, reflecting the egocentric character of the child's preoperational thought. In symbolic play the child "rethinks" the past, perhaps reorganizing it, but the thinking and reorganization are not bounded by real world constraints, social rules, logical classes, and relations. Most certainly, they are not bounded by language, a system of arbitrary and collective signs. Although language and play are each expressions of a broader symbol-sign devising semiotic function, they are independent of one another in development and in actual functioning.

Differences between Vygotsky and Piaget are summarized in Table 9.2. Briefly, Vygotsky stresses the social nature of child thought, the social implications of language, and the culturally stimulated conflicts that press the child to search for substitute sources of gratification. In the course of this search, the child uncovers the principle of signification which then becomes a tool for language acquisition and thinking. It must be stressed, however, that the child's actions of riding on the stick as if it were a horse embodies at the outset the social-cultural practice of riding horses (rather than lions or cows).

TABLE 9.2
Some Comparisons between the Theoretical Positions of Piaget and Vygotsky

	Vygotsky	Piaget
Origins of symbolic play	Emotional press from unrealizable desires force the child to seek substitute sources of gratification	A phase in the development of intelligence marked by the dominance of assimilation over accommodation
Functions of symbolic play	Tension reduction	Consolidation of past experience
Orientation of the player	Social-conceptual	Egocentric-expressive
Developmental outcomes	Major: forces the separation of meaning from object and action; essential mechanism in the development of language and thinking	Minor: temporary mechanism for expressing and reorganizing experiences in order to assimilate them; later supplanted by logical thinking
Signs and symbols	Distinction carries little theoretical significance; both are inherently social	Distinction has crucial theoretical significance; symbols are "motivated" and/or personal; signs are arbitrary and collective
The role of language in symbolic play	Major: play serves a referential function guided by words	Minor: play and language are expressive media, independent of one another in development and in use

By contrast, Piaget stresses the egocentric nature of child thought and its dominance in the early formation of images, symbols, and word meaning. The principle of signification is neither uncovered or discovered. Instead it emerges from the natural relation between imitation and the events that are imitated; imitation is signification. As the actions of imitation become encoded as images, the signifier becomes separated from what is signified. Symbolic play is thereby the assimilation of imaginal signifiers—the incorporation of signified events into systems of meaning constructed during the preceding period of sensorimotor intelligence. In the process of incorporation, the signifiers are susceptible to further distortion, bending, and reshaping to suit the child's momentary preoccupations, and in the process new symbols or signifiers are constructed. On the one hand, Vygotsky calls on forces generated in the domain of emotion to influence development in the domain of language and thought. On the other, Piaget calls on the domain of thought to produce a mechanism for achieving emotional control and stability.

According to Piaget, the forms of symbolic play change between 12 and 24 months in a manner reflecting the development of preoperational thought (Nicolich, 1977); but play representations at any level reflect the child's egocentric, self-preoccupied, and personal orientation. The expressive function of play is served equally well at each level of symbolic development. To Vygotsky, the substitution phenomenon is the crucial event linking language and play. Development is characterized by the gradual emancipation of meaning from physical stimulation.

G. H. MEAD: SOCIODRAMATIC PLAY AND THE GAME AS THE CONSTRUCTION OF A SOCIAL SELF

We have discussed the role of pretend play in contributing to cognitive development, ego development, and the development of imagination. We have not yet discussed play as social and the contribution of play to the development of a social self. To do so, we need to turn to the theory of G. H. Mead (1934). Our starting point is Mead's notion that there is a pretend play stage of development of the social self followed by a game stage. Such a sequence is also proposed by Piaget.

Piaget on Games

Piaget's 1962 account of the major developmental levels of play starts the "practice" play of the sensorimotor period. As the capacity for symbolism develops, play becomes primarily symbolic, a form of play in which activities and objects represent something they are not. Insofar as play involves other children, *symbolic play* is usually termed "sociodramatic" play. According to Piaget, the development of socially organized symbolic play is, first, development in the *coordination of reciprocal social roles*, second, a more exact imitation of social reality, and, third, development in the formation of collective symbols, that is, agreed-on and even conventionalized, representations of shared experiences. These collective symbols embody the "rules" that so impressed Vygotsky. The development of the capacity to play complementary roles occurs first within the child's own solitary role-playing activities (i.e., within the ability to view herself as another) and then in the ability to coordinate this role-playing with that of a partner.

With the transition to concrete-operational thought, sociodramatic play is followed by the development of *games with rules.*

> Games with rules are games with sensorimotor combinations (races, ball games) or intellectual combinations (cards) in which there is competition between individuals (otherwise rules would be useless) which are regulated either by a code handed down from earlier generations or by temporary agreement. (Piaget, 1962, p. 144)

On the one hand, as Piaget (1965/1932) has stressed, experience in games contributes first to a sense of the need for rules (in a heteronomous or moral "Stage 1" sense) and then to an awareness of the function and meaning of rules as agreements for coordinating the activities of equal individuals with varying interests (in an autonomous or moral "Stage 2" sense of rules). As Piaget argues, the child's first sense of rule-making and of the possibility of choosing rules as means to social ends tends to occur in the sphere of the game.*

Piaget then has sketched some of the functions of game participation for sociomoral development. A more complete and vivid sense of the progression and its meaning is given by Mead's discussion which, in turn, builds on Baldwin's theory, already partially discussed.

Baldwin on the Play Stage of Development of the Self

Let us start by noting that sociodramatic play is in part a rendering of how children view adult social reality. In Baldwin's theory, the child generates a social self through imitation. In imitating others, the child is coming to grasp the perspective of the person or role being imitated. Although Baldwin uses the term "imitation," he is not defining imitation as a copy or as social modeling. Rather, the child's rendering is selective and imbued with personal meaning.

The growth of imagination discussed in our section on Baldwin and Vygotsky is primarily an imaginative grasp of the inner reality of oneself and other social beings (people ride horses and I am one of those people). It is through imaginative literature and art that even as adults we come closest to an empathic grasp of the inner life of others. In the child the imaginative grasp is part of the overt rendering

---

*Piaget uses the term competitive in a general way to describe games in which there are ways of winning and losing, even though a person might be competing with herself (such as in solitaire). Piaget's point is that game rules are socially accepted ways of regulating an area of interpersonal discord.

of others' behaviors, or of playing out their roles. As Baldwin points out, in recreating the other, the child is making the role of the other part of himself. This self he then ejects or attributes to others as he constructs a sense of their inner world. In the years from 4 to 8, the child moves from simple behavioral renderings of external others (as a horse rider) to constructing a generalized or ideal self to which he conforms (a heroic cowboy who brings law and order to the west). This is a generalization of the self that obeys common rules whether in the role of the assimilating self acting on others or of the passive self bending to others (Kohlberg, 1969).

Mead on the Play Stage of the Self

This sequence charted by Baldwin is discussed in a richer but compatible theory by G. H. Mead (1934). What Baldwin terms "imitation," Mead terms "role-taking."*

According to Mead, role-taking is a more general process than imitation, one that occurs whenever people communicate. To understand the language or communicative gestures of others, we must implicitly take the role of the other in regard to our own communication gestures. The overt playing of the role of the other is only the tip of the iceberg of taking the role of others.

Within the child's own role-playing activities, social meanings develop through what Mead has called role-taking, which depends on a complementary relationship to the other. In order to "take the role of the other" we must overtly or covertly imagine acting in relationship to the other and so elicit that person's attitudes as reactions to our own responses. Even adults may engage in imaginary dialogue with another individual in order to elaborate both the attitudes of the other they wish to clarify and their own attitudes. In the young child the internal dialogue of thought seems to take the form of "egocentric speech" or "collective monologue" in which the child addresses another but is "really" addressing herself, often asking her companion questions and then answering them herself (see Chapter 5 on thought and language). In play, the dialogue takes explicit form in the enactment of complementary roles. In the child's home, the child behaves as a son or daughter in relation to a parent, but these roles are implicit in the relationship. To explicitly play the child's role, the child must implicitly take the complementary role of the parent even though the child is playing alone. In sociodramatic play, the complementary role of parent, implicitly taken in family life, is explicitly presented in a "dialogue" between the play parent and the play child. As stated by Mead (1934), children organize in this way the responses they call out in other persons and call out also in themselves. Play in this sense,

---

*In this discussion we adhere closely to Mead's language of "role-playing" and "role-taking." Role-playing is the overt enactment of roles in play. Role-taking is the psychological aspect of this behavior. We avoid the term "role adoption" because it refers to the more long-term process whereby the individual reconciles and sorts out the coupled relation between a view of self as a stable individual and a view of self as an individual who adopts shifting roles in relating to others.

especially the stage which precedes the organized games, is a play at something. A child plays at being a mother, at being a teacher, at being a policeman. In Mead's words:

> We have something that suggests this in what we call the play of animals: . . . Two dogs playing with each other will attack and defend, in a process which if carried through would amount to an actual fight. There is a combination of responses which checks the depth of the bite. But we do not have in such a situation the dogs taking the definite role in the sense that a child deliberately takes the role of another. This tendency on the part of the children is what we are working with in the kindergarten where the roles which the children assume are made the basis for training. When a child does assume a role he has in himself the stimuli which call out that particular response or group of responses. He may, of course, run away when he is chased, as the dog does, or he may turn around and strike back just as the dog does in his play. But that is not the same as playing at something. Children get together to "play Indian." This means that the child has a certain set of stimuli which call out in itself the responses that they would call out in others, and which answers to an Indian. In the play period the child utilizes his own responses to these stimuli which he makes use of in building a self. The response which he has a tendency to make to these stimuli organizes them. He plays that he is, for instance, offering himself something, and he buys it; he gives a letter to himself and takes it away; he addresses himself as a parent, as a teacher; he arrests himself as a policeman. He has a set of stimuli which call out in himself the sort of responses they call out in others. He takes this group of responses and organizes them into a certain whole. Such is the simplest form of being another to one's self. It involves a temporal situation. The child says something in one character and responds in another character, and then his responding in another character is a stimulus to himself in the first character, and so the conversation goes on. A certain organized structure arises in him and in his other which replies to it, and these carry on the conversation of gestures between themselves. (1934, p. 213)

Mead then points to a feature of pretend play that is later and more complex than that discussed by either Piaget or Vygotsky. Piaget saw the essence of pretend play as nonserious symbolic gestures (his Type I play; see Table 9.1) and locates its genesis in the second year of life. Vygotsky sees its essence as the separation of the play symbol from the object signified (Piaget's Type II play), and locates its genesis in the third year of life. Mead sees its essence as an organization of collective reciprocal roles (Piaget's Type IV play) and locates its genesis around the fourth year or the beginning of kindergarten.

Mead on the Game Stage of the Self

The next new structure, the game stage, starts later. Of this Mead says:

> If we contrast play with the situation in an organized game, we note the essential difference that the child who plays in a game must be ready to take the attitude of

everyone else involved in that game, and that these different roles must have a definite relationship to each other. In the play stage the child passes from one role to another just as a whim takes him. But in a game where a number of individuals are involved, then the child taking one role must be ready to take the role of everyone else. If he gets in a baseball nine he must have the responses of each position involved in his own position. He must know what everyone else is going to do in order to carry out his own play. He has to take all these roles. They do not all have to be present in consciousness at the same time, but at some moments he has to have three or four individuals present in his own attitude, such as the one who is going to throw the ball, the one who is going to catch it, and so on. . . . In the game, then, there is a set of responses of such others so organized that the attitude of one calls out the appropriate attitudes of the other.

This organization is put in the form of the rules of the game. . . . Part of the enjoyment of the game is to get these rules. Now, the rules are the set of responses which a particular attitude calls out. You can demand a certain response in others if you take a certain attitude. These responses are all in yourself as well. There you get an organized set of such responses. . .which is something more elaborate than the roles found in play. . . . In his game he has to have an organization of these roles; otherwise he cannot play the game. The game represents the passage in the life of the child from taking the role of others in play to the organized part that is essential to self-consciousness in the full sense of the term. (1934, p. 157)

Figure 9.2 schematizes the intricate set of psychological structures involved in the transition from the play stage to the game stage. First, the play stage involves vertical transformations of self into social roles of parent, child, or sibling. These transformations may involve asymmetrical (mother-daughter) or identity (daughter-sister) relations. Second, the play stage involves horizontal transformations. Role-playing with a partner requires complementary or reciprocal relations with another person, mother in relation to father, parent to child, and brother to sister. Both the initial transformation (which establishes the play status of the player) and the consequent reciprocal exchanges require the child to take into account the perspective of others in relation to this play self.

Also schematized in Figure 9.2 is the far more complex and, more important, generalized attitude of the game-playing child. The child as pitcher must also negotiate self transformations (pitcher-batter-team captain) and establish complementary relationships (pitcher with batter, and vice versa). But the game-playing child must also contend with a rule-based system of generalized roles. As pitcher, he must interact with the batter, but simultaneously keep in mind the positions played by members of his own team with respect to spatial location, function, or special skills. As batter, a similar set of relationships are required, but now the other team becomes the generalized other. Finally, as captain of the team, the child must contend with structures describing his own team as well as the other team. Over and above the particulars of personal encounters and individualized team members, the child becomes involved in strategic issues based on the assessment of relative team strengths in relation to game rules.

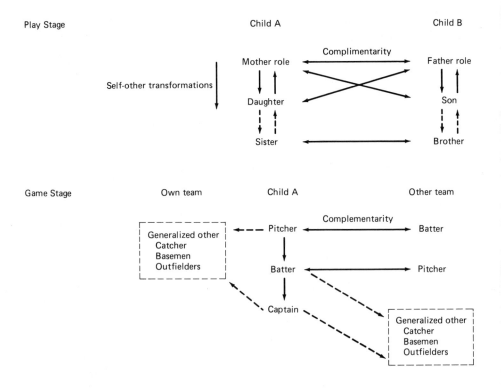

Figure 9.2 Mead's concept of complementarity and the generalized other.

ERIKSON'S THEORY OF PLAY AND WORK

To represent a more clinical mode of theorizing about play, we have selected Erik Erikson, whose general theory we described in Chapter 8. Erikson's thinking about play is worthy of detailed consideration for a number of reasons. One reason important for us is that it is compatible with the cognitive-developmental theories of play just discussed.

Because Erikson writes so beautifully, it is best to let his ideas of the function of play be presented primarily through quotation from the section on "Toys and reasons" in *Childhood and society* (1963) and from the book titled *Toys and reasons* (1977).

Play as Ego-Synthesis

In *Childhood and society*, Erikson presents examples designed to show a continuum from play therapy to the "normal" play of a child with "normal" problems. In all cases Erikson is bent on showing that play involves the ego synthesizing conflicts.

In the case of play therapy, the child requires an understanding adult to engage in successful "self-cure" through play. He says:

> Modern play-therapy is based on the observation that a child made insecure by a secret hate against or fear of the natural protectors of his play in family and neighbourhood seems able to use the protective sanction of an understanding adult to regain some play peace. Grandmothers and favourite aunts may have played that role in the past; its professional elaboration of today is the play therapist. The most obvious condition is that the child has the toys and the adult for himself, and that sibling rivalry, parental nagging, or any kind of sudden interruption does not disturb the unfolding of his play intentions, whatever they may be. For to "play it out" is the most natural self-healing measure childhood affords. (1963, p. 200)

According to Erikson, the normal child uses play for self-cure in a form in which self-cure or ego-synthesis is continuous with pleasurable or recreational activity. He says:

> Paraphrasing Freud, we have called play the royal road to the understanding of the infantile ego's efforts at synthesis...we shall now turn to childhood situations which illustrate the capacity of the ego to find recreation and self-cure in the activity of play; and to therapeutic situations in which we were fortunate enough to be able to help a child's ego to help itself. (1963, p. 188)

The ego helps itself in play by "hallucinating ego mastery and yet also to practice it in an intermediate reality between fantasy and actuality...when man plays he must do something he has chosen to do without being compelled, he must feel free."

This statement of Erikson's is quite close to Vygotsky's statement that play is the expression of unrealizable tendencies in the actual situation in a zone of sensed freedom limited only by self-chosen rules of play.

The example of ego-synthesis through play Erikson chooses is Ben in Mark Twain's Tom Sawyer. He says:

> Let us take as our text for the beginning of this more reassuring chapter a play episode described by a rather well-known psychologist. The occasion, while not pathological, is nevertheless a tragic one: a boy named Tom Sawyer, by verdict of his aunt, must whitewash a fence on an otherwise faultless spring morning. His predicament is intensified by the appearance of an age mate named Ben Rogers, who indulges in a game. It is Ben, the man of leisure, whom we want to observe with the eyes of Tom, the working man.
>
> Ben Rogers hove in sight presently—the very boy, of all boys, whose ridicule he had been dreading. Ben's gait was the hop-skip-and-jump—proof enough that his heart was light and his anticipation high. He was eating an apple, and giving a long, melodious whoop, at intervals, followed by a deep-toned ding-dong-dong, ding-dong-dong, for he was personating a steamboat. As he drew near, he slackened speed, took

the middle of the street, leaned far over to starboard and rounded to ponderously and with laborious pomp and circumstance—for he was personating the Big Missouri, and considered himself to be drawing nine feet of water. He was boat and captain and engine-bells combined, so he had to imagine himself standing on his own hurricane-deck giving the orders and executing them:

...'Stop the stabboard! Ting-a-ling-ling! Stop the labboard! Come ahead on the stabboard! Stop her! Let your outside turn over slow! Ting-a-ling-ling! Chow-ow-ow! Get out that head-line! Lively now! Come—out with your spring-line—what're you about there! Take a turn round that stump with the bight of it! Stand by that stage, now—let her go! Done with the engines, sir! Ting-a-ling-ling! Sh't! sh't sh't!' (trying the gauge-cocks).

Tom went on whitewashing—paid no attention to the steamboat. Ben stared a moment, and then said:

'Hi-yi! You're up a stump, ain't you!...You got to work, hey?'

My clinical impression of Ben Rogers is a most favourable one, and this on all three counts: organism, ego and society. For he takes care of the body by munching an apple; he simultaneously enjoys imaginary control over a number of highly conflicting items (being a steamboat, and parts thereof, as well as being the captain of said steamboat, and the crew obeying said captain); while he loses not a moment in sizing up social reality when, on navigating a corner, he sees Tom at work. By no means reacting as a steamboat would, he knows immediately how to pretend sympathy though he undoubtedly finds his freedom enhanced by Tom's predicament.... In view of Ben's final fate it seems almost rude to add interpretation to defeat, and to ask what Ben's play may mean. (1963, p. 188)

Erikson then goes on to interpret the meaning of Ben's play from a psychoanalytic perspective:

One "meaning" of Ben's play could be that it affords his ego a temporary victory over his gangling body and self by making a well-functioning whole out of brain (captain), the nerves and muscles of will (signal system and engine), and the whole bulk of the body (boat). It permits him to be an entity within which he is his own boss, because *he obeys himself.* At the same time, he chooses his metaphors from the tool world of the young machine age, and anticipates the identity of the machine god of his day: the captain of the Big Missouri. (1963, p. 211)

Whereas Piaget and Vygotsky were concerned with the structure of play symbols—the integration of symbolic elements and the formal relation of symbols to real world events—Erikson is interested in the *content* of symbols, in their specific psychological meanings as personal expressions of universal longings or fears. In this vein, Erikson notes that 'a boat in a mighty stream makes a good symbol of mechanical power, and that a captain is a good symbol of well-delineated patriarchal power. Ben's play then expresses the ego's capacity to marshal symbols and thoughts in an effort to "synchronize the bodily and social processes with the self."

Play as Imagination in Erikson

Echoing J. M. Baldwin's view that play is the childhood form of imaginative planning and hypotheses formation, discussed earlier, Erikson views play as the childhood form of the human ability to deal with experiences by creating model situations and to master reality by experiments and planning.

The meaning of model situations he elaborates as follows:

> The child's play begins with and centres on his own body. This we shall call *autocosmic* play. It begins before we notice it as play, and consists at first in the exploration by repetition of sensual perceptions, of kinaesthetic sensations, of vocalizations, etc. Next, the child plays with available persons and things...
>
> The *microsphere*—i.e., the small world of manageable toys—is a harbour which the child establishes, to return to when he needs to overhaul his ego.... Finally, at nursery-school age playfulness reaches into the *macrosphere*, the world shared with others. First these others are treated as things, are inspected, run into, or forced to "be horsie." Learning is necessary in order to discover what potential play content can be admitted only to fantasy or only to autocosmic play; what content can be successfully represented only in the microcosmic world of toys and things; and what content can be shared with others and foced upon them. (1963, pp. 211–220)

Erikson therefore includes in his thinking about play the functions of play for development discussed by Baldwin and Vygotsky. These functions include not only assimilation of the past but imaginative planning of the future in a world of freedom, a psychological freedom, according to Baldwin, that is created by play.

Play and Erikson's Ego Stages

We have not yet touched on the way in which Erikson's stage theory informs his characterization of play. The "Golden Age" of pretend play are the years between 3 and 6, the period of Erikson's stage of "initiative vs. guilt." To illustrate play in this stage, we have chosen a verbatim episode taken from a study of peer interactions. The episode involves two 5 year olds, a girl named Lil (L) and a boy named Jim (J). As the action begins, Jim is playing with a fire truck and miniature people while Lil is walking back and forth with a broom.

L: Are you the father or the son?*
J: I'm the big brother.
L: OK, then I'll be the big sister.

*Two forms of communication characterize sociodramatic episodes. Metacommunications are communications *about* the play. In these exchanges, the children retain their own identities and, as themselves, talk about the roles and scenes being performed. By contrast, pretend communications are exchanges held *within* the play mode. In these exchanges, the children relate to one another in the roles they have agreed to perform. In the above protocols, metacommunications are underlined.

J: 'Cause fathers don't even play with toys.

L: Well, I'm the big girl, I'm the big sister. Anyway, Mom told me to take care of the two babies, our little brother and sister and you better not touch them or I'm gonna tell Mom on you.

J: You're not gonna tell anybody on me.

L: Huh! I'm gonna tell someone on you, don't you think I'm not. So brother, if you want to say something, keep it to your own self.

J: You know I'm bigger than you.

L: Huh, you're not bigger than anybody.

J: Hey, I'm bigger than you—you're just 9. So you better watch it!

L: You're the biggest 'cause you're just 12 years old. You're even bigger than me.

J: You're just. . .

L: If you want to fight just go fight yourself.

J: You think I'm bigger than you 'cause I'm 12 years old. You, you're just 9. Hey, hey, you better watch it 'cause I'm babysitting for you all.

L: You mean us three?

J: Yeah.

L: One, two, three.

J: There, just. . .

L: One, two, three, four, and your own self. You're a baby: your own self.

J: Hey, I ain't no baby girl, what goes and tattles on you.

(Jim and Lil begin to whisper.)

L: You better watch it 'cause they're waking, brother.

J: Shut up.

L: Well, make me.

J: Shut up before you make me wake the babies up.

L: Then I'll really tell Mom on you.

J: Hey you can't, you cannot tell Mom on me. I'll. . .

L: Then I'll tell Dad on you. Let me tell you; you be the dad and. . .

J: Uh-uh, I ain't playing no dad and I'm certain not no daddy.

L: And I'm certain not no mommy.

J: If you wanna find a daddy, if you wanna find a daddy, ask John (the children's teacher).

This episode can be discussed on at least four levels. At the *manifest* level, Lil skillfully orchestrates and initiates a sibling struggle for dominance. She casts Jim in the role of potential aggressor, controlled by the threat of disclosure to punitive adults. Jim accepts this role, valiantly striving for parity by virtue of age seniority. But Lil can concede the age advantage because she retains greater advantage as the tattling younger sister. Both children accept the premise that the parent will side with sister, and, more important, the premise that Jim will be judged guilty even if someone else made him wake the babies up. For Erikson, these manifest themes mark the period of tension between initiative and guilt. Each child is verbally provocative and abusive—attacking and defending. But, of course, the scene is play—a make-believe rendering of behavior that in real life might bring penalties. As play, the children need experience neither anxiety nor guilt. They can vent anxiety, come to terms with guilt, and, perhaps, practice the verbal skills needed to contend with real siblings in the real world.

At a *latent* level, the scene reflects the concerns of the Oedipal child. Jim is emphatic in his refusal of the paternal role. Even "son" brings him too close to mother for comfort; Jim makes the fine semantic distinction between son and brother, preferring the sibling connection to the filial one. In anticipating the future, Jim settles for being 12 years old—a safe age when boys can still play with toys without either the helplessness of childhood or the tensions of adolescence.

One might also consider the social skill required to negotiate and maintain a sociodramatic play episode in which one plays at hostility without becoming hostile. At least one part of this skill is suggested by Mead—the ability to manage the complementarity of play roles while maintaining the relation of real self to play self and real self to the partner's real self.

Finally, there is the developmental functions served by play. In Erikson's words:

> According to the "traumatic" theory, play serves the compulsion to repeat symboli-
> cally experiences not sufficiently managed in the past and to turn what was passively
> suffered into active mastery.... But if we acknowledge in certain play events the
> working through of some trauma, we may note the very factor of playfulness
> transforms them into acts of renewal. And if play helps the exercise of growing
> faculties, it does so with inventiveness and character. (1963, p. 41)

The virtue that emerges from the ego stage of initiative versus guilt Erikson terms "purpose." This develops largely out of play in the era of the child's personality. Of this, he says:

> It is inherent in man's prolonged immaturity that he must develop in "mere" fantasy
> and play the rudiments of purpose, a temporal perspective giving direction and focus
> to concerted striving. Play is to the child what thinking, planning are to the adult, a
> trial universe in which conditions are simplified and methods exploratory, so that past
> failure can be thought through, expectations tested. In the toy world the child "plays
> out" the past and begins to master the future by anticipating it in countless variations
> of repetitive themes. In taking the various role-images of his elders into his sphere of
> make-believe he can find out how it feels to be like them before fate forces him to
> become, indeed, like some of them. If it seems the child spends on his play a sincere
> purposefulness out of proportion to what he soon must learn, he underestimates the
> evolutionary necessity for representational play in an animal who must learn to bind
> together an inner and an outer world, a remembered past and an anticipated future.
> (1963, p. 43)

Let us summarize what Erikson is saying. First, play is primarily a sphere of ego-synthesis or the resolution of conflicts. Where play themes have a common content in a culture, like Ben as the steamboat, these conflicts are likely to be caused by typical issues of growth. Where play has unique individual meanings these represent resolutions of idiosyncratic forms of conflict, possibly by the repetition of past experiences for the sake of mastery. Such reenactments may be curative, particularly in the presence of an understanding neutral adult. Particularly in the "Golden Age" of pretend play, between 3 and 6 years of age, the conflicts being synthesized involve the attitudes of initiative or "purpose" versus guilt of the Oedipal child. Finally, Erikson notes that with each new stage there is a new element of ritualization contained in play. At the Golden Age of pretend play, focused on themes of initiative versus guilt, the ritualistic element appears in the conflict between archetypal figures of good (representative of the ego-ideal) and evil. In dramatic play, the child explores areas where there can be good initiative without encountering guilt. In a later section, we present a play episode in which two children play-argue. In the play context, aggressiveness can be expressed without penalties.

Erikson shares with Baldwin and Vygotsky the idea that imagination and sociodramatic play serve the functions that in adults are imaginative, the formulating of hypotheses and artistic production and creation. He believes that the play experience is necessary for the accrual of the ego-strength of purpose, with its implied ability to delay gratification stressed by Vygotsky.

Work and Ego Stages for Erikson

For Erikson, positive experiences of initiative or purpose formed through play are a major condition for the accrual of his next virtue, competence or the sense of industry in the face of possible feelings of inferiority. "Competence" is the basic virtue in the sphere of work.

In a sense this virtue represents an overlap of new or salient concerns of this school child, concerns for school learning and achievement, same-sex peer-competition and cooperation, concerns for approval of nonfamilial adults, growing motor mastery of tools, "latency period" interest in competence and work as opposed to fantasy or hedonistic-impulsive gratification. More basically, however, "competence" as a virtue relates to a single concept of "work" and "workmanship" just as "purpose" relates to play. The basic modality of competence for Erikson is the relation of "what works"—what is effective in one's thinking and one's physical coordination as judged by its consequences in materials affected or social cooperations achieved.

The school age, Erikson says,

> adds another element of ritualization, that of *methodical performance*. The mental and emotional eagerness to make material things and facts reveal what can be done

with them in order to create new and lasting forms matures only in the school age. There play is transformed into work and games into competition and cooperation. These basic techniques are thought essential to participation in the economic and technical system, each offering a *ritualization of method.*

The estrangement of the school age is a sense of *inferiority*, of not being able to live up to the demands of physical performance and discipline required for the basic techniques being taught. The other danger of this stage is in overformalization and perfectionism with a ritualism or formalism that pretends that "work makes the man and technique makes the truth." (1977, pp. 103–104)

The thrust of Erikson's thinking is that play and work are not opposed values for the child, but rather that a sense of purpose grounded in play experiences is a precursor or precondition for the virtues of work, of industry and competence.

FROM PLAY TO CONSTRUCTIVE WORK

The major problem in what Erikson calls the development of industry in the early school years is that the work expected of the child is school work, a kind of work that does not seem like true work to the child. For the school child, the experience of satisfying work is more attainable through the making of things, through constructive activity.

In work, the child has a goal in the interests of which he uses objects as means, but he must be continually adjusting his own patterns of activity to the objects to reach these goals. What we call work, then, involves organizing activity in a sequence over time, leading to a goal. It also means revising and refining an initial goal as one selects means to the goal without losing sight of the goal. It involves the reciprocal adjustment of means and ends, of the self's pattern and abilities and the characteristics of objects.

For the young child, "work" in this sense must be concrete, it must be making some*thing*, it must be using tools, or it must involve taking physical parts to construct a whole. The identification of work with the young child's use of tools and construction is expressed by Dewey.

As Dewey and Erikson stress, the disposition to "work" or "industry" is not something imposed on the child by social authority and sanctions (which Dewey calls "labor," not work) but is a natural emergent from what is earlier seen as play. The major difference between play and work lies in the time-span involved or the degree of sequential organization of the activity.

Play also has an end in the sense of a directing idea which gives point to successive acts. Persons who play are trying to do or effect something. The anticipated result, however, is rather a subsequent action than the production of a specific change in things. Consequently play is free and plastic. When a definite external outcome is wanted, the end has to be held with persistence through a series of intermediate adaptations. In play, children like to construct their own toys and appliances. With increasing maturity, activity which does not give back results of tangible and visible achievement loses its interest. Like play, work signifies purposeful activity and differs not in that the activity is subordinated to an external result, but in the fact that a longer course of activity is occasioned by the idea of the result. (Dewey, 1971/1915, p. 202)

According to Dewey, the difference between play and work is a difference in degree of sequential organization of an activity. It is also a difference in degree of organization of means/ends relationships in the extent to which intentions are checked against actual results. The opposition between natural play and "work," Dewey tells us, arises because work is conceived in terms of the traditional school "work" in terms of passive learning of instructional material. "Real or active work," says Dewey, "engages the full spontaneous interest and attention of children. It differs from play not in having a purposed end, but in that the end or purpose is maintained through obstacles and through intermediaries."

Take the example of the little child who wants to make a box. If he stops short with imagination or wish, he will certainly not get discipline. But when he attempts to realize his impulse, it is a question of making his idea definite and into a plan, taking the right kind of wood, of measuring the parts, of knowledge of tools, etc. If the child makes the box, there is plenty of opportunity to gain discipline and perseverance, to exercise effort in overcoming obstacles, to attain information. (Dewey, 1971/1915, p. 55)

The extent to which young children enjoy "work" is evidenced in their efforts at making something. A cognitive-developmental education would surely provide more extensive opportunities to make things that are at the right level of match for the child than exist today.

Two problems exist in the design of approximate work or crafts materials and activities if these are to elicit "work" in the positive sense. The first is the match of the structure of the task inherent in the materials to the child himself. The classical blocks lend themselves to construction that is close to free play. Such material needs supplementation by more "structured" material, for example, blocks designed to be put together to make a definite structure with an end in view. The second problem of design is that of tools satisfactory for the child's psychomotor level. From a safe electric jig saw to potter's wheels, there are many such tools that allow the child to use his or her immediate psychomotor skills to engage in planned construction.

In summary, young children enjoy constructive as well as pretend play. Particularly in the early school years, there is the need for opportunities for constructive work that involves making things. Work need not be equated with academic school work, and should not be if the spontaneous play impulses of children are to grow into the disciplines and forms of work, as Erikson and Dewey suggest.

RESEARCH ON AGE-DEVELOPMENTAL TRENDS IN PLAY

The study of play has mushroomed in the past decade. Space does not permit a comprehensive review here of this vast and growing literature. The interested reader is referred to Fein (1979a & b) and Fein (1981) for reviews of pretend play research, and to Rubin, Fein and Vandenberg (1983), for a review of play research in general. In this section, our aim is to highlight major findings in relation to the theories discussed earlier.

Piaget's outline of major transitions in play has received strong support from empirical studies. First, infants' sensorimotor activities change in ways reflecting their growing ability to combine actions and objects in diverse ways (Fein, 1981). Moreover, the precursors of pretense appear at about 12 months of age, and over the first year early forms are elaborated and extended.

Piaget (1962) cast these empirical observations into a sequence of developmental levels recently replicated by Nicolich (1977). As summarized in Table 9.1, the developmental sequence notes the appearance of new components that become coordinated into increasingly elaborate and flexible representational behavior.

In keeping with the thinking of the developmental theorists discussed earlier, investigators have examined four aspects of the development of pretend play in early childhood: (a) the situational transformations of play, (b) object transformations, (c) self (other) transformations, and (d) the socialization of symbolization and role complementarity in sociodramatic play.

Decontextualization: Situation Transformations

In the earliest appearing form of pretend play, the child's behavior becomes detached from the real-life situation in which it ordinarily occurs (mealtime, bedtime) and the motivational underpinnings ordinarily associated with it (hunger, fatigue). In a sense, a familiar behavior is reframed and placed under voluntary control free of specific situational and motivational demands.

Solitary pretend play is firmly established during the second year of life. Toward the third year of life, there is the beginning of sociodramatic play. It is not until the fourth year of life that children organize their sociodramatic behavior into social roles, that is, in terms of classes of persons who are "supposed" to have certain attributes and who engage in activities with functions defined as functions of these roles.

Recent play episodes, taken from a recent study of peer interactions in children between the ages of 2 and 6 years, confirm these trends (Fein 1979a). In the study, well-acquainted children come in pairs to a well-equipped playroom where their behavior is videotaped through a one-way mirror. Each child is videotaped playing with different peers in four 15-minute sessions. The data illustrate some general features of the pretend play behavior of children within this age range. First, at 2 years of age, sociodramatic episodes are rare, but by 5 years it is not unusual for sociodramatic episodes to occupy an entire 15-minute period. Second, the content of the play changes from simple imitative motor actions (such as one child feeding another) to enactment of full blown social roles (such as sister and brother).

The following episode involves an exchange between two unusually sophisticated 2 and a half year olds, a boy named Herman (H) and a girl named Sally (S). Herman begins the action.

H: (Takes the baby bottle and the spoon) Take your medicine, OK? (said in a coaxing tone)

S: OK, put it on my spoon.

H: (Puts it on her spoon and says) It's not medicine, it's for your nose. Hey, you know what?

S: Yeah, put it in my nose.

H: I put it in your nose, OK? (S. bends head back. H. brings spoon to her nose.)

S: OK (She continues to comb her hair).

H: Drink some of that.

S: OK. (S. pretends to drink what H. is feeding her.)

H: You feed me, OK? (H. puts down the bottle and the spoon.)

S: OK. (S. picks up the bottle and the spoon and feeds H.) It's medicine. It's medicine. Look, it's medicine.

H: It's mine (takes the bottle from S.)

S: OK. Where's my bottle?

H: (Looks in her carriage) Your bottle is down there.

S: Oh, thank you.

H: I'll show you, OK? (Pause) Where's the spoon? (H. takes the spoon from S.)

S: No! (S. reaches for the spoon. H. turns around and pours from the bottle to the spoon.)

H: This is for your nose, OK? This is for your nose.

S: OK.

H: You're gonna be alright.

S: I'll be alright. (Pause) Come here, give me your medicine, I'll feed you, OK? Want me to feed you?

H: You want me to feed you?

S: No, I'll feed you.

H: Unh, unh.

S: Yeah.

H: No. (H. leaves).

S: (Sweetly) it's medicine. You will be OK.

H: Unh, unh.

S: (Sweetly and insistently) Come here, it's medicine. You will be OK. (S. takes a taste of it.) It's Kool-Aid, you want some Kool-Aid?

H: Nods yes, drinks from the spoon, and smiles.

S: (Smiling back) Oh, it's good.

Note that Herman and Sally are preoccupied with the concrete, sensorimotor roles of "giver" and "taker." They are able to negotiate role reversals, and Sally is even able to employ successfully the adult ruse of presenting medicine as Kool-Aid. And yet, although the play lasted for almost 10 minutes, the children never extended either by gesture, clothing, or verbal labeling the sensorimotor roles of "giver" and "taker" to the social roles of parent and child, or doctor and patient. Metacommunications are distinguished from play communications largely by shifts in tone and pacing of the exchange.

Compare this episode to the exchange between the two 5 year olds given earlier. Action roles preoccupy Herman and Sally, whereas social roles are of central importance to Lil and Jim. Father, son, brother, mother, sister, baby, along with the obligations, responsibilities, and privileges that accompany these roles are major issues for older children in defining the boundaries of the play that is to occur. Jim is quite explicit in rejecting the father role because it would not permit him to play with the toys. But as the 12-year-old big brother, he retains some authority even though, as the play unfolds, it becomes clear that this authority must be vigilantly asserted and defended.

Note also that Herman and Sally are unable to maintain conflict in the play frame; the dispute about the bottle or negotiations about the reversal of roles are not embedded in the play until Sally finally pretends to pretend that the medicine is Kool-Aid. In contrast, Lil and Jim are able to play at conflict as well as to argue about the play.

Thus, in the infant, situational transformations appear in the simple acts of eating, drinking, or sleeping. A year or so later they appear in two-person exchanges in which a social situation (giving and taking) is nested within a broader situation, that of giving and taking medicine when you are not "all right." Finally, by 5 years of age, the situational transformation involves the coupled recreation of sibling relationships in the home involving functions such as "baby-sitting", sibling rivalry, and parent-child relations.

Object Substitutions

During the early stages of pretend play, an object must be present in its familiar form if it is to be used as an object in pretense. Initially, the spoon must be "spoonlike," but eventually an object that does not appear to have any apparent spoonlike features (a leaf) can be used as if it were a spoon provided it can be held, lifted, and brought in some fashion to the child's mouth. In our earlier example, a baby bottle became a medicine bottle and the imaginary substance changed from "medicine" to pretending at pretending that the medicine was Kool-Aid. As development progresses, the dependency of pretending on a perceivable object of any sort is reduced and eventually the child is able to produce a purely imaginative object or substance with no apparent reliance on the immediate stimulus field.

Studies of substitutional behavior have been numerous and provocative. In an early study, Fein (1975) argued that the substitution phenomenon as formulated by Piaget and Vygotsky assumed that the child begins with the ability to represent objects as examples of general categories, as cuplike cups or horselike horses. In a sense, the representations are literal, a synthesis of the child's past experience of seeing, touching, smelling, hearing, and acting on such things. By 2 years of age, the child who pretends to feed a horse-like toy horse with a cup-like cup knows that real animals eat and that a cup is for drinking. Pretense is operating insofar as the child behaves as if he were attributing living functions to an inanimate object, adding liquid to an empty cup and, importantly, establishing the relation between horse and cup. In a sense, neither the horse-like horse (a toy) nor the cup (empty) are "real" but the child pretends to "feed the horse" with little difficulty. The scheme developed to describe such an activity is illustrated in Figure 9.1. Note that "object" and "action" are the basic units used to designate the relationships enacted by the child. Now suppose these highly prototypical objects are replaced by less prototypical counterparts—an abstract horse shape and a shell. To initiate a pretense, the child must maintain the action relationships (feeding) with materials that are less horse-like and cup-like. The term transformation is used to designate the process that maintains the relationship and permits one object (a less prototypical object) to be used as if it were another (a highly prototypical object). Note that three categories of transformations are presented: the shift from self to other (the child who is usually fed by another becomes the one who feeds), the transformation of an inanimate object into an animate one (horse shape into horse) and the transformation of one inanimate object into another (a shell into a cup). In the above example, the relation "feeding/eating" would require two transformations by the child if both the "horse" and the "cup" were neither horse-like nor cup-like. If pretending in young children depends on the number of transformations necessary to produce a relation (such as "horse eats from cup"), pretending will vary as a function of the number of transformations required of them. Two of the relationships diagrammed in Figure 9.2 are open to experimental manipulation: a less prototypical cup (or horse) can be substituted for a highly prototypical one. Substitutions can occur singly or jointly. When 2 year olds were asked to "feed the horse" under double, single, or not substitution conditions, the results were in accord with predictions derived from a transformational analysis. Over 90 percent of the children were able to enact the pretense when no substitutions were involved, 70 percent could do so when single substitutions were involved, whereas only 33 percent could do so when a double substitution was involved.

Additional implications of a transformational model have been explored in subsequent research (Elder & Pederson, 1978; Jackowitz & Watson, 1980; Ungerer et al, 1981; Watson & Fischer, 1977). The findings suggest that the child's object transformation abilities develop in a systematic fashion between 1 and 6 years and that, indeed, meaning comes to dominate the immediate and tangible environment. Put another way, the orientation of the child shifts from stimulation to evocation.

Self-Other Transformations

The third strand appearing in the development of pretending concerns how the child as "self" participates in a pretend sequence. Initially, the child's pretend activities are self-related in that the child functions as both agent and recipient (e.g., the child feeds himself). In time, other actors and agents are added to the pretend game and persons as well as things become substitutable (e.g., the child pretends to feed mother or a doll). Eventually, the child becomes a detached generalized "other" who makes the doll feed itself or a parent doll feed a family of dolls.

Again, the evidence is in line with the theoretical positions advanced by Baldwin and Mead. The 12 month old may feed himself with an empty cup or spoon. By 18 months of age the same child may feed a doll or another person (Fein & Apfel, 1979; Fenson & Ramsan, 1980; Watson & Fischer, 1977). Thus between 12 and 30 months, pretense becomes progressively decentered, until these core symbols of "actions with respect to others" can acquire the embellishments of role-taking as described by Mead. Shifts in the elaboration of role-play behavior have been documented by Garvey and Berndt (1977) Iwanaga (1973), and are illustrated in the play episodes presented earlier. Children are fussy about the implications of the roles they enact. Note the stress Jim and Lil give to the distinction between relationship roles (mother-daughter-sister or father-son-brother), age roles (older-younger-baby), and functional roles (baby sitter-parent). The complementarity of the played out relationships are fairly subtle—a sibling fight requires cooperative combatants, baby sitting involves a responsibility to the baby and to the baby's parent's. This brief scene reflects these children's awareness of social rules that specify prerogatives, accountability, dependency, and authority in the ajudication of right and wrong. It is important to note, however, that the role complementarity represented in play is not always restricted to the actual players. For example, in the sibling exchange enacted by Jim and Lil, the daughter-son role was implicit even though the parent role was not actually played by one of the children.

This development of symbolic play into full sociodramatic enactment of reciprocal social roles in the third to the fifth year of life is what Mead terms the "play stage" of the social self. For Erikson, this play stage provides for the expression, without penalty, of conflictual feelings and anger embedded in important real-life relationships.

Symbol Socialization: Collective Transformations

The fourth component in the development of pretend play represents the socialization of symbols. In the study reported by Fein and Apfel (1979), unconventional transformations increased between 12 and 30 months. But, concurrently, the children's pretense became more stereotyped. By 30 months, for example, the children agreed (with few dissenters) that baby dolls are fed with bottles as if by this age children have acquired a collective symbol of infant nurturance. The conventionalization of pretense is seen in the rendering of basic play roles such as mother, father, baby, fireman, or cowboy. In sociodramatic play, these conventions often have the force of "rules"; they may represent on the one hand children's understanding of the rules of social life (as Vygotsky might argue), and, on the other, may constitute the defining criteria of sociodramatic play (as Piaget might argue). Evidence from Garvey and Berndt (1977) suggests that for all the flexibility of sociodramatic play, departures from conventions (e.g., the baby making a phone call) are not tolerated.

In a recent study, Fein & Moorin (1982) demonstrate that the transition from solitary pretense to pretense with a partner follows a stage-like developmental progression that involves backward as well as forward movement. For example, in solitary play, the child might have progressed from sensorimotor activities to multischeme pretend activities. But these phases are reconstituted in social play. The child steps back to functional play with a partner, and then progresses to simple pretense with a partner. Further development in playing social roles (such as mother or baby) or scenes (such as preparing dinner or going shopping) seems to require a return to solitary play. It is as if the child finds it easier to conceptualize the intricate coordinations of social activities when the others are imaginary than when the others are real peers with whom roles and events must be delicately negotiated.

The following episode illustrates the problems children are likely to have in the transitional period between solitary pretense and sociodramatic play. The episode involves two 3 year olds, Bessy and Danny.

B: (Whispers to her doll.) Cover you up. (Covers doll with blanket.) Night-night, night-night. Don't cry. Will you children go to sleep?

D: (Ignores B. Puts truck in buggy.)

B: (To D.) Dad do you want to stay with the baby? Cover her up. Alright, Dad?

D: (Looks at B. Pokes at truck in buggy.)

B: Danny, will you watch my baby? Will you watch my baby so she's not gonna cry?

D: (Sits next to doll. Looks at it.)

B: Alright, Dad?

D: (Feeds doll with bottle.)

B: (Rakes floor, puts rake away.) Thank you, Dad, thank you. Get up now.

D: (Looks at B. Continues to feed doll.)

B: (Stoops down to doll.) Let me see...I hear what you're saying. (Gets blanket.)

D: (Stops feeding doll. Looks at B.)

B: (Takes doll from D. Puts doll and blanket in front of D.) Wrap her up, right there. (Spreads blanket.) Sheet on. Put her right there, OK? (Puts doll on blanket.)

D: (Fiddles with bottle. Looks at B.)

B: (Covers doll.) Good-night, baby. (Appeals to the teacher.) You stay with her, Bea. Stay with her...she'll...so she'll...she'll.

This episode is informative because it illustrates the problem faced by a child who can manage solitary pretense but cannot manage pretense with a willing, but uncomprehending peer. Danny does not respond when asked to play the role of "Dad," but when addressed directly as "Danny," he obediently "watches the baby" by feeding it. But beyond that, even when Bessy patiently illustrates what else "watch the baby" means, Danny seems unable to grasp the significance of the enactment Bessy is trying to promote. Bessy's efforts, for all her persistence, fall short of initiating discussion about the pretense. Recall the episode between Lil and Jim which began with Lil saying, "Are you the father or the son?" One characteristic of children in the transitorial period is the failure to view pretense with a partner as a negotiable effort. It never seems to occur to Bessy to ask Danny whether he would like to be the dad, the brother, or even the baby. Although Bessy is able to step outside herself and take the role of mother with respect to the doll, she seems unable to fully meet Mead's criteria of role-taking in which one takes the role of the other in regard to one's own communicative gestures. Sociodramatic play seems to hinge on at least two types of communicative gestures, one in which children as their real selves communicate about their play selves, and another in which they communicate as play selves about the imagined events.

From Play to Game

For Mead, the development from sociodramatic play into games represents a development of a new structure of role-taking itself, the "game stage" of the self. Both cooperation and game competition require coordination of a number of roles simultaneously. The baseball pitcher in the game stage not only successively plays the roles one after another (pitcher, batter, team captain) as the child did in the play stage, the pitcher in the role of pitcher must simultaneously take the role of each other player on the team to direct his own actions. In so doing, the child must take the role of the "generalized other," the coordination of all the roles included in a team or a social group.

Collective games stimulate and require a structurally more complex awareness of, and coordination of, social roles and perspectives than sociodramatic play which only required the capacity to coordinate parallel or complementary roles. Accompanying this increased organization of role-taking of a generalized other in the game stage is the development of awareness of rules and their functions, since the organization of the generalized other is codified in the rules of the game.

Piaget, Mead, and Erikson expect pretense to be replaced by games and by activities that involve building and making things that increasingly resemble reality. According to Piaget, pretense becomes more realistic—children become more skilled at mimicking adults (e.g., the teacher) and then scenes become increasingly like dramatic presentations vividly capturing the tone and details of classroom events. As Dewey would have it, constructions become more realistic, soon to be replaced by efforts to use real tools in the crafting of wagons, pulleys, and play houses that really function.

Although information about the play of school age children is limited, these theorists are essentially correct in their accounts of this period. For example, Eifermann (1971) reported a decrease in pretend games and an increase in group games between the years of 4 and 8.

RESEARCH ON THE EFFECTS AND SIGNIFICANCE OF PLAY

One implication of cognitive-developmental theories of play is that there are the kinds of qualitative changes in play with age and cognitive maturity we have just summarized. Another is that experiences of pretend play will actually stimulate imaginativeness and role-taking ability.

Play, Imagination, and Creativity

Sutton-Smith (1967) is among those who have argued that play promotes divergent or creative thinking. A recent study by Dansky (1980) nicely illustrates the relations between play (especially pretend play) and divergent thinking. In the study, Dansky first observed children's spontaneous play. Some children pretended a great deal and others did not. He then tested players and nonplayers under three conditions. In one, the children were allowed to play freely with a set of objects, in another, they observed an adult model, and in a third they played a convergent problem-solving game. Subsequently, they were tested for their ability to give novel and imaginative responses on a test of creative thinking. The group that showed the most creative behavior was the group who played imaginatively in the classroom, and who were permitted to play freely in the pretest situation. Moreover, in this pretest condition, children who played pretend games spontaneously in the classroom played more imaginatively with the materials than those who did not. But if these imaginative children were deprived of an opportunity to behave freely in the new situation, they were not more creative on the test than less imaginative children. This study highlights a central principle of cognitive-developmental theory—namely, that there is an intimate connection between a child's competence and the opportunity to exercise that competence. The role of an early childhood educator is to provide ample opportunity.

A linkage between play and creativity is suggested by other studies as well. When children who do not spontaneously play pretend games are offered specific adult encouragement, pretense increases. These children also show improvement on tests of divergent, imaginative thinking (Feitelson & Ross, 1973). Interestingly, pretend play seems to have less of an effect on convergent problem solving (Rubin, Fein, & Vandenberg, 1983). As Piaget's notion of play as assimilation suggests, the exercise and use of information are different from its acquisition. Both exercise and acquisition are necessary for the construction of knowledge.

Play and Role-Taking

As we discussed earlier, Mead stresses the relation between role-playing and the psychological capacity of role-taking. Here, too, the research seems to confirm theory. For example, Burns and Brainerd (1979) compared children in three types of conditions: (a) role-playing dramatic play training (b) block-building play training, and (c) a no training control group. Children were then tested on tasks measuring their ability to take the perspective of another. The results indicate that children in the training groups performed better than those in the control group. But the group who showed the greatest sensitivity to the perspectives of others was the group receiving dramatic play training. Similar findings have been reported by others (see Fein, 1981, and Rubin et al., 1983, for comprehensive reviews of this research).

In sum, the research seems to support the position of cognitive-developmental theorists that play is a significant aspect of early development.

Enhancing Play in the Classroom—Materials

If recent research is beginning to clarify the ways children benefit from play, it is also clarifying the ways adults can enhance play. Properly chosen play materials, sufficient time, a familiar environment, a relaxed home, and supportive teachers promote play in young children.

A deeply held conviction among preschool educators is that playthings with highly realistic details limit the imaginativeness of children's play. Certainly, one aspect of the development of play is the ability to create imaginary situations and objects. If children are able to create such things, they will presumably do so most richly if the environment is neutral and unintrusive. The evidence suggests, however, that the relationship between play objects in the immediate environment may not be so simple.

For young children, the best environment for pretense may be one containing an ample supply of realistic objects. For older children, such an environment may limit rather than enhance play. Pulaski (1973) compared the influence of highly structured and moderately structured materials on the play of middle-class children in kindergarten, first, and second grade. The highly structured set contained costumes designating specific roles, toys, realistic play buildings, and realistic male and female dolls. The moderately structured set contained bolts of fabric, blocks and cartons, and nondescript rag dolls. The amount of play with the two day sets did not differ. Differences appeared in the inventiveness and imaginativeness of the themes generated by the children. Play with the highly structured toy set tended to adhere to the content suggested by the materials whereas play with the moderately structured set was more varied and creative. Moreover, the activity level of the children was higher with the less realistic materials.

In an attempt to extend this issue to architectural aspects of the play environment, Fields (cited in Fein, 1979b) presented 4- and 5-year-old disadvantaged children with two, large enterable play boxes. The boxes were identical in size, openings, and coloring. They differed in only one respect. One box was painted to look like an automotive vehicle, whereas the other was decorated in a simple abstract pattern. Play was observed over 15 consecutive days for approximately one hour each day.

Contrary to Pulaski's findings, children played more imaginatively in the realistic box. The particular themes and variations generated by the children indicate how the boxes were used (see Table 9.3). Clearly, the automotive motif provoked the play theme of transportation, a theme that never occurred when the motif was absent. Motif-specific play elements account for 58 percent of the play elements generated in the realistic box. Although the children imagined several types of vehicles (plane, train, bus, car, and camper), driving, a stereotyped activity, accounted for 61 percent of the transportation play. If motif-specific elements are excluded from the calculation, more play elements appear when children play in the less realistic box. Note also the high occurrence of house play in both boxes. When the children "drove" the camper, the scene shifted rapidly to basic house play activities, eating and sleeping, which occured in 8 of the 24 house episodes in the realistic box and in 15 of the 31 house episodes in the other box. The fire theme occurred only in the nonrealistic box, possibly as an extension of the house play. At any rate, the theme was never developed. In brief, Fields' findings suggest that realistic structures might have a facilitating effect on the pretend play of disadvantaged 4- and 5-year-old children, especially when the structure suggests a theme not likely to occur spontaneously.

TABLE 9.3

Number of Different Play Elements in Enticable Realistic and Nonrealistic Play Boxes

Theme	Realistic Box (Automotive Motif)	Nonrealistic Box (Abstract Motif)
House	17	29
Transportation	39	0
Fire	0	3
Miscellaneous	11	13

Time

In another study, the investigator observed children's play in the housekeeping area over a seven-week period (Enslein, 1979). The area contained wooden play furniture (a stove, refrigerator, cupboard, bed, table, and chairs), a couple of worn rag dolls, some bedding, and little else. Pretend play occurred occasionally during the first two weeks, but decreased steadily thereafter, until by the sixth week it was down to zero. Enslein then added a set of realistic pots, pans, and dishes, dress-up clothes, and empty food containers. During the first day after the new materials were added, the children engaged largely in exploratory activity, rummaging through the boxes of new materials, trying on the new clothes, and so forth. By the second day, exploratory behavior occurred infrequently and pretend play took over. In the presence of a novel object children explore; but when the novelty wears off, they are more likely to play (Hutt, 1970; Nunnally & Lemond, 1973). Limited evidence suggests that novelty may have a positive influence on exploratory behavior and a negative or inhibitory influence on pretense.

Familiar Peers

Just as time serves to reduce the novelty of objects, it also serves to reduce the novelty of people. When children play with unfamiliar children, the activity is restrained and solitary play or simply watching predominates. But as peers become friends, social play increases, exchanges become more extensive, and pretend play begins to unfold (Doyle et al., 1980).

Emotional Security

High levels of arousal and distress disrupt play. In the presence of their mothers, securely attached children play more richly than anxiously attached children (Matas, Arend, & Snoufe, 1978). Children from homes in which the parents are in conflict, separated, or divorced show less mature and more fragmented play than those children from harmonious and stable homes (Hetherington, Cox, & Cox, 1979). The research seems to suggest that a chaotic classroom or one that causes children to feel unsafe or apprehensive will inhibit play.

Teacher Intervention

Encouragement from parents and teachers can also enchance play and its benefits. Smilansky (1968) describes in detail a method for recording on a daily basis the pretend play of individual children. Then, for children who pretend infrequently, the teacher can suggest how a toy can be used more imaginatively or how a pretend game can be elaborated by the addition of new roles or changing scenes. Several studies using such procedures have demonstrated striking changes in the richness and complexity of sociodramatic activities (Smilansky, 1968; Rosen, 1974).

Similansky conducted a study that compared the usage of sociodramatic play by middle-class and disadvantaged kindergarten children. In one type of training, teachers taught specific play *themes* to children. In another type they taught play *techniques*. In a third group they taught both *themes* and *techniques*. A fourth group were *controls*. Dramatic changes occurred in the *theme plus technique group* and smaller changes in the other two training groups.

Modeling

In one study, van den Daele (1968) created an experimental intervention for disadvantaged children in a Headstart program. The assessment of change was based on van den Daele's (1968) stage-developmental assessment of the ego ideal. Van den Daele's ego stages are particularly relevant in assessing developmental change in play since they derive from J. M. Baldwin's theory of the ideal self, an ideal self enhanced in the play mode.

In our Chapter 2, we noted Broughton's description of the child's epistemology using J. M. Baldwin's theoretical stages of epistemology as a framework. As discussed, Baldwin (1906) also devoted great theoretical attention to the development of valuing activity embodied in the construction of an ideal self or ego ideal. Baldwin's thinking was one of the formative influences in our own construction of moral stages as we discussed elsewhere (Kohlberg's chapter in Broughton & Freeman-Moir, 1982). It has, however, most directly influenced van den Daele's (1968) construction of empirical set of levels of the ego ideal.

In addition to the moral judgment interview, van den Daele asked a series of questions about "the kind of person you would like to be in the future and why." The questions were asked with regard to the areas of occupation, material goods, social, community, and body. Groups interviewed included 50 children aged 3 to 5, 108 children who were members of the second, fourth, sixth, eighth, tenth, and twelfth grades, and four adults. By cross referencing age with moral judgment stages and Baldwin's postulations van den Daele arrived at the ten developmental levels summarized in Table 9.4.

In his play study, van den Daele found most of the children on pretest at his Stage 1, egocentric gratification orientation. He reasoned that these children lacked opportunities in which to imitate older same-sex models. Accordingly, he introduced activities in which adults role-played attractive occupations and invited the child to participate and imitate these activities. This, he thought, might stimulate movement to his next stage, the stage of "doing the good thing" and choosing by reference to adult or other valued models. He found indeed that most of his experimental children did move to the next stage. We cannot be sure whether the change induced was simply one in content of choosing (using adult models) or in structure of choice, nor whether this movement facilitated attainment of the next stage. But the findings of the study are very suggestive.

TABLE 9.4

Précis of Ego-Ideal Development

Stage 1: Undifferentiated Incorporation of Powerful or Glamorous Figures.

S emulates "big people" and strives to incorporate behaviors of persons who control, dominate, or manipulate the environment. Vicarious identification and fantasy often involved in reasoning. Little or no concept of the future as a state requiring different role demands. Object choices often conflicting.

Level 1: Ego-Ideal as the "Quick and Agile."

Orientation to the unusual and exciting, individuals or objects possessing speed and motion, physical prowess or agility. Persons evaluated in a way similar to objects. Magical thinking. Gratification of immediate desire. Strives for excitation. Capricious. Confusion of present with future.

Level 2: Ego-Ideal as a "Good Little Boy or Girl."

Orientation to the adult, usually the same-sex parent, as "controller of resources." Little understanding of the function of behavior with which he identifies. Evaluations are usually dichotomous. The world is ordered in terms of the "good and bad," the "nice and not-nice," the "big and little," etc. The good, nice, and big are valued. The adult is good, and when the *S* acts like the adult, he is good, too. The future conceived as an extension of the present.

Stage 2: Naive Identification with Parental Role.

S emulates behavior patterns and choices of parents or same-sex peers. Evaluates choices in terms of immediate products or consequences. *S* displays an elementary pragmatism in "weighing" the utility of behaviors. In an unsophisticated way, child takes over parental or peer goals, as well as means. However, little sense of long-term purpose. Conflict minimized through "mirroring" parental or same-sex peer behaviors.

Level 3: Ego-Ideal as Conflict-Avoidant.

Orientation to parental behavior patterns and choices to avoid trouble, conflict, or punishment. Naive hedonism. Be obedient to parental demands. Choose objects for "fun." Achievement is the product of "working hard."

Level 4: Ego-Ideal as a "Little Man or Little Woman."

Orientation to externalized aspects of sex role. Sex role demands are derived through experience with persons in the immediate environment, including the *S*'s same-sex peers. Proper performance of sex role results in personal and social harmony. Choose objects associated with sex role.

Stage 3: Social Conformity to Expectations and Evaluation by Others.

S emulates behavior which he feels is "mature." Others presumed to think and feel like oneself. Explanation often cliché-ridden. *S* strives to gain other's approval, acceptance, and liking.

TABLE 9.4—Continued

Level 5: Ego-Ideal as One of the Group.

Orientation to peer group behavior. Choice contingent on give-and-take in one-to-one correspondence. Stereotyped, often rigid thinking. Be like others, and thus be liked by others. Object choice may be motivated by interest derived from experience or exposure.

Level 6: Ego-Ideal as a Social Conformist.

Orientation to adult, "mature" behavior. Others viewed as possessing differentiated emotional feelings. Actions which evoke negative feelings, such as envy, jealousy, etc., are to be avoided. Be fair, thoughtful, and considerate, so not to antagonize. Compromise. Object choice derived from role requirements.

Stage 4: Self-Affirmation Through Internalized Values and Beliefs.

S serves internalized values as proscribed by society or self. Self sanctions right or wrong. Others may or may not agree. S distinguishes long-range purpose from external conformity. Be true to one's values. Domains integrated in terms of duty, responsibility, or values.

Level 7: Ego-Ideal as a Social Agent.

Orientation to duty and responsibility as defined by the society. Self-interest and socially defined good coincide. Tolerates differences. Fulfills one's responsibility. Object choices "preferred" as one of several acceptable alternatives. Recognition of personal limitation.

Level 8: Ego-Ideal as an Independent Agent.

Orientation to unique values, beliefs, and preferences of the self. Recognition of individuality of others and their right to their own beliefs and life style. When self and social values clash, S likely to evaluate social values negatively. Accepts differences. Object choice construed as utilitarian to achievement of personal values.

Stage 5: Integrated World View Through Reflective Consideration of Personal or Human Situation.

S patterns thinking upon reflectively derived principles of evaluation. S strives for self-realization in terms of personal-social or transcendent good. Thinking often philosophical or scholarly. Means coequal in importance with ends. Choices highly integrated.

Level 9: Ego-Ideal as Person Striving for Personal-Social Good.

Orientation to principles derived from consideration of self-society relationships. A synthesis of knowledge, often "academic." Welcomes differences. Choices articulate with principles of self-social good.

Level 10: Ego-Ideal as Person Striving for Transcendent Good.

Orientation to philosophy or world view superordinate to self-interest or social value. A creative synthesis of personal experience. Self conceived as an instance in the process of human becoming. Conflict, sorrow, and tragedy viewed as concomitants of human self-realization. Rejoices in differences.

Source: From van den Daele (1968), pp. 251–253.

SUMMARY

In the cognitive-developmental view, much of early education should center on opportunities and stimulation of play. This requires a consideration of the nature of play, stages in the development of play, and the way in which play opportunities lead to intellectual and social development.

From a theoretical perspective, the research evidence gives considerable theoretical support to the Baldwin-Vygotsky-Mead view of sociodramatic play as being related to social environment. It does not, however, suggest that sociodramatic play is a product of simple social learning as opposed to being a cognitive-developmental stage. It does imply, however, that this cognitive-developmental stage is more influenced by language and culture than Piaget's biological model would suggest. The findings appear to be essentially similar to the findings on private speech that we interpreted as supporting the Vygotsky-Mead theory.

On the more practical education side, the studies suggest: (a) that sociodramatic play can be stimulated by educators, and (b) that such stimulation does stimulate ego-development. The findings suggest that both sociodramatic play and private speech may be "golden areas" in educational work stimulating cognitive and ego development in children aged 3 to 6.

Our account of play started with Piaget. For Piaget, play is a necessity in development because it provides much of the symbolism that allows the child to represent the world and the child's own activities and desires. It does not, however, represent a major vehicle for coming to know the world since its activity is one-sided assimilation rather than that balance of accommodation and assimilation Piaget calls intelligence. Being primarily egocentric, play tends to disappear with development except as it finds its place in games with rules and in hobbies of construction that are reality-oriented if miniature. It may survive also in internalized form as daydreaming.

We attempted to supplement and partly contrast Piaget's view with the views of other theorists, especially Vygotsky, G. H. Mead, and Erikson. These latter theorists stress the ways in which play is a precursor or basis of symbolization, but also emphasize that it is the developmental root of later imagination taking the form of art, of hypothesis-making, and industrious construction. They also stress its role in formation of the ego or social self. These differences between Piaget and other theorists are less the result of some basic oppositions of theory than differences in theoretical focus.

Piaget's general concerns are with adaptive intelligence as intelligence moves through a series of structural stages. He is, in other words, concerned with cognition and the epistemic subject. From this point of view, since play is not a straightforward expression of adaptive or operational intelligence, it represents a curious and meaningful anomaly in Piaget's general scheme. To account for it, Piaget interpreted play as the primacy of assimilation and made a brilliant set of observations and interpretations of the development of play from this point of view.

In contrast to Piaget, the other theorists discussed focus on the development of a social self that needs to create a zone of freedom to develop or become an individualized self through imaginatively playing roles the self might become. This interpretation, supported by research on sociodramatic play and the game, gives educational purposes to the cultivation of these activities by the early educator.

REFERENCES

Baldwin, J. M. (1906). *Social and ethical interpretations in mental development* (4th ed.), New York: Macmillan.

Berlyne, D. E. (1966). Curiosity and exploration, *Science, 153,* 25–33.

Broughton, J. M., & Freeman-Moir, D. J. (1982). *The cognitive-developmental psychology of James Mark Baldwin: Current theory and research in genetic epistemology.* Norwood, NJ: Ablex.

Burns, S. M., & Brainerd, C. J. (1979). Effects of constructive and dramatic play on perspective-taking in very young children. *Developmental Psychology, 15,* 512–521.

Dansky, J. L. (1980). Cognitive consequences of sociodramatic play and exploration training for economically disadvantaged preschoolers. *Journal of Child Psychology and Psychiatry, 20,* 47–58.

Dewey, J. (1971). *The child and the curriculum, the school and society.* Chicago: University of Chicago Press (1978). (Originally published 1915.)

Doyle, A. B., Connolly, J., & Rivest, L. P. (1980). The effect of playmate familiarity on the social interactions of young children. *Child Development, 51,* 217–223.

Eifermann, R. R. (1971). Social play in childhood. In R. E. Herron & B. Sutton-Smith (Eds.), *Child's play.* New York: Wiley.

Elder, J., & Pederson, D. Preschool children's use of objects in symbolic play. *Child Development, 49,* 500–504.

Enslein, J. (1979). *An analysis of toy preference, social participation and play activity in preschool-aged children.* Unpublished masters thesis, The Norrill-Palmer Institute.

Erikson, E. (1963). *Childhood and society,* 2nd ed, New York: Norton.

Erikson, E. (1977). *Toys and reasons,* New York: Norton.

Fein, G. G. (1973). Play reconsidered. In G. G. Fein & Clark-Stewart (Eds.), *Day care in context.* New York: Wiley.

Fein, G. G. (1975). A transformational analysis of pretending. *Developmental Psychology, 11,* 291–296.

Fein, G. G. (1979a). Pretend play: New perspectives. *Young Children, 34,* 61–66.

Fein, G. G. (1979b). Play and the acquisition of symbols. In L. Katz (Ed.), *Current topics in early childhood education.* Norwood, NJ: Ablex.

Fein, G. G. (1979c). Piaget, Vygotsky, language and symbolic play. In E. Winner & H. Gardner (Eds.), *New directions in child development.* San Francisco: Jossey Bass. (This chapter itself is an adaptation of Fein, 1979a.)

Fein, G. G. (1981). Pretend play: An integrative review. *Child Development, 52,* 1095–1118.

Fein, G. G., & Apfel, N. (1979). Some preliminary observations on knowing and pretending. In N. Smith & M. B. Franklin (Eds.), *Symbolic functioning in childhood.* Hillsdale, NJ: Erlbaum.

Fein, G. G., & Moorin, E. R. (1982). Symbols, motives, and words. In K. Nelson (Ed.), *Children's language* (Vol. 5), New York: Gardner Press.

Feitelson, W., & Ross, G. S. (1973). The neglected factor—play. *Human Development, 16,* 202–223.

Fenson, L., & Ramsay, D. (1980) Decentration and integration of the child's play in the second year. *Child Development, 51,* 171–178.

Garvey, C., & Berndt, R. (1977). Organization of pretend play. Paper presented at the meeting of the American Psychological Association, Chicago.

Golomb, C. (1977). Symbolic play: The role of substitutions in pretense and puzzle games. *British Journal of Educational Psychology, 47,* 175–186.

Golomb, C., & Cornelius, C. B. (1977). Symbolic play and its cognitive significance. *Developmental Psychology, 13,* 246–252.

Hetherington, E. M., Cox, M. & Cox, R. (1979). Play and social interaction in children following divorce. *Journal of Social Issues, 35,* 26–49.

Hutt, C. (1970). Specific and diverse exploration. In H. Reese & L. Lipsett (Eds.), *Advances in child behavior and development.* New York: Academic Press.

Hutt, C. (1979). Exploration and play. In B. Sutton-Smith (Ed.), *Play and learning.* New York: Gardner Press.

Iwanaga, M. (1973). Development of interpersonal play structures in 3, 4, and 5-year-old children. *Journal of Research and Development in Education, 6,* 71–82.

Jackowitz, E. R., & Watson, M. W. (1980). The development of object transformations in early pretend play. *Developmental Psychology, 16,* 543–549.

Kohlberg, L. (1969). Stage and sequence: The cognitive-developmental approach to socialization. In D. A. Goslin (Ed.), *Handbook of socialization theory and research.* Chicago: Rand McNally.

Matas, L., Arend, R. A., & Snoufe, L. A. (1978). Continuity of adaptation in the second year: The relationship between quality of attachment and later competence. *Child Development, 49,* 547–556.

Mead, G. H. (1934). *Mind, self and society.* Chicago: University of Chicago Press.

Miller, S. N. (1973). Ends, means, and galumphing: Some leitmotifs of play. *American Anthropologist, 75,* 87–98.

Nicolich, L. (1977). Beyond sensorimotor intelligence: Assessment of symbolic maturity through analysis of pretend play. *Merrill-Palmer Quarterly, 23*(2), 89–99.

Nunnally, J. C., & Lemond, L. C. (1973). Exploratory behavior and human development. In H. Reese (Ed.), *Advances in child development and behavior* (Vol. 8). New York: Academic Press.

Parten, M. B. (1933). Social participation in preschool children. *Journal of Abnormal Social Psychology, 28,* 136–147.

Piaget, J. (1962). *Play, dreams and imitation in childhood.* New York: Norton (Originally published 1945).

Piaget, J. (1965). The moral judgment of the child. Glencoe, IL: Free Press (Originally published, 1932).

Piaget, J., & Inhelder, B. (1971). *Mental imagery in the child.* New York: Basic Books.

Pulaski, M. A. (1973). Toys and imaginative play. In J. L. Singer (Ed.), *The child's world of make-believe.* New York: Academic.

Rosen, C. E. (1974). The effects of sociodramatic play on problem-solving behavior among culturally disadvantaged preschool children. *Child Development, 45,* 920–927.

Rubin, K. H., Fein, G. G., & Vandenberg, B. (1983). Play. In P. H. Musson (Ed.), *Handbook of Child Psychology,* 4th ed. (pp. 693–774). New York: Wiley.

Saltz, E., Dixon, D., & Johnson, J. (1977). Training disadvantaged preschoolers on various fantasy activities: Effects on cognitive functioning and impulse control. *Child Development, 48*, 367–380.

Saltz, E., & Johnson, J. (1974). Training for thematic-fantasy play in culturally disadvantaged children: Preliminary results. *Journal of Educational Psychology, 66*, 623–630.

Smilansky, S. (1968). *The effects of sociodramatic play on disadvantaged preschool children.* New York: Wiley.

Sutton-Smith, B. (1967). The role of play in cognitive development. *Young Children, 22*, 361–370.

Sutton-Smith, B. (1971). The role of play in cognitive development. In R. Herson & B. Sutton-Smith (Eds.), *Child's play.* New York: Wiley.

Ungerer, J., Zelazo, P. R., Kearsley, R. B., & O'Leary, K. (1981). Developmental changes in the representation of objects in symbolic play from 18 to 34 months of age, *Child Development, 52*, 186–195.

van den Daele, L. (1968). A developmental study of ego-ideals. *Genetic Psychology Monographs, 78*, 191–256.

Vygotsky, L. S. (1962). *Thought and language.* Cambridge: MIT Press.

Vygotsky, L. S. (1967). Play and its role in the mental development of the child. *Soviet Psychology, 5*(3), 6–18.

Vygotsky, L. S. (1978). *Mind in society: The development of higher psychological processes.* Cambridge: Harvard University Press.

Watson, M. W., & Fischer, K. W. (1977). A developmental sequence of agent use in late infancy. *Child Development, 48*, 828–836.

White, R. (1963). Ego and reality in psychoanalytic theory. *Psychological Issues, 3*(3). New York: International Universities Press.

Index

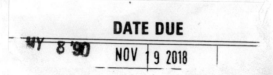